P9-DFJ-568

South-Western

ECONOMICS

J. Holton Wilson
Professor
Central Michigan University

J.R. Clark
Probasco Chair
University of Tennessee/Chattanooga

Editor-in-Chief

Development

Technology and Media

Production

Design

Photos

Marketing and Promotion

Manufacturing

Editorial Support

Library of Congress Cataloging-in-Publication Data

Wilson, J. Holton
Economics / J. Holton Wilson, J.R. Clark. — 4th ed.
p. cm.
Includes index.
ISBN 0-538-65593-3 (alk. paper)
1. Economics. I. Clark, J. R. (Jeff R.) II. Title.
HB171.5.W7413 1996 95-52575
330—dc20 CIP

I(T)P

International Thomson Publishing
South-Western Educational Publishing is a division of International Thomson Publishing Inc.
The ITP trademark is used under license.

ISBN: 0-538-65593-3

2 3 4 5 6 7 8 9 Ki 04 03 02 01 00 99 98 97 96

Printed in the United States of America

PREFACE

ECONOMICS IS ALL AROUND YOU

Economics plays a vital role in society. Trade and exchange reach every aspect of your life through the choices you make in the marketplace and eventually the voting booth. Relationships between nations are likely to revolve as much around economic matters as around everyday political affairs of state.

The role that economics plays in the life of every individual actually is nothing new or different. People always have made choices, and choices always have been the essence of economics. It is true, however, that in the past several decades we have become increasingly aware that much of our decision making is highly economic in nature. You can expect that through the end of the twentieth century and into the new millennium, people throughout the world will be faced with more and more decisions that have important economic components.

One of the primary goals of South-Western ECONOMICS is to explain to you the role that economics plays in improving the quality of your decision-making process. We have brought together a variety of learning tools to help you not only learn about economics but also appreciate the importance of economics in your personal life as well as in the functioning of our domestic and global economies.

COVERAGE OF ECONOMICS

This edition of the text has involved a very major revision; however, it continues to follow the guidelines suggested by the National Council on Economic Education's *Master Curriculum Guide*. This textbook covers every aspect of high school economics.

Part One, Making Economic Decisions, examines the choice process from individual and social viewpoints. A five-step decision process is presented that enables you to make informed and relevant choices in the marketplace, the voting booth, and your own life. You learn to identify the opportunity costs of any choice and to evaluate these costs against the expected benefits. Different economic systems are explained and you learn how these systems answer such economic questions as "What should be produced?," "How should things be produced?," and "For whom should the goods be produced?"

Once the role of choice in economics is firmly established, **Part Two, The Microeconomic Perspective,** explains the choices made by individual

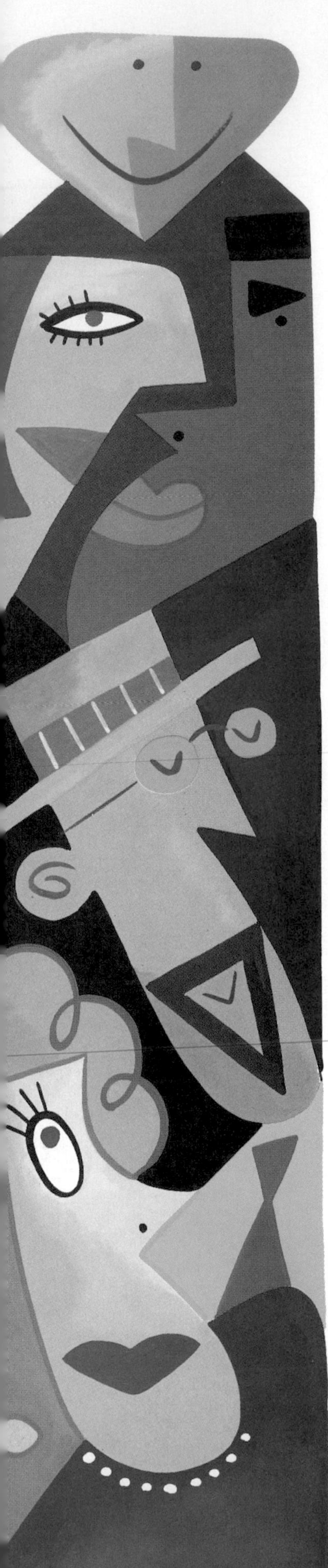

consumers and producers in the marketplace. **Part Two** shows how these individual choices affect supply and demand. It describes the organization of individual business firms and markets, ways to improve the market system, the labor market, and how individual incomes are determined.

Part Three, The Macroeconomic Perspective, explains the choices made by the whole economy. Topics explored include gross domestic product (GDP); unemployment; inflation; the money supply and the banking system; and monetary, tax, and fiscal policies.

Part Four, The World Economy, explores economic topics related to the world economy. These include international trade and the problems of less-developed countries. Again, the role of choice is examined in relation to these topics.

LEARNING WITH ECONOMICS

The world you live in requires people who are well-educated, creative, and determined. Economics is a big part of that world. The following sections identify some of the key features of South-Western ECONOMICS and how you can use this book to get the most out of the time you spend learning about economics.

Preview with the Chapter Opener

The first two pages of each chapter include a unique illustration by Robert de Michiell and clearly defined **Learning Objectives.** Take a moment to view the illustration and see if you can link it to the chapter content. Then read the **Learning Objectives** to preview the economic concepts that you will be learning about in the chapter.

Investigate by Sections

Chapters are divided into several sections, each of which covers an economic concept in its entirety. Within the **Focus** at the start of each section be sure to read the feature entitled ***What Do You Think?*** These are short scenarios that end with a question for you to think about as you read the section. The **Checkpoint** at the end of the section then asks you to reconsider the scenario in light of what you have just learned. When you are asked, ***What Do You Think Now?,*** you might be surprised!

Explore with the Special Features

Every chapter contains the following five features that let you have fun while you explore a diversity of experiences related to the topic of the chapter.

Global Economy. This feature examines the global aspects of economic concepts covered in the chapter. You might learn about current events, important historic events, or activities that have global economic results. Take a look at Chapter 4, where the question "Can We Afford to Save the Environment?" is examined in economic terms.

Economic Spotlight. Individuals who have made important contributions to economics and/or are interesting because of their personal economic activities are highlighted in this feature. Chapter 14 takes a look at why L. L. Bean started a company that has grown into one of the most successful mail-order companies in the United States. (Hint: It has to do with wet feet.)

Internet Connection. This feature provides general information about how the Internet works, as well as economic uses of the Internet. Actual Internet addresses are provided so that you can find sites that have information to supplement what you have read about in the chapter and sites that are just plain fun. Don't miss Chapter 6, where you visit South-Western's ECONOMICS Web page and are given the addresses of many fun sites.

Economic Dilemma. In making economic decisions, you, as an individual or as a member of society, are frequently faced with dilemmas. This feature draws attention to specific situations in which economic dilemmas exist. One dilemma facing you is whether to work or attend college after high school. Chapter 2 gives you some information on the economic trade-offs involved in that critical decision.

Econ & You. This feature relates the concepts in each chapter directly to you. Do you know what type of employee the business is looking for when you apply for a job? Find out in Chapter 7, as you read "Why Should I Hire You?"

As you have read, this book is divided into four parts: **Making Economic Decisions, The Microeconomic Perspective, The Macroeconomic Perspective,** and **The World Economy.** Three special features are included in each of the four parts. **Analyzing Primary Source Documents** presents the original text of an important document for you to read and analyze. **Economic Measurement Concepts** presents examples of how mathematical relationships and measurement tools are used in economic analysis. Finally, **Social Goals of the U.S. Economy** examines how we incorporate the goals of freedom, security, equity, and full employment into our national economic decisions.

Improve Your Vocabulary with Key Terms

Key economic terms are highlighted in bold type and defined in the margins. These are terms to know, because you'll be using them throughout this

course and throughout your life. A complete **Glossary** of all these economic terms is provided at the end of the text, giving you easy access to definitions of any terms you do not understand.

Analyze the Illustrations and Photos

Graphs, tables, photographs, and maps provide graphic representation of the concepts presented. Take some time to look at these, as economic information is often made clearer with graphic images.

Review with the End-of-Chapter Activities

The activities at the end of each chapter are there for your review and assessment. Read **Concepts in Brief** and then review any section of the chapter that remains unclear. The activities provide opportunities for you to demonstrate understanding of and to apply the economic concepts you've studied.

Supplement with the Appendices

Several appendices are available at the end of your book for your use in exploring economic material. Use these appendices to gain an understanding of geography, consumer issues, career options, measurement concepts, and economic data.

Search with the Index

A detailed **Index** is provided at the end of the text. The in-depth nature of this **Index** will be a valuable aid to you when you are trying to find particular concepts in the text.

THE REST OF THE PACKAGE

There are many resources available to support this text and enhance your economic education. On the computer, you may have the opportunity to compete with other students in ***Arctic Express,*** test your knowledge with ***Interactive*** ECONOMICS, hone your math skills with template problems, and even view some video clips from CNBC. These video clips, at least one for every chapter, are also available on VHS and videodisc.

Several workbooks are also available. You can develop your critical-thinking skills when you analyze cases about real companies in the ***Casebook.*** If you would like to improve your math skills, use the ***Economic Measurement Workbook.*** Need to review the chapter content? Try the ***Content Review Workbook.***

ECONOMICS IN YOUR LIFE

Economics is both challenging and interesting. South-Western ECONOMICS will help you understand decision making, economics, and the role of both in business and government. By using this book and the accompanying supplementary materials, you can develop the knowledge and skills needed to become a better citizen, consumer, and worker. This package of learning materials makes learning economics interesting and even fun. Gone are the days of economics as a dismal science. Enjoy your study of economics!

CONTRIBUTORS

The fourth edition of *ECONOMICS* would not be the powerful learning package it is without the feedback received from teachers and students who have used the first three editions. These comments and suggestions are greatly appreciated and encouraged. This edition also has benefited from the observations of high school teachers who had not used the earlier editions, but who generously participated in focus groups and written surveys designed to elicit insight into what works and what doesn't work in helping students learn about economics.

Program Reviewers and Consultants

The following individuals have been instrumental in the development of South-Western *ECONOMICS*.

Eleanor Allen
Foothill High School
Sacramento, California

John Burton
Palm Harbor University High School
Palm Harbor, Florida

Danny L. Cole
Dunedin High School
Dunedin, Florida

Norman B. Cregger
Central Michigan University
Mt. Pleasant, Michigan

Dr. Harlan Day
Purdue University
West Lafayette, Indiana

Dennis Dowling
Lakota High School
West Chester, Ohio

Steven A. Greenlaw
Mary Washington College
Fredericksburg, Virginia

Helen I. Humbert
Kent-Meridian High School
Kent, Washington

Thomas A. Kessinger
Wyoming High School
Wyoming, Ohio

Dr. Usman A. Qureshi
Old Dominion University
Norfolk, Virginia

Holly Sagues
Winter Park High School
Winter Park, Florida

Linda Smith
Clearwater High School
Clearwater, Florida

Jeffrey H. Trout
Mynderse Academy
Seneca Falls, New York

Dr. Mark S. Walbert
Illinois State University
Normal, Illinois

Tom Welch
Jessamine County High School
Nicholasville, Kentucky

Dr. Terry Wilson
Mt. Carmel High School
San Diego, California

THE AUTHORS

Dr. Holt Wilson is a professor at Central Michigan University. Building on his undergraduate degrees in economics and chemistry, Dr. Wilson took major course work and exams in both economics and marketing in his doctoral program. In his nearly 30 years of teaching, Dr. Wilson has taught college and university economics courses in Ohio, Oklahoma, Montana, and Michigan. He was named to Outstanding Educators in America and in 1995 received Central Michigan University's College of Business Administration Dean's Teaching Award.

In addition to his academic credentials, Dr. Wilson has worked in quality control at H. J. Heinz Company and as a partner in a market research firm. He also has consulted with firms in the banking, manufacturing, and chemical industries. Dr. Wilson is a member of the American Economic Association and the National Association of Business Economists. Dr. Wilson has published numerous textbooks and articles on economics and continues his research in the areas of managerial economics, economic forecasting, and economic statistics.

Dr. J. R. Clark holds the Probasco Chair at the University of Tennessee at Chattanooga. In his more than two decades in teaching, Dr. Clark has also been a professor at Fairleigh Dickinson University and the University of Tennessee at Martin. He received the University of Tennessee Outstanding Research Award in 1991 and the Association of Private Enterprise Education Distinguished Scholar Award in 1992.

In addition to his academic credentials, Dr. Clark has consulted in both the public and private sectors, including Fortune 500 companies, government agencies, and universities. He is a member of the American Economic Association and the Secretary/Treasurer of the Association of Private Enterprise Education. Dr. Clark is the author of textbooks and articles in the areas of public choice and economics.

CONTENTS

Special Features

SOCIAL GOALS OF THE U.S. ECONOMY

ECONOMIC MEASUREMENT CONCEPTS

ANALYZING PRIMARY SOURCE DOCUMENTS

ECONOMIC SPOTLIGHT

ECONOMIC DILEMMA

GLOBAL ECONOMY

INTERNET CONNECTION

ECON & YOU

MALL
SCHOOL

PART ONE
Making Economic Decisions

Overview

Section One
Economics and Choice

Section Two
Opportunity Costs and Benefits

Section Three
Basic Economic Questions

Section Four
Economic Systems

The Economic Way of Thinking

Learning Objectives

1-1

Present reasons why it is important for everyone to understand economics.

1-2

Explain why economics is called the science of choices.

1-3

Identify the opportunity cost and the opportunity benefit of an economic choice.

1-4

Relate individual and social choices to microeconomics and macroeconomics.

1-5

Distinguish between the three basic economic questions that must be answered in all societies.

1-6

Analyze market, command, and mixed economic systems by how they answer the three basic economic questions.

1-7

Demonstrate how economic theory is used in economic decision making.

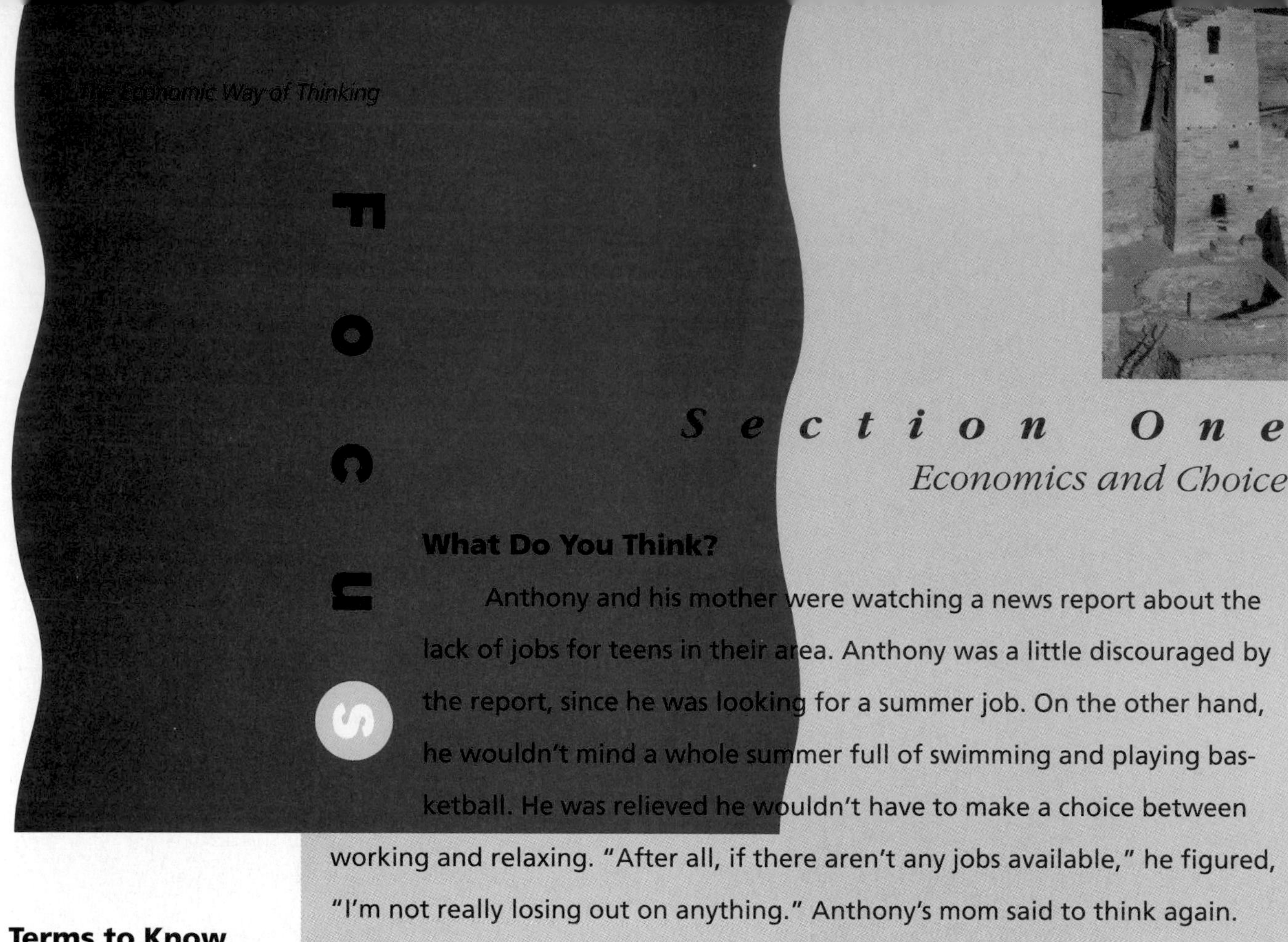

Section One
Economics and Choice

What Do You Think?

Anthony and his mother were watching a news report about the lack of jobs for teens in their area. Anthony was a little discouraged by the report, since he was looking for a summer job. On the other hand, he wouldn't mind a whole summer full of swimming and playing basketball. He was relieved he wouldn't have to make a choice between working and relaxing. "After all, if there aren't any jobs available," he figured, "I'm not really losing out on anything." Anthony's mom said to think again.

Terms to Know

- scarcity
- unlimited wants and needs
- limited resources
- allocation
- economics

What's Ahead?

Economics is important because it affects your life every day. An understanding of economics will help you make more informed decisions and be a more effective citizen. Economics deals with the basic problem of scarcity and how you make tradeoffs between alternatives.

ECONOMICS IS IMPORTANT

Why should you study economics? What will you gain from learning about it? Almost everyone hears something every week about economics. It is difficult to pick up a newspaper, watch television, or have contact with the world outside your home without encountering some economic information. In order to understand the economic information you hear every day, you will need to become familiar with the economic way of thinking.

Economics Affects Your Everyday Life

Economic concerns are the topics of many newspaper headlines: "Teen Unemployment Rate Remains High," "U.S. Auto Makers See Brighter Times Ahead," "College Tuition to Rise," "Concern About Inflation Remains High." You can see that these are topics that affect aspects of your everyday life—cars, school, jobs, and so on. Economics not only identifies economic problems, it provides you with a logical, effective decision-making process. This process helps you make the most of your resources and satisfy many of your wants and needs every day.

Economics Helps You Make More Informed Decisions

As a worker and a consumer, you will have to make many economic decisions. You will have to decide how to spend your income. The cost of all the goods and services you will want to buy will most likely be greater than your income. So, you will have to choose among them carefully. You also will have to choose a career for yourself, and this choice will surely affect your lifetime income, personal happiness, and success. You will make decisions about working, learning, earning, and spending. You can make all these decisions more effectively with a basic understanding of economics.

Economics Makes You a More Effective Citizen

As a citizen in this country, you have the opportunity to vote. You can help decide the future course the economy will take. Do you want to pay higher taxes for more new roads and schools? Or, do you want to pay lower taxes and accept poorer roads and schools? The candidates will have to make these economic choices, and you must decide which candidates to vote for. As you cast your vote, you should understand what these choices will mean to you.

You might even want to become a political candidate yourself. However, before you could take a position on an issue, you would need to understand how it affects the economy. Perhaps you would favor a tax cut that would reduce unemployment. But what if the tax cut also increased inflation? Would you favor free trade with other countries, or would you expect people to buy only U.S.-made products?

The study of economics helps people and societies make better choices. An understanding of economics is vital to your success in the workplace, the marketplace, and the voting booth.

A SCIENCE OF CHOICES

When you think of the term *economics,* many impressions come to mind. Perhaps you associate the term with money, the stock market, inflation, taxes, and unemployment. But, economics is much more. It is a scientific body of knowledge that can analyze, explain, and in many cases predict people's economic behavior. This behavior is centered around the basic economic problem.

The Basic Economic Problem: Scarcity

scarcity
the condition that occurs because people's wants and needs are unlimited, while the resources needed to produce goods and services to meet these wants and needs are limited

The basic economic problem is scarcity. ***Scarcity*** is the condition that occurs because people's wants and needs are unlimited, while the resources needed to produce goods and services to meet these wants and needs are limited.

unlimited wants and needs
the human characteristic of never having all wants and needs satisfied

There are two sides to the scarcity problem. One of the basic human characteristics is that people are never fully satisfied. Psychologists say that as soon as the basic needs for food, clothing, and shelter are met, the mind creates new needs, such as physical security. When this need is fulfilled, the mind finds even more new needs. This need creation and fulfillment process has no end. Every time a need is satisfied, a new need is created. No matter if you are rich, poor, or in between, you probably can think of many things you need right now. ***Unlimited wants and needs*** is the human characteristic of never having all wants and needs satisfied.

Economic Spotlight

CAN YOU TELL A NEED FROM A WANT?

Does Oscar de la Renta's luxurious clothing fulfill a need or a want? Oscar de la Renta dresses some of the most prominent women in the United States for their main events. He is the first American to head a Paris *couture house,* a clothing studio that hand makes clothing to fit each individual customer.

De la Renta is a shrewd, industrious fashion designer who works very hard but does it with grace. According to De la Renta, "I could work harder and have a bigger business, but there is so much more to life." He presents a high-class image in the fashion world—a far cry from his humble beginnings. An orphan, born in Santo Domingo in the Dominican Republic, he is the sixth child in a large family. At 17 years old, this son of an insurance salesman headed to Madrid, Spain, to study art. There he developed an interest in fashion design.

His big break came when he was commissioned to design a debutante gown for the daughter of U.S. politician Henry Cabot Lodge. The gown ended up on the cover of *Life* magazine, giving De la Renta his entry into the world of fashion design. After working for Balenciaga and Elizabeth Arden, he opened his own salon in 1965. He now has more than 45 licensees and three perfumes and sells more than $500 million of products each year.

While De la Renta and his wife Annette Reed may be a wealthy, socially ambitious couple, they still find the time to serve on the boards of many nonprofit organizations. They also have founded and funded an orphanage for 350 children, the only institution of its kind in Santo Domingo. By donating time and money to worthy causes, De la Renta fulfills many people's unmet needs, but does his custom-designed clothing fulfill a need or a want?

Fulfilling most needs requires goods and services of one kind or another. To produce goods and services, resources or the raw materials of production are needed. For example, building houses to fulfill the human need for shelter requires wood, glass, concrete, steel, copper, and the services of builders. However, there is only so much lumber, glass, concrete, steel, and labor available. There is a limit to resources. ***Limited resources*** means that there are never enough resources to fulfill all wants and needs. Limited resources available to satisfy unlimited wants and needs creates *scarcity*, the basic economic problem.

limited resources
the condition of there not being enough resources to fulfill all wants and needs

Definition of Economics

The problem of scarcity results in allocation. ***Allocation*** is the process of choosing which needs will be satisfied and how much of our resources we will use to satisfy them. You must choose which needs to neglect and just how much to neglect them. This allocation process requires making *trade-offs* or choosing among alternatives. When you allocate, you choose among alternatives or make trade-offs in deciding how to use your resources.

allocation
the process of choosing which needs will be satisfied and how much of our resources we will use to satisfy them

Economics, then, is the science of making effective choices or decisions by examining the alternatives. As a social science, economics studies how people interact in their society in an economic way. Broadly defined, ***economics*** is the social science that deals with how society allocates its scarce resources among its unlimited wants and needs.

economics
the social science that deals with how society allocates its scarce resources among its unlimited wants and needs

Checkpoint

Content Check

1. What is the economic way of thinking?
2. Identify the basic economic problem and explain why it occurs in our society.
3. How does allocation apply to the basic economic problem?

What Do You Think Now?

Reread *What Do You Think?* in the Section One Focus. Then answer the following questions:

4. How would a basic understanding of economics help Anthony make a good decision about how to spend his time this summer?
5. What is scarce for Anthony?

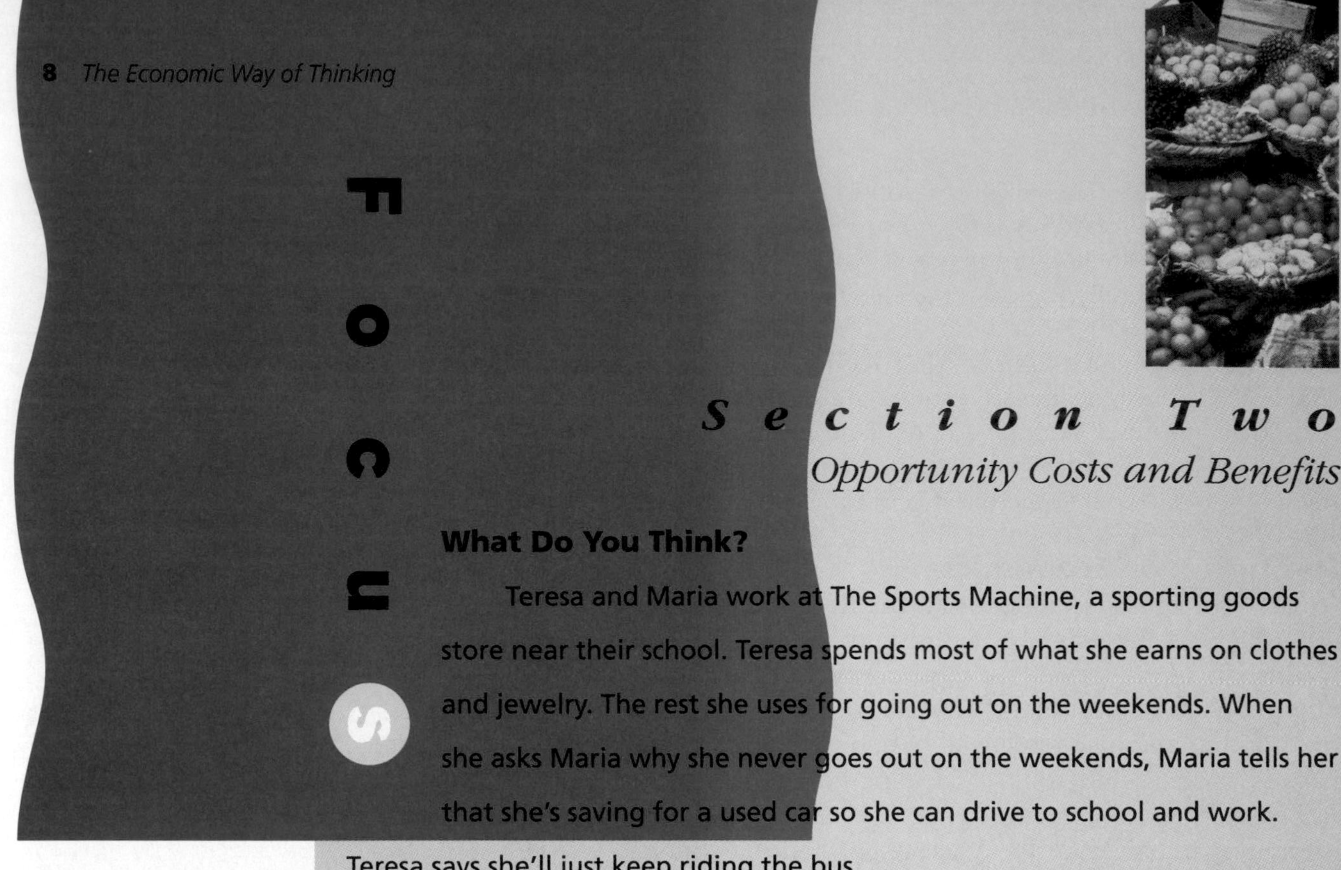

Section Two
Opportunity Costs and Benefits

What Do You Think?

Teresa and Maria work at The Sports Machine, a sporting goods store near their school. Teresa spends most of what she earns on clothes and jewelry. The rest she uses for going out on the weekends. When she asks Maria why she never goes out on the weekends, Maria tells her that she's saving for a used car so she can drive to school and work. Teresa says she'll just keep riding the bus.

Terms to Know

opportunity cost

opportunity benefit

What's Ahead?

Costs and benefits guide the choice process of individuals and countries. They determine what, how, and for whom goods are produced. Every time you make a choice, you give up the value of any alternatives. If you determine the value of what you are giving up, you can make better decisions.

COSTS AND BENEFITS

You have learned that economics is the science of making choices. However, in order to make effective choices, you must understand the costs and the benefits of any given choice. When you make a purchase decision, you weigh the price you must pay against the satisfaction or use you believe you will get from the purchase. There is more to cost, however, than just the dollar price. Economists consider the *opportunity costs* and *opportunity benefits* of each choice.

Opportunity Cost

opportunity cost the value of any alternative that you must give up when you make a choice

Opportunity cost is the value of any alternative that you must give up when you make a choice. In short, the opportunity cost is the value of the opportunity lost. If you choose to study for a test rather than ski, the opportunity cost is the skiing time you must give up to study.

Let's develop another example of opportunity cost and use some of the tools that an economist would use to make a decision. Assume for the moment that you have a weekly income of $30 and that you spend that income on only two different goods: movies and paperback books. To keep the numbers very simple, assume that a movie ticket and snack cost $10 and that books sell for $5 each. Figure 1-1 shows how many of each item you can buy with your income.

As Figure 1-1 shows, you could spend all of your income on three movies or on six books. However, you may wish to have some of both goods. If so, you will spend some of your income on movies and some of your income on books. Of course, how much you spend on movies will determine how much income you have left to spend on books.

Assume you have only two choices. That will make it easier to see the opportunity costs. One choice is to buy four books and use the remaining income to go to one movie. This will be called Combination *A*.

4 books @ $5 = $20	
1 movie @ $10 = $10	Combination *A*
TOTAL = $30	

Another choice is to buy two books and use the remaining income to go to two movies. This will be called Combination *B*.

2 books @ $5 = $10	
2 movies @ $10 = $20	Combination *B*
TOTAL = $30	

Economic Dilemma

NO ONE CAN BE SUPERWOMAN!

Since the early 1960s, women have entered the work force in large numbers. While for families there are many advantages to this situation, including increased income, economics reminds us that there must be an opportunity cost as well.

Some women have attempted to be mother, homemaker, and breadwinner all at the same time, believing they can "have it all." To believe this is to deny that scarcity exists, which is clearly not true. While both women and men have taken on new roles in the 80s and 90s, scarcity will always be with us. Time spent on the job cannot at the same time be spent caring for children, nurturing families, homemaking, and participating in leisure or recreational activities.

It is highly probable that much of the increased stress reported by working women and men today is due to inability or unwillingness to recognize the opportunity costs of a working career. The most basic economic dilemma will always be a part of life because, at least in the sense of opportunity costs, no one can "have it all."

Figure 1-1

Use of Income to Attend Movies and Buy Books

With a fixed income of $30, more movies means fewer books. ***If you buy three books, how many movies can you go see?***

Movies You Can Attend	Price	Total Cost	Your Total Income	Income Left Over
1	$10	$10	$30	$20
2	$10	$20	$30	$10
3	$10	$30	$30	$ 0

Books You Can Buy	Price	Total Cost	Your Total Income	Income Left Over
1	$5	$ 5	$30	$25
2	$5	$10	$30	$20
3	$5	$15	$30	$15
4	$5	$20	$30	$10
5	$5	$25	$30	$ 5
6	$5	$30	$30	$ 0

Either choice is possible since you have $30 to allocate. How, then, will you decide which alternative to choose? Will you choose *A* or *B?* The best way to make that choice is to look at the opportunity cost of each alternative. Suppose you are presently considering Combination *A* with four books and one movie. What, then, will you have to give up to move to Combination *B*, which allows you two books and two movies? As the graph in Figure 1-2 shows, to get the additional movie in Combination *B*, you will have to give up two of the four books you would have had in Combination *A*. Therefore, the opportunity cost of one movie is two books.

You should make your decision based on how much you like movies compared with how much you like books. You need to decide if you like one movie enough to give up two books. On the other hand, you also can con-

Figure 1-2

The Opportunity Benefit and Opportunity Cost of Two Alternatives

As you move from Combination *A* to Combination *B*, you gain one movie (opportunity benefit) and give up two books (opportunity cost). ***Identify two other combinations of books and movies and explain where they are represented on this graph.***

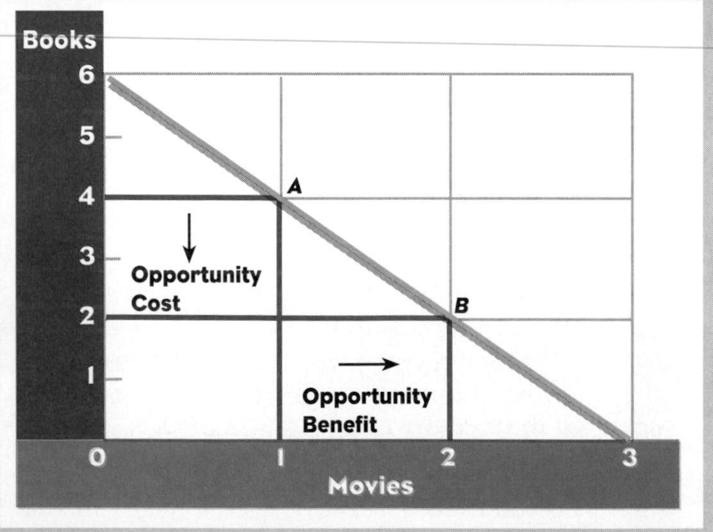

sider whether you like two books enough to give up one movie. What is the opportunity cost of two additional books? It is one movie.

You can now add the concept of opportunity cost to the definition of economics. Economics includes the study of how we make effective choices or decisions by examining the alternatives and considering the opportunity cost of each alternative.

Opportunity Benefit

Another way of making choices is to look at the opportunity benefits of the alternatives. The ***opportunity benefit*** is what is gained by making a particular choice. If, in the previous case, the opportunity cost of moving from Combination *A* to Combination *B* is two books, then the opportunity benefit is one movie. In the case of choosing to study rather than to ski, the opportunity benefit is receiving a better grade on your test.

Every economic choice has an opportunity benefit and an opportunity cost. When you make an informed choice, you compare the opportunity benefit (what you gain) with the opportunity cost (what you lose). This simple concept will serve as a good guide as you further your knowledge of economics. It will also be useful as you make more complicated individual and social decisions.

opportunity benefit
what is gained by making a particular choice

Checkpoint

Content Check

1. What is opportunity cost?

2. What is opportunity benefit?

3. How are opportunity costs and opportunity benefits applied to everyday life?

What Do You Think Now?

Reread *What Do You Think?* in the Section Two Focus. Then answer the following questions:

4. Do you think Maria and Teresa considered the opportunity costs of their choices before they reached decisions?

5. Why do you think Teresa and Maria made different decisions?

6. What would you have decided? Why?

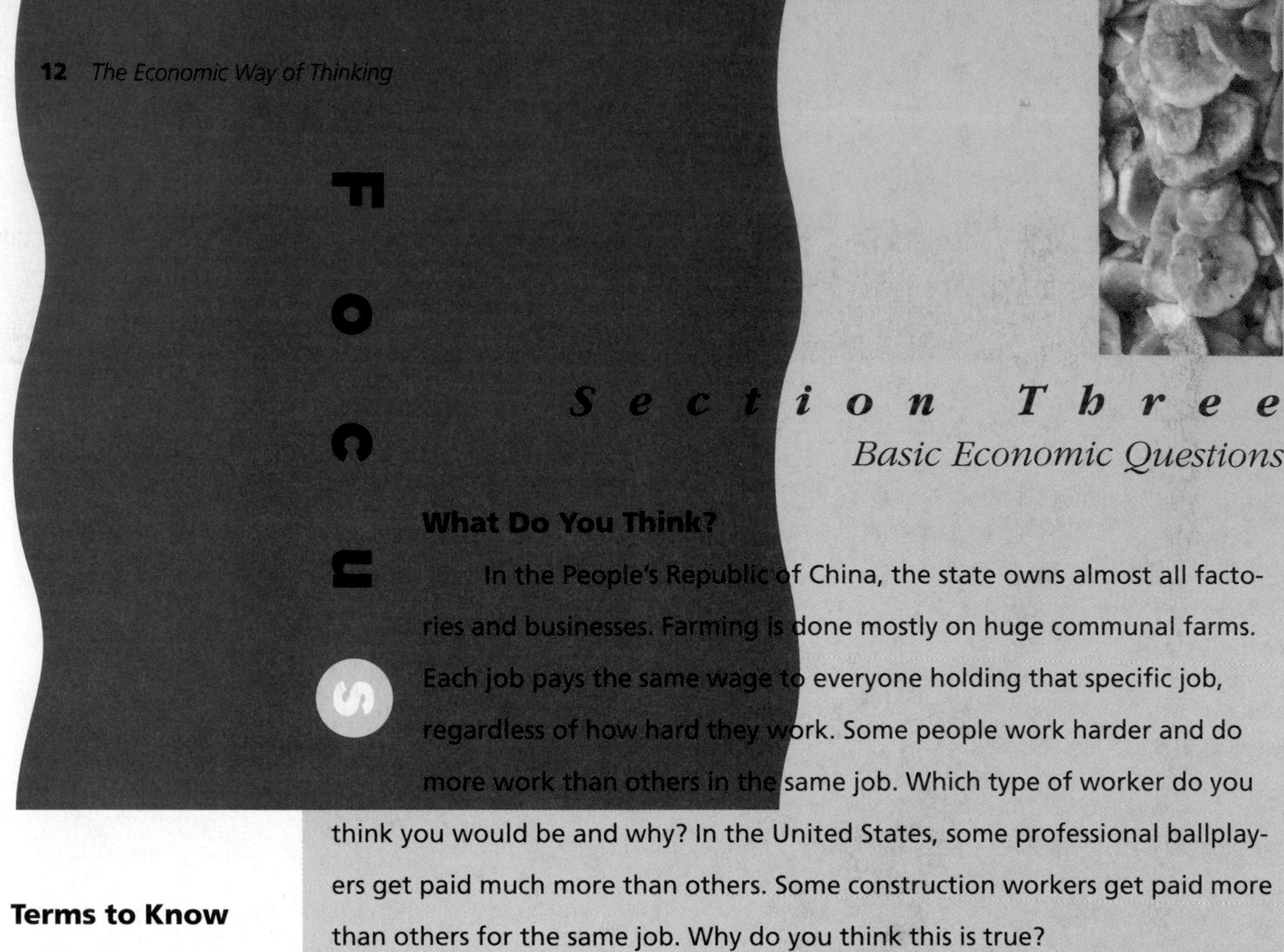

Section Three
Basic Economic Questions

What Do You Think?

In the People's Republic of China, the state owns almost all factories and businesses. Farming is done mostly on huge communal farms. Each job pays the same wage to everyone holding that specific job, regardless of how hard they work. Some people work harder and do more work than others in the same job. Which type of worker do you think you would be and why? In the United States, some professional ballplayers get paid much more than others. Some construction workers get paid more than others for the same job. Why do you think this is true?

Terms to Know

microeconomics

macroeconomics

What's Ahead?

Every society must answer the basic economic questions of what, how, and for whom to produce. These decisions are reached through some combination of individual and social choice. When answering the basic economic questions, societies must balance the needs of individuals with the needs of society as a whole.

INDIVIDUAL AND SOCIAL CHOICES

There are at least two kinds of choices made in a society: individual choices and social choices. First, individuals make choices every day as they try to satisfy their needs with limited resources. Second, society must make social choices to try to satisfy the needs of society as a whole. Some social choices determine how much of society's income is spent on national defense, roads, schools, or cultural affairs for citizens. Individual and social choices play large roles in the functioning of the economy. Economics is divided into two separate branches that deal with these two basic types of choices: microeconomics and macroeconomics.

Individual Choices and Microeconomics

Microeconomics is the branch of economics that examines the choices of individuals concerning one product, one firm, or one industry. It is concerned primarily with individual decision making. The unit of analysis is one person, one product, one firm, or one industry. An example of a microeconomic choice would be how individual beef farmers respond to higher beef prices in the market. Each farmer must decide whether to supply more, less, or the same amount of beef to the market at the new price. Individual consumers of beef must decide whether they wish to buy more, less, or the same amount of beef at the new, higher price. Each individual, both on the buying and selling sides, will make an individual choice.

microeconomics the branch of economics that examines the choices of individuals concerning one product, one firm, or one industry

Social Choices and Macroeconomics

Macroeconomics is the branch of economics that examines the behavior of the whole economy at once. Thus, the unit of analysis is the whole economy.

macroeconomics the branch of economics that examines the behavior of the whole economy at once

Global Economy

SCARCITY WINS THE ARMS RACE

Scarcity, the most basic economic concept, plays many surprising roles in the global economy. For example, in the 1980s under the Reagan administration it was clear that the Soviet Union and the United States were involved in an arms race. Each of the two countries would respond to every new costly weapons system developed by the other country with much larger, frequently more complex, and always more costly weapons systems of its own.

At the same time, the Soviet economy, because of basic economic scarcity, was producing fewer and fewer consumer goods to satisfy the everyday needs of the people. Its resources were going into military production. The command economy of the Soviet Union was much less efficient at producing goods and services in general than were the market economies of other countries. Soviet citizens began to complain bitterly about the lack of consumer goods as their lifestyles declined more each day.

Meanwhile, the Reagan administration announced its Star Wars Defense System or Strategic Defense Initiative. This was the most complex and costly defense system ever conceived. Simultaneously, several other new costly weapons systems were reaching completion in the United States.

These announcements, it is believed, stimulated many huge new costly weapons programs in the Soviet Union that diverted so many resources away from consumer goods into military production that the decline in living standards became unacceptable to the Soviet people. They began to overthrow their communist government and its command economy.

Scarcity is everywhere all the time. It will play an increasingly important role in the global economy of the twenty-first century.

Macroeconomics asks, How much total output is the economy producing? Are the resources of the economy fully employed? How high is the rate of inflation in the economy?

An example of a macroeconomic choice is how the government of a country deals with inflation. The government could cut back its spending, make credit more difficult for consumers to get, and raise taxes to encourage consumers to cut spending. This is a social decision made by government to deal with the macroeconomic issue of inflation.

THREE BASIC ECONOMIC QUESTIONS

Some countries make many more *social* decisions than others because of how their systems of government are designed. Other countries conduct most of their economic affairs through *individual* decision making. Regardless of the relative amounts of social and individual decision making in an economy, all societies use some combination of social and individual decisions to answer three basic economic questions:

1. *What* will be produced with the limited resources?
2. *How* will the goods and services be produced?
3. *For whom* will the goods and services be produced?

What to Produce?

All societies try to produce certain basic goods such as food, clothing, and shelter. The real questions are, How much food? How much clothing? How much shelter? Remember, if more food is produced, there will be an opportunity cost of this additional food. The society must give up some shelter or clothing or something else that is being produced.

The questions get more difficult if the society considers other essentials such as national defense, roads, and schools. If education takes top priority, then perhaps the roads used to get to the schools will not be repaired as often. The society must decide exactly what mix of goods and services to produce. In the United States, this decision is made mostly by the interaction of individual buyers and sellers.

How to Produce?

There are many different ways to produce most goods and services. For instance, a highway can be built with large bulldozers and earth movers. A highway of equal quality can be built with thousands of individual workers using wheelbarrows, picks, and shovels. In the United States, highways are usually constructed with heavy machinery. This does not mean that the use of many laborers and smaller tools is less effective. Decisions about how to produce take into account the resources that are available. A country with a large population and very few machines may decide that the best road building method is *labor intensive;* that is, using many laborers and few machines. In such a country, the opportunity cost of machines is higher than the opportunity cost of labor.

A historical example of this concept occurred in the coal industry. Several decades ago, coal mining in the United States was a relatively low paying profession with many dangers. About 1 million miners worked with picks, shovels, and drills to remove coal from the ground. These coal miners eventually formed unions and demanded higher wages. Thus, it became much cheaper, in many cases, for coal companies to develop and use huge machines, a *capital-intensive* approach, than to hire laborers to mine coal. Today, the coal output of the United States is much greater than it was in the 1940s; yet only half a million workers are employed in mining. Why is coal produced with a capital-intensive process now, when the process used to be labor intensive? Because the opportunity cost of labor (workers) relative to capital (machines) went up.

For Whom to Produce?

Once goods and services are produced, all economies must decide who will use them. Will every citizen get the same quality and amount of goods and services or will there be differences? In the United States, who gets what is decided by consumers and the price system in the market. How individuals choose to spend their income varies according to their personal preferences as well as their income levels. If you can pay the price for a Rolls Royce, you may have one. You also have the option of buying a Ford Taurus or any number of other cars. In the U.S. economy, the question of for whom to produce is primarily an individual choice.

Internet Connection

ECONOMICS ON THE INTERNET

The Internet links more than four million computers in schools, government agencies, and businesses around the world and it's growing everyday. Mainframes, minicomputers, and PCs are connected to small networks connected to even larger networks, making up what we call the Internet.

The economic resources of the Internet include online encyclopedias, studies by economists, economic reports of government agencies, and a wide range of economic statistics. The Clinton administration has adopted a policy of making all government documents, including the text of all bills before Congress, accessible electronically.

The tools of the Internet range from the simple to the powerful. These tools include electronic mail, newsgroups and list serves, file transfer protocol, telnet, gopher, and World Wide Web browsers. There are electronic methods for searching for information, very similar to online catalogs in your local libraries. An additional feature is the ability to communicate easily with anyone connected to the Internet, including the authors of many economic reports and studies. You can use the computer to ask an author a question about his or her work.

You will learn how to use the specific tools of the Internet by completing the applications in each chapter. Here are the first of these applications.

Internet Application: The first step to using the Internet is learning how to connect to a computer on the Internet using a "log-in" procedure. Find out how to log-in to and log-out from the Internet using a user i.d. and password and try it out before the next lesson. If you gain access through a modem, find out the baud rate or speed of the modem. Some high school PCs are automatically connected to an Internet computer via a local area network. If the PCs at your school are like this, you may skip this application.

Economics Application: If the Internet is such a useful tool for education, you might think all schools would have access to it, but many don't. This might be explained by applying the economic principles in Chapter 1. What are the opportunity costs and benefits of having access to the Internet? Use these concepts to explain why some schools do not yet have access.

Other societies allocate goods and services by other means. Some societies provide housing for all workers which, by and large, is identical in design, space, location, and even color. Individuals can't make many choices in this situation. They may choose any housing they desire but only from the location, design, or color that is provided. Here, the social decision to provide identical housing for the whole society takes away much of the individual choice.

Checkpoint

Content Check

1. What are microeconomic choices and macroeconomic choices? Give an example of each.
2. How do social and individual decision making answer each of the three basic economic questions?
3. Why would a company in the United States change from labor-intensive processes to capital-intensive processes?

What Do You Think Now?

Reread *What Do You Think?* in the Section Three Focus. Then answer the following questions:

4. How are decisions about the basic economic questions made in the People's Republic of China?
5. Why do some construction workers in the United States get paid more than others for the same job?
6. Would you want to live and work in the People's Republic of China? Why or why not?

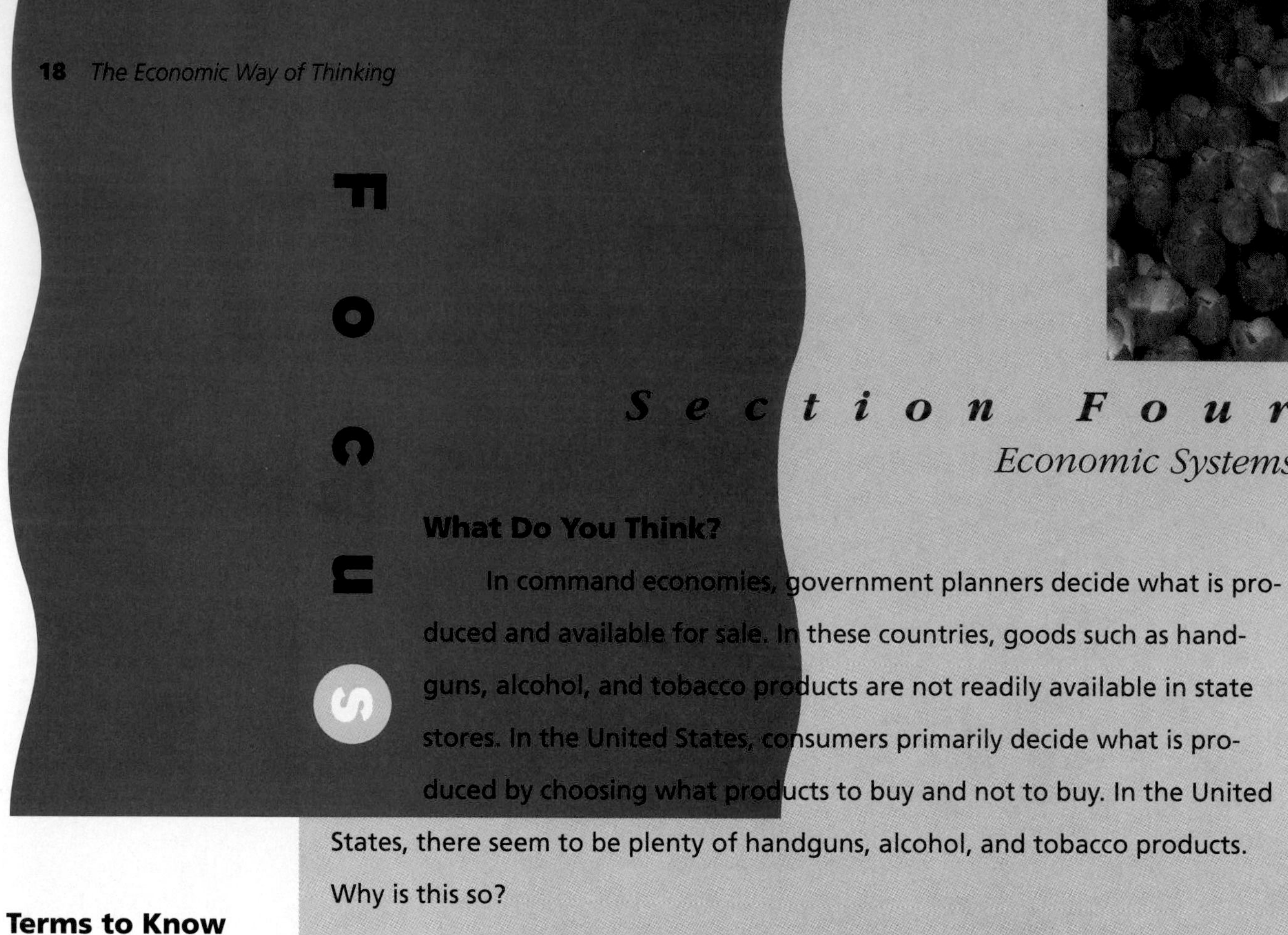

Section Four
Economic Systems

What Do You Think?

In command economies, government planners decide what is produced and available for sale. In these countries, goods such as handguns, alcohol, and tobacco products are not readily available in state stores. In the United States, consumers primarily decide what is produced by choosing what products to buy and not to buy. In the United States, there seem to be plenty of handguns, alcohol, and tobacco products. Why is this so?

Terms to Know

economic system

theory

budget constraint

What's Ahead?

Scarcity and choice exist in all economies. However, societies use different combinations of individual and social choices to allocate resources. That is why traditional, market, command, and mixed economies all answer the three basic economic questions in different ways. Economic theory will help you understand economic systems and the choices they make.

ECONOMIC SYSTEMS ANSWER ECONOMIC QUESTIONS

You have learned that all economies must answer three basic economic questions: what to produce, how to produce, and for whom to produce. The way a society answers these questions determines the kind of economic system it will have. Every society uses a different combination of individual and social choices to answer the economic questions. A society's ***economic system*** is the combination of social and individual decision making it uses to answer the three economic questions.

economic system the combination of social and individual decision making a society uses to answer the three economic questions

There are four basic types of economic systems: traditional economies, market economies, command economies, and mixed economies. These economic systems differ in how the basic economic questions of what, how, and for whom to produce are answered. In traditional economies, the three economic questions are decided mainly by social customs. In market economies, the economic questions are decided mostly by individuals in the marketplace. In command economies, they are decided by government. In mixed economies, they are decided by a combination of market decision making and government order. Many different combinations of these four kinds of economic systems are operating around the world today, with different degrees of success.

Market Economies and Economic Questions

In market economies, the question of what to produce is decided by individual consumers and producers in the marketplace. Consumers, in effect, cast dollar "votes" by spending money in the marketplace. Thus, producers of the products consumers want most are rewarded with profits. Consumers do not buy goods and services that they do not want. Those goods and services do not get as many dollar votes. This tells producers that there are other goods of better quality or lower price that consumers want more. Producers then must respond quickly to consumer desires or lose money and perhaps go out of business.

In market economies, individual producers decide what resources they need and in what amounts. Producers try to use less of the most costly resources and more of the cheapest resources. Individual producers closely monitor their own production processes in an effort to produce the same quality of goods at the least cost. Because producers' profits are the difference between the cost of producing a product and the price consumers will pay for it in the market, each producer has a strong reason to economize, use resources wisely, and buy the right amounts of each resource.

Market economies decide for whom to produce using the price system as well. Usually anyone who can pay the market price of the good gets the good. However, the government makes some decisions about for whom to produce; for example, alcohol and tobacco products cannot be sold legally to those below the legal age. In addition, some goods are only sold to specific legal buyers; for example, some weapons are sold legally only to governments.

Scarcity and Choice Exist in All Economies

Just as individuals make choices because of scarcity, so must economic systems. There simply are not enough of the productive resources to make all of everything everyone wants. For every choice made, there are opportunity costs.

THE IMPORTANCE OF ECONOMIC THEORY

All economic systems are guided in their economic decision making by the use of economic theory. A ***theory*** (also called a *model*) is a simplified description of reality. Theory is not always perfect, however. Sometimes economic decisions do not produce the results that theory might have predicted. Why, then, is it important to understand economic theory?

theory
a simplified description of reality

Economic Theory Simplifies Reality

Earlier, you read about the concept of opportunity cost as applied to buying books or going to the movies. This case used a theoretical tool that

budget constraint
the mix of goods that can be purchased with a limited amount of income

economists call a budget constraint. A ***budget constraint*** is the mix of goods that can be purchased, given a limited amount of income. The budget constraint in the earlier example was that you had $30 to spend on two goods: books and movies.

In reality, an individual can and usually does choose among many goods. Why, then, do we use simplified theoretical tools such as budget constraints? Can they tell us anything about the real economic world? The answer is a definite yes! Remember, theory is merely a simplified description of reality.

To describe reality in detail would be an endless task. If you tried to consider every thought an individual has in making choices about all goods and services, there would be no end to the process. The description would be so complicated that you could not draw any meaningful conclusions from it.

Theory, on the other hand, is like a road map. A road map is a guide to be used for a specific purpose. It does not show every street or even every small town. Trees, rocks, mountains, and fields are not generally part of the road map because they do not affect the decisions of a driver. A road map is helpful to a driver because it simplifies reality.

A hiker, on the other hand, would benefit more from a relief map showing mountains, fields, streams, and landmarks. This kind of map simplifies reality for the purposes of a hiker. Streets are not much help to the hiker and are, therefore, unnecessary information. A theory must include only the useful data. In simplifying reality, it is important to develop the right theory for the problem to be solved.

Economic theory is very much like the map example. To study how individuals make decisions (microeconomic theory), we may need a different theory from the one we use to study how whole societies make decisions

Econ & You

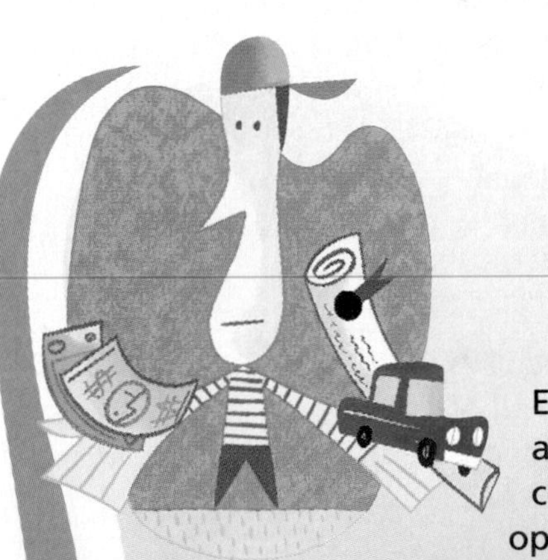

A PERMANENT PAIR

Economics is about scarcity, choice, and opportunity cost, and it touches your life every day in many ways. If you study for your math test for two hours, you cannot at the same time study for your English test. There is a scarcity of time. You must allocate the available time among your competing needs, including study time, leisure, sleeping, eating, and exercising. In the same way, you also must choose how to allocate your limited income among your unlimited wants and needs.

Choosing a career also involves tradeoffs. If you decide to be an economist, you cannot at the same time work as an airline pilot. If and when you choose to marry, you will bear the opportunity cost of not being able to spend time with and enjoy other potential spouses.

You will always be subject to scarcity of some type, and the choices you make will all have an opportunity cost. Econ and you are a permanent pair.

(macroeconomic theory). The theory we use to understand problems such as inflation and unemployment differs from the theory we use to understand gasoline prices. Before we simplify our description of reality, we must know what we are trying to describe.

With the budget constraint for books and movies, we were trying to simplify the process that individuals use in making informed choices between two alternatives. We *assumed* that there were only two choices. This assumption told us under what conditions our theory was valid. We could have used much more complicated theories and not needed this assumption. However, the concept of opportunity cost might not have been as clear.

Economic Theory Is Relevant

As you go through life, you will make economic decisions as a consumer, as a worker, and as a citizen. An understanding of economic theory will be relevant to your everyday life. It will help you to make the most informed decisions possible on every economic issue you will face.

Look for the relevance in every economic theory you learn in this book. Ask yourself how and under what conditions each concept applies. As you do this, you will train your mind in the economic way of thinking.

Checkpoint

Content Check

1. Compare the four basic types of economic systems.
2. How do market economies answer the three basic economic questions?
3. Why is it important to understand economic theory?
4. Why are different economic theories needed to make microeconomic and macroeconomic decisions?

What Do You Think Now?

Reread *What Do You Think?* in the Section Four Focus. Then answer the following questions:

5. How does scarcity affect decisions made in command economies regarding consumer products, such as handguns, alcohol, or tobacco?
6. Do command economies and market economies often make different decisions about allocating limited resources? Why or why not?

Concepts in Brief

1. An understanding of economics is important to your everyday life. Economics helps you make more informed decisions as a consumer, worker, and citizen.
2. Economics is a social science concerned with the basic economic problem of scarcity. Scarcity arises because limited resources are available to satisfy unlimited wants and needs. Because of scarcity, choices must be made to allocate limited resources among unlimited wants and needs.
3. With every decision, there is an opportunity cost and an opportunity benefit. The opportunity cost is the value of the alternative that is not chosen. The opportunity benefit is what is gained by choosing an alternative.
4. Economics is divided into two major types of theory. Microeconomics is concerned with the individual producing or consuming units and generally involves individual decisions. Macroeconomics is concerned with the economy as a whole and generally examines social economic decisions.
5. All economies must answer the three basic economic questions of what to produce, how to produce, and for whom to produce.
6. Countries and their economic systems use a variety of approaches to answer the basic economic questions. Command economies are ruled by social decisions, while market economies operate mostly by individual decisions.
7. Economic theory is a broad description that simplifies reality. Economic theory is not precise in all situations. It is, however, extremely useful and relevant when correctly applied.

Economic Foundations

1. What is the basic economic problem?
2. Why does scarcity occur in a society?
3. What is the solution to the basic economic problem?
4. What is the opportunity cost of asking for a day off from work to attend your cousin's wedding? What is the opportunity benefit?
5. Name the two kinds of choices that societies must make and give an example of each.
6. What are the three basic economic questions?

7. In the United States today, why is coal produced by a capital-intensive process instead of a labor-intensive process?

8. How are the basic economic questions answered in a command economy? How are they answered in a market economy?

Your Economic Vocabulary

Build your economic vocabulary by matching the following terms with their definitions.

1. the social science that deals with how society allocates its scarce resources among its unlimited wants and needs
2. the branch of economics that examines the behavior of the whole economy at once
3. the value of any alternative that you must give up when you make a choice
4. a simplified description of reality
5. the human characteristic of never having all wants and needs satisfied
6. the mix of goods that can be purchased with a limited amount of income
7. the branch of economics that examines the choices of individuals concerning one product, one firm, or one industry
8. the process of choosing which needs will be satisfied and how much of our resources we will use to satisfy them
9. the condition of there not being enough resources to fulfill all wants and needs
10. what is gained by making a particular choice
11. the combination of social and individual decision making a society uses to answer the three economic questions
12. the condition that occurs because people's wants and needs are unlimited, while the resources needed to produce goods and services to meet these wants and needs are limited

allocation
budget constraint
economics
economic system
limited resources
macroeconomics
microeconomics
opportunity benefit
opportunity cost
scarcity
theory
unlimited wants and needs

Thinking Critically About Economics

1. If you had to choose between going swimming or raking your neighbor's lawn for $10, which two economic concepts would enter into your decision? What would you decide and why? If the opportunity to swim were lost, but the offer from the neighbor remained, would your decision change?
2. If you had an income of $1 million a year, would you escape the basic economic problem of scarcity? If so, how? If not, why not?
3. If you were a highly skilled brain surgeon and your brother or sister were a school teacher, which of you would have the larger opportunity cost if drafted into the army? Why? Can opportunity cost be measured only in terms of money?
4. Would you rather live in a country that makes most of its decisions socially or one in which individuals make most of the decisions? In which of these countries would there be more freedom of choice?
5. Candidates for political office often speak of what their administration will give voters if they are elected. Candidate *A* promises more roads, new schools, more public parks, and new fire trucks. From what you have learned in this chapter about scarcity, choices, and cost, what are the obvious questions for you to ask Candidate *A?*
6. Can you develop a simple theory about how much water people drink in the summer relative to how much they drink in the winter? Will your theory always be correct for all people? If not, is your theory worthless in describing human behavior? Is your theory more effective than trying to observe how much water each person drinks in each season? Why or why not?

Economic Enrichment

Read the first section of your local newspaper each day for one week and cut out all the articles that relate directly to economics. You will be surprised at how many there are. Make a collage on poster board with the articles you find. Attach a brief report that contains the following:

1. a list of some of the most frequently discussed economic topics;
2. a summary of an article that you would not have thought was related to economics before you read this chapter; and
3. a paragraph giving your opinion on whether or not the economic way of thinking can be applied to almost any issue.

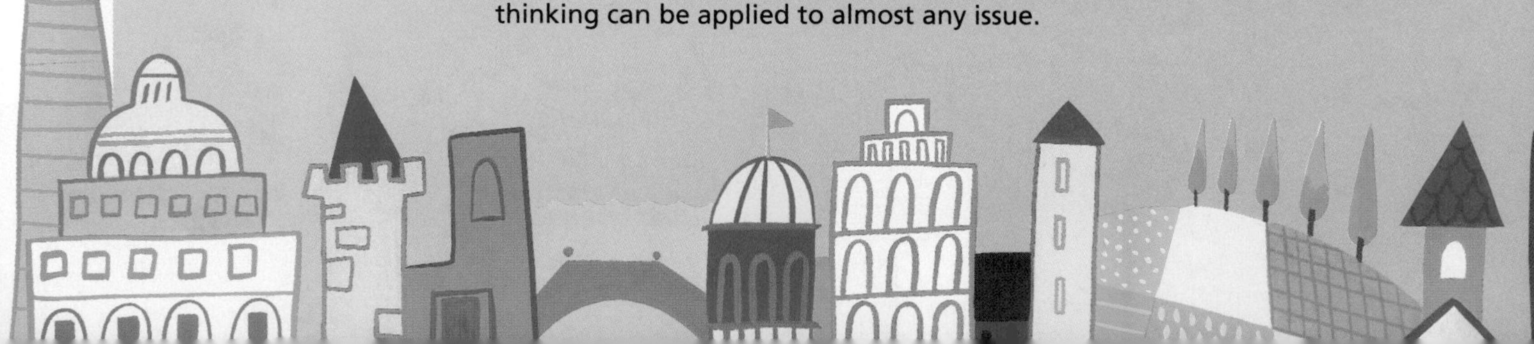

Math and Economics

Assume you have a budget constraint of $90 to spend on new shorts and shirts for the summer. To keep things simple, in this situation shorts cost $10 and shirts cost $15. On a separate sheet of paper, complete the following table to show how many shorts you could buy if you spent all of your money on shorts and how many shirts you could buy if you spent all of your money on shirts.

Shorts You Can Buy	Price	Total Cost	Your Total Income	Income Left Over
1	$10	$10	$90	$80
2	$10	$	$90	$
3	$10	$	$90	$
4	$10	$	$90	$
5	$10	$	$90	$
6	$10	$	$90	$
7	$10	$	$90	$
8	$10	$	$90	$
9	$10	$	$90	$

Shirts You Can Buy	Price	Total Cost	Your Total Income	Income Left Over
1	$15	$15	$90	$75
2	$15	$	$90	$
3	$15	$	$90	$
4	$15	$	$90	$
5	$15	$	$90	$
6	$15	$	$90	$

Before you go shopping, you think you would like to buy three pairs of shorts and four shirts. This is your first choice, Choice *1*. However, when you get to the store, you see six pairs of shorts you really like, leaving only enough money for two shirts. This is Choice *2*. Work through the following tasks to help you decide between Choice *1* and Choice *2*.

1. Sketch a graph that illustrates the many ways you can spend your $90 on shorts and shirts. (See Figure 1-2 for an example of this type of graph.)
2. Use your graph to help calculate the opportunity cost of changing your mind at the store and moving from Choice *1* to Choice *2*.
3. Use your graph to help calculate the opportunity benefit of changing your mind at the store and moving from Choice *1* to Choice *2*.
4. What choice would you make?

Writing About Economics

You are a market analyst for Shelby Oil. Shelby is considering your town as a location for a new gas station. Your job is to analyze your town with regard to current gas station locations and write a memo to the marketing manager, Victor Pumba, summarizing your results.

First, observe and record the prices in your town for regular unleaded gasoline at ten different locations. Are all of the prices the same? Why or why not? Are the prices at locations that are near each other fairly similar?

In your memo to Victor Pumba, present in a table the prices at different locations. Then discuss what role location and transportation costs might play in setting gasoline prices. Include information about the impact of opportunity costs on purchasers' decisions about where to buy gasoline.

Goals 2000: Educate America

Over the last two decades, family incomes have either grown very slowly or actually declined at all income levels. This discouraging picture emerges no matter what statistical measure of compensation or inflation you use. Average real compensation, which is compensation after the effect of inflation is taken out, grew by 3 percent per year between 1948 and 1973. However, it has only grown by seven-tenths of 1 percent per year between 1973 and 1993. To put this into perspective, consider this: If real compensation had grown at the same rate between 1973 and 1993 as it did from 1948 to 1973, the average compensation of a full-time worker in the United States in 1993 would have been $62,400 instead of $40,000.

What growth there has been has not been shared by all Americans. Many studies have shown that workers with more education earn substantially higher wages than those with the same age, experience, race, and gender characteristics who have less education. The average real wage of male high school graduates fell 20 percent from 1973 to 1993. The decline was even steeper for male high school dropouts, whose average real wage fell 27 percent over the same period. The average hourly wage for males with college degrees but no further education fell by 9 percent from 1973 to 1993. Finally, hourly wages of those with college degrees and two or more years of additional education fell by only 2 percent.

In 1994, the federal government enacted *Goals 2000: Educate America. Goals 2000* identifies eight ambitious national education goals to be achieved by the end of the decade:

1. **School readiness.** All children will start school ready to learn.
2. **Improved student achievement.** All students will demonstrate competence in challenging subject matter in core academic subjects.
3. **Best in math and science.** U.S. students will be first in the world in mathematics and science achievement.
4. **Safe, disciplined, and drug-free schools.** Every school will be free from violence, disruptive behavior, and illegal drugs.
5. **Increased graduation rate.** The high school graduation rate will improve to at least 90 percent.
6. **Teacher education and professional development.** All teachers will have the opportunity to acquire the knowledge and skills needed to prepare their students for the next century.
7. **Parental involvement.** Every school will promote parent-teacher partnerships that will increase parents' involvement in the social and academic enrichment of their children.
8. **Adult literacy and lifelong learning.** Every adult will be literate and possess the skills necessary to compete in a global economy.

These goals establish a framework for a lifetime of continuous learning. The hope is that, with these goals and the social choices made in order to effectively and efficiently achieve such goals, Americans will engage in lifelong learning, which ultimately should help rebuild the American dream that working hard and playing by the rules will lead to a higher standard of living.

SOURCE: *Economic Report of the President* (Washington, D.C.: U.S. Government Printing Office, 1995), 172, 174, 184–85.

Overview

Section One
Individual Choice

Section Two
The Decision-Making Model

Section Three
Maximizing Utility

Making Individual Decisions

Learning Objectives

2-1

Explain how economic incentives guide individual decisions in a market economy.

2-2

Discuss how individual self-interest results in decisions that are in the best interest of society.

2-3

Describe how the decision-making model provides a logical approach to problem solving.

2-4

Apply the five-step decision-making model.

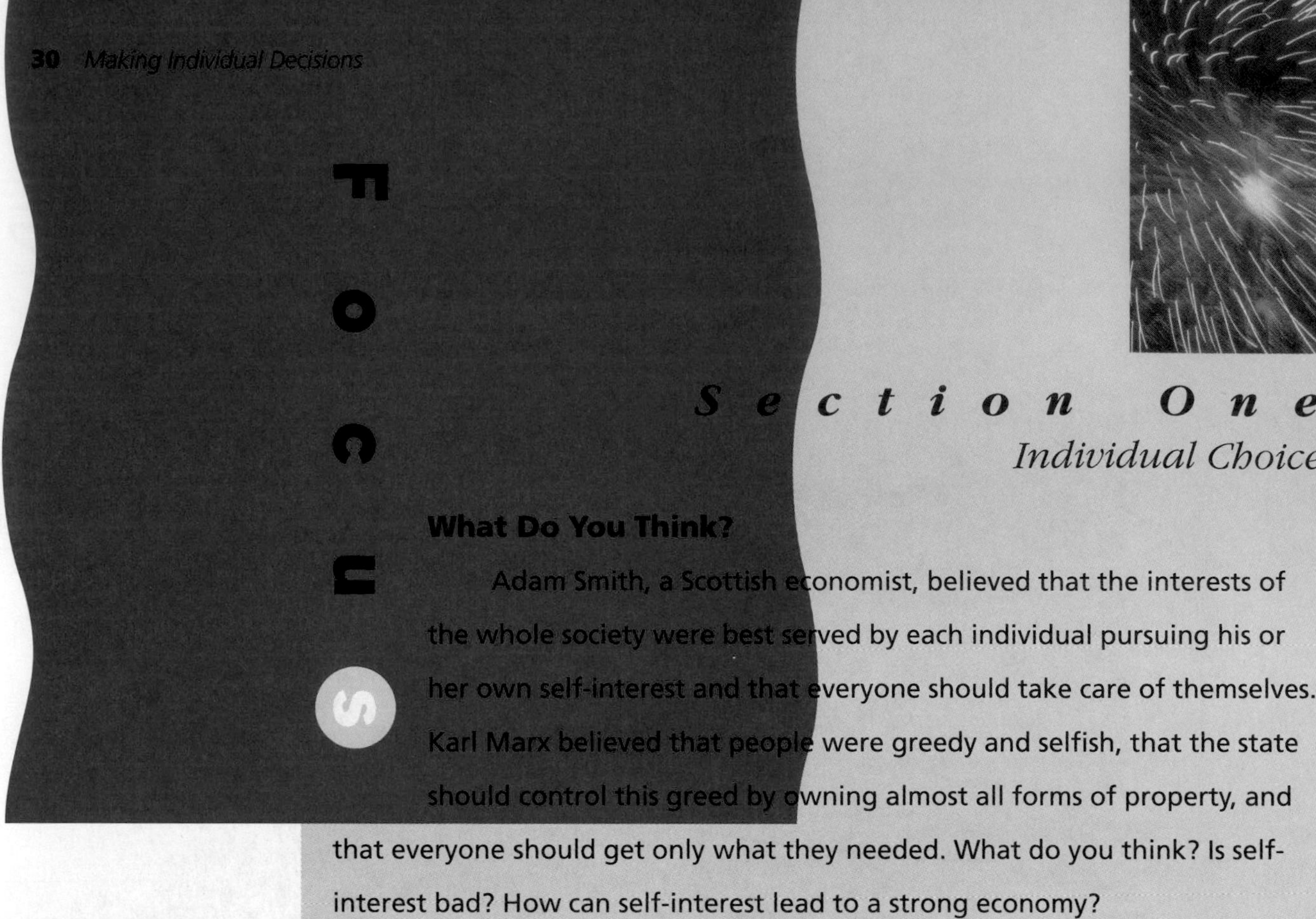

Section One
Individual Choice

What Do You Think?

Adam Smith, a Scottish economist, believed that the interests of the whole society were best served by each individual pursuing his or her own self-interest and that everyone should take care of themselves. Karl Marx believed that people were greedy and selfish, that the state should control this greed by owning almost all forms of property, and that everyone should get only what they needed. What do you think? Is self-interest bad? How can self-interest lead to a strong economy?

Terms to Know

- individual choice
- market economy
- economic incentive
- psychic income
- economic profit
- invisible hand

What's Ahead?

The economic questions of what, how, and for whom to produce are answered by individual choice in a market economy. Individual choice is guided by self-interest and the goal of gaining economic incentives. Individuals must consider the costs and benefits of each choice before making a decision. When individuals directly benefit from their decisions, the whole society benefits. Adam Smith described this effect as the *invisible hand.*

INDIVIDUAL DECISIONS AND THE MARKET ECONOMY

Economics is a science of choices because of scarcity. The economic questions of what, how, and for whom to produce must be answered in every society. Some economies rely mainly on individual choice to answer these economic questions. ***Individual choice*** means decisions are made by people acting separately from one another. To make intelligent choices, individuals must carefully consider the costs and benefits of each choice.

individual choice decisions made by people acting separately

market economy an economy in which the economic questions are decided mostly by individuals in the marketplace

Economic Incentives

An economy in which the economic questions are decided mostly by individuals in the marketplace is called a ***market economy.*** *Capitalist economy* is another name for a market economy. The U.S. economy is an example of a market, or capitalist, economy.

People's actions in a market economy result from their motives or incentives for personal gain. ***Economic incentive*** is the increase in personal satisfaction that may result from some economic activity. This increase in satisfaction may be the result of having more money income; for example, fixing an old bike and selling it for $30. However, money is not the only economic incentive.

economic incentive
the increase in personal satisfaction that may result from some economic activity

Psychic income is the nonmonetary reward we get from taking some action. For example, you may feel a sense of pride from knowing that a child now has a safe bike to ride. You are happier because of that pride and so have some personal gain. The economic incentive of psychic income is very important in determining how economic questions are answered in a market economy.

psychic income
the nonmonetary reward we get from taking some action

Economic Questions

In a market economy, *what to produce* is decided by consumers voting in the marketplace with their dollars. If many individual consumers decide to

Economic Spotlight

WHERE ARE YOU GOING?

Would you like to become the first . . . ? Barbara Brandon, the first nationally syndicated African-American female cartoonist, is stunned that even in the 1990s she still could "become the first black something."

Following in the footsteps of her cartoonist father who created the strip "Luther," about the life of an inner-city child, Brandon knew early on that she wanted to be a cartoonist. As a child, she helped her father by coloring in silhouettes and drawing borders for his strips. Her comic strip was picked up by Universal Press Syndicate in 1991 and now runs in more than 400 newspapers across the country.

Her weekly comic strip "Where I'm Coming From" illustrates difficult life choices that young adults face about relationships, parenthood, and human rights. Brandon takes these difficult choices and, in a lighthearted way, shows the decision-making process that her characters use. Only her characters' heads and arms appear in her strip because she does not want to focus on physical appearances. Brandon wants her readers to learn to look hard at people's faces and gaze into their eyes, so they'll think more about what the person is saying rather than what the person looks like.

Her strip features a range of female characters—from socially conscious to self-absorbed to man obsessed—who shatter many common stereotypes about women. Her main character, Lekesia, is an active, sassy, street-smart African-American woman who battles oppression of all kinds.

Brandon believes that her strip will help people understand themselves better. The artist says she would like, years from now, for "people to read these strips and see what they were going through." So, would you like to become the first . . . ? The choice is up to you.

buy a good or service, the product succeeds in the market. When a product succeeds, its producers earn money and so they have an incentive to provide more of those products consumers want.

However, if many consumers individually choose not to buy a product, the product fails in the market. The producer then faces loss and individually chooses not to produce the item and the product disappears from the market. This process of individual choice by consumers and producers in a marketplace thus determines what will be produced.

How to produce is also decided by individual choice in a market economy. Assume that you are an individual producer in a highly competitive industry such as wheat production. The market price for wheat might be $3.50 a bushel. How will you produce the wheat so that you can make a profit? There are many ways to grow wheat. For instance, you can employ hundreds of farm workers who use hand tools or you can employ fewer workers and more machinery (tractors). How will you choose between these two methods? You will choose the one that produces the greatest amount of wheat at the lowest cost.

It might take 100 hours of plowing with a tractor to cultivate the crop. The tractor might cost $75 an hour to rent and operate. Your cost of plowing with the tractor would then be $7,500. You could do the same amount of plowing in 100 hours with 100 workers each of whom earns $3.25 an hour. Then your plowing cost would be $32,500 (100 hours × 100 workers × $3.25 an hour = $32,500). You would probably choose the method that costs less—using the tractor.

Hundreds of other production decisions will be made the same way. You, as an individual producer, will choose as effectively as you can with the best information you can find. Your incentive will be personal gain. You will want to maximize your income from the production of your product.

For whom to produce also is answered in a market economy by individual choice. Anyone who has enough money can buy any product. Producers will make their products for the people who will be able to buy them.

BENEFITS OF INDIVIDUAL CHOICE

It is important to understand the issues of individual choice and personal gain in order to understand market economies. During the past 50 years, U.S. capitalism has produced a standard of living that is unparalleled. One reason for this high standard of living is that individuals in a market economy directly benefit from their decisions, so their decisions are guided by self-interest. Self-interest is a strong incentive. In other economies, individuals do not necessarily benefit from their own decisions.

Self-Interest

economic profit the difference between the money you obtain from selling a product and the cost of producing the product

In a market economy, if you do not seek out the correct information—and therefore choose poorly—your costs will rise and your profits will decline. ***Economic profit*** is the difference between the money you obtain from selling a product and the cost of producing the product. For example, in the production of wheat, you might have chosen to use laborers instead of a tractor.

Your profits would have been $25,000 more if you had chosen the tractor. You will pay a price in a market economy for choosing poorly.

The power of self-interest cannot be overstated. It is the driving force behind market economies. Self-interest is not merely an advantage to individuals. It is what makes individual choice influence the marketplace. Many economists believe that self-motivated individual choice does the greatest good for society as a whole.

invisible hand
the incentive that guides individuals to choose in the best interest of society by pursuing their own self-interests

The Invisible Hand

When the producer and the consumer meet in the marketplace, they pursue their own self-interests. The producer wants to maximize profits and the consumer wants to minimize costs. The bargain that is struck must benefit both producer and consumer, or they would have no reason to trade or exchange. The incentive that guides individuals to choose in the best interest of society by pursuing their own self-interests is called the ***invisible hand.*** This role of self-interest is best explained in Adam Smith's description of the invisible hand more than 200 years ago:

> An individual neither intends to promote the public interest, nor knows he is promoting it. . . . He intends only his own gain, and he is led by an invisible hand to promote an end which was no part of his intention. . . . It

Global Economy

INDIVIDUALS ARE INTERDEPENDENT

The growing emphasis on global economics comes from the fact that the world's economies are becoming much more interdependent than in the past. World trade is a very important part of the economics of almost all countries now, and the information age is speeding up communication, transportation, specialization, trade, and exchange.

Many decisions made by individuals every day are a part of this global economy. For example, the gasoline for your trip to school, the automobile itself, the TV carrying the morning news, the clothing you are wearing, and the computer game you may play this afternoon all might have been produced in other countries. Your individual decision to use them has direct effects on the foreign producers of those goods and on the livelihood of the employees who work for them.

U.S. investors can now buy and sell shares of stock in foreign companies by phone daily. The same is true of citizens in other countries. They can and do buy U.S. products and invest in U.S. companies, and their individual choices affect the U.S. economy every day.

The world is moving toward a global economy, and the individual choices you make are a part of it. In the future, there will be increased demand for professionals in international business.

is not from the benevolence of the butcher, the brewer, or the baker that we expect our dinner, but from their regard to their self-interest. We address ourselves not to their humanity, but to their self-love and never talk to them of our necessities, but of their advantages.[1]

Individual Incentives and Social Choice

Social choice can reduce the incentive of direct self-interest and therefore, at times, discourage individual productive efforts. Consider the case of wheat production again. This time, however, assume that the government decides workers must work eight hours each day and everyone must be paid equally. What if you, a worker on this farm, work very hard, put in extra hours, and spend your off hours thinking of ways to improve output? As a result of your efforts, the farm increases output by 1,000 bushels. You, however, continue to receive the same pay and rewards as your coworkers who do not try to produce as much. You would have little or no economic incentive to produce more than your coworkers.

The government's decision that the whole society should benefit from the farm equally fails to reward the value of any individual decisions you might make. It is highly likely that you will choose in your own self-interest not to work extra hard to improve. You will still enjoy the same benefits as your coworkers. From the standpoint of productivity, social decisions are generally not as effective as individual decisions.

C h e c k  o i n t

Content Check

1. In a market economy, how do individual choices affect the economic questions of what to produce and how to produce?
2. How does individual self-interest influence the marketplace?
3. How are individuals affected by social choices?

What Do You Think Now?

Reread *What Do You Think?* in the Section One Focus. Then answer the following questions:

4. Do you think Adam Smith's belief that self-interest benefits all of society makes sense in today's economy? Why or why not?
5. Can a government that owns almost all of the economic resources in a country provide economic incentives to workers? If so, how? If not, why not?

[1]Adam Smith, *An Inquiry into the Nature and Causes of the Wealth of Nations*, Edwin Cannan, ed. (Chicago: University of Chicago Press, 1976), 18.

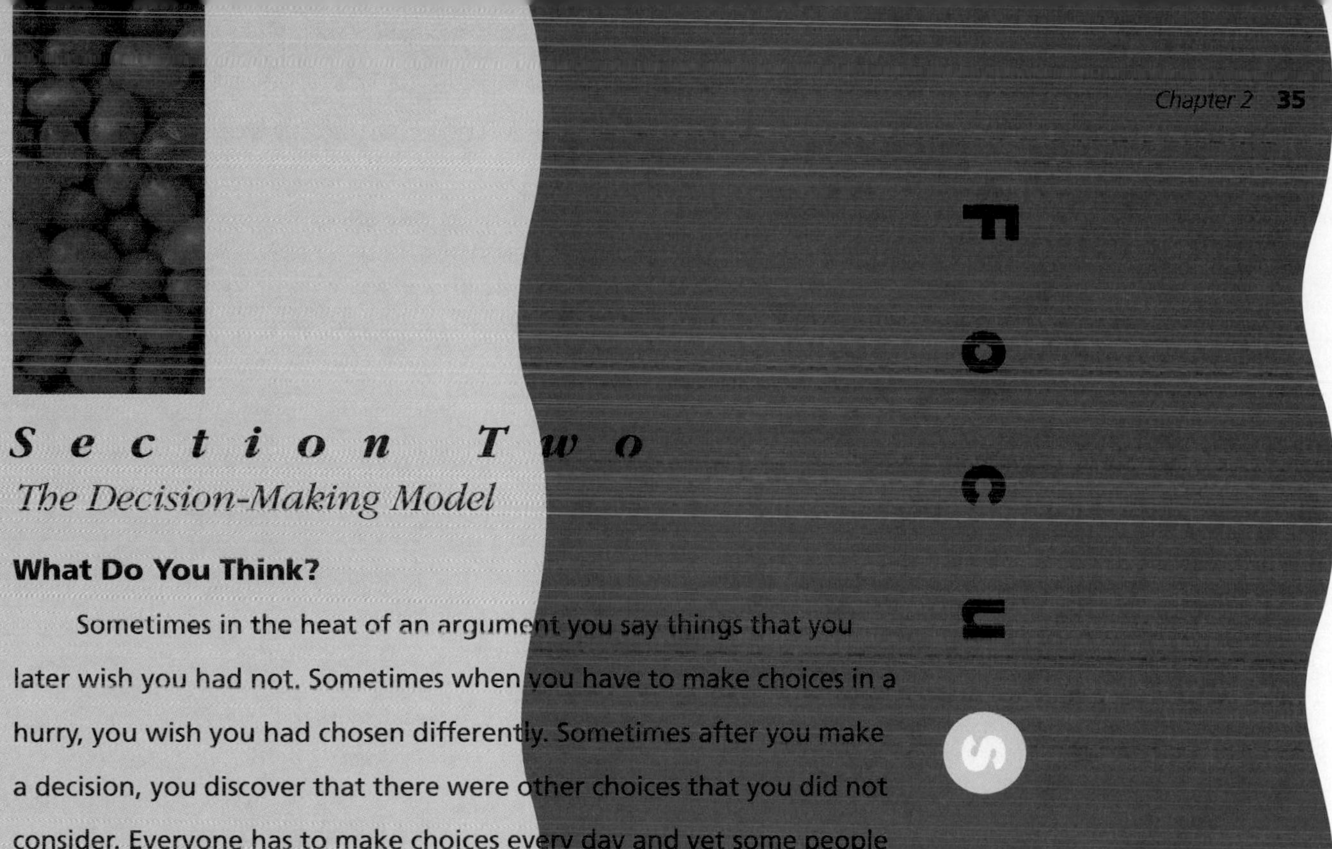

Section Two
The Decision-Making Model

What Do You Think?

Sometimes in the heat of an argument you say things that you later wish you had not. Sometimes when you have to make choices in a hurry, you wish you had chosen differently. Sometimes after you make a decision, you discover that there were other choices that you did not consider. Everyone has to make choices every day and yet some people seem to make better choices than others most of the time. All of these problems revolve around the choice process. What can economics teach you about how to make better choices?

What's Ahead?

Making good decisions increases your satisfaction and the satisfaction of others. Individual decisions are improved with a five-step decision-making model. A clear definition of the problem, well-thought-out alternatives, appropriate criteria, and a careful evaluation process will result in better decisions.

Terms to Know

model
objectivity
alternative
criteria
decision matrix

INDIVIDUAL DECISION-MAKING MODEL

As both consumers and producers of goods and services, your individual or personal decisions affect your own satisfaction as well as the satisfaction of others. Making a correct decision the first time around is always better than trying to correct a poor decision once it has been made. A logical, well-reasoned approach to individual or personal problem solving involves five steps:

1. define the problem;
2. list the alternatives from which you must choose;
3. list the criteria by which you must evaluate the alternatives;
4. evaluate the alternatives based on the criteria you have chosen; and
5. choose the alternative that best meets the criteria you have chosen.

model
a simplified form of reality that shows the relationship between different factors

These five steps make up the decision-making model. A ***model*** is a simplified form of reality that shows the relationship between different factors. For example, a model airplane shows you what a real airplane looks like but does not show every detail. A model decision-making process shows you the general idea of how to go about making well-informed decisions. However, it does not show you every specific detail you have to consider in making a decision.

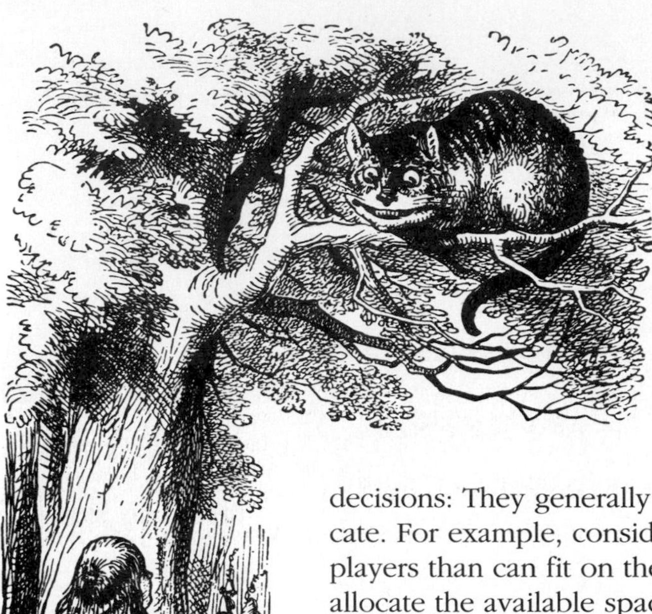

Step 1—Define the Problem

In Lewis Carroll's *Alice's Adventures in Wonderland,* the Cheshire Cat tells Alice: "If you don't know where you are going, any road will take you there."

Individual decision making is often clouded by emotion and misinformation. Instead of plotting a straight path to solve a problem, individuals might take *any road* and hope it is the right one. But *any road* might lead to the wrong solution! Therefore, the first step is to define exactly what the problem is.

Economic decisions are similar to many other decisions: They generally start as a problem of scarcity or the need to allocate. For example, consider the problem of a football team that has more players than can fit on the team bus. This problem can be defined as how to allocate the available spaces to team members. The problem is deciding who will travel and who will not.

As another example, consider the following economic allocation problem. You have just received a tax refund check for $350. You have many uses for this money, but you want to make the best decision about how to use it. The problem can be defined as follows: "How can this income of $350 best be allocated to fulfill my needs?"

objectivity
ruling out aspects of a problem that seem important only because of your strong emotions about them

Be Objective. ***Objectivity*** means ruling out aspects of a problem that seem important only because of your strong emotions about them. In defining the problem, you should be as objective as possible. You should weigh each aspect of the problem in regard to the role it plays. Return to the case of the football team and the bus. What is the real problem here? Is the bus too small? Or is the team too large? The third-string guard may feel that the bus is too small. The starting quarterback, however, may feel that the team is too large.

Both of these problem definitions are affected by the emotions involved with how sure an individual player is of getting a seat on the bus. When the star quarterback's throwing hand gets broken, the quarterback's definition of the problem might change. The quarterback would not be so sure of getting a seat on the bus and might agree that the bus is too small.

Focus on the Issue. After ruling out emotional involvements, you must focus your thoughts on the true issue. For example, individuals without emotional involvement in the problem of the football team's bus will view the issue differently. The school principal may feel that the team is too large. The coach, however, may argue that the team needs to carry as many players as possible in order to train young talent. The problem should be defined objectively and clearly. Buses are limited in size, and most teams usually have more players than seats. The problem definition then becomes how to allocate the limited seats among the players.

Step 2—List the Alternatives

An ***alternative*** is a possible course of action. Once the problem has been defined, the next step in the personal decision-making model is to list the alternatives.

alternative
a possible course of action

Let's take another look at the tax refund problem: "How can this income of $350 best be allocated to fulfill my needs?" To solve the problem, you should make a list of the alternate uses for this income. Remember that your alternate solutions are limited by the amount of the tax refund: $350.

Limit Your Alternatives. There are many ways to use $350. You could consider every item in the world before making your choice. However, that would take more time and effort than you are willing to spend. So, you must list a reasonably small number of alternatives from which to choose.

Economic Dilemma

WORK OR COLLEGE?

One of the first major dilemmas faced by high school students is the choice between taking a job as soon as they graduate or going on to college. College is very expensive; you have to pay for tuition, books, and fees. Attending college for four years or more usually means giving up earnings from a full-time job during that period as well. In other words, the opportunity cost of college can frequently be greater than the financial cost.

With that in mind, it is even more important to consider this decision using the five-step choice process. The alternatives might be immediate full-time college and no work, part-time college with full-time work, or some combination of these. Weighing the opportunity costs and benefits of each alternative will clearly lead to better decisions.

Expect this type of dilemma to come up many times in your life, such as when you graduate from college. There will be decisions about graduate school, marriage, and family. All of these decisions are dealt with best by using the five-step decision process. Better process yields better decisions.

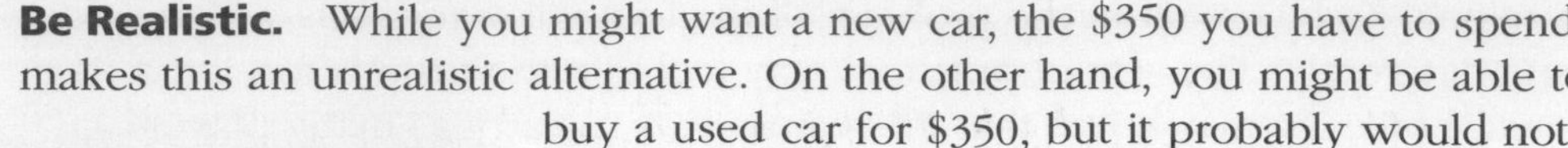

Be Realistic. While you might want a new car, the $350 you have to spend makes this an unrealistic alternative. On the other hand, you might be able to buy a used car for $350, but it probably would not be dependable. Step 2 requires you to list realistic alternatives.

Let's assume that you consider the following four items to be your most important choices:

1. a new CD player;
2. a one-week vacation to Florida during spring break;
3. a new electronic keyboard; and
4. a new 18-speed bike.

Step 3—List the Criteria Used to Evaluate Your Alternatives

Now that you have defined the problem and listed your alternatives, you need some way to evaluate the alternatives. The characteristics that you will use to judge a group of alternatives are called ***criteria.***

criteria
the characteristics of a group of alternatives that will be judged to make a choice

Ask yourself the following questions: "Given these alternatives, on what criteria should I base my choice?" Should I consider cost, usefulness, product life, or some other aspect of the product? The answers will vary from person to person, but you should select your criteria objectively and realistically.

Let's assume that the important criteria in this case include the following:

1. *Durability*—how long the goods or services will last;
2. *Acceptability to authority figures*—how parents, police, school authorities, and others will accept your choice (another way of looking at this criterion is to think about how a given choice will affect your relationship with others);
3. *Related expenses*—The costs of other items that will be needed to enjoy each alternative, such as compact discs, keyboard lessons, or a bike helmet; and
4. *Salvage or trade-in value*—The value, if any, of the alternative when you are finished with it.

Having chosen your criteria, you may also want to rank them in order of importance. For example, you might feel that product durability is more important to you than acceptability to parents because you will be moving into a college dorm soon. However, if you are living at home and working your way through college, other expenses might be the most important criterion.

Step 4—Evaluate the Alternatives

You have now defined the problem, listed the alternatives, and selected some criteria. The next step involves evaluating each alternative using the criteria. To do this, set up a table of alternatives and criteria, such as the one in Figure 2-1. This is sometimes called a decision matrix. A ***decision matrix*** is a table comparing possible decisions.

decision matrix
a table comparing possible decisions

	Alternatives: CD Player	Florida Vacation	Electronic Keyboard	18-Speed Bike
Criteria				
Durability and Product Life	Ten years or more — 4 points	One week; memories good or bad, one lifetime — 2 points	Two years — 2 points	Eight years — 3 points
Acceptability to Authority Figures	Somewhat acceptable — 3 points	Not acceptable — 1 point	Acceptable with volume control — 3 points	Very acceptable — 4 points
Related Expenses	Moderate and flexible; new CDs — 2 points	Some, but flexible; entertainment, shopping, etc. — 3 points	High; lessons, music, electricity — 1 point	Low; bike helmet — 4 points
Salvage or Trade-in Value	Moderate — 3 points	None — 1 point	Low — 2 points	Moderate — 3 points
Final Score and Rank of Alternative	12 points 2nd choice	7 points 4th choice	8 points 3rd choice	14 points 1st choice

Figure 2-1

A Decision Matrix

The four alternatives are listed at the top of the last four columns. The four criteria for evaluating the alternatives are listed in the first column. Note the final score and rank for each alternative. ***Would these ranks vary depending on who assigns the scores?***

Each alternative listed in this decision matrix is given a score for each criterion. A score of four points is given for very desirable alternatives and one point is given for very undesirable alternatives. After the points for each alternative are totaled, final scores are figured. The higher the number of total points, the more desirable the alternative.

This example uses hypothetical scores for each alternative. Your individual evaluation may be different. Every individual places a different and unique value on each good or service in the world. You may listen to music twice as much as you would practice on your keyboard. One of your friends may feel just the opposite. Both of you are entitled to your preference, and both of you are right.

Step 5—Choose the Best Alternative

From the decision matrix in Figure 2-1, you can see that the best alternative is the 18-speed bike. It has the highest total score. Remember, however, that your own final choice depends on the criteria you choose and on your own preferences. If you live only for today, then product durability may not be important to you and your choice might be the vacation. If you get lots of enjoyment from your music, the electronic keyboard may be a better choice for you. There is an important issue here. If you make your personal decisions in the logical, organized, and effective way described, the satisfaction you get probably will be greater than a choice made another way. This will be true no matter what individual preferences enter into your evaluation and no matter what choice you make.

Checkpoint

Content Check

1. What are the five steps in the decision-making model?

2. Why should you define problems in an objective and focused manner?

3. How are alternatives chosen, criteria selected, and alternatives evaluated?

What Do You Think Now?

Reread *What Do You Think?* in the Section Two Focus. Then answer the following questions:

4. Can the decision-making model help you avoid saying things you later regret? Explain.

5. Can the economic concepts you have learned about help you make better choices? Explain.

6. If you combine what you know about economics with what you know about the decision-making model, will you make better choices? Explain.

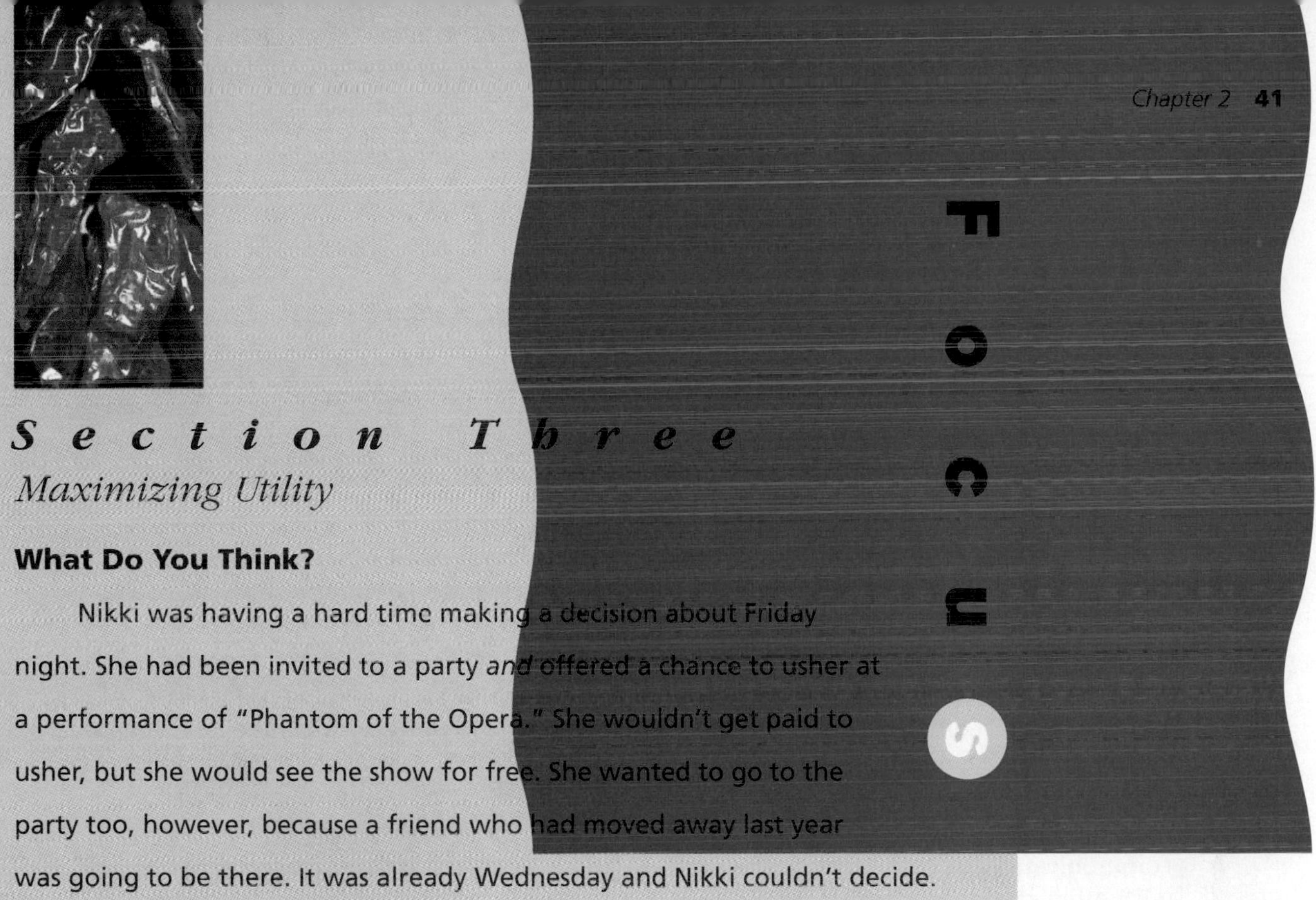

Section Three

Maximizing Utility

What Do You Think?

Nikki was having a hard time making a decision about Friday night. She had been invited to a party and offered a chance to usher at a performance of "Phantom of the Opera." She wouldn't get paid to usher, but she would see the show for free. She wanted to go to the party too, however, because a friend who had moved away last year was going to be there. It was already Wednesday and Nikki couldn't decide. What should Nikki do?

What's Ahead?

The five-step process helps you maximize the utility of your choice and minimize the opportunity cost. Although the decision-making process seems lengthy at first, you will find it can work quickly and easily with practice. You can use it every day to make better choices.

Terms to Know

utility

util

THE DECISION-MAKING PROCESS IN REAL LIFE

It is important to remember that every time you make a choice, there is an opportunity cost. That is, you give up some alternative that you could have chosen. By using the five-step decision-making model to make choices, you can make comparisons between your opportunity costs.

Individual Choice and Opportunity Cost

Economists use the term *utility* to describe the strength of your preference. ***Utility*** is the satisfaction one receives from the consumption, use, or ownership of a good or service. The unit of measurement for utility is the ***util.*** For example, listening to music may have twice as many utils as playing the keyboard.

utility
the satisfaction one receives from the consumption, use, or ownership of a good or service

util
the unit of measurement for utility

Wise choices are those that maximize the utility of the choice. A related concept economists use is psychic income. As you learned earlier in this chapter, *psychic income* is the nonmonetary satisfaction received from taking

Internet Connection

E-MAIL OR SNAILMAIL?

Exploration on the Internet often begins with electronic mail, e-mail. E-mail allows you to send written messages to anyone who has an account on any computer on the Internet or on a commercial network, such as CompuServe, Prodigy, and America Online. You can use e-mail to communicate with your teacher or with other students in your school or in schools around the world.

E-mail is a lot faster than "snail-mail," as the regular postal service is now known to e-mail users. E-mail can arrive from across town or across the globe within minutes. By contrast, snailmail usually takes days to deliver.

E-mail also can be used to obtain Internet resources. However, since there are more sophisticated, easy-to-use tools for that purpose, e-mail is principally used for communication.

E-mail programs have a number of common features. They allow you to create messages using a word processor. You can send e-mail messages to other people and save or print e-mail messages you receive. To take advantage of e-mail communication offerings, you need to know how to address outgoing messages.

Each computer on the Internet, or "Internet host," has a unique name, such as s850.mwc.edu or www.ibm.com or whitehouse.gov. The last block of letters explains the type of organization operating the computer: *edu* represents an educational institution, *com* represents a commercial business, and *gov* represents a government agency. For computers located outside of the United States, the last block of letters is the country code. For example, the *ca* in schoolnet.carleton.ca stands for *Canada.* The next block of letters (reading right to left) identifies the organization: Mary Washington College, or IBM corporation, or the White House. If there are additional blocks of letters, they identify the specific computer at the organization. What is the "host" name of the computer through which your class can access the Internet?

In the last lesson, we described *user-i.d.,* a person's "name" on the Internet. To send e-mail to someone, simply address it to their user i.d. @internet.host.name. For example, suppose a user whose i.d. is "Econ_Connect" can access the Internet through a computer called "swpco.com". Then Econ_Connect@swpco.com is the complete Internet address. (This is pronounced "Econ Connect at swpco dot com.")

Internet Application: Your teacher will assign one or more of the questions at the end of Chapter 2. Do the assignment and turn it in using e-mail instead of paper.

some action. (Psychic income is also called *psychic utility*.) For example, volunteer work at a hospital may not pay anything, but those who do it receive psychic income, or the personal satisfaction or utility from doing such work.

In Figure 2-1, the 18-speed bike was the clear-cut first choice. Owning the bike might also hold some psychic utility. Perhaps it would give you status, peer acceptance, or the attention and admiration of your friends. Psychic utility is another criterion you may want to use to evaluate your alternatives.

If you choose the bike, your opportunity costs are the alternatives you have given up—the vacation, keyboard, and CD player. By using the decision-making model, you have chosen the alternative that will give the most satisfaction and have the lowest possible opportunity costs.

It is possible that prices of bikes may rise. You might find that you cannot buy an 18-speed bike for $350, so you may have to make a second choice. From the decision matrix, note that the CD player follows as a close second choice. Therefore, you may not suffer greatly if you settle for the CD player. Also, note that the vacation and the keyboard, while ranked lower than the bike or CD player, were almost equal choices. They scored only one point apart. If both the bike and the CD player became unavailable, you might have to carefully consider whether to select the vacation or the keyboard. At that point, you might even want to add more criteria to help you decide.

Econ & You

CAREERS IN YOUR ECONOMIC FUTURE

Many personal decisions will affect your own economic future. One of these is your career selection. Clearly, the level of education you obtain will influence your earning power. On average, college graduates earn twice as much each year as people who do not complete high school and about 1.7 times as much as those who stop going to school after graduating from high school.

In considering a career, some of the questions you need to think about include the following:

1. What do you do well?

2. What do you enjoy doing?

3. How much education is required?

4. How will economic trends affect your choices?

5. What careers will most likely have the greatest growth potential for you over your working life?

Your school counselors can probably help you identify answers to the first three questions in this list. Library research and your study of economics will help you with the last two. As you think about different jobs, be sure to include the idea of opportunity costs in your thinking. The decision-making process discussed in this chapter will help you with your career choices.

Making Decisions Every Day

The decision-making process described here may seem very complicated. It seems like a lot of work just to make a choice. However, think about the allocation decisions you make every day. Over and over again, you make decisions concerning how to allocate your limited free time among a variety of activities, such as study, work, and leisure. You also decide how to spend your income and your energy. To make good choices, you must first define each individual problem.

In reality, the first few times you try the process, it may take some time. After a few times, however, you will get accustomed to using the five-step process, and things will move more quickly. In the first few attempts, it might be wise to write out a decision matrix like the one in Figure 2-1. After a few times, this should not be necessary. Just think through the process:

1. define the problem;
2. list the alternatives;
3. list the criteria;
4. evaluate the alternatives; and
5. choose the best alternative.

Remember, the utility received from a particular good, service, or action varies from person to person. The important point here is not how you *feel* about each choice. Instead it is important that you develop an organized, logical approach to making choices.

Checkpoint

Content Check

1. How can the five-step decision-making model result in greater satisfaction from personal decisions?
2. Give an example of individual choice and opportunity cost as they apply to you.
3. Construct and complete a decision matrix like the one in Figure 2-1 to rank the alternatives of driving to a city 500 miles away and flying to the same city. Select appropriate criteria.

What Do You Think Now?

Reread *What Do You Think?* in the Section Three Focus. Then answer the following questions:

4. How would you use the five-step decision-making process to choose between the party and ushering? What criteria would you use to evaluate the alternatives? What would be your choice?

Concepts in Brief

1. Economies must make choices because of scarcity. In a market economy, the economic questions of what, how, and for whom to produce are decided mostly in the marketplace by individual producers and consumers.
2. Self-interest guides individual choices in a market economy. Adam Smith, a Scottish economist, said that self-interest and individual choice would produce the greatest benefit for the individual and the whole economy.
3. Individual choice plays a major role in a market economy. Therefore, it is important to use a well-reasoned decision-making process. To make effective individual choices, five steps can be followed:
   1. define the problem;
   2. list the alternatives;
   3. list the criteria;
   4. evaluate the alternatives; and
   5. choose the best alternative.
4. Every decision results in an opportunity cost. Using the decision-making model in real life allows individuals to minimize opportunity costs. The more the decision-making model is used, the easier it is to make good decisions.

Economic Foundations

1. How are the economic questions of what to produce and how to produce decided in a market economy such as the United States?
2. What is the guiding force behind individual decisions in a market economy?
3. Why are individual decisions important in a market economy?
4. List the five steps in the decision-making model.
5. What two actions should be taken to clearly define a problem?
6. How should alternatives be chosen?
7. How should criteria be selected?
8. How should the criteria be used to evaluate the alternatives?
9. How can you get the most satisfaction from any personal decision you make?

Your Economic Vocabulary

Build your economic vocabulary by matching the following terms with their definitions.

alternative
criteria
decision matrix
economic incentive
economic profit
individual choice
invisible hand
market economy
model
objectivity
psychic income
util
utility

1. the increase in personal satisfaction that may result from some economic activity
2. the difference between the money you obtain from selling a product and the cost of producing the product
3. a possible course of action
4. the satisfaction one receives from the consumption, use, or ownership of a good or service
5. the incentive that guides individuals to choose in the best interest of society by pursuing their own self-interests
6. decisions made by people acting separately
7. the unit of measurement for utility
8. the nonmonetary reward we get from taking some action
9. ruling out aspects of a problem that seem important only because of your strong emotions about them
10. the characteristics of a group of alternatives that will be judged to make a choice
11. a table comparing possible decisions
12. an economy in which the economic questions are decided mostly by individuals in the marketplace
13. a simplified form of reality that shows the relationship between different factors

Thinking Critically About Economics

1. "Self-interest is selfish, greedy, and not in the best interest of our market economy." Do you agree or disagree with this statement? Why?
2. "In a modern society, the government should decide what to produce and how so that enough goods and services are produced to meet everyone's needs." Do you agree or disagree? Why?

3. Assume that you have just ended a dating relationship and now have six more hours of free time per week. You can allocate this time among studying, working, dating others, or spending time with your family. Use the five-step decision-making process to decide how you will spend your time. Select your own criteria and set up a decision matrix.

4. Which do you prefer: an economy based primarily on individual choice or one based on social choice? Why?

Economic Enrichment

In 1995, newspapers and television news broadcasts carried many stories of the continuing struggle between the People's Republic of China and the United States to settle the dispute over copyrights and patents on U.S. goods. The issue had a lot to do with how goods and services are produced in both countries and the incentive those countries provide to producers.

Review articles about this conflict from appropriate editions of *The Wall Street Journal* and other periodicals. Make a brief presentation to your class that answers the following questions: Why was the United States so interested in protecting copyrights and patents? What role do copyrights and patents play in providing incentive to producers?

Math and Economics

Many young people go to camp in the summer. The camp a person chooses depends on many criteria, some of which include the main focus of the camp, the length of the camp, the cost, whether it is a day camp or overnight camp, and the extra activities available at the camp.

Your grandparents have given you $750 to attend a computer camp this summer. Any money you do not spend on camp you get to put in your savings account. You are saving to buy a used car. You have the choice between three summer computer camps: one that teaches you how to produce multimedia reports (audio, video, print), one that teaches you how to navigate the Internet, and one that teaches you to use authoring software to create CD-ROM games. Information about each of these camps is summarized in the decision matrix on page 48.

1. Copy the decision matrix on a separate piece of paper. Based on your own evaluation of the criteria, assign a score to each of the alternatives in the decision matrix. The scores can range from 1 to 5, with 1 being undesirable and 5 being very desirable. Write the scores in the boxes in the bottom right corner of each box.

Criteria	Multimedia Reports	Navigating the Internet	Authoring CD-ROM Games
Cost	$650	$600	$750
Day Camp or Overnight	Overnight	Overnight	Day
Length of Camp	7 Days	7 Days	5 Days
Extra Activities Available	Swimming, boating, tennis, horseback riding	Swimming, tennis, hiking trails	None
Total Score			
Ranking of Alternatives			

2. Add the scores for each camp and complete the Total Score row in the decision matrix. Circle your first choice, the camp with the highest total score.
3. Rank the alternatives, with 1 being your first choice, in the Ranking of Alternatives row in the decision matrix.

Writing About Economics

Observe and record the prices for a half gallon of 2 percent milk at ten different locations in your town. Be sure to include grocery stores, gasoline and convenience stores, milk retailers, and discount grocery outlets.

Summarize your findings in a table that includes the price, location, and type of store. Identify the highest and lowest price. Then prepare a poster that includes your table and a written explanation of the price differences. Consider the following when preparing your explanation: the role of location in setting milk prices and the impact of opportunity costs on purchasers' decisions about where to buy milk.

The Personal Consumption Pie

A useful thing to know about the economy is how people spend their money. Do they spend it on durable goods, such as cars and household furniture? Do they spend it on nondurable goods, such as clothing and gasoline? Or, do they spend it on services, such as housing and medical care? The proportion spent in each of these areas has an impact on what type of jobs are created and what level of wages are earned by people performing those jobs.

The accompanying table shows data on personal consumption expenditures for the United States broken down into three categories: durable goods, nondurable goods, and services.

Total Personal Consumption Expenditures for Durable Goods, Nondurable Goods, and Services (1990–1994)

Year	Total Personal Consumption Expenditures (in billions)	Durable Goods (in billions)	Nondurable Goods (in billions)	Services (in billions)
1990	$3,265.90	$433.20	$1,057.50	$1,775.20
1991	3,265.40	427.70	1,040.40	1,797.30
1992	3,403.40	468.80	1,074.20	1,860.40
1993	3,506.20	510.80	1,088.00	1,907.40
1994	3,625.20	552.40	1,121.10	1,951.70

Although tables are very useful, it is a bit difficult to really see from the table what relationship there might be between the numbers. Another way to look at this information is in a pie chart. The accompanying pie chart presents the same data on total personal consumption expenditures for 1994 as does the table but in a different format. The pie chart shows visually how total personal consumption, on average, is divided among the categories of durable goods, nondurable goods, and services. It is clear from the pie chart that services accounted for the greatest percentage of total personal consumption. Look for pie charts as you read the newspaper or magazines—they can make numbers and their relationships easier to understand.

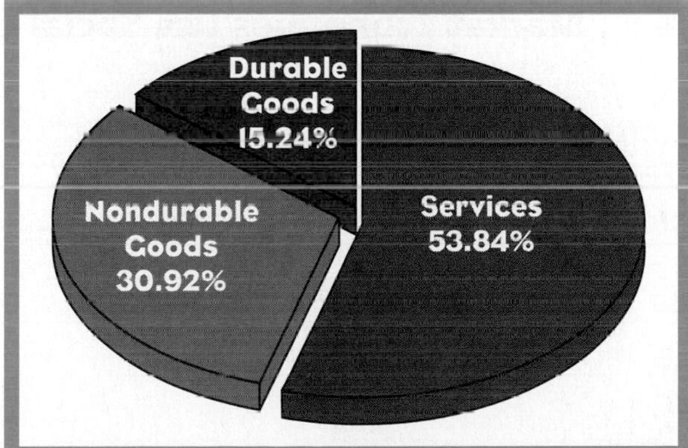

Overview

Section One
Social Choice

Section Two
Market Economies Use Social Choice

Section Three
Effective Social Decisions

Making Social Decisions

Learning Objectives

3-1

Explain how the three basic economic questions are answered in a social economy.

3-2

Discuss the role of personal incentives under social choice.

3-3

Describe the conditions under which social choice is preferable to individual choice.

3-4

Apply the five-step decision-making model to social decisions.

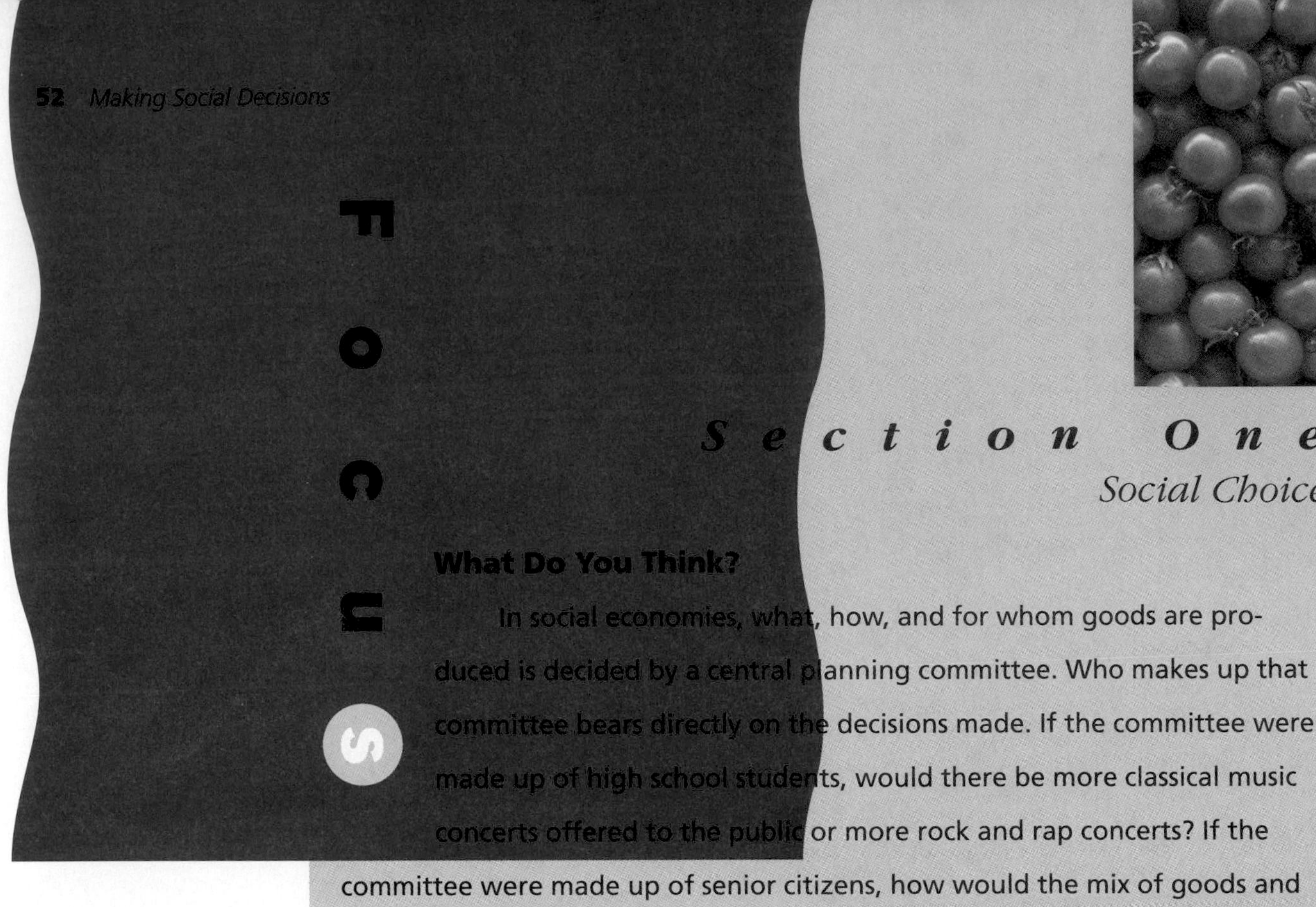

Section One
Social Choice

What Do You Think?

In social economies, what, how, and for whom goods are produced is decided by a central planning committee. Who makes up that committee bears directly on the decisions made. If the committee were made up of high school students, would there be more classical music concerts offered to the public or more rock and rap concerts? If the committee were made up of senior citizens, how would the mix of goods and services produced differ? Why? Do you think it is possible for a small group of people to accurately reflect the diverse preferences of an entire population? Who would you like to choose what goods are available for you: your grandmother or your classmates? Would it make any difference?

Terms to Know
social economy
social choice
equity

What's Ahead?

In social economies, governments make the decisions about what, how, and for whom to produce. Social economies use the social choice process to satisfy most wants and needs with public goods. Karl Marx had a strong influence on the development of socialist ideas.

ECONOMIC QUESTIONS IN SOCIAL ECONOMIES

Some economies in the world operate through mostly *social* decision making. An economy in which the major economic questions of what, how, and for whom to produce are determined by a government representing the interests of the entire society is called a ***social economy.*** A social economy is sometimes called a *command economy.*

social economy an economy in which the major economic questions are determined by a government representing the interests of the entire society

What to Produce?

The question of what to produce with a nation's given stock of resources presents an interesting problem of economic choice. While market economies operate mostly through individual choice, social economies use committees of experts who pool their knowledge.

These central planning committees work out elaborate plans about what the economy will produce. Decisions about what goods and services will be produced are based on what the central planning committee thinks will benefit the whole society. Individuals do not directly make these decisions. Rather, the goods and services are produced by order of the planning committee and appear in the marketplace when completed. The varieties and choices of goods and services in the market are limited to what the central planning committee decides will benefit the whole society. The goods and services produced do not have to pass the difficult test of individual market choice. If they did, many might not survive.

This lack of individual choice in a social economy greatly affects the consumer and the producer. When only one kind of product is made to fill a given need, the consumer still must make a choice; however, the choice is very limited. The consumer can either buy the available product or completely do without it. Producers do not have profit incentives, but it is extremely difficult for their products to fail in the marketplace since there are few competing goods.

Global Economy

SOCIAL DECISIONS VS FREE TRADE

International trade is the life blood of the global economy. Two people decide to engage in trade for the simple reason that each has what the other wants at a price they are both willing to pay. Both parties are better off because of the exchange, or they would not continue to trade. However, social decisions sometimes interfere with the individual decisions of free trade. For example, governments place tariffs (taxes) on international trade to protect domestic industries or to raise revenue for their own benefit. Governments also set quotas (limits) on how much of a certain good can be traded across borders.

These social decisions may be made with good intentions, but they always reduce the amount of trade that takes place. Since trade benefits both trading partners, both trading parties are worse off when tariffs and quotas are imposed. The social decision may well be in the best interest of the whole country, but they are not in the best interest of the individual trading parties.

In times of war or as a result of specific foreign policy, trade with a given country or in specific goods may be prohibited entirely. In 1992, the United Nations prohibited Iraq from selling oil on the world market as a punishment for the Gulf War. This social decision may have been in the best interest of preserving world peace in the future, but it injured not only Iraq but all its trading partners in the process. In the global economy, as in the U.S. economy, when sweeping social decisions are made, the economic impact is felt by individuals.

Economic Spotlight

CAN A FOR-PROFIT COMPANY HAVE A HEART?

What do Princess Di and Oprah Winfrey have in common? They both wear RYKÄ shoes, made specifically for women. Thanks to Sheri Poe, women can now find shoes that really fit their feet. Poe, founder, president, and CEO of RYKÄ, came up with the idea for her product when she couldn't find an athletic shoe that fit her properly. At the time, most women's athletic shoes were only scaled-down versions of men's shoes, so the entrepreneur decided to create a shoe made *for women, by women*.

When Poe tried to find financing to start her athletic shoe company, bankers laughed at her idea. Her small company would be up against the heavy-hitting footwear giants Nike and Reebok, among others. Finally, Poe was given a chance by the Denver-based investment firm R. B. Marich; the "B" in R. B. stood for *Betty,* an aerobics enthusiast who convinced the male members in the firm that there was, indeed, a market for women's athletic shoes. With $25,000 in bank loans and $50,000 from her family, Poe at the age of 34 started RYKÄ in her kitchen in 1987.

Since then, the company has grown into a publicly held, multimillion dollar corporation with distributorships in more than 15 countries. But, even with this phenomenal growth, RYKÄ is a model of a profitable yet socially responsible corporation. Five years after she started RYKÄ, Poe examined her past and found herself reconsidering her silence about being raped when a college student. She wanted to help other women avoid the pain that she experienced as a rape survivor. She decided to give her company a soul and a conscience. In 1992, Poe founded the RYKÄ ROSE (Restore One's Self-Esteem) Foundation, a charitable, nonprofit foundation separate from her shoe company.

RYKÄ ROSE funds programs that battle violence against women. Since RYKÄ was not yet profitable in 1992, Poe pledged $250,000 of her own money to start the foundation, and her principal retail partner, Lady Footlocker, donated additional funding. Now, every time a consumer purchases a pair of RYKÄ shoes at an average retail price of $40 to $75, RYKÄ donates 7 percent of the profits to the RYKÄ ROSE Foundation. According to Poe, "I believe in an ethical *and* a financial bottom line."

The main idea in social economies is that the government, rather than individuals, decides what to produce. This decision-making structure implies that individuals may not be capable of choosing for themselves as well as their government can. ***Social choice,*** then, is decision making by government in the interest of society.

social choice
decision making by government in the interest of society

How to Produce?

The question of how to produce is decided in social economies primarily by government decree. Central planning authorities decide which producers will produce what goods and services. Quantities of resources are allocated to those producers only. Usually, output quotas are set, but producers do not risk market failure since there are few competing goods. Of course, if resources are used wastefully, there is concern. But, with government support, producers cannot incur losses and are not in danger of going out of business.

In a social economy, there is little difference in reward to the producer who is very efficient and to the producer who is only moderately efficient. Profits are not a major goal and self-interest is not a socially acceptable incentive. Therefore, there is no profit incentive. Producers decide how resources are to be used by what is allocated to them, not by what individuals will choose to buy in the marketplace. Producers do not have an extremely accurate resource price system to guide their choices.

For Whom to Produce?

The question of how goods are distributed in a social economy is made primarily in an effort to provide equity. ***Equity*** means dealing fairly and equally with all concerned. All members of the society are supposed to be given a fair share of the fruits of the entire economy's labor. Equity, however, is a difficult objective. What you think is fair or equitable probably is different from what your neighbor thinks is equitable. There are probably as many different opinions about what is equitable in any society as there are citizens.

equity
dealing fairly and equally with all concerned

Social economies try to provide equitable goods and services. This, however, means that individuals do not have the right to choose among many significantly different goods and services. If everyone gets an equitable house, for instance, there certainly cannot be any significant differences among houses. You can choose any house you want, but they all may be alike.

Social Decision Making and Karl Marx

Throughout history, many economists and philosophers have strongly advocated socialism and social decision making. Karl Marx is probably the best known. He certainly had the most influence on the development of socialist ideals.

Marx was born in 1818 and attended the Universities of Bonn and Berlin. He received a doctoral degree from the University of Jena in 1841 and wrote widely about his views on social decision making. Marx believed that the State (entire society) should own the factors of production and make decisions about the production and distribution of wealth. He openly advocated violent revolution by the working class (proletariat) to overthrow the capitalist ruling class (bourgeoisie).

Marx saw communism as a natural evolution of capitalism. He felt that capitalism and individual decision making would lead to the development of a few very wealthy and all-controlling people who would produce nothing. They would live on the labors of the working class. The evolution of a nonproductive bourgeoisie would lead to violent revolution. Then the power and ownership of the society would revert to the common people.

Marx envisioned a classless society of equals. In this society, all people would contribute to the society according to their ability and take from the society according to their needs. He wrote that once the bourgeoisie was overthrown, all power would be in the hands of the State. The State would then gradually distribute power to the people, and the population would make cooperative decisions in the best interest of society.

Marx's most famous writings were *The Communist Manifesto,* written with Friedrich Engels in 1848, and *Das Kapital,* part of which was published in 1867. These books laid much of the groundwork for socialist philosophy.

Checkpoint

Content Check

1. How does a social economy decide what, how, and for whom to produce?
2. What was Karl Marx's vision of how economies would evolve over time?

What Do You Think Now?

Reread *What Do You Think?* in the Section One Focus. Then answer the following questions:

3. What changes would you propose if you were on the central planning committee that makes decisions for your school about how classes are "produced"?
4. What changes would you propose if you were on the central planning committee that made decisions for your city or town about what, how, and for whom community services are produced?

FOCUS

Section Two
Market Economies Use Social Choice

What Do You Think?

Ask your classmates if they watch public television. Now ask if they send donations to public television stations. The number of watchers will probably be larger than the number of contributors. How many people use public parks for ball games and other recreation in other towns? What causes people to choose to use free services without helping to support them? How do we, as a society, deal with this issue?

What's Ahead?

Market economies make some important decisions based on social choice. Public goods that the government provides in a market economy are cheaper due to economies of scale and the public goods rationale. Your views about these social choices are represented by your votes.

Terms to Know

public goods

economies of scale

public goods rationale

free rider

SOCIAL CHOICE IN MARKET ECONOMIES

In market economies such as the United States, most economic decisions are based on individual choice in the marketplace. It is important to note, however, that a number of important decisions are also based on social choice.

The Government Provides Public Goods

As a society, we choose to provide public goods. ***Public goods*** are goods and services available to the whole society. Roads, schools, national defense, and police and fire protection are examples of public goods.

public goods
goods and services available to the whole society

Economies of Scale. There are several important reasons that governments provide public goods. One reason, however, is clearly more valid than the rest. Governments provide public goods because sometimes it is cheaper due to economies of scale. ***Economies of scale*** is the concept that some economic activities become more efficient when done on a large scale. Many people can enjoy a large public park at a lower cost per person than if individuals tried to provide their own parks, for example.

economies of scale
the concept that some economic activities become more efficient when done on a large scale

Public Goods Rationale. Even Adam Smith agreed that government could provide some public goods more efficiently than could individuals. In economics, this is called the public goods rationale (reason) for social choice. The ***public goods rationale*** is the argument that some public goods can be produced more efficiently by the government. Consider a public road. Everyone who uses the road benefits from it. Each individual pays for only a very small part of the total cost of the road. If each of us had to buy or build a road to wherever we wanted to go, no one could afford to travel by road. By joining together, we can realize an economy of scale by spreading the cost of creating the road over everyone in the society.

public goods rationale
the argument that some public goods can be produced more efficiently by the government

The public goods rationale can be applied to police protection or any other public good. For instance, suppose you need a police officer to guard your home from burglars. You could hire a guard to walk around outside your house all day. This would be expensive, however. The mere presence of

Economic Dilemma

WELFARE REFORM

Welfare reform has been a major political issue since the 1980s. Critics contend that huge amounts of federal money are being spent on welfare programs and that the programs themselves take away incentives for people to work and earn their own livelihood. In most welfare programs, recipients are not allowed to work and receive welfare payments at the same time. The government's social choice, in an effort to help welfare recipients, overrode the individual choices recipients might have made to work on their own if they had the opportunity.

Welfare reformers propose that welfare payments be reduced and that recipients without small children be required to work at public service jobs in exchange for their benefits. It is argued that these reforms would create stronger incentives for recipients to find full-time work in the private sector and get off of welfare programs. The dilemma is that some welfare recipients have few job skills, making them unqualified for the required work.

There are many economic dilemmas involving conflict between social choices and individual choices. Most social choices prohibit some individual actions in the belief that society is being protected from the potential of individual harm. For example, while speed limits make driving safer for everyone, they deny the possible thrill of high-speed driving to those who might enjoy it. Smoking is prohibited in many public places in an effort to protect society from secondhand smoke. However, such laws deny the pleasure of smoking to individuals who might enjoy it enough to knowingly endanger their health by doing so. When society makes value judgments for individuals, such as in the case of welfare reform, economic dilemmas are likely to be present.

the officer would probably frighten burglars away from your home and your neighbor's home. The officer might even be protecting the whole block at your expense. Unfortunately, you would be paying the bill individually. How could this situation be improved? You and your neighbor could split the bill. You might offer the police officer's services to everyone in the neighborhood if they would share the cost. One officer could patrol 50 homes and each home owner could pay 1/50 of the expense. All would share in the benefit, and the cost to each individual would be much less. Services such as these are provided more efficiently by a group or society than by an individual.

Internet Connection

PUTTING GOVERNMENT ONLINE

The government is a major contributor to the information superhighway. By making it easier for the government to give information to and receive information from citizens, the Internet may actually enhance social decision making. Many U.S. government agencies—the Commerce Department, the Extension Service of the Agriculture Department, NASA, the National Archives, the U.S. Geological Survey—are making their reports and a variety of statistical information available online.

All U.S. government documents will be published electronically. The current U.S. budget and the latest U.S. census already are obtainable online. The Declaration of Independence, the U.S. Constitution, bills in Congress, committee reports, and the Congressional Record also are available. Even the White House has an Internet site. You can obtain copies of the President's speeches and other press releases.

Let's look at how e-mail has the potential to make government more accessible and responsive to the people. More and more government officials are reachable via e-mail. President@whitehouse.gov and vice.president@whitehouse.gov are e-mail addresses for the president and vice president.

Many senators and members of Congress have e-mail addresses. While many people are reluctant to call or write a letter to a government official, they are willing to communicate via e-mail, because it is so easy to use.

Internet/Economics Application: Effective representative government requires that you inform your elected officials of your views on important issues. Who represents your district in the U.S. House of Representatives? Send e-mail to congress@hr.house.gov with no message to get a list of representatives and their e-mail addresses. If your representative has an e-mail address, send a message letting him or her know what you think is the nation's most pressing economic problem right now. If your representative has no e-mail address, send your message to the President.

The Free Rider Problem

Suppose a society was going to build an army to protect itself. If funding for the army were left to individual choice, there would be a problem. Even if most individuals banded together to pay for the army, some persons would not agree to pay. A person who benefits from a public good without sharing its cost is called a ***free rider.***

free rider
a person who benefits from a public good without sharing its cost

It would be impossible to protect those who did pay without also protecting the free riders. In order to eliminate free riders, it is necessary to back social choice with the power of law. Eliminating free riders is also efficient in spreading the cost of the public good over the whole society.

Social Choice in Representative Government

Now that you know why social decisions are made in market economies, let's look at how your individual view is reflected in the government's social choices. Representative government implies that individual citizens, through their votes, elect government officials. These officials are expected to make social choices for the voters they represent, their constituents. Therefore, you should vote for the candidates who most closely represent your views. If your elected officials choose differently from how you would have, you have the right to vote for other candidates.

Unfortunately, representative government, just like social choice, reduces the number of alternatives you have to choose from. A candidate must vote for or against an issue. You must choose with your vote among two or three candidates. There is little chance that any candidate would vote just as you would on every social choice.

Checkpoint

Content Check

1. Why do governments in market economies provide public goods?
2. What is the public goods rationale?
3. What is the free rider problem and how can it be minimized?

What Do You Think Now?

Reread *What Do You Think?* in the Section Two Focus. Then answer the following questions:

4. Are those who watch public television without financially supporting it free riders? How do public television stations deal with this issue?
5. Describe a situation in your school where there is a problem with free riders. How can this situation be minimized?
6. Is it possible that people who are free riders in one situation provide more than their share of support in another situation? Give an example.

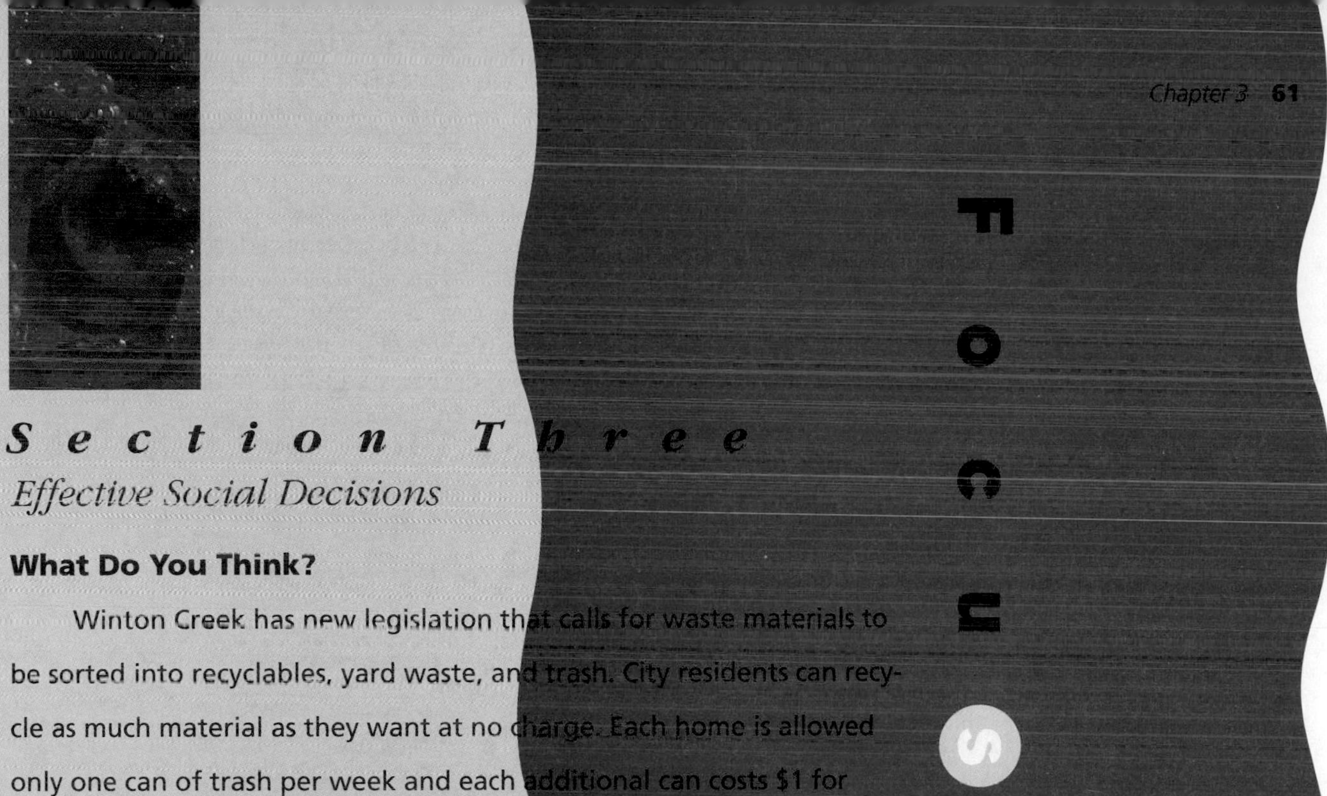

Section Three

Effective Social Decisions

What Do You Think?

Winton Creek has new legislation that calls for waste materials to be sorted into recyclables, yard waste, and trash. City residents can recycle as much material as they want at no charge. Each home is allowed only one can of trash per week and each additional can costs $1 for pickup. Yard waste must be placed in a clearly marked container and pickup costs $0.75. Payment for yard waste and extra trash pickup is made by purchasing stickers and attaching them to containers. Some people are complaining that the system is not fair: They do all the work of sorting and recycling and the city gets all the money. Do you think the system is fair?

What's Ahead?

Social decisions impact many people and should be made very carefully. Decision makers can improve the quality of the choices they make by using the five-step decision-making model. You can use the decision-making process to clarify your position on social issues and communicate the reasons for your social choices.

Terms to Know

distribution effect
social goals
social costs
freedom of choice
social benefits

MAKING EFFECTIVE SOCIAL CHOICES

Representative government concentrates the power to make social decisions in the hands of a very few people. The choices made by a few public officials affect the lives of everyone in a society and so should be made very carefully. It is important to clarify the benefits and the costs of each choice.

Let's look at an example of a social decision at school. Assume that enrollment at your school has increased during the last five years. The parking lot is not big enough to hold the cars of all the students who drive to school. Students have been permitted to park on nearby streets once the lot is full. However, residents of the neighborhood complained. The police chief has notified the school that student cars parked on residential streets will be towed beginning next Monday.

You and five other students have been elected by the student government to make a decision about allocating the parking spaces. In making your social choice, you will follow the five-step decision-making model:

1. define the problem;
2. list the alternatives;
3. list the criteria;
4. evaluate the alternatives; and
5. choose the best alternative.

Step 1—Define the Problem

Presently, there are more cars than spaces available in the parking lot. Students have been distributing the burden of the shortage to private home owners nearby. Thus, residents have been unable to park in front of their own homes. This is called a distribution effect in economics. A ***distribution effect*** is the way the benefit or inconvenience of a social issue is distributed among the members of the society. In this case, the burden was being distributed from students to home owners.

distribution effect the way the benefit or inconvenience of a social issue is spread among the members of the society

In all choices, both individual and social, an allocation of resources is involved. Public officials vote every day on projects and laws. They allocate public money for public projects. More money for one project means less money for other possible projects. Laws define what choices we, as a society and as individuals, can and cannot make. Laws allocate the power to choose. If a law is passed that prohibits nonresident parking on residential streets, the choice or alternative of parking on those streets is no longer available. All choices require us to allocate something.

What is an accurate definition of this problem? Is the parking lot too small? Or, is the number of cars too large? What if the school cannot afford to build another parking lot for students? The problem then becomes how to allocate the available spaces among the students. The problem is defined as how will the limited spaces be allocated among the larger number of students who drive?

Step 2—List the Alternatives

What are some alternate solutions to the parking situation? The current situation is allocation of spaces on a first-come, first-served basis. One alternative is for this policy to continue.

A second alternative is to allocate the spaces by selling school parking permits for each space. Those who could afford the permits could drive, and those who could not afford them would have to walk or find other transportation.

A third alternative is to allocate by need. Students who work, live a long distance from school, are involved in car pools, or are the only drivers in their families might be given use of the lot. Students who have no access to bus service or other transportation would also fall into this category.

A fourth alternative is to allocate parking spaces by seniority. Seniors would have first choice and then juniors and then sophomores. This would, no doubt, be popular among seniors, but sophomores might think it is unfair.

You and the other student representatives decide to consider the following alternatives:

1. first come, first served;
2. selling permits;
3. need; and
4. seniority.

Step 3—List the Criteria

There are advantages and disadvantages to each alternative. In order to evaluate the alternatives, you must select some criteria. In social decision making, the criteria are social goals. ***Social goals*** are the goals of an entire society.

social goals
the goals of an entire society

What social goals should be considered for the parking lot problem? Some of the social goals societies strive for include justice, equality, efficiency, and freedom of choice.

Clearly, your choice should be fair or just. It should not give one group of students advantage over another without a very good reason. Consider, too, that if a decision is easy to understand, more students probably will feel that it is fair.

Equity might also be a part of your considerations. You might think that everyone should have an equal chance to use the parking lot. Remember, however, that equity is a difficult goal, as you will see later.

The costs of the decision, including its enforcement, should also be a criterion. The more efficient the choice is to administer, the lower the social costs. ***Social costs*** are the costs to a society of a social choice. If the decision is easy to understand, more students will probably feel that it is fair.

social costs
the costs to a society of a social choice

Freedom of choice also might be an important goal. ***Freedom of choice*** is the individual power to choose and receive both the costs and the benefits of a choice. Your rule might want to offer students an individual choice rather than simply dictate a course of required action.

freedom of choice
the individual power to choose and receive both the costs and the benefits of a choice

Social benefits could be another criterion. ***Social benefits*** are the benefits received by a society from a social choice. You might want to guide your choice by trying to produce benefits for the largest part of society. Here, a plan that shares the benefits of the choice among many people or groups would be preferable to one that benefits a few individuals or groups. You are trying to do the most good for the most people.

social benefits
the benefits received by a society from a social choice

Step 4—Evaluate the Alternatives

Having defined your problem, determined your alternatives, and established your criteria (social goals), you now must evaluate each alternative. Through evaluation, you will get a clear idea of the advantages and disadvantages of each possible choice.

Figure 3-1 on page 64 is a decision matrix like the one in Chapter 2. In Figure 3-1, the four criteria (social goals) are listed in the first column. The four alternatives are in the first row. Each alternative, beginning with first-come, first-served, is given a score on each criterion. A score of four points is given for very desirable alternatives and one point for very undesirable alternatives. The higher the number of total points, the more desirable the alternative.

Notice that the parking permit alternative in Figure 3-1 scores high on social costs and fairly high on freedom of choice. However, compared to the other alternatives, it is third in social benefit and third in equity. The good aspects of this alternative are that the people who get the benefit of parking spaces are the ones who pay the fees and it allows some individual freedom of choice. In this way, the policy would function a lot like the marketplace. This alternative is weak in equity because those who cannot pay the fee have no opportunity to use the lot. The social benefits also are received only by those who pay the fee. Given its strong and weak points, this alternative ranks second among the four alternatives.

Criteria	Alternatives: First Come First Served	Parking Permits	Need	Seniority
Equity	Everyone has an equal chance 4 points	Limited to those who can afford the fee 2 points	Different treatment for individuals with different needs 3 points	Limited to seniors and some juniors 1 point
Social Cost	No costs—no more room when spaces are full 4 points	Very low; pays for itself through fees 4 points	Difficult to measure and classify individual needs 1 point	Low cost; students easily identified 3 points
Social Benefit	Benefits only those who get there first 2 points	Limited; only those who can pay can benefit 2 points	Limited to those who need it most 4 points	Benefits only older students 2 points
Freedom of Choice	Individuals can choose how early they want to arrive 4 points	Some choice allowed; individuals can choose to pay to drive 3 points	Not much choice; individuals can only change their needs such as by moving farther from school 2 points	No choice 1 point
Final Score and Rank of Alternative	14 points 1st choice	11 points 2nd choice	10 points 3rd choice	7 points 4th choice

Figure 3-1

A Decision Matrix for the Parking Lot Case

In this decision matrix, the criteria are the social goals. ***What social goals would you choose for the criteria?***

The first-come, first-served alternative is the best social choice of the four. This alternative is strong on individual freedom and equity since everyone has an equal chance to try for the available spaces. Students can choose how early they are willing to leave home each day. However, only those who can regularly get to school early can receive the benefits of this choice. Enforcement costs are zero, since when the available spaces are taken no one else can occupy them.

The real shortcoming of the first-come, first-served rule falls under another criterion that we did not consider. What happens if you try for a space and the lot is full? Are the unlucky individuals supposed to take their cars home or do something else with them? Under such a situation, it is likely that some people would park on the streets again and eventually be towed away. This is an example of how difficult it is to include every possible consideration in the social decision-making process. This is probably why some social decisions do not work out as planned.

Allocating parking spaces by need gets high points for equity and social benefit. At first glance, it may seem very fair to let the people who have the greatest need for parking use the spaces. This does the greatest good for as many people as there are parking spaces available. However, need is very difficult to determine. If you are handicapped, you have an obvious need to park near the building. On the other hand, what if you live a half mile closer to school than another student does. Do you have less need than the other student for transportation? This is a matter of judgment. The individual case of every student would have to be considered separately which would require large amounts of time and effort. Individual circumstances would change with time and the judgment process would have to continue for as long as the parking rules were in force. Considering all the criteria, this alternative ranked third.

Assigning space by seniority ranks poorly on almost all social goals. Such a rule would provide no individual choice. All seniors can drive, but few juniors or sophomores have the privilege. The social benefit goes to upper class students only. Since all students do not stay in school until they are seniors, not everyone has an equal chance to park in the school lot. This alternative turns out to be the worst choice, based on the social goals that were established.

Step 5—Choose the Best Alternative

After evaluating the alternatives based on the social goals, the first-come, first-served rule is the best choice. Don't forget, however, that the outcome is based on the alternatives you have considered and the value the society places on each of the social goals. If there were a social goal of trying to provide convenience for student drivers, the outcome might have been different. If the certainty of getting a parking space were very important to students, this might have been a criterion and another alternative might have been chosen. As the values of a society change, its social choices reflect those changes.

The quality of any social choice depends on defining the problem accurately and weighing carefully the costs and benefits of each alternative. Following a logical and well-organized method of decision making will improve your ability to understand and participate in the social decision-making process.

SOCIAL DECISIONS IN REAL LIFE

Remember how the individual decision-making process, described in Chapter 2, seemed very complex at first? After several tries, however, you probably learned to use the process quickly and efficiently. The social decision-making process also may seem complex. If you repeat the process with several different issues, however, you will quickly come to understand its value. The five-step decision-making model will not give you a specific

Econ & You

STANDING BEHIND YOUR DECISIONS

As a social decision maker, once you have decided which alternative is in the best interest of the people, your work is just beginning. You have only worked out the costs and benefits in an understandable form. Your next and most important task is to clearly communicate the costs and benefits of each possible alternative to your constituents. Constituents are the individual citizens or voters in a democracy who are represented by a particular public official.

You must be able to explain your stand on the issue and support it with facts. You have to convince the people that your decision was based on how each possible alternative measured up to the social goals that were considered. You must be sure that the social goals reflect values that most of the constituents have in common. This process should also protect you from criticism regarding acting in your own self-interest.

Once you have communicated the costs and benefits of each alternative to those affected, you must measure the responses. You might try to get a general impression of how people feel about your choice and if your decision was best for the majority. Whether you like it or not, your social choice will override the individual choices of the individuals who disagree with the majority. Your action, by necessity, will take away the power of their individual choice.

With this in mind, your challenge is to convince as many people as possible that your choice is the best for the society. You must exercise your power of social choice with the greatest of care. You must be mindful that when you choose for others, they may not agree with your choice. Thus, in the long run, they may choose some other social decision maker who more closely represents their views.

answer to any problem. But, it will help you organize your thinking and more effectively develop your own solutions to problems involving social choices. The selection of social goals and the value your society places on each goal is up to you to determine.

The five-step decision-making model is, in some respects, more important in making social decisions than it is in making individual decisions. When you choose only for yourself, you usually do not have to justify or explain your choice to others. Your criteria reflect your own values. With social choices, however, you not only will have to make careful decisions, you also will have to clearly communicate to members of the society how and why you make these decisions.

The five-step decision-making process clarifies your decisions and makes it much easier to communicate the *why* and *how* of your decision to society. It also gives you the opportunity to see if your ranking of the criteria (goals) agrees with that of the society. You may have overlooked a major consideration. Through discussions with voters, you might change the outcome of your decision. Finally, if you can communicate the five-step decision-making process to the society, each individual may be able to make more effective decisions in the future. All these outcomes will be to the benefit of the society and to the individuals who belong to it.

Checkpoint

Content Check

1. How can social decisions be improved with the five-step decision-making model?
2. Give examples of social goals, social costs, and social benefits.
3. Why is the five-step decision-making process sometimes more important in making social decisions than in making individual decisions?

What Do You Think Now?

Reread *What Do You Think?* in the Section Three Focus. Then answer the following questions:

4. What criteria would you use to evaluate the waste collection problem in Winton Creek?
5. What other alternatives can you suggest to Winton Creek residents for waste collection?

Concepts in Brief

1. Social economies answer the three basic economic questions of what, how, and for whom to produce mostly by government decree. Central planning committees decide which resources will be used to produce the goods and services selected for production. This process limits the amount of individual choice given to the citizens of social economies.

2. Personal incentives are not as strong in a social economy as they are in a market society. Even in market economies, however, there are many situations in which social choice is more efficient and more equitable than private choice. Decisions about public goods such as roads, schools, and national defense are examples of situations in which public choice may be superior to individual choice.

3. In cases where public choice is preferable to individual choice, the power of law is frequently necessary to deal with the free rider problem. The free rider problem refers to providing a public good to those who do not share in the cost of the good. Laws taxing everyone in a society (regardless of their preference) in order to provide for national defense is an example of such a situation. It is difficult or impossible to defend the society and yet not defend some of its citizens. With this in mind, everyone is taxed by law, whether they wish to be defended or not.

4. A society can make more efficient social choices by applying the five-step decision-making model to its choice process:
    1. define the problem;
    2. list the alternatives;
    3. list the criteria or social goals;
    4. evaluate the alternatives in regard to the criteria; and
    5. choose the best alternative that meets the criteria (social choice).

5. A logical, organized, and effective decision-making process may be even more important in making social decisions than in making individual decisions. Social decision makers must clearly communicate the costs and benefits of each alternative to the society and explain the reasons for their choices. The five-step decision-making model clearly presents these costs and benefits.

Economic Foundations

1. How are the major economic questions of what, how, and for whom to produce answered in a social economy?
2. What personal incentives exist for the producer of goods or services under social choice?
3. Under what conditions is social choice preferable to individual choice?
4. What are the public goods rationale and the free rider problem?
5. How can the five-step decision-making model be applied to social choice?
6. Why is an effective decision making process often more important in social choices than in individual choices?

Your Economic Vocabulary

Build your economic vocabulary by matching the following terms with their definitions.

1. dealing fairly and equally with all concerned
2. the costs to a society of a social choice
3. the way the benefit or inconvenience of a social issue is spread among the members of the society
4. the individual power to choose and receive both the costs and the benefits of a choice
5. the benefits received by a society from a social choice
6. the goals of an entire society
7. an economy in which the major economic questions are determined by a government representing the interests of the entire society
8. decision making by government in the interest of society
9. a person who benefits from a public good without sharing its cost
10. goods and services available to the whole society
11. the argument that some public goods can be produced more efficiently by the government
12. the concept that some economic activities become more efficient when done on a large scale

distribution effect
economies of scale
equity
freedom of choice
free rider
public goods
public goods rationale
social benefits
social choice
social costs
social economy
social goals

Thinking Critically About Economics

1. If you were a producer or worker in a social economy, what personal incentives would motivate you to strive for excellence or efficiency? If you were in the same position in a system of primarily individual decision making, would your incentives be any different? If so, how? If not, why not? Which kind of system do you prefer? Why

2. What do you feel is the strongest argument in favor of social decision making? In what types of situations do you feel social decision making would be better or more efficient than individual decision making?

3. Karl Marx's dream of a socialist economy was a state in which individuals would contribute to society to the fullest of their abilities and take from society only what they needed. Do you believe this to be a workable reality? If so, why? If not, why not?

4. If social decision makers make choices that do not agree with your preferences, what is your recourse under representative government? Can a representative government make social decisions that completely reflect your individual preferences? If so, how? If not, why not? What would you suggest as an alternate form of government?

5. As president of the student council, you and your fellow council members must decide how the council's social events budget will be spent this year. There are sufficient funds for only one event. Alternatives include a junior/senior prom, an all-school picnic, or a recognition banquet for this year's volleyball team. Your criteria or goals might be equity, social benefit, and any other two you feel are important. Use the five-step decision-making process to develop your position on this issue. Once you have decided, clearly communicate your decision and supporting reasons to the class. Do other students agree or disagree and why?

Economic Enrichment

Assume that your school is suffering both from a shortage of parking places in the school parking lot and poor conditions in the girls' locker room. Assume that there definitely are not enough resources to do both projects. Examine this problem using the five-step decision-making process and present your decision to the class. After your arguments and those of other students are presented, the class will vote on which project should be undertaken.

Math and Economics

Your town recently received a donation of land that is located within a growing residential area. There is some disagreement within the town over what is the best use of this land. You are on the town council and have been asked to chair a committee that will make a recommendation about how the land can be used to best meet the needs of the townspeople.

At a series of town meetings, suggestions for alternate uses of the land are received. The final list of alternatives includes selling the land to the state as a site for a new prison; building a multipurpose recreation complex with athletic fields, swimming pool, and gymnasium; or selling the land to the state university for the purpose of building a college branch. Your committee has agreed that the social goals to be used for evaluation should be reducing unemployment, maintaining a clean environment, encouraging economic growth, and striving for economic equity. The following decision matrix summarizes the alternatives and the criteria.

Criteria	Alternatives: State Prison	Recreation Complex	College Branch
Full Employment			
Clean Environment			
Economic Growth			
Economic Equity			
Total Score			
Ranking of Alternatives			

1. Assign a score to each alternative that evaluates how that alternative would affect the criteria. The scores can range from 1 to 5, with 1 representing a very negative impact on the criteria and 5 representing a very positive impact on the criteria. On a separate sheet of paper, copy the decision matrix on page 71 and write the scores in the boxes in the bottom right corner of each box.
2. Within each box, write a brief explanation for your score.
3. Add the scores for each alternative use of the land and complete the Total Score row in the decision matrix. Circle your first choice, which should be the land use with the highest total score.
4. Rank the alternatives, with 1 being your first choice, in the Ranking of Alternatives row in the decision matrix.
5. If you had a chance to choose the criteria, would they be the same as those in the decision matrix? Are there other criteria you think are more important for this decision? If so, what are they? How would different criteria affect your final decision?

Writing About Economics

Collect five to seven newspaper articles about pressing social issues in your city or town. Perhaps the town is raising property taxes or building new roads or schools. Maybe more police are needed or the city is losing an industry that has employed many people for a long time. Prepare a large collage of the articles. Under each article, include a list of alternative solutions and identify the solution you support.

Economic Report of the President

The *Economic Report of the President* contains information on what the president considers to be important social issues that have economic implications for our nation. In addition, this report, published annually, includes many statistical tables relating to income, employment, and production.

The following excerpt from the 1995 *Economic Report of the President* discusses the effects of poverty on children's education and, therefore, on their future ability to earn incomes. This report mentions the Children's Defense Fund, which is a group that lobbies Congress to pass legislation in favor of what the organization believes is in the best interests of children in the United States. The report also refers to a program known as Aid to Families with Dependent Children (AFDC), which provides assistance to families who are below the poverty line in terms of income. Here is the excerpt:

> Our core democratic values affirm that each individual should have the opportunity to reach his or her full potential, regardless of race or the income or educational attainment of his or her parents. Yet numerous studies confirm that our Nation today is far from reaching this ideal. That shortfall imposes great costs both on individual Americans and on the country as a whole.
>
> A recent study by a group of economists chaired by a Nobel laureate and commissioned by the Children's Defense Fund examined the effects of childhood poverty on an individual's future living standards. The study concluded that childhood poverty itself, as distinct from such factors as family structure, race, and parental education, has a significant adverse effect on both the educational attainment and the future wages of the Nation's poor children. The study found that children who experience poverty between the ages of 6 and 15 years are two to three times more likely than those who are never poor to become high school dropouts. Using years of schooling as a predictor of future hourly wages, the study concluded that just 1 year of poverty for the 14.6 million children and their families in poverty in 1992 costs the economy somewhere between $36 billion and $177 billion in reduced future productivity and employment.
>
> Significantly, one of the studies that the group examined concluded that each $1 reduction in monthly assistance through the aid to families with dependent children (AFDC) program may reduce future output by between $0.92 and $1.51 (in present value terms) solely by reducing the educational attainment and future productivity of the children who are AFDC's beneficiaries.

As you can see from this reading, our nation faces some very important social choices regarding poverty and particularly its effects on children. When reading an article such as this, you should be asking yourself a number of questions, such as the following: What is the background of the author? What is the reason for the article? Is there a political agenda behind it? Is the article presenting fact or primarily the author's opinion? What do I think about the subject and the facts or opinion presented?

SOURCE: *Economic Report of the President,* transmitted to the Congress February 1995 (Washington, D.C.: U.S. Government Printing Office, 1995), 31.

Overview

Section One
The Private Sector

Section Two
Private Sector Markets

Section Three
Private Sector Problems

Private Sector Decisions

Learning Objectives

4-1

Explain how economic decisions are affected by private ownership and private choice.

4-2

Describe how competition and individual choice improve the efficiency of exchanges.

4-3

Discuss how markets benefit consumers.

4-4

Identify the role of profits and risk for producers in private sector markets.

4-5

Present three major pitfalls associated with the market system in the private sector.

FOCUS

Section One
The Private Sector

What Do You Think?

Hernandez's fruit orchard is located near a major highway. Despite the signs that clearly identify the orchard as private property, motorists occasionally stop by the side of the road to pick pieces of fruit. Lately, this has become more of a problem. Hernandez's has asked police to increase their patrols and arrest the offenders, even those taking just one or two pieces of fruit. Do you think Hernandez's is overreacting?

Terms to Know

- private sector
- private goods
- public sector
- exchange
- efficiency
- competition

What's Ahead?

The private sector is made up of individuals making private choices for their personal benefit. Exchanges in the private sector contribute to the efficiency of the economy. Individual choice and competition in the private sector improve efficiency.

WHAT IS THE PRIVATE SECTOR?

private sector
the part of an economy that is owned by individuals and operated for their personal benefit

The ***private sector*** is the part of an economy that is owned by individuals and operated for their personal benefit. It is made up of private citizens. You are a member of the private sector.

Private Ownership—Private Benefit

private goods
goods that are privately owned and used to benefit only their owners

In the private sector, individuals own goods for their private gain. If you own a house, you have the right to reside in it. It is not public property and you can exclude the public from using it. You may even sell your house at a profit. As the owner, you, not the public, benefit from the sale. ***Private goods*** are goods that are privately owned and used to benefit only their owners.

Members of the private sector produce private goods and services mostly for the benefit of private owners. For example, General Motors is a private firm that produces automobiles which it then sells to earn profits. These profits are private benefits paid to owners of the company. If you buy a GM car, you own it privately and can use it to your benefit. You control the rights to your private property just as General Motors controls the rights to the private property it owns.

Private institutions also are designed to produce private benefits. If individuals form a private country club, the members bear the cost and enjoy the benefits. The private club, the private auto, and the private company are all private properties that benefit their owners. In general, they are not meant to benefit everyone in society.

There is a public sector in our economy as well. The ***public sector*** is the part of an economy that is owned by the whole society and operated for its benefit. All public goods are found in this sector. All members of the economy own and share the public goods, and no one can exclude anyone from their use. As a citizen, you are part owner of such public goods as roads and schools. You share your classroom with your classmates. You share the use of highways with other drivers. Neither you nor others can exclude anyone from lawful use of the roads and schools.

public sector
the part of an economy that is owned by the whole society and operated for its benefit

Private Choice—Private Benefit

The private sector is controlled by individual or private choice. You individually choose which house or car to buy. Companies, which are owned by one individual or a group of individuals, decide what to produce and how to produce it. Private institutions decide not only who will receive their benefits but also how. Individuals decide how to allocate their time among study, leisure, and work activities so that they receive the maximum benefit.

All these individual choices will be guided by one important principle of economics: Individuals will choose the alternative that produces the maximum private benefit or the minimum private cost to them. This principle is important because it guides the whole private sector. The private sector today produces the majority of all the income in our economy. Therefore, it is reasonable to say that the U.S. economy is primarily an economy of private ownership.

PRIVATE SECTOR EXCHANGES

Economic activity involves exchanges. An ***exchange*** is the giving of one thing in return for some other thing. In economic terms, a voluntary exchange occurs only when both parties benefit from the exchange. In the United States, most property is privately owned. Therefore, most of the economic activity involves the exchange of private property between private individuals, businesses, and institutions. Because private sector decisions involve exchanges, they generally are made in some kind of market situation. Two parties exchange something of value, and both parties are better off because of the exchange.

exchange
giving one thing in return for some other thing

Efficiency and Individual Choice

Individuals make private choices to maximize their benefits or minimize costs. This makes the private sector very efficient. ***Efficiency*** is using a given

efficiency
achieving the maximum benefit from a given amount and combination of resources

Internet Connection

THE PRIVATE SECTOR OF CYBERSPACE

The Internet was developed as a government project by the Defense Department. When the Internet became established, a number of commercial computer networks sprang up to offer similar online services. The largest of these are CompuServe, Prodigy, and America Online.

All three provide the same fundamental services: e-mail, news reports, stock market information, weather forecasts, online encyclopedias, and bulletin boards for special interest group discussions. CompuServe is the oldest and has the most information to offer, but the majority of its resources are text based. Prodigy is more family oriented and uses more graphics. America Online (AOL) is the newest and offers the most extensive Internet access.

Initially, the commercial services were more user friendly than the Internet. However, while they were easier to use, they were less powerful and offered fewer services. Now that the federal government is phasing out financial support for the Internet, the commercial networks and the Internet are converging. Commercial networks are offering more of the Internet services, and with applications such as the World Wide Web, the Internet is getting much easier to use.

To send e-mail from the Internet to a commercial network, you must know the commercial e-mail address. Suppose you have a friend whose e-mail address on Prodigy is "friend." From the Internet, her address should read "friend@prodigy.com." If she subscribed to AOL, her address would be "friend@aol.com." CompuServe is a little more complicated. CompuServe addresses have the form "number,number," or "12345,123," for example. When sending e-mail from the Internet, the address should read "12345.123@compuserve.com". Notice that the comma is replaced with a period.

Internet Application: Since most commercial vendors allow a free trial period, talk with your teacher about setting up a class account. Discuss strengths and weaknesses of the different vendors. Use the account to send an e-mail message to your teacher.

Economics Application: In Chapters 3 and 4, you learned about public and private sector decision making. Use what you have learned to explain the following: Why was the first large-scale network (i.e. the Internet) created by the government and not some private firm? Why then did CompuServe, Prodigy, and America Online get created?

amount and combination of resources to get the maximum amount of benefit. You might say that efficiency is the primary concern of the private sector.

Suppose you are going to make sandwiches. You have a one-pound jar of peanut butter and 24 slices of bread. Each sandwich should have 1⅓ ounces of peanut butter. If you are efficient, you can make 12 sandwiches. If you are not efficient, you may not get 12 sandwiches. If you drop slices of bread on the floor and spoil them, your output (sandwiches) will be less than 12. Spreading more than 1⅓ ounces of peanut butter on the sandwiches will result in an output of less than 12 sandwiches.

Efficiency is not a negative word! In the private sector, firms must try to be efficient to stay in business. When a firm tries to produce at the lowest cost, it is not trying to cheat customers. For example, you buy a pair of jeans because you are willing to pay the price in exchange for the benefit you receive from having the jeans. If the company that makes your favorite jeans reduces the quality of its jeans, you would notice. You would then reevaluate whether the price you must pay is worth the benefit you receive. You might decide to buy another brand of jeans. If another company provides better jeans at the same price, that company is more efficient.

Competition Improves Efficiency

The existence of many individual jeans producers and many individual consumers of jeans contributes to the efficiency of that industry. Levi's, Lee, Wrangler, and all other jeans companies must compete with each other for the consumer's buying decision.

Competition is the rivalry between two or more parties to gain benefits from a third party. Competition forces producers to aim for efficiency. A local tailor shop may not be able to produce jeans that you feel are equal to the major brands at a competitive price. This leaves only two possibilities for that local tailor shop if it wants to compete with such firms as Levi's at the same price. The shop must improve its ability to produce an equal or better pair of jeans at an equal price *or* go out of the jeans business. Competition not only encourages producers to be more efficient; it also forces weaker, less efficient companies out of the industry.

competition
the rivalry between two or more parties to gain benefits from a third party

Competition among producers in the marketplace works to the consumer's advantage. However, there is also competition among consumers. If everyone in the United States wanted a pair of Levi's jeans right away, it is doubtful that Levi's could produce rapidly enough the amount consumers wanted. Prices would rise and only those willing and able to pay the higher price would get the Levi's jeans. Some consumers would be priced out of the market. If the Levi's jeans cost $45, fewer consumers would buy them. Only consumers willing and able to pay $45 would get those particular jeans. The competition among consumers for the available jeans might mean that you must purchase some other brand of jeans instead.

Competition on the consumer side exists all the time, just like competition among producers. Suppose you wanted to buy tickets for a particular concert. However, once you reached the ticket counter you found that there were no tickets left. Because there was a limited number of tickets, not everyone who wanted one received one. Some people settled for less than exactly what they wanted. For example, you might have decided to buy tickets for some other concert.

This competition process causes you to choose so that you get the maximum benefit for a given sacrifice or opportunity cost. It makes you a more efficient consumer. If the sold-out concert had been more important to you, you might have bought your tickets earlier. However, you decided that the benefit was not worth the cost to you of getting there earlier. Therefore, you were forced out of the market for this concert, just as inefficient producers are forced out of their markets. Competition improves the efficiency of both producers and consumers.

Checkpoint

Content Check

1. What is the guiding principle behind private sector decisions?

2. How does individual choice affect efficiency?

3. How does competition affect efficiency?

What Do You Think Now?

Reread *What Do You Think?* in the Section One Focus. Then answer the following questions:

4. Do you think Hernandez's is acting reasonably? If so, why? If not, what actions should be taken?

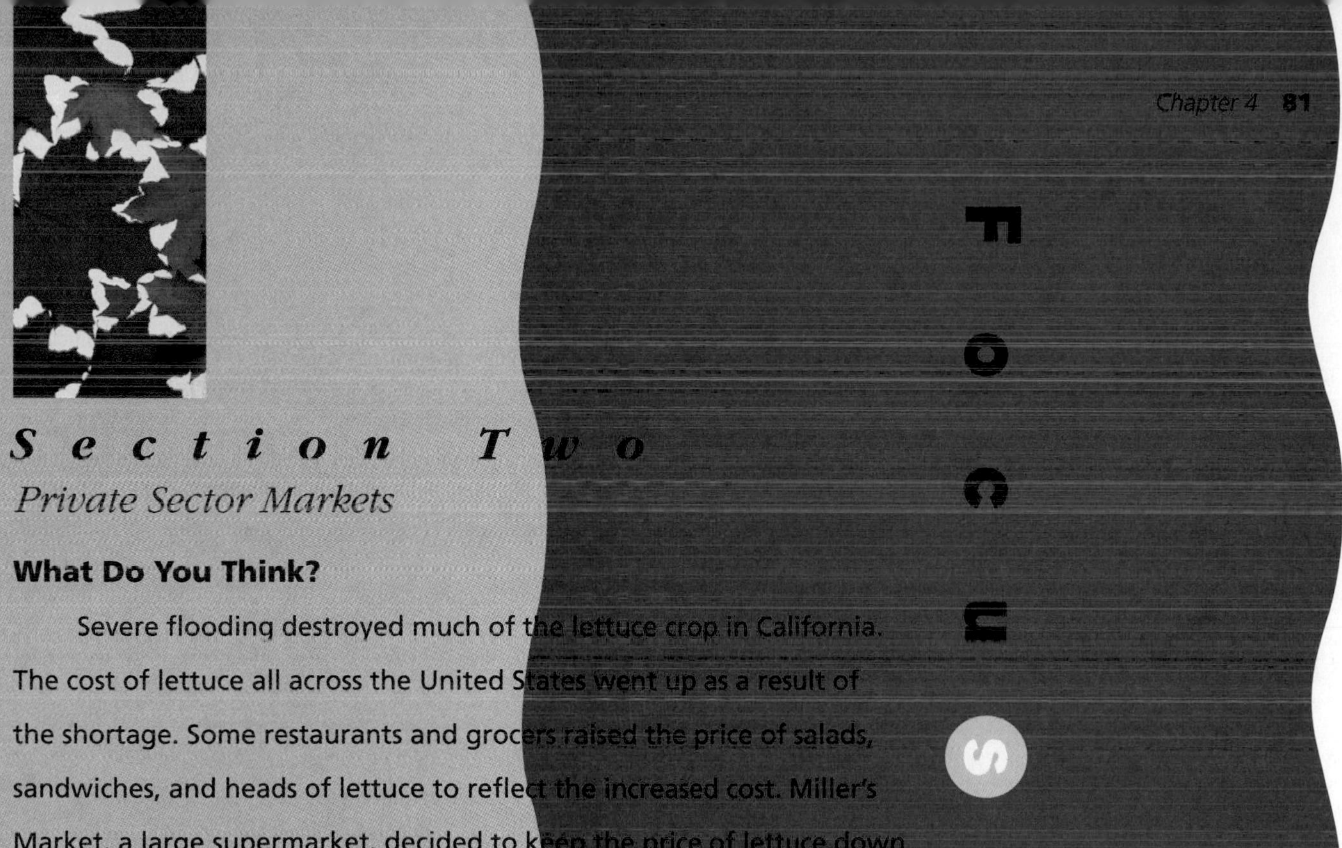

Section Two

Private Sector Markets

What Do You Think?

Severe flooding destroyed much of the lettuce crop in California. The cost of lettuce all across the United States went up as a result of the shortage. Some restaurants and grocers raised the price of salads, sandwiches, and heads of lettuce to reflect the increased cost. Miller's Market, a large supermarket, decided to keep the price of lettuce down by earning a smaller profit. Miller's thought the lettuce shortage was a short-term problem and that keeping the price down would build customer loyalty. Do you think Miller's decision to keep the price down will build customer loyalty?

What's Ahead?

Private sector markets provide price information and a variety of product choices to consumers through competition. The profit motive increases the efficiency of producers and encourages entrepreneurs to take risks. Private markets help you maximize your well-being.

Terms to Know

market

entrepreneurs

private enterprise

PRIVATE SECTOR MARKETS AND CONSUMERS

Exchanges in the private sector usually take place in a market setting. The term ***market*** refers to the exchange activities between buyers and sellers of goods and services. Goods and services of value are exchanged in the market and buyers and sellers benefit from the exchange. Markets provide information through advertising, public relations, promotions, and demonstrations, enabling buyers and sellers to make more efficient private choices.

market
exchange activities between buyers and sellers of goods and services

Markets Give You Price Information

Markets give you important information with which to make your exchange decisions. First of all, markets establish and provide price information. You make your buying decisions based on the price of the item and its benefit to you. A market quickly establishes prices through competition. It takes only a minute to find out the market price of a pair of jeans.

Economic Spotlight

ROAD RUNNER ON THE INFORMATION HIGHWAY

Time Warner Inc. is one of the largest diversified media, entertainment, and publishing companies in the world. Its operations range from publishing to music to movies to cable TV—even to Bugs Bunny and Road Runner cartoons—with a market capitalization of more than $15 billion. The company is an industry leader; in fact, its film entertainment subsidiary, Warner Brothers Studios, was ranked number one at the box office for three consecutive years.

Time Warner is also a major player on the information superhighway, traveling in the fast lane with Richard Parsons, one of the country's most prominent African-American executives, in the driver's seat. As president of Time Warner Inc., Parsons has launched his fourth career after successful careers as a government policy maker, lawyer, and chairman of Dime Bancorp. Parsons is no stranger to the wonders of technology. He attributes much of his success at Dime Bancorp—which he rescued from a three-year struggle with loan problems to make it the fourth-largest savings bank in the country—to technology, which he used to keep his employees informed. He believed that the more informed employees were about the company's numbers, the more effective they would be at their jobs—and his strategy worked!

Brooklyn born, the second of five children, and the son of an electronics technician, Parsons skipped two school grades, graduating from high school at age 16. He ventured on to a fun-filled but academically disastrous experience at the University of Hawaii, leaving school just six credits shy of a degree. Overcoming this "failure" in his life, he was allowed to enroll at Albany Law School in New York without an undergraduate degree. Three years later, he finished first in his class. Parsons attributes his drive for success to his father, who always encouraged him to think for himself.

According to people who know him, Parsons is effective because he is able not only to see the big picture, but also to "grasp the fine point of the details." As Time Warner speeds down the information highway, Parsons sees many challenges ahead. So many, he believes, that "This is the first time I've ever landed somewhere where I think I could be there the rest of my life."

A quick call to several stores will give you this information. If one seller's price is much higher, you may buy somewhere else. If the market price for a pair of jeans is more than you are willing to pay, you might check the market price of other types of pants.

Markets Provide Many Choices

The second important function of markets is that they usually provide many choices. Not only can you get price information, you can also find substitutes to fill your need quickly. If competitive markets did not exist, there might not be a large variety of goods and services from which to choose. There also might not be a range of prices from which to choose.

Suppose you needed a means of transportation to get to school. A quick look in the phone book would turn up references to buses, taxis, trains, automobile dealers, bicycle stores, and other alternatives. Even if you decided to consider just one of these alternatives to fill your transportation needs, the market is still very large. For instance, assume you decided to buy a bicycle. The market for bicycles would offer you everything from a simple one-speed model to racing bikes, with new models entering the market constantly.

Markets usually provide you with many choices to satisfy your needs. You make those choices based on what has the greatest private benefit for you relative to the market price you must pay. The market rewards consumers with the benefits of new and better products to fulfill their wants and needs. Consumers who choose carefully and allocate their incomes efficiently through the market increase their satisfaction. Consumers who choose poorly do not receive the same satisfaction per dollar spent.

PRIVATE SECTOR MARKETS AND PRODUCERS

So far, you have learned mostly about the consumer's view of the private sector. Consumers use market information to make choices that maximize their satisfaction. Now consider the situation from the producer's point of view.

Profit Drives Producers

The success of producers depends on their ability to satisfy the wants and needs of consumers more efficiently than others do. Therefore, producers must find out what consumers want or need. Once the consumer's needs are identified, producers must decide what resources to use and in what quantities to make a product that satisfies these needs. Resource prices guide producers just as final goods prices guide consumers' choices. For example, what if the price of metal buttons rises? Levi's might then change to plastic buttons or some other substitute. Then Levi's could earn the same profit without raising its prices. Profits benefit producers. Therefore, producers in the market try to maximize profits.

Entrepreneurs Take Risks

One major difference between consumer choices and producer decisions is that producers take greater risks in making their decisions. Individuals who organize a company to produce a product for a profit are called ***entrepreneurs.*** Entrepreneurs bring together the inputs of production (raw materials,

entrepreneurs
individuals who take the risk of producing a product for a profit

workers, and machines) to produce a product to satisfy consumer wants and needs. While consumers can see the products that they can buy to satisfy their needs, entrepreneurs cannot see their products until they are produced. Therefore, entrepreneurs must take the risk that their finished products can satisfy a need, be attractive to consumers, and sell at a price that covers the cost of production. Entrepreneurs take the risk that the product will produce profits.

private enterprise a system in which individuals take the risk of producing goods or services to make a profit

Sometimes our economy is referred to as a private enterprise economy. ***Private enterprise*** is a system in which individuals take the risk of producing goods or services to make a profit. In private enterprise, an entrepreneur is willing to take risks or try something that has not been done before. If entrepreneurs did not risk producing new products, you would not have the variety of choices you have today. If reasonable profits were not possible, entrepreneurs would not risk producing new and better products. The market rewards successful entrepreneurs with profits.

On the other hand, the market punishes entrepreneurs who produce products that consumers do not want. In the early 1980s, Adam Osborne identi-

Economic Dilemma

DOES CRIME PAY?

Crime is a social problem that you hear about all the time in the news media. Economists believe that criminals weigh the costs against the benefits when making a decision about committing a particular crime. Remember that this is only a discussion about the economic part of the decision process. Moral and ethical concerns also have a large impact on a person's decision.

Suppose that Sam, who earns $10,400 a year, notices several color television sets on the loading dock at work. These TVs sell for about $800 each. If Sam were to steal a TV, he would gain a piece of property worth $800. However, his decision to steal would not be without its costs. Sam has read that the police apprehend one out of every ten thieves (10 percent). Furthermore, only 10 percent of those apprehended are actually convicted and sentenced to three years in jail. If only 10 percent of the thieves get caught, and only 10 percent of those are convicted and jailed, then Sam's chance of going to jail for stealing is only one in 100 (1 percent).

Sam figures that three years in jail would cost him $31,200, in lost salary ($10,400 × 3). However, if he has only a 1 percent chance of going to jail, the real "cost" is 1 percent of $31,200 or $312. Since the TV is worth $800, from a purely economic standpoint it would be rational for Sam to risk stealing the TV.

Realizing that crime is a costly problem to society, what does economics suggest as a solution? There are many options available to society. To reduce crime, society can (1) raise the opportunity cost of committing the crime, (2) increase the probability of apprehension, (3) increase the probability of conviction, and/or (4) increase the penalties for criminal acts.

fied the need for a small portable computer. At first his idea was very successful in the marketplace. His company, Osborne Computer, became one of the best-known names in technology. However, the company failed to keep up with current market trends. New products introduced by Apple, IBM, and others were favored by consumers. The Osborne computers failed in the eyes of consumers and Osborne Computer eventually filed for bankruptcy.

In summary, the private sector functions primarily through markets. Markets give power to both producer and consumer through competition. The market encourages producers to take risks and to produce new and better products. Markets help producers and consumers make more efficient decisions that maximize their own well-being.

Checkpoint

Content Check

1. What benefits do consumers receive as a result of competition in private sector markets?
2. What is the role of profit in private sector markets?
3. What is the role of entrepreneurs in private sector markets?

What Do You Think Now?

Reread *What Do You Think?* in the Section Two Focus. Then answer the following questions:

4. What other options did Miller's have in response to an increase in the cost of lettuce?
5. What risks is Miller's taking?

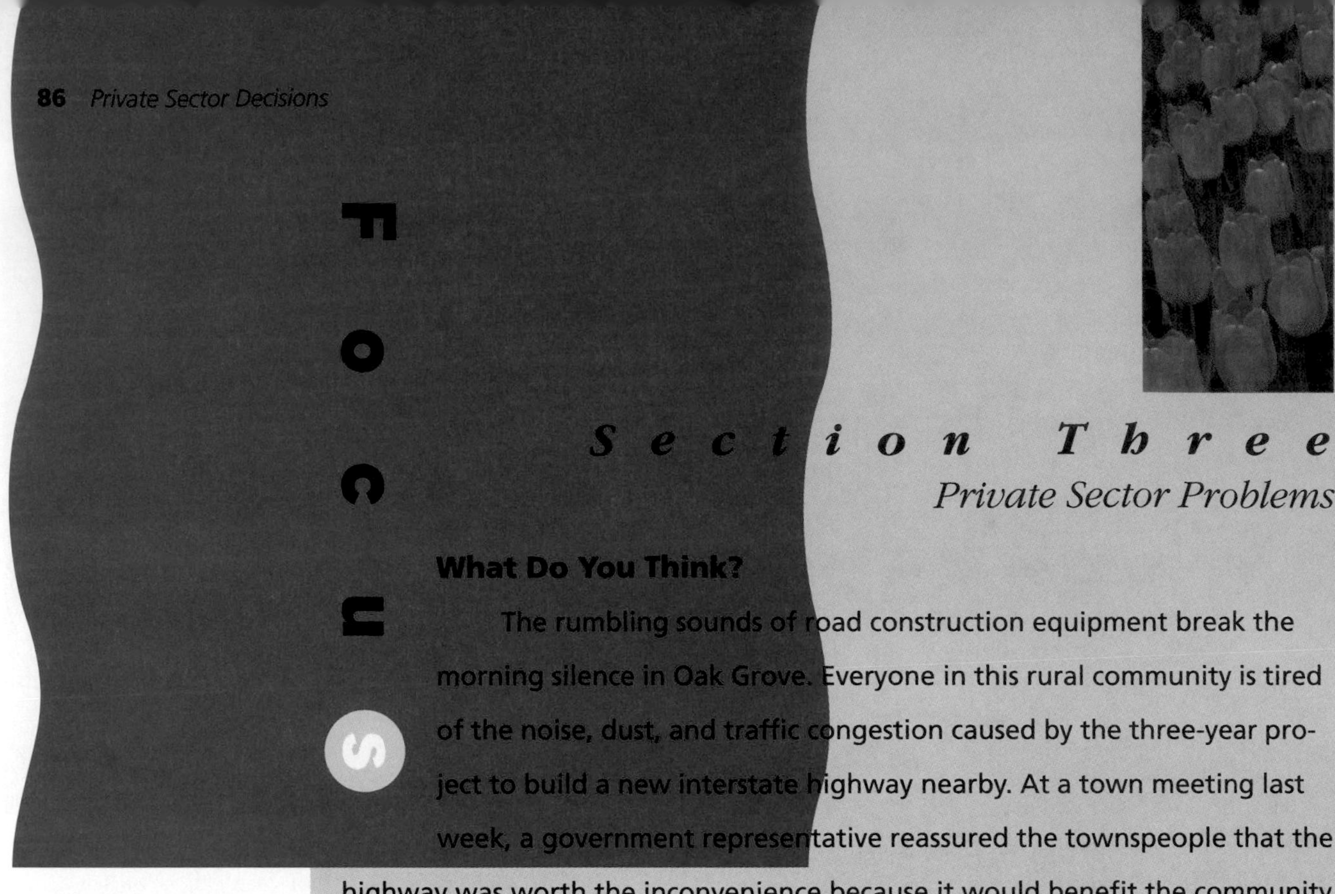

Section Three
Private Sector Problems

What Do You Think?

The rumbling sounds of road construction equipment break the morning silence in Oak Grove. Everyone in this rural community is tired of the noise, dust, and traffic congestion caused by the three-year project to build a new interstate highway nearby. At a town meeting last week, a government representative reassured the townspeople that the highway was worth the inconvenience because it would benefit the community when completed. Some of the farmers agreed because they believe the highway will open new markets for them. Other residents weren't convinced. They feel like they're paying the price for everyone who will eventually use the highway. How would you feel?

Term to Know

externalities

What's Ahead?

Market systems are associated with three major pitfalls. First, producers and consumers can reduce competition within the private sector. Second, public goods are used to support the efficiency of the private sector market. Third, private sector decisions can create costs that spill over to the public sector.

MARKET PITFALLS

The market system and private enterprise have produced one of the highest standards of living in the twentieth century. The efficiency of the private sector can take much of the credit for the large assortment of goods and services you enjoy today. You should be aware, however, that this market system in the private sector does have three major pitfalls: the possibility of reduced competition, the use of public goods for private benefit, and the production of costs that affect individuals outside the market.

Reduced Competition

Competition among buyers and sellers makes private sector markets efficient. However, sometimes competition is not as strong as it could be. Competition can be reduced by both producers and consumers, thus making markets less efficient.

How Producers Reduce Competition. Competition makes producers try to produce at the lowest possible cost the goods that consumers want. Competition among buyers allows producers to offer their goods to many buyers and sell to the highest bidders. Sometimes, however, producers try to swing the forces of the market in their favor. All the producers of milk might get together and agree to set a uniform price higher than the existing market price. If no producer will sell below the agreed-upon price, consumers must

Global Economy

CAN WE AFFORD TO SAVE THE ENVIRONMENT?

The environment is something we all share. Environmental problems, such as depletion of the rain forest and major oil spills, deserve our attention because they have the potential to endanger the future of our lives and our planet. But what can be done and at what cost? Efforts to solve these problems will all have opportunity costs.

Since we do not have unlimited resources, we cannot simultaneously solve all environmental concerns. We must once again allocate our resources among unlimited needs. If a government requires a corporation to install millions of dollar's worth of pollution control equipment, we cannot at the same time use those resources to have cleaner water. The question is not how clean an environment we want, but how clean an environment we are willing and able to pay for.

How many goods and services, how many jobs, and how much income are we willing to give up to get how much more of a clean environment? Individuals must eventually make these choices based upon the costs and benefits of each alternative. This is even more true on a global scale. For example, some less-developed and developing countries who want very much to industrialize and grow are burning off portions of the rain forest. In other words, scarcity in these developing and less-developed countries has lead them to prefer a less clean environment in pursuit of economic development. Some scientists believe this will affect the global climate and have negative effects on agriculture and the quality of life in many other countries, such as the United States. The externality of polluting the environment is producing a global economic issue.

pay the higher price. The choices available to consumers are reduced. If they want milk, they must pay the price. The producers gain at a cost to the consumer.

These same producers can use their extra profits to build larger and more efficient plants, and thus further reduce their costs. They now are able to produce milk at lower costs because of these large plants. Newer and smaller milk producers cannot afford such large plants. They cannot produce milk at as low a cost as the large companies can, and, therefore, they cannot enter or succeed in the market. Competition is reduced.

How Consumers Reduce Competition. Consumers sometimes agree not to buy a particular item from a particular producer. Assume that a dairy is charging the fair market price for milk. However, consumers band together and refuse to buy from that dairy until it lowers its price. Consumers then benefit at the cost of the dairy.

Econ & You

PUBLIC EDUCATION FOR PRIVATE BENEFIT

When students gain a good education, they themselves get the primary benefit. An educated individual has more job skills, is more valuable to an employer, and usually earns more income. Education also adds to the individual's knowledge of many other matters, such as nutrition, health care, and financial security. On average, educated people are healthier, live longer, have more stable marriages, earn higher incomes, and commit fewer crimes than others. It would seem, therefore, that education really does provide significant benefits to the individuals that receive it.

If education produces significant private benefits, why would our government spend billions of tax dollars each year to provide education free of charge to students as a public good? The answer is that education also produces positive externalities for society as a whole. Educated people earn higher incomes so they end up paying higher taxes to support the public sector. Healthier people spread fewer diseases throughout the population. Educated people commit fewer crimes, which decreases the cost of crime on the law abiding population. Stronger and more stable marriages reduce the number of families on welfare.

In reality, education has both private and public benefits, and this is one reason why both society and individuals are willing to spend so much money, time, and effort on good education. As the economy of the future becomes more and more complex, the benefits of an education, both public and private, are sure to increase.

The action of milk producers or the consumers working together to reduce competition destroys the efficiency of the market. It enriches one party in an exchange at the cost of another. Eventually, it leads to inefficient production on the part of producers and inefficient buying decisions on the part of consumers.

Public Sector Reaction to Reduced Competition. The private sector has a definite interest in keeping markets competitive. Both producers and consumers stand to benefit from competitive markets. Unfortunately, neither group is really in a position to force competitive behavior from the other. So far, the only partial solution to the problem has been public laws against noncompetitive behavior. This moves the solution to the problem from the private sector to the public sector. You will learn in the next chapter how the public sector deals with this problem.

Public Goods for Private Benefit

Many aspects of the private sector depend on public goods to operate efficiently. For example, roads, which are public goods, increase the efficiency of shipping goods to markets. Early in our country's history, there were few paved roads. There were just dirt paths and trails for people to use. Farmers drove their pigs, cattle, or sheep to market on foot through these crude trails and paths. The animals lost a great deal of weight on the long journey. This caused farmers to earn smaller profits on their products. Consumers received smaller animals in poorer physical condition in return for the price paid. In this situation, producing a public good, such as a road, was in the interest of both producers and consumers.

Once roads were built, the exchange of private goods between producers and consumers was more efficient. Because the trip to market was not as long, animals didn't lose as much weight, and the farmers got a better price for them. Also, consumers received a better quality animal. In addition, producers, consumers, and the public were able to use the roads for many other purposes besides bringing animals to market. You can see that in this case private sector exchange is made more efficient through public goods.

Public goods, however, do cause problems for the private sector. Public goods cannot easily be provided by the private sector. Private benefits usually are less than private costs. For example, if only farmers pay to have a road built, the cost to each farmer is very large. Their individual use cannot justify such a cost. Also, it is very difficult to keep the public from using a private road. Guards or expensive fences only increase the cost of the road. There is no easy way to exclude those who did not pay to have the road built. If it is difficult to exclude nonpayers, some farmers might even refuse to pay but use the road anyway.

Private goods yield benefits only to their owners. They are goods that exclude the public from their use. Goods such as roads or schools surely contribute to the efficiency of the private sector, but they also benefit the whole economy. Public goods cannot be provided as effectively by the private sector, since individuals cannot keep all the benefits for themselves. The problem is that, to some extent, the public sector supports the efficiency of the private sector.

Costs and Benefits Flow Outside the Market

When producers provide goods and services to the market, sometimes they pass on some costs and benefits to citizens outside the private sector market. Costs or benefits passed on outside of the market system are called ***externalities.*** Another term for externalities is *spillover effect*.

externalities
costs or benefits passed on outside of the market system

Negative Externalities. A new apartment building may be built across from your home on a lot now occupied by a flower garden. When the building is finished, your view will be a concrete wall instead of the flower garden. Your satisfaction or well-being will be reduced by the construction of the building. In effect, a cost will be passed on to you. This is not a cost in dollar terms but a reduction of your satisfaction.

The garbage produced at a local restaurant is another example of costs outside a market. It costs money to clean up and carry away the garbage. The restaurant would save money by cutting back to two garbage pickups a month. As a result, the restaurant could offer lower food prices or enjoy larger profits. However, the garbage would accumulate and pass a cost on to residents of the neighborhood in terms of smell and unsightly appearance. Again, this is not a dollar cost but a reduction of satisfaction. It is an externality, a cost passed on to others outside of the market system.

Figure 4-1

The impact of a negative externality is sometimes hard to measure. ***What negative externalities are illustrated in this editorial cartoon?***

Scott Willis ©1989 San Jose Mercury News

One solution to the restaurant's garbage situation is to have the garbage collected more often, passing the additional cost on to consumers through higher food prices. Getting rid of the garbage is then a true part of the cost of the food. Those who benefit from eating in the restaurant pay the full cost of the benefit. If, on the other hand, garbage collection is reduced to keep food prices low, consumers are not paying the full cost of the food. Local residents are paying part of the cost by enduring the smell and mess.

Positive Externalities. Externalities also can be positive. They can pass on benefits as a by-product of some action. If your neighbor buys a very large dog, it may frighten burglars away from your house, too. You receive a benefit for which you did not have to pay.

In the business world, a positive externality might occur when one company hires guards to patrol its offices and grounds. Other businesses in the area receive some benefit, because the patrol might keep some criminals away from the whole area. Fewer burglaries benefit all companies in the area, not just the company that hired the guards. Whether externalities are positive or negative, they are not reflected in market prices. Therefore, they are a true problem for the market system.

Checkpoint

Content Check

1. How do producers and consumers reduce competition in a market?
2. How do public goods support private sector markets? Give an example in your school.
3. How do externalities spill over to the public sector? Give an example in your community.

What Do You Think Now?

Reread *What Do You Think?* in the Section Three Focus. Then answer the following questions:

4. Who benefits from a new interstate highway?
5. What are some positive and negative externalities of the road construction near Oak Grove?
6. What actions can people who are opposed to the new highway take? What actions could they have taken before construction began?

Concepts in Brief

1. The private sector is that part of the economy owned by and operated for the benefit of private individuals. It includes private business, institutions, and individual citizens. The owners of private property can exclude the public from the use and benefits of their property. The private sector engages in individual choice for private benefit.
2. Efficiency is achieved when individuals make decisions that maximize benefits and minimize costs. Competition in the private sector strongly encourages producers and consumers to be efficient. Each producer attempts to provide at the lowest cost to them goods of a specific quality to the market. This makes producers choose carefully and improves their efficiency. Competition among buyers for the available goods causes buyers to choose carefully as well.
3. Exchanges take place because both parties benefit from the exchange. Markets enable exchange to take place more efficiently by providing price information and a variety of substitutes for consumers.
4. In market situations, producers must take risks in trying to produce goods that they think consumers will buy. Profits are the incentives that encourage producers to take risks and to provide goods and services to consumers.
5. The market system does not solve all economic problems. There are some pitfalls. For one, the competition that encourages efficiency in markets does not always exist. Either buyers or sellers may band together to swing the market in their favor. In some cases, price fixing by producers can force up market prices. In other cases, consumer actions can force market prices down. A second problem is that the private sector depends, in part, on public goods. Some productive parts of our society, therefore, cannot be provided by the private sector. Finally, producing goods and services often results in by-products, such as air or water pollution, that are passed on to consumers outside of the marketplace.

Economic Foundations

1. List some of the differences between the private sector and the public sector.
2. What guides individual choices in the private sector?
3. What is the effect of competition on producers?
4. What is the effect of competition on consumers?

5. How do markets increase the efficiency of individual decisions?
6. How do profits and entrepreneurs benefit consumers?
7. What are three major pitfalls associated with the private sector market system?
8. How can producers reduce competition?
9. How can consumers reduce competition?
10. Why does the private sector avoid producing public goods?
11. Who pays the cost of negative externalities?

Your Economic Vocabulary

Build your economic vocabulary by matching the following terms with their definitions.

1. individuals who take the risk of producing a product for a profit
2. the rivalry between two or more parties to gain benefits from a third party
3. giving one thing in return for some other thing
4. a system in which individuals take the risk of producing goods or services to make a profit
5. achieving the maximum benefit from a given amount and combination of resources
6. goods that are privately owned and used to benefit only their owners
7. exchange activities between buyers and sellers of goods and services
8. costs or benefits passed on outside of the market system
9. the part of an economy that is owned by individuals and operated for their personal benefit
10. the part of an economy that is owned by the whole society and operated for its benefit

competition
efficiency
entrepreneurs
exchange
externalities
market
private enterprise
private goods
private sector
public sector

Thinking Critically About Economics

1. Is it fair that our economy permits private property? Should individuals have the sole benefit of their property? If so, why? If not, why not?
2. What role do markets play in conducting exchanges between private parties?
3. What should be done about markets where producers or consumers band together to swing the market in their favor?
4. Are negative externalities fair to the consumer? Would you feel the same way if the externalities were positive?
5. Should all of our economy be privately owned? If so, why? If not, why not? Can the private sector meet all the needs of the citizens of our society?
6. What are the industries that might be difficult for new entrepreneurs to enter?

Economic Enrichment

Look through some large metropolitan newspapers, such as the *The New York Times* or *Washington Post,* to identify two articles that address negative externalities. Use an online search on your computer or go to the library to find the actual newspapers. Write a one-page report that explains the negative externality and presents two or more proposed solutions. Indicate in the report who you believe will end up paying the price for the externality under each proposed solution. Attach a copy of each article to your report.

Math and Economics

Conduct a market survey to see how market prices affect consumers' willingness to buy. Ask 15 people how many 1-pound bags of Hershey Kisses they would be willing and able to buy at $0.75 per bag. Record the results. Ask the same group of people how many bags they would be willing and able to buy at $1.50 per bag. Record this price and quantity. Now raise the price to $2.00 per bag and record the responses. Finally, raise the price to $4.00 per bag and record the price and quantity. Prepare a table that summarizes the price and quantity combinations from highest price to lowest price.

1. What happens to quantity demanded as price goes up?

2. What happens to quantity demanded as price goes down?

3. What kind of mathematical relationship is there between price and quantity demanded?

Writing About Economics

Markets reward successful professional athletes and entertainers with very large salaries. Teachers, who shape the minds of students around the world, are usually paid much less. Research the average salary for high school teachers, college professors, NBA basketball players, professional soccer players in the United States, and professional actors.

What does this salary information tell you about wages paid to educators, athletes, and entertainers? Write an article for your school newspaper that explains why teachers earn less than professional athletes and entertainers. Be sure to discuss how wages are determined for teachers as well as for athletes and entertainers.

Overview

Section One
The Public Sector

Section Two
Public Sector Contributions

Section Three
Public Sector Problems

Public Sector Decisions

Learning Objectives

5-1

Explain the roles of public institutions and government in the economy.

5-2

Distinguish between the five major functions of the public sector.

5-3

Present three problems with the public sector.

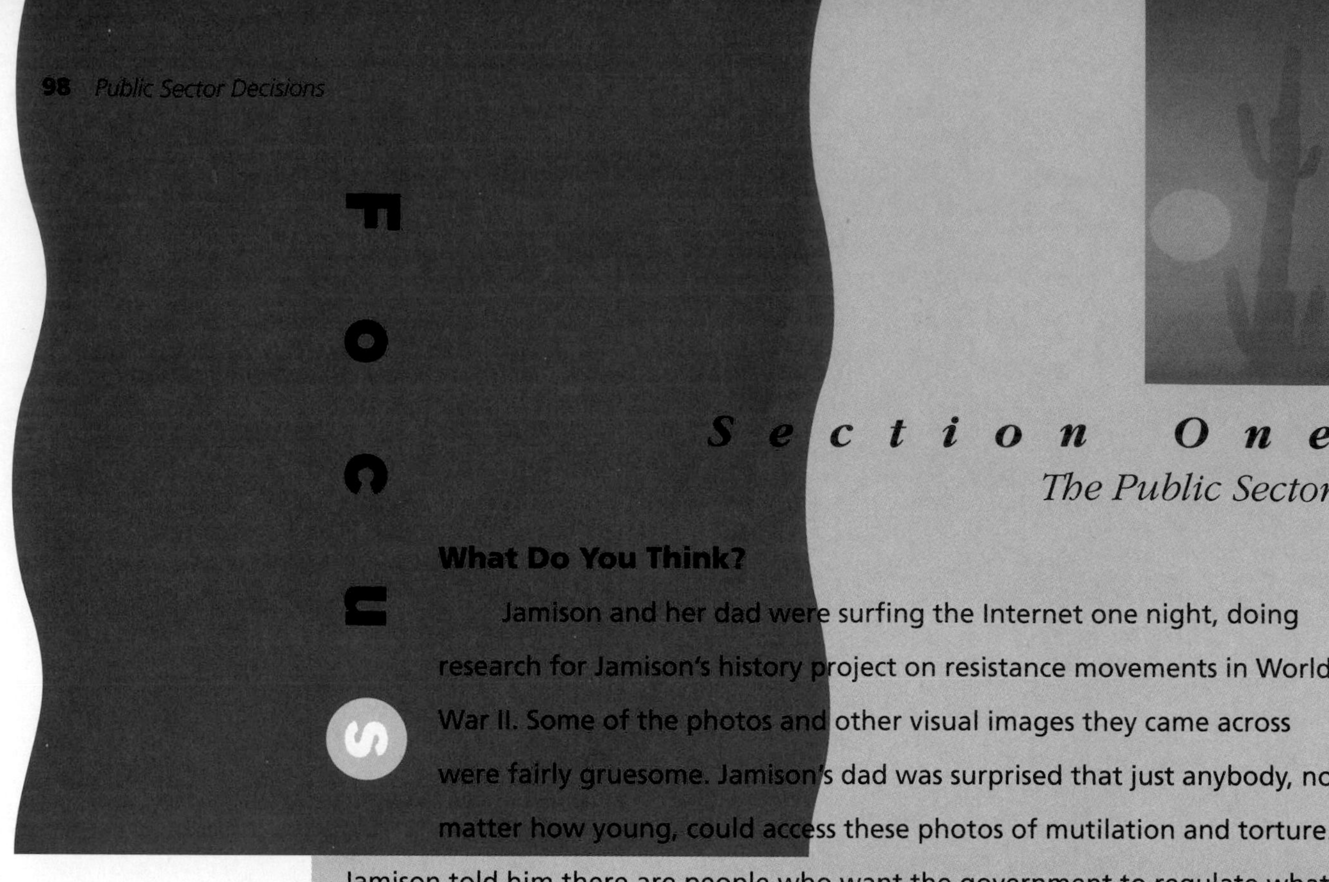

Section One
The Public Sector

What Do You Think?

Jamison and her dad were surfing the Internet one night, doing research for Jamison's history project on resistance movements in World War II. Some of the photos and other visual images they came across were fairly gruesome. Jamison's dad was surprised that just anybody, no matter how young, could access these photos of mutilation and torture. Jamison told him there are people who want the government to regulate what can be carried on the Internet. Jamison's dad said that might not be the best solution—legislation would just get bogged down in regulatory agency rulings and court decisions. Are regulations going to solve this problem?

Terms to Know

public sector

public institutions

What's Ahead?

The public sector is that part of the economy that is owned by and operated for the benefit of the whole society. Government and public institutions at all levels have been given great power to carry out the functions of the public sector. Economists differ in their views about whether the government should play an active or limited role in our economy.

WHAT IS THE PUBLIC SECTOR?

public sector
the part of an economy that is owned by and operated for the benefit of the whole society

The ***public sector*** is the part of an economy that is owned by and operated for the benefit of the whole society. The public sector consists of government at all levels in our economy—federal, state, and local—and public institutions. Individual citizens acting together as a society create the public sector (government) to carry out certain functions. As citizens, we give this vast economic power to government. Therefore, it is important to understand the economic role of government.

Government's Role in the Public Sector

No single force in our economy is more powerful than government. Government makes the laws of the land, thereby establishing rules that all producers and consumers must obey. Our government sets broad limits on what can and cannot be produced and how it can be produced. For example, our government permits and encourages the production of milk. It also sets safety standards and regulations on how milk must be produced. Government also allows the mining of coal. However, it closely regulates the safety and health conditions under which coal is mined. Government creates and enforces the laws by which organizations, such as the miners' unions and the coal companies, must settle their differences.

Government also prohibits the unlicensed production of some goods and services, such as nuclear power, radio and television broadcasts, and military weapons. The government's decisions to regulate or prohibit the production of such items are made by our whole society through our votes. It is government, however, that enforces these decisions.

Public Institutions

Public institutions are publicly owned organizations established by government to serve the wants and needs of a whole society. Our courts, state universities, and Federal Reserve Bank System are examples of public institutions. Government establishes public institutions to help our society function efficiently.

public institutions publicly owned organizations established by government to serve the wants and needs of a whole society

The public sector makes up a large part of our entire economy. By one measure, about 43 percent of U.S. gross domestic product is government expenditures (see Figure 5-1 on page 100).[1]

[1] *Statistical Abstract of the United States: 1994,* 114th ed. (Washington, D.C.: U.S. Bureau of the Census, 1994), 298, 448.

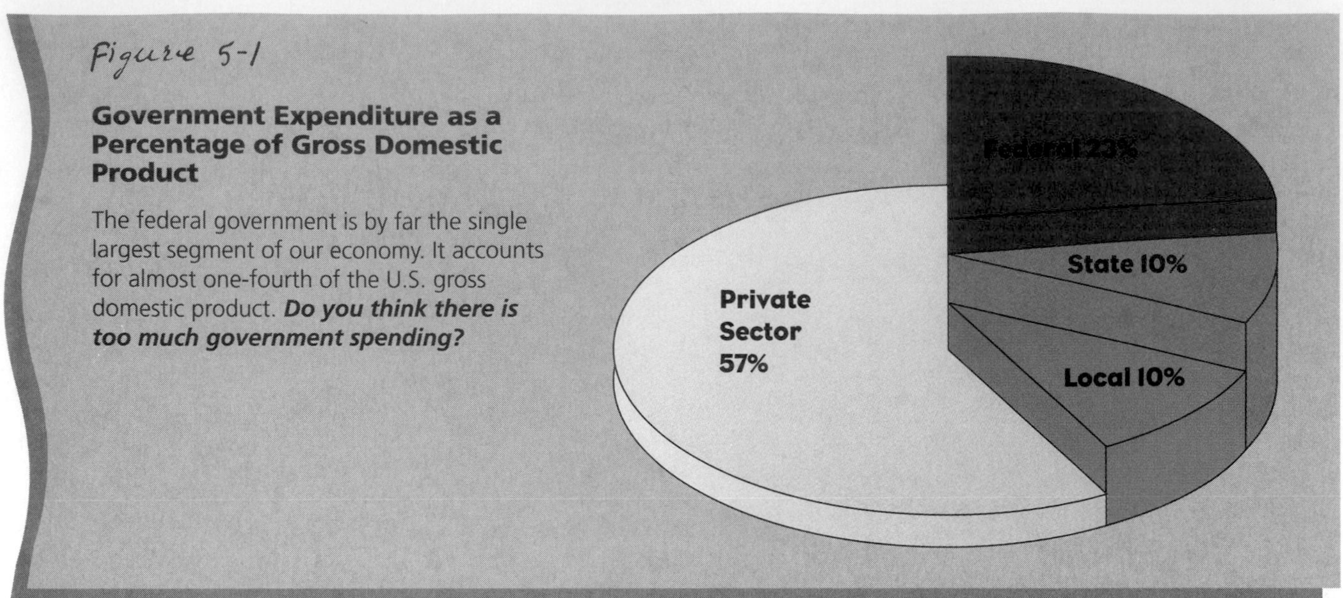

Government Expenditure as a Percentage of Gross Domestic Product

The federal government is by far the single largest segment of our economy. It accounts for almost one-fourth of the U.S. gross domestic product. ***Do you think there is too much government spending?***

While providing an environment in which the private sector can function, the public sector also provides

1. courts to define rights and settle disputes;
2. monetary institutions, such as the Federal Reserve System, to control our system of money; and
3. regulatory agencies to promote competition among producers.

LEADERS IN ECONOMIC THOUGHT

Economic leaders do not always agree on the appropriate role that government and public institutions should play in our economy. Let's see what two leaders in economic thought believe about government involvement in our economy.

Milton Friedman

Milton Friedman is a strong supporter of *laissez-faire*. The concept of laissez-faire means that government involvement in economic matters should be highly limited. Friedman's main argument is that while trying to do good, government actions usually end up doing just the opposite. Most government efforts to protect consumers by regulating business create higher prices or services and goods of lesser quality. Many of the regulatory agencies are not very efficient in promoting competition in markets. They frequently end up representing the interests of the very businesses they regulate. Friedman has contended for more than three decades that minimal government ownership and control in the economy is in everyone's best interest.

Friedman won the Nobel Prize in Economics in 1976 for his work on monetary theory. He is professor emeritus at the University of Chicago and a fellow at Stanford University's Hoover Institute. Milton and his wife, Rose Friedman, have written three books together and are perhaps best known for their television series, "*Free to Choose*."

Economic Spotlight

PUBLIC SERVANT, PRIVATE CONCERNS

One of 11 children of a Dutch-Irish mother and a Cherokee Indian father, Wilma Mankiller spent most of her childhood away from the Cherokee Indian Reservation of her birth. However, she later came back to her roots to help the Cherokees restore their self-sufficiency. As the first female principal chief of the Native-American Cherokee tribe, Mankiller wants to be remembered "as the person who helped us restore faith in ourselves."

As a child, her family fled the reservation for California after a severe drought ruined any chances of eking out a living from the poor Oklahoma soil. After becoming a social worker actively involved in Native-American rights, Wilma Mankiller moved back to the reservation. There she found most of the Cherokees living at the poverty level. On the reservation, she worked hard to revive the Cherokee nation's cultural pride and to restore the people to economic self-sufficiency. She won the respect of male leaders in the tribe by obtaining a grant that enabled rural Cherokees to build their own 26-mile waterline. In 1985, she filled the vacated position of principal chief of the Cherokee Nation. She was subsequently elected to that position in 1987 and 1991, retiring after completion of her 1991 term.

As chief, Mankiller worked 14-hour days to bring national attention to the plight of the Native-American people and to show Cherokees how they can overcome adversity to live productively. Applying the skills that she learned as a social worker, Mankiller's focus as chief was on two issues: self-help as a source of self-esteem and solving economic problems without looking for a handout from the government.

According to Mankiller, "My goal has always been for Indians to solve their own economic problems. Although we have been affected by a lot of historical factors, nobody is going to pull us out but ourselves." She certainly is off to a good start. In 1975, nearly all Cherokee income came from the federal government. But today, more than 50 percent of the tribe's income comes from a Cherokee-owned electronics plant and other private enterprises.

John Kenneth Galbraith

John Kenneth Galbraith urges an affirmative role for government. He argues that because of their size, corporations have too much influence in modern society. This influence is so strong that it sometimes overpowers the classical market forces of supply and demand. Through advertising, corporations tend to *create* wants and needs for consumers. Thus, more private goods are produced, sometimes to the detriment of needed public goods. Galbraith has gained attention and respect in the field of economics.

Economic Dilemma

THE ECONOMICS OF POLITICS AND THE POLITICS OF ECONOMICS

If economists know what policies are good for the economy, why don't those policies always get used? Unfortunately, the system of representative government we have in the United States sometimes links good economics with bad politics and good politics with bad economics. There are at least three major reasons why this is true. The national debt gives us an example of how these three reasons create conflict between good economics and good politics.

First, some voters are rationally ignorant. This means that people make a rational decision to be poorly informed about the national debt. They feel that their individual votes make little difference (little benefit) and it is time consuming to gather information on which to base their votes (high cost). So they rationally decide not to inform themselves about an issue such as the national debt.

Second, special interest groups benefit a great deal from influencing decisions surrounding the national debt. Therefore, they spend a lot of money to influence the government to vote to their advantage, which is often to the disadvantage of the rest of society. Since the cost of the resulting policies is spread over the general public, no one person has too high a cost and there is usually little opposition to special interest groups.

Third, politicians are rationally shortsighted. They are more likely to vote for government spending than against it because it often benefits their voters—in the short run. Rational politicians would rather be in office explaining an increased national debt than defeated and explaining why they did not support spending programs for their state.

When these three effects combine in the political arena, the economic policy that gets voted in is frequently far from what is best for the whole economy. That's when good politics leads to bad economics.

John Kenneth Galbraith has been a professor of economics at Harvard University and president of the American Economic Association. He has served as ambassador to India and provided economic advice to several presidents. His books, *The Affluent Society, The New Industrial State,* and *Economics and the Public Purpose,* have been widely read and have contributed to economic thinking for more than two decades.

Checkpoint

Content Check

1. What makes up the public sector?
2. What are public institutions? Give two examples.
3. How do Milton Friedman's views about the role of government in our economy differ from John Kenneth Galbraith's views?

What Do You Think Now?

Reread *What Do You Think?* in the Section One Focus. Then answer the following questions:

4. Do you think the federal government should play a role in regulating content on the Internet? Why or why not?
5. What other actions, besides government regulation, can be taken to control content and access to the Internet?
6. Do you think any actions need to be taken to oversee information exchanges on the Internet?

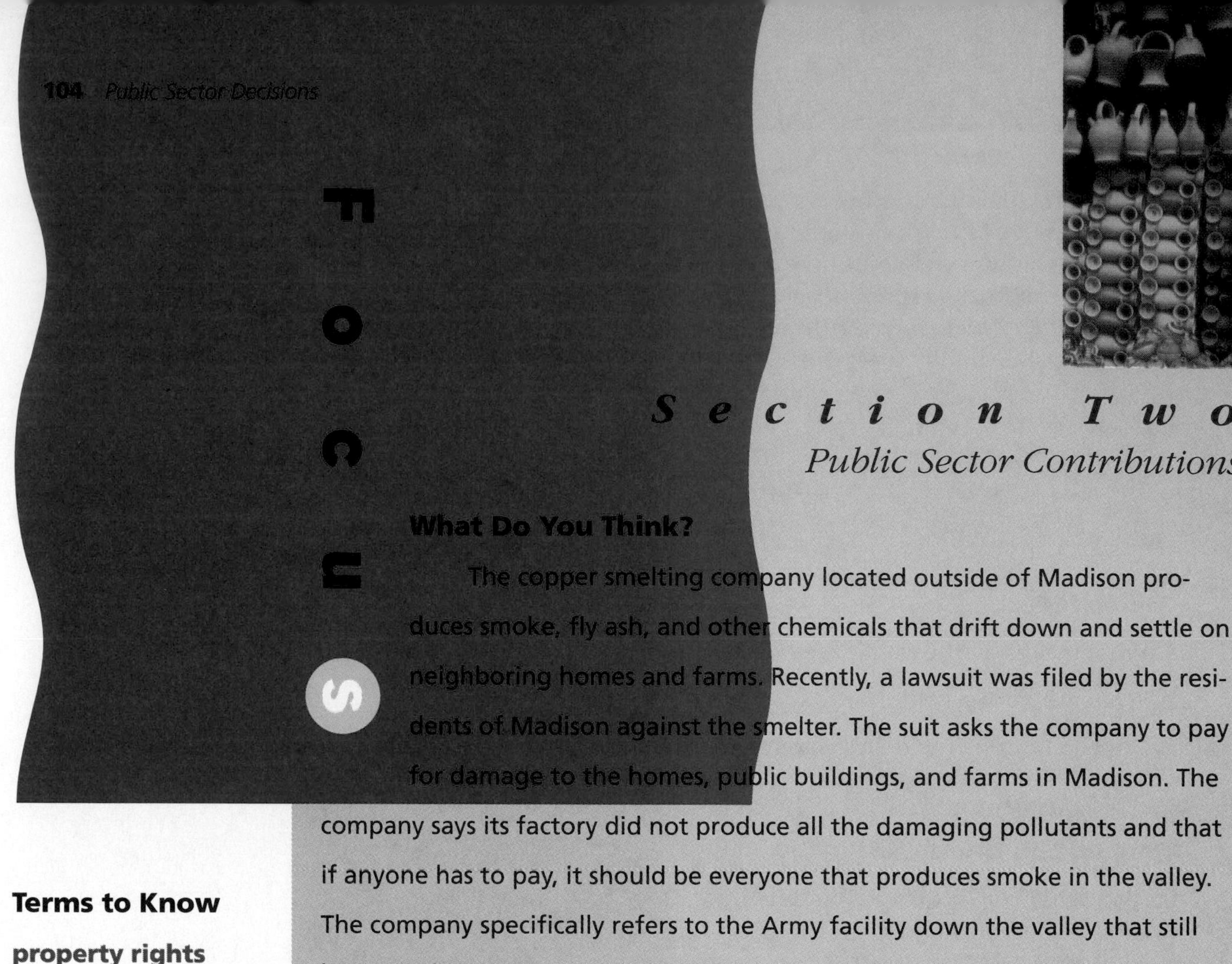

Section Two
Public Sector Contributions

What Do You Think?

The copper smelting company located outside of Madison produces smoke, fly ash, and other chemicals that drift down and settle on neighboring homes and farms. Recently, a lawsuit was filed by the residents of Madison against the smelter. The suit asks the company to pay for damage to the homes, public buildings, and farms in Madison. The company says its factory did not produce all the damaging pollutants and that if anyone has to pay, it should be everyone that produces smoke in the valley. The company specifically refers to the Army facility down the valley that still burns coal in its power plant. What do you think the solution is?

Terms to Know

property rights

contract

What's Ahead?

The public sector performs some tasks more efficiently than the private sector. The public sector also performs some tasks that the private sector is unwilling or unable to perform. Five major tasks of the public sector are to promote competition, define and enforce property rights, provide public goods, reduce negative externalities, and redistribute income.

FIVE MAJOR FUNCTIONS OF THE PUBLIC SECTOR

The public sector often does what the private sector either cannot do or is not willing to do. Let's take a closer look at the five major functions of the public sector. These are tasks that the public sector performs more effectively than the private sector.

Promoting Competition in the Private Sector

The efficiency of the private sector is improved by competition. Producers compete for the consumers' dollar votes by producing the most wanted goods at the lowest possible prices at which they can make a profit. If one company grows so strong in the market that it pushes out all other producers, there will be no competition. The remaining giant company will be the only producer. Then it may not work as hard to produce the goods consumers want most at the lowest possible prices. Once a single producer grows so powerful that it controls an entire market, other producers will not be able to grow strong enough to compete.

Many times in this country's history, several companies joined together to set higher prices or to refuse to compete with each other in certain geographical areas. By joining together, they eliminated competition. The cooperating producers were able to control market forces in their favor. They reduced the supply of goods or services, therefore driving up prices and often profits.

The only force in our economy powerful enough to change this situation is government. In our history, government often has intervened in such cases by passing laws prohibiting companies from working together to dominate a market. The *Clayton Antitrust Act* (1914) is one of many such laws against unfair competition. The government also has established the *Federal Trade Commission* (1914) which promotes competition in industry and prevents unfair competition. The Federal Trade Commission polices the nation's businesses to keep our markets competitive.

Most economists agree that there is a need for government to do this kind of work. However, they do not agree on how it should be done. Government regulation is not always able to do everything that we would like it to do. We can pass laws forbidding producers from cooperating in setting prices. It is difficult, however, to detect this kind of behavior. It is also very expensive to pass and enforce laws against unfair competition. To pass and enforce these laws requires the efforts of many people such as legislators, investigators, judges, and office workers. Your tax dollars pay the salaries of all these people. Therefore, a small price increase may be less costly to you as a consumer than the cost of prosecuting businesses that are cooperating unlawfully.

Defining and Enforcing Property Rights

In our economy, the whole productive process depends on the concept of private property. All productive resources, such as land, labor, capital, and management skills, are owned by people. When you own property, you have certain rights. The government defines and enforces these rights.

property rights the rules that government has established to define who owns what property and how owners may use their property

What Are Property Rights? ***Property rights*** are the rules that government has established to define who owns what property and how owners may use their property. As a worker, you own your own labor and sell that labor to an employer. The employer uses the labor you have sold to produce some good or service. The producer also buys raw materials, such as steel, iron, electric power, lumber, plastic, and glass, to use in producing the good or service. The producers own these goods and services until they sell them.

In most cases, once the goods or services are sold, they become the private property of the buyers. The buyers or owners have the private right to benefit from the ownership and use of these goods or services. They can enjoy

the goods or services, or they have the right to sell them to others. The right to benefit from the use or sale of the items is a private right for the direct benefit of the owner. This system of private property rights strongly influences us to work hard to produce goods and services. We have this incentive because we can benefit directly from our hard work.

How Are Property Rights Protected? How is this system of private property rights enforced? Who is powerful enough to enforce these laws? The answer is *government*. Government defines what rights individuals and producers have. Government establishes and enforces the laws that give us the use and benefit of our private property. Without this system of rights and enforcement, our system of production would not be as efficient as it is.

contract
a legally binding agreement between two or more competent persons

When you sell your labor to an employer, you and your employer enter into a contract. A ***contract*** is a legally binding agreement between two or more competent persons. Suppose you decide to sell your labor to an employer and that employer cheats you or breaks the contract. The employer would be breaking the law, and you would have the power of the law behind you. You could force your employer to live up to the contract under the law.

The law also protects the employer's rights. Suppose your employer paid you in advance for a week's work, and then you only worked two days. The power of the law would be on the employer's side. The employer could force repayment from you through the legal system.

The law establishes a system of property rights and enforces contracts between individuals and businesses. In short, the law defines the rights of all parties and protects those parties equally.

If there were no laws to enforce contracts, individuals and businesses probably would break their agreements more often. Then all businesses would become less efficient because they could not be sure that agreements would be fulfilled. Employers could not depend on employees to fulfill their promise to work. Production would go up and down depending on how many workers decided to work on any given day. A producer could not promise buyers any specific delivery date. Also, workers would not be able to count on an employer to pay the agreed-upon wages. If producers could not deliver goods to buyers, they might not have enough revenues to pay the workers. Therefore, a system of contracts in which all parties must fulfill their legal obligations is extremely important to our economic system.

The legal system defines what you can and cannot do with your property. If you own a piece of residential land, you may legally occupy that land yourself or sell it. You own the private property rights to that land. The law also defines what you and your neighbors cannot do with your land. For example, you may not build a slaughterhouse on your land in a residential neighborhood. You cannot do anything that would injure your neighbors' property rights. And, your neighbors cannot do anything that would injure your property rights. If you decide to build a house on property that you own, there are many legal restrictions. For example, you must follow electrical safety codes. You cannot build a firetrap that might burn down and

Internet Connection

BURROWING FOR INFORMATION WITH GOPHER

The best thing about the Internet is the tremendous amount of information it offers. Gopher allows you to search for and retrieve information.

If you connect to the Internet through a text-based computer (DOS or UNIX), you can access gopher by typing *gopher*. To move around the menu that appears, use the up and down arrow keys or type in the number of an item you wish to examine. Move to a subsequent screen by pressing the space bar. To return to an earlier screen, type *b* for back.

To select a menu item, put the cursor on the item and press *Enter*. Either a new menu will appear or a document will appear. To retrieve a document, type *m* to e-mail yourself a copy or *s* to save a copy in your home directory on the computer that allows you Internet access. To return to a previous menu, type *u* for up. To exit gopher, type *q* for quit.

While you can reach any gopher site on the Internet by moving through the menus from your local gopher, if you know the Internet address of a remote gopher site, it is quicker to access that site directly. To connect directly to a remote gopher, type *gopher remote-gopher-name*.

Economics/Internet Application: One measure of the importance of government is its share of total spending in the economy. Using gopher, connect to the Economics Bulletin Board, **una.hh.lib.umich.edu**. Make the following selections: EBB, National Income and Product Accounts, Latest National Income and Product Account (NIPA) Detail, Latest BEA Annual NIPA (A) Tables. From Table 101, compute the federal government's share of total spending by dividing Government Purchases by Gross Domestic Product. E-mail your answer to your teacher. If you cannot access una.hh.lib.umich.edu, it might be that the address has changed. Connect to gopher.thomson.com. Choose "South-Western Education, Resources, Internet Activities," and then choose "Economics." Print the page that appears and use the address listed for Chapter 5.

spread fire to your neighbors' homes. In general, laws are designed to protect the property rights of all owners. You can do whatever you want with your property as long as it does not threaten or hurt the property rights of others.

The legal system is for your benefit. It protects your rights. Government, by defining these rights, sets up a system in society that helps all of us to live and work together more efficiently. By defining what is fair or equitable, government contributes to the efficiency of an economy. It settles disputes between individuals and forces everyone to fulfill their legal agreements.

Providing Public Goods

As you learned in Chapter 3, many goods and services are produced more efficiently in the public sector. Roads, schools, national defense, and police and fire protection are some of these goods and services. Obviously, it is more efficient for a country to maintain one army than for citizens to try to defend themselves individually. Roads are too expensive to build to be used efficiently by just one individual. The public goods rationale explains why these goods are most efficiently produced by government.

Government also often undertakes activities that the private sector will not. For example, several private railway companies once provided rail service, but they failed financially. They could not generate enough profit to stay in business. The private sector thus stopped providing rail service to some parts of the country. The U.S. government took over much of the railway system in the 1980s and partially paid for its operation through a corporation called Amtrak. Many people in the government tried to eliminate this subsidy in the 1990s, with varying results. Believing that train service is important to our economy, the public sector still spends tax dollars to keep trains running.

Some economists say this is a wasteful and inefficient use of tax dollars. This may be a fair criticism. However, keeping the trains running does provide train service in places where it is vital to our nation's interest. It also provides competition for the trucking industry and other kinds of businesses that transport freight and people. Every government action clearly has both benefits and costs. If train service is important and the private sector cannot provide that service profitably, the public sector must step in.

Dealing with Negative Externalities

Many kinds of costs and benefits are passed on to individuals who are not involved in the market. In Chapter 4, you learned that when these spillover effects are *costs*, they are called *negative externalities*. Negative externalities affect people who are "external" to (or outside of) the market that produces the costs.

Measuring Negative Externalities. When discussing externalities, the term *cost* does not necessarily mean a dollar cost. Instead, cost can be a reduction in individual satisfaction or well-being. For example, assume your neighbors are playing their radio at high volume while you are trying to sleep. Your neighbors are passing on a negative externality to you. They are reducing your satisfaction or well-being by passing on a cost to you outside the market system. There is no dollar price involved, just a reduction in your well-being. A business world equivalent of this is the pollution of a stream by a chemical plant. Air pollution by a coal-burning electric power plant is another example. These activities reduce the quality of life of people downstream or downwind. Clean air and clean water clearly contribute to our health and well-being. Pollution of the environment reduces our satisfaction and quality of life.

Controlling Negative Externalities. Government is often called on to deal with negative externalities in the private sector. If a local chemical plant is polluting the river, you might complain directly to the plant. Many of your neighbors might do the same. However, most plants will not stop polluting if measures needed to stop the pollution are expensive. You and your neighbors will probably need the power of the law behind you. So far, only the public sector has been powerful enough to force companies to spend a large amount of money to stop pollution. It is not that most companies want to pollute. They are simply trying to produce the goods and services consumers desire at the lowest possible price. If a business must spend millions of dollars on pollution control, its costs of production must rise. You and your neighbors, with the help of government, may be successful in forcing a company to clean up its pollution. However, you may end up paying higher prices for goods made by that company.

Pollution and other kinds of externalities are often hard to detect. It is also difficult to find a sole cause of an externality and apply the blame to the proper party. A chemical plant may be the main cause of pollution. On the other hand, every plant that uses the river probably contributes to the pollution in some way. The city sewer system, run by government itself, might be dumping sewage. The large research and monitoring effort needed to control externalities can be provided most efficiently by government.

In controlling externalities, the government defines and enforces property rights. The public sector can deal with this issue more effectively than the private sector. The public sector can protect you by passing laws that prohibit companies or individuals from injuring you by polluting air and water or by making your property less attractive. The public sector also can force companies to buy pollution control equipment. It can even force persons or companies to pay for damages due to externalities they caused. All this effort,

however, will be paid for by the individual in one way or another. The costs to pass and enforce the laws will be paid for through tax dollars. The costs to clean up the pollution or install better equipment will be paid for through higher market prices.

The real choice as to how much externality will be tolerated and at what cost is up to the consumer. The consumer's voice in these matters is heard in two places. First, the consumer's voice reaches producers in the marketplace. What consumers buy and do not buy tells producers how they feel about the goods and services offered at various prices. Second, the consumer's voice reaches government in the voting booth. How individuals vote determines the reactions of the public sector to externalities.

Redistributing Income

In our economy there are some individuals who are unable to earn enough income to survive. Often, this is not their fault. There are members of our society who are handicapped or simply unable to work at a productive job. The public sector taxes the income of those who work and redistributes part of that income to those who cannot earn.

This is more than just an attempt to be compassionate. In our system of private enterprise, the ability to earn income increases with wealth. The more private property you own, the more income you have and the more chances you have of being able to produce. This situation tends to make the rich get richer. By redistributing income, our government attempts to provide equity. It tries to make the opportunity to earn income more equitable, which is a social goal in our society.

This redistribution effort does not give everyone an equal income. However, it does keep all the income in our economy from going only to a few individuals. Income redistribution programs that provide public assistance to low-income households help make more opportunities available. This attempts to break the cycle of poverty.

The United States still has its share of poverty. The distribution of income in this country, however, is more equitable than in many capitalistic countries of the world. Extremely uneven distribution of income in a country is often the cause of revolutions. Much of the political upheaval in Latin America has been due, in part, to an uneven distribution of income. In some Latin American countries, a very small part of the population controls most of the country's income.

We realize, then, that income redistribution may be an equitable and desirable act. To redistribute income on any large scale takes the power of law. Americans give large sums to charity every year, but this is a very small amount compared to the income redistributed by government. Each year, our government redistributes hundreds of billions of dollars to needy people. It is highly unlikely that any individuals or businesses willingly would turn over large parts of their incomes to be redistributed if it were not required by law. You might feel that everyone should do her or his share and that if everyone else chipped in, you would too. However, if everyone did not give their share, you might refuse to bear the redistribution burden alone. Redistribution without the power of law is not likely to be effective. Therefore, the public sector can redistribute income more efficiently than the private sector. The public sector's primary concern is to serve the wants and needs of our society in an equitable manner.

Checkpoint

Content Check

1. What tasks does the public sector perform because it is more efficient than the private sector?
2. What tasks does the public sector perform because the private sector is not able to perform them?
3. Why are property rights important in a market economy?

What Do You Think Now?

Reread *What Do You Think?* in the Section Two Focus. Then answer the following questions:

4. Do you think it is possible to identify everyone responsible for polluting the air? Explain.
5. What functions are the citizens of Madison asking the government to perform?

FOCUS

Section Three
Public Sector Problems

What Do You Think?

Trevor was at the main library looking for books on his favorite subject, the Civil War. As he searched the stacks, he found many books out of place. Two of the Civil War atlases were missing the pages he really wanted to see. One of the very old books about Andersonville had been damaged badly by water and the spine was broken in half. Someone had written notes throughout the margins of a biography of Robert E. Lee. Trevor couldn't understand why some people were so careless with library books. It seemed as if they didn't care that someone else was going to use them later. Do you think that this is a common problem?

Terms to Know

special interest group

lobbying

What's Ahead?

The public sector has some problems carrying out its economic functions. Problems in the public sector include the abuse of public goods, the influence of special interest groups, and a tendency to grow too large. Your actions can help to solve these problems.

PROBLEMS WITH THE PUBLIC SECTOR

You have learned about the five major areas where the public sector plays a major role in a market economy. These five areas seem to function best in the public sector. You should also be aware of some of the major problems that can occur in the public sector.

Abuse of Public Goods

Public goods, such as schools, roads, public housing, parks, and recreational facilities, are goods the whole community or society owns. These goods are provided through public ownership. This is an application of the concept of economies of scale (that some economic activities become more efficient when done on a large scale). People can enjoy a large public park at a lower cost per person than if individuals tried to provide their own parks.

Public Ownership and Individual Responsibility. Public ownership does not always encourage the pride and conscience of individual ownership. Often, individuals do not take care of publicly owned goods as well as they do their own property. For example, graffiti frequently appears on public goods, such as school buildings, but rarely on privately owned property. Individuals who deface or destroy public property usually do not ruin their individually owned property. Other examples of this disregard for public property are litter on highways and destruction of play equipment in parks. These activities detract from the satisfaction we get from the use of public goods. To repair, clean up, and maintain public property is costly. This cost is passed on to all members of society, even though only a few citizens cause the problem.

Global Economy

RIGHTS AROUND THE WORLD

In the mid-1980s, technology that was protected by copyrights and patents in the United States was frequently pirated and sold in other countries. Copyrights and patents are legal property rights granted to those who invest their time, energy, and money to produce new inventions and innovations. The protection of copyrights and patents gives people the right to profit from their invention or innovation for a specified period of time. This provides a strong incentive for entrepreneurs to risk their time, energy, and money to bring new goods and services to market.

The research and development costs of creating new software are very high. Without the protection guaranteed by copyrights and patents, many entrepreneurs would not develop these new products. In a case that drew international attention, it was found that individuals and whole organizations in China frequently copied U.S. computer software and sold it in their country without paying royalties to the copyright holder. When governments allow software to be copied and sold in their countries without paying the proper royalties, they steal from U.S. producers. Since the global market for software is so large, this theft deprives the original producers of royalties, to which they are legally entitled.

In 1995, the Clinton administration notified China that if they did not help protect and enforce U.S. patent and copyright laws, the United States would institute trade restrictions against China. China then agreed to make additional efforts to enforce U.S. copyright and patent laws in China. Just how permanent these efforts will be is not clear. However, the threat of trade restrictions, while potentially injuring individual trading partners, may help all future producers who need the protection of copyrights and patents. Property rights will be a major issue as the world moves toward a single global economy in the future.

Once started, the problem of public property abuse grows. People throw even more garbage on a badly littered highway in the mistaken belief that "everyone does it." Some people who would never throw a soda can in their own front yard think nothing of throwing one out their car window. Many people do not see these acts as the costly activities that they really are. This simply increases the costs all citizens will pay for public goods in the future.

Working Toward a Solution. Abusive private behavior toward public goods has been a problem for many years in our country. Some societies, however, have been able to improve this kind of behavior. The Montreal subway system in Canada is a public good in which many citizens take great pride of ownership. There is almost no graffiti there. The public parks of

Econ & You

EVERYONE'S SPECIAL

Almost all Americans have become part of some type of special interest group. In 1956, there were 4,900 national trade associations in the United States. By 1989, there were 23,000. In 1960, there were 365 paid lobbyists registered with the U.S. Senate, but today there are 40,111.

Lobbyists are highly skilled (and paid) professionals whose function is to promote the well-being of their special interest groups. They represent every kind of interest imaginable in Washington, including every known industry. The Tobacco Lobby openly spends millions of dollars each year in efforts to prevent legislation that would ban smoking. The Automobile Lobby opposes federal legislation that would require higher gasoline mileage and safety standards for cars. If your parents are members of a retirement plan at work, they are represented by lobbyists who work for the securities industry. Your grandparents may be members of the American Association of Retired Persons (AARP). Teachers are represented by the National Federation of Teachers and the National Education Association. The American Bar Association lobbies for lawyers and the American Medical Association lobbies for doctors. The American Lung Association, The American Cancer Society, and many other nonprofit organizations use lobbyists to represent their interests.

It is easy to see why it is difficult to get legislation passed with so many varied interests. It is entirely possible that in the future you may become a member of two special interest groups with completely opposing views on a given law. If, for example, you were a New York teacher who enjoyed hunting, your teachers union would openly advocate more gun control while the National Rifle Association would openly oppose such legislation.

Special interests are something we seem to want to have less of except when it comes to our own individual special interests. The problem of the power of special interest groups is obviously very complex and probably will continue to be a problem for a long time.

Japan are a showplace of public pride. Citizens who foolishly litter or foul the area are quickly reminded by other citizens of their civic responsibility. These examples of changing private behavior show some hope for improving the problem of private abuse of public goods.

Special Interest Groups

Laws are made through our system of representative government in Washington, D.C., that determine how the many functions of the public sector will be carried out. The federal government has tremendous power when it defines and enforces property rights and redistributes income. There will always be people who try to use the system to their own advantage. A ***special interest group*** is an organization of people who are bound together by a common concern. Special interest groups are very active in lobbying. ***Lobbying*** is the act of communicating with government representatives to influence their votes on a specific issue.

special interest group
an organization of people who are bound together by a common concern

lobbying
the act of communicating with government representatives to influence their votes on a specific issue

How Does Lobbying Work? Over the years, many special interest groups have developed to lobby for laws that will benefit them. The National Rifle Association lobbies against gun control. The Sierra Club lobbies in Congress against the use of wilderness lands for public parks and recreation. The National Dairy Association lobbies for higher subsidized, or legally set, minimum prices on dairy products. All these organizations devote large amounts of money and time to make sure that government representatives hear their points of view. If a particular member of Congress votes against laws the organization favors, the organization tries to influence its members against reelecting that representative. These organizations are believed to influence tens of thousands of votes for each candidate.

Individuals do not have the time and resources to lobby for their own interests. It would be difficult for you to write thousands of letters to Congress or to go to Washington to make your views known. So, like all other individual voters, you participate in the process of representative government by electing individuals who represent your views. Perhaps you support with membership dues organizations that will lobby for you.

Lobbying Affects All of Us. Special interest groups are very powerful politically. They strongly influence the passing of laws that will benefit the special interest groups at the cost of all citizens. If the National Dairy Association succeeds in getting laws passed that raise the minimum price of milk, every one pays higher milk prices. The producer of dairy products receives the benefits of such laws. The cost is passed on to every member of the economy who buys milk. The outcome is the same anytime a law benefiting only one particular group in society is passed. The whole society pays for a benefit that is enjoyed by only a small group. This is not necessarily bad. You and others in society may be willing to pay a small price individually to pass on a large benefit to a special interest group. You should be aware, however, that special interest groups number in the thousands. When you pay your taxes or buy the goods and services these groups represent, you are supporting their cause whether you like it or not.

Unfortunately, when political power is concentrated in any organization or group, individual interests of all citizens are sometimes not well represented. There will always be individuals and groups who try to use the public sector to their advantage. There will always be situations where smaller groups and individuals benefit at a cost passed on to everyone in the society. This is very much the nature of the social decision-making process you learned about in Chapter 3.

Problems of Size

Some goods and services are produced in the public sector because of economies of scale. On the other hand, some productive activities can be done more efficiently on a smaller scale. In the private sector, many companies realize this. Therefore, they break their companies down into several smaller subsidiaries or smaller companies. This structure helps to maintain control of a giant company's efforts. However, even with this structure, it is difficult to control any very large organization.

In the past, the public sector has had problems with size. For example, the Department of Agriculture employed 128,595 people in 1981. There were only about 2,434,000 farms in the United States in that year, which means there was nearly one federal employee for every 19 farms. By 1992, the Department of Agriculture served 2,197,000 farms with 128,324 employees, so there was nearly one federal employee for every 18 farms. Many people believe the Department of Agriculture does not need that many employees.

Streamlining government is more difficult than it seems. In the years ahead, we may see a more streamlined and more efficient government. Even though there will always be problems in the public sector, new and innovative solutions are a primary goal of economists.

Checkpoint

Content Check

1. Why are public goods misused by individuals who treat their private property with respect?
2. How does a special interest group influence the law making process?
3. What is the effect of size on the efficiency of the public sector?

What Do You Think Now?

Reread *What Do You Think?* in the Section Three Focus. Then answer the following questions:

4. How can our society minimize the type of abuse of public goods Trevor observed?
5. How would you deal with a situation in which you saw one of your friends destroying public property?

Concepts in Brief

1. The public sector includes all levels of government and its institutions that assist the functioning of the entire economy. The primary concern of the public sector is to provide equity in our system which, in turn, improves efficiency. The public sector undertakes activities that the private sector cannot do or is not willing to do.
2. Some of the functions of the public sector, such as controlling negative externalities, promoting competition, and enforcing property rights, come about because they require the power of law. Other activities of the public sector, such as providing public goods and redistributing income, are undertaken because generally they are not profitable for private industry. The government serves as a referee to encourage competition among firms. The government also sets up the legal system to define and enforce the property rights of individuals and the public. The public sector provides public goods, such as roads and police protection, that improve the efficiency of the private sector. The public sector deals with negative externalities that pass costs on to those outside of the market. Finally, the public sector redistributes income to improve equity within the economy.
3. The public sector encounters problems in performing economic activities. First, public goods are frequently abused by a small number of individuals at the expense of the whole society. Second, special interest groups try to manipulate the process of government to gain benefits for themselves at the cost of all members of the society. Third, the public sector has grown so large that portions of its efforts are not very efficient.

Economic Foundations

1. What are five major functions of the public sector?
2. How does the public sector promote competition?
3. How does the public sector enforce property rights?
4. What can the public sector do about negative externalities?
5. Give one major reason why the public sector redistributes income.
6. Why does abuse of public goods affect all members of a society?
7. How can a special interest group affect those individuals who do not support the cause of the special interest group?
8. How can the size of government affect its ability to carry out economic activities?

Your Economic Vocabulary

Build your economic vocabulary by matching the following terms with their definitions.

contract

lobbying

property rights

public institutions

public sector

special interest group

1. the rules that government has established to define who owns what property and how owners may use their property
2. an organization of people who are bound together by a common concern
3. a legally binding agreement between two or more competent persons
4. publicly owned organizations established by government to serve the wants and needs of a whole society
5. the act of communicating with government representatives to influence their votes on a specific issue
6. the part of an economy that is owned by and operated for the benefit of the whole society

Thinking Critically About Economics

1. Do you think that equity or efficiency is a more important goal for our economy? Why? Do you feel that both are necessary? If so, why? If not, why not?
2. What do you feel is the single most important function of the public sector? Why is this function more important to you than the other major functions provided by the public sector?
3. Are property rights necessary for an advanced industrial society to function efficiently? If so, are private property rights necessary? What do you think is the difference between property rights in general and private property rights? Are there property rights involved with a public good like a park? If so, are they public or private property rights?
4. Are externalities sometimes efficient but not equitable? If so, give an example of an efficient, but inequitable, externality. If not, explain why not.
5. Suggest a solution to each of the three problems of the public sector.
6. Do you feel that the public sector should keep businesses from cooperating to set prices or from competing with each other? If so, explain.

Economic Enrichment

Identify three special interest groups that affect how your school operates. Create a poster that illustrates the beliefs and issues important to each special interest group, the activities the special interest groups undertake to communicate their views, and how the interests of each group might compete with one another.

Math and Economics

Use library resources, commercial online services, or the Internet to find the number of business enterprises in the United States and the number of employees in the U.S. Department of Commerce. Calculate the number of business enterprises for every commerce department employee. How does this number compare with the number of farms in the United States for each employee of the Department of Agriculture?

Writing About Economics

Research a current economic issue that you are interested in, such as government waste, increasing or decreasing taxes, welfare reform, cost of recycling, or education reform. Be sure to examine the facts surrounding the issue and investigate the views of the special interest groups involved. Then write a letter to your senator, representative, or appropriate local political representative that presents your views on the issue and what you think the solution should be. Use the five-step decision-making model to arrive at your proposed solution.

VEG
MAR
AUTORAMA
Sale

PART TWO

The Microeconomic Perspective

Overview

Section One
Demand Schedules and Demand Curves

Section Two
The Law of Demand

Section Three
Determinants of Demand

Section Four
Price Elasticity of Demand

Demand: Achieving Consumer Satisfaction

Learning Objectives

6-1

Read and understand demand schedules and demand curves.

6-2

Explain the relationship between price and quantity demanded.

6-3

Demonstrate how the determinants of demand affect the level of demand.

6-4

Calculate price elasticity of demand and determine its effect on total revenue.

FOCUS

Section One

Demand Schedules and Demand Curves

What Do You Think?

Larry Sanchez makes computer tables out of solid maple. Larry has been selling about five tables a month at a price of $340 each. He has decided to increase his price to $380 so he can make more money. What should Larry consider before he raises his price?

What's Ahead?

Microeconomics is the study of how individual economic units (like a person or a business) behave and make decisions. Individuals buy goods and services to increase satisfaction. These buying decisions are an important factor in determining demand. Demand schedules and demand curves summarize the relationship between the quantity demanded and price.

Terms to Know

demand

demand schedule

demand curve

DEMAND

In this chapter, you begin your study of the branch of economics called *microeconomics*. Microeconomics involves looking at *small* parts of the total economy. It includes the choices we all make as individual consumers. Should we spend our limited amount of money on clothes or on recreation? Or should we spend some money on each? Exactly how we choose to allocate our money is an important factor in determining the demand for various goods and services in the economy.

Economic Meaning of Demand

demand
the quantities of a good that consumers are willing and able to purchase at various prices during a given period of time

Demand refers to the quantities of a good that consumers are willing and able to purchase at various prices during a given period of time. Let's take a closer look at the important elements of this definition.

First, you must be *able* to make a purchase; that is, you must have enough money to make the purchase. There are many items you may want to purchase. For example, you might want to buy a ski lodge in the Colorado Rockies and a private jet to get you there. But, if you do not have the money to purchase these luxuries, you do not have an effective demand for them.

Second, you must be *willing* to make the purchase. There are products that you can afford, but you may not be willing to spend your income on them.

Examples might include a pet snake or prune-flavored yogurt. If you are not willing to purchase these items, you do not have an effective demand for them.

Third, when we discuss demand, we are referring to purchases made during a *given period of time*. For example, you might have a weekly demand for candy bars. If you are willing and able each week to buy four candy bars at a price of $0.50 each, your demand is four candy bars a week.

Fourth, demand represents the *quantities* consumers would purchase at *various prices*. If the price of candy bars drops to $0.25 each, you might increase the number you buy each week from four candy bars to six. If the price rises to $0.90, you might only buy two candy bars a week.

Demand Schedules

It is often convenient to look at demand in the form of a listing of the quantities that would be purchased at various prices. A listing of the quantities that would be purchased at various prices is called a ***demand schedule***. Figure 6-1 shows a demand schedule for the number of hot fudge sundaes Raj Carey would buy per month at different prices. You see that at $2 a sundae, Raj would not be willing to buy any. However, if the price were lower, Raj would have a demand. For example, at a price of $1.80 a sundae, she would buy two sundaes each month. At a price of $1.20, her quantity demanded would increase to eight sundaes a month.

demand schedule
a listing of the quantities that would be purchased at various prices

Demand Curves

A demand schedule shows only a small number of the possible price and quantity combinations. For example, Figure 6-1 shows only eight such combinations. From that table, you can see how many sundaes Raj would buy at certain prices, such as $1.40 or $1.20. But, what if the price of a hot fudge sundae was $1.30? How many sundaes would Raj buy? You cannot answer this question directly from the demand schedule.

Price	Quantity Purchased per Month
$2.00	0
1.80	2
1.60	4
1.40	6
1.20	8
1.00	10
.80	12
.60	14

Figure 6-1

Raj Carey's Demand Schedule for Hot Fudge Sundaes

This table summarizes an individual's demand for hot fudge sundaes at different prices. ***If price fell to $0.40, how many sundaes would Raj want to purchase?***

Economic Spotlight

WHO IS THE #1 ENTREPRENEUR IN AMERICA?

H. Wayne Huizenga knows how to grow a business. Take Blockbuster Entertainment, for example. Huizenga grew the company to more than 4,000 percent of its original value before selling it to the media giant Viacom. A pure entrepreneur at heart, Huizenga gained his business savvy early on in the Illinois Dutch Reform community where he was born and raised. There he learned a strong work ethic and was taught by his father that nobody ever got rich by working for someone else.

As a young man, Huizenga followed in the footsteps of his Dutch immigrant grandfather, entering the garbage-hauling business quietly and then dominating the industry only a few years later. He began by managing a garbage company for a friend of his father. Later, he went out on his own, eventually merging with his grandfather's company to form Waste Management, a global giant generating profits of more than $200 million per year. However, once the company was thriving on its own, Huizenga resigned from the board of Waste Management "to pursue other interests."

In 1987, a friend told Huizenga about a little firm called Blockbuster Video. Blockbuster Entertainment had been founded by Dallas businessman David Cook, who opened the first Blockbuster superstore in October 1985. Cook's display, tracking, and security innovations had eliminated many of the problems associated with the video rental business. But, his company needed money. In short, Cook was looking to expand and Huizenga was looking to invest. Two months after Huizenga invested in Blockbuster, Cook resigned, allowing Huizenga to grow Blockbuster his way—"building by buying" and not by franchising. Huizenga rapidly bought up other video chains that dominated local and regional areas and converted them to Blockbusters. At one point, a new Blockbuster store was opening every 17 hours.

In 1994, Huizenga backed the merger of Blockbuster and Viacom and resigned six months later. Although Huizenga may have stepped out of the video game, the owner of the Florida Marlins and the Miami Dolphins is still playing in the big leagues as the number-one entrepreneur in America.

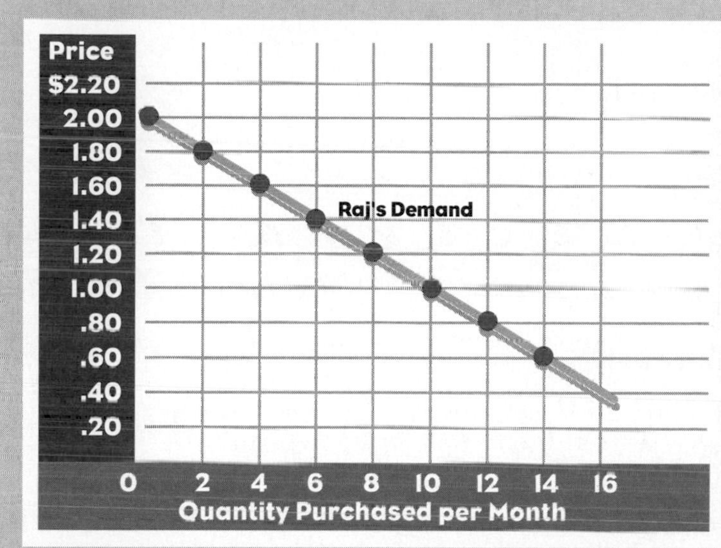

Figure 6-2

Raj Carey's Demand Curve for Hot Fudge Sundaes

This demand curve is based on Raj Carey's demand schedule for hot fudge sundaes. ***How many hot fudge sundaes will Raj purchase at $1.70?***

You can construct a demand curve to help you find the quantity that Raj would demand at any price. A ***demand curve*** is a graphic illustration of the relationship between *price* and the *quantity demanded* at each price. Figure 6-2 is a demand curve that represents Raj Carey's demand for hot fudge sundaes. Prices are measured along the vertical axis. The horizontal axis measures the quantities demanded. Each of the eight price-quantity combinations in Raj's demand schedule (Figure 6-1) is represented as a point in Figure 6-2.

Connecting all the points shows Raj's demand curve for hot fudge sundaes at each possible price. Using this demand curve allows you to determine how many sundaes Raj would buy at prices that are not shown in Figure 6-1. It is reasonable to expect that at a price of $1.30, Raj would buy seven sundaes each month. You can tell this from the demand curve in Figure 6-2 but not from the demand schedule in Figure 6-1.

demand curve
a graphic illustration of the relationship between *price* and the *quantity demanded* at each price

Checkpoint

Content Check

1. Give an example of the economic concept of demand.
2. Make a demand schedule for your favorite dessert for one month.
3. Draw a demand curve for your favorite dessert for one month.

What Do You Think Now?

Reread *What Do You Think?* in the Section One Focus. Then answer the following questions:

4. Can Larry Sanchez expect to sell as many tables per month at $380 as he had been selling at $340? Why or why not?

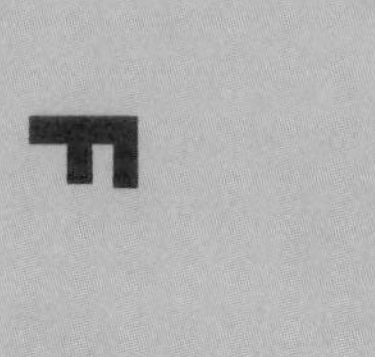

FOCUS

Section Two
The Law of Demand

What Do You Think?

Pat Keats plays on her high school tennis team. She has one Wilson Pro Staff 3.5 racquet and a Prince Extender racquet. A friend called Pat last night to tell her about a great sale on the newest Head tennis racquet at the MX Sports Center in the mall. Pat is trying to decide whether to buy this new racquet. Do you think Pat will buy the racquet?

Terms to Know

- law of demand
- marginal utility
- diminishing marginal utility
- income effect
- substitution effect

What's Ahead?

People tend to buy more of a good or service at a lower price than at a higher price. This is true for individual consumers and the market as a whole. In this section, you will learn three reasons for this relationship between price and quantity demanded.

THE LAW OF DEMAND

For most goods, consumers are willing to purchase more units at a lower price than at a higher price. The relationship between price and quantity demanded holds true as long as other factors, such as income, do not change. You saw this illustrated with Raj's demand for hot fudge sundaes. As the price went down, Raj purchased more and more sundaes.

This pattern is true with most products and services. The inverse relationship between price and the quantity consumers will buy is called the law of demand. The ***law of demand*** states that the quantity demanded of a good will be greater at lower prices than will be the quantity demanded at higher prices (as long as other influences are constant). This movement along the demand curve shows a change in the *quantity demanded* in response to a change in price. Let's look at some reasons the law of demand is true.

law of demand the quantity demanded of a good will be greater at lower prices than will be the quantity demanded at higher prices

Diminishing Marginal Utility

You have already learned that consumers make purchases to increase satisfaction. The amount of satisfaction a person gets from *one* additional unit of a product is called ***marginal utility***. For example, the additional satisfaction Raj gets when she eats the second sundae is the marginal utility of that sundae.

marginal utility the amount of satisfaction a person gets from *one* additional unit of a product

As a person consumes more and more units of a particular product, the satisfaction gained from each *additional* unit starts to lessen. For example, that first hot fudge sundae Raj eats probably tastes wonderful and brings her a lot of satisfaction. By the time she eats 14 hot fudge sundaes, however, one additional sundae does not bring as much satisfaction as the first one did. ***Diminishing marginal utility*** is the principle that as additional units of a product are consumed during a given time period, the additional satisfaction decreases. A person's *total* satisfaction may continue to increase but at a slower rate.

diminishing marginal utility the principle that as additional units of a product are consumed during a given time period, the additional satisfaction decreases

Stop to think about the products that you consume. The principle of diminishing marginal utility applies to most of them. Shoes, sweaters, CDs, and posters all follow this principle. Buying additional units of each good during a given time period provides less and less additional satisfaction.

The Income Effect

A second reason for the inverse relationship between price and quantity demanded is the income effect. The effect that increasing or decreasing prices has on the buying power of income is called the ***income effect.*** As the price of a product changes, your buying power changes as well.

income effect the effect that increasing or decreasing prices has on the buying power of income

If prices go up, your buying power goes down and your income appears to be less. Suppose, for example, that Taylor has a part-time job that pays $30 a week. Taylor collects CDs of her favorite recording artists and usually buys two CDs each week. If the store where she shops has a sale reducing the

price of each CD by $2, Taylor can buy three CDs rather than two. This change in her buying habits results from the fact that her $30 income now goes further. This supports the law of demand: As price goes down, quantity demanded goes up.

The income effect works in the other direction, too. As the price of an item goes up, your income doesn't go as far. You cannot buy as much with a given amount of money since prices are higher. Your buying power and quantity demanded go down as a result of an increase in price.

The Substitution Effect

A third reason for the inverse relationship between price and quantity demanded is the substitution effect. Let's return to our example of the lowered price of CDs. As the price of CDs goes down, CDs become cheaper *relative* to other goods, such as concerts or cassette tapes. Taylor is likely to change her buying habits and purchase more CDs and attend fewer concerts. This is called the substitution effect of a price change. The ***substitution effect*** is the change in the mix of goods purchased as a result of increasing or decreasing relative prices.

substitution effect
the change in the mix of goods purchased as a result of increasing or decreasing relative prices

The substitution effect works in two directions. If the price of a good falls, you may substitute it for other items. But, if the price of a good rises, you may substitute other items for the now relatively more expensive good. This substitution effect is seen relatively often. As the prices of oil and natural gas go up, people substitute wood-burning stoves and solar collectors for heating their homes. When the price of coffee goes up, people substitute with tea and chicory. When the price of beef falls, consumers substitute beef for chicken and pork.

MARKETS AND THE LAW OF DEMAND

You have seen that Raj's demand for hot fudge sundaes follows the law of demand. Raj would eat more sundaes at lower prices than at higher prices. Other consumers in Raj's community also have a demand for hot fudge sundaes. It is reasonable to expect that their individual demand schedules would also follow the law of demand. That is, we would expect them to purchase a greater number of hot fudge sundaes at lower prices than at higher prices.

Let's say that there are 1,000 people in Raj's neighborhood who like hot fudge sundaes. For simplicity, we also will say that each consumer has a demand schedule exactly like Raj's. If the price is $1.40 a sundae, those 1,000 consumers would *each* be willing and able to buy six sundaes a month. In *total,* they would have a demand for 6,000 sundaes at a price of $1.40 a sundae. If the price went down to $1.20 a sundae, the quantity demanded would increase to 8,000. If the price increased to $1.60 a sundae, only 4,000 sundaes would be demanded. When you list the quantities bought at each price for all 1,000 people, you have a market demand schedule. By plotting the market demand schedule on a graph and connecting the points, you have a market demand curve. These are shown in Figure 6-3 on page 132.

Both the market demand schedule and the market demand curve show that the quantity purchased goes up from 2,000 to 12,000 units as price falls from $1.80 to $0.80. As the price falls, a greater quantity is demanded. As the price goes up, a smaller quantity is demanded. A change in quantity demanded is caused by a change in the price of the product for any given demand curve. This is true of an individual consumer's demand, as well as for the market demand.

Internet Connection

SURFING THE NET WITH WORLD WIDE WEB BROWSERS

While the Internet has a huge amount of information and services available, until recently it was not very user-friendly. This changed with World Wide Web. The Web is an easy way of accessing virtually all Internet resources and services.

The Web is a set of resources called *home pages* or *web pages,* located on hundreds of computers around the Internet. Web pages are screens with text and images, with some words and images highlighted. Highlighted items are links to other screens. A web page is like a document with footnotes. A footnote in the middle of a document might give a reference for further information; a link on a web page allows you to jump to a copy of that document. The new document has links to even more documents.

To access World Wide Web, use a program called a *web browser.* There are a variety of browsers available. The major distinction is between those that display text and images (Netscape or Mosaic) and those that only display text (Lynx). This chapter will focus on Netscape. If you have access to Lynx, see your teacher for additional information.

Netscape is a web browser for a Windows environment. If you are familiar with Windows or Macintosh systems, using Netscape will be easy because Netscape uses the same commands. Click on the Netscape icon or select Netscape from a pull-down menu. After a few moments, a home page should appear.

Internet Application: If you have access to WWW, find out what browser you use. Key in **http://www.thomson.com/swpco/internet/hb29da1.html** to check out Thomson Publishing's Economics Internet activities. The Internet Application address is shown as two lines; however, it should be keyed in as one line. Describe some of what you learn in an e-mail message to your teacher.

Economics Application: Once students find out about the Internet, a large number want to use it. Use the law of demand to explain why quantity demanded is so great.

3. changes in the price of a complementary product; and
4. changes in the price of a substitute product.

Some other factors that may influence the level of demand include changes in the size of the population, changes in people's expectations, and even changes in the weather.

Let's look at how the first four factors can bring about increases and decreases in demand.

The Effect of Changing Incomes

As your incomes goes up, you are likely to consume more of almost all goods. People with higher incomes can be expected to buy more clothes, records, theater tickets, and hot fudge sundaes than people with lower incomes. These goods, as well as most others, are what economists refer to as normal goods. ***Normal goods*** are goods for which demand goes up as income goes up. If incomes fall, people cut back on their consumption of normal goods.

normal goods
goods for which demand goes up as income goes up

inferior goods
goods for which demand goes down as income goes up

Goods that are not normal goods are called inferior goods. ***Inferior goods*** are goods for which demand goes down as income goes up. For example, some people think of ground meat as an inferior good. As a family's income goes up, they may buy less ground meat and more steak and other solid meat products. Most goods and services we see in the marketplace, however, can be thought of as normal goods.

The Effect of Changing Attitudes

A change in consumers' attitudes (tastes and preferences) can cause demand to increase or decrease. Perhaps this is most noticeable with respect to clothing fashions. As our ideas about clothing change, so do our purchases of different clothing items. Demand will go up if, for some reason, consumers develop a more favorable attitude about a product.

Our attitudes are influenced by many factors. Family members, friends, classmates, advertisements, television, movies, and many other factors influence our attitudes about various goods and services. Exactly how much influence any of these factors has on our actual purchasing is hard to determine.

The Effect of Changing Prices of Substitute Goods

Changes in the prices of other products can cause a change in the demand for a good. Suppose, for example, that the price of margarine goes up. The law of demand tells us that the amount of margarine demanded would decline. People might substitute butter for the now relatively more expensive margarine. A rise in the price of margarine, then, might cause an increase in the demand for butter. Thus, butter and margarine can be thought of as substitute products. ***Substitute products*** are products whose uses are similar enough that one can replace the other. The same might be true of cassette tapes and CDs. If the price of CDs goes up, the demand for tapes might rise.

substitute products
products whose uses are similar enough that one can replace the other

complementary products
products that are used together

The Effect of Changing Prices of Complementary Goods

Complementary products are products that are used together. If two goods are complementary products, a decrease in the price of one can increase the demand for the other. For example, suppose that the price of snow skis goes down. More people could afford to buy skis. Thus, the demand for ski clothing and ski facilities would go up.

If the price of a product goes up, the demand for the complementary product would go down. Consider the effect of gasoline prices on the demand for automobile tires. As the price of gas goes up, people may reduce the number of miles they drive. This will result in less overall tire wear; therefore, tire demand will go down.

Global Economy

GROWING COFFEE IN THAILAND

Nestlé is a Swiss company you may know best for its chocolate candy products. This is a company that is very familiar with global markets. But, trying to sell a hot coffee beverage in a tropical country where tea is a favorite drink posed a real challenge. It took about ten years to establish coffee as a breakfast drink in Thailand, where Nestlé focused its attention mainly on the cities.

To do this Nestlé had to abandon its usual western advertising themes that centered on coffee taste and aroma as well as on its use as a stimulant. In Thailand, Nestlé found it more effective to focus on coffee as a relaxing beverage used to reduce the stresses caused by hectic traffic and the other pressures of life in Thailand's large cities.

Nestlé also borrowed a concept that had been developed by Nestlé Greece: promotion of a cold coffee beverage called the *Nescafe Shake.* As a result of these strategies, Nestlé captured 80 percent of the growing coffee market in Thailand, with sales increasing from $25 million to $100 million in a seven-year period.

How did Nestlé influence consumer choices in a country where coffee was not a popular beverage at one time? How does the concept of substitute goods relate to this discussion?

Graphing Increases in Demand

An increase in demand causes the entire demand curve to shift to the right. This is shown as a move from the demand curve *D* to the demand curve D_H in Figure 6-4. Demand curve *D* is the market demand curve for hot fudge sundaes first shown in Figure 6-3. As shown in Figure 6-4, at a price of $1.30, the initial level of demand for hot fudge sundaes is 7,000. If the incomes of consumers in this market area went up, the demand for hot fudge sundaes might rise from *D* to D_H. If demand increases to D_H, consumers would purchase 11,000 units at a price of $1.30 rather than the 7,000 units along the demand curve *D*.

Graphing Decreases in Demand

A decrease in demand can be illustrated by a shift of the whole demand curve to the left. In Figure 6-4, this is represented by a move from the original demand *D* to a lower demand D_L. If the price of strawberries decreased,

Economic Dilemma

WE DEMAND HEALTH CARE!

As the age distribution in the United States shifts toward a more elderly population, what are the consequences in terms of consumer demand? The demand for certain types of products and services will certainly increase. Examples abound but would include nursing home space, home health care, elderly day care, wheelchairs, various medications, and other health-related products and services. Some people suggest that as a society we spend too much on often futile medical treatment for people who have short life expectancies. Others point out that the potential savings by reducing such treatments is only about 3 percent of total health care expenditures.

There are ethical considerations that impinge on our decisions about who gets health care and how it is paid for. Should a 60-year-old woman who does not have a large savings account or medical insurance be prohibited from having a life-saving heart transplant? Should health care for the elderly be allowed to so deplete a family's savings that the entire family must take a substantial cut in their standard of living?

What are some other products or services, beyond health care, for which you think demand will increase due to the aging of the population? What choices in terms of costs and benefits must we, as a society, make to answer the questions raised in this discussion?

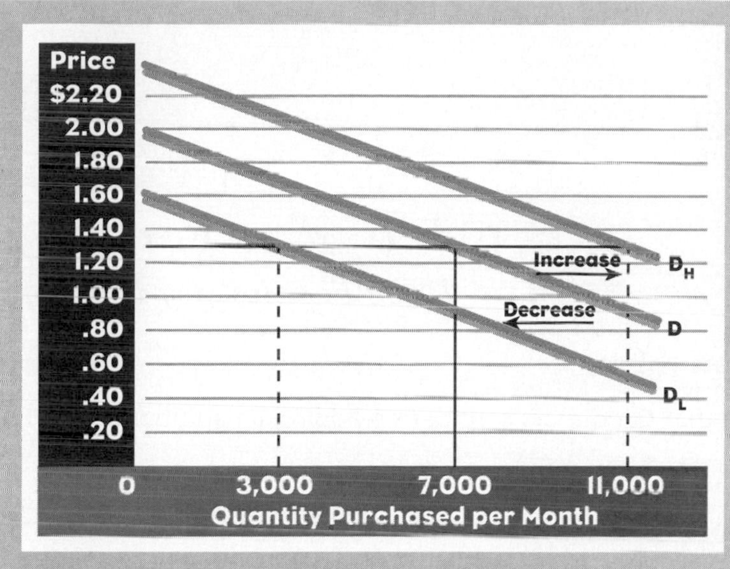

Figure 6-4

Shifts in the Market Demand for Hot Fudge Sundaes

An increase in overall demand is represented by a shift of the entire demand curve to the right, such as from D to D_H. A decrease in demand is shown by a shift to the left, such as from D to D_L. ***What might cause the demand to shift from D to D_L?***

thus making strawberry sundaes less expensive, the demand for hot fudge sundaes might fall from D to D_L. Hot fudge sundaes and strawberry sundaes are substitute goods. Given the lower level of demand, just 3,000 hot fudge sundaes would be purchased at $1.30 each.

Checkpoint

Content Check

1. How does a *change in demand* differ from a *change in the quantity demanded*?
2. Give an example of four determinants of demand.
3. Show how the demand curve for Ice Melt would be affected by an extremely long and severe winter.

What Do You Think Now?

Reread *What Do You Think?* in the Section Three Focus. Then answer the following questions:

4. How will Vincent Pisoni's promotion affect his demand for normal goods?
5. Name some products for which Vincent's tastes and preferences might be influenced by his promotion.

FOCUS

Section Four
Price Elasticity of Demand

What Do You Think?

Suppose that Congress is considering adding an additional $0.10 per gallon tax on gasoline. Your senators are supporting this tax because they say reduced consumption of gasoline will improve air quality and reduce our oil imports. Do you agree with your senators?

What's Ahead?

It is important for business people and government officials to be able to measure the effect a price change will have on the quantity demanded. In this section, you will learn about the relationship between price, unit sales, and the revenue a firm receives.

Terms to Know

price elasticity of demand

total revenue

PRICE ELASTICITY OF DEMAND

It is often useful to be able to measure the sensitivity of the quantity demanded to a change in the product's price. Price elasticity is the measure that is used for this purpose. The ***price elasticity of demand*** measures the relative responsiveness of the change in quantity demanded as a result of a change in the product's price. It can be calculated as the ratio of the percentage change in quantity demanded to the percentage change in price. The formula for price elasticity of demand is as follows:

price elasticity of demand measures the relative responsiveness of the change in quantity demanded as a result of a change in the product's price

$$\text{Price Elasticity of Demand} = \frac{\text{Percentage Change in Quantity Demanded}}{\text{Percentage Change in Price}}$$

Elastic Demand with Respect to Price

The term *elastic* implies responsiveness. If something is elastic, it is responsive. Thus, when economists say that a product is price elastic, they mean that the quantity demanded is quite responsive to a change in price. If the calculated value of a price elasticity is greater than 1, we classify demand as being *price elastic*.

CD players may be a good example of a product for which demand is elastic. Since there are many substitutes (radios, tape players, and other forms of entertainment), the consumer demand for CD players may be quite elastic. The number of substitute products available is one important determinant of price elasticity. The more substitutes that are available, the more price elastic is demand. Another important influence is the size of the purchase in relation to the buyer's total income. Demand for an expensive item is more likely to be price elastic than demand for an inexpensive item.

Suppose that a 5 percent decrease in the price of CDs stimulated a 10 percent increase in the quantity demanded. Economists would say this demand was quite elastic with respect to price. The price elasticity of demand would be 2:

$$\text{Price Elasticity of Demand} = \frac{\text{10\% Change in Quantity Demanded}}{\text{5\% Change in Price}}$$

$$= 10\% \div 5\%$$
$$= 2$$

Think of some other products that you consider to be price elastic. That is, try to think of products for which you would expect the quantity demanded to be very responsive to a price change.

Inelastic Demand with Respect to Price

When the quantity demanded is not very sensitive to a change in price, we say that demand is *price inelastic*. Table salt is a good example of a product that has an inelastic demand. There are few good substitutes and spending on salt is a small part of total household spending. Thus, people are not very sensitive to the price of salt.

When a product has an inelastic demand, the percentage change in quantity is less than the percentage change in price. This results in a calculated value of price elasticity that is less than 1. For example, suppose that a 4 percent increase in price for salt caused the quantity demanded to fall by just 1 percent. The numeric value of the price elasticity would be calculated as follows:

$$\textbf{Price Elasticity of Demand} = \frac{\textbf{1\% Change in Quantity Demanded}}{\textbf{4\% Change in Price}}$$

$$= 1\% \div 4\%$$
$$= 0.25$$

A price elasticity of 0.25 signifies that the quantity demanded is not very responsive to a price change. Gasoline is another product for which demand is price inelastic. The price elasticity for gasoline is close to 0.1.

Unitary Price Elasticity

It is possible that the percentage change in quantity demanded would exactly equal the percentage change in price. In such a case, the calculated value of the price elasticity would equal 1. For example, suppose that a 3 percent decrease in price caused a 3 percent increase in the quantity demanded. The price elasticity of demand would be calculated as follows:

$$\textbf{Price Elasticity of Demand} = \frac{\textbf{3\% Change in Quantity Demanded}}{\textbf{3\% Change in Price}}$$

$$= 3\% \div 3\%$$
$$= 1$$

This is a case of unitary price elasticity because the calculated value is equal to 1 (or unity).

WHAT DETERMINES THE PRICE ELASTICITY OF DEMAND?

It is possible to make some predictions about the price elasticity for a product. The following three factors are generally considered important in determining the price elasticity of demand:

1. number of substitute products;
2. importance of the product in the consumer's budget; and
3. time period considered.

Number of Substitute Products

The most important factor in determining the elasticity of a product with respect to the price is the number of substitute products available. The more substitutes available, the more price elastic we can expect demand to be. If there are few substitute products available, we would expect demand to be inelastic.

Consider some specific examples to illustrate this point. As noted earlier, the demand for gasoline in the United States has been estimated to have a price elasticity of about 0.10. Thus, we would classify gas as price inelastic. How does this fit with our explanation of the number of substitute products available? Given the current state of technology, there are virtually no substitutes for gasoline. Gasohol and even electric-powered cars may one day provide important substitutes. Until then, the only real substitute is to use other forms of transportation that use no gas or that conserve on gas. Bicycles use no gas. Riding on buses, in car pools, or in more efficient cars also conserves gas. Americans have shown that they are not willing to reduce gas consumption by very much as the price increases.

There are products that are much more sensitive to price changes. It has been found, for example, that the demand for haddock (an Atlantic fish) is quite price elastic. The price elasticity for haddock has been estimated to be 2.2. There are many substitutes for haddock, such as codfish and other fish. Even meats such as beef, lamb, pork, chicken, and turkey are substitutes for haddock.

Importance of the Product in the Consumer's Budget

A second factor that often influences the price elasticity of demand is the importance of the product in the consumer's budget. If expenditures on a product are a small fraction of a consumer's budget, demand will tend to be price inelastic. If the product represents a large fraction of consumer spending, demand will tend to be more elastic. For example, it is reasonable to expect table salt to have a very inelastic demand. Few consumers purchase enough salt to even remember if it is \$0.20 per pound or \$0.60 per pound. At either price, a pound of table salt would be a small fraction of a consumer's budget. On the other hand, products that represent major purchases would be expected to have a more elastic demand. Examples include appliances such as refrigerators, ranges, or microwave ovens.

Time Period Considered

Finally, price elasticity may depend on the length of the time period being considered. The shorter the time period, the more inelastic demand will be. As the time period considered increases, estimates of demand will usually be more elastic. Consumers will have more time to adjust to price changes and perhaps to find substitute products. If your home is heated with fuel oil and its price doubles, you may not be able to do much about it this winter. You can keep the house cooler, but you cannot do much more. Over a longer period of time, you may be able to convert to other energy sources, such as natural gas, wood, or solar heating.

TOTAL REVENUE AND DEMAND

So far, we have looked at demand from a consumer's point of view. Let's now shift our attention to the seller. Sellers of products have a strong interest

Econ & You

INELASTIC CIGARETTES

There is a great deal of debate about the health effects of smoking on those who smoke and on those who are subjected to second-hand smoke. Various policies have been enforced, by both the private and public sectors, to eliminate smoking in many places where smoking was once common. Excise taxes have been placed on cigarettes to raise revenues for the public sector, to reduce consumption, or both, depending on which argument one happens to believe.

Some economic concepts can help you decide which argument makes the most sense. The price elasticity of demand for cigarettes has been estimated to be about 0.4, which means the demand is quite price inelastic. Thus, policy makers are well aware that raising price (via a tax) will have only a slight effect on consumption. However, as a result of the tax, there will be a considerable increase in tax revenues. In Canada, for example, cigarette taxes were increased by 152 percent over a ten-year period spanning parts of the 1980s and 1990s. As a result, cigarette tax revenues increased by nearly 400 percent, while consumption dropped by only 38 percent.

What do you see as some of the costs and benefits of placing a higher tax on cigarettes? Are there both private and public costs and benefits? Why is a knowledge of price elasticity useful to those who must deal with this issue?

in understanding the demand for products. In particular, the sellers of a product are interested in the amount of money they can obtain from various levels of sales.

Measuring Total Revenue

The total amount of money a company receives from sales of a product is called ***total revenue.*** The formula for calculating total revenue is as follows:

total revenue
the total amount of money a company receives from sales of a product

Total Revenue = (Price) × (Quantity Sold)

Let's go back to the hot fudge sundae example. Suzanne's shop gets one-fifth (20 percent) of the market demand presented in Figure 6-3. The total revenue for hot fudge sundaes is the price multiplied by the quantity sold at that price. At a price of $1.40 per sundae, Suzanne's total revenue, $1,680, would be equal to the price, $1.40, times the quantity sold, 1,200. The demand schedule for Suzanne's Sundae Shop is shown in Figure 6-5. The total revenue at each price is presented in the third column.

Price x	Quantity Sold per Month =	Total Revenue
$2.00	0	$ 0
1.80	400	720
1.60	800	1,280
1.40	1,200	1,680
1.20	1,600	1,920
1.00	2,000	2,000
.80	2,400	1,920
.60	2,800	1,680

Figure 6-5

Demand and Total Revenue for Hot Fudge Sundaes at Suzanne's

As Suzanne lowers her price for hot fudge sundaes, the quantity that she can sell increases. ***What happens to total revenue as Suzanne lowers the price of sundaes?***

Relationship Between Price and Total Revenue

You already know that the quantity sold is determined in part by the product's price. Figure 6-5 shows some interesting relationships. You see that, at first, price cuts stimulate enough new sales that total revenue goes up. But, note that this is not always the case. Down to a price of $1, total revenue rises as price falls and quantity goes up. However, if price is reduced below $1, the additional sales do not compensate for the lower price per unit. This results in lower total revenue.

When considering what price to charge it is important for a business to think about the price elasticity of demand. You know that according to the law of demand, lowering price will always increase unit sales. But, lowering price may cause total revenue to either increase or decrease depending on the price elasticity of demand. This important relationship is summarized in Figure 6-6.

Figure 6-6

The Relationship Between Price, Elasticity, and Total Revenue

This figure summarizes how price, price elasticity, and total revenue are related. ***If the demand for movie tickets is price elastic, would a theater get more or less total revenue if it lowered the price of tickets?***

Elastic Demand	Inelastic Demand
Decreasing price increases total revenue.	**Decreasing price decreases total revenue.**
Increasing price decreases total revenue.	**Increasing price increases total revenue.**

You can see from the relationships in Figure 6-6 that you should consider price elasticity carefully when thinking about changing price. If you have an objective of increasing total revenue, you need to decide if a price decrease or a price increase would have that effect.

Checkpoint

Content Check

1. What does price elasticity of demand measure?
2. Name three factors that affect the price elasticity of demand and give an example of each.
3. Using the following table, calculate total revenue at each price:

Price	Quantity Demanded per Month
$1.60	4,000
1.20	8,000
.80	12,000

4. If a product has a price elasticity of 1.3, what would happen to total revenue if the price decreased?

What Do You Think Now?

Reread *What Do You Think?* in the Section Four Focus. Then answer the following questions:

5. Explain whether you agree or disagree with your senators' analysis. Will people cut back on their consumption of gas, reducing pollution and oil imports?
6. Will this tax provide much additional revenue to the government?

Concepts in Brief

1. The relationship between price and quantity demanded can be shown in a table as a demand schedule or in a graph as a demand curve. A change in quantity demanded can be caused by only one factor: a change in the product's price. A change in quantity demanded can be shown in a graph by movement along a given demand curve.
2. Most goods that you consume give you diminishing marginal satisfaction. As you consume a greater number of units (in a given time period), each *additional unit* gives less *additional satisfaction.* This is one reason that people will buy a greater quantity of a good only at lower prices. The inverse relationship between price and the quantity demanded is called the *law of demand.*
3. The overall level of demand can be affected by many factors. Four very important factors are consumers' incomes, consumers' tastes and preferences (attitudes), the prices of substitute products, and the prices of complementary products. Changes in any of these factors can cause a change in demand. A change in demand can be represented on a graph as a shift of the demand curve. An increase in demand is shown as a shift of the demand curve to the right. A shift of the demand curve to the left indicates a decrease in demand.
4. It is important to measure the sensitivity of demand to changes in price. Price elasticity measures the responsiveness of the quantity demanded to price changes. A business usually is concerned with the effect a price change will have on its total revenue. The price elasticity of a product can help to predict how a change in price will affect total revenue. A company can always increase sales of a product by lowering price, but total revenue may increase or decrease as a result.

Economic Foundations

1. How does the economic meaning of demand differ from the everyday use of the word *demand*?
2. What is the advantage of a demand curve over a demand schedule?
3. What happens to quantity demanded as a result of the substitution effect?
4. What happens to quantity demanded as a result of the income effect?
5. How does changing income affect demand?
6. How do changing attitudes affect demand?

7. How do the changing prices of other goods affect demand?
8. Explain the differences between the three kinds of price elasticity of demand.
9. What three major factors influence the price elasticity of demand?

Your Economic Vocabulary

Build your economic vocabulary by matching the following terms with their definitions.

complementary products
demand
demand curve
demand schedule
determinants of demand
diminishing marginal utility
income effect
inferior goods
law of demand
marginal utility
normal goods
price elasticity of demand
substitute products
substitution effect
total revenue

1. the effect that increasing or decreasing prices has on the buying power of income
2. a listing of the quantities that would be purchased at various prices
3. products whose uses are similar enough that one can replace the other
4. the total amount of money a company receives from sales of a product
5. a graphic illustration of the relationship between *price* and the *quantity demanded* at each price
6. products that are used together
7. the change in the mix of goods purchased as a result of increasing or decreasing relative prices
8. goods for which demand goes down as income goes up
9. measures the relative responsiveness of the change in quantity demanded as a result of a change in the product's price
10. the quantity demanded of a good will be greater at lower prices than will be the quantity demanded at higher prices
11. the quantities of a good that consumers are willing and able to purchase at various prices during a given period of time
12. the amount of satisfaction a person gets from *one* additional unit of a product
13. goods for which demand goes up as income goes up
14. the principle that as additional units of a product are consumed during a given time period, the additional satisfaction decreases
15. the factors that determine how much will be purchased at any given price

Thinking Critically About Economics

1. Why are people willing to pay a price for the right to consume any product or service? Why would you be willing to pay for a cassette tape?
2. Explain how the principle of diminishing marginal utility would influence your consumption of hot fudge sundaes. Give several other examples of goods you buy that have diminishing marginal utility.
3. Explain the difference between a demand schedule and a demand curve. Construct an example of each.
4. What factors have influenced the demand for bicycles in the last few years? Focus your attention on income, attitudes, and the prices of other products. Explain how changes in these factors would either increase or decrease the demand for bicycles.
5. If the price of housing (rent or house payments) goes up, there may be an income effect on your family. What does this mean? What is the relationship between prices and income?
6. Since the early 1970s, much public attention has been focused on the demand for gasoline. Economists have found that the demand for gas Is inelastic with respect to price. What does this mean? Why would the demand for gasoline be price inelastic?
7. A simple demand schedule for a company follows:

Price	Quantity
$6	0
$5	1
$4	2
$3	3
$2	4
$1	5

   Find the dollar value of total revenue at each of the six prices. At what price will total revenue be the greatest? How many units will sell at that price?
8. Choose two products and explain why you think their demand is price elastic or price inelastic. Be sure to consider the three factors that determine price elasticity in preparing your answer.
9. Explain the difference between a change in quantity demanded and a change in demand. Draw a graph to show this difference.

Economic Enrichment

LearnComp is a new company that is making pocket-sized computers that weigh just 5 ounces and are specifically designed to aid learning. These little computers run on solar power or on a single AAA battery if enough light is not available to power the system. Each of the computers has a slot where the user can slide in "LearnCards." Each LearnCard has an active learning exercise for a specific subject area. For example, there are LearnCards for basic algebra, geography, grammar, and biology.

You have been asked to develop the contents for the "Demand" unit on an economics LearnCard. There is limited space available so you cannot include everything you have learned about demand. Identify four concepts that you think would be the most important to include. Write a short learning exercise that could be used to illustrate each of the concepts you select.

Math and Economics

You have seen that consumers' demand is affected by their level of income. Current income can, however, be supplemented by the use of credit (borrowing). Often, the availability of credit makes it easy for people to spend more than they really can afford. You need to be careful about how much you borrow. How much credit can you afford? As a rule of thumb, the amount of credit payments you make each month should be less than 20 percent of your take-home pay. Thus, if you have take-home pay of $1,500, you should not have more than $300 a month in credit payments ($1,500 × 0.2 = $300). This amount does not include housing.

A family has an after-tax (take-home) income of $3,600 per month after paying for their housing. Currently, the family's monthly payment on their Sear's charge is $122. They also have a VISA payment of $110 per month. Last week, they decided to replace the family car with a new minivan. Assuming that they have no other credit payments, how large a monthly car payment can they afford?

Writing About Economics

Look at advertisements in a local newspaper and a national magazine. From each publication, pick two advertisements for products or services a typical household might buy. Write a short report explaining the kind of information in each ad and discussing how that information may affect the demand for that product or service. In your report, cover the following: What differences in the kind of information did you find? What substitute and complementary goods also may be affected by each of the ads? How might the demand for these goods be affected by advertising?

Seasonality at the GAP

Sales in many types of retail establishments are seasonal. This means that sales during some parts of the year are consistently higher or lower than they are during other parts of the year. In the case of the GAP, we find that fourth-quarter sales are considerably stronger than sales the rest of the year.

Managers need to look at how much of the increased (or decreased) sales in any quarter is due to actual sales trends and how much of it is due to seasonality. When you think of the clothing industry, think of any reasons that might cause sales to be greater in some parts of the year than others. Some reasons to consider are people's decision to buy clothes at the beginning of the school year, clothing purchases in November and December for Christmas gifts, and the fact that sweaters, jackets, and heavier fall and winter clothing cost more than do shorts and T-shirts.

If you look closely at the accompanying line graph of the GAP's quarterly sales, you will see that the trend over time is toward increasing sales but with noticeable upward spikes (increases in sales) in the fourth quarter of the year followed by a steep decline in sales for the first quarter. Managers must be aware of this factor, which is called *seasonality,* and make allowances for it in decision making. As you read the newspaper or magazines and come across other line graphs, look for indications of seasonality.

Seasonality of GAP Sales

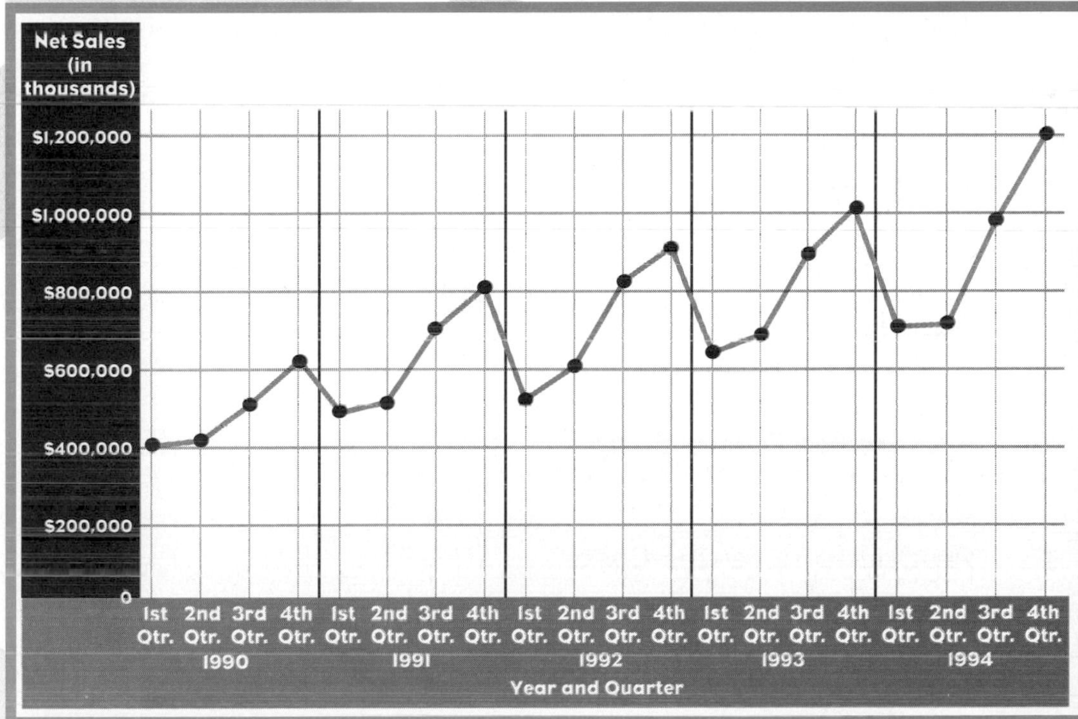

SOURCE: GAP, Inc., Annual Reports 1990–1994.

Overview

Section One
Supply

Section Two
Production Drives Supply

Section Three
Production Creates Costs

Supply: Producing Goods and Services

Learning Objectives

7-1

Explain the relationship between price and quantity supplied.

7-2

Distinguish between a change in quantity supplied and a change in supply.

7-3

Discuss how and why people produce goods and services.

7-4

Recognize the impact of diminishing marginal product on production costs and the supply curve.

7-5

Understand the relationship between scale of production and production costs.

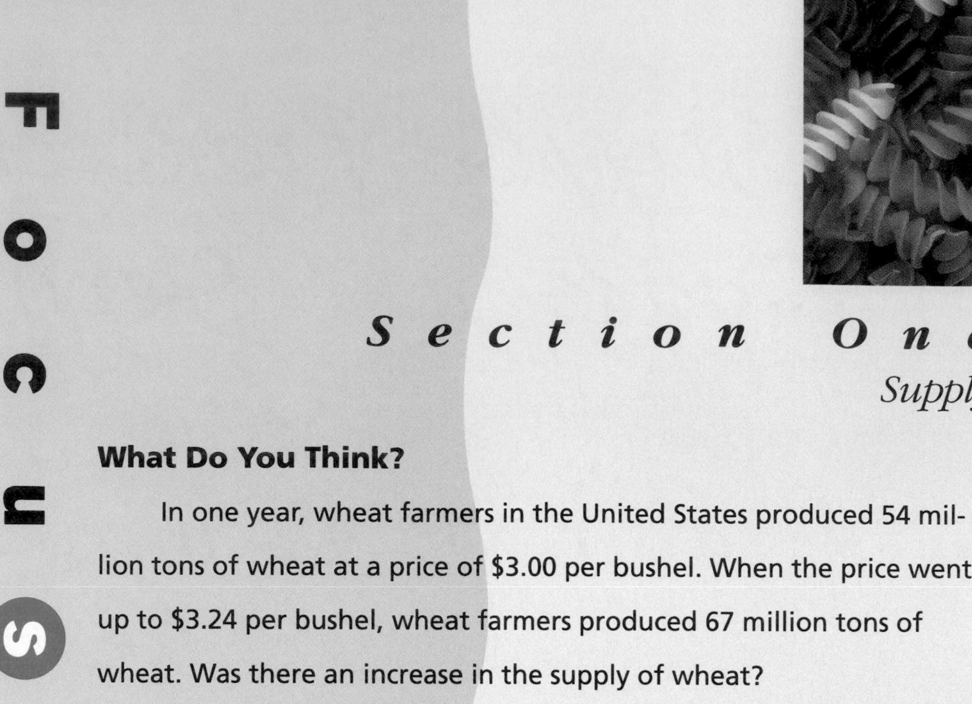

Section One
Supply

What Do You Think?

In one year, wheat farmers in the United States produced 54 million tons of wheat at a price of $3.00 per bushel. When the price went up to $3.24 per bushel, wheat farmers produced 67 million tons of wheat. Was there an increase in the supply of wheat?

What's Ahead?

Businesses are successful when they supply the goods or services that people demand at a fair price. As the price increases, the quantity of goods supplied increases too. If there is a change in productivity or production costs, the quantity supplied at every price might change.

Terms to Know

supply

supply schedule

supply curve

law of supply

change in the quantity supplied

price elasticity of supply

change in supply

SUPPLY FOR THE INDIVIDUAL FIRM

In our economy, people produce goods and services to gain certain benefits. These benefits include money income and psychic income. One goal of firms is to make money for the owners of the business. So, firms will only produce goods and services that sell at prices that cover the cost of making those goods available. ***Supply*** is the quantities of a product or service that a firm is willing and able to make available for sale at different prices.

supply
the quantities of a product or service that a firm is willing and able to make available for sale at different prices

Supply Schedules

A list of the various prices of a product and the quantities made available for sale at those prices can be summarized in a table. A ***supply schedule*** is a table that shows the quantities of a good or service that would be supplied by a firm at different prices. A supply schedule for Ramano's Sandwich Shop, located in Sycamore Bend, is shown in Figure 7-1.

supply schedule
a table that shows the quantities of a good or service that would be supplied by a firm at different prices

At a price of $2 per sandwich, Ramano's is willing to make 120 sandwiches each day. But, at higher prices, Ramano's is willing to make a greater quantity. For example, if the price went up to $4, Ramano's would supply 160 sandwiches each day. At a price of $7, Ramano's would be willing to make 220 sandwiches per day.

Price	Quantity Supplied per Day
$2.00	120
$3.00	140
$4.00	160
$5.00	180
$6.00	200
$7.00	220

Figure 7-1

Supply Schedule for Ramano's Sandwich Shop

This supply schedule summarizes the number of sandwiches Ramano's will supply at six different prices. ***Is Ramano's willing to supply more or fewer sandwiches as the price goes up?***

Supply Curves

The supply schedule for Ramano's also can be illustrated as a graph. A ***supply curve*** is a graphic representation of the quantities that would be supplied at each price. A supply curve shows the quantity supplied at every price, not just the prices in a supply schedule. A supply curve depicts price and the quantity supplied in a way that makes the relationship between them easy to see. Ramano's supply curve is shown in Figure 7-2.

supply curve a graphic representation of the quantities that would be supplied at each price

You can read any price/quantity supplied combination from this supply curve. For example, the quantity of sandwiches supplied at a price of $2 is identified by the dashed lines. To find a price/quantity supplied combination that is not in the table in Figure 7-1, do the following:

1. Find the price on the vertical axis.
2. Go from that point straight across to the supply curve.
3. Go straight down from the supply curve to the horizontal axis to find the quantity supplied.

Using Figure 7-2, find out how many sandwiches Ramano's would supply if the price were $5.50 each.

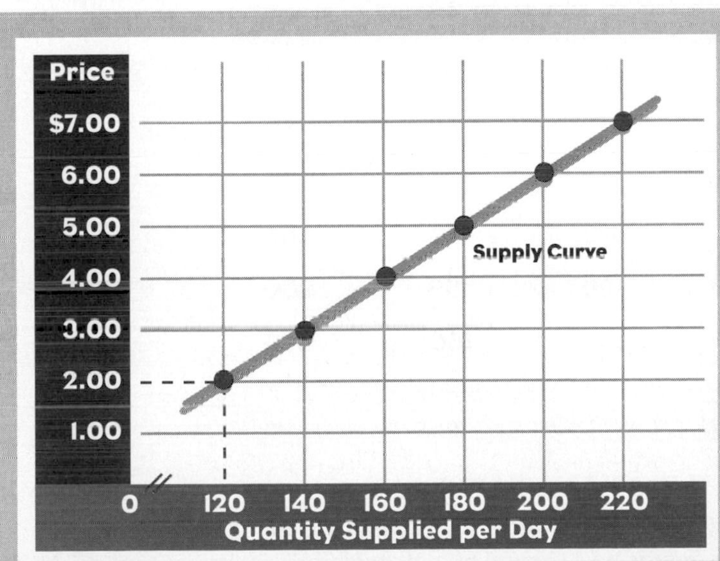

Figure 7-2

Supply Curve for Ramano's Sandwich Shop

This supply curve, based on the information in Figure 7-1, illustrates how quantity supplied increases with price. ***How many sandwiches do you think Ramano's will be willing to make each day at a price of $4.50?***

MARKET SUPPLY

Market supply is the total quantity of a product or service that all firms in a market will make available for sale at various prices. To get the market supply, you add up all the quantities that each firm in the market would supply at each price.

The Market Supply Schedule

In Sycamore Bend, the market served by Ramano's Sandwich Shop, there are four other restaurants that serve sandwiches: The Food Emporium, The Village Deli, Singh's Subs, and Damon's Diner. The supply schedules for these four firms are given in Figure 7-3, along with Ramano's supply schedule. The last column of Figure 7-3 is the market supply schedule for sandwiches in Sycamore Bend, which is the sum of columns two through six.

Price	Ramano's Sandwich Shop	+	The Food Emporium	+	The Village Deli	+	Singh's Subs	+	Damon's Diner	=	Total Market Supply
$2.00	120		90		115		140		135		600
$3.00	140		100		120		150		140		650
$4.00	160		110		125		160		145		700
$5.00	180		120		130		170		150		750
$6.00	200		130		135		180		155		800
$7.00	220		140		140		190		160		850

Figure 7-3

Market Supply Schedule for Sandwiches in Sycamore Bend

This market supply schedule summarizes the individual supply schedules for five sandwich shops in Sycamore Bend. ***What is the relationship between price and the quantity supplied by the market?***

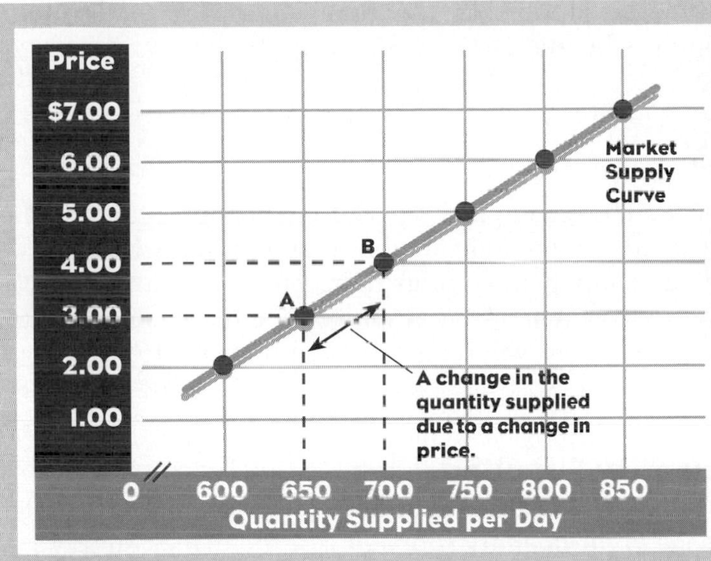

Figure 7-4

Market Supply Curve for Sandwiches in Sycamore Bend

The market supply curve for sandwiches is the sum of the supply curves for all firms in the market. ***How many sandwiches do you think would be supplied by this market if the price were $3.50?***

The Market Supply Curve

The market supply curve is a graph of the information contained in the market supply schedule. The market supply curve for sandwiches is illustrated in Figure 7-4. You can use the market supply curve to identify the quantity

Econ & You

WHY SHOULD I HIRE YOU?

Businesses find it increasingly important to maintain a highly productive work force. As a result, they expect more and more from the people they hire to help in the production of their products or services. It is very likely that you will be asked questions such as "What have you done?" and "What do you know?" at some point in your job search.

Education and training are critical to being a productive participant in today's fast-moving economy. The skills you have today won't be sufficient tomorrow. Continual learning is an important element of success. In the last two decades, the real wages of high school dropouts have dropped nearly 24 percent. For those workers with only high school educations, the decline has been more than 12 percent.

Business Week reported what a variety of workers suggested as important personal skills. Here are some examples:

- ability to communicate;
- positive attitude;
- ability to listen;
- willingness to work overtime; and
- self-confidence.

These personal skills, along with a good education, may be your keys to success.

of sandwiches that would be supplied by the market at a price that is not represented in the supply schedule.

LAW OF SUPPLY

law of supply
states that the quantity of goods supplied will be greater at a higher price than it will at a lower price

You have learned that a change in price will cause a change in the number of units supplied. This is true for the individual firm and for the whole market as well. Firms are willing to supply more units if the price goes up. If the price goes down, fewer units will be made available. The ***law of supply*** states that the quantity of goods supplied will be greater at a higher price than it will at a lower price.

Change in the Quantity Supplied

change in the quantity supplied
change in the number of units made available for sale due to a *price change*

This change in the number of units made available for sale due to a *price change* is called a ***change in the quantity supplied***. For the market supply curve in Figure 7-4, movement from Point *A* to Point *B* is an example of a change in quantity supplied. When price goes from $3 to $4, the quantity supplied goes up from 650 to 700 sandwiches per day. If the price fell again from $4 to $3, firms in the marketplace would cut production from a total of 700 to 650 per day.

A change in the quantity supplied is always shown as a change *along* a given supply curve. The change in quantity supplied in response to a price rise will be upward along the supply curve. For a fall in price, the change in quantity supplied will be downward along the supply curve. This is illustrated by the double-headed arrow between Points *A* and *B* in Figure 7-4.

Price Elasticity of Supply

price elasticity of supply
measures the responsiveness of the quantity supplied to changes in the product's price

The ***price elasticity of supply*** measures the responsiveness of the quantity supplied to changes in the product's price. This concept is very similar to the price elasticity of demand. The price elasticity of supply is calculated as the ratio of the percentage change in the quantity supplied to the percentage change in the product's price. The formula for price elasticity of supply follows:

$$\text{Price Elasticity of Supply} = \frac{\text{Percentage Change in Quantity Supplied}}{\text{Percentage Change in Price}}$$

When the quantity supplied is very responsive to price changes, supply is elastic and the price elasticity of supply is greater than 1. If a certain percentage change in price brings about a relatively small percentage change in the quantity supplied, supply is considered inelastic and the price elasticity of supply is less than 1. Supply is said to be unitarily price elastic if the calculated price elasticity of supply equals 1. Unitary price elasticity indicates that the percentage change in quantity supplied exactly equals the percentage change in price.

CHANGE IN SUPPLY

A ***change in supply*** means a change in the number of units supplied at every price. An increase in supply means *more* units will be supplied at *each* price. A decrease in supply means *fewer* units will be supplied at *each* price.

change in supply
a change in the number of units supplied at every price

Shifts in the Supply Curve

A change in supply means a shift of the whole supply curve. Changes in the supply of sandwiches in Sycamore Bend are illustrated in Figure 7-5.

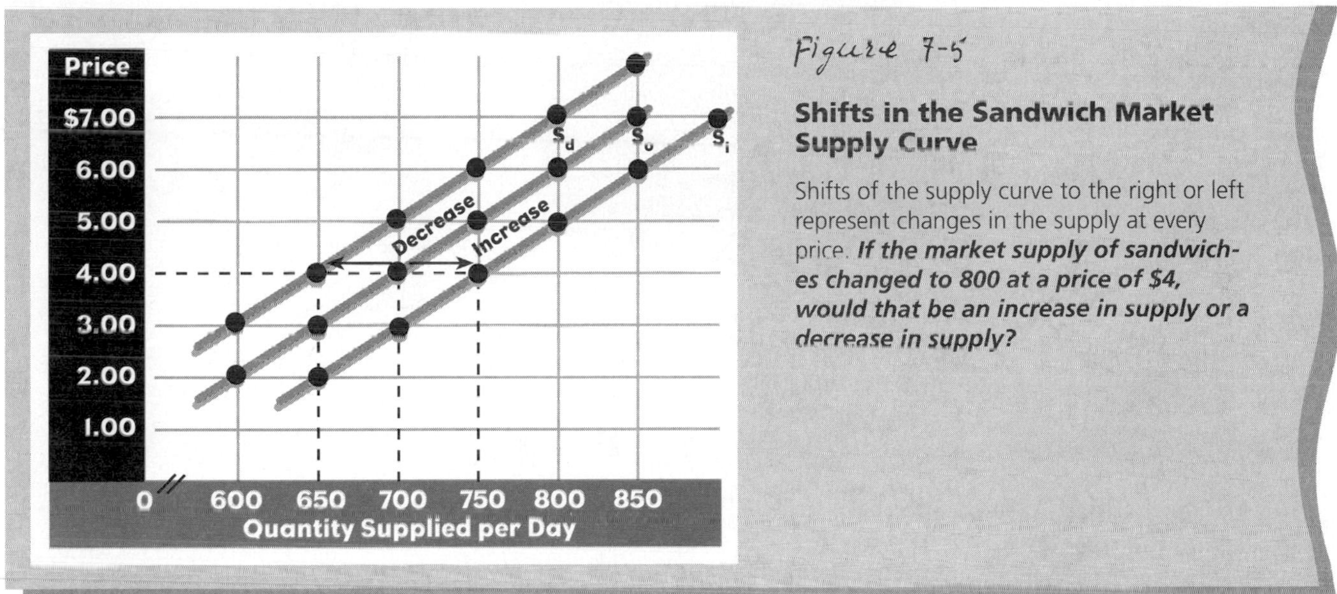

Shifts in the Sandwich Market Supply Curve

Shifts of the supply curve to the right or left represent changes in the supply at every price. ***If the market supply of sandwiches changed to 800 at a price of $4, would that be an increase in supply or a decrease in supply?***

An increase in the market supply of sandwiches is shown by supply curve S_i, which is to the right of the original supply curve S_o. For example, at a price of $4, originally there were 700 units supplied. Curve S_i reflects that at the same $4 price, 750 units were supplied. More is supplied at each price along S_i than along S_o.

A decrease in supply is shown by curve S_d, which is to the left of the original supply curve. For example, at a price of $4, the original supply was 700 units. After the decrease in supply, only 650 units were supplied at that same price. Less would be supplied at each price along S_d than along S_o.

What Causes a Change in Supply?

Changes in supply can be caused by a number of factors. The two most common causes are technological change and a change in the cost of inputs. Technological changes generally increase productivity. This in turn lowers the cost of production. If the cost of production is lower, firms can sell more output at any given level of price. For example, a technological change that increases productivity and lowers cost may allow firms to sell 650 units at a price of $2 rather than 600.

A change in the cost of inputs often causes costs to rise. Higher labor costs, a rise in the cost of raw materials used in production, and higher energy costs all cause the cost of production to increase. If production costs go up, firms may either charge a higher price for the same level of output or cut production back at the present price. That is, there would be a decrease in supply. If input costs fall, the reverse would be true and supply would increase.

Checkpoint

Content Check

1. Draw a graph of the relationship between price and quantity supplied for sport utility vehicles.
2. How would magazine publishers probably respond to an increase in the price of paper? Draw an illustration to support your answer.
3. What does the price elasticity of supply measure?
4. Explain the difference between a change in quantity supplied and a change in supply.

What Do You Think Now?

Reread *What Do You Think?* in the Section One Focus. Then answer the following questions:

5. Was there an increase in the *supply* of wheat or in the *quantity supplied* of wheat between the two years? Explain.
6. Describe what may cause a change in supply and a change in quantity supplied. Could both have happened in this case? Explain.

F

O

U

Section Two

Production Drives Supply

What Do You Think?

Gerry Lamdon owns the Shaggy Dog grooming business. Over the past five years, Gerry has employed between one and five groomers, depending on the season. The following table summarizes the number of groomers at Shaggy Dog and the total number of dogs they groomed per month.

Number of Groomers	Number of Dogs Groomed per Month
1	140
2	270
3	370
4	420
5	410

Gerry currently has four groomers. They have been complaining that they can't get all the dogs groomed on time. Do you think Gerry should hire another groomer?

What's Ahead?

To understand economics, you must understand concepts related to production. In this section, you will learn about why people get involved in production and how production is measured.

Terms to Know

- factor of production
- land
- labor
- capital
- entrepreneurship
- total product
- average product
- marginal product
- short run
- diminishing marginal product
- long run
- scale of production
- returns to scale

PRODUCING GOODS AND SERVICES

Production is the act of providing the supply of goods and services to the market. Production is what makes it possible to meet consumer demand. It is often said that the desire to make money fuels the great engine of a productive economy. But, you know that earning money involves opportunity costs.

Most of us would rather play tennis, dance, hike, or enjoy some activity other than work. To make up for those opportunity costs, we must get some benefits from working. We work because of the compensation, particularly money, that we receive for our efforts. We then use this money to buy the goods and services we need and enjoy.

The Four Factors of Production

factor of production anything used to produce a good or service

land a broad measure representing all the basic natural resources that contribute to production

labor the human factor of production

capital previously produced goods used to produce other goods

entrepreneurship the managerial ability and risk taking that contribute so much to a productive economy

A ***factor of production*** is anything used to produce a good or service. There are four broad categories of factors of production or productive resources: land, labor, capital, and entrepreneurship. ***Land*** is a broad measure representing all the basic natural resources that contribute to production. A Midwestern farm, a coal field in Wyoming, a Florida orange orchard, and natural gas in Oklahoma are all examples of the factor of production called *land.*

Labor represents the human factor of production. Each of us is free to follow our own best interests in using our productive abilities. Truck drivers, nurses, dockworkers, baseball players, teachers, and authors are all part of the factor of production called *labor.* The jobs and skills are very different, but they all fall into this broad category of labor.

Capital includes previously produced goods used to produce other goods. For example, a sewing machine used in making jeans is a form of capital. Office buildings, schools, factories, automobiles, tractors, and computers are all forms of capital equipment. Look around and you will note other kinds of capital equipment.

Entrepreneurship includes the managerial ability and risk taking that contribute so much to a productive economy. Few people can organize, direct, and control other people and resources efficiently and productively. Only an able person who is willing to accept risks will be a successful entrepreneur. We all benefit from the work of such people.

Ownership and Control of Factors of Production

In a free enterprise economy, most factors of production are owned or controlled by individuals. In such an economy, you can use your labor and the other factors you control to produce goods and services in exchange for monetary and nonmonetary rewards. If you own a large truck, you can use it to haul any goods you wish. You probably will choose to haul those items for which you can receive the most money. However, even in a free enterprise economy, there may be legal limits on how you use your productive resources.

Production takes place as owners of the factors of production allocate their land, labor, capital, and entrepreneurship in a manner that maximizes their expected returns. Thus, the profit motive is of great importance in guiding the production of goods and services in the economy.

MEASURING PRODUCTION

Businesses measure how much is produced or supplied during different time periods. For example, a company may keep track of how much is produced on a yearly, monthly, weekly, or even hourly basis. Without accurate measures of production, it is impossible to manage a business well.

Counting Units Versus Counting Dollars

Output can be measured in units or dollars. Using units makes it easier to compare sales from one time period to another. To see why this is so, consider the example of the Lumin Company. Lumin produces table lamps. Figure 7-6 shows Lumin Company's sales of table lamps for six years.

Year	Unit Sales	Dollar Sales
1	121,292	$6,082,662.00
2	128,570	6,360,358.00
3	124,998	6,492,834.00
4	121,747	6,576,924.00
5	126,253	6,956,750.00
6	124,727	7,078,885.00

Figure 7-6

Lumin Company Lamp Sales (Years 1–6)

A company can measure production in units and dollars. ***How would you describe this company's sales history during these six years?***

A sales pattern such as this is fairly common and can be misleading. If you look at the dollar amount of sales, the company seems to be doing quite well. As measured in dollars, sales have increased every year. But what has really happened? The number of units produced and sold has increased in some years and decreased in other years. Part of the year-to-year increase in dollar sales must have been due to price changes, not changes in actual units produced. Measuring production only in dollars would have given the misleading impression that the company has been selling more and more every year. Thus, it is better to measure output in units than in dollars.

Total Product

The production and sales listed in units for the Lumin Company represent a measure of output called *total product*. ***Total product*** is all the units of a product produced in a given period of time. For the Lumin Company, 124,727 lamps represent the total product for Year 6.

total product
all the units of a product produced in a given period of time

Average Product

Average product is an important measure of output. ***Average product*** is the number of units of output produced per unit of input.

average product
the number of units of output produced per unit of input

$$\text{Average Product} = \frac{\text{Units of Output}}{\text{Units of Input}}$$

To calculate the average product of labor for the Lumin Company, first you would determine the units of input for labor. Think of one workday as one labor unit. During Year 6, 88 people worked for Lumin for five days each week for 50 weeks a year. Therefore, the number of labor units used in Year 6 would be (88 workers) × (5 days/week) × (50 weeks/year) = 22,000 workdays.

The average product per labor unit would be total output for Year 6 divided by 22,000 labor units. Since 124,727 lamps were produced in Year 6, average product is 124,727 lamps ÷ 22,000 workdays = 5.67 lamps per workday. Thus, each worker produced an average of almost six lamps per day.

Marginal Product

marginal product
the amount that total product increases or decreases as a result of adding one additional unit of input

Another measure of production that is very important for economists is marginal product. ***Marginal product*** is the amount that total product increases or decreases as a result of adding one additional unit of an input. Marginal product is calculated as follows:

$$\text{Marginal Product} = \frac{\text{Change in Output}}{\text{Change in Input}}$$

Suppose that Lumin employed 90 workers each day last week and produced 510 lamps per day. When the company hired one additional worker, the total product increased to 515 lamps. The marginal product of that additional worker is five lamps.

Marginal product is very important in making production decisions. The dollar value of additional output should always be compared with the dollar cost of the additional input. The Lumin Company would have to compare how much it has to pay the additional worker with how much the company makes from the increased output. If the dollar value of the added output is more than the cost of the added input, then the firm's profit will increase.

DIMINISHING MARGINAL PRODUCT IN THE SHORT RUN

Production has two time frames: the short run and the long run. A firm's ability to change the quantity supplied varies depending on whether it is operating in the short run or in the long run.

The Short Run

short run
any period during which the usable amount of at least one input is fixed while the usable amount of a least one other input can change

The ***short run*** is any period during which the usable amount of at least one input is fixed while the usable amount of at least one other input can change. The short run is not a time period that is determined by the calendar. The short run is a period that is determined by whether one or more of the factors of production can be changed.

Lumin has a 5,000-square-foot building for the production and assembly of lamps. Lumin is limited to the existing building space, conveyor systems, and other equipment, so this input is fixed. However, the number of workers, another input, might be changed. In this scenario, Lumin is operating in the short run.

If sales are good, Lumin might hire more assemblers to increase production. But, adding more workers will not continue to increase output for long. Eventually, Lumin will need extra space and more equipment. As all factors of production begin to change, Lumin will move out of the short run.

Diminishing Marginal Product

Marginal product is a short-run measure because there is some base of fixed factors of production and one variable factor of production. Calculating the marginal product of labor, for example, assumes that the other factors are not changing.

Diminishing marginal product is the principle that as more of one input is added to a fixed amount of other inputs, the marginal product decreases. This does not mean that total output necessarily declines as more of the input is used. It means that output increases less and less rapidly as additional units of the input are used.

diminishing marginal product the principle that as more of one input is added to a fixed amount of other inputs, the marginal product decreases

Suppose that Lumin has decided to open a small retail store named Lights Unlimited. If the store hires no labor (clerks, cashiers), no sales can be made. If only one person is hired, not many customers can be served. But, as more people are hired, more customers can be served and more sales can result.

Will each extra employee increase Lights Unlimited's sales by an equal amount? Even if you assume that each worker is equally skilled, the answer is *no*. As more and more workers are added, the amount they add to total output (sales) decreases. Indeed, Lights Unlimited could hire so many workers that sales per worker would decrease. If there were 60 employees in the store, there would be no room for customers. Sales would fall to zero, just as if the store had hired no workers. Figure 7-7 summarizes the marginal product of labor for Lights Unlimited.

Number of Employees	Total Product	Marginal Product (Change in Output / Change in Input)
0	0	*
10	100	100 ÷ 10 = 10
20	160	60 ÷ 10 = 6
30	180	20 ÷ 10 = 2
40	160	-20 ÷ 10 = -2
50	100	-60 ÷ 10 = -6

*** A value cannot be determined at this point.**

Figure 7-7

Marginal Product of Labor for Lights Unlimited

In the short run, adding additional workers causes total product to increase for a while, but by a decreasing amount. Eventually, even total product begins to decrease. ***Why doesn't total product always increase as more workers are hired?***

Notice in Figure 7-7 that marginal product can be negative. This happens when total output declines as additional units of the input are used. This could happen if too many workers were hired. The concept of diminishing marginal product is very important. It is not possible to go on adding any one factor of production without getting less and less *additional* output. This is true in the short run in nearly all situations, from farming to retailing to education to steel production.

Figure 7-8 is a graph of the information in the table in Figure 7-7. Notice that total output increases rapidly at first when labor units are increased. Then as more labor units are added, output increases less rapidly and finally declines.

Figure 7-8

Graph of Diminishing Marginal Product for Lights Unlimited

Total product increases rapidly at first when labor usage is increased. Output increases less rapidly when the number of employees goes from 10 to 20 and from 20 to 30. After hiring 30 people, output actually declines. ***If you knew the information in this figure, would you hire the 45th unit of labor?***

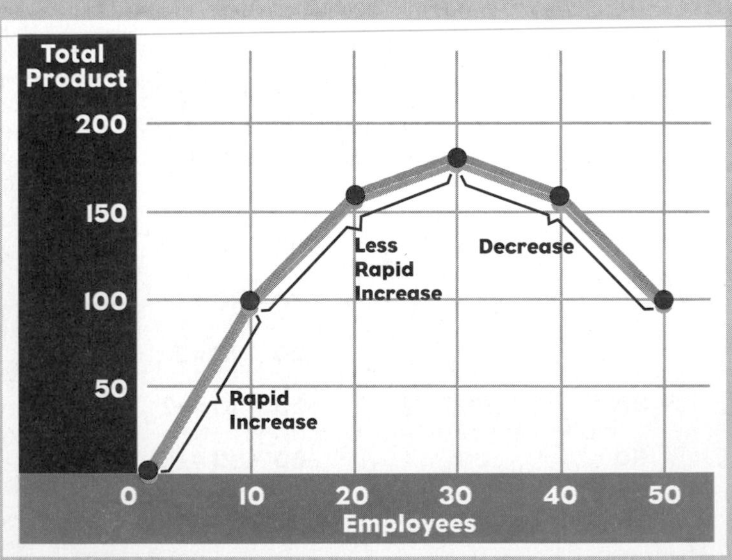

CHANGING PRODUCTION IN THE LONG RUN

Remember that in the short run, only one of the factors of production can change. The rest are fixed or constant. What happens if a producer can change more than one of the factors of production? Does the principle of diminishing marginal product still hold true?

The Long Run

The ***long run*** is a period during which the amounts of all inputs can be changed. None of the factors of production are fixed in the long run. The long run, like the short run, is not based on the calendar. Lights Unlimited might be able to expand its retail store and get additional space, equipment, and employees in place in two or three months, changing all of its inputs. For some firms it would take much longer. A power company, for example, might need ten years or more to increase plant capacity.

long run
a period during which the amounts of all inputs can be changed

Scale of Production

The ***scale of production*** is the overall level of use of all factors of production. When all inputs are increased, the scale of production increases. If all inputs are increased, the principle of diminishing marginal product is no longer valid. For example, if Lights Unlimited kept enlarging its store, more employees could be hired without the problem of crowding described earlier.

scale of production
the overall level of use of all factors of production

Global Economy

WHO HAS THE MOST QUALIFIED WORKFORCE?

In today's economy, the playing field is global. You compete for jobs not only with others in the United States but with everyone everywhere. A *Business Week* article asked, "Where will workers be best prepared?" Where do you think? Based on quality of public education, levels of secondary schooling, on-the-job training, computer literacy, and worker motivation, *Business Week* reported the following ranking of national workforces:

1. Singapore
2. Denmark
3. Germany
4. Japan
5. Norway
6. United States
7. Austria
8. Sweden
9. Netherlands
10. Finland

Being able to compete in the global marketplace is crucial to maintaining a healthy domestic economy. Many businesses are increasingly flexible in terms of where they locate and it is likely that many will gravitate to those economies that have the most productive workforces.

Returns to Scale

returns to scale
the relationship between changes in the scale of production and the corresponding change in the amount of output

Returns to scale is a term used to describe what happens when the scale of production changes. ***Returns to scale*** is the relationship between changes in the scale of production and the corresponding change in the amount of output. Returns to scale may be increasing, decreasing, or constant.

Many products, such as cars, steel, and home appliances, are produced more efficiently on a large scale. Production is characterized by *increasing returns to scale* when the level of output increases more rapidly than the rate of increase in the use of inputs. For example, if the use of all inputs is doubled and output more than doubles, there are increasing returns to scale.

In some forms of production, doubling all inputs results in exactly twice as much output. That is, output increases at the same rate as all inputs are increased. Using 20 percent more inputs would cause 20 percent more output to be produced. When this is true, there are *constant returns to scale.*

In other situations, output may increase less rapidly than the rate at which input usage increases. This situation involves *decreasing returns to scale*. For example, if the use of all inputs were increased by 50 percent but output increased by only 30 percent, there would be decreasing returns to scale.

Checkpoint

Content Check

1. What is the motivation for people to use their land, labor, capital, and entrepreneurship to produce goods and services?
2. What is the relationship between total product and marginal product?
3. How is the short run different from the long run in economic terms?
4. Why is the principle of diminishing marginal product only valid in the short run?
5. Explain the relationship between the scale of production and returns to scale in the long run.

What Do You Think Now?

Reread *What Do You Think?* in the Section Two Focus. Then answer the following questions:

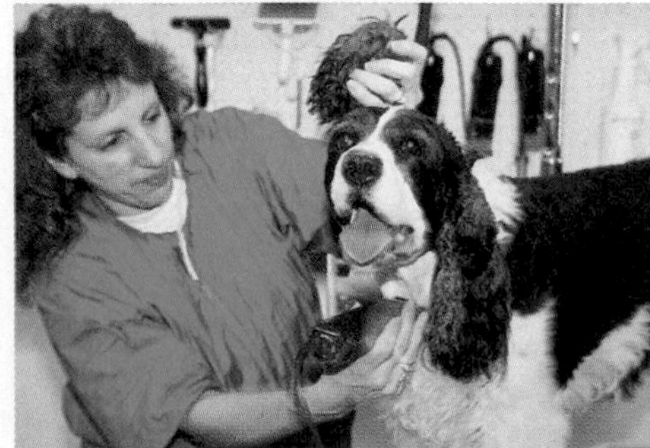

6. What happens to the marginal product of labor for Shaggy Dog as groomers are added? Why?
7. Will hiring another worker solve Gerry's problem? Why or why not?
8. What do you think Gerry should do?

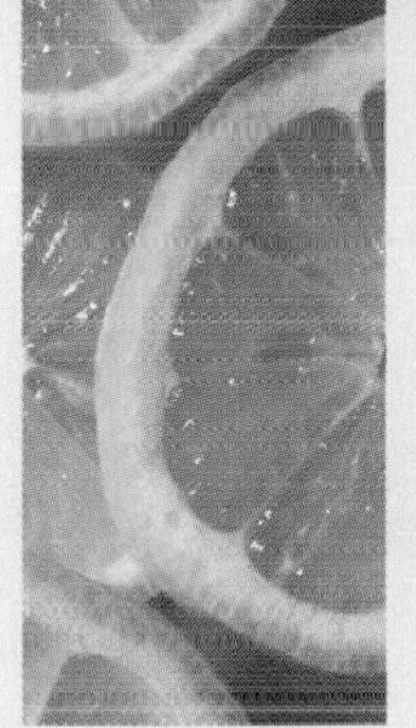

FOCUS

Section Three

Production Creates Costs

What Do You Think?

Billy Joe quit his job at Wal-Mart, where he made $5 an hour. He quit so that he could work full time painting portraits of children. Billy Joe gets $20 for each portrait. The paint, canvas, and brushes cost him about $12 per painting, and it usually takes him two hours to complete a portrait. Billy Joe is looking forward to the extra money he is going to make. Do you think Billy Joe made a good decision?

What's Ahead?

People who are involved in economic activity in both the private and the public sectors are usually concerned with controlling costs. Therefore, it is important to understand what determines costs. In this section, you will see that it is the process of producing a good or service that results in costs.

Terms to Know

explicit costs

opportunity costs

COSTS REPRESENT PAYMENTS TO FACTORS OF PRODUCTION

When businesspeople are asked about the problems they face, their answers almost always include dealing with rising costs. Government officials also talk about rising costs in the public sector of the economy.

Costs are incurred through the production process. The costs that a company incurs represent payments to factors of production or to the supplier of some intermediate good, such as the steel used in making a car. Payments to the factors of production of land, labor, capital, and entrepreneurship are called *rent, wages, interest,* and *profit,* respectively. The four factors of production and their payments are shown in Figure 7-9.

Figure 7-9

Payments for the Four Factors of Production

Payments for the factors of production result in costs. ***Which of these payments describes the salary that your economics teacher gets from the school system?***

Payment		Factor of Production
Rent	in exchange for	Land
Wages	in exchange for	Labor
Interest	in exchange for	Capital
Profit	in exchange for	Entrepreneurship

Dollars that are spent for intermediate goods, such as the steel in a car, are eventually used for these same factors of production. Thus, all costs are related to the factors of production at some stage in the production process.

Explicit Costs

Some costs are easy to see and account for. For example, Suzanne and Ben Kanoza have always wanted to own a business. Now that they are both about 40 years old, they have decided to start a business that customizes personal computers for home use. After looking into this type of business, they believe that they can get one started for $110,000. They will use $50,000 of their own money from savings accounts and stock and borrow $60,000 from the bank. The Kanozas figure their new business, Unitech, will have the monthly costs shown in Figure 7-10.

The costs in Figure 7-10 are the explicit costs of running Unitech every month. ***Explicit costs*** are payments made to others as a cost of running a business.

explicit costs payments made to others as a cost of running a business

Opportunity Costs

When the Kanozas show their cost estimates to the loan officer at the bank, they are surprised by the response they get. The loan officer tells the Kanozas that they have left out some very important costs: salaries to themselves and lost earnings on their $50,000 in savings and stock. These are the opportunity costs of starting and running Unitech.

Item	Monthly Cost
Rent	**$ 1,200.00**
Loan payment	**1,500.00**
Wages to technician	**2,000.00**
Electricity	**500.00**
Telephone	**100.00**
Advertising	**160.00**
Total monthly costs	**$5,460.00**

Figure 7-10

Monthly Cost Estimates for Unitech

The Kanozas can count on these monthly costs to run Unitech. ***What other costs might they have?***

Economic Dilemma

THE PRICE OF GREEN

Some businesses are actively considering alternate methods of production that are more environmentally friendly. This effort is sometimes referred to as *Green Marketing* because of the reduced environmental damage that can result. If you go to a local card shop and look at various greeting cards, you will see on the backs of some that they are printed on recycled paper (in whole or in part). At a bookstore, you also may find books that claim in the opening pages to be printed on recycled paper. The use of recycled paper may reduce the cutting of trees and thus help maintain more forested land. However, it also may be more costly.

It is possible in some parts of the country to produce electricity in an environmentally friendly manner using wind power. However, doing so may result in production costs that are higher per kilowatt hour than the costs of more conventional methods. This possibility raises some economic questions. Would people be willing to pay an extra $0.10 for a greeting card that was printed on recycled paper? Would you? Would people be willing to pay the higher price for electricity if it meant having cleaner air? Would you? Should the choice of whether to use wind power to produce electricity be left to the power companies or should it be made by the regulatory agencies that have oversight responsibility in this industry?

Economic Spotlight

A FAMILY WHO WORKS TOGETHER, STAYS TOGETHER

Through six decades, Goya Foods has managed to keep its business all in the family. Goya was originally founded as Unanue & Sons in a Manhattan warehouse in 1936. Goya is now the second largest Hispanic-owned company in the United States. The eight Unanues who run Goya, including the president, Joseph Unanue, strongly believe in preserving the family ownership of the business. The company was founded by husband and wife Prudencio Unanue and Carolina Casal because they missed the foods of their native lands of Spain and Puerto Rico.

Goya quickly became known for producing everything from rice and beans to octopus in hot sauce (an Hispanic delicacy), traditional foods that Hispanics in this country sorely missed. Over the years, Goya's business has expanded its product line into broader markets to include such items as frozen foods, desserts, and breads. Today, Goya is taking expansion one step further. The company is introducing Hispanic foods to non-Hispanic communities through coupons and recipes in newspapers and magazine ads and by running television spots.

But this expansion hasn't always been easy. As Goya has built a broader customer base, it has encountered language problems—even within the Hispanic community. For example, beans may be called *frijoles* by Cubans or *habichuelas* by Puerto Ricans. Hispanics have different names for fruits, vegetables, and other products, which poses a labeling problem. Consumers who call a product by a different name might not recognize the product they are looking for, so its identity must be made very clear.

When entering new markets, the Unanue family strategy has been to move more like a tortoise than a hare—approaching one new market at a time. By using this market-to-market strategy, Goya has been able to capture 80 percent of the Hispanic food business in the northeastern United States and 75 percent in Florida. It appears that Goya is one family-owned company that won't be stopped.

The Kanozas make a total of $5,000 each month at their present jobs. This is income that they would give up by leaving their current jobs, and so it is a cost of the new business. In addition, if the Kanozas didn't use their $50,000 to start the business, it would still be invested and earning about $375 per month. This $375 per month is also an opportunity cost that should be included as part of the cost of Unitech. Adding the lost salaries and earnings on savings to the explicit costs in Figure 7-10 bring the total monthly costs for Unitech to $10,835 ($5,460 + $5,000 + $375).

You can see the importance of the Kanozas considering both explicit costs and opportunity costs in their decision to open Unitech. If projected sales were enough to cover both explicit costs and opportunity costs ($10,835), Unitech would appear to be a worthwhile business. If projected sales were less than $10,835 per month, the Kanozas would have to reconsider their decision. If the Kanozas thought they would get a lot of psychic income from owning their business, they might still do so even if they earned less money.

COSTS AND DIMINISHING MARGINAL PRODUCT

You have seen that in the short run, production is subject to the principle of diminishing marginal product. That is, as added units of labor (or other variable inputs) are used, the marginal product decreases. Each new worker adds less to total output than does the previous one.

This means that in the short run, each added dollar's worth of input adds fewer units to output. So, the added cost per unit of output goes up. Firms that want to increase production without increasing all inputs will find that the additional cost per unit of output becomes greater. Remember the relationship between price and the quantity supplied? The law of supply states that as price goes up, so does quantity supplied. You can see now that this relationship is based on the principle of diminishing marginal product. As the cost per unit of output becomes greater, firms must get a higher price. So, the supply curve is determined by the level of cost. Thus, the supply curve is positively sloped because, in the short run, production is subject to the principle of diminishing marginal product.

COSTS AND THE SCALE OF PRODUCTION

As businesses enter the long run and change the scale of production, the cost of producing each unit is likely to change. Over the long run, costs per unit of output may fall, rise, or stay the same. What happens depends on whether the type of production has increasing, decreasing, or constant returns to scale (see Figure 7-11).

Increasing Returns to Scale	Decreasing Returns to Scale	Constant Returns to Scale
Production Cost per Unit Decreases	Production Cost per Unit Increases	Production Cost per Unit Remains Constant

Figure 7-11

Relationship Between Returns to Scale and Cost of Production

The cost of production per unit of output depends on the type of returns to scale experienced by the production process. ***What type of returns to scale do you think a manufacturer would like to have?***

Internet Connection

Browsing and Burrowing with Bookmarks

When you explore the World Wide Web or Gopherspace, it is easy to lose track of where you are. Suppose you follow a series of Web links or gopher menus, and you discover something interesting. How do you figure out where you are and how can you return there easily?

To figure out where you are, you need to understand Uniform Resource Locators (URLs), which indicate the address of a Web page, Gopher site, or any other Internet site. Examples of URLs include **http://alfred.econ.lsa.umich.edu** and **gopher://niord.shsu.edu/11gopher_root%3a%5b_DATA.ECONOMICS%5d**.

The information to the left of the "://" indicates the type of Internet resource. Web pages begin with "http". Gopher sites begin with "gopher". The information to the right of the "://" indicates the Internet address.

If you are using Netscape, finding out your location is easy. The "Location:" box gives the URL of the current document. The address changes as you move through Web space. If you are using Gopher, place your cursor on the item you are interested in and type =.

You can skip burrowing and connect directly to a remote Web page by *opening a URL.* Click on the OPEN icon on the toolbar and enter the URL of the remote Web page. An even better way is to use a bookmark list that stores the addresses of interesting Internet resources. Click on the Bookmarks menu item to view your bookmark list, select an item from the list, or add/delete an item.

To create a bookmark in gopher, select an item and type *a* (add). Gopher will prompt you for a bookmark name. To view your bookmarks, type *v* (view). To delete, select the appropriate bookmark and type *d* (delete).

Internet Application: Find an interesting Web or gopher site somewhere on the Internet. Create a bookmark. E-mail the URL for the site to your teacher.

Economics Application: Use what you have learned about production and supply to answer the following: How have Gopher and WWW affected the productivity of workers whose jobs involve using the Internet? How have they affected the supply of the firms who employ those workers?

If doubling all inputs produced more than twice as much output, then the cost per unit of output would fall. This is the case with increasing returns to scale. If doubling all inputs produced less than twice as much output, then the unit cost of the output would rise. This would represent decreasing returns to scale. In those cases in which there are constant returns to scale, the cost per unit of output would remain constant. Doubling all inputs would exactly double output.

Checkpoint

Content Check

1. Name the payments to land, labor, capital, and entrepreneurship and give an example of each.
2. Why should you consider opportunity costs when making a production decision?
3. In the short run, what happens to the cost of additional production when inputs are added? Why?
4. The rate of output for a product was 1,000 units per month. The company increased all inputs by 20 percent and output increased to 1,500 units per month. Are the returns to scale increasing, decreasing, or constant for this product? What should happen to the production cost per unit?

What Do You Think Now?

Reread *What Do You Think?* in the Section Three Focus. Then answer the following question:

5. What do you think now about Billy Joe's decision to quit his job at Wal-Mart and paint portraits? Consider both explicit costs and opportunity costs in your answer

Concepts in Brief

1. In a market economy, production decisions are made primarily by individuals acting in their own self-interest. We work in some form of production for the money and psychic income we get in exchange for our work effort.
2. The amount of a good or service that is supplied by a firm or market is related to the price at which the product can be sold. The higher the price, the greater the quantity supplied. This relationship is identified as a *change in the quantity supplied* and can be illustrated in either a supply schedule or a supply curve. The responsiveness of the amount supplied to changes in the product's price can be measured by the price elasticity of supply.
3. If the supply of a good or service at each and every price changes, this is called a *change in supply.* A change in supply is not the result of a change in price. Rather, it is the result of a change in technology or input costs.
4. Individuals own and/or control nearly all the factors of production in a market economy. These factors of production include land, labor, capital, and entrepreneurship. The output that results from production can be measured in units or in dollars. It is better to use units because the dollar measure can be misleading if prices change over time.
5. In the short run, there is at least one factor of production that is fixed in terms of availability. Almost all production is subject to diminishing marginal product in the short run. This means that as the use of a variable input (such as labor) increases, output will increase at a decreasing rate. A point can be reached at which so much of the input is used that output actually declines.
6. In the long run, all factors of production can be varied in terms of the amounts used in production. If all inputs can be increased at the same time, production may become more efficient due to increasing returns to scale. This is true in the production of cars, household appliances, steel, aluminum, and many other products. In some forms of production, there may be constant or even decreasing returns to scale. However, increasing returns to scale is the most common situation.

7. Costs are a natural result of the production process. It is important to consider both explicit costs and the opportunity costs when making economic decisions. Failure to do so will often result in bad decisions with undesirable results. Because of the principle of diminishing marginal product, the cost of production per unit of output increases as the rate of production increases in the short run. In the long run, the production cost per unit of output depends on whether there are increasing, decreasing, or constant returns to scale.

Economic Foundations

1. Market supply of a product is 1,000 units at $8 and 1,200 units at $9. Calculate the price elasticity of supply.
2. Explain the difference between a change in quantity supplied and a change in supply.
3. Who controls the factors of production in a market economy?
4. The total product for a company is 10,565 golf balls. If the company can produce 10,580 golf balls by adding one more worker, what is the marginal product of labor?
5. What distinguishes the short run from the long run in economic terms?
6. Explain the relationship between costs and level of production in the short run.
7. Explain the relationship between costs and level of production in the long run.
8. What payments are made to the four basic factors of production?
9. Differentiate between the three kinds of returns to scale.

Your Economic Vocabulary

Build your economic vocabulary by matching the following terms with their definitions.

- average product
- capital
- change in supply
- change in the quantity supplied
- diminishing marginal product
- entrepreneurship
- explicit costs
- factor of production
- labor
- land
- law of supply
- long run
- marginal product
- price elasticity of supply
- returns to scale
- scale of production
- short run
- supply
- supply curve
- supply schedule
- total product

1. a table that shows the quantities of a good or service that would be supplied by a firm at different prices
2. a graphic representation of the quantities that would be supplied at each price
3. the human factor of production
4. the quantities of a product or service that a firm is willing and able to make available for sale at different prices
5. a change in the number of units made available for sale due to a *price change*
6. measures the responsiveness of the quantity supplied to changes in the product's price
7. the managerial ability and risk taking that contribute so much to a productive economy
8. a change in the number of units supplied at every price
9. anything used to produce a good or service
10. previously produced goods used to produce other goods
11. a broad measure representing all the basic natural resources that contribute to production
12. the amount that total product increases or decreases as a result of adding one additional unit of an input
13. all the units of a product produced in a given period of time
14. any period during which the usable amount of at least one input is fixed while the usable amount of at least one other input can change
15. states that the quantity of goods supplied will be greater at a higher price than it will at a lower price
16. the principle that as more of one input is added to a fixed amount of other inputs, the marginal product decreases
17. a period during which the amounts of all inputs can be changed
18. the overall level of use of all factors of production
19. the relationship between changes in the scale of production and the corresponding change in the amount of output

20. payments made to others as a cost of running a business

21. the number of units of output produced per unit of input

Thinking Critically About Economics

1. Why do people work if it is not a pleasurable activity? Why would someone choose a lower paying job over a higher paying one?

2. Why are supply curves generally positively sloped? What relevance do production and cost concepts have in this regard?

3. Camcorder sales have been increasing. What factors do you think have contributed to the increase in supply and/or quantity supplied of this product? Can you think of some other products for which supply has increased recently?

4. Why might an increase in gasoline and diesel fuel costs cause a decrease in the supply of wheat in the United States? What technological changes might offset this effect?

5. Explain how the principle of diminishing marginal product relates to studying for a test.

6. Why do increasing returns to scale result in a lower cost per unit of output?

7. Suppose you decide to start a housecleaning business with some friends next summer. List the types of costs you would expect in this new business. Which of the costs would be explicit costs and which would be opportunity costs?

Economic Enrichment

You and a friend are designing a newsletter for your school's Spanish club using graphics and word processing programs on the computer in the school library. In the process, you come up with the idea to provide customized newsletters to businesses in your area. Each business could send the newsletter to its employees and customers.

Make a table of the factors of production that you would need in order to start producing these newsletters. Classify each factor as labor, capital, land, or entrepreneurship. In a short paragraph, explain whether you would expect to see diminishing marginal product from the factors you classify as labor and why.

Math and Economics

In Figure 7-6, you saw the following sales data for Lumin Company:

Year	Unit Sales	Dollar Sales
1	121,292	$6,082,662.00
2	128,570	6,360,358.00
3	124,998	6,492,834.00
4	121,747	6,576,924.00
5	126,253	6,956,750.00
6	124,727	7,078,885.00

Sketch a graph showing the dollar sales for Lumin. The vertical axis should indicate dollars and the horizontal axis should indicate years. Then sketch a second graph that shows unit sales for Lumin. Place unit sales on the vertical axis and years along the horizontal axis. Compare these two graphs and provide a written explanation for the differences you see.

Writing About Economics

Inez LaRoosa, the owner of Mama Mía's Pizzeria, is trying to determine how many cooks are needed in the main kitchen. The main kitchen prepares the sauce, dough, pasta, and specialty items for three pizzerias. LaRoosa was doing just fine until she opened the third pizzeria. Now she can't seem to produce enough food. She hired two more cooks, but matters only got worse.

You have been hired as a consultant to Mama Mía's Pizzeria. LaRoosa says she knows how to make a good Italian dinner, but she doesn't understand much about economics. Write a three-part proposal to LaRoosa in which you explain (1) how you plan to analyze this problem (use plenty of creativity here), (2) what data you will need for your analysis, and (3) how supply and production at Mama Mía's are linked. Cover the following areas in your explanation of how supply and production are linked: total product, marginal product, diminishing marginal product in the short run, and the relationship between returns to scale and production costs in the long run.

Economic Freedom on the Internet

Bob and Arminda Alexander ran a coffee store on Maui. Their shop was located on Front Street in Lahaina, a prime tourist spot. By all accounts, things were going well. Then Bob discovered the Internet.

"After exploring the Internet for three days, I thought, 'We could put the shop online,'" recalls Bob. For $1,000 in design and setup fees and $200 a month to a firm to manage their home page, the Alexanders did just that. The online business, Hawaii's Best Espresso Company (**http://hoohana.aloha.net/~bec/**), broke even in less than one month.

This is one example of a successful business enterprise being started on the Internet by two individuals. However, running a business over the Internet brings up several issues. How does the business get paid for its goods and services? If the customer decides to pay by credit card, how is the customer's credit card number kept secure? What are other forms of payment over the Internet?

To help resolve some of these payment and security issues, David Chaum founded DigiCash. The purpose of DigiCash is to provide a safe, secure, private means of conducting business transactions on the Internet. An online payment transaction generally involves three parties. The customer pays, the merchant receives the payment, and a bank does the accounting, making sure that money from the customer ends up in the merchant's account.

In the case of DigiCash's E-cash, the customer buys E-cash coins from the bank for his or her digital wallet. When the customer places an order over the Internet, the merchant's computer sends a payment request to the customer's computer. The E-cash software pops up, the customer approves the payment, and the software sends E-cash coins in the proper amount to the merchant. The merchant then connects with the bank payment server and sends the E-cash coins to the bank. The bank verifies the transaction and then transfers the money to the merchant.

Solutions such as DigiCash's E-cash have made it easier and more practical for people to start up businesses on the Internet. No longer is it necessary for merchants to worry about whether they will get paid for their goods and services. Nor do customers have to worry about sending their credit card numbers over the Internet. Everyone wins, because anything that makes it easier to start a business encourages a greater degree of competition, which should give consumers better prices and/or service.

SOURCE: Furger, Roberta, "Gold Rush on the Digital Frontier," in *PC World* (October 1995): 260.

Overview

Section One
Market Equilibrium

Section Two
The Market out of Balance

Section Three
Governments Impact Market Equilibrium

Demand, Supply, and Prices

Learning Objectives

8-1
Explain the equilibrium between demand and supply.

8-2
Graph equilibrium price and equilibrium quantity.

8-3
Demonstrate how price acts as a rationing device.

8-4
Analyze the effects of a shortage or a surplus and how they are eliminated.

8-5
Determine the effects of a change in demand on the market equilibrium.

8-6
Determine the effects of a change in supply on the market equilibrium.

8-7
Show how price floors and price ceilings are used to block the market system.

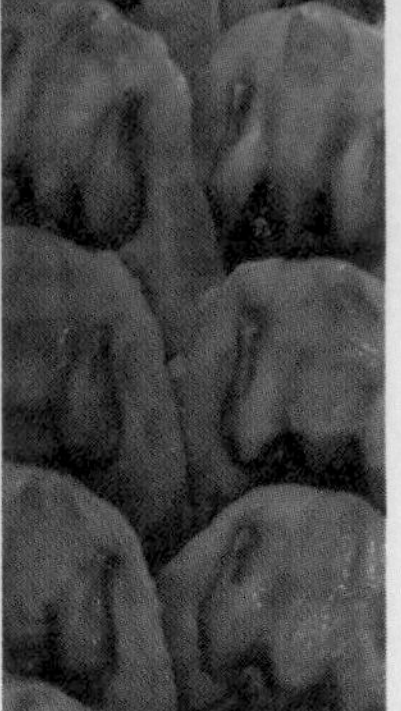

FOCUS

Section One
Market Equilibrium

What Do You Think?

When the price of hiking boots was $70, producers made 1.8 million pairs. At that price, people in the United States would want to buy 1.2 million pairs of hiking boots. Jocelyn Aders watched as the price of the hiking boots she wanted went down from $70.00 to $67.50 to $65.00. She decided to wait until it dropped to $55.00 before she bought, since that price would be within her budget.

Terms to Know

equilibrium price

equilibrium quantity

What's Ahead?

Individual producers and consumers direct the workings of a market economy. Each participant in the market economy acts in his or her own best interests in giving direction to the economy. In this section, you will review some important concepts about supply and demand. You will learn how the equilibrium price and quantity are determined in the marketplace.

THE MARKET SYSTEM

In a market system, people acting in their own self-interests make the decisions that guide the economy. Every time you make a purchase, you guide the direction of the economy. If you buy a new wool sweater, you signal to producers that people want wool sweaters. You do not buy a wool sweater with the idea of increasing employment in woolen mills or adding to the profits of mill owners. You buy a wool sweater because you know you will like wearing it or giving it as a gift. Your decision to buy the sweater is based on your own self-interest. No one makes you buy it.

Meanwhile, producers of wool sweaters respond to consumers' signals by employing more factors of production to make more sweaters. Producers don't have to make more sweaters. No government agency tells them to do so. They make more because they expect to make money. The producers

make more sweaters because it is in their own self-interest to do so.

A system of markets, such as the market for wool sweaters, is the heart of our economic system. We depend on free markets to communicate information between consumers and producers. Markets provide the mechanism for exchange, as illustrated in Figure 8-1. Consumers exchange money for goods and services from producers. Producers then exchange that money for factors of production used in making their products. The owners of these factors use that money in their own roles as consumers. So, the exchange process starts over again. At each stage, the exchange is made more efficient because of the existence of the market system.

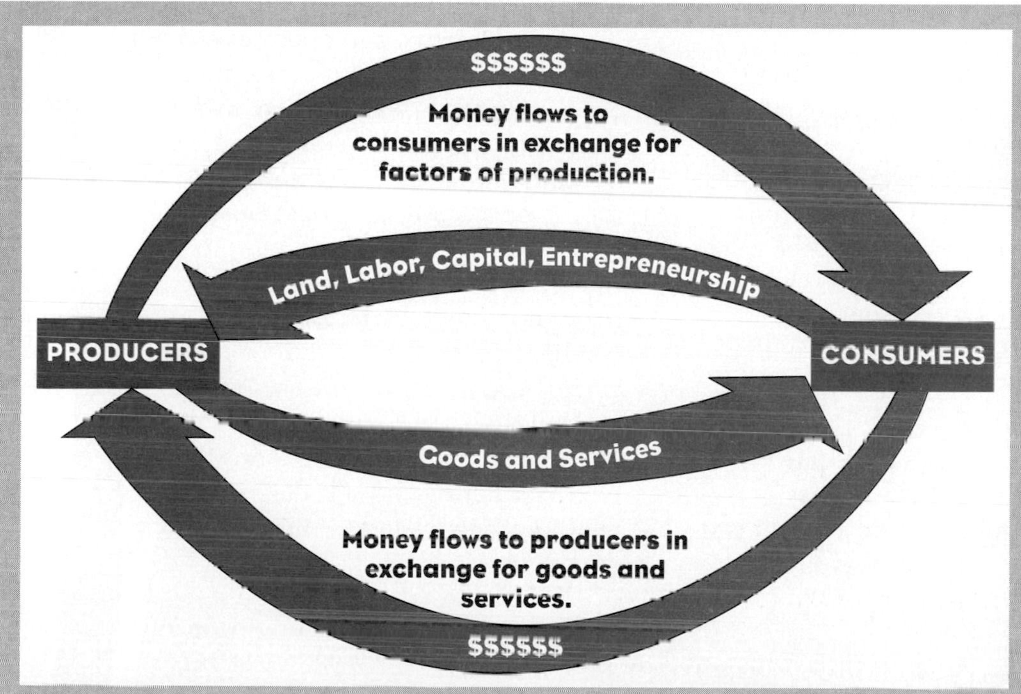

Figure 8-1

Markets Facilitate Exchanges

Money flows between consumers and producers in a circular fashion. Consumers pay money to producers in exchange for goods and services. Producers make payments to land, labor, capital, and entrepreneurship as they produce goods and services. ***What else is exchanged in a market system, such as the one illustrated here?***

Economic Spotlight

WHERE DID THE NINE-CENT COOKIE GO?

You probably don't remember the nine-cent cookie: a cold, small cookie handed to you over the counter in a paper bag. In fact, you probably don't even remember the 25-cent cookie! In the late 1970s, Debbi Fields introduced the 25-cent cookie, which was much larger than the old "nine center" and was served on a napkin while it was still warm from the oven.

Today, Americans spend a couple million dollars a year on chocolate chip cookies. Nobody knew how well Mrs. Fields cookies would catch on, however. Not even Fields herself. In 1977, she borrowed $50,000 from a bank to open her first cookie store. By noon on the first day of business, she began to fear that her first day would also be her last. Not a single cookie had been sold. To make matters worse, her husband had bet her that she wouldn't have $50 in the cash register at the end of the day. So, Fields decided to take matters into her own hands. She called a friend to watch the store. Then, she took her cookies out to the street in search of customers. Fields gave away all of her unsold cookies so she could bake more fresh ones. It was love at first bite! The people who sampled her cookies came back looking to buy more. By the end of the first day, she had exactly $50 in the till! Within a week, her store was profitable.

The demand for Mrs. Fields Cookies was so great, she opened more stores. That meant borrowing more money, which was difficult because most bankers believed that the cookie business wouldn't last. Today, Fields owns and operates a chain of more than 700 cookie stores throughout the United States, Europe, and the Far East. Fields moved slowly and kept her commitment to quality and customer service. She continues to sell freshly baked cookies, donating to charity any cookies that are more than two hours old. According to Fields, success has come from doing what she loves to do. She says that she never set out to make lots of money, just the best cookies possible. With her resulting success, you might say Debbi Fields is one "smart cookie."

The function of a market is to bring consumers and producers together. The interaction of demand and supply is an essential part of a market system. Because demand and supply are so important, we will briefly review these concepts. Then we will look at how demand and supply interact in a market system.

A Review of Demand

Demand is defined as the quantities of a product that consumers are willing and able to buy at various prices. The law of demand is that consumers will buy a greater quantity at a lower price than at a higher price. The market demand for a product is the sum of all individual consumers' demands. So, the market demand represents the total amount that all consumers are willing and able to buy at each price.

The market demand can be shown by either a table or a graph. Figure 8-2 illustrates a hypothetical demand schedule and demand curve for wheat. Note that wheat follows the law of demand. The quantity demanded becomes less as the price goes up. Looking at the demand curve, you quickly see the inverse relationship between price and quantity. At high prices such as $4.40 per bushel, the amount demanded is fairly low (1,600 million bushels). At lower prices, the amount demanded goes up.

A Review of Supply

Supply is the quantities of a product firms are willing and able to make available for sale at various prices. How much a firm supplies at any price depends on the firm's cost of production. Because of diminishing marginal product, the cost per unit of output rises as more is produced in the short run. The price a firm gets for a product must cover production costs. So, we can expect that firms will increase the amount supplied if price goes up.

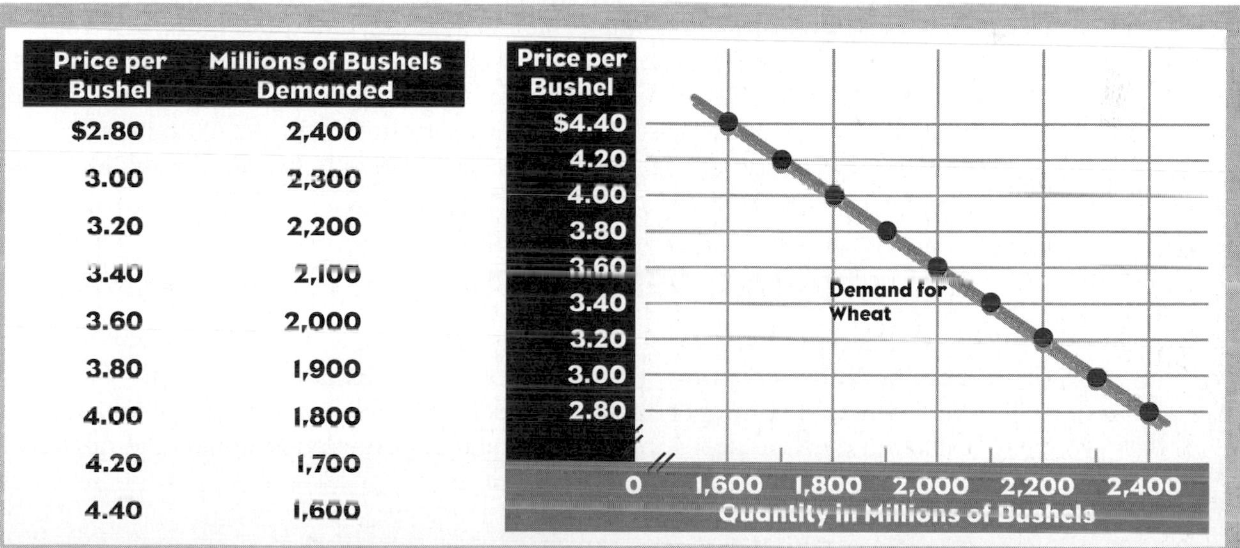

Price per Bushel	Millions of Bushels Demanded
$2.80	2,400
3.00	2,300
3.20	2,200
3.40	2,100
3.60	2,000
3.80	1,900
4.00	1,800
4.20	1,700
4.40	1,600

Figure 8-2

Hypothetical Demand Schedule and Demand Curve for Wheat

Each of the nine price and quantity combinations given in the demand schedule are represented by dots on the demand curve. Connecting these points allows you to estimate quantity demanded at prices not listed in the demand schedule. ***How many bushels of wheat would be demanded at a price of $3.70?***

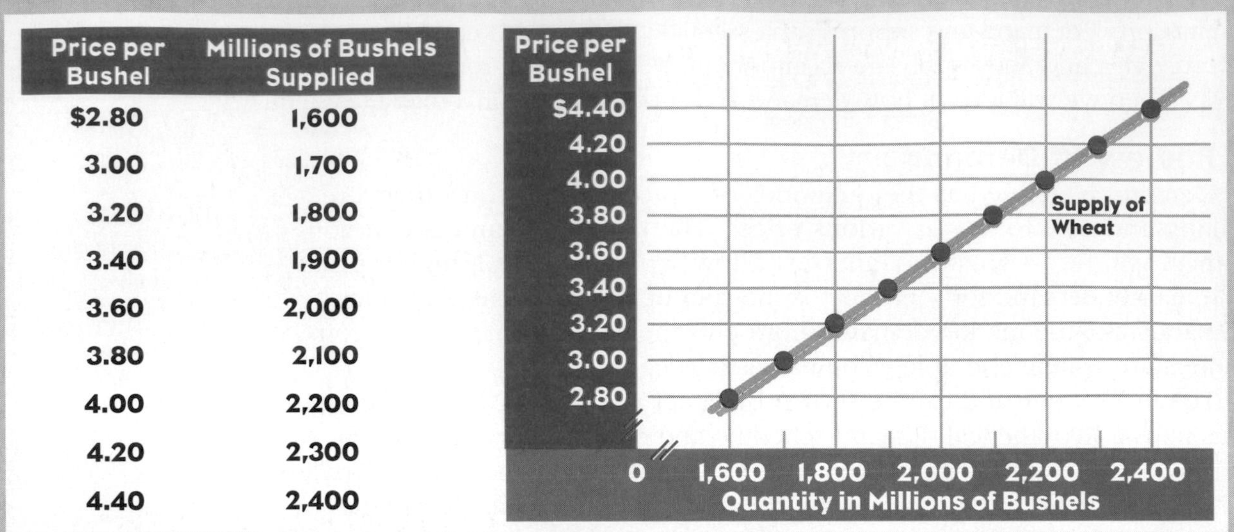

Price per Bushel	Millions of Bushels Supplied
$2.80	1,600
3.00	1,700
3.20	1,800
3.40	1,900
3.60	2,000
3.80	2,100
4.00	2,200
4.20	2,300
4.40	2,400

Hypothetical Supply Schedule and Supply Curve for Wheat

Each of the nine price and quantity combinations given in the supply schedule are represented by dots on the supply curve. Connecting these points allows you to estimate quantity supplied at prices not listed in the supply schedule. ***How many bushels of wheat would be supplied at a price of $3.70?***

If each producer produces more at a higher price than at a lower price, the same will be true for all firms combined. Adding together the quantities supplied by all firms at each price gives the market supply of the product.

A hypothetical market supply of wheat is illustrated in Figure 8-3. You can see the positive relationship between price and the quantity supplied in both the supply schedule and supply curve. As price goes up from $2.80 to $4.40 per bushel, the quantity supplied goes up from 1,600 to 2,400 million bushels. The slope of the supply curve is positive because, in total, all firms supply a greater quantity the higher the price.

EQUILIBRIUM: DEMAND AND SUPPLY IN BALANCE

The condition of two forces exactly balancing one another is called equilibrium. In the economy, those two forces are demand and supply. In a market economy, natural economic forces lead to an equilibrium, or balance, between demand and supply. If the quantity demanded equals the quantity supplied, the market is in equilibrium.

Finding Equilibrium

In Figure 8-4, the demand and supply schedules we have been working with are shown in a single table. You can see in the table that at prices higher than $3.60, the quantity supplied is greater than the quantity demanded. At every price less than $3.60, the quantity demanded is greater than the quantity supplied. Only at a price of $3.60 is there equilibrium in the market, with the quantity supplied equal to the quantity demanded. The price at

Price	Quantity Demanded	Quantity Supplied
$2.80	2,400	1,600
3.00	2,300	1,700
3.20	2,200	1,800
3.40	2,100	1,900
3.60	2,000	2,000
3.80	1,900	2,100
4.00	1,800	2,200
4.20	1,700	2,300
4.40	1,600	2,400

Figure 8-4

Hypothetical Demand and Supply Schedules for Wheat

Putting the supply and demand schedules together in one table allows you to see the price at which quantity supplied equals quantity demanded. ***At a price of $3, what is the relationship between supply and demand?***

which the quantity demanded equals the quantity supplied is called the ***equilibrium price*** (or market price). In this case, then, the equilibrium price is $3.60.

At the $3.60 price, the quantity demanded is 2,000 units, as is the quantity supplied. Thus, 2,000 units represent the equilibrium quantity. The ***equilibrium quantity*** is the quantity that is both demanded and supplied at the equilibrium price.

equilibrium price
the price at which the quantity demanded equals the quantity supplied

equilibrium quantity
the quantity that is both demanded and supplied at the equilibrium price

Graphing Equilibrium

Figure 8-5 shows the supply and demand curves for wheat on the same graph. You will see these curves several times throughout the rest of this chapter.

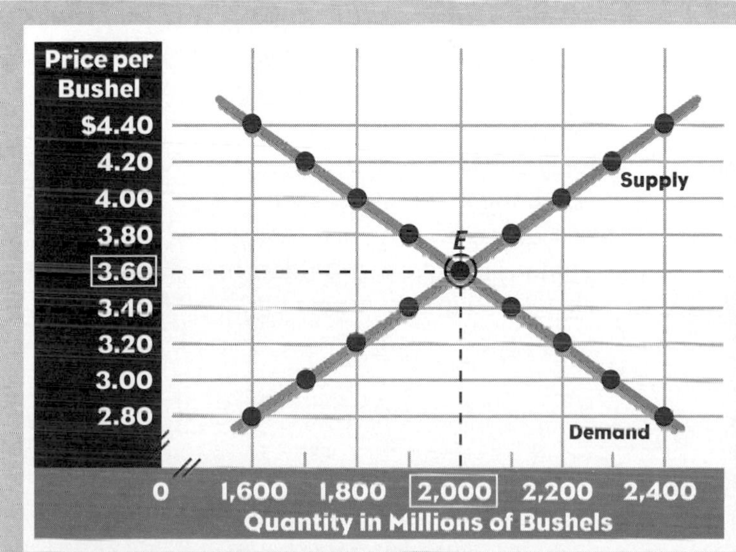

Figure 8-5

Balance Between Demand and Supply

Equilibrium occurs at the point where the supply and demand curves intersect. ***Would there be equilibrium at a price of $4.20?***

Internet Connection

POWER SEARCHES USING GOPHER AND THE WEB BROWSERS

As you have learned, the Internet is a great research tool. The Internet offers a tremendous amount of information from libraries, schools, government agencies, and businesses. Two good locations to start any research project are the Global Electronic Library at **gopher://marvel.loc.gov/11/global** and the WWW Virtual Library at **http://www.w3.org/hypertext/DataSources/bySubject/Overview.html**.

To find the information you need, you could browse through Gopher menus or Web pages, but a more efficient way is to use one of the electronic search methods available on the Internet. There are a variety of such methods, but we will focus on two: Veronica for Gopher and WebCrawler for the World Wide Web.

Most Gopher servers have menu items labeled *Veronica Searches* or something similar. You select appropriate keywords to search for and follow directions. Veronica searches through the menu titles in Gopher space to find titles that contain the specified keywords. The results come in the form of a Gopher menu. You then select from the menu to access them.

The easy way to access WebCrawler using Netscape is to click on the directory button *Net Search,* which is located under the *Location* box. If you use a different browser and you don't appear to have direct access to WebCrawler, you can open the URL at **http://webcrawler.com/WebCrawler/**.

WebCrawler asks you to choose keywords; it returns a list of Web pages with the specified keywords that ranks the items on a scale of 1 to 1,000. Clicking on any item in the list connects you to that Web page.

Internet Application: Pick a topic on some aspect of economics that interests you. Try both a Veronica search (even via browser) and a WebCrawler search. Do they give you the same results? Which do you prefer?

Economics Application: Now that the government is no longer subsidizing the Internet, more and more people are getting access to the Internet through commercial Internet providers. Use the theory of supply and demand to explain why, despite the increased demand for Internet access, the price charged by commercial Internet providers has fallen. Use a graph, if possible.

What does market equilibrium look like on a graph? In Figure 8-5, the equilibrium price and quantity are shown in boxes. From this graph, you can see that equilibrium occurs at the point where the demand curve crosses the supply curve. That is, the quantity demanded and the quantity supplied are equal where the two lines cross. This is an important point that you will see again and again as you study economics.

The equilibrium point, or the intersection of the demand and supply curves, is labeled *E* (for equilibrium) in Figure 8-5. Only at this point does the quantity demanded equal the quantity supplied. At any price above $3.60, the quantity supplied is greater than the quantity demanded. At any price below $3.60, the quantity demanded is greater than the quantity supplied.

This relationship between the quantity supplied and the quantity demanded is true in all markets. Any market is in equilibrium, or balance, when the quantity demanded equals the quantity supplied. In a graph, this is the point where the demand curve crosses the supply curve. To find the equilibrium price and equilibrium quantity for a market, you first find the point where demand crosses supply. Then read over to the price axis to find the equilibrium price. The equilibrium quantity is found from the quantity axis directly below where the two curves cross.

Checkpoint

Content Check

1. How does your purchase of a bicycle helmet guide the market?
2. If there is equilibrium in the market for oats to feed horses, what do you know about the quantity supplied and the quantity demanded?
3. Graph the supply and demand curves to represent a market equilibrium for corn.

What Do You Think Now?

Reread *What Do You Think?* in the Section One Focus. Then answer the following questions:

4. What determines how far the price of hiking boots will drop?
5. Do you think the price of hiking boots will ever get to $55 so that Jocelyn can buy a pair?

F O C U S

Section Two

The Market out of Balance

What Do You Think?

Alonzo Borland, a Kansas wheat farmer, is talking on the phone to his sister Grace in New Jersey. "It's been a great year. We got the plowing done on schedule, we had perfect rainfall and sunshine, and the harvest is better than we expected. In fact, all around the country, total wheat production is way up. I just hope I can make some money this year." Grace is not sure why Alonzo is worried after such a great year.

Terms to Know

shortage

surplus

What's Ahead?

The market is in equilibrium when the quantity supplied equals the quantity demanded. What happens when the market is not in equilibrium? In this section, you will see what happens to the market when there is either a shortage or a surplus in the market. You will also see what happens to equilibrium when either demand or supply change.

PRICE AS A RATIONING DEVICE

You know that price is important in determining both the quantity demanded and the quantity supplied. Consumers look at prices as they decide how to spend their money. Producers look at prices as they decide what goods or services to produce. So, price acts as a signal for both consumers and producers. In this way, prices help to distribute both finished goods and raw materials among competing uses. You will see that when there is a shortage of something, price tends to rise. When there is a surplus, price tends to fall. In the following sections, you will examine how price changes help to eliminate either a shortage or a surplus.

A Shortage in the Market

What does it mean to say there is a shortage of some product? What does it mean when a newscaster announces that there is likely to be a shortage of heating oil next winter? When cold weather hits the orange groves of Florida, people in New York experience a shortage of orange juice in the grocery stores. What does that mean?

What Is a Shortage? A shortage exists when people are willing to buy more than producers have for sale at a particular price. A ***shortage*** is the condition in which the quantity demanded is greater than the quantity supplied at a certain price. A shortage of orange juice means that consumers want to buy more at the present price than is available for sale. That is, there is a shortage when the quantity demanded at a certain price is greater than the quantity supplied.

shortage
the condition in which the quantity demanded is greater than the quantity supplied at a certain price

What Does a Shortage Look Like on a Graph? Figure 8-6 takes another look at the wheat market. You can use Figure 8-6 to understand a shortage. At a price of $3.20, the quantity supplied is 1,800 units. This can be found by following the dashed line from the price of $3.20 to the supply curve at the point marked *A*. Then from *A*, follow the dashed line down to the quantity axis at 1,800 units. You can verify that 1,800 units would be supplied at a price of $3.20 by checking the supply schedule in Figure 8-4.

But, what about the quantity demanded at that price? From the demand curve, you can see that 2,200 units are demanded at a price of $3.20. You can find this quantity by extending the dashed line from the $3.20 price over to the demand curve at *B*. Then from *B*, follow the line down to the quantity axis at 2,200 units. Looking back to the demand schedule in Figure 8-4, you also can see that 2,200 units are demanded at a price of $3.20.

At a price of $3.20, there is a shortage of wheat. Consumers would want to purchase 2,200 units, but suppliers are willing to supply only 1,800 units. The quantity demanded is greater than the quantity supplied at that price. Not everyone who wants to buy wheat at that price is able to do so. There is a shortage of 400 units. This is the distance between *A* and *B*.

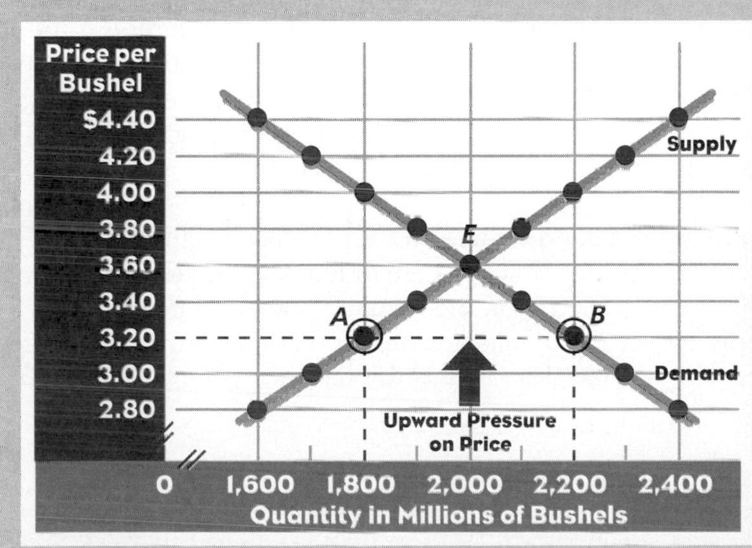

Figure 8-6

Shortage in the Wheat Market

A shortage results when the quantity demanded is greater than the quantity supplied at a certain price. The distance between *A* and *B* (400 units) is a measure of the amount of the shortage. ***What do you think happens to price when there is a shortage of a product in the marketplace?***

How Is a Shortage Eliminated? Some people are willing to pay more than $3.20 per bushel for their wheat. You can see this is true by looking at the demand curve. For example, enough consumers are willing to pay $4.20 per bushel for 1,700 units to be sold at that price. So, there are consumers who stand ready to buy wheat at prices above $3.20. Some of them are likely to pay more than $3.20, rather than do without the wheat.

Suppliers are likely to know when the quantity demanded is greater than the quantity supplied and that some people are willing to pay a higher price. The suppliers in such a situation will probably raise their prices. Thus, a shortage causes upward pressure on the price. This is shown by the arrow pointing up in Figure 8-6. This upward pressure is due to natural economic forces on both the demand and supply sides of the marketplace.

As price rises, the amount demanded becomes less. Some consumers may drop out of the market while others will cut back on their use of the product. At the same time, producers will increase the amount they supply as price rises. As the amount demanded decreases and the amount supplied increases, the shortage is reduced.

As long as the quantity demanded is greater than the quantity supplied, this process continues. There is upward pressure on price. This, in turn, decreases the amount demanded and increases the amount supplied. Only when there is no shortage is there no longer upward pressure on price.

A Surplus in the Market

At times, U.S. car manufacturers have produced more cars than people have been willing to buy at existing prices. When weather and other conditions cooperate, the agricultural sector may produce more wheat or corn than consumers wish to purchase. You probably can guess that these conditions represent a surplus. What does that mean in the market?

surplus
the condition in which the quantity supplied is greater than the quantity demanded at a certain price

What Is a Surplus? A surplus is the opposite of a shortage. A ***surplus*** is the condition in which the quantity supplied is greater than the quantity demanded at a certain price. There is a surplus of a product when people are not willing to buy as much as is produced at a given price. That is, if the amount demanded is less than the amount supplied at any price, there is a surplus.

What Does a Surplus Look Like on a Graph? A surplus is illustrated in Figure 8-7. At a price of $4.20, the amount demanded is 1,700 units. This is determined from the point labeled *C* on the demand curve. As indicated by Point *D* on the supply curve, 2,300 units are supplied at that price. There is a surplus of 600 units. This surplus is shown as the distance between *C* and *D* in Figure 8-7.

How Is a Surplus Eliminated? Suppliers have more of the product than they can sell at this high price. They are likely to reduce price to try to increase sales. At the same time, consumers are likely to know about the

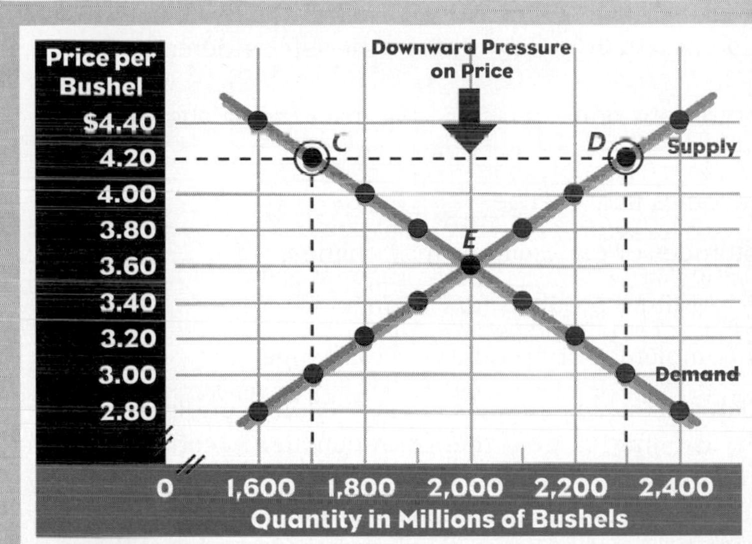

Figure 8-7

Surplus in the Wheat Market

A surplus results when the quantity supplied is greater than the quantity demanded. The distance between *C* and *D* (600 units) is a measure of the amount of the surplus. ***What would you expect to happen to price when the quantity supplied is more than the quantity demanded?***

surplus. They may recognize that they have greater bargaining power and may offer to buy the product, but only at a reduced price. Thus, when there is a surplus, there is downward pressure on price. This is shown by the arrow pointing down in Figure 8-7.

When car companies produce too many cars, they frequently offer rebates to improve sales. A rebate is a lowering of price. If you get back a $500 check from the company after buying a car, that is like having the price reduced by $500. In fact, the rebate often can be deducted from the price at the time of purchase.

Forces on both the demand and supply sides of the market react with downward pressure on price when there is a surplus. As price comes down, the amount demanded increases. This helps reduce the surplus. Also, as price falls, the amount supplied decreases as firms reduce production. This also acts to reduce the surplus.

As long as the quantity demanded is less than the quantity supplied, price continues to fall. As price falls, the amount demanded increases and the amount supplied decreases. When there is no longer a surplus, the downward pressure on price is eliminated.

CHANGES IN DEMAND

You have seen that, in a market economy, natural economic forces lead to a balance between demand and supply. But, in Chapter 6, you learned that demand may change. The demand curve may not stay in the same place. It may shift to the right as demand for the product increases. Or, the demand curve may shift to the left as demand for the product falls.

To review, there are four primary factors that can cause a change in demand:

1. Consumers' incomes may change.
2. Consumers' attitudes or expectations may change.
3. The prices of substitute products may change.
4. The prices of complementary products may change.

Other factors, such as consumer expectations, weather conditions, and population changes, also may cause a change in demand in certain situations.

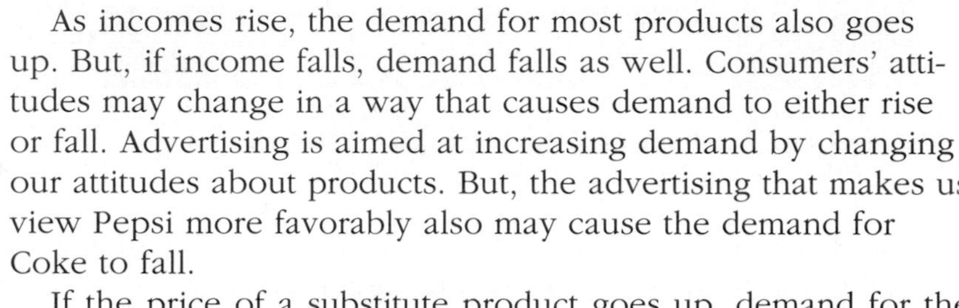

As incomes rise, the demand for most products also goes up. But, if income falls, demand falls as well. Consumers' attitudes may change in a way that causes demand to either rise or fall. Advertising is aimed at increasing demand by changing our attitudes about products. But, the advertising that makes us view Pepsi more favorably also may cause the demand for Coke to fall.

If the price of a substitute product goes up, demand for the other product increases. For example, if the price of Pepsi goes up, the demand for Coke rises. This also works in the other direction. If the price of Pepsi comes down, the demand for Coke falls. Changes in the prices of complementary products also affect demand. As the price of gas goes up, the demand for car tires goes down. Gas and tires are complementary because the use of one increases the use of the other. This works in reverse, too. If the price of gas falls, people drive more and the demand for tires goes up.

What Happens to Equilibrium If Demand Increases?

When the demand for a product goes up, the equilibrium price and quantity are affected. An *increase in demand* means that consumers are willing to buy more at each price than they would have before the rise in demand. If the supply does not change, price will surely rise. The original quantity supplied no longer satisfies demand at the original price. There is a shortage at the original price. As you have seen, price is pushed up when there is a shortage. But, remember that if price goes up, the quantity supplied goes up also as producers respond to the higher price.

Figure 8-8 will help you see exactly what happens. The supply curve and original demand curve shown in Figure 8-8 are the same as the supply and demand curves used earlier in this chapter. They cross at Point *E* at a price of $3.60 and a quantity of 2,000 units. This is the original equilibrium.

Suppose that demand goes up and consumers now are willing to buy 100 more units of wheat at each price. This is shown by the new, higher demand curve. With this higher demand, consumers want to buy 2,100 units rather than 2,000 units at a price of $3.60 (Point *E*). There will be a shortage of 100 units if the amount supplied does not change. This shortage is represented by the distance between Points *E* and *F*.

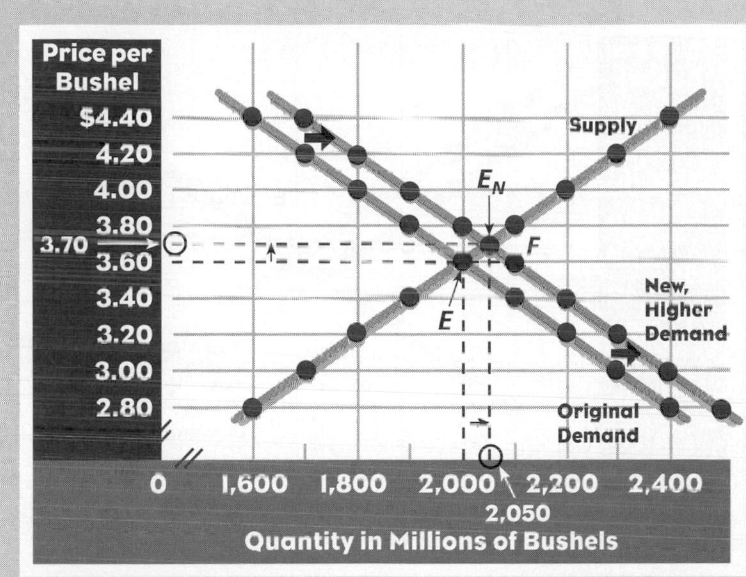

Figure 8-8

Effects of an Increase in Demand

When demand shifts to the right, the equilibrium price and quantity both go up. ***What might cause an increase in the demand for wheat?***

This is not the new equilibrium, however. Remember that when there is a shortage, there is upward pressure on price. As price rises, the quantity supplied goes up as well. A new equilibrium price is reached when the new, higher demand curve crosses the supply curve. This is at Point E_N in the middle of Figure 8-8. The new equilibrium price is $3.70. This is found by following the dashed line to the left from the point where the new, higher demand curve crosses the supply curve.

At a price of $3.70, consumers want to purchase 2,050 units. This is the quantity directly below the intersection of the new, higher demand and supply curves. This quantity demanded is exactly the same as the amount that would be supplied at a price of $3.70.

So, there are two important changes when there is an increase in demand. If demand goes up and the supply curve remains the same, the following occurs:

1. Prices rise.

2. Quantity exchanged rises.

What Happens to Equilibrium If Demand Decreases?

When the demand for a product falls, consumers are willing to buy fewer units at each price. This affects both equilibrium price and equilibrium quantity. With a lower level of demand, there is a surplus if the supply does not change. A surplus puts downward pressure on price. As price falls, the quantity supplied by producers also falls. This process goes on until the quantity supplied and the quantity demanded are once more in balance.

You can use Figure 8-9 on page 196 to see how this happens. The original equilibrium is at a price of $3.60 and a quantity of 2,000 (Point *E*). Demand and supply are in balance. But suppose that demand falls to the level given by the new, lower demand curve. The first effect is a surplus of 100 units at the $3.60 price. Consumers now are willing to buy only

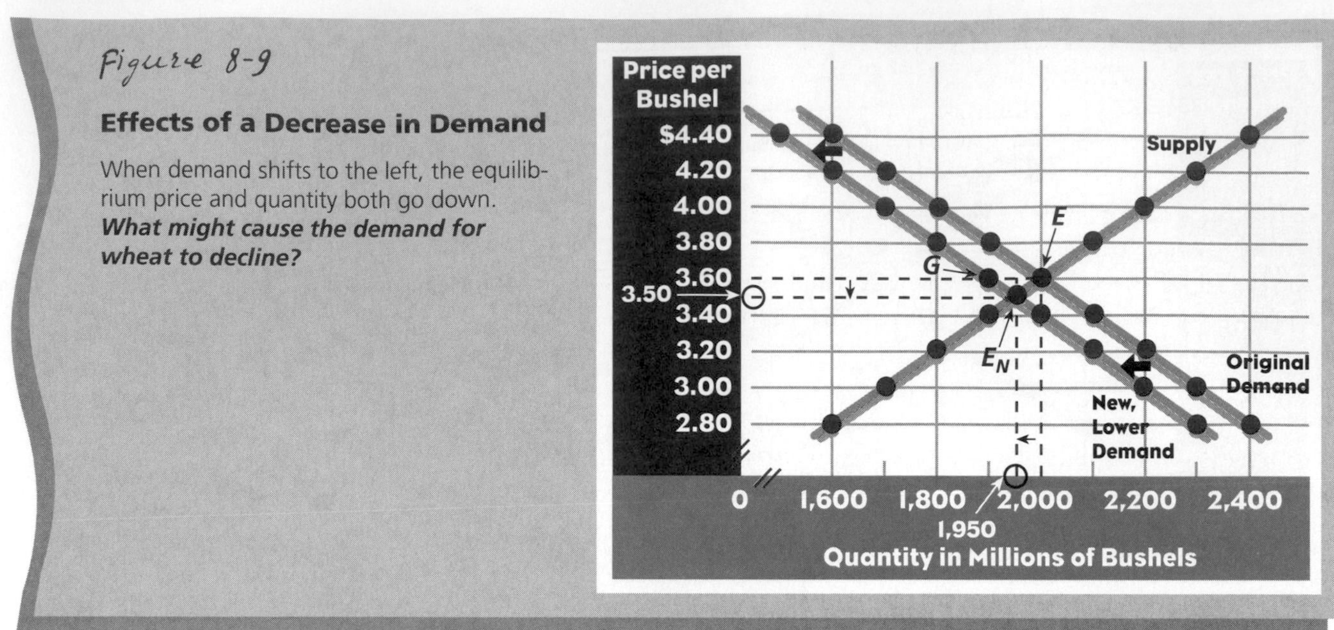

Figure 8-9

Effects of a Decrease in Demand

When demand shifts to the left, the equilibrium price and quantity both go down. ***What might cause the demand for wheat to decline?***

1,900 units, while producers still are supplying 2,000 units. This surplus is shown as the distance between Points *E* and *G* in Figure 8-9.

This surplus results in downward pressure on price. As the price falls, producers cut back on the amount supplied. Price goes on falling, and the amount supplied falls until a new equilibrium is reached. This is at the point where the new, lower demand crosses the supply curve. In Figure 8-9, this is Point E_N.

The price at this new equilibrium is $3.50, and the quantity is 1,950 units. The 1,950 units satisfy consumers at a price of $3.50. Also, suppliers only want to supply 1,950 units at a price of $3.50. The market is once more in balance.

Thus, if demand falls while the supply curve stays the same, the following occurs:

1. Prices fall.
2. Quantity exchanged falls.

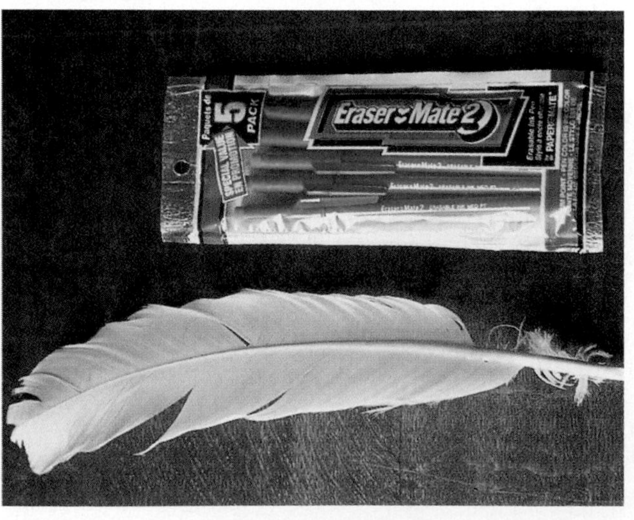

CHANGES IN SUPPLY

A shift of the supply curve also can upset the balance between demand and supply. Remember that the two main causes of a change in supply are a technological change and a change of input prices. If input prices go up, the firm's costs go up. Therefore, the quantity the firm supplies at each price is less. Higher costs result in a decrease in supply. This shifts the supply curve to the left.

Technological changes usually result in a greater supply. Using a more advanced technology increases productivity. As productivity increases, the cost per unit of output goes down. Supply increases as shown by shifting the supply curve to the right.

What Happens to Equilibrium If Supply Increases?

An *increase in supply* means that producers are willing to supply more at each price. If there is an increase in the supply of wheat, the supply curve shifts from the original supply to the new, greater supply, as shown in Figure 8-10. This shift shows that firms supply 100 more units at each price. For example, at the original equilibrium price of $3.60, firms now supply 2,100 units rather than 2,000 units.

At the $3.60 price, there now is a surplus. Producers still supply 2,100 units, but consumers only want to buy 2,000 units. This surplus of 100 units is shown as the distance from *E* to *F*. The existence of the surplus means that there is downward pressure on price.

As the price begins to fall, the amount demanded goes up. This follows from the law of demand. Consumers are willing and able to purchase more at lower prices than at higher prices. As the amount demanded goes up, the surplus is reduced.

At the same time, producers are cutting back on the amount supplied, due to the fall in price. This further helps to lower the amount of the surplus. After all changes, the price has fallen just enough that the quantity demanded and quantity supplied are balanced again.

In the example shown in Figure 8-10, the new equilibrium price is $3.50. At this price, consumers want to buy 2,050 units, as shown by their demand curve. Given the new greater supply, we see that producers want to supply 2,050 units at a price of $3.50. Thus, the quantity demanded and the quantity supplied are once more in balance at Point E_N.

If supply increases while the demand curve remains the same, the following results can be expected:

1. Prices fall.
2. Quantity exchanged rises.

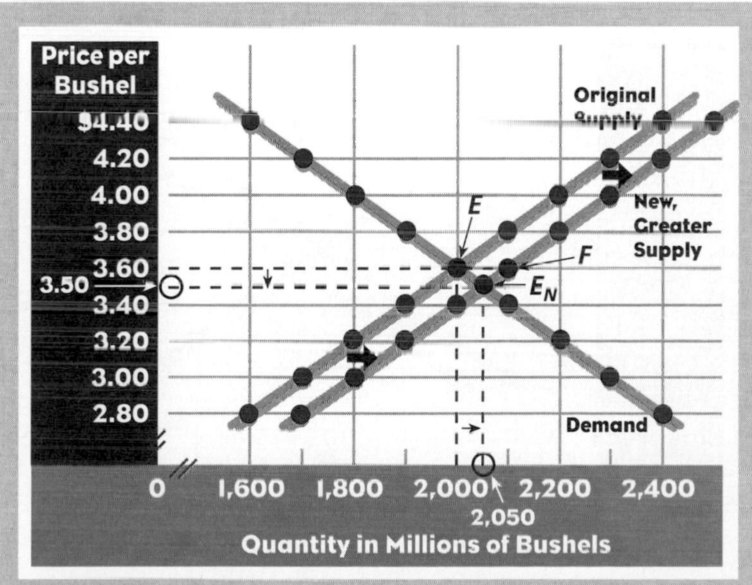

Figure 8-10

Effects of an Increase in Supply

When supply shifts to the right, price falls and the quantity exchanged rises. ***Why might the supply of wheat increase?***

What Happens to Equilibrium If Supply Decreases?

Supply shifts to the left when the cost of production goes up. This often is caused by a rise in the costs of inputs to the firm. Higher costs for labor, fertilizer, fuel, and machines might combine to cause a reduction in the supply of wheat. This is shown in Figure 8-11 as the shift from the original supply to the new, lower supply. The first effect of this drop in supply is a 100-unit shortage of wheat. At the original equilibrium price of $3.60, consumers want to buy 2,000 units. But now with the reduced supply, producers only want to supply 1,900 units. This 100-unit shortage is shown as the distance from *E* to *G*.

We know that when there is a shortage there is upward pressure on price. As the price rises, consumers reduce the quantity they demand in keeping with the law of demand. This helps to reduce the shortage. As price goes up, producers expand production along the new, lower supply curve. This process goes on until the market is in balance again.

Figure 8-11

Effects of a Decrease in Supply

When supply shifts to the left, prices rise and the quantity exchanged falls. ***What might cause the supply of wheat to fall?***

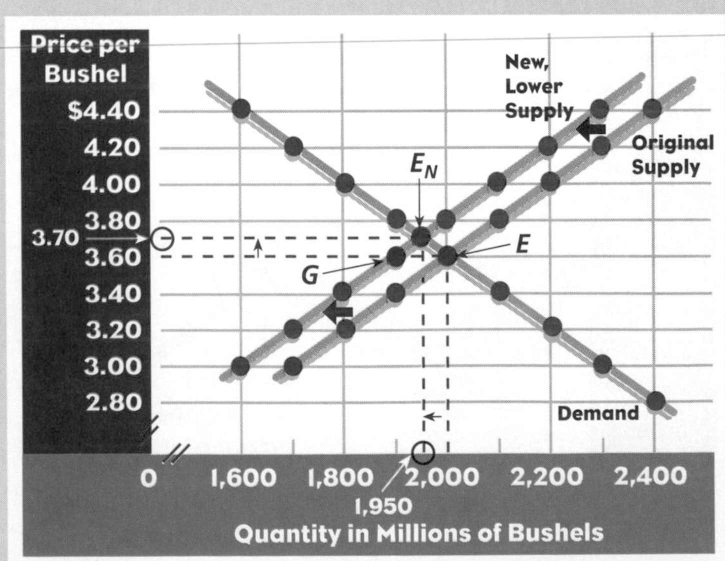

In the case we have shown, the new equilibrium is where the demand curve crosses the new lower supply curve at Point E_N. The price at this level is $3.70. At this new equilibrium price, consumers want to buy 1,950 units. Producers want to supply this same amount at that price. So, at a price of $3.70, the market is in balance. The quantity demanded and the quantity supplied are both 1,950 units.

If demand stays the same and supply decreases, we can expect the following results:

1. Prices go up
2. Quantity exchanged is less.

Checkpoint

Content Check

1. Prepare a graph of a shortage and describe how the market will work to eliminate the shortage.
2. Prepare a graph of a surplus and describe how the market will work to eliminate the surplus.
3. Complete the following chart by identifying the effects each change in demand and supply will have on equilibrium price and quantity:

	If Only Demand		If Only Supply	
	Increases	Decreases	Increases	Decreases
Price Will:				
Quantity Exchanged Will:				

What Do You Think Now?

Reread *What Do You Think?* in the Section Two Focus. Then answer the following questions:

4. Why is Alonzo worried about making money after such a good harvest? Think about the effect of an increase in supply on the price farmers get for the wheat. Is it possible that a good crop year could mean lower incomes for farmers?

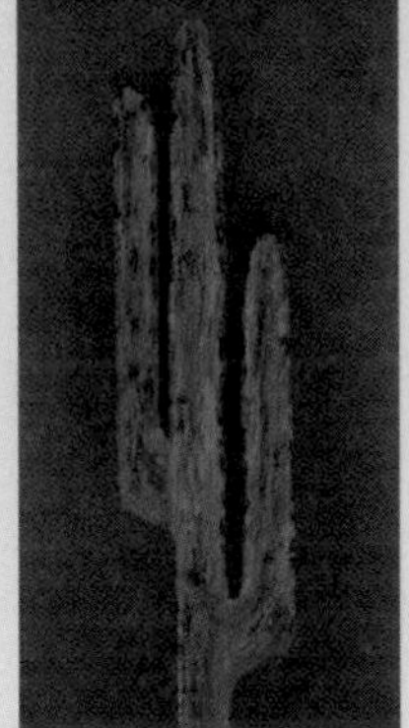

FOCUS

Section Three
Governments Impact Market Equilibrium

What Do You Think?

Every so often, political debate in Washington, D.C., turns to the question of whether the mandatory minimum wage should be increased. Some of your representatives and senators suggest raising the minimum wage to help young people earn more money to help with their educational expenses. Would you support an attempt to increase the minimum wage knowing that Congress wants to do so in part to help you earn more at your after-school job?

Terms to Know

price floor

price ceiling

What's Ahead?

Sometimes political forces cause politicians to want to alter the results of the market system in terms of the prices that result. In this section, you will learn how the government may try to hold prices down with a price ceiling. You also will see how the government may try to raise some prices by using a price floor.

THE GOVERNMENT MAY BLOCK THE MARKET SYSTEM

There are times when the government may act to block the market system, thus preventing a balance between the quantity demanded and the quantity supplied. Elected officials may give in to special interest groups who believe the market price is either too high or too low. The following are just a few examples of how the government may prevent a balance between the quantity demanded and the quantity supplied. There are many other examples in our economy:

- The government may allow only a certain amount of imported steel to enter the economy. This cuts down on supply and, as you have seen, results in a higher steel price.
- The government may buy grain products. This increases the demand and results in a higher price.

- The government may set rent controls to keep apartment rents below the market level.
- The government may set a minimum wage to keep wages higher than they would be otherwise.

Programs that block the market often can be evaluated using demand and supply concepts. Looking at two types of government actions will illustrate how such programs can be analyzed. First, you will see how a price floor may be used to keep prices higher than the market system would allow. Then, you will see how a price ceiling can keep price down.

A Price Floor

A ***price floor*** is a minimum price set by government that is *above* the market equilibrium price. In our example, if there is no interference with the wheat market, an equilibrium price of $3.60 results. But, what if wheat farmers convince the government that $3.60 is too low a price? The farmers and government might agree that $4.00 per bushel is a better price (at least for some wheat growers). If the government decided that no wheat will be sold below that price, the $4.00 becomes a price floor. A price floor is illustrated in Figure 8-12.

price floor
a minimum price set by government that is *above* the market equilibrium price

Why do we use the term price floor? If you were on the second floor of a building and dropped your pencil, where would it stop? On the floor. The floor would keep your pencil from falling farther. Similarly, a price floor keeps price from falling below a certain level. To be effective, a price floor must be above the equilibrium price. If a price floor were lower than equilibrium price, it would not be useful. Such a price floor would already be below the natural market price.

If the government said that there would be a price floor of $4 per bushel of wheat, how would the amount supplied compare to the amount demanded? From Figure 8-12, you see that the amount supplied would be 2,200 units.

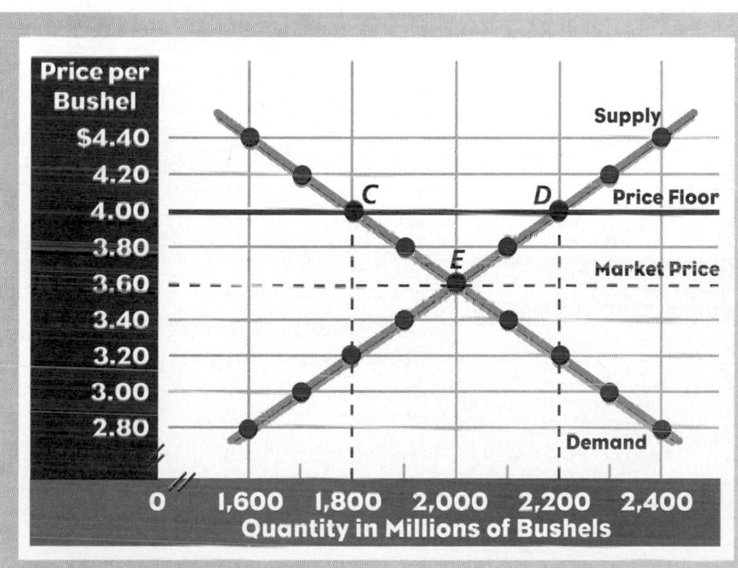

Figure 8-12

A Price Floor Is Set Above Equilibrium

A price floor at $4.00 prevents the market from balancing the quantity demanded and the quantity supplied at $3.60. A surplus results, consumers pay a higher price, and they buy less. ***As a producer how would you feel about this price floor?***

Econ & You

Rationing Concert Tickets

How much would you pay for a ticket to see a concert by your favorite band? Ticket prices for concerts vary depending on the performer and the number of seats available for each show. The primary determinant of ticket prices is the interaction between supply and demand. In many cases, the supply of tickets is limited by the capacity of the facility in which the concert is to be held. Thus, the supply can be represented as a vertical line at the number of seats available. In the following graph, this supply curve is labeled *Capacity Quantity.*

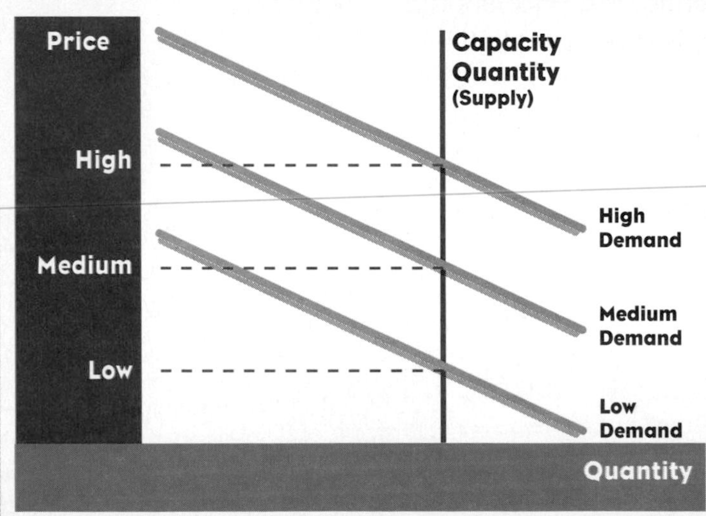

The Supply and Demand of Concert Tickets

The demand depends on the popularity of performers. For some performers in some areas, the demand is relatively low. This would be true for a band that is just starting and is not widely recognized. For some, the demand might be very high and for others there might be a mid-level demand. These possibilities are represented by the three demand curves in the graph. When demand is low and supply is at capacity quantity, you can see that price is low. At the medium demand, you see that price is somewhat higher. Finally, when demand is high the price is high as well.

Suppose a very popular singer is going to appear in your area and tickets are priced at $300. Will you go? It depends on your willingness and ability to pay that high a price.

This price will block some people from even thinking about attending such a concert. However, tickets to shows for a Barbra Streisand tour sold out at about this level. The high price acted as a rationing device to allocate the limited supply of tickets to those with the ability and willingness to pay that much. Do you think this is fair? Why or why not?

But, the amount demanded at $4 is 1,800 units. The quantity supplied would be greater than the quantity demanded by 400 units. This 400-unit surplus is shown as the distance from *C* to *D* in Figure 8-12.

In a free market, you know that when there is a surplus, price is pushed down. The amount demanded increases, and the amount supplied decreases. This continues until price falls enough so that the quantity demanded and the quantity supplied are balanced. But, with a price floor, such a free market adjustment is blocked. The market is kept from working.

We are left with an unbalanced market situation. The quantity supplied is greater than the quantity demanded at the government's set price. Producers produce more than consumers buy. What happens to the extra production? The government must either buy up the surplus or keep producers from producing so much. To cut down on production, firms must be kept from producing more than the government wants them to by some type of penalty. When the government buys the surplus, it is really we who buy it since our tax dollars are used for the purchase. Taxpayers often pay to store the surplus as well.

Look at the result of the price floor for consumers. At the free market equilibrium, price is $3.60, and consumers purchase 2,000 units. With the price floor at $4.00, consumers purchase less (1,800 units) but pay a higher price ($4.00).

A Price Ceiling

A ***price ceiling*** is a maximum price set by government that is *below* the market equilibrium price. A price ceiling is the opposite of a price floor. It keeps the price from going above some upper limit. If you threw your pencil up in the air as hard as you could, it would hit the ceiling. The pencil would not go any higher because the ceiling would limit how high it could go. A price ceiling keeps price down to the level the government thinks is right. To be effective, a price ceiling must be below the equilibrium price. If it were above the equilibrium price, the natural market price would already be below the ceiling.

price ceiling
a maximum price set by government that is *below* the market equilibrium price

Suppose the government thought that wheat producers were making too much money at the expense of consumers. The government might set a ceiling price of $3.20 per bushel. This is shown by the horizontal line at $3.20 in Figure 8-13.

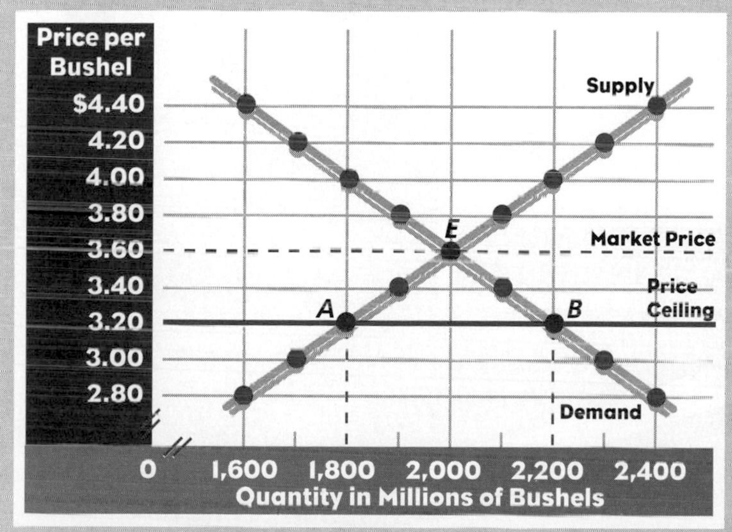

Figure 8-13

A Price Ceiling Is Set Below Equilibrium

A price ceiling at $3.20 blocks the market from working and balancing the quantity demanded and the quantity supplied at a price of $3.60. A shortage results. Consumers pay less but cannot purchase as much as they want at that lower price. ***As a consumer how would you feel about this price ceiling?***

Economic Dilemma

THE MINIMUM WAGE PRICE FLOOR

The minimum wage was first instituted in the United States in 1938 when it was $0.25 per hour. Since that time, it has been increased from time to time and always with considerable public debate. At the start of 1995, about 2.5 million Americans were earning the minimum wage. Would raising the minimum wage help the poor of the country? That is the issue of much of the political debate.

The minimum wage is an example of a price floor, where the wage is the price paid for labor services. The effects of a minimum wage can be seen with the help of the following supply and demand diagram.

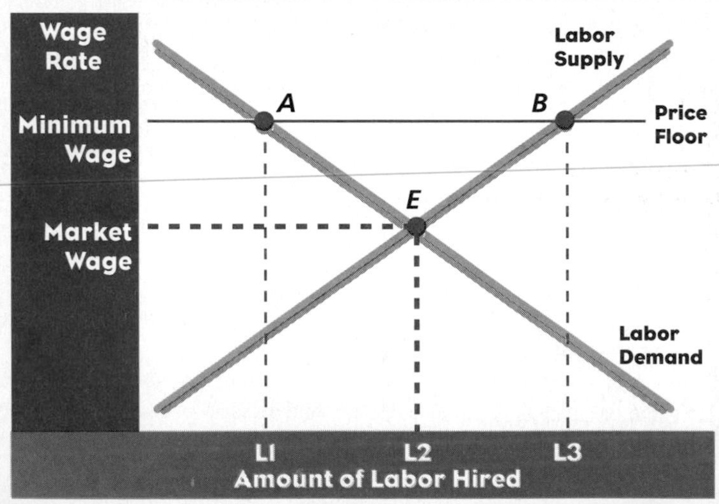

Minimum Wage

Market equilibrium is shown at the intersection of the Labor Supply and Labor Demand curves. Market Wage is the equilibrium price, and *L*2 is the equilibrium amount of labor. Raising the minimum wage clearly reduces the amount of labor hired (employment). The decrease is shown as the drop from *L*2 to *L*1 in the diagram. David Neumark of Michigan State University has found evidence that there may be a 1 to 2 percent drop in employment for every 10 percent increase in the minimum wage. The job losses hit the hardest among the already poor—low-skilled workers, teenagers, and welfare mothers. These are all groups that supporters of minimum wages talk about wanting to support. Yet, economics would suggest that raising the minimum wage may have an effect that is the opposite of what is intended. The debate goes on.

At a price of $3.20, consumers want to buy 2,200 units. Producers, on the other hand, are willing to supply only 1,800 units. A 400-unit shortage results. This is shown as the distance from *A* to *B* in Figure 8-13. You have seen that a shortage normally results in upward pressure on price. In a free market, price rises. The amount supplied increases, and the amount demanded decreases. When the price rises to $3.60, there is no shortage. The quantity demanded and the quantity supplied balance at that price.

But, this cannot happen if there is a price ceiling. If the $3.20 price is enforced, the quantity supplied is less than the quantity demanded. The government would have to find a different way to allocate the 1,800 units among consumers who want to buy 2,200 units at that price. Ration coupons are sometimes used in cases like this. However, a large system of people

Global Economy

WHAT'S A DOLLAR WORTH?

The U.S. economy is only one part of the global economy, but it is a very important and influential part. Evidence of this is seen in the market for U.S. dollars. Fluctuations in the value of the U.S. dollar make headlines in newspapers around the world. This is because the dollar is the dominant world currency. What determines the value of the dollar in the worldwide money market?

The value of the dollar compared to other currencies is determined by supply and demand conditions in the global economy. An increase in the demand for dollars raises the value of the dollar, while decreases in demand lower its value.

A weak dollar is a dollar with a low exchange value. Because the U.S. dollar is used around the world, its value affects not only the U.S. economy but the economies of other countries. After one period in which the value of the dollar had fallen, *The Wall Street Journal* reported that, "The Dow Jones Industrial Average dropped 3.7% and Japan's Nikkei stock index fell 3.4%. Stocks fell 4.8% in Britain, 2.2% in Germany and 1.5% in France. Global bond markets also sustained losses, pushing up long term interest rates in the U.S. and abroad." ("The Unloved Buck." *The Wall Street Journal* (June 27, 1994): A1, A8.)

Such events can have widespread effects. Here are three examples:

- An increase in interest rates can slow economic growth in all the major economies of the world.
- A lower value for the dollar increases the cost of items that we import which can cause inflationary pressure in the U.S. economy.
- A weaker dollar may have a positive effect on our balance of payments and unemployment rate because it shifts consumer demand more to goods produced in the United States and away from goods that we import from abroad.

usually is needed to issue and keep track of the use of the coupons. This can be very costly. It is sometimes possible for the government to produce enough of the product to make up for the shortage. However, this also costs taxpayers money. Finally, the government can set the price ceiling and let the consumers and producers deal with the shortage problem. In this case, many illegal nonmarket transactions are likely to take place. Those consumers who can afford to pay more will offer secret payments to suppliers to get the product.

Checkpoint

Content Check

1. Using Figure 8-12 as a guide, draw a graph of a price floor at $4.20. Identify the quantity supplied, the quantity demanded, and the amount of surplus. Explain the effects on consumers of a price floor of $4.20.
2. Using Figure 8-13 as a guide, draw a graph of a price ceiling at $3. Identify the quantity supplied, the quantity demanded, and the amount of surplus. Explain the effects of a price ceiling of $3 on consumers.

What Do You Think Now?

Reread *What Do You Think?* in the Section Three Focus. Then answer the following questions:

3. Is the minimum wage an example of a price floor or a price ceiling?
4. Consider the effect of the minimum wage on wages and employment. Would you support an attempt to increase the minimum wage knowing that Congress wants to do so in part to help you earn more at your after-school job?

Concepts in Brief

1. In a free market economy, individuals make the decisions that guide the direction of the economy. Demand and supply are the key factors involved in the working of a market economy. When the market is in balance, the quantity supplied equals the quantity demanded. This balance is called *equilibrium*. The price at which this balance is reached is called the *equilibrium price*. In a graph, the equilibrium is determined where the demand curve crosses the supply curve.
2. Price acts as a rationing mechanism in a market economy. If there is a surplus because the quantity supplied is greater than the quantity demanded, there will be natural downward pressure on price. This pressure decreases the quantity supplied and increases the quantity demanded. The eventual result is the elimination of the surplus.
3. This rationing role of price also acts to eliminate a shortage. A shortage exists when the quantity demanded is greater than the quantity supplied. When this is true, natural economic forces put upward pressure on price. This pressure decreases the quantity demanded and increases the quantity supplied. The shortage is eventually eliminated.
4. Changes in demand affect market equilibrium. If demand increases while supply stays the same, price rises as does the quantity bought and sold. If demand decreases while supply stays the same, price falls, as does the quantity bought and sold.
5. Changes in supply affect market equilibrium. If supply increases while demand stays the same, price falls, but the quantity bought and sold increases. If supply decreases while demand stays the same, price rises and the quantity bought and sold decreases.
6. For various reasons, the government may block the functioning of the market system with a price floor or a price ceiling. A price floor is set above the equilibrium price and keeps price from reaching equilibrium. A surplus results from a price floor. This causes other problems for government to handle.
7. A price ceiling is the opposite of a price floor. A price ceiling is set below the market price to keep price from rising. This results in a shortage of the product. Illegal nonmarket transactions are likely to result, and the government must find some nonprice mechanism for allocating the limited product.

Economic Foundations

1. When a market is in equilibrium, what is the relationship between the quantities supplied and demanded?
2. What happens to price and the quantities supplied and demanded when there is a shortage?
3. What happens to price and the quantities supplied and demanded when there is a surplus?
4. If demand increases, what is the effect on equilibrium price and quantity?
5. If demand decreases, what is the effect on equilibrium price and quantity?
6. If supply increases, what is the effect on equilibrium price and quantity?
7. If supply decreases, what is the effect on equilibrium price and quantity?
8. When government sets a price floor, what is the effect on the market? on consumers? on taxpayers?
9. When government sets a price ceiling, what is the effect on the market? on consumers? on taxpayers?

Your Economic Vocabulary

Build your economic vocabulary by matching the following terms with their definitions.

equilibrium price

equilibrium quantity

price ceiling

price floor

shortage

surplus

1. a maximum price set by government that is *below* the market equilibrium price
2. the price at which the quantity demanded equals the quantity supplied
3. the condition in which the quantity demanded is greater than the quantity supplied at a certain price
4. a minimum price set by government that is *above* the market equilibrium price
5. the condition in which the quantity supplied is greater than the quantity demanded at a certain price
6. the quantity that is both demanded and supplied at the equilibrium price

Thinking Critically About Economics

1. What is meant by the concept of a market system? What roles do demand and supply play in such a system?

2. "When the quantity demanded and the quantity supplied are in balance, the market is in equilibrium." Explain what this statement means.

3. Suppose that there is a news report of a shortage of gasoline. What does this mean? If the market system were left alone, how would this shortage be eliminated?

4. If growing conditions were ideal in the next crop season, a surplus of wheat might be produced. What does the phrase *surplus of wheat* mean in this context? How would a market system reduce or eliminate this surplus?

5. Some years ago, there was a "cranberry scare" in the United States. In the fall of the year, there were widespread stories that cranberries had been contaminated by a cancer-causing chemical. This affected consumers' attitudes and reduced the demand for cranberries. Use your knowledge of supply and demand to analyze this situation. What probably happened to price? What probably happened to the quantity sold that holiday season? Use a graph to help explain your answer. (You may assume that supply did not change.)

6. The wage rate is the price that is paid per labor hour for the use of a person's labor skills. A minimum wage enacted by government is then a type of price floor. Explain how the minimum wage affects the labor market. Begin by drawing a graph of the demand and supply of labor. Assume that demand will have a negative slope and supply will have a positive slope.

7. Rent controls are often suggested as a method for keeping housing costs down. Explain how this type of price ceiling affects the rental housing market.

8. Pick some product or service that you buy on a regular basis and explain how the concepts of demand and supply relate to that product. Can you identify any changes in demand and/or supply that have influenced the price and the quantity people consume?

Economic Enrichment

Coffee houses may seem new to some people because of the boom in this business over the last decade. However, coffee houses probably first appeared in the seventeenth century. There is evidence of coffee houses in Italy at that time, and the first U.S. coffee house was the London Coffee House in Boston which opened in 1689. Today, there are more than 4,500 coffee houses and the number is growing rapidly with expectations there will be close to 10,000 by the year 2000. What do you think might be some of the supply and demand changes that are affecting this market?

Math and Economics

Grace Hopkins works at a local grocery store after school and on weekends. She currently works 20 hours a week and earns minimum wage. She is excited because she has heard that Congress plans to pass an increase of $0.50 per hour in the minimum wage. If Grace continues to work 20 hours a week, how much will her earnings go up? (Do not consider taxes in your calculations.) Suppose that due to the higher wage, the store reduces the number of work hours for each employee by 15 percent. What would be the net effect on Grace's earnings considering the lost hours and the higher wage?

Writing About Economics

General Motors, Ford, Chrysler, and Honda are among the car companies that have offered special finance rates and/or rebates on selected vehicles in recent years. Look for three current print advertisements for special financing rates or rebates on cars. Cut these out or make photocopies. Prepare a booklet that includes the advertisements, an explanation of why the car makers would make these offers, and an explanation of how you think the makers decide on the cars that will receive such incentives. Prepare a cover for your booklet that is illustrated and includes a title that reflects the content.

Price Determination—The Equilibrium of Demand and Supply

Alfred Marshall (1842–1924) was a highly influential teacher of economics at both Oxford and Cambridge universities in England. He received acclaim with the publication of *Principles of Economics* in 1890. Prior to the publication of this book, some economists believed that price was determined by the cost of producing goods. These economists focused on the supply side of markets. Other economists thought that price was dependent on the usefulness of the goods. This approach focused only on demand. Marshall argued that price was determined by both cost (supply) and utility (demand).

In explaining this relationship between cost of production and utility (or supply and demand), Marshall compared the situation to a pair of scissors. In *Principles of Economics,* he wrote,

> We might as reasonably dispute whether it is the upper or the under blade of a pair of scissors that cuts a piece of paper, as whether value is governed by utility or cost of production. It is true that when one blade is held still, and the cutting is effected by moving the other, we may say with careless brevity that the cutting is done by the second; but the statement is not strictly accurate and is to be excused only so long as it claims to be merely a popular and not a strictly scientific account of what happens.

The accompanying figure illustrates the analogy Marshall was using. Supply can be thought of as one blade of a scissors and demand as the other blade. You need both blades of a scissors to effectively cut a piece of paper. Likewise, you need both supply and demand to determine prices in a market economy. In Marshall's time, this theory suggested a new way of looking at price. Today, the relationship between supply and demand as described by Marshall is at the core of many important economic concepts.

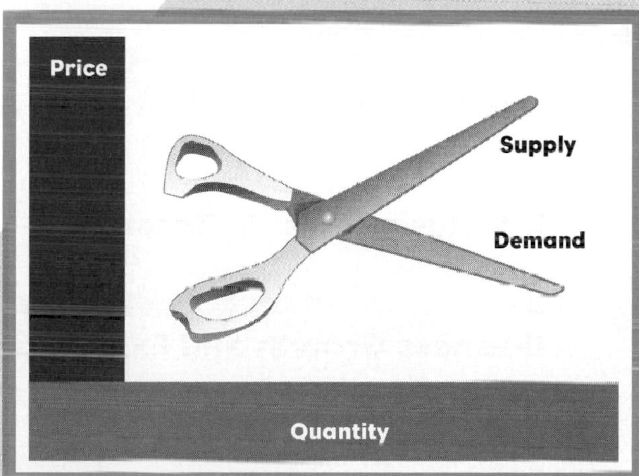

SOURCE: Marshall, Alfred, *Principles of Economics,* 8th ed. (New York: Macmillan, 1920), 348.

Analyzing Primary Source Documents

Overview

Section One
Proprietorships, Partnerships, and Corporations

Section Two
U.S. Businesses: A Closer Look

Section Three
Business Growth and Expansion

Business Firms in the Economy

Learning Objectives

9-1
Compare the advantages and disadvantages of proprietorships, partnerships, and corporations.

9-2
Explain why private organizations must pass the test of the market in a market economy.

9-3
Describe the relative importance of the three forms of business organizations in the U.S. economy.

9-4
Distinguish between the major forms of business financing.

9-5
Contrast the three kinds of mergers and how they are viewed by government.

FOCUS

Section One
Proprietorships, Partnerships, and Corporations

What Do You Think?

Maria and Maurine Vanuta worked in their uncle's bakery when they were in high school. Now the sisters have started a partnership, MMV Muffins. The Vanutas borrowed money to start the business, using their homes and savings to guarantee a bank loan. At first, business was good, but in the last year competition from a new supermarket has caused a big drop in sales. MMV Muffins is behind on loan payments, owes money for utility bills, owes money to suppliers of baking supplies, and is behind on worker's compensation payments to the government. It looks as if MMV will go out of business. Maria and Maurine are worried that creditors will force them to turn over their personal savings and sell their homes to get the money to pay for MMV's business debts.

What's Ahead?

Knowing the different ways in which businesses can be organized can help you understand how businesses function in the economy. In this section, you will learn about three forms of business organization: proprietorships, partnerships, and corporations.

Terms to Know

- proprietorship
- unlimited liability
- partnership
- partnership agreement
- corporation
- articles of incorporation
- charter
- stock
- limited liability
- dividends
- test of the market

FORMS OF BUSINESS ORGANIZATION

Imagine that you want to open a bicycle repair shop. You will do so only if you think you can provide a service for which customers are willing to pay. You will find out how many people own bicycles in your area of the city and how often they repair them. Once you assure yourself of a demand for repair services, you need to know if you can provide the service needed. You check on the cost of tools and supplies. You find out what space is available for your shop and how much it costs. Don't forget that you have to include the opportunity cost of your time. When you determine that the business can be successful, you are ready to start.

But what form of organization should your business take? Should it be a proprietorship, a partnership, or a corporation? Before you can answer this question, you must understand each form. Each form has certain advantages. If that weren't the case, all three would not exist. Each form also has very important disadvantages of which you should be aware.

Proprietorships

A ***proprietorship*** is a form of business in which there is one owner. If you want to open a bicycle repair shop as a proprietorship, the process is simple. You check to be sure that you satisfy any state or local laws and then you open the shop. Few regulations govern proprietorships. You can borrow the money you need, buy tools and supplies, and hire any necessary labor.

proprietorship
a form of business in which there is one owner

In a proprietorship, the owner and the business are one and the same. The money that the shop makes is your money. But, you also suffer any losses. If business is bad and you can't pay your bills, the bank (and others) can collect from any source of money you have. You feel the pride of ownership and success. But, you also bear the burden of failure.

Advantages of a Proprietorship. Setting up a proprietorship has many advantages. Check this list and compare a proprietorship with other forms of organization:

1. *Easy to start.* There is usually little red tape involved in starting a proprietorship. Almost anyone with a good idea and the willingness to accept some risk can start a business as a proprietorship.
2. *Little government regulation.* Once started, a proprietorship does not face much regulation. Accurate tax records must be kept and there are certain employment guidelines that must be met. But, there are not many regulations in most cases.
3. *Profits stay with owner.* The owner does not have to share money from the business with anyone else. All of the profit stays with the owner.
4. *Pride of ownership.* A proprietor usually has a lot of pride in the business. The owner can see the progress of the business and feel proud to run it.
5. *Complete control.* The owner has complete authority over business decisions. The owner decides which product or service to sell, the hours the firm should be open, and all other aspects of the business. The owner is boss.
6. *Lower taxes.* The taxes for a proprietorship are the same as for personal income. Remember that the business and the owner are the same. In many cases, taxes are lower than if the business were a corporation, particularly if the business has a low profit.

Disadvantages of a Proprietorship. A proprietorship may sound very attractive as a form of business organization. But, there are some important disadvantages that must be considered. Sometimes these disadvantages outweigh the advantages:

unlimited liability the concept that an owner's personal assets can be used to pay bills of the business

1. *Unlimited liability.* ***Unlimited liability*** is the concept that an owner's personal assets can be used to pay bills of the business. The owner's personal assets, which may include the owner's home, car, or savings account, may be used to pay debts of the business. This means that the owner risks all the money put into the business, plus all other savings or assets.
2. *Limited life of the business.* The business stops when the owner dies or becomes unable to run it any longer. Once more, the business and the owner are one. If the owner dies, the business ceases to exist. The assets can be sold or assigned to someone else who may start the business again. But, then it becomes a new firm with different ownership.
3. *Difficult to raise money.* It is difficult and expensive to raise money for a proprietorship. This is particularly true when the business is just getting started and has no record of success. But, even a successful proprietorship may be seen as risky by lenders. Often the owner of a proprietorship has difficulty borrowing money. When the owner is able to get a loan, it is often at a high rate of interest and is thus expensive for the business.
4. *Risk of loss is not shared.* In a proprietorship, the owner bears the entire risk of loss.

Partnerships

A ***partnership*** is a type of business organization in which there are two or more owners. Each person involved agrees to provide some portion of the work and start-up money and then to share the profits or losses. For example, you alone might not have enough money to open your bicycle repair shop. In this case, you can form a partnership with someone else who can bring more money into the business. Often a partnership is formed by one person who has the skill to run the business and another who has the money to get it started.

partnership
a type of business organization in which there are two or more owners

Taking on partners is often how a proprietorship grows. Each new partner brings something to the business and shares in the good or bad fortune of the firm. New partners may contribute their personal skills, money, or even ideas to the business. Suppose that two of your friends come into your repair shop with a new idea. They have figured a way to change old one-speed bikes into 18-speed mountain bikes at a much lower cost than that of build ing new mountain bikes. You might offer them partnerships in the firm in exchange for their idea. They will then share in the profits and operations of the firm. They will also share responsibility for the losses. You will no longer have complete control. The three of you together will make decisions about the partnership.

The partners in a partnership must agree on their respective responsibilities and on how the profits or losses from the business will be split between them. These issues are usually specified in a ***partnership agreement*** that becomes a legally binding document. This agreement lasts for the life of the partnership, unless the partners agree to make changes. While it is not necessary to have a lawyer familiar with partnerships write the agreement, it is a good idea.

partnership agreement
a legally binding document that specifies how the responsibilities and profits or losses from a partnership will be split between the partners

Advantages of a Partnership. A business organized as a partnership has many of the same advantages as a proprietorship. The following are the main advantages of organizing a business as a partnership:

1. *Easy to start.* As in a proprietorship, there is usually little red tape involved in starting a partnership. The partners need only agree about how they will share both responsibilities and rewards.
2. *Little government regulation.* Like proprietorships, most partnerships do not face many regulations. But, they must keep good records for tax purposes and meet guidelines related to employment practices.
3. *Not difficult to raise funds.* It is easier to raise funds for the operation of a partnership than for the operation of a proprietorship. All partners' financial assets are considered by a bank or other lender. This makes it possible for the partners to borrow more together than any one of them could alone. Also, each partner may have some money available to put into the business directly.
4. *Combination of skills.* Partnerships are often more efficient than proprietorships. Using the different skills of each partner may increase the efficiency of the firm. One partner may be good at

selling and the other better at record keeping. The first, then, should have sales responsibilities and the second should handle accounting and taxes. The owner of a proprietorship is not likely to have as many skills as the two or more people in a partnership.

Disadvantages of a Partnership. There also are disadvantages to forming a partnership. While some resemble the disadvantages of proprietorships, others result from the partnership itself. There are four major disadvantages of a partnership:

1. *Unlimited liability.* The members of the partnership have unlimited liability for the debts of the business. Just as with a proprietorship, the owners' personal assets can be used to pay debts of the firm. Even a partner who has not put any money into the business is subject to unlimited liability.
2. *Profits are shared.* The partners must share the profits according to their original agreement. Even if one of the members of the partnership puts in more work than originally agreed on, the split of profits will follow the original agreement. This also works in reverse. A partner who doesn't work as much as is expected still gets the share of profits specified in the agreement.
3. *Limited life of business.* The business stops when any one of the partners dies or is unable to participate. Thus, a successful business may have to be ended even though other partners may want to continue it. A new partnership often can be formed to continue the business, but sometimes this is not easy. Part of the firm's assets may have to be sold to pay off the deceased partner's share.
4. *Disagreements.* There is always the potential for disagreement among the partners. Unlike a proprietorship in which one owner makes all decisions, partners must reach an agreement. While they all may have the same plan, their choices of how to carry it out may differ. These disagreements can lead to inefficient operations and even to the end of the partnership.

corporation
an organization of people legally bound together by a charter to conduct some type of business

articles of incorporation
a written application to the state requesting permission to form a corporation

Corporations

A ***corporation*** is an organization of people legally bound together by a charter to conduct some type of business. It is a legal entity separate from its owners. The types of business a corporation can participate in are determined by the articles of incorporation. ***Articles of incorporation*** are a written application to the state requesting permission to form a corporation. The articles of incorporation give the name, address, and type of business for the corporation; the names of the initial directors of the firm; and the amount of money being put into the business.

If the articles of incorporation satisfy state and federal laws, a charter will be issued and the corporation becomes a legal entity. A ***charter*** is the legal authorization to organize a business as a corporation. A lawyer familiar with the laws concerning corporations should be hired to write the articles of incorporation.

charter
the legal authorization to organize a business as a corporation

Suppose that your bicycle repair and conversion business continues to grow. You find that if you had the money to buy some new equipment, you could increase production. You may even consider making your own brand of bikes. You might consider forming a corporation. Doing so would allow you to sell stock to raise more money. Shares of ownership in a corporation are called ***stock.*** The sale of stock is one way a corporation can raise money. More will be said about stock later in this chapter.

stock
shares of ownership in a corporation

You could trade your share of the business for some of the stock. Your partners could do the same. And other people could buy some of your company's stock. Then, all the stockholders would elect a board of directors. The board of directors supervises the operation of the business but usually does not take an active part in running it. The board of directors also selects the people who run the company. In your case, you would be the most likely choice for president. Your original partners would be wise choices for other corporate officers such as vice president and treasurer. You would continue to run the business, but now you would be responsible to all the stockholders.

Some of the advantages and disadvantages to forming a corporation are clear from the previous discussion. After reading the following information about the advantages and disadvantages of corporations, you will be able to compare corporations with the other kinds of business organization.

Advantages of a Corporation. There are more than 2 million corporations in the United States. You might expect, then, that there are some real advantages to this form of business organization. Here are the most important advantages:

1. *Easy to raise funds*. The corporate form is the most effective for raising money. This is particularly true if large amounts of money are needed to run the business. Corporations have more alternate methods of getting money than either proprietorships or partnerships.

2. *Limited liability*. ***Limited liability*** is the concept that owners of a business are only responsible for its debts up to the amount they invest in the business. This means that the stockholders (owners) only risk the money they paid for their stock. If the corporation goes bankrupt or is sued, the owners' other assets cannot be used to pay the debts of the business.

limited liability
the concept that owners of a business are only responsible for its debts up to the amount they invest in the business

3. *Unlimited life*. The corporation does not cease to exist if a major stockholder dies. Even if all the owners of stock died, the corporation would continue. For example, USX, formerly U.S. Steel, has outlived Andrew Carnegie, its founder, and J. P. Morgan, its second owner. It almost certainly will exist long after all the present stockholders have died.

Economic Spotlight

ROLE MODEL, ENTREPRENEUR, AND PHILANTHROPIST

It's hard to believe that the first woman to become the world's highest paid entertainer was, at age 13, turned away from a juvenile detention home due to a lack of beds. That entertainer, Oprah Winfrey, has come a long way since then, but she hasn't forgotten her roots. Today, Winfrey is dedicated to giving much of her time and money back to society. From a multimillion-dollar grant to help people get off welfare to a one-million-dollar donation to Morehouse College to a never-ending crusade against child abuse, Winfrey's dedication to helping others is legendary. According to this philanthropist, herself a victim of abuse, "No one makes it alone. Everyone who has achieved success in life was able to do so because something or someone serves as a beacon to light the way."

Winfrey says, "My father turned my life around by insisting I be more than I was and by believing I could be more." Just like her father, she has served as a beacon to others by succeeding against the odds. After enduring an abusive childhood that resulted in an unwanted pregnancy and juvenile detention, the future talk-show queen set her sights on broadcasting. Her first experience was in high school, working after school at WVOL radio. She worked her way through college as a TV reporter. Then, after college, she became a street reporter at WJZ-TV in Baltimore, where she eventually took over the role of coanchor of the evening news. This news experience led Winfrey to her first talk-show opportunity as cohost of WJZ-TV's "People Are Talking." Seven years later, she was offered the job of hosting "AM Chicago Show," a talk show that was at the bottom of the ratings and up against talk-show king Phil Donahue. According to Winfrey, almost everyone except her best friend thought she would fail because "I was black, female, and overweight." In two short months, Winfrey overtook Donahue in the local ratings. The show was expanded from a half-hour to a one-hour format, and the name was changed to "The Oprah Winfrey Show." The rest, as they say, is history.

Winfrey attributes much of her success as a talk-show host to her willingness to share her inner feelings with the audience, talking freely about matters such as her abusive childhood, her weight problem, and her bout with drugs. No doubt Oprah Winfrey's intelligence, ambition, and concern for others have also contributed to her success.

4. *Specialized management.* Most corporations are big businesses. They can afford to have specialized managers in all parts of the business. They can hire people who are experts in marketing, accounting, and forecasting. Smaller businesses just cannot afford such specialization.

5. *Risks are shared.* In a corporation, the risks of the business are spread among many owners. Each stockholder takes some risk. But, no one person has to accept all the risk.

Disadvantages of a Corporation. Our economy depends heavily on corporations, but there are some disadvantages to this form of business organization:

1. *Difficult to start.* It is easier to start a proprietorship or partnership than a corporation. Government approval must be obtained to form a corporation.

2. *Less direct control.* In large corporations, the owners are usually far from the day-to-day operation of the business. Professional managers actually run the business and are in charge of the firm's operations. This is more common in large corporations than in small ones.

3. *Double taxation.* To some extent, most corporations are subject to double taxation. The corporation's profits are taxed by corporate income taxes. The corporation pays dividends to stockholders out of the firm's after-tax income. ***Dividends*** are that part of a corporation's income paid to its stockholders. The stockholders then pay personal income taxes on the dividends. So, each dollar of a corporation's earnings may get taxed twice.

dividends
that part of a corporation's income paid to its stockholders

4. *Limited activities.* Corporations are limited to activities stated in their articles of incorporation. The articles of incorporation state the purpose of the business. Unless these are written carefully and in broad terms, the corporation's activities can be limited. This is not a problem for proprietorships or partnerships.

BUSINESSES MUST SURVIVE THE TEST OF THE MARKET

In our market economy, we depend a great deal on the private sector to produce goods and services. More than 80 percent of our total production comes from private businesses. These businesses are guided by supply and demand in deciding what to produce and how to produce it.

All firms, large or small, must satisfy the test of the market. The ***test of the market*** is being able to provide goods that satisfy consumers' needs and desires at prices consumers are willing to pay. And, the business must be able to pay all the necessary factors of production in doing so. Small firms are more likely than large firms to fail this market test. Small firms, and new firms especially, have little money to spend on a product that may fail in the

test of the market
being able to provide goods that satisfy consumers' needs and desires at prices consumers are willing to pay

marketplace. A large firm can afford to try some risky products, because one failure out of many products may not ruin the company.

Each year, thousands of firms fail the test of the market and go out of business. At the same time, other new firms start up. You probably notice start-ups in your community such as clothing stores, restaurants, bakeries, bicycle shops, automotive repair shops, and sporting goods stores. You probably also know of some businesses that have recently closed. The market economy is ever-changing. Some businesses fail, while others succeed. In recent years, there have been about 90,000 business failures each year in the United States.

As long as we rely on the market system and the private sector, these changes will continue. The market system tends to respond fairly to consumers' wishes. It may not always respond perfectly. It may not always respond the way you personally would like. But, it certainly provides goods and services more in line with what consumers want than command-oriented economies do.

Checkpoint

Content Check

1. Compare the advantages of proprietorships to the advantages of corporations.
2. Compare the disadvantages of partnerships to the disadvantages of corporations.
3. What happens to a company if it does not pass the test of the market?

What Do You Think Now?

Reread *What Do You Think?* in the Section One Focus. Then answer the following questions:

4. Can MMV Muffins' creditors force Maria and Maurine Vanuta to turn over their personal savings and sell their homes to pay the debts? Why or why not?
5. Do you think this is fair to the Vanutas? Do you think this is fair to the creditors? Explain.

FOCUS

Section Two

U.S. Businesses: A Closer Look

What Do You Think?

In the nineteenth century, a young immigrant to the United States was disappointed to find that land was so expensive he couldn't follow his dream of becoming a successful farmer in New Jersey. As he searched for another way to earn a living, he thought there might be a good market for gun powder. He had enough knowledge in chemistry to produce gun powder, so he found a site on the Brandywine River, close to Philadelphia, and started a new business. Now that gun powder is relatively less important in our economy, do you think this company would still be in business today?

What's Ahead?

There are more proprietorships, by far, than partnerships or corporations in the United States. However, sales by corporations represent the vast majority of total sales in the United States. Both large and small companies are redefining the term *multinational business*. In this section, you will learn about the size and number of firms in the United States and be introduced to the topics of nonprofits, multinationals, and franchises.

Terms to Know

multinational business

nonprofit organization

franchise

DISTRIBUTION OF THE THREE FORMS OF BUSINESS

Think about the last time you went shopping. As you walked down the street or through the shopping center, what kinds of stores did you see? Some were probably small proprietorships or partnerships, such as some shoe stores, hardware stores, or bookstores. Many of the larger stores were probably corporations, such as Sears, J. C. Penney, Wal-Mart, or Kmart.

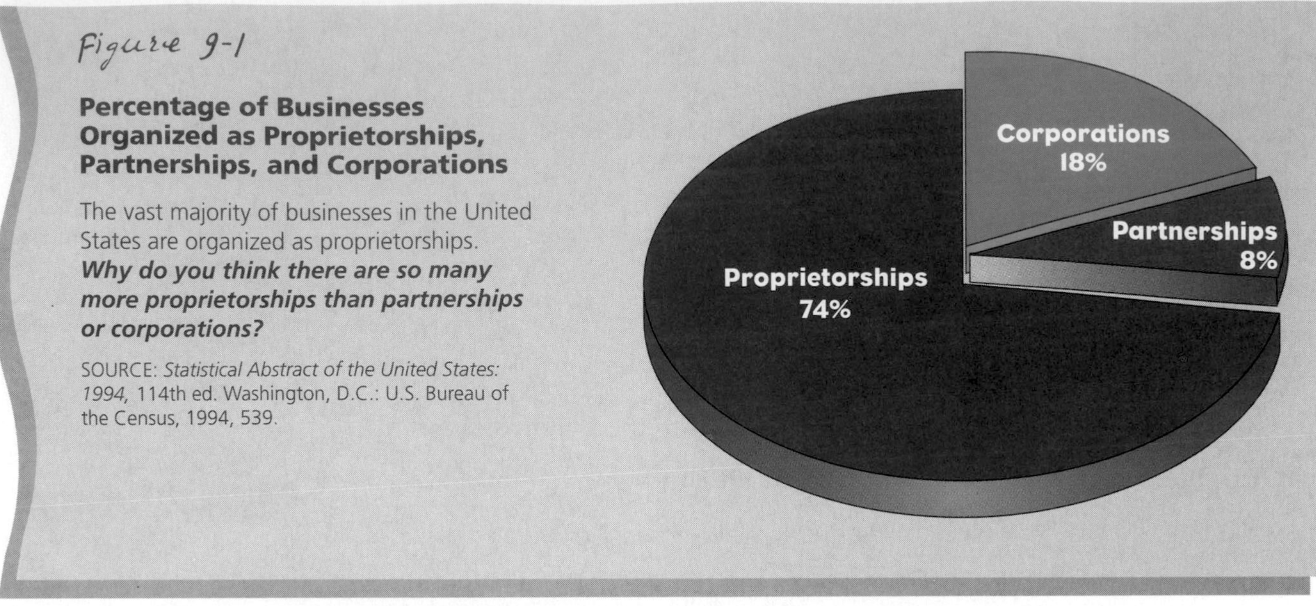

Percentage of Businesses Organized as Proprietorships, Partnerships, and Corporations

The vast majority of businesses in the United States are organized as proprietorships. ***Why do you think there are so many more proprietorships than partnerships or corporations?***

SOURCE: *Statistical Abstract of the United States: 1994,* 114th ed. Washington, D.C.: U.S. Bureau of the Census, 1994, 539.

Number of Firms

Our economy often appears to be dominated by very large businesses. Names such as General Motors, Mobil, Pepsi, and Wal-Mart are familiar to everyone. Yet, there exist many more small firms than large ones. Small firms remain unknown outside of a relatively small geographic area. However, they are an important part of our economy. New firms almost always start out small. If successful, they may grow to become large firms with national reputations.

As Figure 9-1 shows, the majority of companies in the United States are proprietorships. In 1994, there were almost 15 million proprietorships compared to more than 3.7 million corporations and roughly 1.6 million partnerships. Proprietorships represent about 74 percent of all companies; corporations, 19 percent; and partnerships, 8 percent. These proportions have been about the same since 1960.

Size of Firms

Many retail stores are fairly small and are proprietorships or partnerships. But, what about the products they sell? Compaq computers, Levi's jeans, Head tennis racquets, Pioneer stereos, and almost all other products come from corporations. In manufacturing, corporations are the dominant form of business organization.

If you look at sales, rather than the number of firms, proprietorships and partnerships appear much less important. Corporations clearly produce a greater dollar value of sales than the other two combined. The sales of corporations are measured in trillions of dollars. Such numbers are too high to be meaningful to most of us. Perhaps it would mean more to note that the sales of corporations amount to more than $43,000 for each person in the United States. Figure 9-2 uses a pie chart to show the percentage distributions of the dollar value of sales for corporations, partnerships, and proprietorships.

In the pie chart in Figure 9-1, the number of proprietorships is far larger than the other two types of organizations. But, the pie chart in Figure 9-2 tells a different story. There you see that corporations account for most of the sales. You can see that the proprietorships are fairly small businesses, and the real giants of business are the corporations.

To see how big corporations are, look at Figure 9-3 on page 226. It lists the 20 largest corporations with headquarters in the United States. The dollar value of sales for these firms is huge. In total, these 20 firms had sales of more than $1 trillion. For just these 20 corporations, sales represent more than $4,000 per person in the United States. These firms employed a total of 4,456,400 people. That represents more than 3 percent of the total labor force. The employment of just those 20 firms is about the same as the entire population of the Detroit metropolitan area.

In 1994, the largest U.S. corporation, as measured by sales, was General Motors. GM had sales of $138,222,000,000. That represented about $540 per person in the United States. Comparing the sizes of corporations with the

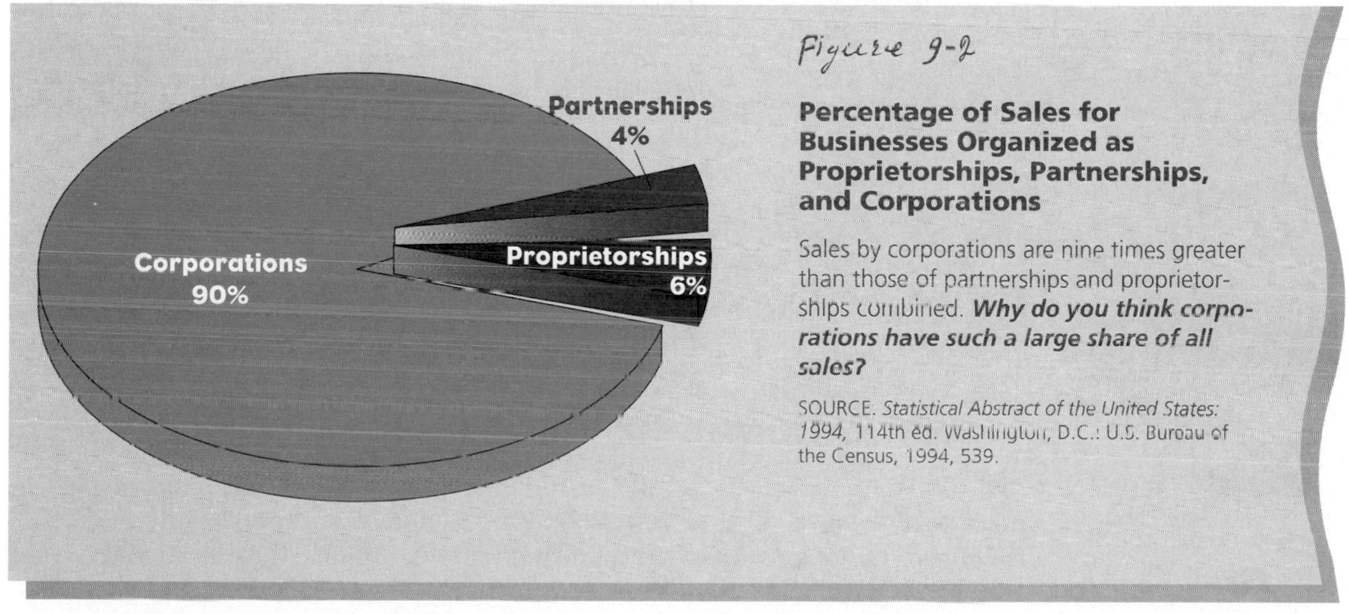

Percentage of Sales for Businesses Organized as Proprietorships, Partnerships, and Corporations

Sales by corporations are nine times greater than those of partnerships and proprietorships combined. ***Why do you think corporations have such a large share of all sales?***

SOURCE. *Statistical Abstract of the United States: 1994,* 114th ed. Washington, D.C.: U.S. Bureau of the Census, 1994, 539.

Company	Sales	Employment	Corporate Headquarters
General Motors	$138,220,000,000	710,800	Detroit, MI
Ford Motor	$108,521,000,000	322,200	Dearborn, MI
Exxon Corp.	$97,825,000,000	93,000	Irving, TX
Wal-Mart Stores	$67,435,000,000	472,500	Bentonville, AR
AT&T	$67,156,000,000	310,700	New York, NY
IBM	$62,716,000,000	278,900	Armonk, NY
General Electric Co.	$60,562,000,000	226,500	Fairfield, CT
Mobil Corp.	$56,576,000,000	62,800	Fairfax, VA
Sears, Roebuck	$50,838,000,000	382,500	Chicago, IL
Philip Morris Co.	$50,621,000,000	167,000	New York, NY
Chrysler	$43,600,000,000	115,900	Highland Park, MI
Kmart	$34,557,000,000	320,000	Troy, MI
Texaco	$33,245,000,000	33,700	White Plains, NY
duPont de Nemours	$32,621,000,000	119,500	Wilmington, DE
Citicorp	$32,196,000,000	81,300	New York, NY
Chevron	$32,123,000,000	48,400	San Francisco, CA
Proctor & Gamble	$30,067,000,000	104,800	Cincinnati, OH
Boeing	$25,438,000,000	161,700	Seattle, WA
Amoco Corp.	$25,336,000,000	46,700	Chicago, IL
PepsiCo, Inc.	$25,021,000,000	397,500	Purchase, NY

Figure 9-3

Sales and Employment for 20 Largest U.S. Corporations

These U.S. corporations are enormous, both in dollar sales and in the number of people they employ. ***Which of these companies is the largest employer?***

SOURCE: *Forbes* 153, no. 9 (April 25, 1994): 199, 202, 215–17.

sizes of selected countries also helps you to understand how large some corporations are. For example, in Figure 9-4 you can see that sales of some U.S. companies are greater than the total production of Portugal, Colombia, and Morocco, as well as some other countries not listed.

MULTINATIONAL BUSINESSES

The world of business today is the entire world. Many large and small companies based in the United States sell and produce products in markets around the globe. Not long ago, when people thought of international business, they thought of selling to consumers in other countries. That concept

Country or Corporation	Total Production (Countries) or Sales (Corporations)*
Japan	$3,386,000,000,000
United Kingdom	$1,002,000,000,000
France	$1,191,000,000,000
Austria	$288,000,000,000
General Motors	$138,220,000,000
Ford Motor	$108,521,000,000
Exxon Corp.	$97,825,000,000
Portugal	$65,000,000,000
IBM	$62,716,000,000
Sears, Roebuck	$50,838,000,000
Colombia	$40,000,000,000
Kmart	$34,557,000,000
Morocco	$27,000,000,000

* Data are 1993 sales for corporations and 1991 GNP for countries

Figure 9-4

Economic Sizes of Selected Countries and U.S. Corporations

You can see that by these measures, Exxon Corp. is bigger than Portugal. ***Find out how they compare in terms of employees versus population.***

SOURCES: For corporations: *Forbes* 153, no. 9 (April 25, 1994): 199, 202. For countries: *Statistical Abstract of the United States: 1994*, 114th ed. Washington, D.C.: U.S. Bureau of the Census, 1994, 862.

has become broader and the terms *multinational business* or *global business* are more common than *international business*. A ***multinational*** (or global) ***business*** is one that sells and produces products in multiple countries.

multinational business
a firm that sells and produces products in multiple countries

While many U.S. companies, such as Coca-Cola, General Motors, KFC, and Whirlpool are multinational, there are many non-U.S. multinationals as well. The automotive market is a good example. Companies such as Toyota and Honda sell and produce cars outside of Japan. In fact, most of the cars they sell in this country are now produced in the United States. Honda even exports cars that are produced in the United States to other countries.

Whirlpool is an excellent example of a multinational company. It produces in Europe, South America, and Asia, in addition to the United States. Whirlpool has taken products developed in Europe and adapted them for other markets around the globe. For example, Whirlpool took a type of microwave oven manufactured in Sweden that can cook crispy products and introduced it to other markets in Asia and the United States. Whirlpool's corporate attitude is that there are "no foreigners." There is one large global market with varying product needs.

NONPROFIT ORGANIZATIONS

So far, you have been reading about organizations that are driven largely by the profit motive. But, there is another type of organization, called a ***nonprofit organization,*** that does not have profit as its objective. Examples

nonprofit organization
an organization that does not have profit as its objective

include the American Red Cross, most museums, most educational institutions, and religious institutions. There are well over 20,000 nonprofit organizations in the United States.

FRANCHISES

franchise
a contract between a parent company (franchisor) and some other business or individual (franchisee) that details the terms under which the franchisee does business with products, names, or other services of the franchisor

A ***franchise*** is a contract between a parent company (franchisor) and some other business or individual (franchisee) that details the terms under which the franchisee does business with products, names, or other services of the franchisor. There are essentially three types of franchise operations.

The first is a retail franchise granted by a manufacturer. Automotive dealerships are good examples of this type of franchise. The second type is a wholesale franchise granted by a manufacturer. For example, Coca-Cola grants franchises to bottlers who buy Coca-Cola syrup, add other ingredients, and then bottle and sell the product to retailers.

Economic Dilemma

GOING OUT OF BUSINESS—AGAIN?

You may have seen advertisements for going-out-of-business sales. Or, you may have walked past a retail store that had a big sign in the window that said, "GOING OUT OF BUSINESS," with other wording to lead a shopper to believe that great savings could be had by making a purchase at that store. But, does this mean the store is really closing?

In some cities, you can walk by certain stores and see such signs that are yellowed with age. Some stores have been going out of business for years and years, but they open up shop every day. Could it be that some stores use "going out of business" as a ploy to attract customers into the store and to give them a sense, perhaps false, that prices are greatly reduced? In one midwestern town, two jewelry stores put up "going out of business" signs at about the same time. One store closed up about six weeks after announcing that it was quitting business. It really was. The other store is still operating—and apparently has "gone out of business" several times before.

Should such behavior be allowed? Is it ethical for a business to mislead customers in this manner? Should customers be on guard against such practices? If they are fooled, is it their own fault for not shopping around to be sure they get the best price?

The third type of franchise is probably the one with which you are most familiar. These are service-sponsored retail franchises. Local business people are granted the right to provide specific service sector products. McDonald's fast-food restaurants are perhaps one of the most visible examples of service-sponsored retail franchises. Others would include H&R Block tax preparation offices, gasoline stations, car rental agencies, and many motel chains. About 40 percent of all franchises are restaurants or gasoline stations.

Checkpoint

Content Check

1. What type of business organization is represented by the largest number of firms in the United States? Why?
2. What type of business organization is responsible for the largest volume of dollar sales in the United States? Why?
3. In what types of business are franchises most common?

What Do You Think Now?

Reread *What Do You Think?* in the Section Two Focus. Then answer the following questions:

4. The business started by the farmer turned gun powder maker eventually became duPont de Nemours, a corporation featured in Figure 9-3. Do you think the owners of most proprietorships have the goal of growing their businesses into giant corporations someday? Why or why not?

FOCUS

Section Three
Business Growth and Expansion

What Do You Think?

Remember the problems facing Maria and Maurine Vanuta's business, MMV Muffins? The business is behind on loan payments, owes money for utility bills, owes money to suppliers of baking supplies, and is behind on worker's compensation payments. The Vanutas are afraid they will have to go out of business if they can't make the payments. But, the sisters are optimistic that they can compete with the large grocery on a quality basis in the long run—if they just can hold on for awhile. MMV Muffins needs to obtain additional money to get over this difficult period. But how?

Terms to Know

line of credit
bond
interest
common stock
merger
horizontal merger
vertical merger
conglomerate merger
conglomerate

What's Ahead?

All types of business firms find at times that they need to have access to more money than they have on hand. Sometimes they may need money to get the business going. Sometimes they may need it to help run the business when sales revenue is low. And, sometimes they may need it to help the company merge with another company. In this section, you will learn about ways a business can obtain money. You will also learn about different types of mergers.

FINANCING A BUSINESS

Every business needs money to get started and to run day-to-day operations. Start-up money for most proprietorships and partnerships comes from the savings of the people involved and some funds borrowed from banks or friends. Borrowing from a bank usually requires some form of collateral as security to back up the loan. The people starting the company may pledge their homes and/or other assets as security. If business is bad and they are unable to repay the loan, they risk having to sell their property to pay the loan.

Line of Credit

Once the business has been established, money that comes in from sales is often enough to meet the cash needs of running the business. But, this is not always the case. Sometimes businesses need additional cash to help them get through a period of low sales. For this reason, partnerships and proprietorships try to establish a line of credit with a local bank. A ***line of credit*** is an arrangement through which the business can access needed cash quickly. Obtaining a line of credit is similar to getting a loan. The business files an application with the bank for approval to borrow up to some limit, such as $100,000. Once the application is approved, the business can access the money as needed without going through the time-consuming loan application process each time.

line of credit
an arrangement through which a business can quickly access needed cash from a bank

Global Economy

ECONOMIES IN TRANSITION—AND CONFUSION

The term *economies in transition* refers to economies that are trying to make a relatively rapid leap from command economies to free-market economies. An example is Russia. In countries such as Russia, nearly all business activity used to take place in government-owned enterprises. But, as many such economies have moved more to market-based economies, the way in which businesses are organized has become a source of much confusion.

After the country's economic transition began, private businesses in Russia sprang up almost spontaneously as people recognized the opportunity to make money. For example, small stands, many perhaps only 10 feet by 15 feet in size, started to appear as free-standing shops. These businesses sold a variety of items, from Coke products; to candy bars from the United States and western European countries; to knockoffs of brand name radios, CD players, and watches that were imported from Asia and Poland.

A major problem emerged for all kinds of businesses. There was no legal structure in place to guide the conduct of business. There weren't adequate laws relating to contracts, for example. So, a surprising amount of business was settled on a handshake rather than a formal contract. Even when contracts between parties were made, they were difficult to enforce because of a lack of clear contract law. Issues were decided on a case-by-case basis by a vastly overloaded court system that was not designed to handle such matters. Transactions were made based on a handshake because contracts were essentially meaningless and getting a dispute heard in court could take so long that it would not be worth the wait.

Bond

bond
a certificate stating the amount the corporation has borrowed from the holder and the terms of repayment

Corporations can issue bonds to raise funds. A ***bond*** is a certificate stating the amount the corporation has borrowed from the holder and the terms of repayment. Bonds can be issued for any amount, but bonds of $1,000, $5,000, and $10,000 are very common. If a firm wanted to raise $1 million by selling bonds, it might offer to sell a thousand $1,000 bonds.

interest
the payment for using some else's money

People who buy bonds get a yearly payment in exchange for the corporation's use of their money. A $1,000 bond paying 6 percent would give the lender $60 per year in interest. In financial dealings, ***interest*** is the payment for using someone else's money.

Each bond has a maturity date. That is, each bond has a date when the amount of the bond must be paid back to the buyer. Suppose you bought a $1,000 bond that paid 9 percent and had a 10-year maturity. You would get $90 each year in interest and, at the end of 10 years, you would get your $1,000 back.

Stock

common stock
a type of stock that gives the holder a partial ownership of the corporation

Corporations also can sell stock. There are several types of stock, but the most important is common stock. ***Common stock*** is a type of stock that gives the holder a partial ownership of the corporation. If a corporation issued 10,000 shares of common stock and you bought 1,000 of them, you would own one-tenth of the business. In turn, the corporation would have use of the money you paid for the stock.

Econ & You

IS SERVICE IN YOUR FUTURE?

The greatest growth in jobs in recent decades has been in the service sector. Projections for the future see this trend continuing. In the late 1970s, about 30 percent of all nonfarm jobs were in goods-producing activities. These include such things as mining, construction, and manufacturing. The other 70 percent were in service-producing activities.

By the mid-1990s, the percentage of jobs in goods-producing sectors had fallen to 21 percent, while service-producing jobs had increased to 79 percent of the total. By the year 2005, the mix is expected to be 18 percent goods-producing and 82 percent service-producing jobs. It is likely that your career will find you producing some type of service, not some type of product. But, what are the service sector activities? The largest category is retail trade. Some other service sectors that employ a lot of people are finance, insurance, real estate, advertising, computer-related services, health services, and government employment.

Owners of common stock are not guaranteed any payment. They may receive dividends if the company is successful, and the market value of the stock may go up. For example, shares that were purchased for $15 may go up to $20, $25, or more. If the company is not successful, the owners of common stock lose money. If a corporation goes out of business, bondholders' interest will be paid and bonds will be repaid before common stockholders receive anything.

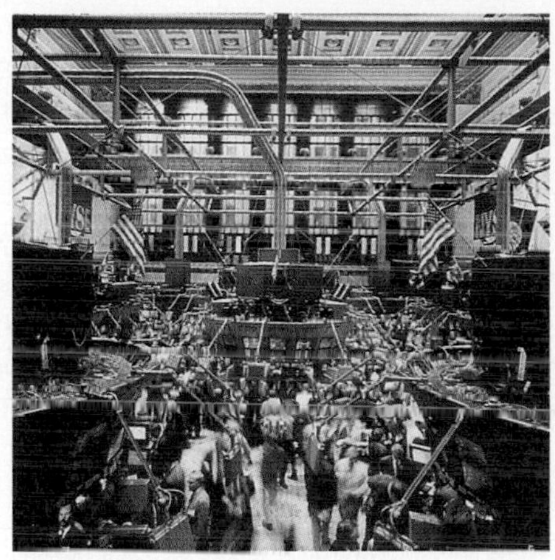

MERGERS: ONE WAY BUSINESSES GET BIGGER

In addition to growing by selling more, many firms grow by buying other businesses. A corporation buys another corporation by buying its stock. This could be all of a corporation's stock or just enough to control the company. When two firms combine in this way, they have merged. A ***merger*** is the combining of one company with another company it buys. There are three kinds of mergers: horizontal, vertical, and conglomerate.

merger
the combining of one company with another company it buys

Horizontal Mergers

A ***horizontal merger*** is a merger of two companies in the same industry. An example would be a merger between two large retailing corporations, such as Kmart and Sears. The term *horizontal merger* indicates that the two firms operate at the same level, or stage, in the production process. Sears and Kmart are both at the retail sales level. Other examples of horizontal mergers are the merger of two coal mining companies, or two airlines, or two companies that make bicycles.

horizontal merger
a merger of two companies in the same industry

Horizontal mergers are watched carefully by the Antitrust Division of the Federal Justice Department. If horizontal mergers reduce competition in an industry, they may not be in the public interest. The merging of two small companies would probably cause little harm. There even could be benefits to the public if as a result products could be produced at a lower cost because of the merger. However, if the companies already had a large share of the market, the government would probably block the merger. For example, if General Motors and Ford wanted to merge, the government probably would not allow them to do so. Such a merger would give the new firm too much control over the automobile industry.

Vertical Mergers

A ***vertical merger*** is a merger of two companies that are at different stages in the same production process. For example, a merger between a steel company and a car manufacturer would be a vertical merger. The steel would be an input to making cars. A merger between a department store chain and an appliance manufacturer would be a vertical merger, because the appliances could be sold through the department stores. The appliance manufacturer

vertical merger
a merger of two companies that are at different stages in the same production process

and the department store chain operate at different levels, or stages, in the process that moves appliances from the manufacturer to individual buyers.

The Antitrust Division of the Justice Department also keeps a close eye on vertical mergers. If such a merger might reduce competition, the government may block the merger. Suppose there were many firms that made steel but only a few that mined iron ore. Now suppose that one of the steel producers merged with one or more of the ore companies. The steel company could then restrict the flow of ore to the other steel companies. This could reduce competition in steel production. Therefore, the government might not permit this merger.

Conglomerate Mergers

conglomerate merger
a merger of two companies that are in different businesses

A ***conglomerate merger*** is a merger of two companies that are in different businesses. One example of a conglomerate merger was the purchase of Montgomery Ward (a large retail sales firm) by Mobil (an oil firm). The two businesses have little in common. Some people were alarmed by this conglomerate merger because they thought Mobil should use its money to expand oil production. But, remember that horizontal and vertical mergers are often discouraged by the government. Had Mobil tried to use its money to expand in the energy field, the merger may well have been blocked.

conglomerate
a firm made up of many divisions and/or subsidiaries that may not have much in common in their lines of business

This type of merger results in the formation of large conglomerates. A ***conglomerate*** is a firm made up of many divisions and/or subsidiaries that may not have much in common in their lines of business. What they have in common is that they are owned by one firm. An example of a conglomerate that almost everyone knows is PepsiCo. PepsiCo owns divisions and subsidiaries such as Pepsi-Cola North America, Frito-Lay, KFC, Pizza Hut Worldwide, and Taco Bell Worldwide.

The government less actively opposes conglomerate mergers because it is not certain that they reduce competition. For example, Frito-Lay would not be in competition with Pepsi-Cola or other parts of PepsiCo. KFC, Pizza Hut, and Taco Bell are all in the same fast-food sector of the economy. However, each of these has a small enough market share that their joint ownership probably does little to reduce competition.

Internet Connection

COMMERCIAL USE OF THE INTERNET

The Internet was originally the domain of government and educational institutions, but it hasn't taken long for businesses to become involved. Firms have begun to use the Internet for commercial purposes: to provide product and company information, customer service, and even direct sales. More than 25,000 firms have Internet addresses.

For marketing purposes, firms ranging from Microsoft to Volvo have created company Web pages. Several of the top 20 U.S. corporations, listed in Figure 9-3 of this chapter, have them.

AT&T	**http://www.att.com**
IBM	**http://www.ibm.com**
General Electric	**http://www.ge.com**
Citicorp	**http://www.tti.com**

There are now more than 700 electronic shopping sites selling a wide range of items including CDs, books, and software. Virtually anything sold by mail order can be obtained from cyberspace. Two electronic shopping sites are CyberMalls at **http://www.cybermalls.com/index.htm** and Hello Direct at **http://www.hello-direct.com/hd/**.

Many newpapers and magazines are being published in online versions. Most of these are available from the online services but many have sites on the Web. Two Web versions of newspapers are the *Raleigh News & Observer* at **http://merlin.nando.net** and the *San Francisco Examiner* at **http://cyber.sfgate.com/examiner/**.

Internet Application: One way to find companies with Gopher sites or Web pages is to search with Veronica or WebCrawler for the company name. The Web also has at least one list of commercial Web sites at **http://www.directory.net/dir/directory.html**.

Find a Web page or Gopher site of some interesting business. E-mail a description of the site, including its URL, to your teacher.

Economics Application: Most people begin to use the Internet through school or a job. After graduation or job change, many users lose their access. To satisfy demand for continued access, a growing number of commercial Internet providers have sprung up. These providers are not the same as the online services that we covered in Chapter 4. These small firms give the same type of Internet access as was provided through schools and employers but without the user-friendliness of the online services. Do you think commercial Internet providers are more likely to be proprietorships, partnerships, or corporations? What about commercial online services?

Why do you think one company would want to buy another company that is in an unrelated type of business? One reason is that most companies try to increase the value of their assets for the owners (stockholders). If it appears that they can make a larger return on their investment in a different industry, it may make sense to do so. A company has to be careful, however. Just because managers have the expertise to manage a large car company, for example, doesn't mean they will be equally successful managing a food processing company.

Another reason for merging with a company in an unrelated business is to stabilize stockholder returns. By having assets in a number of different industries, the company is less likely to be hurt when there is a downturn in one part of the economy.

Checkpoint

Content Check

1. Which would give you some ownership of a corporation: buying a corporate bond or shares of the corporation's common stock?
2. How would you classify the merger of a personal computer manufacturer with a discount electronics retail chain?
3. If a clothing company, such as Levi Strauss, were to merge with a beverage company, such as PepsiCo, what type of merger would it be?
4. If the Zeos computer company merged will Dell computers, would it be a conglomerate merger? Explain.

What Do You Think Now?

Reread *What Do You Think?* in the Section Three Focus. Then answer the following question:

5. What can the Vanutas do to obtain additional money to get over this difficult period for MMV Muffins?

Concepts in Brief

1. A proprietorship is a form of business owned entirely by one person. There are more proprietorships than any other form of business in the United States. In part, this is because they are easy to start. The major disadvantage of a proprietorship is that the owner faces unlimited liability. This means that the owner's personal assets can be used to pay debts of the firm should the business fail.
2. A partnership is very similar to a proprietorship. In a partnership, two or more people own the business together. They agree to share in the work and in the profits of the business. Each partner's share of the work or profits need not be equal. Partnerships are easy to start. With more than one owner, it is usually easier to raise money for the firm's operations. The major disadvantage of a partnership is that the partners are subject to unlimited liability.
3. A corporation is a form of business that is itself a legal entity. The owners are people who have purchased common stock in the business. In a corporation, these owners are usually separate from the managers who run the daily affairs of the business. A corporation becomes a legal entity when its articles of incorporation have been approved and it receives a charter. The articles of incorporation specify the corporation's purpose, how it is financed, and other details about its formation. Two major advantages of a corporation are limited liability for the owners and the availability of more ways to raise money.
4. All businesses must meet the test of the market if they are to survive. This means they must provide goods or services for which consumers are willing to pay. Therefore, the goods must give consumers satisfaction, and they must be affordable. Firms that are not able to do this will eventually go out of business.
5. While proprietorships represent more than 70 percent of all U.S. firms, they make less than 10 percent of all sales. This means that most proprietorships are fairly small firms. Fewer than 20 percent of the businesses in the United States are corporations, but they account for about 90 percent of all sales. Therefore, most corporations are fairly large firms.
6. The 20 largest firms in the United States have sales of more than $1 trillion a year. This equals more than $4,000 for every man, woman, and child in the country. Those same 20 firms employ more than 4 million people. That is about the same as the population of the Detroit metropolitan area.

7. Multinational businesses view the world as their marketplace. They produce and sell in countries all over the world. Franchising is a means of doing business whereby a franchisee uses products, names, or other services of the franchisor. Some organizations, called nonprofits, do not have profit as their main objective.
8. Money to start or run a business can be obtained from several sources. Proprietorships and partnerships use money mostly from the owner(s) and from bank loans. Corporations also can raise money by issuing bonds or selling stock.
9. Mergers are one way in which firms can grow and expand. A merger takes place when one firm buys all the stock in another firm (or enough to control the company being bought). When one firm buys another that is in the same line of business, it is a horizontal merger. When the two firms are at different stages in one production process, it is a vertical merger. If the firms are in unrelated types of businesses, it is a conglomerate merger.

Economic Foundations

1. What are the three kinds of business organization?
2. What are the advantages and disadvantages of organizing a business as a proprietorship?
3. What are the advantages and disadvantages of organizing a business as a partnership?
4. What are the advantages and disadvantages of organizing a business as a corporation?
5. What is meant by *test of the market*?
6. Compare the sizes of the three kinds of business organizations. Use both the number of businesses in each category and the sales volume of each.
7. How has the definition of *multinational business* changed over the years?
8. What is the relationship between a franchisor and a franchisee?
9. How do the three kinds of business organizations raise money?
10. Why does government watch horizontal mergers closely?
11. Why might government prevent a vertical merger?
12. Why does government usually not oppose conglomerate mergers?

Your Economic Vocabulary

Build your economic vocabulary by matching the following terms with their definitions.

1. a firm made up of many divisions and/or subsidiaries that may not have much in common in their lines of business
2. a type of stock that gives the holder a partial ownership of the corporation
3. the concept that an owner's personal assets can be used to pay bills of the business
4. the concept that owners of a business are only responsible for its debts up to the amount they invest in the business
5. a type of business organization in which there are two or more owners
6. a written application to the state requesting permission to form a corporation
7. that part of a corporation's income paid to its stockholders
8. an arrangement through which a business can quickly access needed cash from a bank
9. an organization of people legally bound together by a charter to conduct some type of business
10. a certificate stating the amount the corporation has borrowed from the holder and the terms of repayment
11. the payment for using someone else's money
12. shares of ownership in a corporation
13. the combining of one company with another company it buys
14. a merger of two companies in the same industry
15. a merger of two companies that are at different stages in the same production process
16. a form of business in which there is one owner
17. a merger of two companies that are in different businesses
18. a legally binding document that specifies how the responsibilities and profits or losses from a partnership will be split between the partners
19. being able to provide goods that satisfy consumers' needs and desires at prices consumers are willing to pay

articles of incorporation

bond

charter

common stock

conglomerate

conglomerate merger

corporation

dividends

franchise

horizontal merger

interest

limited liability

line of credit

merger

multinational business

nonprofit organization

partnership

partnership agreement

proprietorship

stock

test of the market

unlimited liability

vertical merger

20. a firm that sells and produces products in multiple countries
21. the legal authorization to organize a business as a corporation
22. a contract between a parent company (franchisor) and some other business or individual (franchisee) that details the terms under which the franchisee does business with products, names, or other services of the franchisor
23. an organization that does not have profit as its objective

Thinking Critically About Economics

1. List three businesses in your city that you think are proprietorships. Then talk to the owner or manager of one of these to see if you are correct. Ask why the business is operated as a proprietorship and write a paragraph summarizing the owner's answer.
2. Why would some businesses use the partnership form of organization rather than operate as proprietorships? Are there any disadvantages to doing so? If so, what are they?
3. Why do you think most very big businesses are corporations?
4. Choose a corporation that you are familiar with, either because you buy its products or because you know someone who works there. Then go to the library and use *Forbes* magazine's latest list of the Forbes 500 (the Forbes 500 is always in a late spring issue of the magazine) to find out the following information: (a) sales, (b) number of employees, (c) location of home office (city and state), and (d) rank within the 500 by sales volume. Finally, from the *Directory of Corporate Affiliations (Who Owns Whom),* find out either what other companies the firm owns or who owns the firm.
5. Do corporations, partnerships, and proprietorships all have to meet the test of the market? What happens if they fail the test?
6. Think of an example, either actual or hypothetical, of each of the three kinds of mergers. Explain why you classify the examples as you do.
7. Compare the three types of business organizations in terms of the volume of sales each has and how many of each there are in the United States. Why do you think the number of firms and sales are distributed in the way they are?

8. What is the difference between raising money by issuing bonds versus by selling stock? Which would you rather own: $10,000 worth of General Motors stock or a bond issued by General Motors with a value of $10,000? What do you think is important in making this decision?

Economic Enrichment

You may be one of many people who decide to start your own business rather than work for someone else. More than one-half million new firms are started each year. Both the risks and rewards of opening your own business can be quite high. You might have considerable financial success, but, equally important, you may gain a great deal of personal satisfaction or psychic income.

Pick a type of business you might be interested in starting in your community (for example, a secondhand sporting goods store). Prepare an outline of how you would start up your business. Include the planning steps you would go through, what type of business organization you would use, how you would obtain funding, where you would locate, and, if appropriate, who you would ask to become part of your business.

Math and Economics

In Figure 9-1, you saw that corporations have sales of about $10,914,000,000,000 (written as $10,914 billion). There are about 96,400,000 households in the United States. How many dollars of corporate sales are there per household? If the average household has 2.63 people, is your answer consistent with the information in this book that indicated that corporate sales are about $43,000 per person?

Writing About Economics

Pick a business in a shopping area near where you live. Write a short paragraph describing the business in terms of types of products or services offered, approximate number of employees, hours of operation, and location. Then write a second paragraph that explains what type of business organization you think the business represents and why. Illustrate your paper with a small sketch of the firm and entitle your paper "Organizing for Business."

Overview

Section One
Market Characteristics

Section Two
Many Firms, Homogeneous Product

Section Three
Single Seller, Unique Product

Perfect Competition and Monopoly

Learning Objectives

10-1
Describe the five characteristics of market organizations.

10-2
Identify the four kinds of market organization.

10-3
Describe the five characteristics of perfectly competitive markets.

10-4
Draw the demand curve and explain the level of output and price for a firm in perfect competition.

10-5
Describe the five characteristics of monopolistic markets.

10-6
Draw the demand curve and explain the level of output and price for a monopoly.

FOCUS

Section One
Market Characteristics

What Do You Think?

When you walk into a store to buy a new shirt with your favorite college or sports team logo, the price is clearly marked. The seller has set the price and you can either buy at that price or do without the shirt. It seems that the sellers of products have total control over the price. Is that always true?

Terms to Know

market organization

price taker

price setter

What's Ahead?

There are four types of market organizations: perfect competition, monopolistic competition, oligopoly, and monopoly. These market organizations are defined by five characteristics. In this section, you will learn about these five characteristics and how they are used to identify market organizations. Knowing how businesses are organized in relation to one another is helpful in understanding firms' economic decisions and public policy issues.

HOW MARKETS DIFFER

You have seen that firms can be organized as proprietorships, partnerships, or corporations. These three kinds of business organization refer to ownership and internal control of the business. To understand the workings of a market economy, you also need to know how firms are organized with respect to each other. In this chapter, you will begin your study of the organization of firms within the economy.

Market Organization

Every firm is part of some market. General Motors, Ford, Honda, and Chrysler are four of the firms that make up the seller's side of the automobile market. Wheat farmers from Montana, Iowa, Ohio, and Nebraska are part of the wheat market. Cannondale, Specialized, Huffy, and Peugeot are active in the bicycle market. Kroger, Safeway, and IGA all sell products in the retail grocery market. When the term *market* is used this way, it refers to the industry or activity that represents the firm's most important line of business. ***Market organization*** refers to the way participants in markets are organized and how many participants there are. The word *industry* often means the same as *market*.

Forms of Market Organization

Firms can be placed in one of four major types of market organization: perfect competition, monopolistic competition, oligopoly, and monopoly. You will see that firms behave differently depending on their type of market organization. In later sections of this chapter and then in Chapter 11, you will take an in-depth look at each of the types of market organization and learn about the characteristics that define them.

market organization the way participants in markets are organized and how many participants there are

Economic Dilemma

SUBSIDIES ON TRIAL

Should the government subsidize the agricultural sector of the economy? And, if so, by how much? These questions have been debated for years, on family farms and in the halls of Congress. The Commodity Credit Corporation, a part of the Department of Agriculture, is involved with various farm subsidy programs. In a recent year, it spent more than $16 billion to subsidize agriculture.

Some in favor of subsidizing agriculture would argue that these expenditures are important to preserve a way of life that has a rich heritage in the United States. They also might argue that it is important to our national interest to have a healthy and stable agricultural sector because of the valuable food products and raw materials that agriculture provides.

Others suggest that this industry should not be subsidized because doing so promotes inefficiency. They argue that it does not make sense to pay people not to produce, which is what some programs do. Others emphasize that we should be more selective in our decisions about what products should be subsidized. For instance, there is probably less debate about $2 million in subsidies for wheat than a $235 million subsidy for tobacco. Of course, if you live in North Carolina, or another tobacco producing state, you may well have reason to favor subsidies that flow to tobacco growers.

CHARACTERISTICS OF MARKET ORGANIZATION

There are five characteristics that can be used to differentiate between the forms of market organization. You will explore each the following five market characteristics in the next few pages:

1. number of firms;
2. type of product sold;
3. ease of entering or leaving the industry;
4. amount of information about the market; and
5. degree of price control.

Number of Firms

The number of firms that are active in the market differs from industry to industry. Compare the number of firms selling electric power in your hometown with the number of firms selling groceries. In some markets, there are many firms trying to get your business. In others, there may be just a few firms or even just one firm. The number of firms in active competition with

Global Economy

CATTLE FROM CANADA AND MEXICO

Many people think of the United States as a country with sophisticated manufacturing industries and a wide array of services. But, we also have a strong agricultural sector that is a reasonable example of perfect competition. The United States produces about 10 percent of the world's wheat, 20 percent of the world's cotton, 40 percent of the world's corn, and about 50 percent of the world's soybeans.

These products and others are exported primarily to Canada, the European Union (EU), Japan, Mexico, Russia, South Korea, and Taiwan. The United States also exports agricultural products to other countries. For example, cotton, soybeans, and fresh fruit are imported to Indonesia. Total U.S. exports of agricultural products exceed $40 billion per year.

The United States is also a major importer of agricultural products, mainly from Canada, the EU, and Mexico. Our main agricultural imports from Canada are cattle, pork, beef, and canola. Our primary imports from the EU include wine, beer, dairy products, and processed vegetables. From Mexico we import fresh vegetables and fruit, as well as cattle. Agricultural imports from other countries include coffee from Brazil and Columbia. Our total imports of agricultural products are typically between $20 billion and $25 billion per year.

each other influences how each one behaves. This is especially true with respect to how each firm prices its product, what services each firm offers, and how much each produces.

Type of Product Sold

In some markets, the products offered by every firm are very similar. Wheat from one farm is very much like wheat from another farm. Gasoline from Shell is nearly identical to gasoline from Mobil. However, in other markets, the product of one firm may be quite different from that of another firm. A Bic pen is very different from a Cross pen. A Cadillac is very different from a Ford. The extent to which products differ among sellers also influences each seller's behavior.

Ease of Entering or Leaving the Industry

It is relatively easy to enter some industries but very hard to get started in others. If you wanted to open a ice-cream shop, it would not be too difficult. This is not to say it would be easy to operate a successful ice-cream shop. However, it would be relatively easy to get started. You would need just a small amount of space and some fairly inexpensive, low-tech equipment.

The same is true for growing corn, wheat, tomatoes, or most other agricultural products. Although agriculture is becoming a more complex industry and uses more sophisticated capital equipment every year, it is still easier to enter this industry than many others. Businesses that are easy to enter are also usually easy to leave. You can quit and sell your buildings, machines, and land fairly easily and without too much loss of value.

On the other hand, some businesses are very difficult to enter. To successfully enter the automobile industry, for example, you would probably have to spend hundreds of millions of dollars. The amount of technical knowledge and sophisticated equipment necessary would be huge. The same is true for the steel and telephone communications industries. In the phone industry, entry is further restricted by government controls.

Industries—such as metal engraving or newspaper printing—that use a lot of sophisticated equipment also can be difficult to leave. The equipment is usually highly specialized; so it has few, if any, other uses. This makes it hard to sell the equipment without a substantial financial loss. So, once a firm such as this is in business, there is a lot of pressure not to leave.

Amount of Information About the Market

In some industries, firms know a great deal about their markets. They know how much rival firms pay for inputs, how other firms operate, and how much others charge for their products. Wheat farmers, for example, know how much other wheat farmers pay for seed, fertilizer, tractors, and fuel. They also know the selling price for the wheat produced. In fact, television stations in agricultural areas generally report prices for wheat and other products on regular newscasts.

The flow of information among firms is not always this complete. In the production of computers, cars, tents, radios, and most other products, there is not a perfect flow of information among firms. Each firm has some trade secrets it tries to protect. When one firm finds a new and better method of production, it keeps it a secret as long as possible.

One firm might not even know exactly what prices the other firms charge. The list price for a product often does not represent the actual sales price. Sellers may find it difficult to determine what price is actually charged by another seller. For example, a car buyer may look at the same car at different dealers. The sticker price might be identical at each dealer, but the actual price offered might vary quite a bit among the different dealers.

Degree of Price Control

Some firms have a good deal of control over the prices they charge, while others have very little control. The degree of control a firm has over price is determined in part by the other four market characteristics you just read about. You will see this as you study the major forms of market organization in this chapter and in Chapter 11.

price taker
a firm that takes a price determined by forces outside the firm's control

price setter
a firm that has some control over the price at which its product sells

If a firm has no control over price, we say the firm is a price taker. A ***price taker*** is a firm that takes a price determined by forces outside the firm's control. On the other hand, a ***price setter*** is a firm that has some control over the price at which its product sells. There are different degrees to which a firm that is a price setter can determine price. In some situations, the firm may have a great deal of control over price. In other cases, there is only a very small degree of control in the hands of a single firm. You will see examples of these situations as you read the rest of Chapter 10 and Chapter 11.

Market Characteristic	Market Organization			
	Perfect Competition	Monopolistic Competition	Oligopoly	Monopoly
Number of Firms				
Type of Product Sold				
Ease of Entry and Exit				
Amount of Information				
Degree of Price Control				

Figure 10-1

Market Organizations and their Characteristics

This matrix summarizes the five market characteristics that are used to define the four types of market organization. You can draw this matrix on a piece of paper and fill it in as you learn more about the various types of market organization. ***How do you think perfect competition is defined by each of the five market characteristics?***

Identifying Markets by Their Characteristics

The four types of market organization and their five defining characteristics are summarized in the matrix in Figure 10-1. As you move through this chapter and the next, you will learn how each type of market organization is defined by the five characteristics.

The most important defining characteristic of markets is the number of firms selling in the market. In perfect competition, there are a great many firms, while in a monopoly, there is just one firm. Monopolistic competition and oligopoly lie between these two extremes. Most business in the United States takes place in these last two market structures: monopolistic competition and oligopoly. In terms of total sales in the economy, monopoly and perfect competition are not as important. However, it is very important for you to understand perfect competition and monopoly because they are referred to in many public policy debates.

Checkpoint

Content Check

1. What is the difference between market organization and forms of business organization (as described in Chapter 9)?
2. How are the four forms of market organization related to the five characteristics of market organizations?
3. Explain what is meant by the characteristic called *degree of price control.*

What Do You Think Now?

Reread *What Do You Think?* in the Section One Focus. Then answer the following question:

4. Do sellers always have total control over price?

FOCUS

Section Two
Many Firms, Homogeneous Product

What Do You Think?

Jacky Barber owns a farm in northern Indiana. Like many of the owners of the almost 2 million farms in the United States, Jacky produces products for which the forces of supply and demand determine price. If the current market price for wheat is $3.50 a bushel, that is what Jacky will get when she sells her crop. The individual farmer has no control over price. Does this sound like a perfectly competitive market to you?

Terms to Know

perfect competition

homogeneous product

economic profit

What's Ahead?

In some ways, perfect competition is held as an ideal form of market organization. Agriculture is an industry that comes close to perfect competition. In this section, you will learn to identify the characteristics of perfectly competitive markets. You also will earn about market forces in a perfectly competitive market and how they affect output and price levels for producers.

PERFECT COMPETITION

perfect competition a form of market organization in which a great many small firms produce a homogeneous product

Perfect competition is a form of market organization in which a great many small firms produce a homogeneous product. Let's examine perfect competition in terms of the five characteristics of market organization.

Great Many Sellers

In a perfectly competitive market, there are a great many sellers of a product. An industry that comes close to satisfying the characteristics of perfect competition is agriculture. There certainly are many farms in the United States. Although the number varies from year to year, there are about 2.2 million firms involved in agriculture.

Most of these firms are small farms operated as proprietorships. Even big farms are very small in relation to the entire market. For example, there are about 2.4 billion bushels of wheat grown each year in the United States. A farmer with 50,000 acres, with each acre yielding 40 bushels of wheat, would produce 2,000,000 bushels of wheat (50,000 acres × 40 bushels per acre). This is less than one-tenth of 1 percent of total wheat production (2,000,000/2,400,000,000). A 50,000-acre wheat farm certainly is considered to be very large. So, even a very large farm is likely to produce only a very small fraction of total output.

Homogeneous Product

Each firm in a perfectly competitive market produces a product that is just like the output of other firms in that market. A bushel of wheat from one farm is very much like a bushel of wheat from any other farm. A buyer of the wheat, such as General Mills, would not care whether the wheat had been grown on the Myers farm in North Dakota or on the Durkin farm in Montana. General Mills not only wouldn't care, but it also would have almost no way of knowing which farm produced which bushel of wheat.

When the output of one firm so closely resembles that of other firms, we say the product is homogeneous. A ***homogeneous product*** is a good or service that varies little from producer to producer. That is, the products of all producers are exactly the same. There is no way to tell them apart. There are no brands or trademarks. In such a case, buyers do not care from which firm they buy.

homogeneous product
a good or service that varies little from producer to producer

Complete Freedom to Enter or Leave the Industry

In perfect competition, there must be complete freedom for new firms to enter the industry as well as for exiting firms to leave. The entering and exiting also must be fairly easy to do. Each year, some farmers leave farming while others start farming. In recent years, more people have been leaving than entering agriculture, so the number of farms has been declining.

No one forces a person to start or to quit farming. This decision is made by individuals. Farmers do not try to block others from starting in or from leaving the industry. The amount of money necessary to get started in agriculture on a small scale is not great. At least, the amount is not large when compared with the cost of entering many other industries.

Perfect Information About the Market

In perfect competition, information flows freely and completely among participants in the market. *All buyers and sellers have perfect information.* Each seller knows the prices others charge for products as well as the prices paid for inputs. Each producer can have the same information regarding production methods.

Internet Connection

Moving Files with FTP

A great deal of information available on the Internet cannot be found in Gopherspace or the WWW. It can only be found in File Transfer Protocol (FTP) archives. Many computers on the Internet have FTP sites containing collections of text files, free software, and other data. Like Gopher sites and Web pages, these sites are open to the public.

FTP is a powerful way for you to transfer files from a remote computer to your local computer. Before Gopher and WWW, the major data archives on the Internet were FTP sites. FTP was the original way to send and receive Internet files. While many items from FTP sites are being made available via Gopher or WWW, there may come a time when you need to obtain a file only available via FTP.

If you access the Internet through a text-based computer, DOS, or UNIX, you can use FTP by typing **ftp ftp.site.name** where ftp.site.name is the Internet address. If your computer uses a graphical interface, Windows, or a Macintosh system, click on *FTP* and enter ftp.site.name. When you get a log-in prompt, type *anonymous.* When you get a password prompt, type in your e-mail address. After a few moments, you should get an "ftp>/" prompt.

FTP sites have one or more public access directories through which you can browse by using DOS commands (dir for a listing of files; cd to change directory.) Once you find a text file you are interested in, you can retrieve it by typing *get file-name* and pressing "Enter." When you are finished browsing and retrieving, you can exit FTP by typing *quit* "Enter."

If you don't have access to FTP, you can still access FTP archives with a Web browser. Use your browser to open a URL with **ftp://ftp.site.name**.

Internet Application: Connect to the FTP site at **ftp.eff.org** **(ftp://ftp.eff.org)**. Browse around to find something interesting. E-mail the document to your teacher and explain why you liked it.

Economics Application: Based on what you learned in Chapter 10 about market organization, would you describe the commercial Internet providers as an example of perfect competition or monopoly? Why?

In agriculture, for example, firms have nearly perfect information about the market. There is a wide network of sources that provides information to farmers. Farm cooperatives, university agriculture extension programs, seed and fertilizer companies, equipment dealers, and many government agencies help to spread information throughout the industry.

A great deal of information also is available to farmers through the news media. Radio, television, and newspapers give daily information about prices, sales, and factors expected to influence the market in the future. The daily papers in cities such as Minneapolis, Chicago, Bismarck, Great Falls, and hundreds of others list such information. Newspapers often list prices, price changes from the previous day, and volume for such products as wheat, oats, barley, and soybeans, as well as hogs, cattle and calves, and sheep. For many of these products, information will be given for several subgroups, too. Different types of wheat and different weight classes of cattle, for example, will be included.

No Price Control

You have now seen that in perfect competition there are a great many firms selling products that are perfect substitutes for each other. There is free entry into, or exit from, the industry. And, all firms have complete knowledge about the market. From these characteristics of perfect competition, you should expect that *no one firm has any control over the market price for its output.*

Once more, think about the example of agriculture. Suppose the market price for No. 1 hard winter wheat is $3.50 per bushel. No buyer will pay more and no seller will sell for less. Suppose you went to the grain market with 5,000 bushels and said you wanted $4.00 per bushel. Buyers would likely tell you to move your trucks aside so the next seller could unload. They would not pay more than the $3.50 market price because they could buy as much as they wished at $3.50. Keeping your 5,000 bushels from the market would have no effect since they would be such a small part of total wheat production.

On the other hand, the seller has no reason to offer to sell below the market price. If you were willing to sell the 5,000 bushels of wheat at $3.00, buyers would gladly buy it from you at that price. They would save $0.50 per bushel. But, you would lose $0.50 per bushel, or $2,500. Assuming that you are raising wheat to earn money, it is most unlikely that you would sell it for less than buyers would be willing to pay. This is especially true since you would know exactly what buyers were willing to pay.

PRODUCING IN A PERFECTLY COMPETITIVE MARKET

Producers in a perfectly competitive industry sell at the market price. The sellers take that price as given. They cannot sell anything at a higher price and have no reason to sell at a lower price. For this reason, perfectly competitive firms are price takers. They must accept a price that is determined by market conditions that are outside of their control and sell whatever amount they wish at that price.

The Demand Curve for the Firm

What determines the price in such cases? Price is determined by the interaction of market demand and market supply, as you saw in Chapter 8. The left-hand side of Figure 10-2 shows a diagram of the market demand and supply for wheat. The equilibrium price of $3.50 per bushel is determined at the point where the demand curve crosses the supply curve.

The demand for the output of any one firm is shown on the right-hand side of Figure 10-2. At the $3.50 market price, buyers are willing to purchase all that each producer wishes to sell. *In perfect competition, the demand for any firm's output is therefore a horizontal line at the market price.* Every seller takes the market price and sells all that is produced at that price.

Output and Price Levels

economic profit total revenue minus total costs

Because of the characteristics of perfect competition, firms will be led to produce an amount of output at which economic profit is zero. ***Economic profit*** is defined as total revenue minus total costs. A perfectly competitive firm will be led by market forces to produce so that total revenue equals total

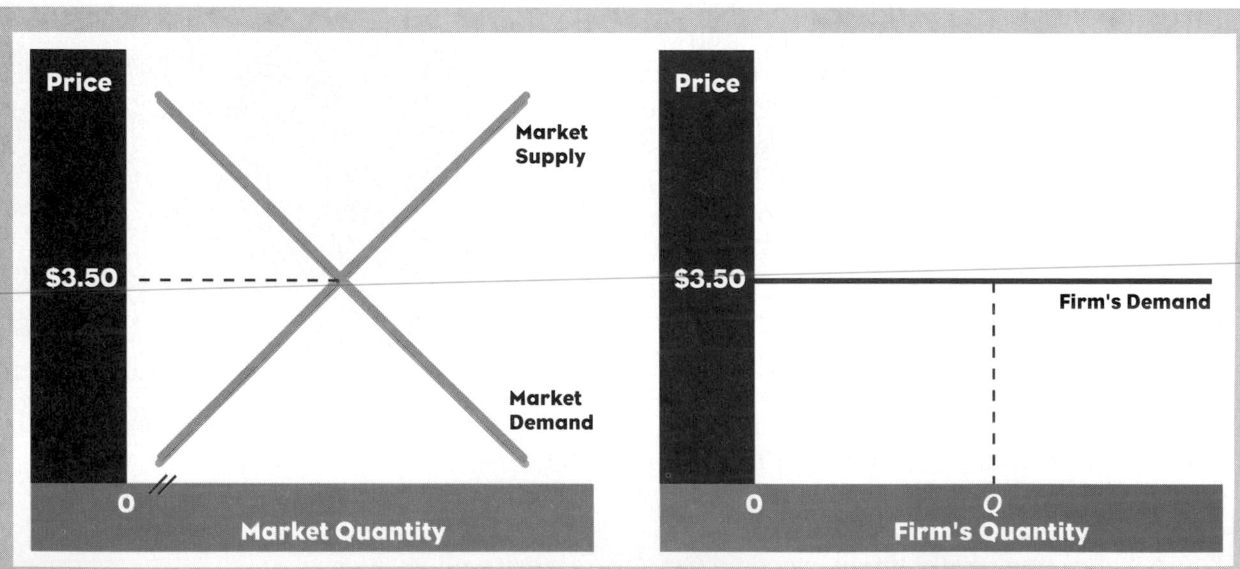

Supply and Demand in Perfect Competition

The demand curve for the output of a perfectly competitive firm is a horizontal line at the level of the market price. ***What could cause the market price to change?***

Econ & You

THE COST OF ENTRY FOR APPLES

The agricultural sector of the economy is often used as an example of a perfectly competitive market. One of the characteristics of a perfectly competitive industry is that entry is relatively easy. Suppose that your family decides that it wants to enter the segment of the agricultural market that grows apples. You may be in for a big surprise. Some library research may tell you that to make a living growing apples you need to have a minimum of 140 acres of producing apple trees. A mature, producing orchard, without living quarters on the property, can easily cost $1,800 an acre or more. That means that for a 140-acre orchard you are likely to have to pay $252,000 for the land and the trees.

At a cost of entry of a quarter of a million dollars, this may not seem an easy industry to enter, especially when this cost covers only one of the factors of production. You would still need to purchase a fair amount of equipment to run the orchard. So, agriculture may not be as easy to enter as one might think.

cost. This does not mean that the owner (a farmer, for example) will not make a good living. A farmer's income is a part of the cost of running the business and is included in the firm's total cost. However, there is no excess return to people in that form of production.

If profit were above zero, new firms would enter the industry. This would increase supply—thus, price would fall, and profit would be reduced. If profit were less than zero (negative profit, or a loss), firms would leave the industry. This would decrease supply. Price would rise and profits would rise (losses would become less). These natural economic forces would direct each firm to produce at a level such as *Q* in Figure 10-2. At *Q*, the firm would have a zero economic profit. Remember, though, that each firm would still have enough revenue to pay for all inputs including the owner's salary. But, there would be no excess returns.

This rate of output has several important results. First, price is equal to the average cost of producing each unit of output. This again means that profit must be zero and that there is no excess return to the owners or workers in the industry.

Second, at this level of production, the average cost of production is as low as possible. This is often taken as a measure of economic efficiency. Since perfectly competitive firms produce at the lowest possible unit cost, they are said to be economically efficient.

Third, at this level of output, price is just equal to the additional cost of producing that unit of output. If one more unit were produced, the added cost would be greater than the price. But, if one less unit were produced, price would be greater than the added cost. The equality of price and the additional cost of producing one more unit of output is considered a measure of the ideal (optimum) allocation of resources in production. So, in perfect competition, just the right level of resource use is allocated to produce each good.

Checkpoint

Content Check

1. What is the effect of having a great number of firms in an industry?
2. Give an example of a homogeneous product (other than wheat).
3. Why is it easy for a producer to enter a perfectly competitive market?
4. Using the following hypothetical industry supply and demand curves for soybeans, draw a demand curve for an individual soybean farmer.

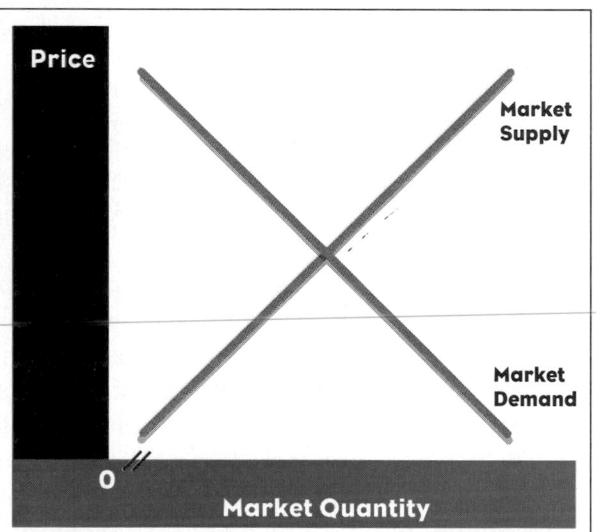

5. Explain three important results of perfectly competitive markets.

What Do You Think Now?

Reread *What Do You Think?* in the Section Two Focus. Then answer the following questions:

6. How does wheat fit the characteristics of a perfectly competitive market?
7. Is Jacky Barber a price taker or a price setter? Why?

FOCUS

Section Three

Single Seller, Unique Product

What Do You Think?

Isaiah's water is supplied by the Madeira Water Works. The water meter at his house is read once every three months to determine his water bill. Isaiah's most recent bill was much higher than the previous one for the same amount of water. He thinks it is unfair that Madeira Water Works can just raise the rates and everyone has to pay. After all, it is the only water supplier in Madeira so people don't have a choice. What do you think?

What's Ahead?

There are situations in which buyers have only one seller from whom a product or service can be purchased. This type of situation is called a *monopoly*. In this section, you will learn about the characteristics of monopolies, how they are regulated, and how they are affected by market forces.

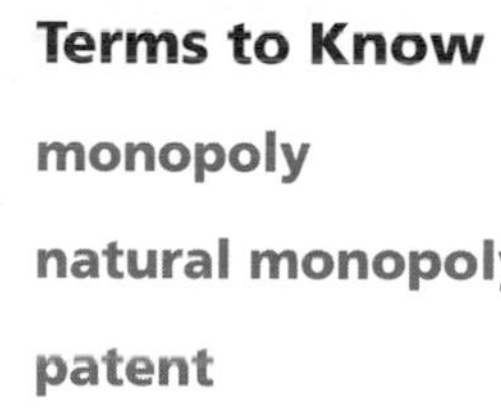

Terms to Know

monopoly

natural monopoly

patent

MONOPOLY

A ***monopoly*** is a form of market organization in which there is only one seller of a product. Electricity, water, natural gas, and local telephone service are examples of goods and services that in most communities are provided by monopolies. You can use the five characteristics of market organization to examine monopolies.

monopoly
a form of market organization in which there is only one seller of a product

Single Seller

Monopoly *refers to a situation in which there is a single seller of a good or service.* For most households, there is a single source of electric power. You buy electricity from the local power company, or you don't buy it at all. Just one seller is available to you. True, there are many firms from coast to coast that sell electricity. Montana Power, Ohio Edison, and Consolidated Edison are examples of such firms. But, you cannot shop around for your supplier. In almost any geographic area, there is just one seller of electricity. The same

is usually true of local phone services, natural gas for home heating, and water piped to your home. In each case, there is a single seller.

There are still other cases in which local monopolies may exist. In many smaller cities and towns, there is just one taxi company, one movie theater, one hospital, and one grocery store. As long as the buyer cannot obtain the good or service (or a close substitute) elsewhere, the owners of these lone businesses have local monopolies.

Unique Product

The product of a monopolist is unique. This means that there are no products that are directly comparable. There are no good substitutes. In perfect competition, the product of one firm is a perfect substitute for the product of any other firm. But, in monopoly this is not true. There is no close substitute for electrical power or local telephone access. If you want the kind of satisfaction that comes from consuming such a product, you must buy it from the monopolist who sells it.

Very Difficult to Enter or Leave the Industry

In monopoly, the entry of new firms or the ability of firms to leave is very difficult, if not impossible. There are several reasons for this, and they are at the heart of why monopolies develop in the first place.

First, there usually are very high costs in obtaining machines and other equipment necessary for production. For example, producing electrical power requires a generating plant and a transmission system, plus office and related equipment. These necessary factors of production add up to hundreds of millions of dollars for even a small electric company. This much cost in equipment can prohibit entry into an industry.

A related aspect helps to keep such industries monopolies. Once one firm gets started, it can sell its product at a lower price because costs are spread over a large number of units of output and customers. A new firm entering such an industry starts out with fewer customers and has a higher cost of production per unit of output. The new firm's price has to be higher than the existing firm's price to cover those higher costs.

natural monopoly
a situation in which it is not practical to have competition

patent
a legal protection for the inventor of a product or process that gives that person or company the sole right to produce the product or use the process for up to 17 years

In many monopolistic industries, the unit costs of production decrease with every additional unit produced. When this is true, it is more efficient (less costly) for one firm to operate than it is for several or many firms to do so. It may be impractical to have more than one firm. For example, having more than one electric power company in a community is not practical and is not in the public interest. A situation such as this in which competition is not practical is called a ***natural monopoly.***

In some industries, competition can be prevented through use of a patent. A ***patent*** is a legal protection for the inventor of a product or process that gives that person or company the sole right to produce the product or use the process for up to 17 years. This protection can keep other firms from entering a new industry.

Economic Spotlight

YOUNGEST BILLIONAIRE: KING OF THE SOFTWARE MARKET?

In 1975 at the age of 19, Bill Gates cofounded Microsoft, the first personal computer software company. An over-$10-billion company employing more than 8,000 people, Microsoft towers above other software companies.

Gates scored a perfect 800 on the math section of the Scholastic Aptitude Test (SAT) in high school and enrolled in Harvard University's pre-law program. When Gates and his college friend, Paul Allen, read an article about the first microcomputer, they decided to jointly write a program for it. They adapted the already available mainframe language, BASIC, to this new microcomputer without even having access to the actual hardware. Amazingly, the language worked! The BASIC language that Gates and Allen wrote went on to set the industry standard for more than six years.

Deciding to devote his time to computers, Gates dropped out of Harvard at the end of his sophomore year. Together with Allen, he started a partnership called Microsoft. In 1980, IBM hired Microsoft to design an operating system for its new personal computer. To fill this need, Gates bought the rights to a program named *Q-DOS*. Gates adapted Q-DOS, creating his own MS-DOS (Microsoft Disk Operating System). He then masterminded a deal in which IBM gave up its secret design specifications. This allowed other software makers to create software compatible with the IBM system—and Gates would be paid a licensing fee every time a computer that ran on MS-DOS was sold. Today, Gates receives more than $200 million a year in royalties from this deal.

The contract with IBM made the company vulnerable to antitrust suits. In 1995, the U.S. Department of Justice became convinced that Microsoft's royalty on any machine that is capable of running MS-DOS, whether it uses it or not, violates antitrust law. Considering that eight out of every ten IBM-compatible computers run Microsoft software, many people believe that the company is a monopoly. Microsoft thinks not, contending that it's merely a tough competitor. Is Microsoft doing anything illegal? The judge and jury are still out.

In some cases, one firm may control access to critical raw material for producing a product. For some years, ALCOA controlled access to bauxite, which is used in the aluminum industry. During that time, ALCOA had a near monopoly in producing aluminum, mostly because it controlled this raw material.

A monopoly may also be maintained by government regulations. Suppose that you could raise enough money to start an electric power company or a telephone company. To start your business, you would have to get approval from one or more regulatory agencies. It is very doubtful that you could get such approval. In most regulated monopoly cases, it is believed that the public interest is best served by having just one firm. If we had two electric companies, there would be twice as many lines running along our highways and through our cities. Each company would have separate electricity generating plants. And, each would have to operate at a smaller rate of output, if the market were shared. This almost certainly would mean higher electricity prices for consumers. So, the government often restricts entry and maintains a monopoly.

Leaving an industry in which a firm has a monopoly may be equally difficult. The equipment is usually highly specialized. Therefore, it may not be possible to sell it except at a very large loss. If the product is considered necessary for consumers, the government may not allow the firm to leave or go out of business. It is hard to imagine an entire city without electricity. Therefore, government would not allow a major electric power company to go out of business.

Complete Information About the Market

The monopolist is the only firm in a market. So, you should expect that *the monopolist knows as much as can be known about the market.* The firm knows how much it pays for inputs, how it produces the product, the selling price, and the number of customers. Local monopolies that are part of a larger industry get a good deal of additional information through trade publications and corporate associations.

A lot of information about regulated monopolies becomes a matter of public record and is available to all other firms. We can say, then, that monopolists generally have very good information about the market in which they sell.

Great Deal of Price Control

In a monopoly, the firm has a great deal of control over price, since the monopolist is the only available seller of the product. With no other firms to supply a substitute product, consumers must either pay the price set by the monopolist or do without the product.

This leads to an important point. The monopolist can set the price but cannot force consumers to buy any particular amount at that price. The firm cannot raise the price and make consumers buy more of the product. Consumers are likely to buy less at a higher price. Even for a product such as electricity, consumers have a choice about how much they buy. Most households could be far more careful about unnecessary use of electricity. Leaving lights on in an empty room and doing laundry in small loads are common wastes of electricity. There are many ways consumers can reduce

the amount of electricity they use. Consumers also can switch, in part at least, to other forms of energy if electricity prices become too high.

Most monopolies are subject to government regulation, so prices are not set just by the firm. Some regulatory agency, such as the Public Service Commission, must approve all prices. Open public hearings usually allow consumers to have some voice in this process along with the company, stockholders, and other interested parties. Therefore, you can see that both consumers and the government have some power to limit the control a monopolist has over price.

PRODUCING AS A MONOPOLY

You now know that monopolists are called *price setters*. This is because they set a price and allow consumers to buy as much as they want at that price. Even when a monopolist is regulated, the firm has considerable input into decisions regarding price.

The Demand Curve for a Monopolist

You also know that a monopolist is the only firm selling the product in a given market. So, it stands to reason that *the demand curve for the output of a monopolist equals the market demand curve for the product.* This is illustrated in Figure 10-3 on page 262. The market demand curve is on the left-hand side, and the monopolist's demand curve is on the right-hand side. These two demand curves are identical.

At the price shown as *P*, the monopolist would sell *Q* units. At that price, the market demand curve also shows that consumers would buy *Q* units. This would be true of any price chosen. The monopolist's demand, then, must be the same as the market demand.

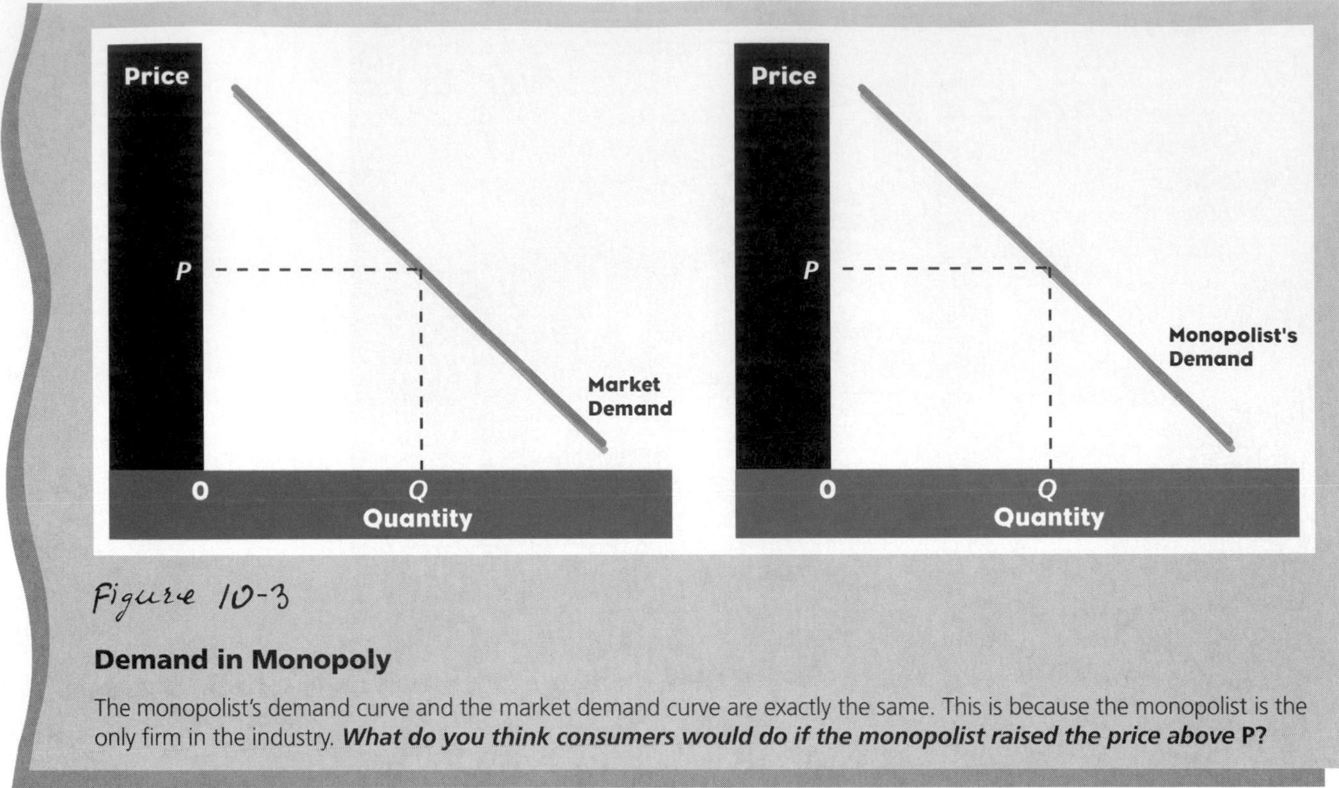

Figure 10-3

Demand in Monopoly

The monopolist's demand curve and the market demand curve are exactly the same. This is because the monopolist is the only firm in the industry. ***What do you think consumers would do if the monopolist raised the price above* P?**

Output and Price Levels

Managers of a monopoly, like those of other firms, will try to produce at a level at which they can make as much money as possible. At low levels of production and sales, the added revenue from increasing sales is normally greater than the added cost of producing the extra output. For example, $20 of added revenue might be obtained by spending $8 in added cost. If so, the firm's profit will increase by $12. As long as the added revenue from new sales is greater than the added cost to produce the output, expansion is favorable.

As a firm expands, the added revenue from sales tends to fall and the added cost from production tends to rise. Firms try to select the level of output with the greatest difference between total revenue from sales and total cost of production. This level of output occurs when added revenue from selling one more unit equals the added cost of producing that unit. Once added revenue and added cost are equal, it is not profitable to expand any more.

So, the monopolist determines the best and most profitable level of output by finding where the added revenue from sales equals the added cost of producing that output. This would be some level such as *Q* in Figure 10-3. The price that corresponds to *Q* along the demand curve becomes the best price to set. This is the price *P*. At *P*, consumers will purchase the *Q* units the monopolist wishes to sell.

Often, a regulatory agency will not permit the monopolist to charge this price. Rather, the agency may force the monopolist to set a price that equals the per-unit cost of production. This will result in a zero economic profit to the monopolist. Even so, production costs will be covered and stockholders will earn dividends since dividends are considered part of the cost of doing business. However, there will not be any excess return to the monopoly. Such a regulated price is illustrated in Figure 10-4 as P_R, which is lower than P. The corresponding quantity produced and sold is Q_R, which is greater than Q.

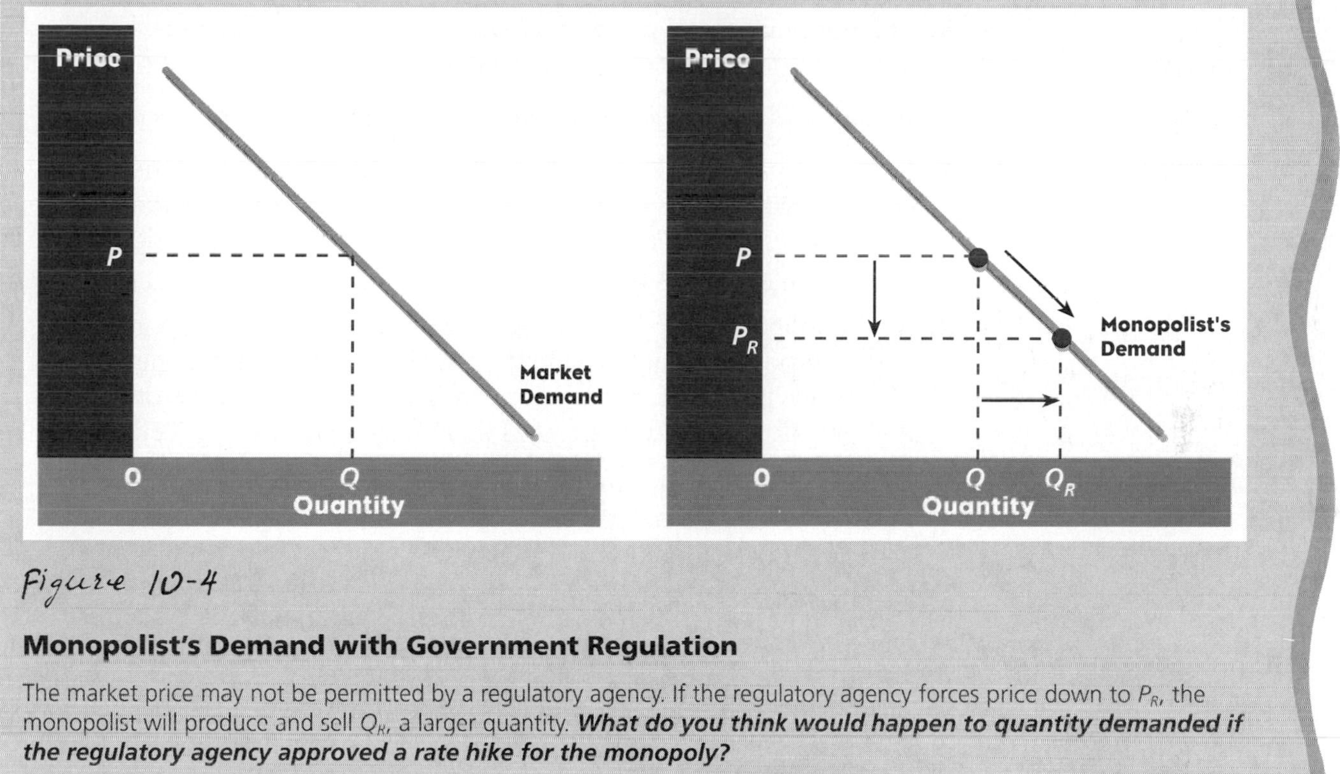

Figure 10-4

Monopolist's Demand with Government Regulation

The market price may not be permitted by a regulatory agency. If the regulatory agency forces price down to P_R, the monopolist will produce and sell Q_R, a larger quantity. ***What do you think would happen to quantity demanded if the regulatory agency approved a rate hike for the monopoly?***

COMPARISON OF MONOPOLY AND PERFECT COMPETITION

If an industry is a constant cost industry (one that can expand or contract without changing the production cost per unit of output), the price charged by a monopolist will be higher than if the industry were perfectly competitive. If the monopolist's price is higher, you should expect that the total quantity purchased by consumers will be less than if the industry were perfectly competitive and price was lower. So, for some monopolies we can expect price to be higher, but the quantity produced to be lower than in perfect competition.

In many monopolistic industries, however, prices are lower than they would be if the same industries were perfectly competitive. This is true when monopolies afford greater economies of scale in production. Electric power is a good example. If there were a great many firms supplying electric power to any area, the cost (and price) of electricity would be much higher.

In studying perfect competition, you learned that market forces work to assure the following conditions:

1. Price would equal the per-unit cost of production, so there would be no excess profit.
2. Price would equal the added cost of increasing output by one unit, so there would be a desirable allocation of resources in production.
3. The per-unit cost of production would be as low as possible, so there would be efficiency in production.

How does a monopoly compare on these counts?

1. In a monopoly, price generally will be greater than the per-unit cost of production, so some excess profit results. An exception occurs when the monopoly is regulated and forced to set price equal to the per-unit production cost.
2. In a monopoly, price will almost always be greater than the added cost of producing one more unit of output. From society's view, this means that too few resources are allocated to this type of production. More should be produced and sold at a lower price.
3. If there are not significant economies of scale, a monopolist normally produces where per-unit costs are higher than the lowest possible level. When this is true, some economic efficiency is lost. However, if there are economies of scale, per-unit costs will be lower with a monopoly than with perfect competition.

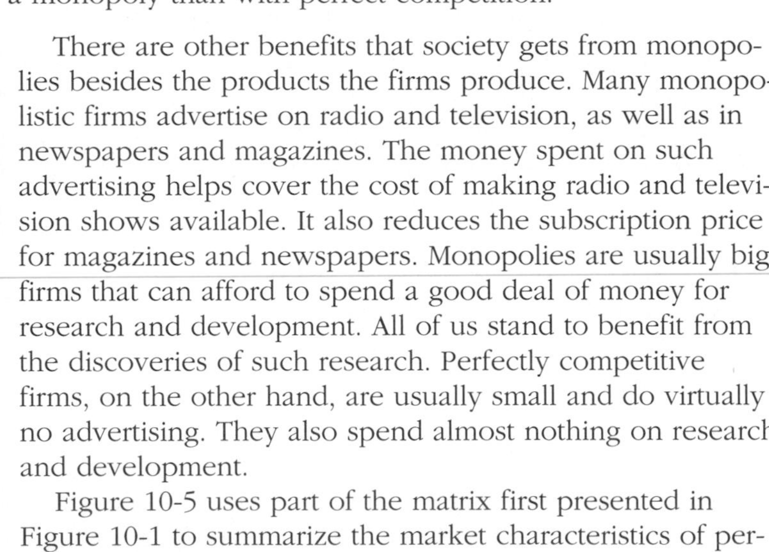

There are other benefits that society gets from monopolies besides the products the firms produce. Many monopolistic firms advertise on radio and television, as well as in newspapers and magazines. The money spent on such advertising helps cover the cost of making radio and television shows available. It also reduces the subscription price for magazines and newspapers. Monopolies are usually big firms that can afford to spend a good deal of money for research and development. All of us stand to benefit from the discoveries of such research. Perfectly competitive firms, on the other hand, are usually small and do virtually no advertising. They also spend almost nothing on research and development.

Figure 10-5 uses part of the matrix first presented in Figure 10-1 to summarize the market characteristics of perfect competition and monopoly. You will be able to complete the matrix after reading Chapter 11 by entering the market characteristics for monopolistic competition and oligopoly.

Market Organization

Market Characteristic	Perfect Competition	Monopolistic Competition	Oligopoly	Monopoly
Number of Firms	great many			one
Type of Product Sold	homogeneous			unique
Ease of Entry and Exit	very easy			very difficult
Amount of Information	complete			complete
Degree of Price Control	none			great deal

Figure 10-5

Market Characteristics of Perfect Competition and Monopoly

This matrix summarizes the five characteristics of perfect competition and monopoly markets. ***For perfect competition and monopoly, name one example that was not used in your textbook.***

Checkpoint

Content Check

1. How does a monopoly compare to a firm in a perfectly competitive market on the five characteristics?
2. Why is it hard to enter and exit a monopolistic market?
3. Explain why a monopolist has complete information about the market.
4. Show how a monopolist's demand curve compares to the market demand curve.
5. Name some benefits society receives from monopolies.

What Do You Think Now?

Reread *What Do You Think?* in the Section Three Focus. Then answer the following questions:

6. Do residents of Madeira have any control over their water bills? Why or why not?
7. Can utility companies charge any price they want? Why or why not?

Concepts in Brief

1. *Market organization* refers to the way in which participants in an industry are organized and how many participants there are. The four types of market organization are perfect competition, monopolistic competition, oligopoly, and monopoly. From the producer's side, market organization is determined by five characteristics: number of firms, type of product sold, ease of entering or leaving the industry, amount of information about the market, and degree of price control.
2. Perfect competition is a form of market organization in which there are a great many firms producing products that are exactly the same. There is a very good flow of information among firms, and it is easy to enter or leave the industry. No one has any control over price.
3. In perfect competition, a firm's demand curve is a horizontal line at the market price. There are three important results of perfectly competitive markets. First, price equals the per-unit cost of production, so there is no excess return to firms in that industry. Second, output is produced at the lowest possible unit cost, so there is economic efficiency. And third, price equals the added cost of producing the last unit of output, so society's resources are allocated well.
4. Monopoly is a form of market organization in which there is just one firm from which a consumer can buy the product. The monopolist has considerable control over price. But, monopolies are usually regulated by the government to prevent misuse of their power.
5. Since there is only one firm in a monopoly, the firm's demand curve is the market demand curve. A monopolist can be expected to produce at a level at which price is greater than the per-unit cost. This means that excess economic returns result. The monopolist is not likely to produce at the lowest possible cost per unit of output. So, production is not as efficient as it could be. Also, since price is above the added cost of producing one more unit of output, the monopolist allocates too few resources to production.
6. In some ways, monopolies can benefit a market society. Due to economies of scale, many products are produced at a lower cost than could be done otherwise. Monopolists also do a good deal of research and development. And, monopolists' support of the media through advertising helps make radio and television shows available and lowers subscription prices for newspapers and magazines.

Economic Foundations

1. List four kinds of market organization.
2. Identify five characteristics that differentiate among forms of market organizations.
3. Describe *perfect competition* by using the five characteristics of market organization.
4. Draw the demand curve for the perfectly competitive firm. How does it compare with the market demand curve?
5. What is the level of output and price for the perfectly competitive firm?
6. Describe *monopoly* by using the five characteristics of market organization.
7. Draw the demand curve for the monopolistic firm. How does it compare with the market demand curve?
8. What is the level of output and price for the monopolistic firm?

Your Economic Vocabulary

Build your economic vocabulary by matching the following terms with their definitions.

1. a good or service that varies little from producer to producer
2. total revenue minus total costs
3. a firm that takes a price determined by forces outside the firm's control
4. a legal protection for the inventor of a product or process that gives that person or company the sole right to produce the product or use the process for up to 17 years
5. a form of market organization in which there is only one seller of a product
6. the way participants in markets are organized and how many participants there are
7. a firm that has some control over the price at which its product sells
8. a form of market organization in which a great many small firms produce a homogeneous product
9. a situation in which it is not practical to have competition

economic profit
homogeneous product
market organization
monopoly
natural monopoly
patent
perfect competition
price setter
price taker

Thinking Critically About Economics

1. Consider the characteristics of a perfectly competitive market. Why do you think governmental policy generally tries to promote competition?
2. What are the good and bad features of a monopoly? Give examples of two goods or services your household buys from firms that have a monopoly. Why do you think those firms have a monopoly?
3. Explain why the demand curve for a perfectly competitive firm is a horizontal line at the market price. Why does the demand curve in the case of a monopoly have a negative slope?

Economic Enrichment

Shelly Egan and her brother Bob have decided to start a business next summer so they can earn money to help with college expenses that fall. They need to choose a business for which entry is easy and inexpensive. It also will be important for them to leave the business easily once college begins. They decide on a house cleaning and lawn care business. They currently have one lawn mower, one electric weed eater, and a small truck. They plan to hire friends as needed to meet the demand if the two of them can't do all the work themselves.

Develop a plan for Bob's and Shelly's business. Include a list of the things Bob and Shelly will need to start and operate their business. Consider the following issues in the plan you develop: How easy will it be to get started? How much money will they need? How will they distribute information to potential customers? Will they have a lot of competition? What will their demand curve look like? Are they more likely to be "price setters" or "price takers"?

Math and Economics

In a recent year, about 62,600,000 acres of wheat were harvested in the United States. The average yield per acre was 38.3 bushels. What was the total production of wheat in that year? The average price per bushel that year was $3.20 per bushel. How much revenue went to farmers for their wheat production that year?

Writing About Economics

In many areas, cable television companies have a local monopoly. Research the pros and cons of having multiple suppliers of cable in any one geographic area. Then, write a short play that depicts an exchange between owners of a cable television company and government representatives. The play could take place in a courtroom setting, at a city council meeting, or at a congressional committee meeting.

Your script should accurately reflect the following positions: The cable company wants to have a local monopoly and the government wants to promote competition. The dialogue should cover pricing, production costs, benefits to society, and any other areas you think are important to this issue.

Overview

Section One
Many Firms, Differentiated Products

Section Two
Few Interdependent Firms

Monopolistic Competition and Oligopoly

Learning Objectives

11-1
Describe monopolistic competition in terms of the five characteristics of market organization.

11-2
Draw the demand curve and explain the level of output and price for the monopolistically competitive firm.

11-3
Describe oligopoly in terms of the five characteristics of market organization.

11-4
Draw the demand curve and explain the level of output and price for the oligopolistic firm.

11-5
Compare the four forms of market organization.

FOCUS

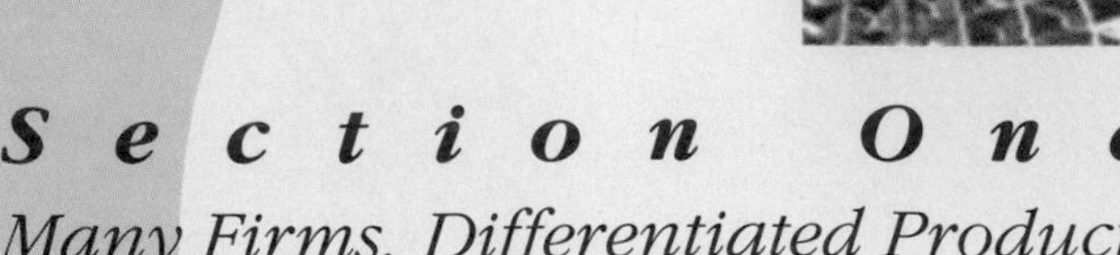

Section One
Many Firms, Differentiated Products

What Do You Think?

Weiss, Inc., makes ketchup and distributes it to retail supermarkets. The ketchup is sold as Weiss ketchup in grocery stores throughout the country. The same ketchup is also bottled as the private store brand for the Bates Supermarket chain, which includes 30 stores. So, the same ketchup is sold under two different brands: Weiss and Bates. Do you think these products are the same in the eyes of consumers?

Terms to Know

monopolistic competition

product differentiation

What's Ahead?

Most of the economic activity in the United States takes place in markets that are either monopolistically competitive or oligopolistic. In this section, you will learn about the market characteristics of firms that operate in monopolistic competition. You will see how these firms differ from both monopolies and perfectly competitive firms.

CHARACTERISTICS OF MONOPOLISTIC COMPETITION

monopolistic competition
a market organization in which many firms produce goods that are different but similar enough to be substitutes

Monopolistic competition is a market organization in which many firms produce goods that are different but similar enough to be substitutes. You learned in Chapter 10 that five characteristics can be used to classify market organization: number of firms in the market, type of product sold, ease of entering or leaving the industry, amount of information about the market, and degree of price control. In the last chapter, you also learned about perfect competition and monopoly. As the name implies, monopolistic competition has some characteristics of monopoly and some of perfect competition. Overall, it is closer to perfect competition than to monopoly. Now you will learn how monopolistic competition is defined in terms of the characteristics of market organization.

Many Sellers

In monopolistic competition, there are many firms from which a given type of product can be bought. Although there are more firms in an industry classified as perfectly competitive, monopolistic competition does provide many different suppliers from which to choose.

Imagine, for example, that you want a haircut. You have many choices about where to buy that service. If you look in the *Yellow Pages* of your local phone book, you will find many listings under the headings *Barbers* and *Beauty Salons*. Even in fairly small cities, the combined listings can run more than 10 pages. In almost any city, there are many places where you can get a haircut.

Differentiated Product

In monopolistic competition there is product differentiation. **Product differentiation** is the concept that the product of one firm can be distinguished from the products of other firms. There may be actual physical differences between products, or the differences may be superficial. This can be illustrated in the market for breakfast cereals. There are very clear taste and physical differences among corn flakes, raisin bran, and puffed rice, for example. Almost anyone would be able to taste the differences among these cereals. And, anyone with reasonably good eyesight could tell them apart on the store shelf. The containers' colors and brand names make them clearly different.

product differentiation
the concept that the product of one firm can be distinguished from the products of other firms

Product differences may not always be so clear. Consider two different brands of the same kind of breakfast cereal: Post Raisin Bran and Kellogg's Raisin Bran. Many people have a strong preference for one brand over the other. Others claim to have no preference at all. There is not as much physical and chemical difference between these cereals as between raisin bran, corn flakes, and puffed rice. Why, then, do some people form such strong brand preferences? The answer involves psychological reasons. To some people, the ads for Kellogg's Raisin Bran may be more appealing. Other consumers may like the color and design of the Post Raisin Bran box better than the other box. The reason for brand preferences is not as important as the simple fact that preferences do exist and are sometimes very strong.

For products to be considered differentiated, consumers must be able to tell one product from another. The differences may be in physical characteristics, function, quality, or just in the brand, trademark, or package. Consider the example of a haircut. In a sense, one haircut is just like any other haircut. It makes little difference where you go. On the other hand, we know that people develop very strong preferences and loyalties to particular businesses and even to specific hairstylists. This appears to be true for both men and women.

Here are ten representative names from one phone book of places where a person can get a haircut:

1. Bell Hair Designs
2. Campus Barber Shop
3. Mirror's Image
4. Razor's Edge
5. The Squire Barber Salon
6. Creative Hair Designers
7. Luau's Salon of Beauty
8. Star Barber Shop
9. Sande's Hair Shoppe
10. Guy's and Gal's Hair Styling

Knowing only that each place takes both female and male customers, which would you choose? If you ask 100 people this question, probably each of the ten choices will be selected. Firm names alone will create some kind of preference. "Luau's Salon of Beauty" has a different image than "Star Barber Shop." Some of the names may appeal more to women than to men and vice versa. Some will appeal more to young people, while others will appeal more to older consumers.

The important point is that the product (or service in this example) becomes differentiated in our minds as soon as we know the producer's name. This service also may be differentiated by the shop's location, its cleanliness and design, and the quality of the haircuts. The fact that products are differentiated in monopolistic competition is the most important characteristic separating this form of market organization from perfect competition.

Relatively Easy to Enter or Leave the Industry

With respect to the ability of firms to enter or leave the industry, monopolistic competition is much closer to perfect competition than to monopoly. *Entry into and exit from monopolistically competitive industries is relatively easy.* Usually, there are few, if any, regulations imposed by the government. Getting started in business in monopolistic competition requires less money than, say, steel production or the production of electric power.

For example, think about the restaurant industry. Look in the *Yellow Pages* for your area under the heading *Restaurants.* You probably will find many firms listed. They all have at least one thing in common. They are all places where prepared meals can be bought. But, they also may be very different from one another. At some restaurants, the meals may be eaten only in the restaurant; while at others, the meals may be taken out. In some cases, either choice is possible. The types of food available may differ quite a bit: from salads and sandwiches to lobster and prime rib. Many of the restaurants in your area may be fairly new. Perhaps they opened within the past five years. Other restaurants may have gone out of business in the past five years. Businesses in monopolistic competition enter and leave the industry with relative ease and freedom.

Reasonably Complete Information About the Market

Firms in a monopolistically competitive industry have reasonably complete information about conditions that may affect the business. Each firm knows approximately how much other firms pay for labor, raw materials, and other inputs. All firms can find out the prices that the others charge. They all have the same access to existing technology. Through trade associations, government publications, and private sources, all firms can learn a great deal about the demand for the product or service produced.

Think about restaurants again. If you opened a sandwich shop, you would know approximately how much other similar firms paid for bread, meats, cheeses, labor, rent, and other inputs. You could find out what prices they charged for similar products by watching their ads or visiting them. You could get information from government publications about how much money local residents spend at restaurants. And, you could get a more personal feel for demand by observing business at other similar restaurants.

Economic Dilemma

BUSINESS OR BRIBE?

The textbook industry at all levels of education is a pretty competitive business. There are lots of publishers involved and many publishers print more than one title for each subject. This means that the people who decide which books will be purchased (mostly teachers) have a lot of choices. For most subjects, there are several to many quality texts available. That's certainly quite true in the subject area of economics—and we think you got the best of the best.

In today's changing world, texts are increasingly being integrated with technology-based supplements. Examples include CD-ROMs, computer simulations, Internet connections, and videotapes and disks. Unfortunately, some schools do not have the hardware or equipment to fully utilize these supplements. This restricts the level of sales for the supplements and/or the entire text package. In turn, the lower sales make it harder for publishers to justify the very high cost of producing good simulations, CDs, and other quality learning aids.

In the past, some publishers have told schools that if they order the text package the publishers will provide all or part of the necessary equipment. Is this ethical? Is it a bribe? Or, is it a mechanism to get state-of-the-art learning packages into the hands of students? What do you think?

Some Price Control

Firms in monopolistic competition have some control over price but not very much. This is mainly because there are many firms producing products that are good substitutes for each other. If the price of Coke were much higher than the price of Pepsi, few cola drinkers would buy Coke. The degree of price control any firm has depends on how different the consumers think its product is. If buyers view two products as very different, the price difference between them can be greater. For example, economic reasoning would suggest that the price difference between Kellogg's Raisin Bran and Post Raisin Bran would be less than the price difference between Kellogg's Raisin Bran and a box of generic raisin bran cereal. Kellogg's and Post Raisin Bran cereals are generally seen as more alike than Kellogg's and a generic box of the same type of cereal.

The same situation can be observed in the restaurant business. Those that serve similar meals usually have prices that are close. A spaghetti dinner will not differ much in price from one family restaurant to another. A breakfast of two eggs, bacon, hash browns, and juice costs about the same regardless of where you buy it as long as the restaurants are of a similar type. As the type of meal or the type of restaurant becomes more different, price difference also increases. A steak dinner at an elegant restaurant will cost more than the same dinner at a cafeteria-style steak restaurant. But, as long as the products and services are close substitutes, individual firms cannot exert much price control.

PRODUCING IN A MONOPOLISTICALLY COMPETITIVE MARKET

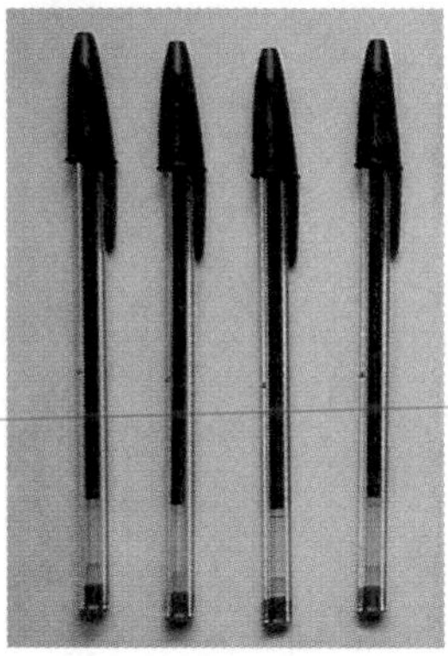

There are many close substitutes in a monopolistically competitive market. Remember, though, that even the closest substitute products are not exactly the same. There is some product differentiation. In fact, if we defined products narrowly, each firm would have a monopoly. You could not produce jeans and sell them under the Levi's name. If you wanted to open a fast-food restaurant, you could not construct a building with golden arches and call it McDonald's. These two firms have a legal monopoly over the use of those names. Bic has a monopoly in the production of Bic pens. There are other pens that are very similar, but they do not carry the Bic name. So, all such firms have some monopoly power. They are the only ones that can make and sell those exact products.

The Demand Curve for a Monopolistically Competitive Firm

As Figure 11-1 shows, the demand curve for a firm in monopolistic competition will have a negative slope. More can be sold at lower prices than at higher prices. The small amount of monopoly power resulting from product differentiation is what gives the firm some slight control over price. This control over price is reflected in the negative slope of the demand curve.

The demand curve for the firm looks flatter than the market demand curve. This is because for the individual firm, the quantity demanded is likely to be fairly responsive to changes in price. If Mobil raised the price

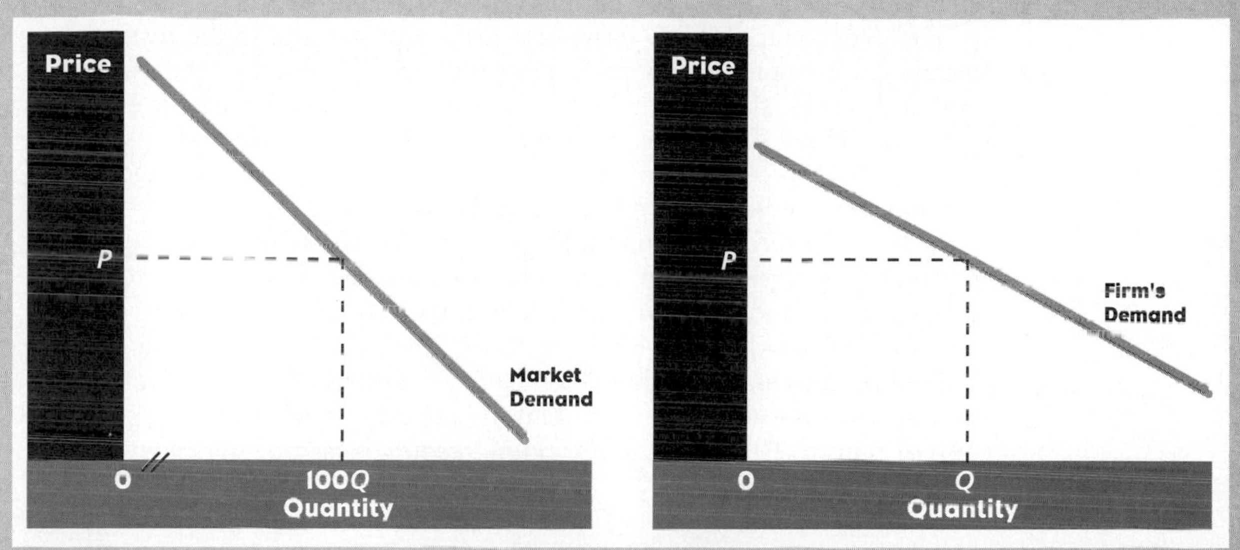

Figure 11-1

The Demand Curve for Monopolistic Competition

The left-hand diagram shows the demand curve for the market. The demand curve for a monopolistically competitive firm is shown in the right-hand diagram. The firm's demand curve is less steep than the market demand curve because the firm's sales are more sensitive to price changes than is the market in general. ***What do you think would happen to a firm's sales if it lowered price below the current level* P?**

of a gallon of regular gas to $0.05 above what others are charging, it would lose some sales but not all of its sales. In comparison, wheat farmers asking $0.05 more than the market price per bushel would lose all their sales. People with a strong brand preference for Mobil gas probably would pay the higher price. But people don't form a brand preference for wheat. What if Mobil raised its price to $1 more than what other gas stations charge per gallon? Do you think many people would have a strong enough brand preference to continue buying Mobil?

Output and Price Levels

In determining how much to produce and what price to charge, firms in monopolistic competition act much like monopolists. If the sale of an added amount increases revenue more than it increases costs, the firm is well-advised to do so. If the added costs go up more than the added revenue, the firm should not sell more. By making such comparisons, the firm might settle on Q in Figure 11-1 as the best amount. And, from the demand curve, you know that Q units can be sold at the price P. Therefore, P is the best price to charge.

Suppose that the firm represented by the demand curve in the right-hand side of Figure 11-1 sells 1 percent of the total industry sales. That is, that firm has 1/100 of the total market. If the average price for the industry is also at P, all firms in total will sell 100 times Q. This is the amount labeled $100Q$ on the left-hand side of Figure 11-1, which represents the market demand.

Suppose prices become very high in such an industry and there are large profits. Since entry is fairly easy, new firms will start up. In the restaurant industry, for example, new restaurants will open. Then, the total market demand will be shared by more firms. Therefore, the demand for each firm's product will fall some. This will cause price to drop. As price drops, so will profits. When profits fall to an equilibrium level, there will no longer be incentive for new firms to enter the business.

In the long run, this equilibrium price will equal (or be very close to) the per-unit cost of production. Remember that this means no excess returns go to people in this industry. In addition, the cost of the quantity produced and sold will tend to be fairly close to the lowest possible per-unit cost. Therefore, reasonable economic efficiency is approached. However, as with monopoly, price will be greater than the added cost of producing an added unit of output. This means that too few resources may be allocated to that industry.

Econ & You

CREDIT UP CLOSE

The market for credit cards can be described as monopolistically competitive. There are many companies offering credit cards to consumers and each card has some differentiating feature(s). Many are very nearly identical except for the name of the issuing institution. In a recent year, more than 6,000 issuers of credit cards sent about 2 billion pieces of mail soliciting business. So, there are lots of firms offering cards that are pretty close substitutes for one another.

Which card is best? That depends. Maybe you want one with your photo on the front and would pay more to have such a card. Maybe you want one with no annual fee but a higher interest rate on unpaid balances. There is a big array of choices to pick from and you are not limited to just one credit card. You can have many, but be careful. Credit card debt can rise quickly if you are not careful and soon you may have trouble paying all those monthly bills that seemed far away when you said, "Charge it." Many people have ten or more bank, gas, and store credit cards ,and the average balance for bank cards runs about $1,700. You can see how people can get into debt too far by using credit cards.

You can get a free and informative booklet about credit cards from the Board of Governors of the Federal Reserve System. The booklet title is "Shop: The Card You Pick Can Save You Money." To request one, write to Board of Governors of the Federal Reserve System, Washington, D.C. 20551-0001.

COMPARISON OF MONOPOLISTIC COMPETITION WITH MONOPOLY AND PERFECT COMPETITION

A firm in monopolistic competition has some monopoly power due to product differentiation. But, that power is not very strong since there are many substitute products available. While firms have some control over price, they don't have nearly as much control as monopolists. Because there are so many other firms in the same market, firms in monopolistic competition also have some characteristics of perfect competition. In fact, they often have so little control over price that they are fairly close to perfectly competitive firms. Figure 11-2 provides an update to the matrix first presented in Chapter 10 that compares the four forms of market organization.

Market Characteristic	Market Organization: Perfect Competition	Monopolistic Competition	Oligopoly	Monopoly
Number of Firms	great many	many		one
Type of Product Sold	homogeneous	differentiated		unique
Ease of Entry and Exit	very easy	relatively easy		very difficult
Amount of Information	complete	reasonably complete		complete
Degree of Price Control	none	some		great deal

Figure 11-2

Market Characteristics of Perfect Competition, Monopolistic Competition, and Monopoly

This matrix summarizes the five characteristics of perfect competition, monopolistic competition, and monopoly markets. ***Can you predict the market characteristics for oligopoly?***

Checkpoint

Content Check

1. Compare the type of products sold in a perfectly competitive market to the type sold in a monopolistically competitive market.
2. Compare the degree of price control in a perfectly competitive market to the degree in a monopolistically competitive market.
3. Draw the demand curve for a monopolistically competitive firm and explain how it relates to the market demand curve.
4. How does a monopolistically competitive firm decide how much to produce and what price to charge?
5. Is monopolistic competition closer to perfect competition or to monopoly? Why?

What Do You Think Now?

Reread *What Do You Think?* in the Section One Focus. Then answer the following questions:

6. Do you think consumers would be willing to pay a higher price for Weiss ketchup? Why or why not?
7. Check prices on a national brand ketchup and a store brand ketchup. Was your original thinking correct?

FOCUS

Section Two
Few Interdependent Firms

What Do You Think?

Reggie and her grandmother were looking at used cars. Reggie needed a car to drive between school and work. They looked at Buicks, Fords, Chryslers, Toyotas, Acuras, Mercuries, Audis, Chevrolets, Nissans, and Volkswagens. There were so many models and styles and colors to choose from they had to keep track of what they liked by making notes. Do you think the auto industry is monopolistically competitive?

What's Ahead?

In some industries, there are relatively few firms or a few dominant firms with many smaller firms selling similar products. These industries are called *oligopolies.* In this section, you will learn about the market characteristics of oligopoly, how firms determine output levels and price, and how oligopolies compare to the other three market organizations.

Terms to Know

oligopoly
pure oligopoly
differentiated oligopoly
collusion
cartel

OLIGOPOLY

Oligopoly is a form of market organization in which there are relatively few firms. There is no absolute number of firms that separates oligopoly from monopolistic competition. In some industries that are oligopolies, there may be quite a few firms.

oligopoly
a form of market organization in which there are relatively few firms

Like monopolistic competition, oligopoly has some characteristics of both perfect competition and monopoly. Overall, the industries that would be classified as oligopolies are closer to monopolies in terms of how the firms behave. Most economic activity in the United States takes place in industries that are classified either as oligopolies or as monopolistically competitive. In the next few pages, you will read about oligopoly in terms of the five characteristics of market organization.

Internet Connection

GOVERNMENT ANTITRUST POLICY AND THE INTERNET

In Chapter 5, you learned that promoting competition in the private sector is one of the major functions of government. In the real world, most industries are less than perfectly competitive. Promoting competition is a serious concern for government policy makers. Most monopolies in the United States today are regulated monopolies. This means that they are allowed to be the sole suppliers, but they are supervised by some government agency to make sure that they do not restrict supply and charge excessively high prices. In addition, the government is always wary of mergers between businesses in monopolistically competitive or oligopolistic industries. If an agency weren't watching over mergers in these types of industries, there would be increased concentration and monopoly power.

Two government agencies with responsibilities in the area of promoting competition are the Antitrust Division of the Justice Department, which enforces antitrust law, and the Federal Trade Commission, which protects against unfair business practices.

The Antitrust Division has a Web page, **http://gopher.usdoj.gov/atr/atr.html**, which provides policy statements of the agency and descriptions of current cases. This information is also available from the agency's Gopher site, **gopher://gopher.usdoj.gov/1/atr**.

Vanderbilt University has a very interesting Web page on antitrust policy, **http://www.vanderbilt.edu/Owen/froeb/antitrust/antitrust.html**. It includes a collection of business merger case studies, a summary of antitrust/merger law, and a regularly updated link called "In the News," which describes current merger activities.

The Federal Trade Commission has a Web page that provides a description of the agency, news releases, and an explanation of how the FTC begins an investigation, how the investigation proceeds, and the various ways an investigation is concluded, such as consent orders, cease and desist orders, and penalties. The URL is **http://www.ftc.gov**.

Internet Application: Visit the Vanderbilt Antitrust Policy Web page to find an interesting merger case in the news. E-mail the names of the firms involved to your teacher. Are these firms oligopolies or monopolistically competitive?

Economics Application: Based on what you learned in Chapter 11 about market organization, would you describe the commercial on-line services (CompuServe, America Online, Prodigy) as examples of monopolistic competition or oligopoly? Why?

Few Interdependent Sellers

We usually think of an oligopoly as an industry in which there are few firms. But, it is hard to assign an absolute number to the term *few*. The degree to which firms act independently of one another is more important than the exact number of firms. If there are a great many firms, such as in wheat production, we expect each to act on its own. That is, each firm will act independently of the others. But, think about the car industry where a relatively small number of firms dominate the industry. Each firm takes the actions and reactions of the other firms into account when making economic decisions. This interdependence that influences economic behavior is one key element of oligopoly.

Identical or Differentiated Products

In oligopoly, the products produced by different firms can be either nearly identical or differentiated. Consider the case of steel beams used in building bridges. The product is very much the same whether it is produced by Bethlehem Steel, USX (formerly U.S. Steel), or any other steel producer. In this case, the industry is a pure oligopoly. A ***pure oligopoly*** is an oligopoly in which the products are the same for all firms. The aluminum industry is also a pure oligopoly.

pure oligopoly
an oligopoly in which the products are the same for all firms

In other oligopolistic industries, there is considerable product differentiation. As with monopolistic competition, this product differentiation can be actual physical differences or differences perceived by the consumer due to brands, trademarks, packages, or other factors. Consider, for example, the car industry. The products are clearly differentiated. A Jeep is very different from a Cadillac. A Buick is different from a Toyota. Even products that are very similar in a strict physical sense may be viewed as very different by consumers. The Mercury Sable and Ford Taurus are very similar, yet some people would buy one and not the other. Thus, the two cars are considered differentiated. An industry such as this is called a *differentiated oligopoly*. A ***differentiated oligopoly*** is an oligopoly in which the product is differentiated.

differentiated oligopoly
an oligopoly in which the product is differentiated

Difficult to Enter or Leave the Industry

It is fairly difficult to enter an industry that is oligopolistic. There are a couple of reasons for this.

First, most oligopolistic industries use very expensive and sophisticated equipment. It would cost a great deal of money to enter the car or steel industries at a scale that would be economically efficient. Hundreds of millions of dollars would be necessary to make even a serious attempt.

Second, because the products have a brand, buyers develop brand preferences that can be quite strong. Some people have always bought the same brand of car. This is true of many other products including televisions, stereo equipment, and other home appliances. The buyer for a large construction firm may prefer one company's steel beams because of the product's past performance. This might happen even though other companies produce very similar steel beams. A new firm would have a hard time overcoming people's existing brand preferences. Therefore, it would be difficult to get those important first-time sales.

Global Economy

MADE IN ______?

There was a time when U.S. companies dominated car sales in this country. There were very few imports and there were no foreign companies producing cars in the United States. This changed quite rapidly during the last half of the twentieth century. Foreign imports came in at lower prices, with models more to the liking of the modern consumer and with better quality ratings. Detroit, the one time auto capital of the world, was stunned and caught by surprise.

As we move toward the third millennium, this industry is in a continued state of change. It has become a truly global market. Japanese and German manufacturers are making cars in the United States. U.S. companies are selling and making cars and trucks in Europe and elsewhere. For example, in the early 1990s, I was personally surprised when the first car I saw upon walking out of the Moscow (Russia) airport was a Chevrolet Astro Van that was pretty similar to the one in my driveway thousands of miles away.

There are many joint ventures between U.S. companies and their foreign competitors. It is now hard to say whether some vehicles are foreign or domestic. Companies sell transmissions, engines, and even body designs to their competitors. Parts may be made anywhere in the world and assembled in the United States. How much of the final product is domestic is hard to determine, and trying to make such a determination probably is becoming less and less important.

Leaving oligopolistic industries also can be pretty difficult. Because most of these industries use highly specialized machines, it is often very hard for a firm to exit and sell the equipment without great loss. When a firm does leave, it commonly does so by selling out to another firm. If the firm is in the same line of business, this creates a horizontal merger. An example of this occurred when Chrysler bought American Motors primarily to acquire the Jeep line of vehicles.

Incomplete Information About the Market

In oligopolistic industries, firms have less complete information about the market than in other forms of industry organization. Firms usually know how much other firms pay for labor, but there is much less reliable information for other inputs. One car company may pay more for steel than another car company does. This can be true even though the published list price for the steel is the same for all car companies. Because of their size, some oligopolistic firms can get a price reduction that other firms cannot get. This is true even in the money markets. When two firms go to a major bank, they may find that the interest rate to borrow money is not the same for both of them.

More trade secrets exist in oligopolistic industries than in any other type. Each car company will try to keep new designs, new advertising programs, and even major personnel changes secret as long as possible. Chemical companies such as Dow or Monsanto closely guard new product development, sales, and cost information. However, it is very difficult for these firms to prevent information from leaking out. People change jobs and move from one company to another. The firms are likely to buy things from the same suppliers and sell to the same buyers. So, information that either a supplier or a buyer may obtain can leak out (even accidentally) to other firms in the industry.

Varying Degree of Price Control

Firms in a differentiated oligopoly have a great deal of control over price. These large firms spend a lot of money on advertising to create and maintain consumer brand preferences. The car buyer who has bought a new Buick every three years since 1980 is not likely to change now. Therefore, that buyer is probably not very sensitive to price. And, surely the difference in price between a Buick and a Chevrolet will not be important to a buyer with such a strong brand preference.

Firms in a pure oligopoly have some control over price, but they usually have less control than firms in a differentiated oligopoly. A manufacturer of steel beams cannot price the beams much higher than other manufacturers do. Any firm's steel beams are likely to be satisfactory. In many cases, such products are bought solely on the basis of price. So, even favorable company preferences based on past performance may not give any one firm the ability to charge a higher price without hurting sales.

Economic Spotlight

THE OVERNIGHT SENSATION

How did a 1965 "C" term paper in Economics 43A at Yale University turn into FedEx, Frederick Smith's "overnight" sensation? Smith was given a "C" on his economics paper because his professor thought that Smith had thrown it together at the last minute. Smith based his paper on the hub-and-spoke concept used today by most major airlines. With this concept, a hub, or central, office in a middle-America location such as Little Rock or Memphis serves as a "feeder" to spoke cities in the far reaches of the country.

Smith didn't let the "C" convince him that his idea wouldn't fly. In April 1973, the former Marine pilot bought 14 small aircraft housed at Memphis International Airport and launched the overnight package delivery industry. Somewhere between 7 and 18 packages were shipped the first night. (No one knows the exact number because tracking wasn't an issue back then.) Overcoming great skepticism and on-going loan problems, Smith quickly grew FedEx into a phenomenal success. His company, then named Federal Express, was the first in U.S. history to report $1 billion in revenues within 10 years of start-up without the benefit of mergers or acquisitions. Today, the company's 5,000 employees ship 1 million to 1.5 million packages a night on more than 400 airplanes and thousands of trucks from 93 airports and several hundred smaller hubs. At the Memphis Superhub, computer monitors outnumber people by five to one, and more than 250 video cameras monitor packages moving over 171 miles of conveyer belts. The Superhub even has its own meteorology department to track the weather in 165 FedEx regions twice a day.

In 1994, the Federal Express Corporation officially changed the company name to FedEx to reflect customers' widely used nickname for the company. In fact, the public has coined a new verb inspired by Federal Express. To "FedEx" is now nationally understood to mean to "ship overnight." The name change was also a response to the needs of the company's fastest growing segment: international business. Non-native English speakers who had difficulty pronouncing "Federal Express" have found the new name much easier to pronounce. In fact, customers in almost 200 countries around the world have learned to "FedEx" with great enthusiasm. As a result, FedEx is able to bill itself as the world's largest express company.

Collusion and Cartels. Because there are relatively few separate firms in an oligopoly, there is often incentive for them to make joint decisions. This is especially true of pricing decisions. ***Collusion*** is the situation of firms acting together rather than separately. So, if two or more firms make joint decisions, we say there is collusion between the firms. If this collusive behavior becomes formal and well organized, the firms become what is called a *cartel*. A ***cartel*** is a formal organization of firms in the same industry acting together to make decisions.

collusion
the situation of firms acting together rather than separately

cartel
a formal organization of firms in the same industry acting together to make decisions

The objective of having collusion and/or forming a cartel is to give the group of firms the power of a monopoly. All of the firms then can act as one and earn greater profits than if they acted separately. To consumers, this usually means a higher price and a lower level of output for purchase.

The most famous cartel probably is the international cartel known as OPEC (Organization of Petroleum Exporting Countries). This cartel has controlled oil prices and output throughout the world. In the United States, cartels are illegal. This does not mean firms do not practice collusion. However, it is often done secretly and is very hard to prove.

Price Leadership. In some oligopolistic industries, cooperation between firms exists but falls short of being a full cartel. Price leadership, for example, happens when one firm in an industry sets a price and other firms follow. The other firms then sell their product at the price set by the leader rather than set their own prices. It is illegal in the United States for managers of firms to decide collectively on a pricing strategy. Such action is considered collusion and is viewed as an attempt to form a cartel. However, it is not illegal for one firm to react to the price set independently by another firm.

The firm that acts as the price leader may vary from year to year. Often, the largest firm in the industry will be the price leader, but this is not necessarily the case. As long as all the other firms will follow, any firm can act as the leader.

PRODUCING AS AN OLIGOPOLIST

Managers in oligopolistic businesses probably pay more attention to the actions and reactions of other firms than do managers in any other industrial setting. You can see this in the car industry, in the steel industry, in banking, and in other oligopolistic industries. In the car industry, consumers see the result in terms of similar prices, similar designs, and similar timing of the release of new models.

The Demand Curve for an Oligopolist

The demand curve for an oligopolist is negatively sloped. As with monopolistically competitive firms, this is due mainly to the product differentiation that exists between firms. Unlike in the other forms of industry organization, there is not one type of demand curve that is good for all oligopoly cases. Probably the most famous type is a *kinked demand curve* such as the one shown in Figure 11-3 on page 288.

The demand curve is kinked because the responsiveness of the quantity demanded to a price change differs depending on whether the firm raises or

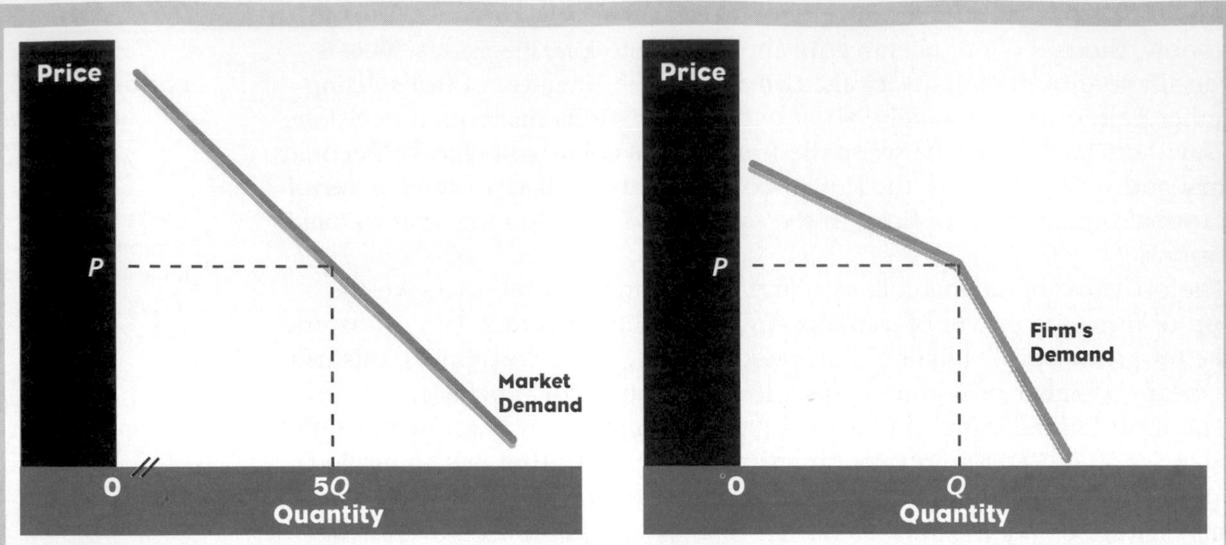

Figure 11-3

The Demand Curve for an Oligopolist

The demand curve for an oligopolistic firm is shown to the right of the market demand curve. The firm's demand is often drawn as a kinked demand curve. This shows that sales may be more responsive to a price rise than to a drop in the firm's price. ***Would you say that the demand curve for the oligopolist in the right-hand graph is more or less price elastic above the kink than below the kink?***

lowers price. Suppose the current price is at the level marked *P* in Figure 11-3. At *P*, the firm shown in the graph has 20 percent, or one-fifth of the total market. The firm's sales are *Q* units. In the left-hand graph, you can see that sales by all of the firms in the market are five times *Q* (5*Q*).

Suppose the firm lowers price to try to get a greater share of the market. The kinked demand curve shows that other firms will also cut price to prevent this firm from getting part of their sales. Therefore, the firm in the right-hand graph will not have much of an increase in sales by lowering price. So, its demand curve is very steep below the existing price *P*.

Now suppose this firm raises price. Other firms will not necessarily follow. If the others do not increase price, the firm that does will likely experience a large drop in sales. For this reason, the demand curve for the firm is very flat above the existing price *P*.

The kinked demand curve approach to an oligopolist's demand and pricing behavior does not explain all cases of oligopoly. It does, however, help to explain why some oligopoly prices do not change as frequently as prices in other industries. Many other approaches to oligopoly explain demand for the firm when the kinked demand curve is not appropriate.

Output and Price Levels

In deciding the levels of output and price, oligopolistic firms behave very much like firms in other situations discussed earlier. If selling an added unit of output makes revenue go up more than costs go up, it will be profitable to sell that added output. On the other hand, if the added costs go up more than the added revenue, it will be better not to sell more.

In cases in which a cartel is formed or price leadership is followed, these principles may be altered by individual firms. Some firms may produce and sell less while others may produce and sell more. As a result of their decision, some firms may sacrifice profit for the overall good of the industry.

COMPARISON OF OLIGOPOLY WITH OTHER MARKET STRUCTURES

Firms in oligopolistic markets have some amount of monopoly power. Generally they have more monopoly power than do firms in monopolistic competition. This is due largely to the smaller number of substitute products available in oligopolies. There are fewer firms to provide competition.

This monopoly power, along with the relatively difficult entry of new firms, means that high profits may result. There is no guarantee of high profits, of course. In the automotive sector, we sometimes see that even with relatively few firms in a large market it is possible to lose money. In an oligopoly, however, prices will stay high enough to be profitable for most, if not all, firms involved.

In oligopoly, production is likely to occur at a level where the per-unit cost of output is not as low as possible. This means that the product is not produced as efficiently as is technically possible. In this regard, oligopoly is very similar to monopoly. The similarity continues if we compare price to the extra cost of producing an added unit of the product. As in monopoly, price is higher than this added cost, so we can conclude that too few resources are used in producing that product. For society to be best served, more should be produced and it should be sold at a lower price.

Firms in oligopolistic industries do benefit society, however. Pharmaceutical companies, car companies, petroleum companies, chemical companies, and others spend a great deal of money on research and development. Some of that money does not pay off since the research does not always produce usable products. But, much of the spending supports successful research that may benefit the whole society in the long run. In this respect, oligopolies are like monopolies.

Firms in oligopolistic industries, like those in monopolistic and monopolistically competitive industries, also spend a lot of money for advertising. Many of the television specials and sports broadcasts are paid for by oligopolistic firms through advertising. Magazines with national distributions are full of ads by these companies. These firms also support broadcasts on public radio and television through donations.

Figure 11-4 gives a complete summary of the characteristics of the four forms of market organization. An example of each type of market structure is also included in this chart.

Market Organization

Market Characteristic	Perfect Competition	Monopolistic Competition	Oligopoly	Monopoly
Number of Firms	great many	many	few and interdependent	one
Type of Product Sold	homogeneous	differentiated	differentiated or homogeneous	unique
Ease of Entry and Exit	very easy	relatively easy	difficult	very difficult
Amount of Information	complete	reasonably complete	incomplete	complete
Degree of Price Control	none	some	varying degree—often considerable	great deal
Example	wheat	hair cuts	steel	electric power

Figure 11-4

Market Characteristics of Perfect Competition, Monopolistic Competition, Oligopoly, and Monopoly

This matrix summarizes the five characteristics of all four forms of market organization. ***Name an industry, besides the one given, that belongs in each group.***

Checkpoint

Content Check

1. Use the five characteristics of market structure to describe oligopoly.
2. Explain why the demand curve for an oligopolistic firm may be kinked.
3. How does an oligopolistic firm decide how much to produce and what price to charge?
4. Is oligopoly closer to perfect competition or to monopoly? Why?

What Do You Think Now?

Reread *What Do You Think?* in the Section Two Focus. Then answer the following questions:

5. Describe the auto industry in terms of the five market characteristics.
6. What market organization do you think the auto industry fits into?

Concepts in Brief

1. Monopolistic competition is a form of market organization in which firms create products that, while different in some ways, are good substitutes for one another. Firms have good information about the market, and it is fairly easy to enter or leave the industry.
2. In monopolistic competition, price is usually very close to the unit cost of producing the product, so there is little, if any, excess return. The degree of economic inefficiency is small since output is produced close to the lowest possible cost. There is some misallocation of resources since price is greater than the cost of producing one additional unit.
3. Oligopoly is a form of market organization in which there are just a few firms. In some cases, the output is very much the same no matter which firm it comes from. In other cases, products are very different between firms. It is usually quite difficult to enter or leave an industry that is oligopolistic.
4. In oligopoly, price is likely to be greater than the cost per unit of output, so excess profits result in the industry. At the level of output that is best for the firm, price is greater than the added cost of producing one more unit of the product. So, too few resources are allocated to production. Also, oligopolistic firms are not likely to produce at the lowest unit cost and therefore some economic efficiency can be lost.
5. Firms in oligopolistic industries tend to advertise heavily and thus help support newspapers, magazines, radio, and television. Oligopolists also spend a great deal of money on research and development, which is often of great benefit to society in the long run.

Economic Foundations

1. Describe monopolistic competition using the five characteristics of market organization.
2. Draw the demand curve for the monopolistically competitive firm. How does it compare with the market demand curve?
3. What determines the level of output and price for the monopolistically competitive firm?

4. Describe oligopoly using the five characteristics of market organization.
5. Draw the demand curve for the oligopolistic firm. How does it compare with the market demand curve?
6. What is collusion and how is it used by cartels?
7. What determines the level of output and price for the oligopolistic firm?
8. What is the difference between a pure oligopoly and a differentiated oligopoly?

Your Economic Vocabulary

Build your economic vocabulary by matching the following terms with their definitions.

1. the situation of firms acting together rather than separately
2. a form of market organization in which there are relatively few firms
3. a market organization in which many firms produce goods that are different but similar enough to be substitutes
4. an oligopoly in which the products are the same for all firms
5. the concept that the product of one firm can be distinguished from the products of other firms
6. a formal organization of firms in the same industry acting together to make decisions
7. an oligopoly in which the product is differentiated

cartel

collusion

differentiated oligopoly

monopolistic competition

oligopoly

product differentiation

pure oligopoly

Thinking Critically About Economics

1. Review what is meant by the term *monopolistic competition.* How does this form of market organization resemble a monopoly? How does it resemble perfect competition?
2. From a recent issue of *Time* (or any other weekly news magazine) pick out ads for industries you consider oligopolies. Explain your choices, using the characteristics of oligopoly as a guide.

3. Using news magazines and reference materials, write a brief history of the OPEC oil cartel. In your report, indicate how key world events, such as the Persian Gulf War, have affected the strength of OPEC throughout its life.

4. Explain why the demand curve for a perfectly competitive firm is a horizontal line at the market price, while demand curves for firms in the other market structures all have negative slopes.

Economic Enrichment

Picture the intersection of two busy streets. On two of the four corner lots there are gas stations. One is a Shell station, a national brand, and the other is Gary's Gas and Go, a local company that is a combination convenience store and gas station. The price of regular unleaded gas at the Shell station is $1.39 per gallon, while at Gary's the comparable price is $1.35. You have probably experienced situations such as this many times. The product itself, unleaded regular gas, is essentially the same at the two stations. In fact, it comes from the same refinery in a nearby city. Why does anyone buy their gas at the Shell station, where ten gallons of gas costs an extra $0.40?

Math and Economics

A firm has determined that a 10 percent price cut would increase sales by 8 percent, whereas a 10 percent price increase would cause sales to drop by 12 percent. Remember from Chapter 6 that price elasticity is calculated as the percentage change in quantity demanded divided by the corresponding percentage change in price. What is the price elasticity for a price cut? What is the price elasticity for a price increase? What do your calculations for these two price elasticities tell you about the likely market structure in which this firm operates?

Writing About Economics

Go to the cereal aisle at a local supermarket and make a list of all the brands of cold cereals that you find. In addition to writing down the brand name (for example, Cheerios), write down the name of the company that markets the product (for example, General Mills).

When you get home, make two separate lists based on what you found. The first list should group the cereals into broad product types (for example, put all raisin brans together). In the second list, put the brands into groups according to the company that markets each cereal (for example, Cheerios would go in the General Mills group). Write a report of your findings. Include the two lists, a description of the market structure of the cold cereal industry, and an explanation for your choice of market structure.

Overview

Improving the Market Economy

Learning Objectives

12-1

Explain the relationships between marginal private costs and supply and between marginal private benefits and demand.

12-2

Analyze negative externalities in terms of marginal costs and benefits.

12-3

Describe how the effects of negative externalities on the market system can be controlled.

12-4

Analyze positive externalities in terms of marginal costs and benefits.

12-5

Describe how the effects of positive externalities on the market system can be encouraged.

12-6

Recognize how the government improves the market economy by providing public goods and controlling natural monopolies.

Section One
Markets May Not Always Work Well

What Do You Think?

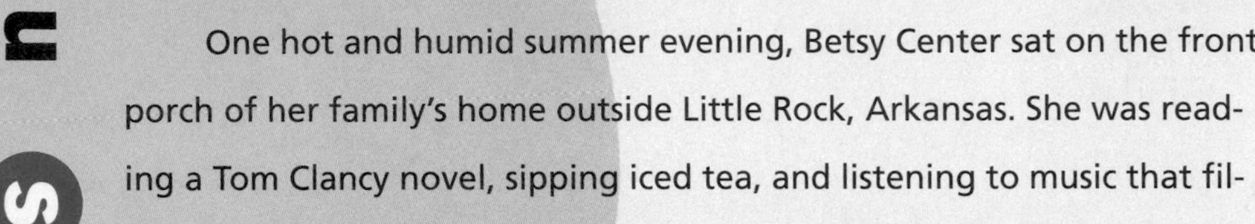

One hot and humid summer evening, Betsy Center sat on the front porch of her family's home outside Little Rock, Arkansas. She was reading a Tom Clancy novel, sipping iced tea, and listening to music that filtered through an open living room window. How might this event have affected other people in the neighborhood?

Terms to Know

marginal private benefit (MPB)

marginal private cost (MPC)

externality

What's Ahead?

In a free market economy, the quantity of a product that is produced and consumed depends on a balance between private costs and private benefits. However, the costs or benefits of people's actions sometimes are greater than what they may seem. This creates what economists refer to as *externalities.* In this section, you will learn about how a market economy reaches a balance between marginal private costs and marginal private benefits but fails when externalities are involved.

THE MARKET CAN BE SUCCESSFUL

When a market is perfectly competitive, the economy benefits in three ways:

1. Economic efficiency results. This means that products are produced at the lowest possible cost per unit.
2. Firms in the industry do not make excessive profits. This is because price equals the cost per unit of producing the product.
3. There is the best possible allocation of resources to production in the industry. For the good of society, neither too much nor too little is produced because price equals the added cost of producing an added unit.

A graph of supply and demand helps explain why just the right amount is produced when markets are competitive. The graph in Figure 12-1 shows

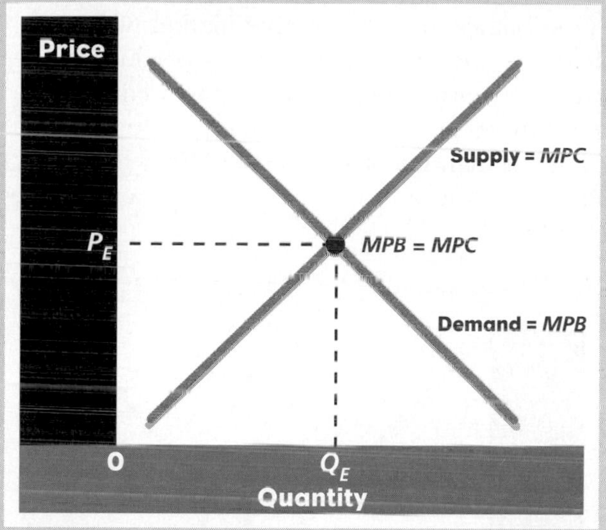

Figure 12-1

Demand and Supply Curves for Bicycles

The demand curve represents the marginal private benefit of consuming one more unit. The supply curve represents the marginal private cost of producing one more unit. The market is in equilibrium when the marginal private benefit equals the marginal private cost at the price P_E. This is where the demand and supply curves cross. ***How many bicycles are demanded and produced when this market is in equilibrium?***

demand and supply curves for bicycles. Here's a quick review of what demand and supply curves show:

Demand: A demand curve shows the quantities that people are willing and able to purchase at various prices.

Supply: A supply curve shows the quantities that producers are willing and able to make available for sale at various prices.

marginal private benefit (MPB) the added benefit that individuals directly involved in an activity get from increasing the activity by one unit

marginal private cost (MPC) the added cost individuals directly involved in an activity pay to increase the activity by one unit

Marginal Private Benefit (MPB)

The demand curve reflects willingness of individuals in the marketplace to buy. Think of it as showing the added benefit received from each unit. This is called *marginal private benefit*. ***Marginal private benefit*** **(MPB)** is the added benefit that individuals directly involved in an activity get from increasing the activity by one unit. It is *marginal* because it shows the benefit from each added unit. It is *private* because you consider only your own personal satisfaction, or benefit, in deciding whether to buy. You can see that marginal private benefits decrease as more units are consumed. This is due to diminishing marginal utility.

Marginal Private Cost (MPC)

The supply curve shows the firm's cost of producing each added unit. This cost is called the *marginal private cost*. ***Marginal private cost*** **(MPC)** is the added cost individuals directly involved in an activity pay to increase the activity by one unit. It is *marginal* because it is the cost of producing one more unit. It is *private* because the only costs included are those that the individual producer must pay. Marginal private costs increase as more units are produced because of the effect of diminishing marginal product.

Best Rate of Production

Figure 12-2 illustrates three possibilities in a competitive market with only private costs and benefits. In Graph *A*, the number of bicycles produced is represented by Q_1. At that rate, consumers would be willing to pay a fairly high price for the product. That is, consumers get a high marginal private benefit (MPB_1). But, you can also see that the marginal private cost (MPC_1) to produce that output is lower. Should the added unit of output given by Q_1 be produced?

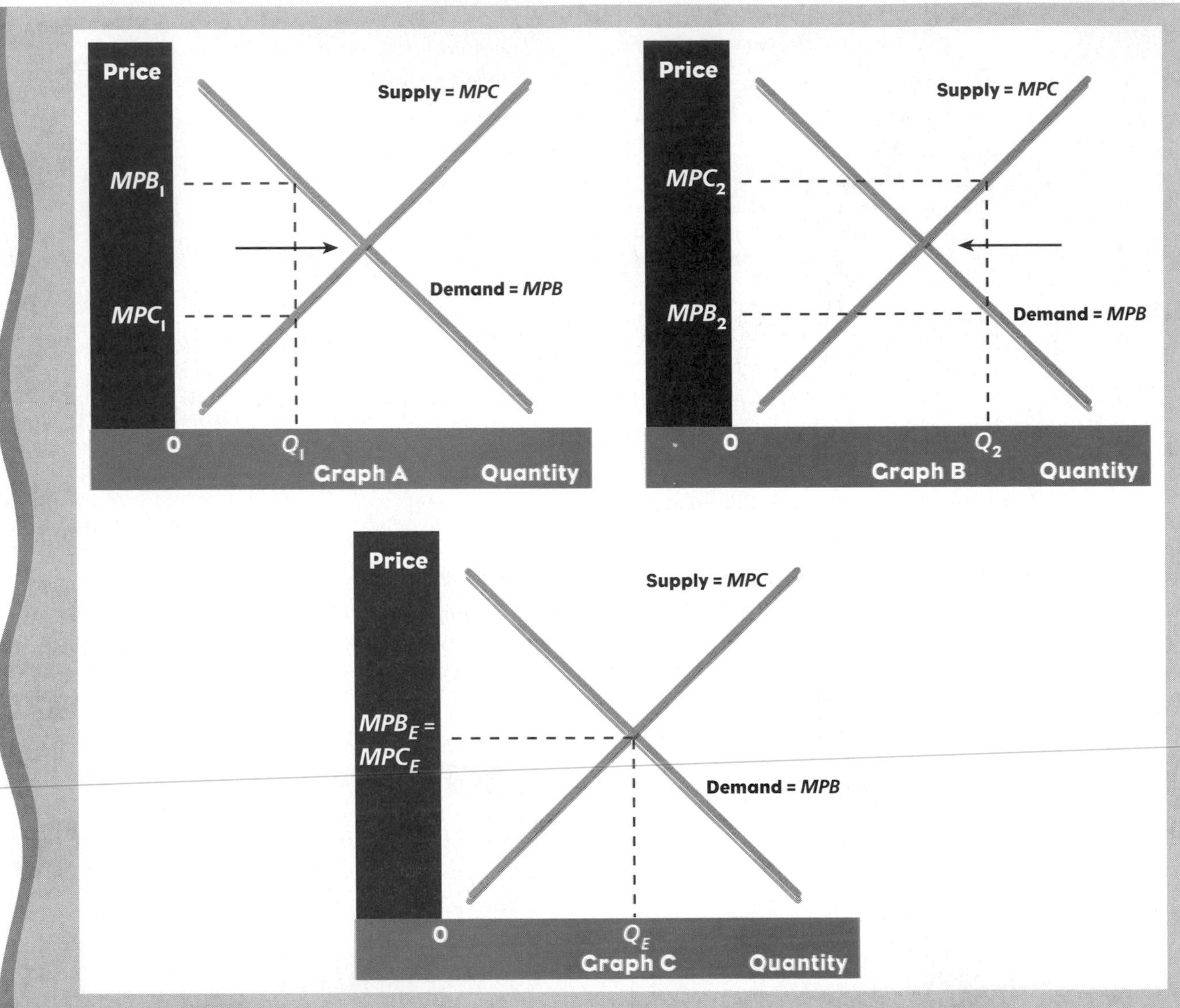

The Relationship Between MPB and MPC in a Competitive Market

If marginal private benefits are greater than marginal private costs, as in Graph *A*, output should be increased. If marginal private costs are greater than marginal private benefits, as in Graph *B*, less should be produced. The best rate of production and the best allocation of resources occur when marginal private costs equal marginal private benefits, as in Graph C. ***In Graph C, if more than Q_E units were produced, how would the marginal private costs and marginal private benefits compare?***

YOUR EXTERNALITIES ARE SHOWING

It would be rare to find an individual who does not contribute to pollution in some way. Answer the following questions for yourself:

1. Do you ever leave a light on when you are not using it?
2. Do you ever play a radio or similar device loudly enough that it could interfere with someone else?
3. Do you ever drive or catch a ride when you could walk or ride a bike?
4. Do you actively try to conserve on heating and/or air conditioning use?
5. Do you personally recycle paper, bottles, and cans?
6. Have you ever littered?

Identify other similar questions that might be relevant.

The answer is *yes*. The added benefit from consuming the product is greater than the added cost of making it available. So, it is desirable to produce that bicycle.

Now look at Graph *B* in Figure 12-2. The added cost of producing the unit given by Q_2 is MPC_2. This is a high cost. But, the added benefit consumers would get from that unit is just MPB_2. You can see that MPB_2 is much less than MPC_2. So, for Q_2, the added cost would be greater than the added benefit. It would not be desirable to produce that many bicycles.

It is desirable to produce Q_1 but not Q_2. Think again about why this is true. For Q_1, the added benefit is greater than the added cost. But, for Q_2, the added cost is greater than the added benefits. This leads to a general conclusion: *It is only desirable to produce an additional unit if the added benefit that results is greater than or equal to the added cost.*

In Graph *C* of Figure 12-2, Q_E represents the best rate of production. For units to the left of Q_E (less than Q_E), the added benefit is greater than the added cost. Those units would be worth producing. For units to the right of Q_E (greater than Q_E), the added cost is higher than the added benefit. So, it would not be desirable to produce those units. At Q_E, which is the best rate of production, the added costs are exactly equal to the added benefit. That is, at Q_E, MPC = MPB.

When all costs and benefits are private, the economy's scarce resources are allocated in the best possible way when *MPB* = *MPC*. This happens when price equals the added cost of producing the last unit. In perfectly competitive markets, this is a natural result. The market system is successful in providing the best possible allocation of resources.

SOMETIMES THE MARKET CAN FAIL

So far in this and previous chapters, it has been assumed that all costs and benefits are private. The benefits all go to the people who buy the product. The costs are all paid for by the producers. When this is true, all the costs and benefits go only to people involved in market transactions. In such cases, we say that all costs and benefits are *internalized*. None of the benefits or costs spill over to people who are not involved in the market transaction.

In some cases, however, this assumption is not correct. It is possible that some of the benefits or costs will go to third parties. Third parties are people not directly involved in the production or purchase of the product. When all the benefits or costs are not internalized, externalities exist. As you recall, an ***externality*** is a cost or benefit passed on to people not directly involved in a transaction. Three terms are used to describe these cases, and any of the three is correct: *spillovers, third-party effects,* or *externalities*. Each of these terms refers to cases in which all the costs of production or the benefits of consumption do not go to the people directly involved in producing or using the product.

externality
a cost or benefit passed on to people not directly involved in a transaction

The market system does not work well when there are spillovers. Resources are not allocated to different types of production in the best possible way. In the following sections, you will look more closely at the effects of such externalities. You will also look at some examples of spillover benefits and costs. In addition, you will consider some ways to correct this failure of the market system to allocate resources in the best possible way.

Checkpoint

Content Check

1. Explain why the demand curve is the same as the marginal private benefits curve.
2. Explain why the supply curve is the same as the marginal private costs curve.
3. What happens to the market system when there are externalities?

What Do You Think Now?

Reread *What Do You Think?* in the Section One Focus. Then answer the following question:

4. Might Betsy's activities have any spillover effect on others?

FOCUS

Section Two
The Shifting of Costs

What Do You Think?

The Millikin Paper Company operates in the beautiful foothills of the northern Rocky Mountains. It has been in business at this location for more than 60 years. Recently, EPA (Environmental Protection Agency) officials found that the company has been discharging waste water into the Grey Wolf River, resulting in fish kills and a reduction of recreational activities on the river. Should the government step in and shut down the plant?

What's Ahead?

There are times when individuals, families, social groups, and businesses do not bear the full cost of their activities. This creates various forms of pollution. In this section, you will learn how economists analyze such situations and about how to develop possible solutions.

Terms to Know

negative externality

marginal social benefit (MSB)

marginal social cost (MSC)

NEGATIVE EXTERNALITIES

A ***negative externality*** is the result when *costs* are shifted to people who are not directly involved with the production or consumption of a good. When the costs of externalities shift to third parties, producers and consumers of the good do not pay the full cost to society of providing the good. In other words, the social costs of providing the good are greater than the private costs. The social costs include all costs: the private costs plus the costs that are shifted to third parties in the form of externalities. Therefore, the social costs are higher than the private costs. The difference between the social costs and the private costs is a measure of the cost of the externality.

negative externality the result when *costs* are shifted to people who are not directly involved with the production or consumption of a good

Water Pollution Is a Negative Externality

Suppose the Sulfa Chemical Company builds a new plant on the banks of the Green River. The company uses pure water from the river in the production of chemicals. Waste water containing various chemical impurities is

dumped back into the river downstream. As a result, fish die. The town of Greenville, which is downstream from Sulfa Chemical, has to add new equipment for water treatment because the Green River is the town's main source of water. People for the next 50 miles downstream find that the Green River is no longer safe for recreation. The river can no longer be used for boating, fishing, swimming, or water skiing.

To whom does the Sulfa Chemical Company shift part of the production costs? Who are the third parties in this case? People who used to enjoy fishing in the river have to go elsewhere. This creates a cost to all of them. Every resident of Greenville has to pay more for water because of the added cost of water treatment. Some people are affected by both these added costs.

Society as a whole bears some of the cost of producing the chemicals. The private costs of making the chemicals, as shown by the company's records, are less than the true total costs. Some of the costs are shifted to third parties. So, the social cost is greater than the private cost. There are costs to society in addition to the costs to the company. If the water returned to the river had been as clean as the water the company took out, there would have been no spillover to other people. The company would have internalized all the costs. The private costs would then have been the total cost to society of making the products. There would be no negative externality, and private costs would be the same as society costs.

Examples of such water pollution are very common. Indeed, it is hard to find a major river or lake that has not been polluted in some way. Almost all major industries have dumped wastes into our water. Producers of steel, coal, cars, chemicals, wood products, paper, and food are only a few. Lake Erie and the Ohio River are highly polluted. But, the problem is not found just in the industrial Northeast and Midwest. The Yellowstone River at some locations is also polluted.

Air Pollution Is a Negative Externality

Another common type of negative externality is air pollution. Industries all too often treat the atmosphere as a free "dump" for waste products. Each year, hundreds of millions of tons of air pollutants are released into the air. Almost everyone shares in creating this problem, including you. One of the biggest sources of air pollution is the exhaust of cars and trucks. Industrial plants, many electric power plants, agricultural burning, and solid waste disposal also contribute to air pollution.

Air pollution causes an increase in health costs for many people. In some cities, air pollution sometimes gets so bad that people are warned to stay indoors and refrain from heavy physical activity. Air pollution also damages vegetation and personal property. For example, people living near a source of air pollution may have to paint their homes more often. In all these cases, as with water pollution, the firms or people involved shift part of the cost of activities to other members of society. Once more, the social cost is greater than the private cost.

Individual Activities Can Result in Negative Externalities

Negative externalities can take less obvious forms. Consider, for example, how one family can affect a neighborhood. They have a horse trailer that sits in the street in front of the house and makes an otherwise very pretty street less attractive. They have a disassembled car in their driveway. Their six-year-old son leaves his bike and other toys in their side yard and in neighbors' yards. Their house needs painting, and the yard is overgrown with weeds. Their two dogs bark throughout the night, keeping even people living several houses away awake. This family allows part of the cost of enjoying their lifestyle to spill over to others in the neighborhood. You can plant a nice hedge to separate your yard from theirs and to give you a more pleasant view. But, this is a cost you have that is due to someone else's activities.

When people in an apartment play their stereo and television loudly, other people who live in the same building are affected. There is a negative externality. Due to the activities of others, some people incur a cost in the form of psychological discomfort, loss of sleep, or even moving to a quieter place.

ANALYSIS OF NEGATIVE EXTERNALITIES

Negative externalities result in the social costs of some activity being greater than the private costs. So far in our analysis, it has been assumed that private costs and social costs are equal, and that no costs are shifted to third parties. Figure 12-2 on page 300 assumes that this is the case and that the competitive market system will yield the best allocation of resources.

Marginal Social Benefit (MSB)

What is the economic impact of negative externalities? The demand curve in Figure 12-3 shows the diminishing marginal private benefits *(MPB)* from consumption. For now, assume that all the benefits are private. The only benefits to society are internalized to private individuals. So, you can say that society's benefits *are the same as private benefits*. ***Marginal social benefit* (MSB)** is the added benefit that society gets from increasing an activity by one unit. Marginal social benefit is the same idea as marginal private benefit, which was defined earlier in this chapter, except that it applies to society instead of individuals. In Figure 12-3, the demand curve, *MPB,* can be labeled *MSB* as well because all benefits are internalized.

marginal social benefit (MSB)
the added benefit that society gets from increasing an activity by one unit

Figure 12-3

Negative Externalities and Marginal Costs

Negative externalities result in marginal social costs *(MSC)* that are greater than marginal private costs *(MPC)*. The market system leads to more production than is desirable. ***Name two situations in which you think the marginal social costs are higher than the marginal private costs.***

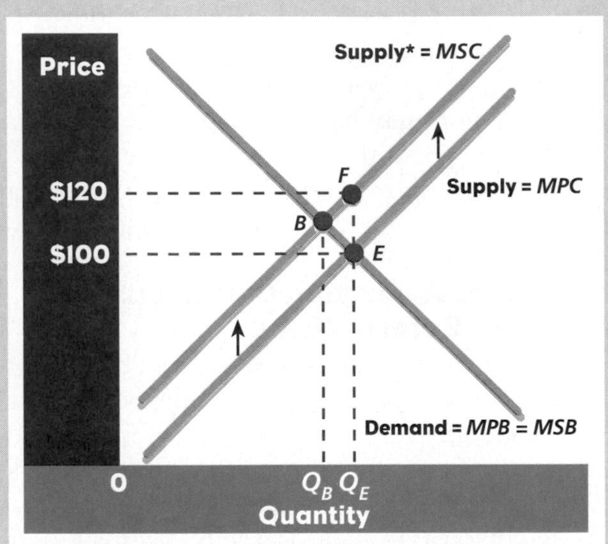

Marginal Social Cost (MSC)

The curve labeled *Supply = MPC* in Figure 12-3 shows the quantities that producers are willing and able to make available for sale, considering only private costs. This is the supply (or marginal private cost) curve that firms use to determine the rate of production. In Figure 12-3, another supply curve is drawn above the firm's own supply. This new supply curve, labeled *Supply* = MSC,* reflects the full cost of producing the good. Since all costs are included in this higher supply curve, it is the marginal social cost *(MSC)* curve. ***Marginal social cost* (MSC)** is the added cost that society pays to increase an activity by one unit. The vertical distance between the two supply curves is the amount of the full cost that is shifted to third parties for each unit produced. This is the distance labeled *FE* in Figure 12-3.

marginal social cost (MSC)
the added cost that society pays to increase an activity by one unit

Spillover Costs

Left to competitive market forces, Q_E units would be produced and sold. The last unit produced would cost the firm that produced it $100. But, the full cost of that unit would be $120. The difference, or $20, would be shifted to third parties in the form of pollution costs. In this case, the distance *FE* equals \$20 per unit. Suppose 1 million units are produced (Q_E = 1 million). The total pollution cost to society will be \$20 million. That is, the cost of this negative externality will be \$20 million.

Most people would agree that such a spillover of costs is not in the public interest. Let's compare the full cost of producing Q_E units with the price people are willing to pay for those Q_E units. The full cost is \$120 per unit. That is, the marginal private cost (*MPC*) of \$100 plus the pollution cost of \$20 is the full marginal cost to society (*MSC*) of \$120. According to consumer demand, people will be willing to pay only \$100 per unit for Q_E units. The cost to society of producing the last unit is greater than the benefit received from the last unit. Therefore, society will be better served if fewer than Q_E units are produced.

Best Rate of Output

How many units should be produced? What is the best rate of output? The best rate is found on the graph where the full marginal cost is just equal to the full marginal benefit. In Figure 12-3, this is where *MSC* crosses *MSB* (which equals *MPB*) at Point *B*. At this point, the marginal social cost of supplying the last unit is exactly the same as the marginal social benefit obtained from that unit. This best rate of output is labeled Q_B on the horizontal axis.

Suppose firms did pay the full cost of making products. If they did, the *MPC* curve would be the same as the *MSC* curve. No costs would be shifted to third parties. The competitive market would naturally lead to the production of the best rate of output, Q_B. Knowing this best rate of output is helpful in deciding what should be done to control negative externalities.

PUBLIC POLICY FOR NEGATIVE EXTERNALITIES

When negative externalities are present, *MSC* is greater than *MPC*. For now, continue to assume that all the benefits are private, or *MSB* = *MPB*. You now know that the best rate of output is found on the graph where marginal social cost is the same as marginal social benefit. That is, the best rate of output, Q_B, is where *MSC* = *MSB*. The question is, "How can you get firms to produce Q_B units?" If you can do this, the best possible allocation of our scarce resources will result.

Making Pollution Illegal

One way for government to control negative externalities is to pass laws making pollution illegal. Of course, there would have to be some penalty for people who broke the law. To avoid this penalty, owners and managers of businesses would have to buy machines to clean the air and water they use before discharging either back into the environment. More labor and other inputs probably would be necessary, too. So, the firms' costs would go up. As costs went up, the prices the firms would have to charge for each unit produced would go up as well. That is, the firms' supply curves would shift upward. If no externalities were left, marginal social cost and marginal private cost would be the same.

This situation is shown in Figure 12-4. The *Original Supply* curve shows the quantities that firms would produce at each price before the passage of laws against pollution. This curve also represents the marginal private cost of production if firms did contribute to pollution problems. If firms did obey the antipollution laws, the supply curve would shift to the curve labeled *New Supply* due to the added costs of complying. With this new supply curve, firms would charge a higher price for each unit because of the higher production costs. All the costs would be internalized. Marginal private costs *(MPC)* and marginal social costs *(MSC)* would be the same. There would be no negative externalities. Having decided to obey the laws against pollution, firms naturally would be led to produce the best amount of output (Q_B).

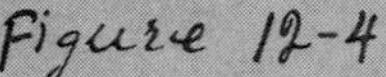

The Effect of Antipollution Laws

If the government passed a law prohibiting pollution, firms would have to clean up waste products. This would raise production costs so that marginal private costs *(MPC)* would be the same as marginal social costs *(MSC)*. The new supply curve would be above the original supply curve, and the best rate of output, Q_B, would be produced. ***What would be the rate of production if there were no laws prohibiting pollution?***

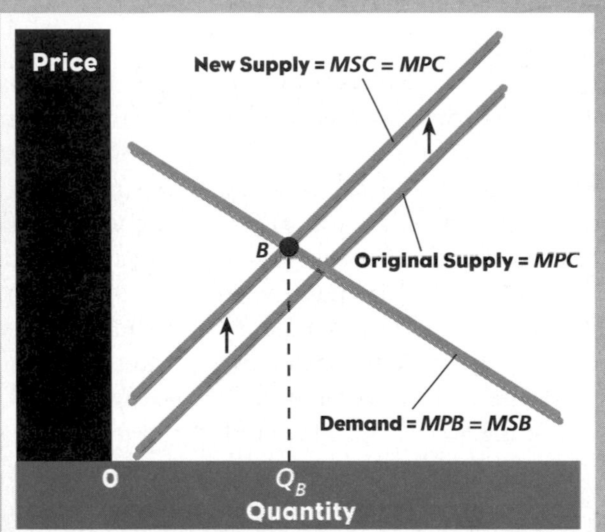

Using a Tax to Curb Pollution

A second common way to deal with the problem of negative spillovers is to use taxes. Any tax that is in some way tied to the rate of output could be used. The tax could be on the output itself or on an input. The tax even could be on the actual pollution. The easiest tax to use, however, is usually a tax on output.

To understand how such a tax would work, look at Figure 12-5. To start, suppose that firms only consider the private costs of production. Also, continue to assume that all of the benefits are internalized—that is, that $MPB = MSB$.

The free, competitive market system would ignore any negative externalities. Production would take place where marginal private costs were equal to marginal private benefits. This is at the point labeled *E* in Figure 12-5. The number of units produced would be Q_E units.

But, suppose there are negative externalities that equal $25 per unit of output. The marginal social costs then would be $25 more than the marginal private costs. This is shown by the distance *FE* in Figure 12-5, as well as by the difference between $85 and $60 on the vertical axis. If firms had to internalize that pollution cost of $25 per unit of output, less would be produced.

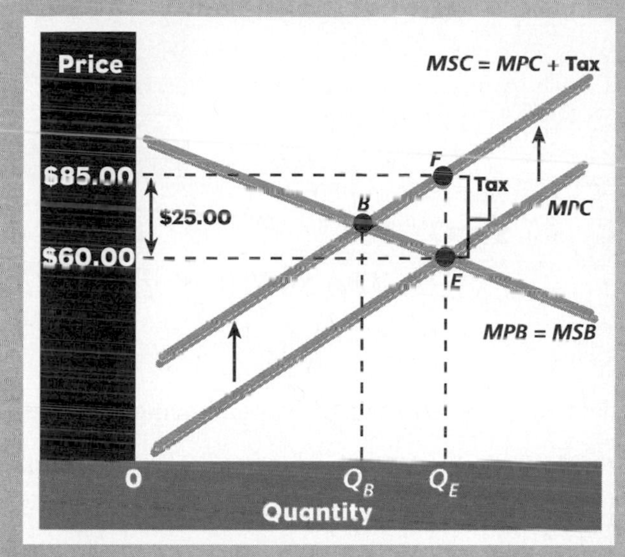

Figure 12-5

The Effect of a Tax on Output

When there are negative externalities, a tax on output can be used to decrease production from Q_E to Q_B units, which is the best rate of production. In this example, the amount of the tax is $25. ***Why is Q_B a better rate of production for society than Q_E?***

The government could put a tax on each unit of output equal to the pollution cost per unit, $25. Firms would have to pay the tax plus the cost of producing each unit. The cost for each additional unit of output would then be equal to *MPC* + *Tax*. Since the tax equals the pollution cost, the sum *MPC* + *Tax* would equal *MSC*. Firms would then base output decisions on the *MPC* + *Tax* curve, which is exactly the same as the *MSC* curve.

The result is that firms would find Q_B to be the best output rate. And, as you have seen before, Q_B is the best amount from the viewpoint of the entire society. That is, at Q_B, the *MSC* curve crosses the *MSB* curve. Marginal social costs are equal to marginal social benefits and resources are allocated in the best possible way.

Checkpoint

Content Check

1. Explain the difference between marginal social cost and marginal private cost.
2. How do laws that make pollution illegal affect a supplier's level of production?
3. How do taxes on output affect a firm's output decision?

What Do You Think Now?

Reread *What Do You Think?* in the Section Two Focus. Then answer the following questions:

4. If a company is polluting the environment, should it be forced to shut down? Why or why not?

FOCUS

Section Three

The Shifting of Benefits

What Do You Think?

The Kelinsky family across the street just finished having a professional landscaping firm redo their yard. The new trees and shrubs and flowers make quite a showplace. The Kelinsky's are very happy with the results and their increased enjoyment of their yard. How might others benefit as well?

What's Ahead?

There are times when the overall benefits from an activity are greater than the benefits to just those who are directly involved. Economics can help you understand such situations and how governments encourage these positive externalities.

Terms to Know

positive externality

subsidy

POSITIVE EXTERNALITIES

positive externality the result when *benefits* are shifted to people who are not directly involved with the production or consumption of a good

A ***positive externality*** is the result when *benefits* are shifted to people who are not directly involved with the production or consumption of a good. There are situations when third parties benefit from an economic activity, even though they are not directly involved in it. This means that the social benefits of the activity are higher than the private benefits. It may be hard to believe that you ever get something for nothing, but it is possible. Unfortunately, though, there may be fewer cases of positive externalities than of negative ones.

Mass Transportation Can Create Positive Externalities

People who live in big cities that have mass transportation systems may enjoy a positive spillover from these systems. When people use the mass transit system rather than driving private cars, there is less air pollution. Other people in the city, even those who don't use the mass transportation system, benefit because of the cleaner air. The benefit from the system is greater than just the benefit to direct users. This positive externality results in social benefits that are greater than private benefits.

Individual Activities Can Create Positive Externalities

Consider again the family next door. Suppose they decide to spend some of their time and money fixing up their house and yard. They build a garage big enough for their trailer and their son's bicycle and other toys. They paint the outside of the house and improve their yard. They get some benefits from doing these things. The property is more enjoyable for their personal use, and the value of their property goes up. But, there is a spillover of benefits to others as well. Your family and other neighbors will get some benefits. You will enjoy the use of your own yard more if there is a more pleasant view next door. If the people next door improve their house and property, the neighborhood is improved and your house becomes more valuable. So, the social benefits of the improvements made by one household are greater than just the private benefits.

Education and Health Care Create Positive Externalities

You will get many private benefits from your education. You are more likely to enjoy a wider variety of activities as you get more education. You will have a better understanding of the world around you, and you probably will earn more money. But, education also provides some external benefits. As more people are educated, the number of crimes tends to decrease. There is a likelihood that welfare payments will decrease. And, the democratic process works better when people are better educated, because they are more able to understand issues. While you get private benefits from your education, the rest of society gets some benefits, too. So, the social benefits are higher than the private benefits.

There also are positive externalities from many types of medical care. When one person is inoculated against an illness, that person clearly gets a private benefit. But, other members of society benefit, too, because there will be less chance of their getting that illness. Again, the social benefits are higher than the private benefits that go just to the person who is inoculated.

Economic Dilemma

HO-HO-HO OR BAH HUMBUG?

Every year in December during the Christmas season, many families decorate the outside of their homes with lights and other displays. It is not uncommon to find one or more homes in a given area that really "go all out." They may hang thousands of lights, display an animated Santa Claus, or play Christmas music over a loud speaker.

Some people so enjoy seeing such displays that they drive for miles to see what displays people have put up. Occasionally, these drives lead to massive traffic jams. People sometimes have trouble getting to their own homes due to the congestion. Some residents complain about the noise, the light, and the damage to their own property caused by the spectators who come to view the displays of a few neighbors.

Should such displays be encouraged or discouraged? Think about both the positive and the negative externalities that are involved. What suggestions do you have for solving this dilemma?

ANALYSIS OF POSITIVE EXTERNALITIES

In this section on positive externalities, assume that the only costs involved are private costs. That is, assume that marginal social costs and marginal private costs are exactly the same *(MSC = MPC)*. When there are positive spillovers, the social benefits are greater than the private benefits. So, the marginal social benefits curve is above the marginal private benefits curve. This is shown in Figure 12-6.

Figure 12-6

Positive Externalities and Marginal Benefits

Positive externalities cause marginal social benefits *(MSB)* to be greater than marginal private benefits *(MPB)*. The market system allocates too few resources to the production of this product. Only Q_E units are produced when the best rate of output is Q_B. ***Why is the Q_E rate of output too small?***

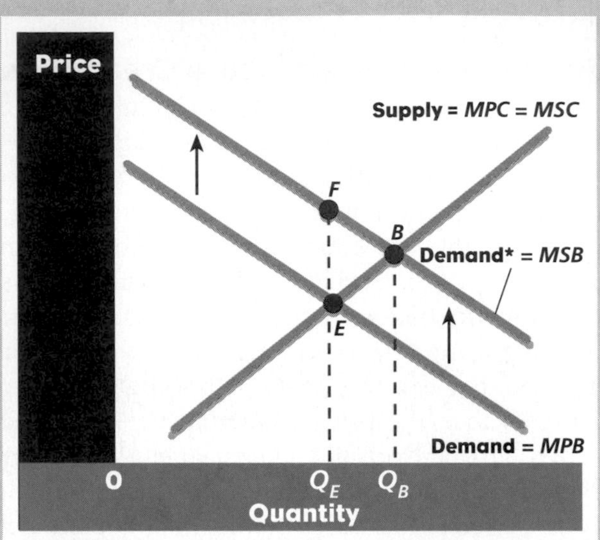

The competitive market economy will fail to take the social benefits into account. Only private benefits will be considered. The result is that firms will produce, and people will buy, the amount shown as Q_E in Figure 12-6. This is where marginal private benefits and costs are equal.

But, from the view of the whole society, Q_E is too little of the good. The marginal benefits to society are greater than the marginal costs of producing the amount represented by Q_E. As you saw in Figure 12-2, this means that more resources should be allocated to this type of production. In Figure 12-6, the amount by which the marginal social benefit is greater than the marginal social cost is the distance *FE*.

The best rate of output can be found only by comparing the marginal social cost with the marginal social benefit. The demand curve labeled *Demand* = MSB* shows the demand that would result if all of society were included, including third parties. Since there are benefits to third parties in cases of positive spillovers, *Demand** is above the demand curve that includes only private benefits.

When you compare the marginal social cost with the marginal social benefit, you see that the best rate of production is Q_B units. This is the rate where *Demand** crosses the supply curve at Point *B*. Society's resources are allocated in the best way when Q_B units are produced.

PUBLIC POLICY FOR POSITIVE EXTERNALITIES

subsidy
a payment made by the government to encourage some activity

Activities that have positive externalities should be encouraged by society. The government can encourage such activities by subsidizing them. A ***subsidy*** is a payment made by the government to encourage some activity. A subsidy is the opposite of a tax. For example, participants in a market transaction can be given money to get them to make or buy more of the goods that yield positive externalities.

Subsidies are given for a number of activities. Think about the examples used for positive spillovers. Education gets very big subsidies. Education in public schools from kindergarten through high school is nearly free for most people. Even postsecondary education in technical schools, nursing schools, and colleges is subsidized. Tuition fees usually do not cover the full costs of education in such schools. Sometimes the subsidy goes directly to the supplier, such as a public school system. But, it can also go to the consumer through student loan programs, for example. The government also provides large subsidies for medical programs and mass transit. In many geographical areas, government programs have been used to help families or businesses pay for the costs of improving property.

In Figure 12-7 on page 314, you can see how subsidies can work on either the supply side or the demand side. Graph *A* shows a subsidy of *BC* dollars per unit for consumers. With the subsidy, consumers get benefits from consuming the product and from the subsidy. This shifts the demand curve to *Demand**, and the best rate of output (Q_B) results.

Graph *B* of Figure 12-7 shows what would happen if the subsidy were given to suppliers instead. The subsidy to suppliers would lower the cost of production so that the supply curve would shift to *Supply**. *Supply** crosses the original

Global Economy

POLLUTION WITHOUT BORDERS

In 1978, researchers predicted "that the frozen continent would be the world's canary-in-a-coal-mine, showing the early signs that the climate is warming." In 1995, a chunk of ice the size of Rhode Island broke off the Larsen ice shelf on the Antarctic peninsula. A few months later, a large crack, 30 feet wide and 40 miles long, appeared in the ice shelf, another ominous sign to scientists who worry about global warming.

There is concern that as the ice shelves of Antarctica melt, the winds that blow over the ice of Antarctica will be warmer and potentially melt a portion of the continents' ice cover. If only 10 percent of that ice melts, it is predicted that sea levels worldwide could rise by 12 to 30 feet. Think about what this would mean for the thousands of cities around the world in coastal areas.

Perhaps the greatest cause of global warming (if indeed it is taking place—which is not certain) is the accumulation of carbon dioxide and other gases. These gases stem mainly from the burning of coal, gas, and oil. Pollution does not recognize political boundaries between countries. The air pollution caused by traffic in Detroit drifts readily into Canada. The emission of greenhouse gases such as carbon dioxide, methane, and chlorofluorocarbons, may contribute to global warming no matter whether they come from Germany, Japan, the United States, or Brazil.

demand at Point *A*. So, with the subsidy to suppliers, market forces would make sure Q_B units would be produced. And, as you have seen several times now, Q_B is the best rate of output. At that rate, resources are allocated in the best way.

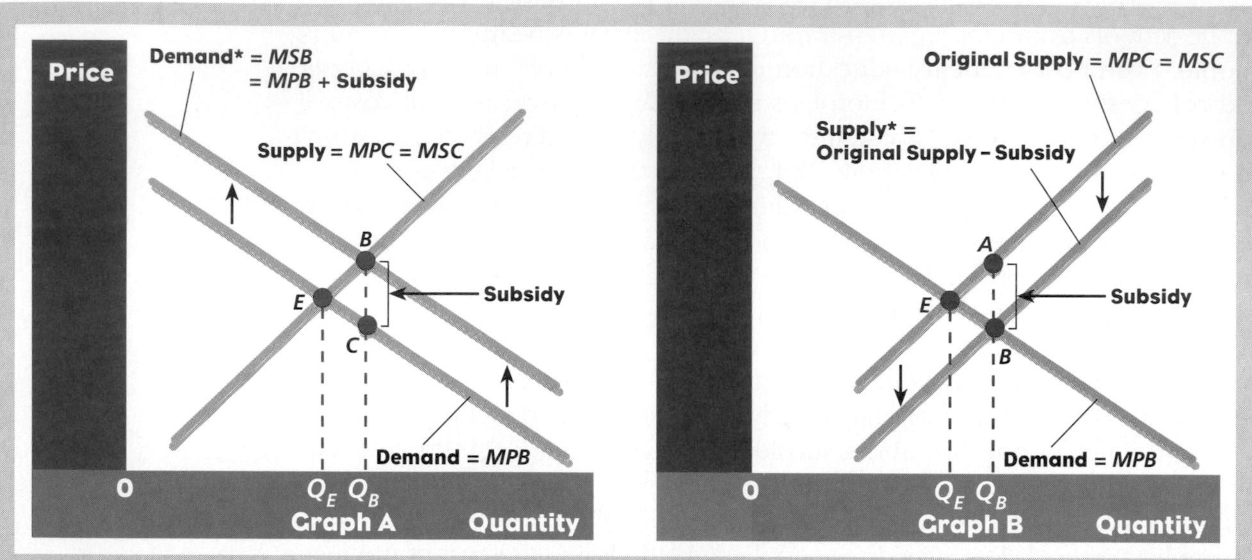

A Subsidy Will Affect the Amount Produced and Consumed

A government subsidy to consumers, Graph *A*, or to producers, Graph *B*, can correct the misallocation of resources due to a positive externality. In either case, output would be increased from Q_E units to the best rate of output, Q_B. ***If too great of a subsidy were given in the cases described in these graphs, what would be the result?***

Checkpoint

Content Check

1. Explain the difference between marginal social benefits and marginal private benefits.
2. How do subsidies to suppliers affect a supplier's level of production?
3. How do subsidies to consumers encourage activities that have positive externalities?

What Do You Think Now?

Reread *What Do You Think?* in the Section Three Focus. Then answer the following question:

4. When one family makes its property more attractive, how might others benefit as well?

F O C U S

Section Four

Sometimes Having a Single Supplier Is Best

What Do You Think?

For most households there is a single supplier of electric power. This is due, in part, to the high cost of the equipment that is necessary to generate and distribute electricity. Would you, or society in general, be better served by having competition in the supply of electric power?

What's Ahead?

In the United States, we generally have favored a competitive free market economy. Overall, the results have been good. However, there are times when a single supplier and no competition may be better. In this section, you will learn about two such situations: the provision of public goods and the case of natural monopolies.

Term to Know

exclusion principle

PUBLIC GOODS

The market system does not always give good signals about how much should be produced. Either too much or too little may be produced if the market is left alone. A special class of goods that if left alone the market would fail to provide at all, even though society wants them, are public goods.

Everyone Benefits from Public Goods

You will recall that public goods and services are used by the whole society. To expand on this definition a little, public goods are goods that cannot be sold one unit at a time to individuals. Once the good is available for one person to consume, it is available for everyone to consume. An example of a public good is national defense. Everyone gets some benefit from national defense. Some people get more and some get less, but the same amount of benefit is available for everyone.

FOCUS

Section One
The Labor Market

Terms to Know
- demand for labor
- wage rate
- derived demand
- supply of labor
- equilibrium wage

What Do You Think?

Bill and Sheri Lati own a messenger service in a large city. They hire people to ride bikes throughout the city to deliver small parcels to various offices. Most of the deliveries involve the medical, legal, and financial sectors of the economy, so confidentiality and reliability are important to the success of the business. The work demands good physical fitness and a thorough knowledge of the city. Lately, the Latis have been having trouble hiring enough messengers to meet the delivery demands of their customers. What might cause this difficulty and how might Bill and Sheri hire more people?

What's Ahead?

Labor is one of the four factors of production in the economy. Each company has some demand for labor to use in the production of the products or services it sells. There is also a supply of labor. Each of us has an equal amount of time to use (24 hours a day). We must decide how much of that time to use for work and how much to use for other activities. In this section, you will see how the forces of demand and supply determine how much labor is hired and at what wage rate labor is paid.

THE DEMAND FOR LABOR

Just as there is a market for cars or stereos, so is there a labor market. People are not bought and sold, but their time and skills are. Suppose a restaurant hires you to wait on customers. The manager doesn't buy you but does buy (pay for) some of your time and ability to take and process orders correctly. So it is with all jobs. A school buys someone's time and ability to act as a teacher. A steel mill buys an engineer's time and ability to watch over a production process.

Determining the Demand for Labor

The ***demand for labor*** is the amount of labor that firms would want to hire at various wage rates. The ***wage rate*** is the price paid for each unit of labor. The amount of labor demanded depends on the demand for the good or service produced. One hundred years ago, when people used horses instead of cars for transportation, blacksmiths were in high demand. As cars came into use, fewer services of blacksmiths were needed. Thus, the demand for blacksmiths declined. But, at the same time, the need for skilled workers in the automobile factories rose. Due to the higher demand for cars, there was a higher demand for workers to make those cars.

demand for labor
the amount of labor that firms would want to hire at various wage rates

wage rate
the price paid for each unit of labor

The demand for labor is called *derived demand*. ***Derived demand*** is a demand for an input that is dependent on the demand for the product that the input helps to produce. Demand for the company's product clearly determines the company's demand for labor. If consumers do not want to buy the product, the company will not need to hire any labor. The firm needs labor to produce what it wants to sell.

derived demand
demand for an input that is dependent on the demand for the product that the input helps to produce

The level of productivity of the workers themselves also helps determine the demand for labor. *Labor productivity* is measured by the amount of output produced per hour of labor input. Productive labor will be more in demand than unproductive labor. Keep this important point in mind. Anything you can do that will increase your productivity will help you in the labor market. Education and training programs are two means of increasing your productivity.

Wage Rate and Quantity of Labor Demanded

An inverse relationship exists between the quantity of labor a business will hire and the wage rate it must pay. If the wage rate is high, businesses will hire less labor. Perhaps you can already guess why this is true. First, at a high wage, it is cheaper to use methods of production that employ less labor. More equipment, more machines, and even robots may be used. Second, as the wage level goes up, the cost of production goes up and the product's price is likely to rise. As the product's price goes up, fewer units will be demanded. This means there will be less demand for labor to produce the product. The inverse relationship between the wage rate and the quantity of labor demanded is illustrated in Figure 13-1 on page 328.

active in the labor force. You can see that the height of the bars for women has been rising. For men, the height of the bars has been falling.

BALANCING LABOR DEMAND AND SUPPLY

You have learned that product markets are in balance, or equilibrium, when the quantity demanded and quantity supplied are equal. The same is true in the labor market. When the quantity of labor demanded equals the quantity of labor supplied, the labor market is in balance. That is, the labor market is in equilibrium where the demand curve crosses the supply curve.

Remember that the demand curve for labor slopes downward to the right. Companies will demand more labor hours at a lower wage than at a higher wage. For supply, the relationship is reversed. The supply curve for labor slopes upward from left to right. More labor will be offered at a higher wage than at a lower wage.

Look at Figure 13-4. Suppose that the wage rate is $8 an hour. You see that the distance between the points marked *A* and *B* shows the excess of the quantity of labor supplied over the quantity demanded. In other words, the amount of labor demanded is less than the amount of labor supplied. When this happens, there is downward pressure on the wage rate, as indicated by the large arrow pointing down. As the wage rate falls, the quantity of labor demanded goes up (movement to the right *along* the demand curve). At the same time, the quantity of labor supplied falls (movement to the left *along* the supply curve).

Now suppose the wage rate is $3 an hour. Can you explain what will happen at this relatively low wage? Think about it step by step just as you did for the high $8 wage. At $3 an hour, companies will want to hire more labor hours than people will be willing to offer. The distance between points *C* and *D* shows how much greater the quantity demanded is than the quantity supplied at the $3 wage. Businesses will not be able to hire all the labor they want. Some companies will start to offer a higher wage to attract workers. This will cause upward pressure on the wage rate, as indicated by the large

Figure 13-4

Market Equilibrium for Labor

The market equilibrium wage is found where the supply of labor curve crosses the demand for labor curve at Point *E*. The equilibrium wage is $6, and the amount of labor employed is 7,000 labor hours. At a wage above equilibrium ($8), the quantity of labor supplied is greater than the quantity of labor demanded. There is downward pressure on the wage rate. At a wage below equilibrium ($3), the quantity of labor demanded is greater than the quantity supplied. Thus, there is upward pressure on the wage rate. ***What will happen in the labor market if the wage rate is $7?***

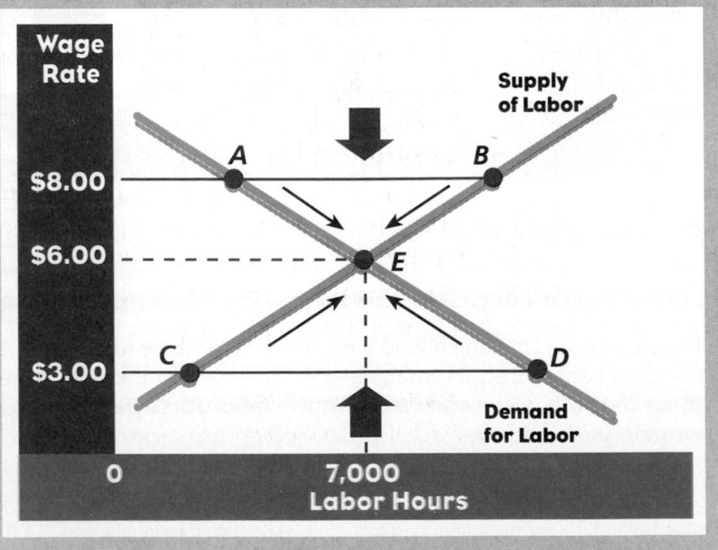

arrow pointing up. As wage goes up, more hours of labor will be offered (movement to the right *along* the supply curve). At the same time, less labor will be demanded (movement to the left *along* the demand curve).

At the high wage, there is downward pressure on the wage rate. At the low wage, there is upward pressure on the wage rate. You should expect that, somewhere in between these two wage rates, there is a balance between the quantity demanded and the quantity supplied. Look at the wage rate of $6 an hour. At that wage, the amount of labor demanded is 7,000 hours. And, at the $6 wage, the amount of labor supplied is also 7,000 hours. Demand and supply are in balance. The labor market is in equilibrium at the wage where the amount of labor demanded is equal to the amount of labor supplied. So, the labor market equilibrium is found where the supply and demand curves cross. This is Point *E* in Figure 13-4. The ***equilibrium wage*** is the wage rate at which the quantity of labor demanded equals the quantity of labor supplied.

equilibrium wage the wage rate at which the quantity of labor demanded equals the quantity of labor supplied

Checkpoint

Content Check

1. Why do you think there has been a rise in the demand for workers with good computer skills?
2. A city official in New Orleans commented in the mid-1990s that it is impossible to hire good police officers for what was the current wage. What could the city have done to attract more people to this job market?
3. Draw fictitious labor demand and labor supply curves to illustrate a labor market. Label your graph carefully and indicate the equilibrium wage as well as the amount of labor that would be employed.

What Do You Think Now?

Reread *What Do You Think?* in the Section One Focus. Then answer the following questions:

4. Do you think that if Bill and Sheri increase the wage rate they offer for new employees it will help their problem? Explain.
5. What else, besides increasing wages, could Sheri and Bill do to find more messengers?

FOCUS

Section Two
Other Factors Affecting the Labor Market

What Do You Think?

Students at Northview High School recently participated in a letter writing campaign to members of Congress concerning the minimum wage. They urged the members of Congress who represent them to push for an increase of $2 an hour in the minimum wage because they feel that student workers in their community do not earn enough. Do you agree with the students at Northview?

Terms to Know

- monopsony
- minimum wage law
- labor union
- collective bargaining
- injunction
- closed shop
- union shop

What's Ahead?

Under certain conditions, wages may stay above or below the equilibrium that would be established by a free and competitive labor market. We have been assuming that the labor market functions in a free and competitive way. But, this may not always be true. A variety of noncompetitive forces may cause wages to be higher or lower than this equilibrium. In this section, you will learn about three such forces.

MONOPSONY IN THE LABOR MARKET

One noncompetitive force in the labor market occurs when a given labor market is dominated by one employer. That single employer may have enough influence over the market to keep wages low, since laborers either work for that employer or not at all. This influence is sometimes called a *monopsonistic influence*. A ***monopsony*** is a market in which there is only one buyer. (It is similar to the word *monopoly* which means one seller.) If there is only one buyer of labor (one employer) in a labor market, that employer can influence wage rates considerably.

monopsony
a market in which there is only one buyer

This often happens in university towns where the community is small relative to the size of the university. When this is true, an abundant supply of people want sales, clerical, and other such jobs. Students, spouses of students and faculty, and other people from the town compete for jobs. Most jobs in such an area are with the university. A university may employ as much as 50 or 60 percent of the labor force of a town.

As a result of the abundant labor supply in university-dominated towns, nonprofessional jobs with universities tend to be low paying. In large cities where a university represents a small part of the total population, wages for university workers are likely to be more competitive.

MINIMUM WAGE LAWS

The second noncompetitive force that can affect the wage rate is a minimum wage law. A ***minimum wage law*** is a law that sets the lowest wage that can be paid for certain kinds of work. The Fair Labor Standards Act of 1938 marked the beginning of a national minimum wage in the United States. Some states had their own minimum wage laws even before 1938. In 1950, the minimum wage was just $0.75 an hour. In 1956, it was increased to $1.00 an hour. By the late 1960s, the minimum wage was $1.60 an hour. Starting in 1974, there were increases nearly every year that resulted in a minimum wage of $4.25 an hour beginning April 1, 1991. There is considerable debate about increasing the minimum wage above this level.

minimum wage law
a law that sets the lowest wage that can be paid for certain kinds of work

The Reasoning Behind Minimum Wage Laws

Why would Congress want to set a minimum wage? One reason usually given is that a minimum wage helps provide low-income families with more money to spend. The reasoning Congress seems to use is as follows. If the market wage is $4 an hour and a person works 40 hours per week, the income earned will be $160 (40 hours × $4/hour). But, if the government forces employers to pay $4.25 an hour, the income earned will be $170 (40 hours × $4.25/hour).

At this point in your study of economics, perhaps you already can see a problem with the reasoning that a higher minimum wage means more money to spend. You now know that the demand curve for labor slopes down to the right. This means that if the wage increases, the amount of labor that companies will demand decreases. Fewer labor hours will be employed at a higher wage than at a lower wage. So, when Congress forces the minimum wage up, you should expect that some low-wage workers will be laid off and some may end up working fewer hours. Those who keep their jobs with no cut in their work hours will earn more. But, some workers will earn less or even nothing at all.

Analyzing the Effect of Minimum Wage Laws

To analyze this problem, draw a graph on a piece of paper. Label the vertical axis *wage rate* and the horizontal axis *labor hours*. Draw a downward sloping line for the demand for labor and an upward sloping line for the supply of labor. Make a small circle where these two lines cross and label it *E*. This is the equilibrium point where the labor demand and supply are in balance. Draw a line from Point *E* to the vertical axis. This shows the equilibrium wage, or the market wage. Drawing a line down from *E* to the horizontal axis shows the amount of labor hired at that wage.

Now draw a horizontal line across the graph above the equilibrium wage (that is, above where demand crosses supply). This line represents the government's minimum wage. How much labor will firms want to hire at this wage? You can tell from your demand curve. It is less than the number hired at the equilibrium wage, isn't it? Thus, fewer labor hours would be employed with the minimum wage than without it.

Compare your graph with the one in Figure 13-5. The size and exact shape of the curves may differ, but your graph should look very much like Figure 13-5.

Figure 13-5

Minimum Wage and Supply and Demand for Labor

The minimum wage (W_M) is set by government above the market equilibrium wage (W_E). At the minimum wage, fewer units of labor will be employed, but those who still have jobs get a higher wage per hour. ***If the government mandates a minimum wage at W_M, how much unemployment will result?***

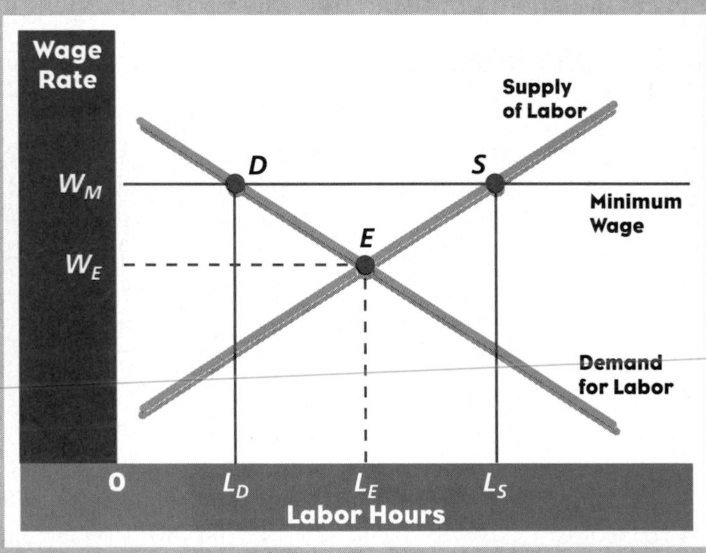

In Figure 13-5 you see that at the minimum wage (W_M) the quantity of labor demanded will be at Point *D*. This is L_D labor hours on the horizontal axis. But, at that wage, the quantity of labor supplied will be at Point *S*, or L_S labor hours on the horizontal axis. The quantity of labor supplied will be greater than the quantity demanded, so there will be unemployment. Some people who have jobs at the market wage (W_E) are pushed out of those jobs.

What groups of people will be hurt the most? Those who are not skilled, that is, the less productive workers. Young people make up a large part of this group. They have yet to learn productive and marketable skills. This is why unemployment is particularly high among teenagers. And, the minimum wage makes this problem worse than it would be otherwise.

LABOR UNIONS

Labor unions represent a third noncompetitive force that can affect the wage rate. The labor movement came about because workers wanted more control over working conditions and other job-related matters. Many workers felt that the market system gave too much power to management and not enough to labor. Employees had only their own labor with which to bargain. Laborers had to work for whatever management would pay or quit. Each employee acting alone had very little bargaining power. If management decided fewer workers were needed, some were fired. Workers had the choice of either accepting the working conditions and hours set by management or not working at all. Often, the choices were not good ones for the workers. Because they had to support themselves and their families, they were forced to work despite the conditions or wages.

Workers Band Together

How did workers try to solve their problem? They started to band together in groups called *labor unions.* A ***labor union*** is an organization of workers formed to give workers greater bargaining power in their dealings with management. The first labor union was a group of tailors in Philadelphia. They called themselves the Noble and Holy Order of the Knights of Labor.

labor union
an organization of workers formed to give workers greater bargaining power in their dealings with management

Economic Dilemma

FAIR PAY OR FOUL?

It is generally accepted that there should not be pay discrimination according to factors, such as gender or race, that do not directly relate to the ability to perform a specific job. Thus, a male teacher and a female teacher with similar experience and training should earn the same amount for the same work. A male nurse should earn the same as a female nurse with a comparable background.

Yet it is well documented that, on average, women earn less than men. Some people have argued that the differential is caused by women being employed predominately in lower paying occupations. But, how can we arrive at a fair compensation mechanism when the jobs are different?

The concept of "comparable worth" has been suggested as a solution to this problem. This approach says that the pay for various jobs should be based on the skills required for a job, the level of responsibility that the job entails, and the amount of effort required to perform the job. While it is difficult to quantify these three aspects of a job, doing so is seen as a step in the right direction. A number of states now have comparable worth laws, most notably the state of Washington, where much of the original impetus for this approach began.

Fairness is a hard goal to achieve because our definitions of what is fair often differ. As we try to reach for fairness in compensation of employees, the stumbling block will be the difficulty in identifying and comparing required job skills, responsibility, and effort.

Economic Spotlight

THE ENDORSEMENT GAME SLAM DUNKS OR SLIPUPS?

It bounced up, then down, and then back up again. No, it's not a basketball. It's Michael Jordan's marketability as a high-powered endorser. When Jordan decided to hang up his basketball shoes and go looking for new challenges, he sent Nike Corporation stock prices on a roller-coaster ride that would last for a year and a half. Nike, which had signed Jordan to a lucrative, multiyear athletic-shoe endorsement, watched its stock drop from $80 to $42 a share when the superstar decided he had shot his last free-throw.

On October 6, 1993, Jordan retired the Chicago Bull's number 23 jersey that had seen him through three consecutive NBA championships. His decision also threatened to send Nike's highly profitable "Air Jordan" marketing campaign into retirement. Stating that he was no longer challenged by basketball (and that he wished to shelter his family from the media circus surrounding the tragic murder of his father), Jordan said good-bye to basketball.

But, only a few months into his "retirement," Jordan sent Nike stocks on the rebound when he announced that he would try his hand at major league baseball. Jordan's career decision came just before the onset of the longest major league baseball strike in history. Refusing to cross the picket line, Jordan returned to basketball, rejoining the Chicago Bulls in 1995. Jordan's double-dribble from basketball to baseball and back again to basketball had sent advertisers and their stockholders into a frenzy.

Much of the wild speculation subsided with Jordan's return to basketball. Today, the hoopster is among the world's highest paid advertising endorsers, influencing $300 million to $400 million in annual sales at his peak and making $31 million a year from commercials and other endorsement deals. But, why is Michael Jordan such a moneymaker for advertisers? Could it be because of his charm and quiet confidence? Could it be because he takes seriously his status as a role model for youth everywhere? The truth is it's Michael Jordan the person that is so appealing to consumers.

The superstar refuses to let fame go to his head. "My mother is my root, my foundation," says Jordan. "She planted the seed that I base my life on, and that is the belief that the ability to achieve starts in your mind." Apparently, Michael Jordan has made up his mind to be a winner —on and off the court.

In 1869, the union was founded in secret. But, the union gradually came into the open, and by 1886, it had nearly 1 million members. Also in 1886, Samuel Gompers founded the American Federation of Labor (AFL). The AFL was formed as a voluntary association of craft unions such as carpenters' and bricklayers' unions. Even though the Knights of Labor died out by 1917, the AFL has survived to this day. In 1955, the AFL merged with the Congress of Industrial Organizations (CIO). The CIO had been formed 20 years earlier during the Great Depression under the leadership of John L. Lewis. The CIO was made up of industrial unions such as the steelworkers' and the rubber workers' unions.

The formation of unions helped to balance out the bargaining power between labor and management. While management didn't need any one worker, it did need workers as a group. While a single worker had little power, workers as a group did have economic power. When workers belonged to a union, individual workers no longer negotiated working conditions with management. Benefits such as wages, hours, vacation time, and insurance coverage were determined through collective bargaining. ***Collective bargaining*** is the process of having the union negotiate with management to determine the terms of employment for all workers rather than having each worker negotiate separately. If management did not listen to workers' demands, workers could threaten a strike—the ultimate union weapon.

collective bargaining
the process of having the union negotiate with management to determine the terms of employment for all workers rather than having each worker negotiate separately

Management Responds

Management, of course, did not like the formation of unions. It struck back by asking the courts to say that unions were conspiracies and should be outlawed. The courts, however, ruled that unions were not illegal. Employers then turned to other weapons of their own, such as injunctions, yellow-dog contracts, and the use of antitrust laws.

An ***injunction*** is a court order to stop someone from doing something (or to make someone *do* something). If unions acted in ways management did not like, management would try to have an injunction issued against the union. And, management usually succeeded. The penalties for violating an injunction included fines and jail sentences. Management also forced workers to sign agreements before they were hired. A *yellow-dog contract* was a contract workers had to sign before they were hired saying that they would not join a union. Anyone who wouldn't sign did not get hired.

injunction
a court order to stop someone from doing something (or to make someone *do* something)

Finally, management used the Sherman Antitrust Act to stop unions. The Sherman Antitrust Act was passed partially to make combinations that were in restraint of trade illegal. The law was aimed at big corporate businesses. But, much of its early use was against unions that used strikes to fight management. Management claimed that the unions' strike activities were in restraint of trade because the strikes limited the flow of goods across state lines.

Legislation Is Passed

By the early 1930s, public opinion began to favor labor unions. Public opinion was against business, because many people blamed business for the Depression. As a result, the Norris-LaGuardia Act was passed in 1932. The act held that labor activity was not in violation of antitrust laws and that yellow-dog contracts were illegal. The act also greatly limited business use of injunctions against unions. This opened the door for the development of labor unions. The stress between labor and management, however, increased. Armed conflicts between labor and the people hired by management to keep unions in check were common.

Partly as a result of such conflicts, the National Labor Relations Act, also called the Wagner Act, was passed in 1935. One of the most important pieces of labor legislation, this bill defined management practices that were unfair to labor. Management could no longer interfere with or restrain union activities. It could not discriminate against workers who wanted to join unions and could not act against workers who filed charges against business. Employers had to recognize and bargain with unions that were properly formed. The law also established the National Labor Relations Board that set up procedures for conducting union elections.

As a result of the National Labor Relations Act, union activity grew. There were restraints on management but almost none on unions. But, after World War II, unions began a flurry of strike activity and public opinion started to turn against unions. In 1947, the Taft-Hartley Act was passed. This act specified which union actions were unfair labor practices. For example, the closed shop was made illegal. A ***closed shop*** is a business that agrees to hire only those workers who are members of a union. A union shop was and is still legal, however. A ***union shop*** is a business that requires workers to join a union shortly after taking a job. The Taft-Hartley Act also set up emergency procedures to allow government to interfere with union activity if labor problems threatened national security.

closed shop
a business that agrees to hire only those workers who are members of a union

union shop
a business that requires workers to join a union shortly after taking a job

Today, there is a better balance between the power of unions and the power of management. People still join unions, and union growth is greatest in white-collar jobs such as teaching. Overall, however, the percentage of all nonagricultural workers who belong to unions has declined.

Checkoint

Content Check

1. Under what conditions might there be a monopsony in the labor market?
2. Why do labor unions exist?
3. How does collective bargaining work?

What Do You Think Now?

Reread *What Do You Think?* in the Section Two Focus. Then answer the following questions:

4. Who ends up being hurt the most by a minimum wage?
5. Who ends up benefiting from a minimum wage?

F O C U S

Section Three
Interest: A Source of Income and an Expense

What Do You Think?

Many of you may have elderly grandparents who have savings from which they get interest payments. For some people, this interest is an important source of income. The higher the interest rate, the higher the income of people with interest income. Do you think high interest rates are a good thing?

What's Ahead?

The income that individuals get depends on the quality and quantity of the factors of production over which they have control. We can work for wages to earn income. In fact, most of the income earned in the United States is labor income. We also may own stocks in corporations. This allows us to share in the profits earned by those firms. We may own land or the right to natural resources which gives us rental income. We also can get interest income from lending money to people who invest it in productive machinery or from investing the money ourselves. Interest income is the second most important source of income in the United States. In this section, you will learn about different ways of looking at interest and its role in the economy.

Terms to Know

interest

inflation

prime rate

corporate bond rate

federal funds rate

discount rate

INTEREST INCOME

Interest is the price paid for the use of money. The concept of interest dates back at least to biblical times when all payments for the use of money were considered evil. Money was thought of as useless and non-productive. The collection of money for the use of money was called *usury,* and it was considered sinful and illegal. Not until the development of modern business did people accept interest as a justifiable charge for the use of money. Modern businesses often must borrow large sums of

interest
the price paid for the use of money

Factors That Influence the Interest Rate

On television and radio, as well as in newspapers and magazines, we see and hear many articles and reports about the rate of interest. Actually, there are many different interest rates in the economy. You may have heard of the prime rate, the corporate bond rate, or the federal funds rate. Every lending market has its own interest rate. The rate in each market depends upon many factors. Among these are the time period involved, the risk, the rate of inflation, the costs of making the loan, and the tax treatment of interest.

In general, the shorter the time period of the loan, the lower the interest rate. Lenders prefer a shorter time period because there is less chance of changes that would affect the profitability of the loan. Loans that extend over long periods of time reduce the lender's ability to change and to adjust to changing economic events.

Global Economy

NAFTA DRIVES DEMAND FOR LABOR

The long-term consequences of the North American Free Trade Agreement (NAFTA) may not be known fully until well into the twenty-first century. But, it appears that this agreement, passed in the mid-1990s, is having the beneficial effects that were widely anticipated. There have been ups and downs, especially in the case of Mexico's emerging economy. But, overall, the positive outcomes have dominated.

In Canada, increased employment has resulted as Canadian exports have risen. In addition, the demand for labor in Canada has been bolstered by big expansion in the automotive sector. For example, Ford spent about $2.2 billion to expand production of minivans, trucks, and engines in Ontario. Chrysler also expanded production in Canada. In 1994, Chrysler produced in Canadian facilities a record 695,000 vehicles, mostly minivans and LH models.

Similar events have unfolded in the Mexican economy. In the first eight months of NAFTA, U.S. and Canadian firms invested $2.4 billion in Mexico. Ford spent $60 million to revamp its Cuautitlán plant near Mexico City to produce small cars and trucks for global sales. Ford's export of cars from Mexico to the United States and its export of vehicles from the United States to Mexico were up dramatically in the first year of NAFTA. The president of Ford's Mexico operations commented, "We've created jobs here and in the U.S."

Other positive results have been evident for the United States. Food and beverage producers, manufacturers of consumer goods, and agricultural businesses have benefited. For example, Proctor & Gamble experienced a 75 percent increase in exports to Mexico in the first six months of NAFTA, and the exports to Mexico of Archer-Daniels-Midland tripled in NAFTA's first year.

Risk is another factor that influences interest rates. For example, suppose you have the choice of lending your money to IBM or to the Wickey Wackey Widget Corporation. Because IBM is a large, well-established firm, it is more likely that it will repay your money in full and on time. You might then lend money to IBM at a relatively low interest rate. But, you will charge the Wickey Wackey Widget Corporation more since you can't be as sure of repayment in full and on time. There is a general rule in lending money: The higher the risk, the higher the interest.

The rate of inflation also influences interest rates. We will discuss inflation in more detail later, but for now we will define it in broad terms. ***Inflation*** is a rise in the average level of prices. You can see quickly why inflation influences interest rates. Suppose the average level of prices increases 10 percent a year. Next year it will take $110 to buy what $100 buys today. If you are loaned $100 today at 5 percent interest, you will owe $105 a year from now. But, that $105 a year from now won't even be enough to buy what the $100 buys today. It will take $110 to do so. So, the lender will not earn any real interest and, in fact, will lose buying power. It follows, then, that lenders will not want to lend money unless the interest rate is greater than the inflation rate. This means that in times of high inflation, we should expect high interest rates.

inflation
a rise in the average level of prices

The costs a lender has in making a loan will also influence the interest rate. There are costs involved in checking the borrower's credit and in administering the loan.

Finally, the ways in which tax laws treat different forms of interest can influence the interest rate. If a lender can get tax benefits by loaning money in some market, that market's interest rate is likely to be lower. Most of the time, a lender must pay taxes on interest that is collected. For example, if you lend IBM money by buying its bonds, you pay taxes on that interest income. But, if you lend money to the city of Tulsa by buying a bond the city issues, the interest income is tax free. So, you might be willing to lend money to Tulsa at a lower interest rate than you would to IBM. People will be more likely to lend money if the interest income is not taxed.

As you study macroeconomics in Part Three, you will see some ways that national economic policy can influence interest rates. You also will see how interest rates influence investment, productivity, and economic growth.

Particular Interest Rates

What do people in the news media mean when they refer to rising or falling interest rates? Usually, they are referring to the prime rate. The ***prime rate*** is the interest rate that banks charge their best corporate customers. Companies such as General Motors, IBM, and AT&T may be

prime rate
the interest rate that banks charge their best corporate customers

charged the prime rate. The risk involved in lending money to those firms is very small. Therefore, the prime rate is usually lower than most other interest rates. It also is often used as a standard indicator of changes in interest rates in general.

corporate bond rate
the interest rate paid on corporate bonds

Another interest rate that is commonly talked about is the corporate bond rate. As the name implies, the ***corporate bond rate*** is the interest rate paid on corporate bonds. A corporate bond is a certificate issued by a corporation promising to pay bondholders a specific amount of money by a specific date.

federal funds rate
the interest rate that banks pay to borrow from each other on a short-term basis

A third interest rate that is often reported in the news is the federal funds rate. The ***federal funds rate*** is the interest rate that banks pay to borrow from each other on a short-term basis. The time may be as short as overnight. Such loans have little risk and last for a very short time. Therefore, the federal funds rate usually stays low, even lower than the prime rate.

discount rate
the interest rate that banks must pay to borrow from the Federal Reserve System

Another rate we hear about often is the discount rate. The ***discount rate*** is the interest rate that banks must pay to borrow from the Federal Reserve System. (The Federal Reserve System and the discount rate will be discussed more fully later in this text.) The discount rate is lower than the prime rate and the other rates mentioned, but it is not available to private individuals and businesses except banks.

CONSUMER CREDIT AND INTEREST RATES

The rates charged for consumer credit are usually higher than other rates. There are three reasons for these higher rates:

1. Consumer loans have higher risk.
2. Consumer loans are costly to set up.
3. Consumer loans often run over a relatively long period of time.

Most consumer loans involve much more risk than do loans to corporations that qualify for the prime rate. The costs of checking credit and handling loan accounts are also higher for individuals. This is particularly true in comparison to the dollar amount of a loan. There may be high costs in trying to collect the balance due if the person fails to keep up with the pay ments. Also, many consumer loans are made for three or more years. It is not uncommon for people to have car loans that run four or even five years.

Consumer credit comes from credit unions, life insurance companies, commercial banks, savings and loan associations, finance companies, charge accounts, and credit cards. The interest charged by these lenders varies, so you should shop around when looking to borrow money. It will always cost you money to borrow money. But, by shopping around, you often can save. Let's look at two common examples of how it pays to shop for interest rates: buying a car and buying a house.

Buying a Car

Suppose that you have saved enough money for a down payment on a car, but you need to borrow $5,000 to make the purchase. You investigate two loan sources. A credit union will lend you the money at a 9 percent interest rate. A local finance company will lend you the same amount at a 12 percent interest rate. (A difference of 3 percent or more on a car loan is not uncommon.) Both loans are for four years. Your monthly payments and total payments for the $5,000 loan would be as follows:

	Monthly Payment	Total Payment
Finance Company (12% Interest)	$ 131.67	$6,320.16
Credit Union (9% Interest)	124.43	5,972.64
Difference in Payment	$ 7.24	$ 347.52

As you can see, there is a $347.52 savings over the four years at the lower interest rate. But, if you don't shop around, you might not borrow at the lowest rate.

Buying a House

At some point, you may want to buy a house, and finding the lowest interest rate will be important. Assume that you want to borrow $90,000 to buy a house. A home loan may be for as long as 30 years, so we will use that time period. You go to a bank and to a savings and loan to see about borrowing the money. The bank will lend you the money at 10.5 percent, and the savings and loan will lend you the money at 10 percent. This does not seem like much of a difference. But is it? Your payments on the $90,000 are summarized as follows:

	Monthly Payment	Total Payment
Bank (10.5% Interest)	$ 823.27	$296,377.20
Savings and Loan (10% Interest)...........	789.81	284,331.60
Difference in Payment..........................	$ 33.46	$ 12,045.60

A one-half of 1 percent difference in the interest rate means a difference in total payments of $12,045.60 over the 30-year loan. It may surprise you to see that even at the lower rate, you will have to pay $284,331.60 for the $90,000 home loan. The interest payments will total $194,331.60, which is more than twice the amount you will borrow. Interest can add up to a large amount of money. So, it is as important to shop around when you borrow money as it is when you make purchases.

Checkoint

Content Check

1. Why do you think people are willing to pay a price (interest) to borrow money?

2. Name three factors that may influence the rate of interest charged for a loan.

3. Would you expect the rate of interest for a family's car loan to be higher or lower than the rate paid by General Motors on a loan to expand a factory? Why?

What Do You Think Now?

Reread *What Do You Think?* in the Section Three Focus. Then answer the following questions:

4. How would the rate of interest affect the income of a retired couple who rely on their savings as a primary source of income?

5. As a potential borrower would you like to see lower interest rates? Why or why not?

Concepts in Brief

1. Labor is bought and sold in a market, very much as goods and services are bought and sold. People are not bought or sold, but their labor, skills, and time are.
2. The demand for labor can be represented by a negatively sloped labor demand curve. This means that firms will hire more units of labor at a lower wage than they will at a higher wage.
3. The supply of labor can be represented by a positively sloped labor supply curve. This means that more units of labor will be made available for work at a higher wage than will at a lower wage.
4. When the quantity of labor demanded equals the quantity of labor supplied, the labor market is in balance. This is called an *equilibrium* in the labor market. If the wage is above the market equilibrium, more labor will be supplied than will be demanded. If the wage is below the market equilibrium, the quantity of labor demanded will be greater than the quantity supplied. In either case, economic forces will push the wage toward the equilibrium.
5. The government may set a minimum wage to prevent firms from paying a wage that is considered too low. Congress periodically votes to increase the minimum wage. This puts some people out of work and reduces the hours that others work. This is particularly hard on teenagers and people with less-developed labor skills. If minimum wage earners are not laid off or do not have their hours cut back, they do earn more after increases in the minimum wage than they did before the increase.
6. Labor unions developed because management seemed to have too much control over labor. Since the late 1800s, much conflict has occurred between business managers and unions. Laws favoring both sides have been passed by Congress. Power between unions and management appears better balanced now than 100 years ago.
7. People's incomes depend on the quantity and quality of the factors of production that they control. We all have our own labor to use in whatever form of production we wish. Some people own land and capital, while others have none of these resources within their control.

PART THREE

The Macroeconomic Perspective

Overview

Section One
Macroeconomics—The Big Picture

Section Two
Composition and Uses of GDP

Section Three
A More Complete Picture of the Macroeconomy

Measuring Aggregate Economic Activity

Learning Objectives

14-1
Draw a circular flow diagram of the economy.

14-2
Identify some problems with using GDP as a measure of economic well-being.

14-3
Show how production possibilities curves represent trade-offs within GDP.

14-4
Categorize production as either consumer goods, investment goods, or government purchases.

14-5
Discuss the various uses of income.

14-6
Illustrate how government, savings, and investment fit into the circular flow diagram.

14-7
Describe how aggregate supply and aggregate demand determine macroeconomic equilibrium.

FOCUS

Section One
Macroeconomics—The Big Picture

What Do You Think?

In a certain year, the GDP of Alfrea was $4,000,000,000. Alfrea's population in that year was 200,000. Kwandera had a GDP of $6,000,000,000 in the same year. Kwandera's population was 280,000 people. Which country do you think was better off in economic terms?

What's Ahead?

In this chapter, you begin your study of the branch of economics called *macroeconomics.* In learning about macroeconomics, you will look at the total level of economic activity as well as ways of measuring and evaluating that activity. You will start in this section by learning about gross domestic product as a measure of the circular flow of economic activity. Then, you will learn about some problems with using GDP as a measure of economic well-being.

Terms to Know

macroeconomics

gross domestic product (GDP)

inflation

constant dollar GDP

barter

THE CIRCULAR FLOW OF ECONOMIC ACTIVITY

macroeconomics that part of economics that examines the behavior of the whole economy at once

Recall that ***macroeconomics*** is defined as that part of economics that examines the behavior of the whole economy at once. Think of the national economy as a circular flow, as shown in Figure 14-1. The box on the right represents households like yours. The box on the left represents the business sector of the economy. Households spend money to buy goods and services from businesses. For example, you buy CDs and tapes, ice cream, cars, radios, jeans, haircuts, and many other services and products. In each case, an exchange of money for the good or service takes place. Look at the two flows in the upper loop of the circular flow diagram. Goods and services flow from businesses to households. In exchange, money flows, in the form of consumer spending, from households to businesses. This upper loop shows the total dollar value of all the goods and services produced and sold.

What would happen if these two were the only flows in the economy? Soon households would run out of money! Businesses would have all the money, and we would have many goods and services. But, as soon as we spent all the money we had, there could be no more economic activity. The economy would quickly grind to a stop, and everyone would soon be unemployed. There would

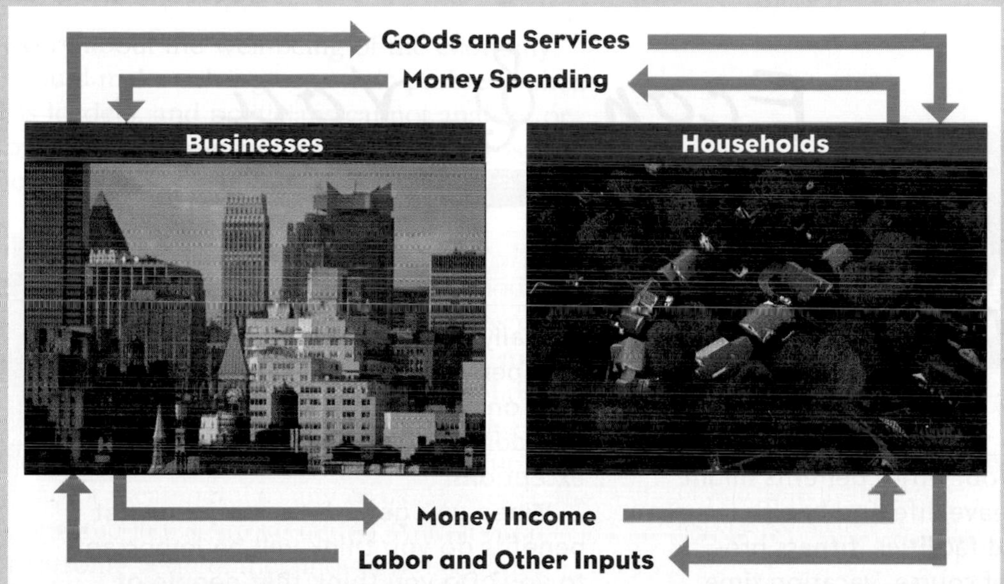

Figure 14-1

A Circular Flow Diagram of the Economy

Money flows from households to businesses in exchange for goods and services. Money flows from businesses to households in exchange for labor and other productive inputs. ***Which of these flows would include your purchase of a pair of hiking boots?***

be no production and, of course, no consumption. But, this is not what really happens. Year after year, these two flows continue, and they tend to get bigger.

The reason the flows do not stop is shown by the lower loop. You can see in Figure 14-1 that the lower loop also has two flows. One is a money flow from businesses to households. Every company has an outflow of money to individuals who provide companies with productive resources. The most obvious resource is the labor individuals provide. When people work for a business, they expect to be paid. That pay is almost always in the form of money income.

The bottom loop of the circular flow represents all the money income that is earned in the economy. It is the income earned by the people who produce the goods and services in the upper loop. This circular flow view of the national economy is a simple yet fairly accurate model of how the entire economy works. This model shows the kinds of exchanges that keep the economy going.

As we progress through this chapter, we will add to this simple model of the economy. You will see that consumers do not spend all their income. They save some of it, and you will see what happens to those savings. You will discover that businesses not only produce goods but also buy goods. You will also see that there is a very active government sector in our economy. Taxes and government spending are important parts of our economy. And, our economy operates within the context of a global economy. Near the end of this chapter, you will see a more complete circular flow model of the economy that includes these ideas.

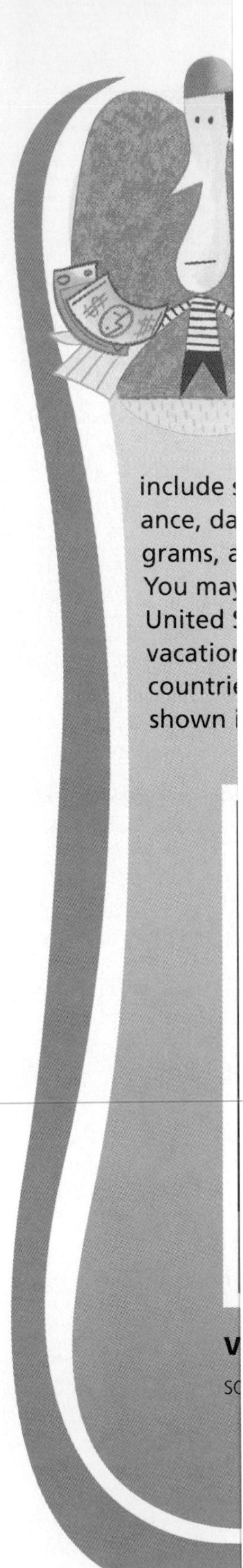

States also has a productive labor force. We have used these resources to become one of the most productive countries in the world, as measured by GDP. Many other countries, such as Pakistan, have fewer natural resources and produce much smaller levels of output.

Even countries with the same number of people and the same amount of natural resources can have very different levels of GDP. One reason is that the countries may have different amounts and qualities of machines and equipment available. The country with more and better machines and equipment will be able to produce a higher GDP. Also, the skill of labor forces in various countries may differ. The country with a better skilled and more educated labor force will be able to produce more. Over the years, the United States has had very good equipment and a well-educated, highly skilled labor force. This, along with large supplies of natural resources, has made the United States one of the world's leaders in terms of GDP.

GDP IS NOT A PERFECT MEASURE

There are some problems with using GDP as a measure of well-being. In using it, or in evaluating other people's use of it, you should know about these problems. Then you can make better economic judgments than you could have made otherwise.

GDP Doesn't Consider Kinds of Items Produced

The composition of GDP makes a big difference to a country's well-being. Consider two countries that are the same size. We'll call them Terrastan and Hydrostan. In our example, Terrastan and Hydrostan have the same number of people who like the same kinds of goods. However, the two countries differ in the size of their GDP. Terrastan has a GDP of $250 billion, and Hydrostan has a GDP of $140 billion. At first glance, Terrastan appears to be economically better off.

However, suppose that in Terrastan a great deal of the GDP is made up of military goods. Tanks, planes, and bombs are a very big part of what is produced. Also, suppose that Terrastan cannot trade these products for the food and clothing needed to support its people.

On the other hand, Hydrostan's GDP includes less military goods and more of goods such as cars, corn, clothes, movies, houses, and milk. Hydrostan's mix of goods and services produced balances the economic well-being of its society better than does Terrastan's. The mix of products that makes up the GDP of a country may be more important to individual well-being than the dollar volume of output.

Consider a government's decision to produce a number of new military fighter planes. The dollar cost of the planes will count in GDP, even if it does not show the true value the people place on having such planes. GDP increases when the planes are made, and this may indicate to some that people in the economy are better off. However, if the people do not want the planes, then they are economically worse off when the planes are produced. This is one of the major weaknesses of GDP: It does not take into account the *kinds* of goods produced.

This matters most when economic decisions are made in the public sector. When the market system allocates resources, our purchases determine which products survive the test of the market. When governments decide what to produce, we have some influence through voting, but politicians do not always act in the best interest of the entire country.

GDP Doesn't Measure Amount Produced per Person

Another problem in using just the dollar value of GDP as a measure of well-being is that it doesn't tell us how much is available per person. To show this, take another look at Hydrostan. Hydrostan has a GDP of $140 billion and a population of 10 million. A neighboring country, Sunya, also has a GDP of $140 billion, but it has a population of 20 million. This means that in Hydrostan there are twice as many goods per person as in Sunya. In Hydrostan, the $140 billion of GDP must be divided among only half as many people as in Sunya. In Hydrostan, there are $14,000 worth of GDP per person. But, in Sunya, there are just $7,500 worth of GDP per person. The people in Hydrostan are better off than the people in Sunya, even thought the total value of GDP is the same for both countries. The amount of GDP per person is often called *GDP per capita*.

To show the importance of comparing GDP on a per-person basis, let's look at two real countries, Turkey and Austria. In one recent year, the GDP of Turkey was about $201 billion. Austria's GDP was just under $135 billion. So, Turkey's GDP was about 1.5 times as large as Austria's. However, Turkey has a much larger population than Austria. It is so much larger that the GDP per person in Austria was more than five times as much as that in Turkey. GDP per person in Austria was $17,280, but in Turkey it was only $3,491. In the same year, GDP per person in the United States was $22,204.[1]

GDP Doesn't Measure How Goods Are Distributed

An additional problem in using GDP as a measure of well-being involves the distribution of goods among different people in a country. Suppose that most of a country's GDP is consumed by a small fraction of the people. In this case, there are few very rich people and many poor people. On the other hand, suppose that the GDP of another country is more evenly distributed. In that country, a smaller number of people are poor. But, there also are fewer very rich people.

A more equal distribution of income means there is a large middle class, and few people are very rich or very poor. Most people in the United States seem to favor a distribution of national income

[1]U.S. Bureau of the Census, *Statistical Abstract of the United States,* 1994, 114th ed. (Washington, D.C., 1994), 864.

so that there is a large middle class and relatively few poor people. At the same time, we want to make it possible for people to achieve high incomes as an incentive for being productive. Severe economic problems could result if the distribution of GDP were exactly equal among all people in a country.

GDP Doesn't Allow for Changing Price Levels

We often want to compare GDP figures from year to year. Many people think that we are economically better off if GDP goes up from one year to the next. But, we need to be very careful about making this kind of comparison. GDP figures usually express the current dollar values of the goods and services produced. If prices change, then this unit of measure (current dollar values) can change, even if the actual amount produced does not change.

inflation
the economic condition in which the average level of prices goes up

Since about 1940, the average level of prices has gone up pretty steadily in the United States. ***Inflation,*** as discussed briefly in Chapter 13, is the economic condition in which the average level of prices goes up. If the average level of prices goes up, the reported value of GDP goes up even if there is no added production.

Suppose, for example, that in 1996 a pair of jeans costs $22. The same jeans in 1997 cost $26. When the jeans are counted in GDP in 1997, each pair adds $4 more to GDP than it would have in 1996. So, even if the same number of jeans are sold, GDP goes up in 1997. The actual amount of goods available in the economy does not go up, but the dollar measure increases. In this example, the GDP does not show a growth in goods available but a rise in prices. When we use GDP to judge growth, we must be sure to understand that part of the growth may be due to inflation.

Suppose that GDP in one year was $800 billion. Suppose that the next year's GDP was reported to be $891 billion. Did the rise in GDP really increase the well-being of society by $91 billion? No, not if some of the increase was due to inflation. If the rate of inflation was 8 percent (0.08), then prices in the second year were 1.08 times the prices in the first year just due to inflation. How can the effect of inflation be taken out so that only real changes remain?

constant dollar GDP
the value of gross domestic product after taking out the effect of price changes

Dividing the second year's GDP by 1.08 gives the constant dollar GDP for the second year. ***Constant dollar GDP*** is the value of gross domestic product after taking out the effect of price changes. For this example,

$$\text{Constant Dollar GDP} = \frac{\text{Current Dollar GDP}}{\text{Adjustment for Inflation}}$$

$$= \frac{\$891 \text{ billion}}{1.08}$$

$$= \$825 \text{ billion}$$

So, using a comparable price measure, GDP in the second year was only $825 billion. The goods and services available increased by $25 billion rather than by $91 billion. When we convert any dollar measure to constant dollar terms, we take out the effect of price changes. Only actual, or real, changes remain. For this reason, we often use the terms *real GDP* or *GDP in real terms* when disccussing GDP that has been adjusted for price changes.

When GDP is adjusted in this way, any changes that remain represent actual changes in the volume of goods and services produced. Unadjusted or *current dollar GDP* is not nearly as meaningful. Unfortunately, however, current dollar GDP is often reported in the media.

The graph in Figure 14-2 shows what happened to GDP from 1960 to 1994 in the United States. The **yellow** line shows GDP in current dollars (the actual dollars in a particular year). The **orange** line shows GDP in constant dollars, or in real terms. GDP, measured either way, has increased steadily during this period.

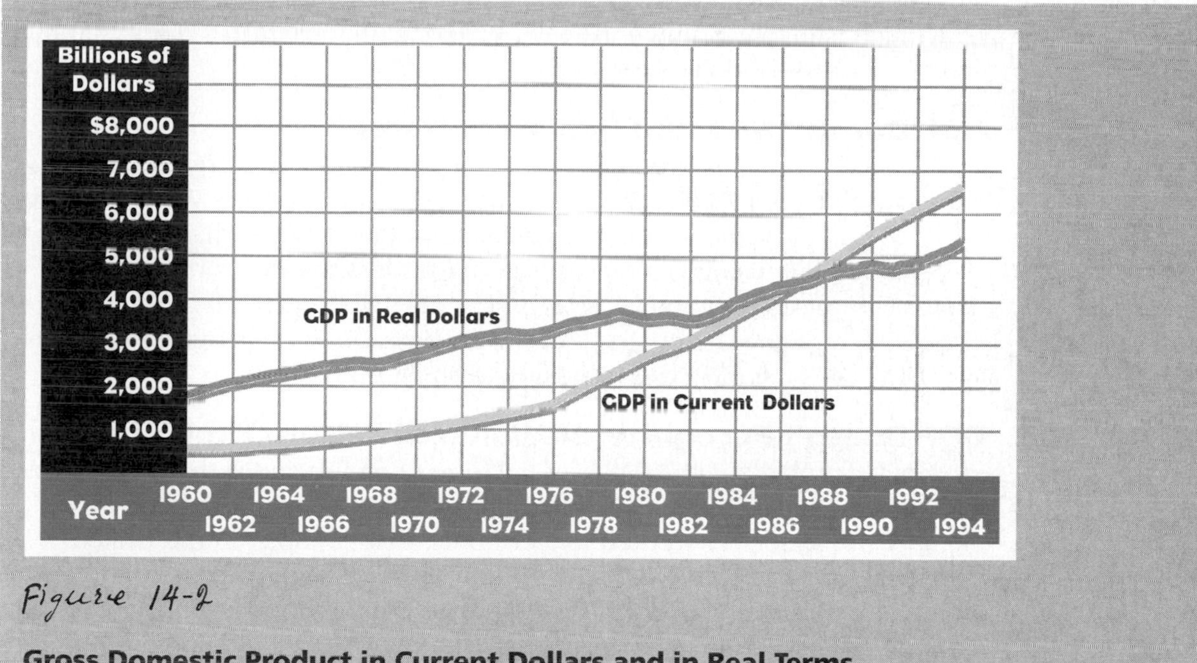

Figure 14-2

Gross Domestic Product in Current Dollars and in Real Terms

Due to inflation, current dollar GDP goes up more rapidly than real GDP. ***Do you think real GDP will continue to increase?***

GDP Doesn't Include Unpaid Household Work

People who maintain homes for their families produce many goods and services. They prepare meals, drive children to school and to other activities, clean house, paint, cut the lawn, wash clothes, and provide many other valuable services. Yet, the value of this work is not counted in GDP. As long as such jobs as housecleaning, lawn care, and painting are done by household members, these jobs don't add to GDP. But, if Service-Master is hired to clean the house, Lawn-Green to care for the lawn, and Wilcott Co. to paint, then the value of the work is added to GDP. Either way, the total production in society is the same. However, in order for these jobs to count in GDP, there must be a market exchange.

GDP Doesn't Include Barter

There is growing interest in a similar problem with reported GDP figures. To avoid taxes, some people are finding ways to exchange goods without going through the normal market. For example, a dentist might provide dental services for a car mechanic in exchange for car repairs. An accountant might do the accounting free of charge for a law firm in exchange for legal services. In such cases, no one declares any income from the services, and so the income tax owed for the year is reduced.

barter
a direct trade of goods or services

Such activities are called barters. A ***barter*** is a direct trade of goods or services. Barter translations are part of what is often called the *underground economy* or the *irregular economy*. The irregular economy is the economy consisting of economic activity that purposely avoids the market system in order to avoid reporting income for tax purposes. Since barter translations and other activities in the irregular economy do not show in GDP, the value of GDP must understate our true economic well-being. It is hard to know how much is involved in the irregular economy, but estimates run in the hundreds of billions of dollars each year.

GDP Doesn't Measure Quality of Items

The quality of items produced is also not measured in GDP. An electronic calculator that cost $400 in 1975 can be bought today for less than $40. Due to product improvements, the $40 calculator today is better than the $400 1975 model. But, using GDP measures, it adds less to our economic well-being. The price of color televisions today does not greatly differ from the price 20 years ago. The quality today is far better, however. But, again, there is no way for such increases in quality to show up in GDP.

GDP Doesn't Recognize the Value of Leisure Time

Another problem with GDP as a measure of well-being is that leisure time has no value in GDP. The GDP of a country could be increased if every member of the society worked longer hours. For example, in the United States, we could return to 60- and 80-hour workweeks. (The current, average workweek is about 35 hours.) If we did increase the number of hours we all worked, GDP would increase. But, our well-being probably would not go up. Leisure time is highly valued, and we would suffer if it were cut. Yet, the value of leisure time is not included in GDP.

Checkpoint

Content Check

1. How is macroeconomics different from microeconomics?

2. Describe how the economy is a circular flow of activities.

3. How does inflation affect GDP?

What Do You Think Now?

Reread *What Do You Think?* in the Section One Focus. Then answer the following questions:

4. Given the information on the two countries' GDPs and populations, which country do you think is better off in economic terms?

5. What other factors might you consider in comparing the economic well-being of the two countries?

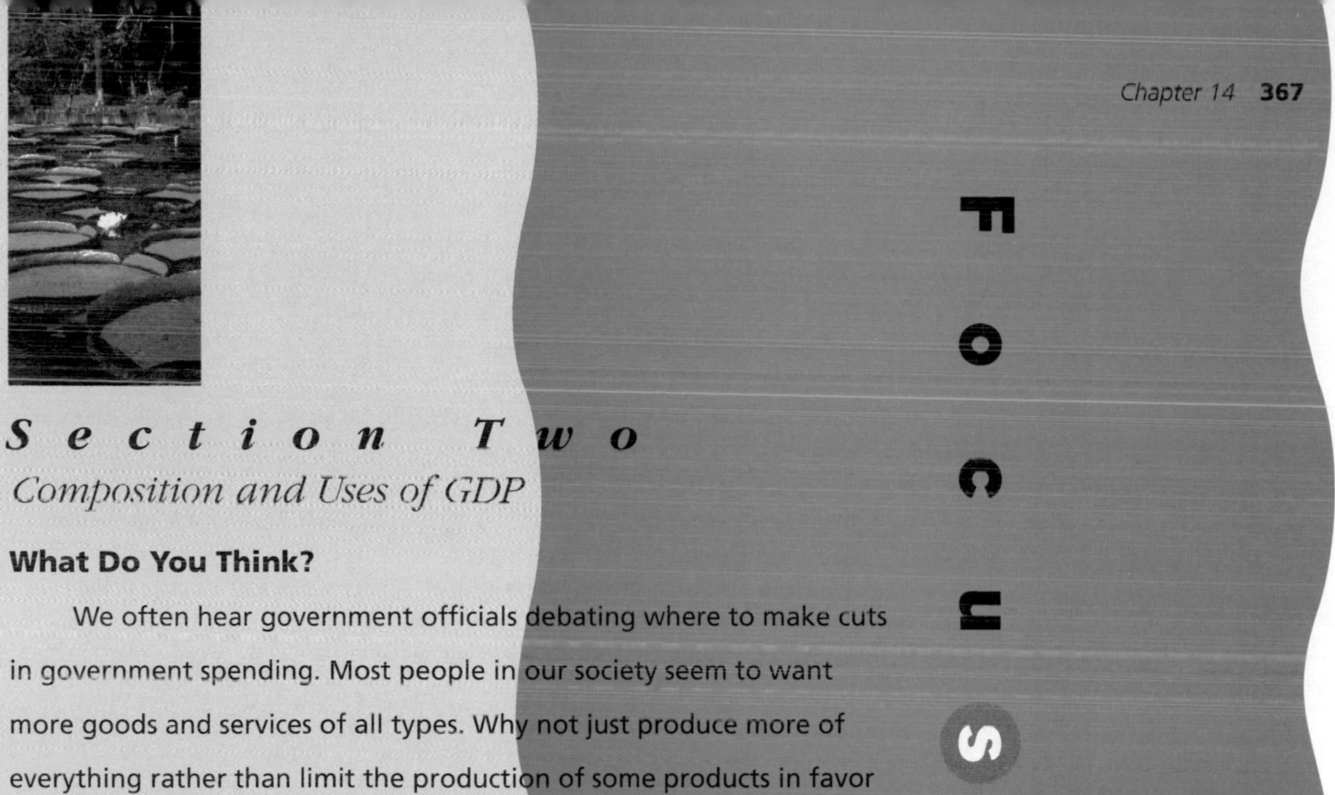

Section Two

Composition and Uses of GDP

What Do You Think?

We often hear government officials debating where to make cuts in government spending. Most people in our society seem to want more goods and services of all types. Why not just produce more of everything rather than limit the production of some products in favor of others?

What's Ahead?

Many types of goods and services make up our gross domestic product. You have already seen that the makeup of GDP can determine how much benefit we get from it. Society has to make many choices about how to allocate resources. We can make many different goods and services or we can concentrate production on just a few kinds of goods. In this section, you will learn about how different types of production are classified and about the trade-offs we make among goods.

Terms to Know

production possibilities curve

consumer goods

investment

capital

PRODUCT TRADE-OFFS WITHIN GDP

There are always trade-offs to be made. In the United States, we use many resources to produce cars and items used by car owners. These include highways, parking lots, garages, gasoline, and other products or services that are used along with a car. The trade off of doing this is, at least in part, that we have spent less on other forms of passenger transportation. It has been said that if railroads had as much government support for railroad tracks as the car industry has for road construction, railroads would be more useful today. You have seen several times now that resources used in one type of production have an opportunity cost in terms of other products that could have been made.

Resources that are used by governments are not available for production in the private sector. Resources used to make goods for consumers cannot be used to make machines for business use. Such trade-offs can be represented using the concept of a production possibilities curve.

Efficient Production Possibilities

production possibilities curve a graphic illustration of the combinations of output an economy can produce if all of its resources are utilized and utilized efficiently, given the state of technology

A ***production possibilities curve*** is a graphic illustration of the combinations of output an economy can produce if all of its resources are utilized and utilized efficiently, given the state of technology. Resources include natural resources, labor, and capital. In Figure 14-3, the **gray** curve represents one production possibilities curve. In this figure, we have assumed that all of the production in an economy functions as either a private good or a public good. All of the country's resources can be used to produce either private goods only or public goods only. These two extremes are represented by Points *A* and *B*.

Figure 14-3

Two Production Possibilities Curves

The curve *AB* shows the possible amounts of private and public goods a society can produce at a given time. With some economic growth, the production possibilities curve would shift to curve *A'B'*. ***If the economy were at Point F and you proposed trying to move to a position of producing more private goods, would you be advocating a move toward Point D or Point C?***

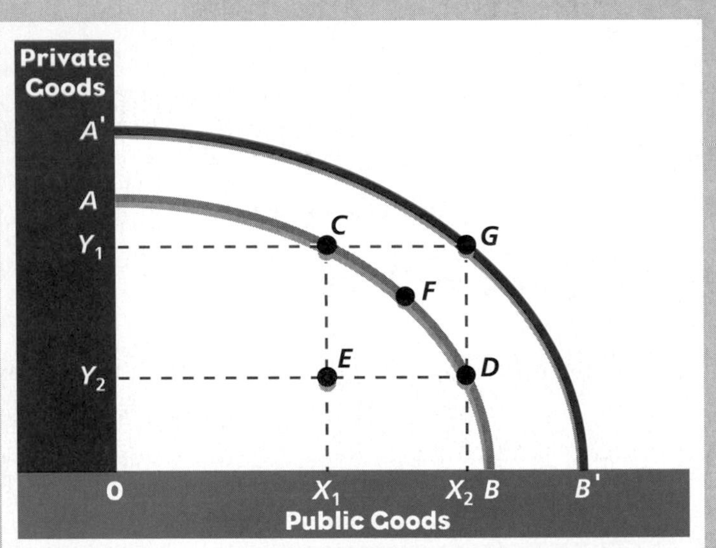

No economy would produce only one type of good and nothing else. Some combination will be produced. For example, Point *C* on the production possibilities curve represents Y_1 amount of private goods and X_1 amount of public goods. Point *D* also represents full use of the country's resources but with greater production of public goods (X_2) and less production of private goods (Y_2). This is an important point. If an economy is using all of its resources efficiently, to increase production of one good the production of another good must be decreased. The cost of adding more production of public goods (from X_1 to X_2) is a decrease in the production of private goods (from Y_1 to Y_2). This is an example of an opportunity cost.

Inefficient Production Possibilities

Suppose that the economy shown in Figure 14-3 produced Y_2 amount of private goods and X_1 amount of public goods. This combination of production would be represented by Point *E* in the figure. Point *E* could represent two cases: (1) the economy is not using all of its resources (there are unemployed resources) or (2) the economy is using its resources inefficiently. Economists refer to this situation as *underemployment of resources*. If the economy is at Point *E*, a gap exists between what is being produced and what could be produced. With the same resources and technology, the economy could produce more private goods by moving to Point *C* or more public goods by moving to Point *D*. It could also produce more of both goods by moving from *E* to any point on the production possibilities curve between *C* and *D*. An example would be movement to Point *F*.

Increasing Production Possibilities

Suppose that the people of the economy wanted to have Y_1 of private goods and X_2 of public goods produced. That combination of output would be represented at Point *G*. But, Point *G* lies outside the gray production possibilities curve and thus is impossible to reach, given the resources and technology available. Points beyond the production possibilities curve are called *unattainable levels of production*. However, with new resources or advanced technology, the production possibilities curve would shift outward. Such a case is represented by the **purple** curve in Figure 14-3. With this new production possibilities curve, Y_1 amount of private goods and X_2 amount of public goods could be produced. So, Point *G* would become an attainable level of production.

THE COMPOSITION OF GDP

The trade-offs we have to deal with as a society involve more than just public versus private goods. The total production in the economy can be divided into several classes of goods. The most important are consumer goods, investment goods, and the government sector.

Each of these can be further divided into more specific kinds of goods. The following list shows some important categories:

Consumer Goods	Investment Goods	The Government Sector
• Durable Goods	• New Plants and Equipment	• Federal Government
• Nondurable Goods	• Private Housing	• State Government
• Services	• Inventories	• Local Government

All production in the economy can be put into one of these categories. We will briefly look at each of these in the following sections.

Consumer Goods

Consumer goods are items that are made for final consumption. Most of the goods and services you use are consumer goods. To list all of them would be an almost endless job. A few examples of consumer goods and services are sweaters, cars, eyeglasses, haircuts, and magazines. You can see that there is a good deal of variety just in this list. About two-thirds of our gross domestic product is allocated to consumer goods and services.

consumer goods
items that are made for final consumption

Internet Connection

THE STATE OF THE ECONOMY

How is the economy doing? How do you tell? Economic statistics can help you make a decision. You can gather the major macroeconomic indicators online.

Official statistics about the economy are called the National Income and Product Accounts (NIPA) and are collected by the Bureau of Economic Analysis of the Commerce Department. These data are available from the Economic Bulletin Board (EBB) at **gopher://una.hh.lib.umich.edu/00/ebb/nipa/nipacurr/nipa-a.prn**.

The broadest measure of economic activity is Gross Domestic Product (GDP). Other important statistics include the inflation rate, the unemployment rate, the index of industrial production, the capacity utilization rate, interest rates, the money supply, and the Dow Jones Industrial Average (a measure of stock prices).

Different economic indicators tell different stories. To draw a conclusion, you use the "art" of economics. Use your best judgment to weigh the different economic indicators. A formal way of doing this is by using an index number. You may have heard of the Index of Leading Economic Indicators. This is an average of eleven major economic statistics. An increase suggests good times are coming and a decrease suggests the opposite. Data for the percent change in the index can be found on the EBB at **gopher://una.hh.lib.umich.edu/00/ebb/indicators/ei.prn**. This file gives the title of the data series, followed by the last seven months of data, beginning with the most recent month. For some variables, there is no data for the last month. In September 1995, the file read, "Composite Index of Leading Indicators, '',-0.2,0.2,-0.2,-0.6,-0.4,0.3." There was no data for August (''). In July, the index fell 0.2 percent.

Internet Application: A key theme of Chapter 14 is the importance of the composition of real GDP. Access the Economic Bulletin Board and determine the values for real GDP, real consumer spending, real investment spending, and real government spending for the most recent year available. What fraction of GDP is made up of consumer spending, investment spending, and government spending?

Economics Application: Figure 14-7 shows equilibrium in the economy at the intersection of the aggregate supply and aggregate demand curves. What real world concepts are shown on the horizontal and vertical axes of the graph? How would you measure average price level and total output?

Some consumer goods last for a fairly long time. These are called *durable goods.* Durable goods can be used over and over again. We benefit from them for a number of years. Bicycles, cars, washing machines, refrigerators, and furniture are some examples of consumer durable goods. Because these products last for some time, consumers often delay buying them during periods of economic hard times. This means that durable goods industries such as the car industry are more sensitive to national economic problems than many other industries.

Other products are entirely consumed almost as soon as they are purchased. These are called *nondurable goods.* Nondurable goods are goods that do not last a long time. Food products clearly are nondurable goods. We usually eat food items within a few days or weeks after we buy them. The clothes we buy wear out more quickly than a freezer or other appliance does. A magazine becomes old within a few days or weeks, but a bicycle does not.

Still other forms of production result in services that have value to us. We get some satisfaction from consuming services just as we do from physical products. A haircut is a service for which many of us pay. Other services include those of a doctor, a dentist, a travel agent, and a lawyer. The service sector of the economy is a growing part of GDP. In 1950, the services part of personal consumption spending was about 33 percent of GDP. As shown in Figure 14-4, the percentage of total consumer spending on services has increased since then to about 54 percent.

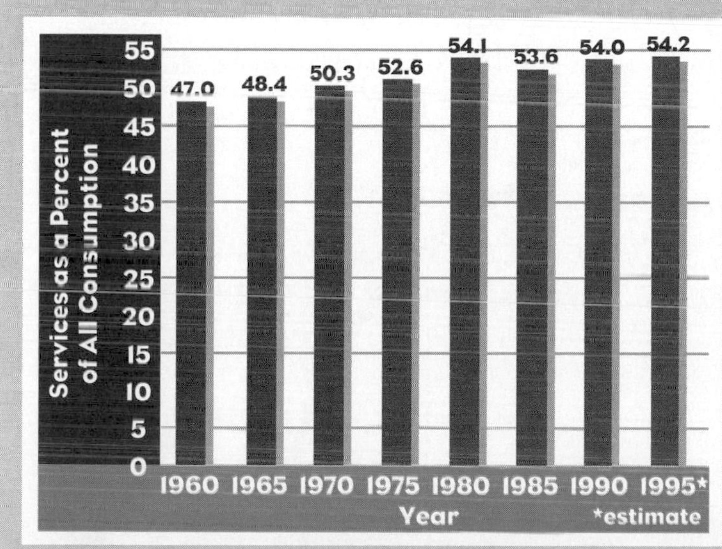

Figure 14-4

Percentage of Consumer Spending for Services

There has been growth in the service part of the economy. We not only spend more money on services, but we also spend a greater percentage of our money for services. ***Name some services you consumed last week.***

SOURCE: Calculated from values in *Economic Report of the President 1995* (Washington, D.C.: U.S. Government Printing Office, 1995), 276.

Investment Goods

Investment goods make up the second category of GDP. But, before we learn about the different kinds of investment goods, we need to know the difference between two uses of the word *investment:* physical investment and financial investment.

If you buy stock in a company such as IBM, you have invested in IBM. This is a form of financial investment. Normally, when people discuss their investments, they are referring to financial investments.

However, when economists use the term *investment,* they are referring to physical investment. If the investment part of GDP goes up, physical investment has increased. Physical investment refers to an increase in the amount of productive capital in the economy. Therefore, in economic terms,

Economic Dilemma

GUNS AND BUTTER

Throughout most of the last half of the twentieth century, economics texts have discussed the trade-off between "guns and butter." The phrase *guns and butter* was used as a generalization for the trade-off between producing goods that were designed for national defense (like war planes) and goods that were for personal consumption. Some people felt that we would have to sacrifice some personal consumption goods in order to have an adequate military base. The accompanying graph of the trade-off is similar to the production possibilities curve shown in Figure 14-3. Point *A*, corresponding to G_1 of guns and B_1 of butter, represents one possible allocation of resources.

While the political debate today may be phrased somewhat differently, the issues are similar. We must still decide how much of our resources should be allocated to the public sector (guns) and how much to the private sector (butter). The news media frequently report on debates about this issue in the halls of government. It is an economic and political dilemma that will probably be the focus of attention for many years to come.

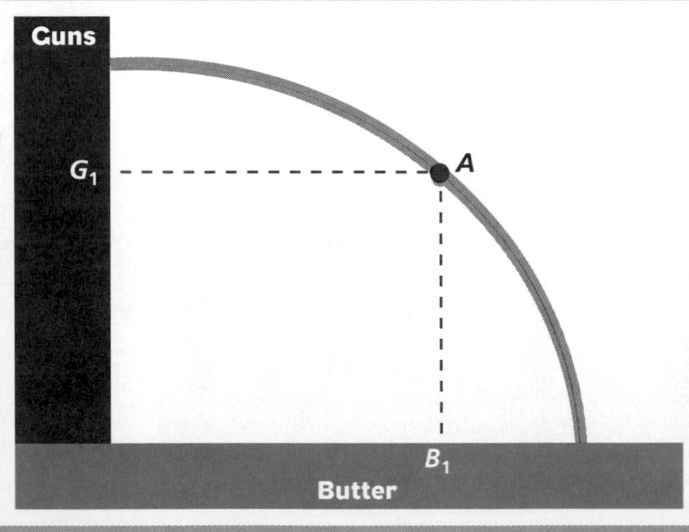

investment is an increase in the amount of productive capital in an economy. It is an increase in the number of factories, office buildings, stores, and machines or equipment used in producing goods and services.

investment
an increase in the amount of productive capital in an economy

We also need to know the difference between the two uses of the word *capital:* financial capital and physical capital. To someone in business, the word *capital* means money to pay bills and make purchases. The owner of a small business often worries about having enough working capital. This means the owner worries about having enough money to pay employees, to pay bank loans, and to buy supplies.

But, capital has another meaning in economics. ***Capital*** means goods that are produced and can be used as inputs for further production. It refers to the machines, factories, and computers that help in producing other goods. This is physical capital. When the amount of physical capital has increased, there has been some physical investment. When economists use the words *investment* or *capital,* they mean physical investment or physical capital.

capital
goods that are produced and can be used as inputs for further production

Just as we could divide consumer goods into several parts, we could study three kinds of investment. New plants and equipment use the majority of investment money. When a firm buys a new computer or puts in a new assembly line, this is one type of investment. Building a new steel mill or a new office building is the same type of investment.

The second type of investment is in housing. A new house is a type of physical investment. (Buying a new house is a financial investment, too.) The building of a new house is a physical investment because the house will produce housing benefits for a long period of time. Each year, the house will provide the people who live in it a new amount of housing satisfaction. A house continues to be productive in this sense until no one uses it anymore.

Finally, an increase in business inventory is considered an investment. A company's inventory is the amount of goods it has on hand. Suppose a business makes 100,000 washing machines during the year but only sells 90,000. The 90,000 that are sold show up in GDP as consumer durable goods. The 10,000 that are not sold do not count as consumption, but since they were made they should be part of that year's GDP. To solve this problem, the 10,000 machines that are not sold to consumers are thought of as being sold to the company itself. Therefore, when a company adds to its inventory, that inventory is counted in GDP as its own investment. This way, all production gets counted.

The Government Sector

The third major part of our GDP measures the government sector of the economy. The government sector includes all government purchases of goods and services. Federal, state, and local governments belong to this sector. The total of government purchases has increased steadily over the last half of the twentieth century, reaching more than $1 trillion by the mid 1990s.

The percentage of GDP accounted for by the government sector has fluctuated over the years. During World War II, the percentage was more than 46 percent. By 1950, it had dropped to 13.5 percent. After 1950, the percentage of GDP in the government sector increased steadily and reached more than 22 percent during the Vietnam War period. In 1990, total government purchases were about 20 percent of that year's GDP. By the mid-1990s that percentage had dropped to about 17 percent.

State and local government spending has increased. In 1960, state and local governments spent about $44.5 billion, which was about 45 percent of total government purchases. By 1980, this spending was about $298 billion, about 59 percent of all government purchases. By the mid-1990s, state and local governments were spending about $738 billion, which was nearly 63 percent of all government spending.

The Makeup of GDP: A Quick Review

Gross domestic product is composed of three components: personal consumption expenditures, investment spending, and the spending of governmental units. The process of producing goods for each sector results in people earning some income. If you worked in a factory making radios, you would earn money from making a consumer good. If you worked on the construction of a new steel mill, your income would come from making an investment good. And, if you were a public school teacher, your income would come from the government sector. The composition of GDP can be expressed in an equation as follows:

GDP = Personal Consumption + Investments + Government Purchases

C h e c k  o i n t

Content Check

1. What are the three primary components of spending in our economy?
2. Give an example of a consumer durable good.
3. What has happened to state and local government spending as a percentage of total government spending over the last three decades?

What Do You Think Now?

Reread *What Do You Think?* in the Section Two Focus. Then answer the following questions:

4. Why doesn't the government produce more of everything rather than debate what should be provided by the government sector?
5. How does the problem faced by the government sector relate to the concept of a production possibilities curve?

F

O

Section Three

A More Complete Picture of the Macroeconomy

What Do You Think?

The United States is a country that is rich in many economic resources. Do you think that this allows our economy to function independently of the other economies of the world?

What's Ahead?

Early in this chapter, you saw a diagram that represented the economy as a circular flow of exchanges between the household and business sectors (Figure 14-1). Now you will see how the government sector, savings, and investment spending can be added to the circular flow model. This provides a more complete view of how our macroeconomy works.

Terms to Know

disposable income

macroeconomic equilibrium

aggregate demand

aggregate supply

USES OF INCOME

By working and being productive, we earn an income. Where does that income go? How do we (as a nation) use our income? You will see that we use most of our income for consumption—that is, we use it to buy goods and services. But, we also use some of our income to pay taxes and we save some of it. Let us look at each of these uses in turn.

Consumption

Most of our income is used for consumption—that is, we *spend* most of it. Think about how your family spends its money. A large part of the total income probably pays for housing. For most families, the rent or mortgage payment is the biggest single part of the family budget. Food also takes a big part of our income. Spending on housing, food, and clothing is often thought of as necessary spending.

We also spend money on items that are unnecessary. Examples include candy, movies, tennis, and CDs. We often spend a good deal of money on these luxuries because we get a lot of satisfaction from them. What do you spend money on? Make a list of items you and your family have purchased in the last few weeks. It will probably be a long list and include many different kinds of goods and services.

Global Economy

FILL 'ER UP!

The following table shows some international differences in the levels of gross domestic product per person as well as how people in different countries spend some of that income.

The last column is included so that you can see how much more of your income it would take to drive in many other countries. People often complain about the high price of gas without knowing how little we pay per gallon in comparison to people in other countries. This is especially true if you compare gas prices in each country to GDP per person in the same country.

Country	GDP per Person (Adjusted for Purchasing Power Differences)	Total Health Spending as a Percent of GDP	Public Health Spending as a Percent of Total Health Spending	Public Spending on Education as a Percent of GDP	Persons per Car	Price of Premium Gasoline (U.S. Dollar per Gallon)
United States	$22,204	13.4	43.9	5.5	1.7	1.31
Germany	$19,500	8.4	71.8	4.0	2.1	3.25
Japan	$19,107	6.8	70.1	3.7	3.3	4.55
United Kingdom	$15,720	6.6	83.3	5.3	NA	2.77
France	$18,227	9.1	73.9	5.4	2.4	3.41
Canada	$19,178	10.0	72.2	6.7	2.1	1.85
Italy	$16,896	8.3	77.5	NA	2.0	3.77
Denmark	$17,621	6.5	81.5	6.1	3.2	3.38
Australia	$16,085	8.6	67.8	4.7	2.2	1.83

SOURCE: U.S. Bureau of the Census, *Statistical Abstract of the United States,* 1994, 114th ed. (Washington, D.C., 1994), 859, 860, 864, 865, 876.

NA indicates data not available.

Taxes

We cannot spend all our earnings on consumer goods. Part of our income must go toward different kinds of taxes. Only disposable income is available to spend on consumer goods. ***Disposable income*** is the income that is left after deducting tax payments. We pay income taxes to the federal government. Most states and many cities and counties also have income taxes. State and local governments also use sales taxes to pay for their programs. In addition to paying income and sales taxes, property owners pay property taxes to local governments.

disposable income
the income that is left after deducting tax payments

Savings

Even after paying taxes, most people do not spend all of their income for consumption. Part of their income is put aside as savings to be used for consumption at a later time. Some families or individuals do spend all of their income, but, for the total of all people in the society, some fraction of income is saved.

How do we save our money? Much goes into some kind of savings account. We put our savings in banks, savings and loan associations, and credit unions. We may use passbook accounts or other forms of savings that pay us a higher rate of interest on our money. We also save money when we invest in stocks and bonds. (Remember, these are financial investments.) Various types of life insurance also include some savings.

In all these forms of savings, the money we save does not sit in a bank vault but returns to the spending flow of the economy. This spending may be some kind of investment, government spending, or spending by other consumers. If you buy a corporate bond with your savings, the money is likely to be used by the company to invest in new capital (physical capital). If you buy government bonds, the money will be spent for government programs. It might help build a school or highway. If you put savings in a savings and loan association, it will likely be lent to someone to build or buy a house. Money saved in a credit union will probably be loaned to someone else to buy a consumer good, perhaps a new car. Savings put into a bank may be loaned for almost any of these uses.

Figure 14-5 on page 378 shows the percentage of disposable personal income that has gone into savings since 1950. Look at what happened to savings starting in the mid-1980s. The percentage of disposable personal income that we saved became fairly low. This meant that less money was available for business firms to invest in new capital than if savings had been higher. The low rate of savings in the United States has been a matter of concern to economists as well as to business and political leaders.

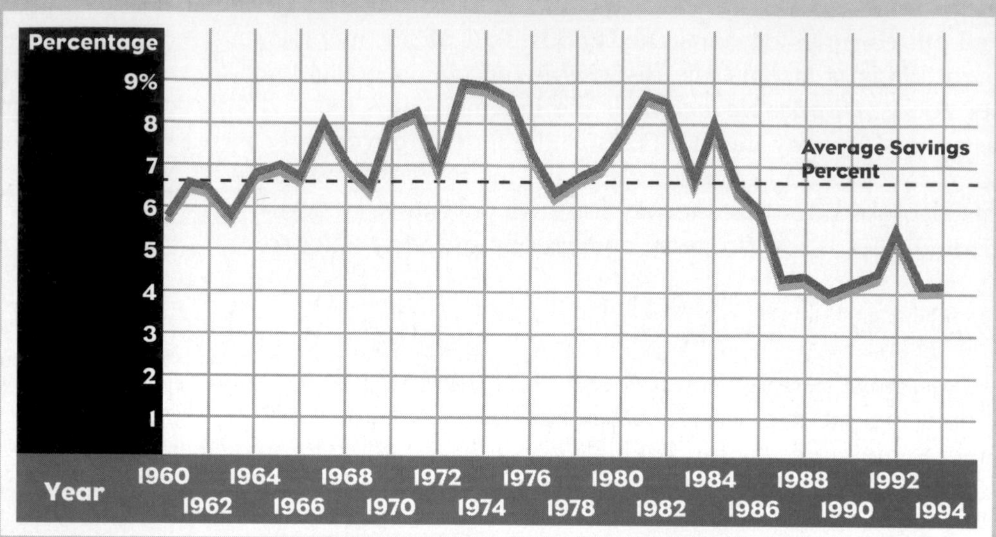

Figure 14-5

Savings as a Percentage of Disposable Personal Income

For the period shown, the average percent saved was 6.6 percent. Notice that recently we have had savings below this long-run average. ***What does the level of savings in a country have to do with how much is invested in new productive facilities?***

Source: *Economic Report of the President 1995* (Washington, D.C.: U.S. Government Printing Office, 1995), 306.

Occasionally, you hear of someone who has saved hundreds of thousands of dollars in an attic or basement. But, only a very small part of our savings is in the form of cash hidden in the home. Most of our savings gets right back into the spending flows in the economy.

A MORE COMPLETE VIEW OF THE CIRCULAR FLOW OF THE ECONOMY

Figure 14-6 shows another circular flow diagram of the economy. This figure is very much like Figure 14-1, but it is more detailed and more realistic because government is added and both savings and investment are included. And, you will note that in Figure 14-6 our economy works within the context of a global economic environment.

Flow of Savings

We have just discussed savings, which is a leakage out of the flow of consumer spending. It is a part of income that does not immediately get back into the flow of the economy. But, the money we save does get back into the economy when banks, savings and loans, or other such institutions lend money to others. In Figure 14-6 this process is shown by the flow labeled *Savings* that comes out of the household sector. Savings is funneled through various financial intermediaries (such as banks) back into the flow of economic activity. As this money flows into the business sector, it is used for investment. Investment functions as an injection back into the economy. For the total economy, this investment is limited to only as much as individuals are willing to save.

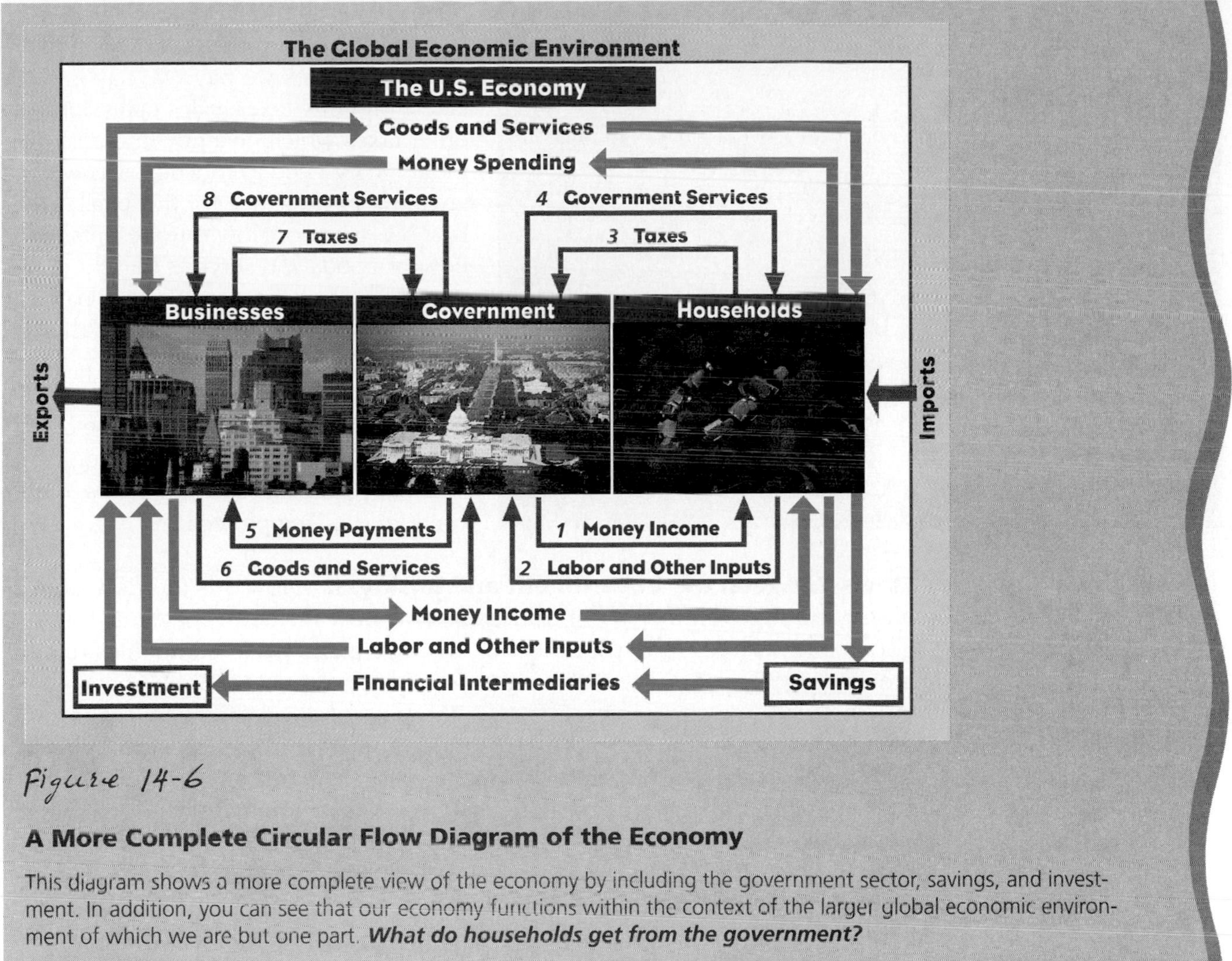

Figure 14-6

A More Complete Circular Flow Diagram of the Economy

This diagram shows a more complete view of the economy by including the government sector, savings, and investment. In addition, you can see that our economy functions within the context of the larger global economic environment of which we are but one part. ***What do households get from the government?***

Flow Between Government, Households, and Business

The government sector is added to the circular flow in the middle of Figure 14-6. What kinds of flows run between governments and households or between governments and businesses? A full description could fill an entire chapter or even a whole book. Here's a look at the eight most important flows, identified by the numbers 1 through 8 in the diagram.

Flows Between the Government and Households. Flow 1 is the flow of money from governments to households. Examples include a teacher's paycheck, a senator's paycheck, or a welfare payment. Flow 2 is the flow of labor and other inputs to governments from households. In exchange for the paycheck, a teacher provides labor skills for educational services. A senator works in exchange for the money payment.

In general, Flows 1 and 2 work like the loop that connects households and businesses in which money is exchanged for labor and other inputs. However, the government does make some payments to people for which nothing is given in exchange. Welfare payments are one example.

Flow 3 is the flow of money from households to governments. This flow is mainly the taxes we pay. We pay income taxes, property taxes, sales taxes, and other taxes which give governments the money they need to function. Do we get anything in exchange for those tax dollars? We sure do. Flow 4 represents the flow of goods and services that the government provides to us. We may pay a small part of the cost for some of these goods and services directly. But, without government backing, we would not have as many of them as we have come to expect. A sample includes schools, national parks, museums, libraries, highways, and police protection.

Flows Between the Government and Business. Flow 5 is the flow of money from governments to businesses. This flow includes payments for goods and services from IBM, Boeing, Rockwell, and other companies that are awarded government contracts. Governments provide the major source of income for some companies. Flow 6 is the flow of goods and services from businesses to governments. The government buys tanks, planes, food, paper clips, pencils, cars, books, and thousands of other goods and services. In the United States, the government does not produce very many of these items. It buys almost all it needs from businesses in the private sector. So, these goods flow to governments in exchange for the dollar flow in Flow 5.

Flow 7 is the flow of money from businesses to governments. This flow is made up mainly of taxes, particularly corporate income taxes and property taxes. Flow 8 is the flow of goods and services to the business sector in exchange for the tax dollars. Basically, these are the same goods and services that we listed in Flow 4. Just think how much the car industry benefits from having the system of roads provided by governments. Companies benefit from national defense, police and fire protection, and an educated labor force. Also, the legal system makes it possible to enforce contracts. This helps business to run smoothly.

BALANCE IN THE MACROECONOMY

What would happen to our economy if savings leaked out of the spending flow and never got back into it? Suppose that each year, $100 billion were stuffed into our pillows or hidden in attics. This money would not be spent; therefore, fewer goods would be bought. Fewer workers would need to be hired. Less income would be earned. With less income, there would be even less spending, less production, and still fewer jobs. The economy would slowly become drained and weakened. The same thing could happen if tax dollars did not get back into the flow of spending.

But, as you saw in Figure 14-6, savings does work its way back into the spending stream as a financial investment. Banks and other financial intermediaries help our savings get to others who need that money for current spending.

Economic Spotlight

THE SECRET TO SUCCESS: GET YOUR FEET WET!

While working part-time in his brother's dry goods store, Leon Leonwood (L. L.) Bean had some free time to hunt and fish. But, after each trip into the woods, Bean would come home with wet feet. Instead of complaining, Bean decided to solve the problem himself. He took a pair of rubber galoshes and sewed leather tops on them to get the protection of galoshes with the comfort and fit of leather boots.

After successfully field-testing the boots himself, Bean figured that others might be interested in purchasing a pair. He kicked off his marketing strategy by obtaining a mailing list of all the people in Maine with hunting licenses. Then, Bean, a highly effective writer of advertising copy, mailed a letter to each person on the list, describing his new boot as "light as a moccasin, with the protection of a heavy hunting boot." In addition, Bean's letter offered something that no other producer had ever offered—a written guarantee that if buyers were not satisfied, they could return the product for a full refund. This process of field-testing each and every product and then offering a money-back guarantee served as the foundation for the company he would later found in 1912, L. L. Bean.

Because of his personal experiences and his own need for a lightweight, waterproof boot, Bean knew what would appeal to consumers. He used this personal interest to write his highly successful sales brochures. Today, L. L. Bean's grandson, Leon A. Gorman, who became president of L. L. Bean in 1967, carries on this tradition himself. Daily, Gorman sends out workers to hike, fly-fish, bike, and ski using L. L. Bean clothing and gear. He upholds his grandfather's founding beliefs that a company should personally test a product before selling it and that the customer should be completely satisfied with every purchase.

Gorman believes it is this extra effort that gives the L. L. Bean catalog authenticity and a competitive edge—and there's plenty of competition out there. Although the L. L. Bean catalog started out as the only company of its type, it now has many competitors, including Lands' End, Eddie Bauer, and J. Crew. However, Gorman refuses to get too caught up in competition, stating, "We've no intention of being the hottest or trendiest. The soundest strategy is to be more like L. L. Bean."

Our tax dollars get back into the spending stream as the government provides goods and services. Because investment and government spending put this money back into the economic system, we call such spending an *injection*. Money is injected back into the circular flow of the economy by investment and government spending.

So, money leaks out of the circular flow in the form of savings and taxes. But, these leakages become injections back into the system in the form of investment and government spending. There is a macroeconomic balance (or equilibrium) when the leakages equal the injections. That is, ***macroeconomic equilibrium*** results when the sum of savings and taxes equals the sum of investment and government spending. Macroeconomic equilibrium results when

macroeconomic equilibrium
what results when the sum of savings and taxes equals the sum of investment and government spending

Savings + Taxes = Investment + Government Spending

AGGREGATE DEMAND AND SUPPLY

Each person has a demand for many different goods and services. When everyone's demands for all products are added together, the result is aggregate demand. ***Aggregate demand*** is the total demand of all people for all goods and services produced in an economy. This aggregate, or total, demand is graphed in Figure 14-7. Since we are adding together many different kinds of products, their dollar value is used to represent quantity in Figure 14-7. To keep out the effect of inflation, this quantity is in *real* terms, or in *constant* dollars. As you should expect from your study of demand, the lower the price, the more real output demanded. So, the aggregate demand curve slopes down to the right.

aggregate demand
the total demand of all people for all goods and services produced in an economy

Many firms produce a wide variety of goods and services in our economy. ***Aggregate supply*** is the total supply of all goods and services in an economy. Aggregate supply is also graphed in Figure 14-7. You know that individual company and market supply curves slope up to the right—more will be

aggregate supply
the total supply of all goods and services in an economy

Figure 14-7

Aggregate Demand and Aggregate Supply

The economy is in equilibrium when aggregate demand equals aggregate supply. This is where the aggregate demand curve crosses the aggregate supply curve. This intersection determines the equilibrium price level and output for the economy. ***What would happen to the average price level if aggregate demand increased (the curve shifted to the right) while the aggregate supply curve stayed the same?***

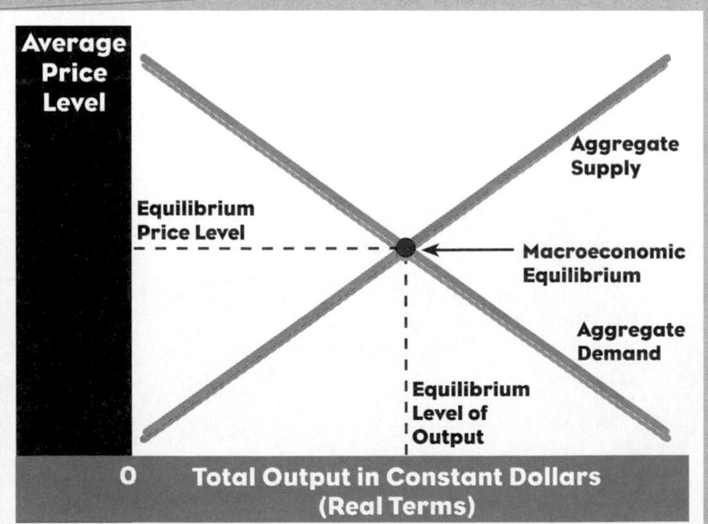

supplied at higher prices than at lower prices. This is also true of the aggregate supply for the whole economy, as shown in Figure 14-7.

We have said that the economy is in equilibrium when leakages out of the spending flow equal injections into the spending flow. We can also think of macroeconomic equilibrium using aggregate demand and aggregate supply. The economy is in equilibrium when aggregate demand equals aggregate supply. This is where the two lines cross in Figure 14-7.

Checkpoint

Content Check

1. How does the rate of savings in the 1990s compare with the long-term average savings rate?
2. Households pay taxes to various levels of government. What do we get from the government?
3. How does savings get back into the flow of economic activity?
4. When is the macroeconomy in equilibrium (or in balance)?

What Do You Think Now?

Reread *What Do You Think?* in the Section Three Focus. Then answer the following question:

5. Does the U.S. economy function independently of the rest of the world?

Concepts in Brief

1. Macroeconomics involves the study of the entire economy. Microeconomics looks at the output of individual firms and workers, but macroeconomics looks at the total output for the whole economy. One measure of economic well-being is gross domestic product (GDP). GDP is the total current dollar value of all final goods and services produced by resources located in the United States during a year.

2. The size of GDP for any country depends on many factors. These include the amount of natural resources the country has, the amount of capital (machines and equipment) it has, and the skills of its labor force.

3. There are some problems with using GDP as a measure of well-being. GDP does not describe what kinds of goods are produced, how much is produced per person, or how GDP is distributed per person. Are there many poor people and a few rich people? Or, is the GDP well distributed among all of the people? Also, only GDP in real terms, after taking out the effects of price changes, should be used for comparisons. Finally, GDP figures do not reflect production that does not go through a formal market, the value of leisure time, or the quality of what is produced.

4. Every society decides which goods should be produced. A production possibilities curve can help show and evaluate the trade-offs that must be made. Producing one item involves some opportunity cost in terms of other items that cannot be made with the same resources.

5. Consumer goods are goods that are made for final consumption. Consumer durable goods are goods that last a fairly long time in normal use, such as cars, refrigerators, and furniture. Consumer nondurable goods are those that are consumed more quickly, such as food, clothing, and magazines. Services, such as haircuts or radio repair, are intangible forms of production.

6. When economists use the term *investment* they mean physical investment. This is an increase in the amount of capital that can be used in making goods and services. Capital, in this context, means machines and equipment that are made for use in further production.

7. The government sector of the economy includes the federal government as well as state and local governments. The total dollar value of this sector has increased almost every year for the past 40 years. GDP is equal to the sum of spending for consumer goods and investment goods and the value of production in the government sector.

8. Income is earned in the process of producing GDP. That income is used to buy goods and services, to pay taxes, and as savings.
9. Savings and taxes can be thought of as leakages out of the flow of spending in the economy. Only if those leakages of money get back into the economy will the economy continue to run. The injections of investment and government spending get this money back into the flow of the economy. When savings plus taxes equal investment plus government spending, the economy is in equilibrium. Macroeconomic equilibrium occurs when aggregate demand equals aggregate supply.
10. The economy can be illustrated in a circular flow diagram that includes the flows among business, households, and government. The flows include labor, income, goods and services, savings, and investment.

Economic Foundations

1. Why is GDP an important economic measure to understand?
2. How does the amount of natural resources in a country affect its GDP?
3. List the major problems with using GDP as a measure of economic well-being.
4. In an economy that is using all its resources efficiently, what happens if production of one good is increased?
5. List three examples of consumer goods.
6. What three sectors make up GDP?
7. What are the three flows of money between households and businesses?
8. Draw the flows of money and goods and services between households and governments.
9. Draw the flows of money and goods and services between businesses and governments.
10. Describe two ways of looking at macroeconomic equilibrium.

Your Economic Vocabulary

Build your economic vocabulary by matching the following terms with their definitions.

aggregate demand
aggregate supply
barter
capital
constant dollar GDP
consumer goods
disposable income
gross domestic product (GDP)
inflation
investment
macroeconomics
macroeconomic equilibrium
production possibilities curve

1. an increase in the amount of productive capital in an economy
2. the total demand of all people for all goods and services produced in an economy
3. what results when the sum of savings and taxes equals the sum of investment and government spending
4. goods that are produced and can be used as inputs for further production
5. a graphic illustration of the combinations of output an economy can produce if all of its resources are utilized and utilized efficiently, given the state of technology
6. the total supply of all goods and services in an economy
7. the total dollar value of all final goods and services produced by resources located in the United States (regardless of who owns them) during one year's time
8. that part of economics that examines the behavior of the whole economy at once
9. items that are made for final consumption
10. a direct trade of goods or services
11. the income that is left after deducting tax payments
12. the value of gross domestic product after taking out the effect of price changes
13. the economic condition in which the average level of prices goes up

Thinking Critically About Economics

1. Describe how macroeconomics is different from microeconomics.
2. Make a list of ten consumer goods and explain why you think they are consumer goods. Mark the durable goods with a *D* and the nondurable goods with *ND.* Briefly explain why some are durable and others are nondurable.
3. Why is gross domestic product measured in dollars rather than in units?
4. Why are only final goods counted in GDP?

5. Draw a production possibilities curve to show the trade-off between producing consumer goods and capital goods (use Figure 14-3 as a model). Explain what happens when society chooses to produce more of either type of good.

6. What are capital goods? List four examples of such goods and explain why you think they are capital goods.

7. Explain the difference between the following pairs of terms:

   - physical investment versus financial investment
   - physical capital versus financial capital

   In your explanation include an example of each type of good.

8. Write a short explanation of the three ways that people use their incomes. Into which category would you put the use of money for a charitable contribution?

9. Differentiate between *real GDP* and *GDP in current dollars* and explain why *real GDP* is the better measure to use in comparing the economy from one year to another.

10. What do economists mean when they talk about leakages and injections in the economy? What are the major leakages? What are the major injections? Why is it important for leakages to equal injections?

Economic Enrichment

Make a list of at least ten services or products that you have used in the past month that were provided, completely or in part, by government. Copy the following Venn diagram on a separate sheet of paper and write the name of each product or service in the appropriate place depending on which level of government (national, state, or local) provided it. Then write a brief essay in which you state your personal thoughts about what goods and services should be provided by the government and what goods and services should not.

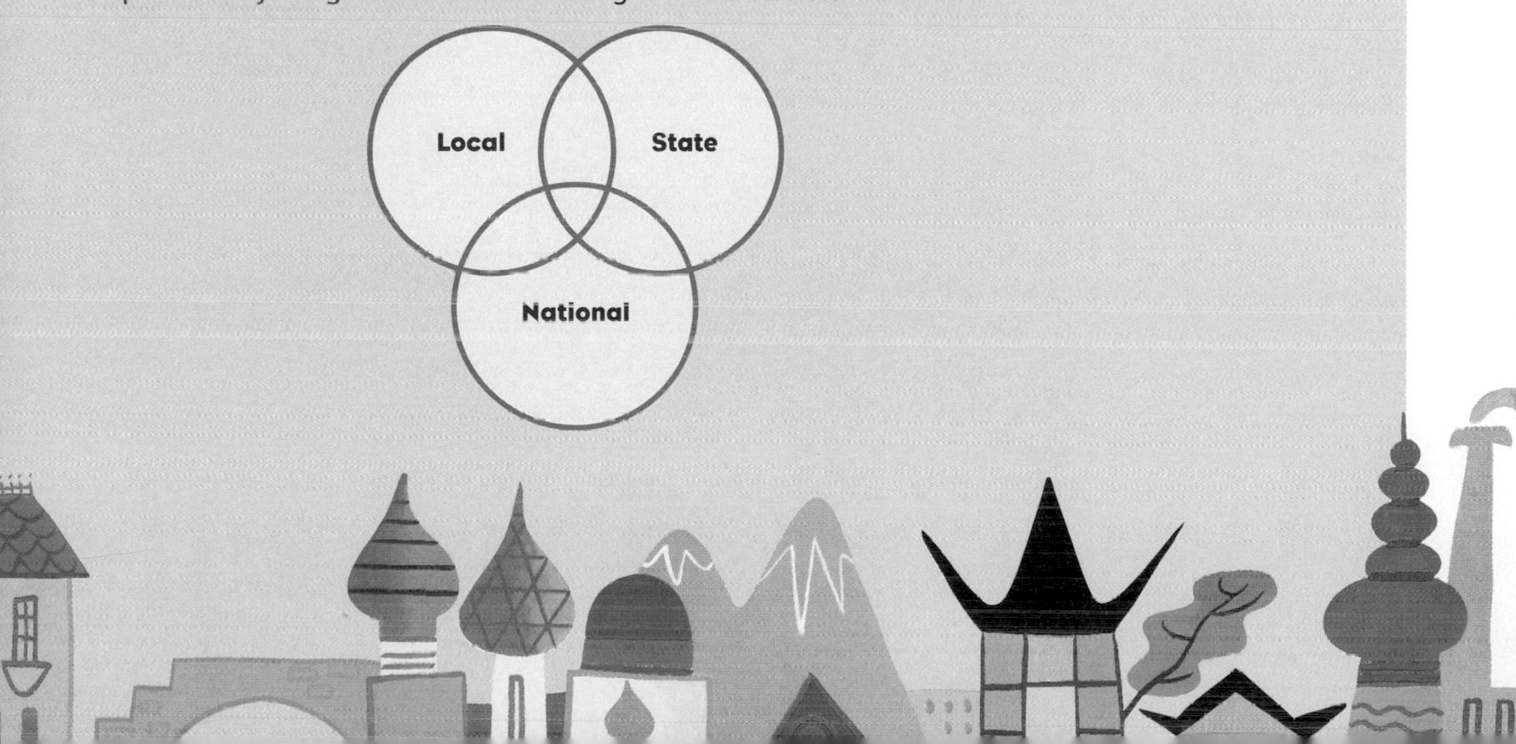

Math and Economics

Data for the current dollar value of GDP (in billions of dollars) for the United States at the start of each decade beginning with 1960 and continuing to 1990 are shown in the following table. The adjustment factor for converting GDP to real terms is also given.

Year	Current Dollar GDP	Adjustment Factor
1960	$ 513.3	0.260
1970	1,010.7	0.352
1980	2,708.0	0.717
1990	5,546.1	1.132

Use these data to calculate the constant dollar value of GDP for the four years shown. Does constant dollar or current dollar GDP give you a better idea about the growth in the economy during this period? Explain.

Writing About Economics

Go to a library and find a current issue of *Business Week* magazine. In that issue you will find a table of contents (usually about the fourth or fifth page). In the contents there will be a heading for a section on economic analysis. Read an article from that section that relates to some of the ideas in this chapter. Then write a summary of the article and about how it relates to some aspect of what you studied in this chapter.

Analyzing Primary Source Documents

"The Republican Contract with America"

The "Republican Contract with America" was introduced in the mid-1990s. It is made up of a short introductory contract and ten proposed congressional bills. This "Contract" sparked much debate between and among Republicans and Democrats across the nation. As you read through these proposed congressional bills, think of which group or groups might benefit from each of the proposals. Which groups might be hurt? Are some groups harmed and helped by different proposals? Overall, do these proposals seem fair from an economic standpoint?

Here is an excerpt from the "Contract" and the text of six of the ten bills to be proposed in Congress.

> As Republican Members of the House of Representatives and as citizens seeking to join that body we propose not just to change its policies, but even more important, to restore the bonds of trust between the people and their elected representatives.
>
> That is why, in this era of official evasion and posturing, we offer instead a detailed agenda for national renewal, a written commitment with no fine print. . . .

1. THE FISCAL RESPONSIBILITY ACT
A balanced budget/tax limitation amendment and a legislative line-item veto to restore fiscal responsibility to an out-of-control Congress, requiring them to live under the same budget constraints as families and businesses. (. . .)

3. THE PERSONAL RESPONSIBILITY ACT
Discourage illegitimacy and teen pregnancy by prohibiting welfare to minor mothers and denying increased AFDC for additional children while on welfare, cut spending for welfare programs, and enact a tough two-years-and-out provision with work requirements to promote individual responsibility.

4. THE FAMILY REINFORCEMENT ACT
Child support enforcement, tax incentives for adoption, strengthening rights of parents in their children's education, stronger child pornography laws, and an elderly dependent care tax credit to reinforce the central role of families in American society.

5. THE AMERICAN DREAM RESTORATION ACT
A $500 per child tax credit, begin repeal of the marriage tax penalty, and creation of American Dream Savings Accounts to provide middle class tax relief. (. . .)

7. THE SENIOR CITIZENS FAIRNESS ACT
Raise the Social Security earnings limit which currently forces seniors out of the work force, repeal the 1993 tax hikes on Social Security benefits, and provide tax incentives for private long-term care insurance to let Older Americans keep more of what they have earned over the years.

8. THE JOB CREATION AND WAGE ENHANCEMENT ACT
Small business incentives, capital gains cut and indexation, neutral cost recovery, risk assessment/cost-benefit analysis, strengthening the Regulatory Flexibility Act, and unfunded mandate reform to create jobs and raise worker wages. (. . .)

SOURCE: "The Republican Contract with America," **http://edf.www.media.mit.edu/conttex.html**.

Overview

Section One
We Are a Rich Nation

Section Two
Measuring the Degree of Income Inequality

Section Three
Poverty in the Midst of Riches

The Distribution of Income

Learning Objectives

15-1
Explain why the distribution of income by industry has changed over the years.

15-2
Illustrate how the distribution of income by function is related to the factors of production.

15-3
Describe the personal distribution of income in the United States.

15-4
Analyze a Lorenz curve of income distribution.

15-5
List six characteristics of the poor.

15-6
Discuss the causes of poverty.

15-7
Identify some solutions to poverty.

income were divided evenly among all the people in the United States, each person would get about $22,000. This includes the old and the young, people with jobs, and people without jobs. Many people have incomes much higher than this, and many have incomes much lower.

The Personal Distribution of Income

personal distribution of income
how income is shared among people in our society

How income is shared among people in our society is called the ***personal distribution of income.*** We all know some families who appear to have a lot of money to spend. We also know others that have little income. How much economic inequality exists? In the mid-1990s, about 16 percent of the

Econ & You

LEARN MORE TO EARN MORE

How valuable is a college education? In order to answer this difficult question, you need to consider many factors. The dollar value of a degree in terms of increased earning power is one consideration. However, there are many other benefits to a college education. Some students attend college because they want to learn a skill and some because they enjoy learning: They can develop political and social awareness and a more positive self-image as a result of their education.

The following figure shows how educational level affects income. You can see that people with lower levels of education are also likely to have lower incomes. Having a college degree does not assure you of a high income, but it certainly improves your chances.

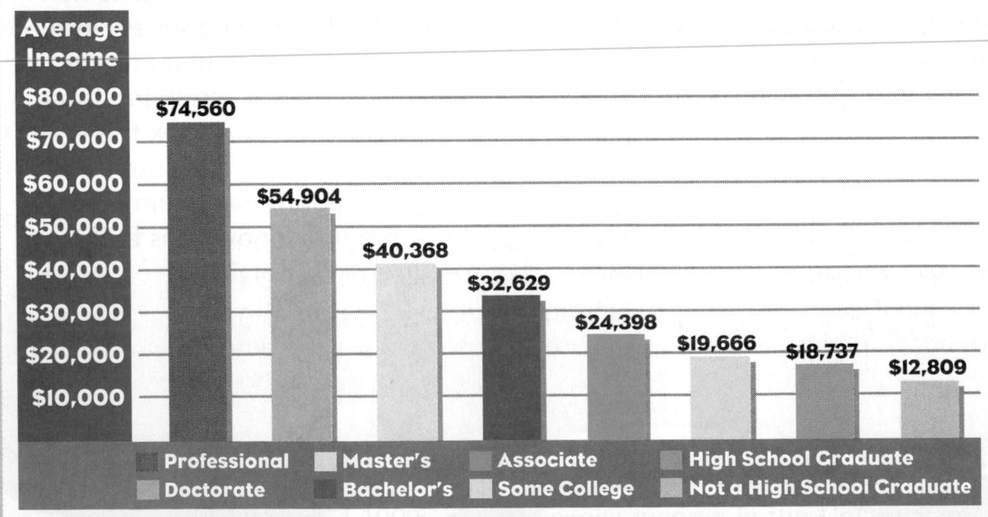

SOURCE: *More Education Means Higher Career Earnings,* U.S. Bureau of the Census Statistical Brief SB/94-17 (1994).

families in the United States had less than $15,000 in total annual family income. And, 8.9 percent had under $10,000 per year, or less than $835 a month. This is not much to live on. For this low income group, the level of education of the head of the household typically was low. Most of the heads of such households never completed high school.

About 30 percent of the families in the United States in the mid-1990s had incomes between $15,000 and $35,000. The typical head of the household in this income bracket had finished high school plus some further education. Education after high school can include college, trade school, nursing school, and secretarial school.

About 39 percent of the families in the United States at that time had incomes in the $35,000 to $75,000 range. The heads of the families in this group had even more education. At the upper end of the income ladder, more than 14 percent of families had incomes of more than $75,000. It shouldn't surprise you that most of the heads of these households were professionals with considerable education.

Equality of Income Distribution

You often see news stories about the very poor or the very rich. We also have a very large and fairly wealthy middle class. This is evidenced by the 39 percent of the families that in the mid-1990s had incomes in the $35,000 to $75,000 range. This is a wide income range. This large middle income class is considered a very good feature of our economic system.

Two opinions about the distribution of personal income are generally shared in the United States. First, it is not good to force an equal income distribution on the economy. In order to keep people's work efforts high, they should have the chance to earn more income. If all people were guaranteed an equal share of national income, there would be less incentive for them to work hard. They might not even work at all. This would cause production and incomes to fall so we would have less to share.

Second, there should not be too much inequality in the distribution of income. A lot of inequality can create social problems. This is especially true if people at the lower end think they have little chance to improve their economic standing. But, how much is too much inequality? There is no clear answer to this question. People have different feelings about what the best distribution is. Public policy has favored making the income distribution more equal but not completely equal. Our tax and welfare programs are, in part, a result of this thinking.

On the average, we are rich. But, the average includes the very rich and the very poor. As a country, we have concern for the poor. We spend a lot of time and money working to assist the poor. But, it is hard to think of ways to help that are fair to rich and poor alike. Probably the best way to help the poor is to have a healthy, growing economy. In such an economy, there would be enough well-paying jobs for everyone. Furthermore, we need to make sure that everyone has an equal chance for those jobs. Equality of opportunity is even more important than equality of income.

Checkpoint

Content Check

1. What are the major trends in the distribution of national income by industry since 1955?
2. What factor of production earns most of our national income?
3. What is the difference between per capita income and the personal distribution of income?

What Do You Think Now?

Reread *What Do You Think?* in the Section One Focus. Then answer the following question:

4. With per capita income of about $22,000, explain how there can be families in the United States that earn less than $10,000 a year.

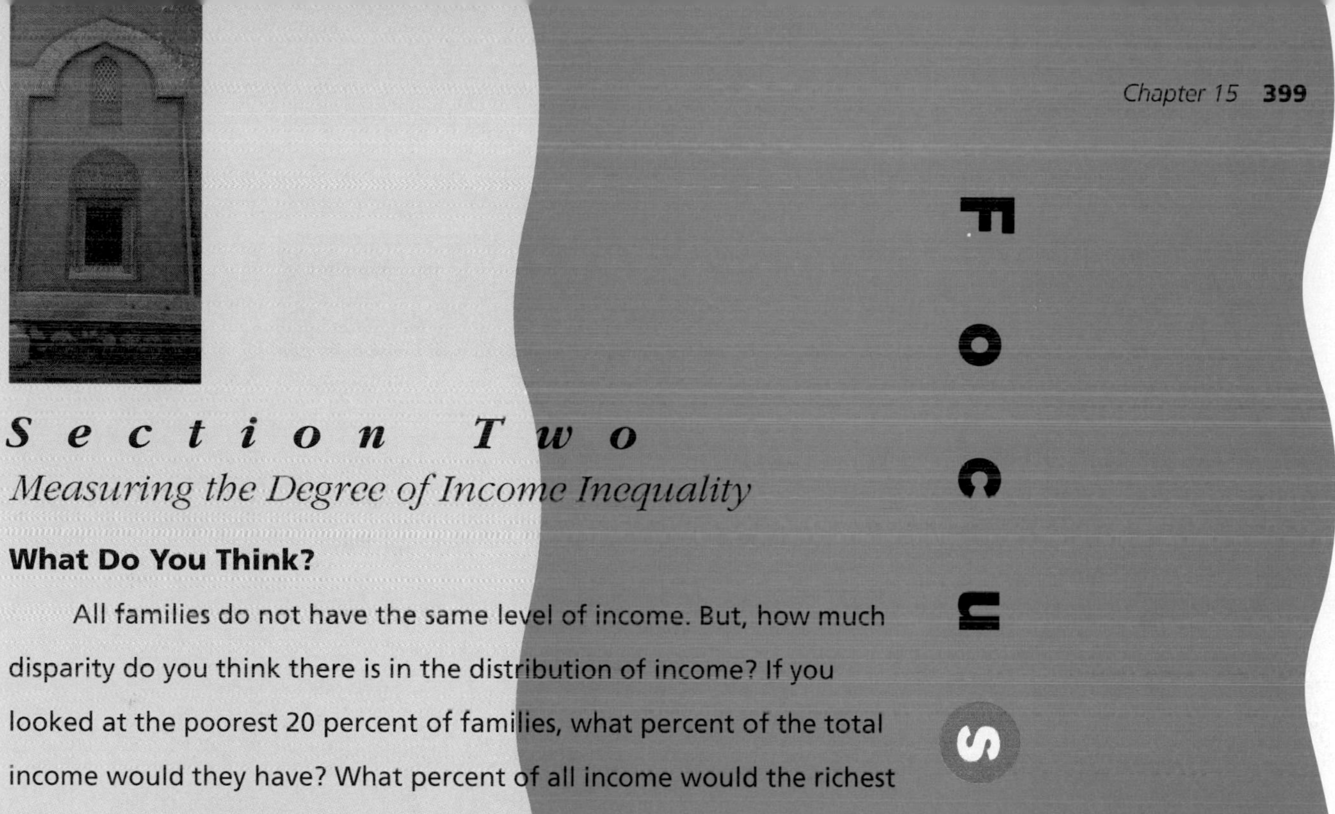

Section Two

Measuring the Degree of Income Inequality

What Do You Think?

All families do not have the same level of income. But, how much disparity do you think there is in the distribution of income? If you looked at the poorest 20 percent of families, what percent of the total income would they have? What percent of all income would the richest 20 percent of all the families have?

What's Ahead?

In order to know how income is distributed, you need some way to measure the amount of inequality that exists. In this section, you will learn about one way in which income inequality can be measured using a graph.

Term to Know

Lorenz curve

THE LORENZ CURVE

One popular way to measure income inequality is to use a Lorenz curve of income distribution. A ***Lorenz curve*** of income distribution is a graphic method of showing the amount of income inequality that exists in society at any point in time. By comparing Lorenz curves for different time periods, you can tell whether income inequality is becoming less or greater. In the United States, there is a slight trend toward greater income equality. But the changes from year to year, or even from decade to decade, are relatively small. This is because for years our income distribution has included the large middle class mentioned earlier.

Lorenz curve
a graphic method of showing the amount of income inequality that exists in society at any point in time

In order to graph the Lorenz curve, we need some information about the distribution of income. If you ranked all households in the United States from the poorest to the richest, you would find a distribution like that shown in columns two and three in Figure 15-3 on page 400.

You can see that the richest 20.0 percent of the households has 46.8 percent of the nation's income. But, the poorest 20.0 percent of the households shares a much smaller fraction of national income—only 3.8 percent. The middle 60.0 percent of households has 49.4 percent of the income.

Point	Percentage of U.S. Households	Percentage of National Income	Cumulative Percentage of U.S. Households	Cumulative Percentage of National Income
A	Poorest 20%	3.8%	20%	3.8%
B	Lower Middle 20%	9.4%	40%	13.2%
C	Middle 20%	15.9%	60%	29.1%
D	Upper Middle 20%	24.1%	80%	53.2%
E	Richest 20%	46.8%	100%	100%

Figure 15-3

Personal Distribution of Income in the United States (Based on money income before taxes)

The values in this table help you see the degree of inequality in the distribution of income. ***What percent of income do the richest 40 percent of households have?***

These data about income distribution form the basis for a Lorenz curve. In a Lorenz curve, the cumulative percentage of income is measured along the vertical axis. The cumulative percentage of households is measured on the horizontal axis. To draw a Lorenz curve, you need to find cumulative percentages. The cumulative percentages are shown in the last two columns of Figure 15-3.

This gives five points to graph: *A, B, C, D,* and *E.* These five points are graphed in Figure 15-4. When all five of these points are connected, they

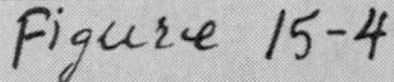

The Lorenz Curve of Income Distribution in the United States

The curved line through Points *A, B, C, D,* and *E* shows how income is distributed in the United States. ***What percent of income would the lowest 40 percent of the households have?***

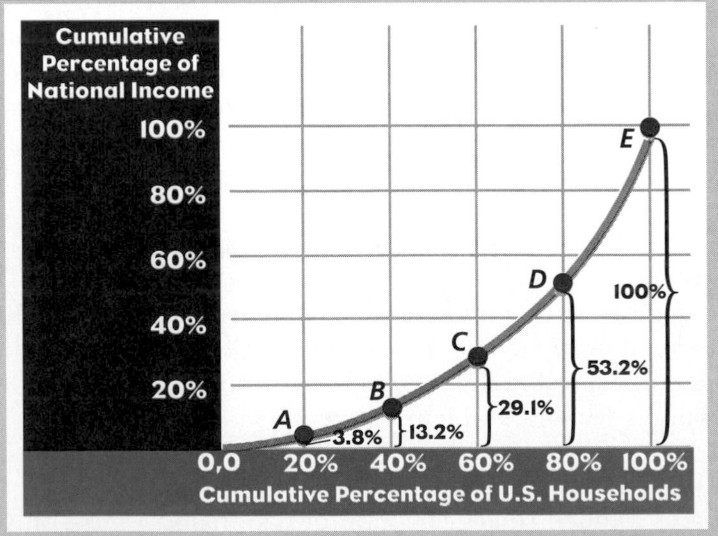

represent the Lorenz curve for income distribution. The curve starts at the origin (0,0) since 0 percent of the households would have 0 percent of the income. It ends at the point *E* where 100 percent of the families have all of the income (100 percent of the income).

To be sure you understand what each point in the graph in Figure 15-4 represents, let's look at two of them in detail. The point marked *A* is directly above 20 percent on the horizontal axis, so it represents 20 percent of the households. Reading directly from *A* over to the vertical axis, you find that *A* represents 3.8 percent of the national income. Therefore, Point *A* shows that the poorest 20.0 percent of all U.S. households shares just 3.8 percent of our national income. Now look at Point *C*. Point *C* shows that the lowest 60.0 percent of all U.S. households shares 29.1 percent of the national income.

Global Economy

EDUCATION MEETS DEVELOPMENT IN MALAYSIA

Malaysia, a country in southeast Asia, has a land area of about 130,000 square miles—somewhat smaller than the state of Montana. It has a population of about 19 million people—about the same as the state of New York. Its population density is 144 people per square mile—in Montana there are less than six people per square mile and in New York there are 337 people per square mile.

The average income per person in Malaysia is about $2,790 compared to about $22,000 in the United States. You know that this means that Malaysians have, on average, less ability to buy goods and services than we do. For example, in the United States there are 814 televisions per thousand people. In Malaysia that figure is 149. In Malaysia there are 11 phone lines per 100 people, whereas in the United States there are 56.

To help with economic development, Malaysia is investing in education and training. Between 1970 and 1990, the percent of children of elementary school age enrolled in school increased from 87 percent to 93 percent. During the same period, secondary school enrollment increased from 34 to 58 percent. According to a World Bank publication, the government of Malaysia has made education and training a priority because such an investment is necessary to increase the standard of living for Malaysian families.

THE LINE OF EQUALITY

What would the Lorenz curve look like if there were perfect equality in the distribution of income? To find out, first look at the percentage distribution of income if there were complete equality.

1. The lowest 20 percent of all U.S. households would have 20 percent of the income.
2. The lowest 40 percent of all U.S. households would have 40 percent of the income.
3. The lowest 60 percent of all U.S. households would have 60 percent of the income.
4. The lowest 80 percent of all U.S. households would have 80 percent of the income.
5. The entire 100 percent of all U.S. households would have 100 percent of the income.

When these points are graphed, they form a straight line from the origin to Point *E*, as shown in Figure 15-5.

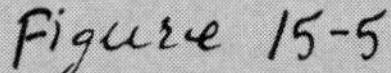

The Line of Equality

The straight line from the origin to Point *E* shows a perfectly equal distribution of income. The curved line through *A, B, C, D,* and *E* shows the actual distribution of income in the United States. A move to the dashed line would show a change to a more equal distribution of income. ***What would the Lorenz curve look like for a less equal distribution of income?***

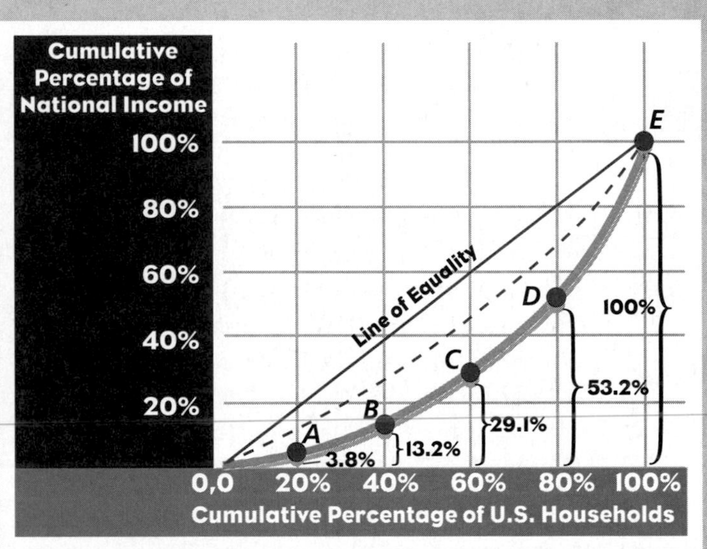

The straight line from the origin to Point *E* would be the Lorenz curve if there were a perfectly equal distribution of income. So we call the line from the origin to Point *E* the *line of equality*. When income is not shared equally, the Lorenz curve is below this line. The line joining Points *A, B, C, D,* and *E,* the actual Lorenz curve for the distribution of income in the United States, is below the line of equality. The farther the actual Lorenz curve is below the line of equality, the greater the inequality of the distribution of income.

Economic Dilemma

CAN A NEGATIVE INCOME TAX BE POSITIVE?

Criticism of our public assistance or welfare programs has led to discussions of other ways to help the poor. Some plans that have been proposed by well-known economists, such as Milton Friedman and James Tobin, include a negative income tax program. The term *negative income tax* describes poverty programs in which a person or family below some income level receives a *payment* from the government rather than pays taxes. The payment, or subsidy, is the opposite of a tax and thus is called a negative tax.

Negative income tax proposals have three important characteristics: (1) minimum income, (2) cut-off income, and (3) tax rate. The minimum income is the amount of income that every family is guaranteed. That amount usually is determined by finding out the amount of money necessary to support the basic necessities of life and adjusting it for family size and local cost of living.

The income at which the individual must begin to pay positive taxes and thus lose benefits (negative taxes) is called the *cut-off income.* Under most negative income tax plans, each family gets the basic minimum income grant from the government. But, if family members work and earn other income, their subsidy is lowered by some percentage of their earnings. That percentage is the tax rate. At the cut-off point, the reduction in the subsidy due to earnings equals the initial subsidy. Therefore, no government payment is forthcoming. If a family earns above the cut-off level, it owes tax to the government.

Traditionally, we have used different welfare programs, such as food stamps and subsidized housing, to guarantee a minimum standard of living rather than income subsidies. Many people believe that there would be less waste with a negative income tax plan than with our current programs. Some people also argue that with a negative income tax program people would have more choice in obtaining the specific things that their families need.

There is continuing debate about whether it is better to relieve poverty by providing cash payments through a negative income tax or by providing specific items, such as food stamps or public housing. What do you think?

Suppose the government starts a new program to make the distribution of income more equal. We want to be able to measure the success or failure of the program. This can be done by drawing Lorenz curves for income distribution before and after the program. If the *after* curve is closer to the line of equality, the program successfully made the distribution of income more equal. For example, suppose the Lorenz curve moves from the line drawn for the United States to the dashed line in Figure 15-5. This shows more equality in the distribution of income.

Checkpoint

Content Check

1. What does the Lorenz curve represent?
2. What does the line of equality represent?
3. How can the Lorenz curve and the line of equality be used to evaluate the success or failure of an income redistribution plan?
4. If the distribution of income became less equal over time, would the Lorenz curve become straighter or more curved?

What Do You Think Now?

Reread *What Do You Think?* in the Section Two Focus. Then answer the following questions:

5. How much disparity is there in the distribution of income?
6. Is the amount of inequality in the distribution of income more or less than you thought before reading this section?

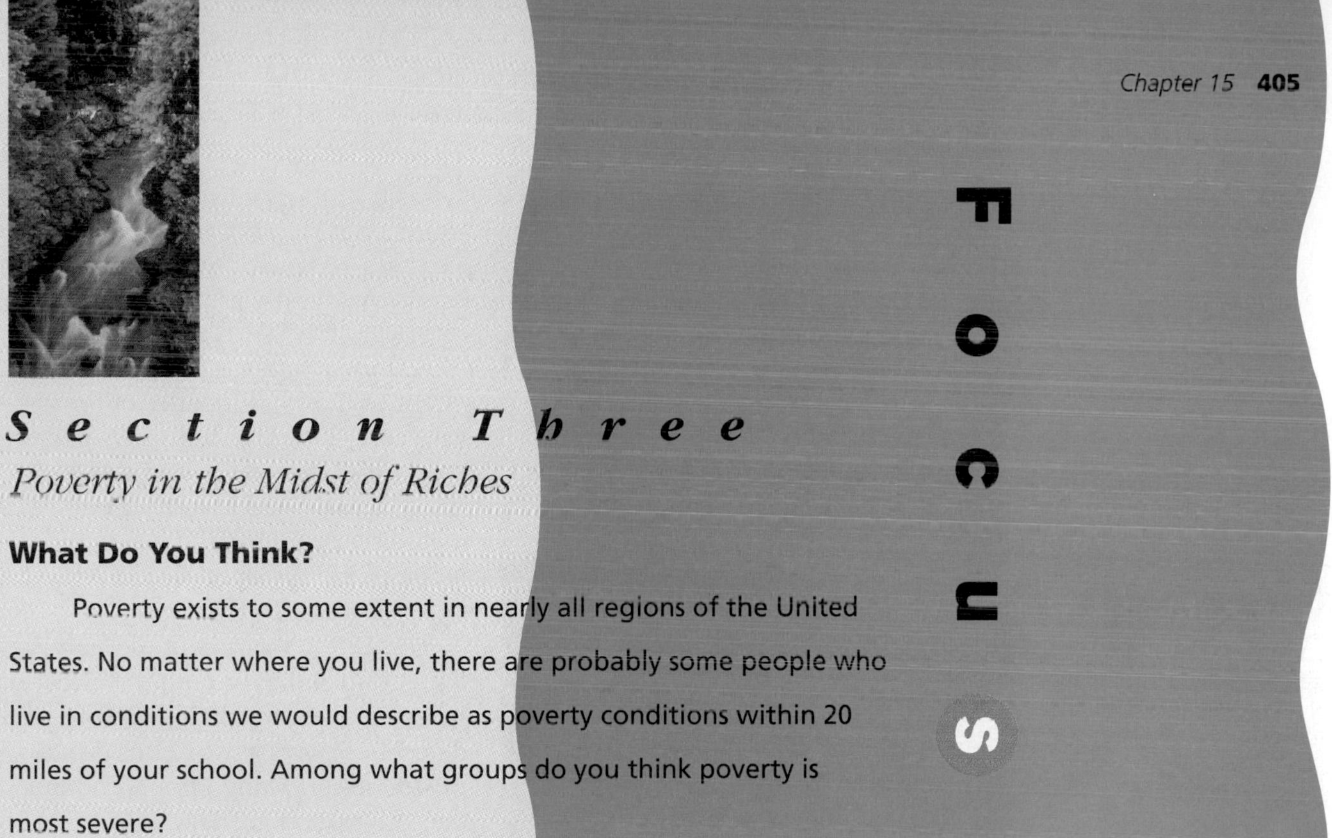

Section Three
Poverty in the Midst of Riches

What Do You Think?

Poverty exists to some extent in nearly all regions of the United States. No matter where you live, there are probably some people who live in conditions we would describe as poverty conditions within 20 miles of your school. Among what groups do you think poverty is most severe?

What's Ahead?

People's ideas and feelings about poverty are many and varied. Some people think that the poor are lazy and worthless people who live on government handouts and deserve little or no assistance. Others feel that people are poor predominantly due to factors outside their personal control and that the rest of society should do more to help alleviate their condition. In this section, you will learn about poverty in the United States and will then be in a better position to form your own opinions about related issues.

Terms to Know

poverty

job discrimination

AN OVERVIEW OF POVERTY

When we speak of ***poverty,*** we are referring to the condition in which people do not have enough income to provide for their basic needs, such as food, clothing, and shelter. But, it is difficult to settle on a universal definition of poverty.

poverty
the condition in which people do not have enough income to provide for their basic needs, such as food, clothing, and shelter

Poverty in the United States

Poverty often brings to mind images of starving children in Africa, Asia, and Latin America. But it also exists in the United States. You may have seen photos of the bloated bellies and skinny limbs of some children in scattered low income rural sections of this country or in certain crowded city tenements. It is difficult to understand why poverty exists in a country where the overall standard of living is high.

In some very poor countries, poverty is bound to occur because of the low level of total income coupled with a very large population. In the United States, there is enough total income that poverty is not a necessary outcome.

We produce enough food, clothing, and shelter for all of our people to live well. But, some Americans are very poor and do not share in the national prosperity. In the United States, we have plenty of income, but that income is distributed unevenly. Our poverty problem is thus partly a problem of income distribution.

You have seen that if the population of the United States is divided into fifths, the bottom fifth receives only 3.8 percent of the total income of the country. The second fifth receives only 9.4 percent; the third fifth, 15.9 percent; the fourth fifth, 24.1 percent; and the top fifth, 46.8 percent of the money. These figures only represent income. If actual wealth were used, including property and assets plus income, the distribution would be even more lopsided.

The U.S. government did very little about poverty until the Great Depression of the 1930s. Before that time, poverty was considered a private affair. Many people thought that the poor were lazy and so deserved to be poor. However, the high rates of unemployment in the 1930s added millions to the ranks of the poor. It became clear that not all people were poor because they were lazy. Many were poor because the economic system did not provide enough jobs. Therefore, the government took some responsibility for the care of the poor during this period. Government programs included public works projects, bank reform, and support of labor unions. Perhaps the most important legislation was the Social Security Act, which provided income for older citizens past employment age.

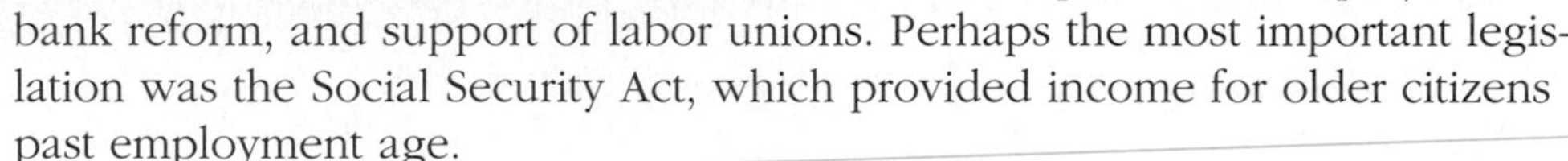

During the 1940s and 1950s, the United States prospered, and the issue of poverty dropped into the background. However, it was brought back to public attention in the 1960s and 1970s. The civil rights movement, the War on Poverty, and President Johnson's Great Society Program all helped refocus our attention on poverty.

The Poverty Line

Some people think about poverty in terms of a fixed income level, such as $5,000 per year. But, this is not a good measure of poverty because, as prices change, the buying power of $5,000 also changes. For example, suppose the poverty level had been set at $5,000 in 1975. By 1985, after adjusting for price changes, it would have taken about $10,000 to buy as much as you could buy for $5,000 in 1975. By 1995, an income of more than $14,000 was needed to buy the same things that $5,000 bought 20 years before. So, using a fixed income level is not a good way to define the poverty level.

The U.S. government defines poverty in terms of a *poverty line*. To determine the poverty line, the U.S. Department of Agriculture first figures the cost of a year's nutritious, low-cost diet. This figure is then adjusted for family size and composition. For example, in the mid-1990s the poverty line for a family of four was close to $15,000. Different poverty lines are determined for different areas based on varying food prices.

There are some problems with this definition of the poverty line. First, the low-budget diet that forms the basis of the definition is not necessarily the least expensive nutritious diet. The government's standard diet allows for variety and choice. But, people could provide a basic diet for less money by having less variety. Second, the definition considers only current money income. The savings and assets of a family are not evaluated by the official definition of poverty. Therefore, some people who do not seem poor may sometimes qualify for poverty assistance programs such as the food stamp program. Despite a low current income, these people may have money in the bank or even own homes.

To help remedy the measurement problems caused by changing prices, the poverty level is changed every year. As prices go up, so does the official definition of the poverty level. The increase in the poverty level since 1960 for a family of four is shown in Figure 15-6.

Year	Poverty Income Level
1960	$ 3,022
1965	3,223
1970	3,968
1975	5,500
1980	8,414
1985	10,989
1990	13,359
1992	14,335
1995*	15,000

***This is an estimate.**

Figure 15-6

Increases in Poverty Level for Families of Four

These values show how much the official poverty level has increased since 1960. ***Do you think that the poverty level will continue to go up?***

SOURCE: U.S. Bureau of the Census, *Statistical Abstract of the United States, 1994,* 114th ed. (Washington, D.C., 1994), 480, Table 739.

CHARACTERISTICS OF THE POOR

In the mid-1990s, nearly 40 million people in the United States were judged to be poor by the government. Those 40 million represented about 15 percent of the population. That is, about one in every seven people in the United States lived in poverty conditions. Poverty can be found in all ethnic and racial groups. About 11.6 percent of all white families are below the poverty line. For African-American families, this figure is 33.3 percent and for Hispanic families, it is 29.3 percent.

Poverty can be found all over the United States. When you look at the poor as a percentage of an area's population, the greatest concentrations of the poor live in southern rural areas and in Appalachia. Small cities and towns have the next highest percentage of poor. Many people are surprised that, in terms of percentages, large cities have fewer poor people than rural

areas or small cities and towns. It is not surprising, however, that the lowest percentage of poverty is in the suburbs.

Families with one or more of the following characteristics are most likely to be poor:

1. The family belongs to a minority group.
2. The head of the family is female.
3. The head of the family has no high school diploma.
4. The head of the family is handicapped by illness or physical or mental problems.
5. The family lives in a rural area.
6. The family has seven or more members.

The data in Figure 15-7 illustrate some of these characteristics. You can see that 16.9 percent of people in the South were living in poverty, but only 12.3 percent of people in the Northeast lived in poverty. You also can see that the percentage of the young and old who are living in poverty is higher than the percentage of people between 35 and 64 years of age.

Age	Percent in Poverty
Under 18 years	21.9
18–24 years	18.0
25–34 years	13.2
35–44 years	9.8
45–54 years	7.9
55–59 years	10.0
60–64 years	10.6
65 years and older	12.9

Race	Percent in Poverty
African American	33.3
Hispanic	29.3
White	11.6

Education	Percent in Poverty
No high school diploma	24.1
High school diploma—no college	11.0
Some college—less than four-year degree	7.2
Four-year college degree or more	2.2

Region	Percent in Poverty
Northeast	12.3
Midwest	13.1
South	16.9
West	14.4

Figure 15-7

Percentage of Persons Below Poverty Level by Age, Race, Region, and Education

These data show that those people in poverty are likely to be among the youngest and oldest people, are likely to be non-white, are likely to live in the South, and/or are likely to have little formal education. ***In what region of the country is the percent of people who live in poverty the lowest?***

SOURCE: U.S. Bureau of the Census, *Statistical Abstract of the United States, 1994*, 114th ed. (Washington, D.C., 1994), 476, 478.

CAUSES OF POVERTY

Most causes of poverty can be classified into one of the following categories:

1. unemployment,

2. low productivity, and

3. restrictions on job entry.

During the Depression of the 1930s, the largest cause of poverty was unemployment. The economic system failed, and there was not enough total demand to provide jobs for all those who were willing to work. Poverty caused by low total demand, such as the poverty of the 1930s, is a direct result of unemployment. This can be fought by applying the necessary tools of monetary and fiscal policy to reach a full-employment economy. Monetary and fiscal policies represent government actions designed to influence the level of national economic activity. These policies are discussed in detail later in this text. However, because of the way we define a full-employment economy, poverty is not eliminated by these policies. We say the economy is *fully employed* when about 95 percent of the labor force is employed. Even when there is full employment, there still may be unemployed persons and poverty.

A second cause of poverty is *low productivity*. Many people have characteristics that contribute to low productivity. These characteristics include low educational levels, physical and mental handicaps, and old age. Those who have jobs but do not make enough money to go over the poverty line also are considered to have low productivity. These people are called the "working poor." Low productivity is the major cause of poverty among these groups.

In our economy, labor, capital (machinery), and land are productive. All three are used to produce goods. The more of these three factors that people own, the more income they are likely to have. Usually the poor own neither capital nor land. All they have is their own labor, and their labor often is not very skilled. Thus, a low skill level leads to low productivity, which often results in poverty.

Restrictions on job entry also contribute to poverty by reducing the number of people who have access to skilled jobs. Many of the poor work in unskilled jobs, such as janitorial jobs and certain types of assembly-line work. In fact, the way out of poverty for many is to learn a skill and enter the skilled labor market. The skilled labor market includes such workers as electricians, plumbers, and millwrights. However, obtaining training in a skilled trade may be difficult. Some trade unions have very restrictive apprenticeship programs. Some unions allow only a few new workers to learn the trade, and they make the apprenticeship period very long. These trade unions may

limit the number of skilled workers and thereby keep their wages high. Thus, the trade unions protect their members. However, this prevents others from getting jobs.

job discrimination the refusal to hire certain people because of their gender, race, or other characteristics that have nothing to do with their ability to do a job

Another form of restriction is job discrimination. ***Job discrimination*** is the refusal to hire certain people because of their gender, race, or other characteristics that have nothing to do with their ability to do a job. For example, at one time, women rarely became doctors or business executives. Today, women can enter these fields much more easily. Although there is still discrimination, minority groups and women have far more freedom to choose careers that they want than they ever had before.

The poor are caught in a vicious circle of poverty. They do not have the skills to earn a living in today's society, and many have handicaps that prevent them from learning such skills. Since they lack skills, they don't have the money it takes to learn these skills even if they are able. They are trapped and often they stay poor.

POVERTY PROGRAMS

Since the 1930s, the government's attempts to help the poor have taken three major directions: (1) creating jobs for the poor, (2) setting up education and retraining programs for the poor, and (3) providing income support programs.

Creating Jobs

The Works Progress Administration (WPA) and the Public Works Administration (PWA) were set up to create jobs for the poor during the 1930s. Both programs involved public projects such as the building of roads, sidewalks, schools, and parks. Despite their many useful and desirable results, the WPA and the PWA received criticism as make-work projects. That is, much of the work was created only to keep people busy. As unemployment decreased with the approach of World War II, these programs phased out.

The Economic Opportunity Act of 1964 also provided jobs for the poor through the Job Corps, the Neighborhood Youth Corps Work Training Program, and the Work-Study Program. Only one out of nine people who joined the Job Corps stayed in the program for a full year, and one-third quit within three months. The Neighborhood Youth Corps subsidized 500,000 jobs for young people. The Work-Study Program continues to provide part-time work for college students from poor families.

In 1971, the Emergency Employment Act provided $2.25 billion for public service jobs for the unemployed and the underemployed. Job creation programs have helped our unemployment problems. However, the kinds of jobs created generally have provided little training or opportunity to improve skills. Often, these jobs do not lead to permanent employment.

Education and Retraining

The second way to help the poor is to provide for their education and retraining. Instead of creating jobs to fit the skills of the poor, the poor learn skills that will fit the available jobs. The Manpower Development Training Act, the Work-Study program, and the CETA program used this approach in their attempts to reduce poverty. In general, the training given under these programs succeeded. More than 90 percent of those who received aid in the Manpower programs stayed with the jobs they were trained for.

Economic Spotlight

CAN SHE MAKE WORK PAY?

Who has the second-hardest job after the President? Donna Shalala, Secretary of the Department of Health and Human Services, believes she does. Why is her job so difficult? Because Shalala has to tackle the enormous challenge of reforming the U.S. welfare and health care systems. As head of a federal department that has a bigger budget than that of the Pentagon, Shalala controls 40 percent of all federal government spending.

Growing up in a working-class neighborhood in Cleveland, Ohio, helped this policy maker keep her priorities straight. Shalala says that every woman in her family, from her mother to her aunts, held a job to put food on the table. Shalala says it is this upbringing that shaped her view that all welfare recipients—including mothers of young children—should get jobs within two years. Her goal is to put everyone who *can* work to work. Part of Shalala's plan is to make work "pay"—that is, to raise the minimum wage so that it is more desirable for people to work than to stay on welfare.

Today's welfare system supports more than 14 million parents and children, with the number of welfare recipients climbing every year. One welfare program alone, Aid to Families with Dependent Children (AFDC), costs the United States $22 billion a year. Shalala believes that, with all this money, the system has failed to break the cycle of poverty. It discourages people from working and encourages dependence on the government. She wants to change the nature of welfare to make it a temporary measure to help people get back on their feet and back into the workforce.

This kind of reform requires money for training and education. But, it's hard to explain to Americans that cutting welfare will initially take more tax money, not less. To win support, Shalala believes, "You have to demonstrate that, in the long run, it will save us money, that the cost of doing nothing is very high. It's a much larger cost for our society of keeping people their whole lives on welfare."

Throughout her career, Shalala has demonstrated that she knows how to get results. As the only woman on the Municipal Assistance Corporation (MAC), she helped rescue New York City from financial disaster in the 1970s. She also served as assistant secretary of the Department of Housing and Urban Development (HUD), was president of Hunter College in New York, and was the first woman to head a Big Ten university—the University of Wisconsin. As for her current job, Shalala says she "wanted to be where the action is." Somehow, it seems more accurate to say that "the action" is wherever Donna Shalala is.

Income Supplements

The third way to help the poor is through income supplement programs. Many people believe that income supplements are crucial to eliminating poverty. There are people who are poor because they cannot work (and cannot be trained for productive jobs) for reasons of handicaps or age. In addition, regardless of our success in educating and retraining the poor, some poverty will continue because of a lack of jobs. In the United States, our current programs of income supplements have developed in a piecemeal pattern. These programs include Old Age and Survivors Insurance (OASI), Medicaid, Medicare, Aid to Families with Dependent Children (AFDC), and food stamps. These programs are not aimed specifically at the poor. They are aimed at people in certain categories, such as low-income families with dependent children, the aged, and the disabled.

Problems with Poverty Programs

There are problems with the poverty programs in the United States. Even when a lot of money supports these programs, the results often are not good. Some people argue that these programs discourage the poor from working and being productive. And, it is true that some people get more money from welfare programs than they can earn by working. This is usually only true for people with low skill levels. They cannot qualify for jobs that pay very much, and so they are better off financially getting welfare benefits.

A great many people are employed in government agencies that run our welfare programs. Of course, these jobs cost taxpayers money. Many people think that it takes far too much money to run these programs. But, many employees are needed to keep track of all the rules that determine who should have different benefits. There is a trade-off between our desire to make sure only the eligible poor get aid and our desire to keep welfare costs down.

Checkpoint

Content Check

1. Why are the less educated more likely to be in poverty?

2. Are minorities more or less likely to live in poverty than the rest of society?

3. What are three causes of poverty?

What Do You Think Now?

Reread *What Do You Think?* in the Section Three Focus. Then answer the following questions:

4. Among what groups do you think poverty is most severe? Why?

Concepts in Brief

1. The United States is a rich nation. Our national income is so high that nearly all families have cars. Almost every household has at least one television and many other expensive goods. We earn our incomes by producing goods and services. Historically, manufacturing was the biggest income-earning sector of the economy. However, this sector has been shrinking and now the services and finance, insurance, and real estate sectors account for the largest percentage of our national income.

2. The functional distribution of income is the way in which income is divided by economic functions. Most of our income is earned by our personal labor effort. Other income comes from rent, profits, and interest.

3. In the United States, there is a large middle income class. There also are the very poor and the very rich. But, our economic system has enough economic opportunity that the majority of people belong to a large middle class. The average level of income goes up as a person's educational level increases. In the lowest income bracket, the typical head of the household did not complete high school. At the upper end of the income distribution, the average years of education include a college degree.

4. A Lorenz curve can show graphically the amount of inequality in the distribution of income. The Lorenz curve bows down away from the line of equality. The more it bows, the greater the amount of inequality shown. The Lorenz curve can be used to measure the success of programs to make income distribution more equal.

5. The very poor in this country are likely to have one or more of the following characteristics: the family belongs to a minority group, the head of the family is female, the head of the family has eight years or less of formal education, the head of the family is handicapped by illness or by physical or mental problems, the family lives in a rural area, and/or the family has seven or more members.

6. Some people are poor because there are not enough good jobs for everyone who wants one. Some are poor because they lack skills and training. And, some people are poor because of restrictions, due to unionization or prejudice, to entry into high-skill and high-paying jobs.

7. Our country has used many programs over the years to help the poor. Some programs create jobs for the poor. Some help the poor get better job skills. Other programs transfer money or goods to the poor from the rest of the society.

Economic Foundations

1. What three industry sectors have increased the most in the distribution of income since 1955?
2. What two industry sectors have decreased the most in the distribution of income since 1955?
3. Explain the difference between personal and functional distribution of income.
4. What does the space between the Lorenz curve and the line of equality represent?
5. List six characteristics that increase the chances of being poor.
6. Identify three factors that are considered to be causes of poverty.
7. Describe three approaches to helping the poor.

Your Economic Vocabulary

Build your economic vocabulary by matching the following terms with their definitions.

functional distribution of income

job discrimination

Lorenz curve

per capita income

personal distribution of income

poverty

1. a graphic method of showing the amount of income inequality that exists in society at any point in time
2. the condition in which people do not have enough income to provide for their basic needs, such as food, clothing, and shelter
3. how income is shared among people in our society
4. the refusal to hire certain people because of their gender, race, or other characteristics that have nothing to do with their ability to do a job
5. the way in which income is divided by economic functions
6. the average income per person

Thinking Critically About Economics

1. The following statement appeared in this chapter: "Equality of opportunity is even more important than equality of income." Do you agree or disagree with this statement? Why? What do you think a poor person would say about it? What would a rich person say about it?
2. Study the following two Lorenz curves that show the distribution of income in Countries *A* and *B*. Which country has the most inequality in the distribution of income? How can you tell? In which country would you rather live? Why?

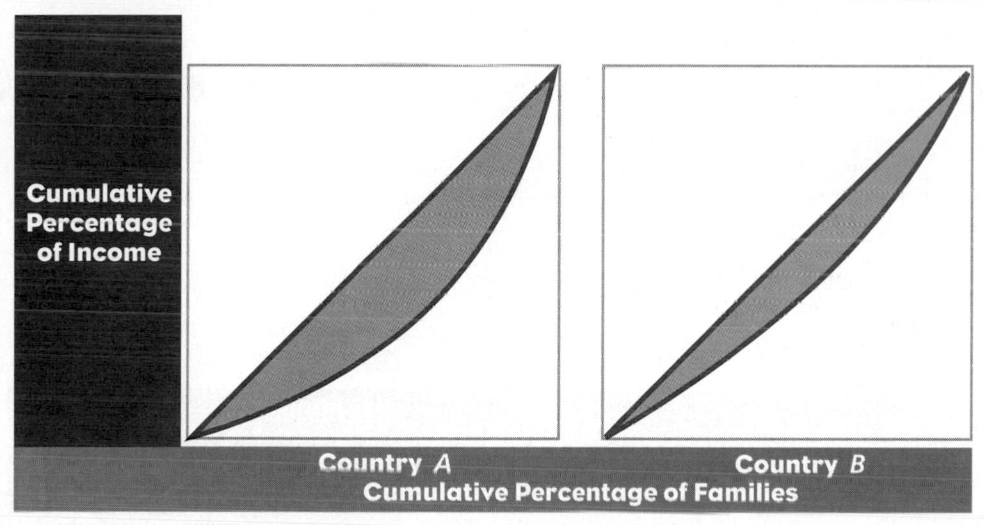

3. Write a paragraph describing what poverty in the United States means to you. Why does a rich country like ours have a poverty problem?
4. Do you agree with the way our government defines poverty? Why or why not? Would it be better or worse to use a fixed income level, such as $12,000, to define poverty? Why?
5. How is low productivity related to poverty? What does this suggest about a person getting as much training and education as possible? Should you be selective in the skills you develop, or should you develop as many as you can? Why?
6. What are some of the causes of poverty in the United States? Which do you think are the most important?
7. What kinds of programs have been used to fight poverty in the United States? Which kind do you think is best? Why?

Economic Enrichment

At some time in your life, you will have to choose a career. You could become a plumber, a dentist, a homemaker, a sales clerk, a teacher, an artist. The list of choices is almost endless. You have a great deal of freedom to choose a career. You probably have more freedom to choose now than at any time in our country's history.

What type of career do you want to have? Have you considered the current and future demand for people in that career? What are some economic and noneconomic factors to consider? Go to the library or use the Internet to research a career of your choice. Find out the following about your career choice: educational requirements, training requirements, future market demand for that career, work environment, and average earnings.

Math and Economics

The following data represent the distribution of income in the United States about ten years prior to the data given in Figure 15-3.

Personal Distribution of Income in the United States

(Based on money income before taxes)

Point	Percentage of U.S. Households	Percentage of National Income	Cumulative Percentage of U.S. Households	Cumulative Percentage of National Income
A	Poorest 20%	5%	20%	%
B	Lower Middle 20%	11%	40%	%
C	Middle 20%	17%	60%	%
D	Upper Middle 20%	24%	80%	%
E	Richest 20%	43%	100%	%

Copy this table on a separate sheet of paper and complete the last column by calculating the cumulative percentage of national income for U.S. households. Refer to Figure 15-3 if you need help. Then create a graph, plot the points, and connect the points to create a Lorenz curve. Add a line of equality that begins at the origin and ends at Point *E*. Finally, draw on the same graph the Lorenz curve for the data in Figure 15-3. In a short paragraph, describe the relationship between the two Lorenz curves you have drawn and discuss the movement in the distribution of income in the United States over the ten-year period.

Writing About Economics

Mollie Orshansky, an economist, developed the current approach to establishing the poverty level of income. She found that a typical family spent one-third of its income on food. From this, she reasoned that the minimum cost of living could be calculated by multiplying a minimally adequate food budget by three. This market basket of food products is now called the *Thrifty Food Plan*. Each year, the poverty level determined in this way is increased by the amount of the increase in the Consumer Price Index for urban consumers (CPI-U).

This determination of the poverty level is an *absolute* measure. It is absolute because it defines poverty using a subsistence level of income; that is, it determines the income level on which it is possible for a family to survive. For an economy with a rising living standard and a rising average income, this kind of absolute measure causes the poverty level to fall further and further behind the average household.

A *relative* measure of poverty is often suggested to get around this problem of the growing gap in living standards. More than 200 years ago, Adam Smith suggested that "the custom of the country" should be used as the standard. A recent study by the joint Economic Committee of Congress supported this type of relative measure. It recommended raising the poverty level in line with the growth in median family income.

Think about the impact of using an absolute measure versus a relative measure for determining the poverty level. Then, write a letter to your congressional representatives explaining why you think an absolute or a relative measure should be used to determine the poverty line. Have your teacher review your letters before you mail them.

Overview

Unemployment

Learning Objectives

16-1
Define unemployment.

16-2
Explain how the unemployment rate is determined.

16-3
Measure unemployment for various groups, based on age, gender, and race.

16-4
Analyze the economic, social, and personal costs of unemployment.

16-5
Identify ways the government can help soften the effects of unemployment.

16-6
Describe four kinds of unemployment.

However, both government and news reports use this measure of unemployment.

Unemployment during the Great Depression rose to as high as 25 percent. However, the unemployment rate since 1950 has generally been between 3 percent and 8 percent. Most of the periods when unemployment was near 8 percent were during recessions and usually lasted for only a short time. In the 1974 to 1975 recession, unemployment reached a high of 9.2 percent in May, 1975. In 1982, again during a recession, unemployment was more than 10 percent by the end of the year. Thus far in the 1990s, the highest unemployment rate was 7.7 percent in June of 1992. By the following June, it had fallen to under 7 percent.

GEOGRAPHIC DIFFERENCES IN UNEMPLOYMENT

The Department of Labor gathers unemployment figures from a wide geographic area. These figures show that different regions of the country have different unemployment rates. The map in Figure 16-1 shows how the unemployment rate differs from one state to another. Official unemployment rates are even available for about 150 smaller but important labor areas. In the smaller area data, some labor markets are nearly always well below the national rate of unemployment. Other areas are usually above the national rate. What was the unemployment rate in your state? How does that compare with the national average of 6.8 percent?

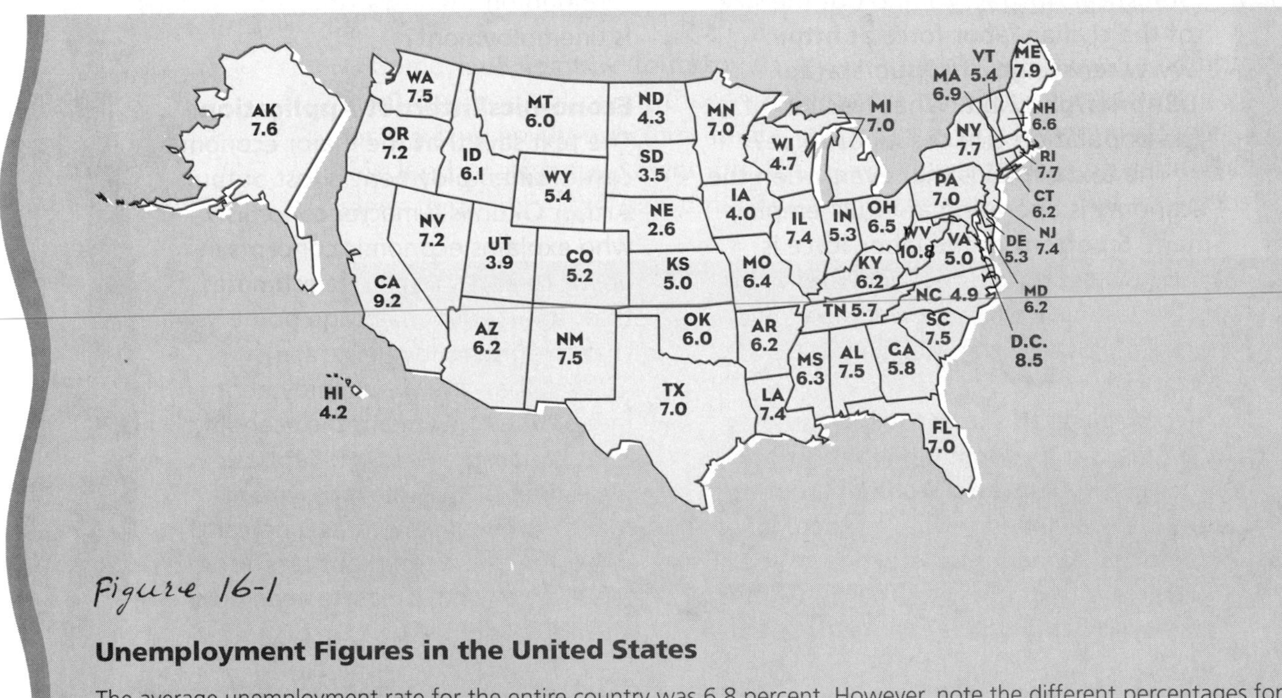

Figure 16-1

Unemployment Figures in the United States

The average unemployment rate for the entire country was 6.8 percent. However, note the different percentages for each state. ***What economic and social factors would make unemployment higher or lower in one area of the country than in another?***

SOURCE: U.S. Bureau of the Census, *Statistical Abstract of the United States:* 1994, 114th ed. (Washington, D.C., 1994), 399.

UNEMPLOYMENT DIFFERENCES BY AGE, RACE, AND GENDER

Look at Figure 16-2 before reading further. You can see that unemployment rates are different for different groups of people. Young people between the ages of 16 and 19 are hit hardest by unemployment. Their unemployment rate is often close to three times greater than the general unemployment rate. The unemployment rate among nonwhite workers is the next highest—often close to twice as high as the general unemployment rate.

There are many explanations for the differences in unemployment rates by gender, age, and race. The relative skill and educational levels of the different

Years	All Workers	Workers 16–19	Male Workers 20 or Older	Female Workers 20 or Older	White Workers	Nonwhite Workers
1950	5.3%	12.2%	4.7%	5.1%	4.9%	9.0%
1955	4.4%	11.0%	3.8%	4.4%	3.9%	8.7%
1960	5.5%	14.7%	4.7%	5.1%	5.0%	10.2%
1965	4.5%	14.8%	3.2%	4.5%	4.1%	8.1%
1970	4.9%	15.3%	3.5%	4.8%	4.5%	8.2%
1975	8.5%	19.9%	6.8%	8.0%	7.8%	13.8%
1980	7.1%	17.8%	5.9%	6.4%	6.3%	13.1%
1985	7.2%	18.6%	6.2%	6.6%	6.2%	13.7%
1990	5.5%	15.5%	4.9%	4.8%	4.7%	10.1%
1991	6.7%	18.6%	6.3%	5.7%	6.0%	11.1%
1992	7.4%	20.0%	7.0%	6.3%	6.5%	12.7%
1993	6.8%	19.0%	6.4%	5.9%	6.0%	11.7%
1994	6.1%	17.6%	5.4%	5.4%	5.3%	10.5%

Figure 16-2

U.S. Unemployment Rates for Selected Years by Gender, Age, and Race

These data will help you see how much variation there is in the unemployment rate among different groups. ***What pattern do you see in the unemployment rates for male and female workers in the 20 or older age groups?***

SOURCE: *Economic Report of the President: 1995* (Washington, D.C.: U.S. Government Printing Office, 1995), 320.

age groups cause differences in unemployment rates. Skill and education may contribute to gender and racial differences as well. But, much of the problem in these cases stems from discriminatory patterns with deep historical roots. Fortunately, these discriminatory patterns are changing even if slowly.

By closely examining statistical data, such as the data presented in Figure 16-2, you can learn a lot about who is unemployed. You can also learn about long-term employment trends when you examine the employment rates for different groups of workers over time.

Check  oint

Content Check

1. Who is not a member of the civilian labor force?

2. What does the term *unemployment* mean?

3. Do all groups of people experience the same rates of unemployment? Why or why not?

What Do You Think Now?

Reread *What Do You Think?* in the Section One Focus. Then answer the following question:

4. Would the Bureau of Labor Statistics include Bob Ohn in the number of unemployed?

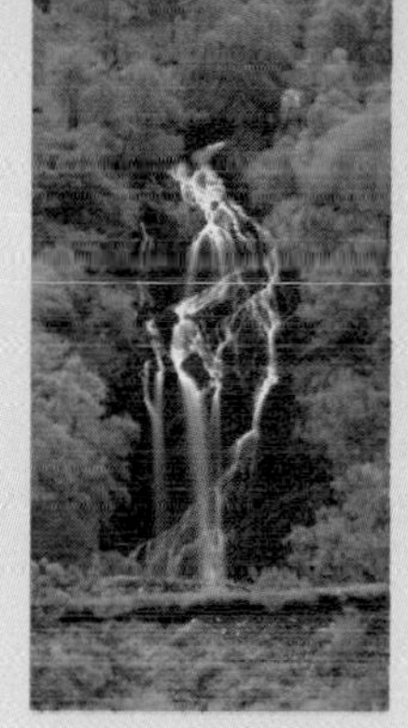

FOCUS

Section Two

Unemployment Has Social as well as Economic Costs

What Do You Think?

Caitlin Duffin has been unemployed and looking for work for almost 18 months. She cannot pay her bills and has moved in with her sister and her sister's family. Caitlin knows that if only she could get another job, she wouldn't feel so depressed. Who should be responsible for making sure there is enough work for everyone who wants a job?

What's Ahead?

The unemployment rate in the United States has varied a great deal during this century. In the 1930s, there were very high rates of unemployment. For example, in 1933, the unemployment rate was 24.9 percent. In 1944, during World War II, the unemployment rate fell to 1.2 percent. In this section, you will learn about some of the effects of unemployment and the role of the federal government with regard to unemployment.

Terms to Know

Employment Act of 1946

recession

THE PERSONAL, SOCIAL, AND ECONOMIC COSTS OF UNEMPLOYMENT

Unemployment hurts the economy, the family, and society. In economic terms, unemployed persons do not add to our gross domestic product (GDP). The difference between GDP when everyone works and GDP when many are unemployed is the major cost of unemployment to the economy. This reduction in GDP means that there are fewer goods and services available for people to consume as a result of unemployment.

But, in many ways, unemployment hits hardest in the home. The entire family suffers when a main wage earner is unemployed. When paychecks stop coming in, families must worry about how to pay the rent and other bills and how to buy food. Unhappiness and tension result. It has been found that visits to psychiatrists and other mental health facilities increase in times of high unemployment. This is in part because unemployment often destroys self-respect and self-confidence. Bill collection agencies try to

collect payments, which adds to the unemployed person's stress. Even after a job is found, the struggle to pay old bills goes on. Unemployment causes much personal damage that can have a lasting effect.

In addition to these economic and personal costs, there are serious social costs. Unemployment may lead some people to crime in order to support themselves and their families. Others may turn to crime because they have too much free time. Unemployment may also cause people to do without certain medical treatments, which can cause a higher rate of disease.

THE FEDERAL GOVERNMENT AND UNEMPLOYMENT

Unemployment hurts everybody in our society. Because of the negative impacts of unemployment, many people believe that the federal government should take responsibility for the overall health of the economy, including maintaining full employment.

Economic Dilemma

IS UNEMPLOYMENT ALL BAD?

The base rate of unemployment is the lowest rate that unemployment can go. Some people think that this rate is about 6 percent. However, others are convinced that the unemployment rate can drop to as low as 4.5 percent without causing other economic problems. If a lower base rate of unemployment were achievable, that certainly would be good news for the workforce.

There are those who argue that anything less than full employment is unacceptable in our society. They suggest that everyone who wants a job and is able to work should be able to find a suitable job. For anyone who is unemployed this would be great. But, is it feasible to have an objective of absolutely full employment or does it make more sense to target some relatively low rate of unemployment as a national objective? In the next chapter, you will see some reasons why the goal of a low rate may be preferable. You will see that doing what would be necessary to reduce the unemployment rate to near zero could harm the economy in other ways.

Employment Act of 1946

The ***Employment Act of 1946*** states that the federal government should take responsibility for full employment, price stability, and economic growth. The Employment Act also established the President's Council of Economic Advisors to give the president advice on matters of economic policy.

Employment Act of 1946
states that the federal government should take responsibility for full employment, price stability, and economic growth

The Employment Act of 1946 said the following:

> The Congress hereby declares that it is the continuing policy and responsibility of the Federal Government to use all practicable means . . . for the purpose of creating and maintaining . . . conditions under which there will be afforded useful employment opportunities . . . for those able, willing, and seeking to work and to promote maximum employment, production, and purchasing power.

This act required government to try to keep the economy strong enough to provide jobs for all who want them and are able to work.

Fluctuations in Unemployment

In the 1950s and 1960s, economic policy appeared to work fairly well. Unemployment averaged less than 5 percent. The 1970s brought quite another situation. During that time, unemployment averaged roughly 6.2 percent. Then, in the 1980s, there were times when the unemployment rate was close to 10 percent. In the 1990s, it has generally been under 7 percent, with the exception of 1992. So, you can see that unemployment is a problem that is not easy to solve. We seem to go through good times and bad, with unemployment falling only to one day rise again.

Recession

A slowdown in economic activity can cause an increase in unemployment. When GDP falls and there is high unemployment, the economy is in a recession.

Economic Spotlight

WHAT DOES IT TAKE TO STAND AND DELIVER?

For more than 20 years, Edward James Olmos has been giving "pep talks" to the down-and-out. This strong commitment to helping others has overshadowed everything else in his career, even though he is an award-winning actor. In his talks, Olmos shares a message with his audiences that is strong and inspiring—that "by discipline, determination, perseverance, and patience, anyone can reach the highest goals."

Olmos stands as one who has followed his own advice. The inspirational speaker and activist grew up in East Los Angeles in a house with dirt floors. To take refuge from the gangs and drugs in his neighborhood, he became absorbed in baseball. In fact, Olmos worked so hard at the sport that as a young boy he became the Golden State batting champ.

Today, it's easy to see that he has applied that same determination to other areas in his life. The actor, who, over the years, has won an Emmy and been nominated for a Tony and an Academy Award, wasn't born with an award-winning script in his hand. "I made a choice," states Olmos, and he has pursued that choice with a vengeance. As a young man, Olmos attended college by day and performed with a band by night as the lead vocalist. Later, he started taking acting lessons to improve his performance and quickly discovered that the spoken word suited him better. From there, he turned to Hollywood, eventually winning the role of police lieutenant Martin Castillo on TV's *Miami Vice* and starring as teacher Jaime Escalante in the motion picture *Stand and Deliver*.

Olmos says that his role in *Stand and Deliver* made him realize that teachers like Escalante are national heroes. "I felt honored and proud to be able to depict this inspirational role model," says Olmos. The movie tells the true story of how a group of East L.A. math students beat the odds to pass a crucial calculus test. The film's tough-love message challenges students to *learn* their way out of the barrio and has become a symbol of hope and renewed self-esteem to Hispanics across the country.

Inspired by the effect of the movie on troubled and underprivileged youth, Olmos has gone on to become what might be referred to as a positive activist. Today, he spends more than half of his time visiting prisons, juvenile detention centers, high schools, and community halls spreading the message that if individuals only have the desire, they can become anything they want to be.

Recession is the condition in which unemployment is high and GDP falls for two or more consecutive quarters. The government tries to soften the unemployment effects of recession when they happen. Unemployment compensation (payments to the unemployed) gives unemployed persons a minimal level of income for a certain period of time. In most states, unemployment benefits last 26 weeks.

Eligibility requirements and the amount of payments received differ from one state to another. However, most people who have worked for 26 weeks out of the past year can receive benefits. The Labor Department has estimated the average payment to unemployed workers to be about 40 percent of those workers' previous pay. Living on 40 percent of your previous income is not easy, but it keeps starvation from the door.

recession
the condition in which unemployment is high and GDP falls for two or more consecutive quarters

Checkpoint

Content Check

1. When was the unemployment rate especially high in the United States?
2. What is the effect on the economy of periods of high unemployment?
3. When was the unemployment rate especially low in the United States?
4. What are the effects on society and the family when unemployment is low?

What Do You Think Now?

Reread *What Do You Think?* in the Section Two Focus. Then answer the following questions:

5. Do you think the federal government should be responsible for helping Caitlin become employed? Why or why not?
6. What did the Employment Act of 1946 say about the role of the federal government in regard to unemployment?

FOCUS

Section Three
Kinds of Unemployment

What Do You Think?

Warren Chambers is a golf pro at a golf and tennis club near Albany, New York. This is a good job that pays very well. In their spring, summer, and early fall season, he earns almost $50,000 in salary and from giving private golf lessons. Unfortunately for Warren, the golf season is the only time that the club needs his services and he is laid off from November first until the middle of March. Is Warren considered unemployed during that period?

Terms to Know

structural unemployment

cyclical unemployment

frictional unemployment

seasonal unemployment

full employment

What's Ahead?

All unemployment is not the same. Unemployment can be divided into four kinds. These divisions can help us better understand the causes of unemployment. Then programs can be planned to help ease the burden caused by unemployment. In this section, you will see that some kinds of unemployment are not as important a problem as others.

STRUCTURAL UNEMPLOYMENT

structural unemployment unemployment resulting from skills that do not match what employers require or from being geographically separated from job opportunities

Structural unemployment is unemployment resulting from skills that do not match what employers require or from being geographically separated from job opportunities. One form of structural unemployment results when people remain unemployed because they are not qualified for the available jobs. In our complex society, very few jobs exist for those who cannot read or do simple arithmetic. However, not only the uneducated find that their qualifications do not match the jobs available. For example, a NASA engineer has highly specialized skills in space shuttle building. Due to changes in the economy, such a person may find that no jobs call for those skills, either because of less demand for space shuttles or a change in the skills needed in space shuttle production. Economists consider this kind of unemployment to be structural unemployment. It represents a mismatch between workers' skills and the skills needed in the economy.

Another kind of structural unemployment occurs when there are jobs in one part of the country but the people with the skills for those jobs live somewhere else. Many people do not like to move. The costs of moving, fear of the unknown, and family ties make moving very difficult for some. If labor moved more easily from place to place, the unemployment rate would even out throughout the United States. However, as the map in Figure 16-1 shows, the rate of unemployment differs from state to state. There are even greater differences among individual cities than among states. For example, at one point in time when the national unemployment rate was 6.8 percent, it was 10.5 percent in Riverside, California, and 3.6 percent in Salt Lake City, Utah.

Both skill and location problems are generally long-term problems. This is one reason that structural unemployment is often considered the most serious form of unemployment.

CYCLICAL UNEMPLOYMENT

Cyclical unemployment is unemployment resulting from too low a level of aggregate demand. Another name for cyclical unemployment is *demand deficiency unemployment.* The unemployment that occurs during recessions is usually cyclical or demand deficiency unemployment. Demand deficiency unemployment results from too little demand for goods and services in the economy. As you know, a low demand for goods and services means a low demand for labor. Remember that the demand for labor is a *derived demand.* It is derived from the demand for goods and services.

cyclical unemployment
unemployment resulting from too low a level of aggregate demand

There was a time after the 1930s until sometime in the 1970s when economists believed it was possible to eliminate this kind of unemployment. More recently, this idea has become less accepted.

FRICTIONAL UNEMPLOYMENT

Some people are unemployed because they cannot, at present, find work that matches their qualifications. They have skills and training that are useful in the economy, but, in the short term, they are unable to find the right match in terms of a job. Economists refer to this kind of unemployment as frictional unemployment. ***Frictional unemployment*** is unemployment of people who are temporarily between jobs. Probably between 3 and 5 percent of all unemployment is frictional.

frictional unemployment
unemployment of people who are temporarily between jobs

For example, think of a class of vocational technical students. When they finish school, they will look for jobs that use their skills, but finding such jobs may take time. However, since the skills they have acquired are useful, the students are likely to find jobs fairly soon. Their unemployment is temporary. Another example of frictional unemployment is the case of an employee who has an argument with the boss and quits. Until another job is found, the person is unemployed. Because such unemployment is temporary, it is not of much concern to economists dealing with the national unemployment problem.

Econ & You

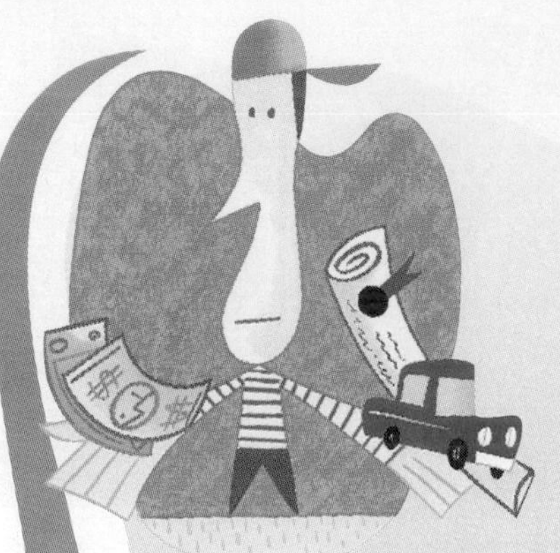

So You Want to Be a Doctor?

In the 1980s and early 1990s, anesthesiology was an attractive field from a financial standpoint. Average earnings of anesthesiologists had risen to $228,500 in 1992. As a result, many young people sought this out as a career, and medical schools responded by providing the opportunity to train in this specialty at a rapid and accelerating rate.

Anesthesiologists' lives and profession have been influenced by demand and supply changes in the medical services industry. There has been a slowdown in the demand for labor throughout the medical industry. Anesthesiologists are dependent on the volume of surgery in hospitals, which has been shrinking due to various cost-cutting programs in the medical industry. The effect of these reductions in demand has been exacerbated by changes on the supply side, as shown by the accompanying graph. As the diagram illustrates, these demand and supply changes have caused a drop in wages for anesthesiologists, such as from W_1 to W_2. As you might expect, the supply is now dropping. Hospitals reported declines of 30 percent to 50 percent in the number of applicants for anesthesiology residencies during 1995.

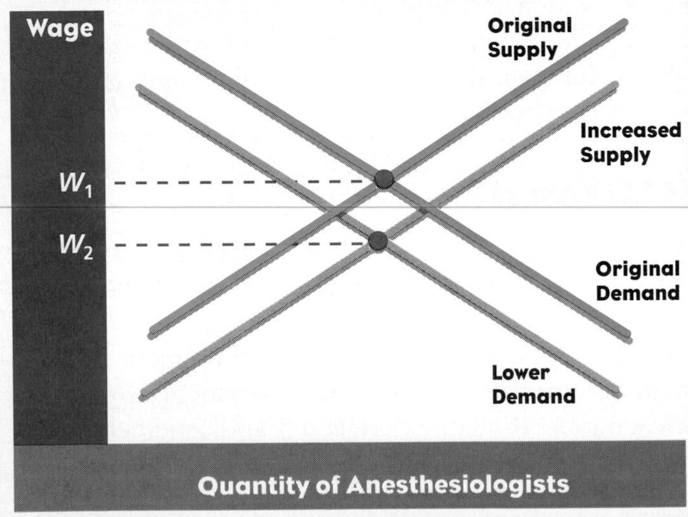

SEASONAL UNEMPLOYMENT

Seasonal unemployment is unemployment of people who are out of work because of factors that vary with the time of year. People are often unemployed because their jobs depend on seasonal factors. For example, many people in ski resort areas are unemployed when there is no snow. Farm workers also suffer seasonal unemployment because few crops need to be harvested or planted in the winter. Work in the food processing industry also is seasonal. Many workers are employed to can tomatoes, peaches, pickles, and other foods during the summer months. But, during the rest of the year, food-processing plants hire only a few workers. Thus, many of the seasonal workers lose their jobs until the next season. This kind of unemployment is usually short-term and so it, too, is not the subject of much government unemployment policy.

seasonal unemployment unemployment of people who are out of work because of factors that vary with the time of year

REDUCING UNEMPLOYMENT

There are several ways to reduce unemployment. In general, economists and politicians do not worry about frictional and seasonal unemployment. In fact, they usually define ***full employment*** as employment of about 95 percent of the labor force (allowing about 5 percent for frictional and seasonal unemployment).

full employment employment of about 95 percent of the labor force

Education and Training

Structural unemployment, which results from lack of needed skills or from problems in geographical location, is a more serious and difficult problem. One way to counteract this problem involves education and training (or reeducation and retraining) of workers. Programs organized by the Office of Economic Opportunity or programs sponsored by agencies such as Goodwill are examples of this kind of approach. Sometimes colleges and universities even help faculty members retrain so they may keep their jobs.

Match Skill Requirements to Job

Another way to reduce unemployment is to lower the skill requirements for specific jobs. For example, many employers will not hire an applicant who has no education beyond high school. But, the actual skills needed for a job may not include anything more than a high school education. However, the applicants are barred from the jobs because they do not have the qualifications, even though those qualifications may not be needed to do the work. Labor unions and other employee groups also may restrict entry into some jobs. Restricted entry into jobs, unnecessarily long apprenticeships, and pressure for higher wages without increased productivity are examples of actions that may contribute to unemployment.

Lower Minimum Wage

A third way to reduce structural unemployment is to lower the minimum wage. Minimum wage rates add to structural unemployment because they block many workers from getting jobs in the labor market. They also may discourage on-the-job training programs. Even unskilled and unproductive workers must be paid the minimum wage if they are hired. If employers could pay such workers lower rates during their training (when they are less productive), the workers might soon become more productive and deserve a pay increase. A reduction in race and gender discrimination also could reduce structural unemployment.

Increase Aggregate Demand

Demand deficiency, or cyclical, unemployment is often to blame when the unemployment rate rises. Several strategies that increase the total level of aggregate demand can reduce this type of unemployment. We will look at these in detail when we discuss monetary policy and fiscal policy.

RISING EMPLOYMENT RATES

On the brighter side, today's economy employs more people than ever before. Not only are more people employed today, but people also have greater total buying power. Their standard of living has improved greatly. Despite unemployment, the economy as a whole has provided a comfortable and even luxurious standard of living for most Americans.

A Look at the Past

Figure 16-3 shows the employment rates in the United States, at five-year intervals, since 1960. The first column shows the number of people employed in the economy. You can see that more and more people have jobs in each year shown. Occasionally, the number of people employed has dropped from one year to the next. For example, between 1981 and 1982, the number dropped from 100,397,000 to 99,526,000. However, the overall trend has been upward.

Figure 16-3

Civilian Employment and Employment Rates in the United States

The number of people employed in our economy has been increasing over time. The percent of the population who are employed has also been increasing. ***Do you think the percent of the population who are employed can continue to increase?***

SOURCE: *Economic Report of the President: 1995* (Washington. D.C.: U.S. Government Printing Office, 1995), 312.

Years	Number Employed	Percent of Population Employed
1960	65,778,000	56.1%
1965	71,088,000	56.2%
1970	78,678,000	57.4%
1975	85,846,000	56.1%
1980	99,303,000	59.2%
1985	107,150,000	60.1%
1990	117,914,000	62.7%
1995*	125,222,000	63.0%

***Values for 1995 are estimates made by the author.**

The second column of Figure 16-3 shows the percent of the population who are employed. This number has fluctuated over the years but has generally risen. The first year that more than 60 percent of this age group was employed was 1985.

A Look to the Future

Historically, we have been influenced greatly by the work ethic. Most Americans believe that worthwhile people work and pull their own weight. Because of technological advances, the productivity of each worker has greatly increased. In fact, in the future, we may be able to maintain our standard of living with increasingly smaller numbers of workers. Also, it may become increasingly difficult for our economy to supply enough jobs for all potential workers.

The future may bring more three- and four-day workweeks, more workers who share shifts with other workers, and other forms of job sharing. There even may be an increase in voluntary unemployment. It may be necessary for Americans to change their opinions regarding work. We may have to stop thinking of people as less worthy because they do not work a 40-hour week at a traditional job. There may be more public service jobs, such as cleaning up a public park, for people not employed in traditional jobs.

Checkpoint

Content Check

1. What are the four kinds of unemployment?

2. What two types of unemployment are the most important unemployment problems in our economy?

3. How do frictional and seasonal unemployment differ?

What Do You Think Now?

Reread *What Do You Think?* in the Section Three Focus. Then answer the following question:

4. Is Warren Chambers considered unemployed?

Concepts in Brief

1. The number of unemployed people 16 years of age and older is determined by a monthly survey of about 50,000 households. The unemployment rate is found by dividing the number of unemployed persons by the civilian labor force. The unemployment rate is reported frequently in the news and is the focal point of much public attention.
2. Unemployment does not spread evenly among different groups of people. There is considerable variation in unemployment rates among states and other geographic regions. Also, young people and nonwhite workers are hard hit by unemployment.
3. Unemployment has several costs. There is a loss of output when people are unemployed. This costs society because there are fewer goods and services for consumption. There are also social and personal costs due to unemployment. These social and personal costs can be long lasting and very damaging. The Employment Act of 1946 made it a responsibility of the federal government to try to keep the economy operating at full employment.
4. There are four major types of unemployment: structural, cyclical, frictional, and seasonal. The first two are of more social concern because they usually last longer. Most public attention is focused on the structural and cyclical types of unemployment.
5. Programs to help soften the hurt of unemployment are conducted by state, local, and federal government agencies. Some programs give financial aid to the unemployed and some help people learn skills that are in greater demand in the economy.

Economic Foundations

1. How is the unemployment rate determined?
2. Which groups of people are most likely to be unemployed?
3. What is the major economic cost of unemployment?
4. What are the major personal costs of unemployment?
5. What are the major social costs of unemployment?
6. What did the Employment Act of 1946 require the federal government to do?
7. Of the four kinds of unemployment, which two usually receive the most public attention? Why?
8. Identify four ways of reducing unemployment.

Your Economic Vocabulary

Build your economic vocabulary by matching the following terms with their definitions.

1. the percentage of the civilian labor force that is considered unemployed
2. unemployment of people who are temporarily between jobs
3. the total number of people in the working age group (16 years and over) who are either employed or actively seeking work
4. unemployment of people who are out of work because of factors that vary with the time of year
5. employment of about 95 percent of the labor force
6. unemployment resulting from too low a level of aggregate demand
7. the condition of those who are willing and able to work and are actively seeking work but who do not currently work
8. unemployment resulting from skills that do not match what employers require or from being geographically separated from job opportunities
9. the condition in which unemployment is high and GDP falls for two or more consecutive quarters
10. states that the federal government should take responsibility for full employment, price stability, and economic growth

civilian labor force

cyclical unemployment

Employment Act of 1946

frictional unemployment

full employment

recession

seasonal unemployment

structural unemployment

unemployment

unemployment rate

Thinking Critically About Economics

1. Determine what the current unemployment rate is and whether it has gone up or down in recent months. (For this task, you will need to find current statistics on population and employment from an economic or government publication.)
2. Write an essay in which you summarize the economic, social, and personal costs of unemployment. Which of these do you consider the most severe? Why?
3. List several characteristics that you think would increase a person's chances of being unemployed. Explain your choice of each characteristic. Suggest some ways to change these factors or to reduce their effect.

4. How does the government help to soften the effects of unemployment? What kind of unemployment program do you think is best? Why?

5. Explain each of the four types of unemployment presented in the text. Give at least one example of each type.

Economic Enrichment

"We must change our attitudes toward unemployment. Since the economy may not be able to provide jobs for everyone who wants one, we must stop measuring people's worth by their work." Do you agree or disagree with this statement? Explain your answer.

Math and Economics

The following table summarizes the size of the labor force and employment data for a local economy for five consecutive years. Use these data to calculate the number of people unemployed and the unemployment rate for each of the five years.

Year	Size of Labor Force	Number Employed	Number Unemployed	Unemployment Rate
1	62,208	58,918		
2	69,628	65,778		
3	82,771	78,678		
4	106,940	99,303		
5	124,787	117,914		

Writing About Economics

Each month, *The Wall Street Journal* publishes the employment data provided by the Bureau of Labor Statistics. These data usually appear in *The Wall Street Journal* on Monday of the second week of each month. A graph of the unemployment rate normally appears at the top of column four on the front page and a detailed story typically follows on the second page, A2.

In a recent edition of *The Wall Street Journal*, find a table that lists the following: the civilian labor force, the amount of employment, the amount of unemployment, the unemployment rates for various groups, and average hours in the work week. Write a short essay in which you relate what you find in that current issue of *The Wall Street Journal* to the historic data given in this chapter.

Overview

inflation

Learning Objectives

17-1

Describe the impact of inflation on the economy.

17-2

Identify those who benefit from inflation and those who are hurt by inflation.

17-3

Show how the Consumer Price Index is figured.

17-4

Calculate the rate of inflation using the Consumer Price Index.

17-5

Present the limitations of the Consumer Price Index.

17-6

Differentiate between demand-pull inflation and cost-push inflation.

17-7

Analyze various ways of controlling inflation.

FOCUS

Section One
The Cost of Living Changes over Time

What Do You Think?

Claudia Jennings has $5,600 in a savings account at a local bank, where it earns an annual interest rate of 4.5 percent. Claudia is happy when she thinks about the added interest she will get in the coming year. She realizes that with the interest, her savings balance will increase to $5,852 at the end of one year. Do you think Claudia is earning money?

Terms to Know
inflation
speculation
debtors
fixed income
creditors

What's Ahead?

Inflation is as much an economic problem as is unemployment. It can cause uncertainty about the economy, which can affect the economic decisions made by businesses and households. In this section, you will learn what inflation is, as well as who it benefits and hurts.

WHAT IS INFLATION?

inflation
a sustained rise in the general level of prices

A sustained rise in the general level of prices is called ***inflation.*** During an inflationary period, the average level of prices rises. Some prices may rise rapidly, some may rise only slightly, and some prices may even fall. For example, during recent inflationary periods, the price of small calculators fell while most other prices rose rapidly. In an inflationary period, rising prices outweigh falling prices. An upward movement of the general, or average, price level results. We often call this a *rise in the cost of living.*

Inflation causes uncertainty in the marketplace for both consumers and businesses. Shortly after World War I, Germany fell victim to runaway inflation. Prices were so uncertain that people in restaurants paid the bill as they ordered rather than paying when they finished eating because prices could go up during their meal. People wanted to be paid at the end of each workday so they could spend their money before prices rose. Money lost its value so quickly that people would no longer use it as a medium of exchange. During this period, Germany suffered from extreme inflation. The uncertainty it produced was devastating to the German economy.

Less extreme inflation of perhaps 2 percent to 3 percent actually can stimulate an economy. During a mildly inflationary period, wages often rise more slowly than the prices of products. This means that the price for products sold is high in relation to the cost of labor. In such an environment, producers make higher real profits and tend to expand production and hire more people. The newly employed workers increase spending, and the total demand in the economy goes up. This may result in increased economic growth and prosperity.

Global Economy

THE MANY FACES OF INFLATION

As the accompanying graphic illustrates, there is inflation in countries all around the world. The inflation rate given is the average for each country in a recent year. These averages hide some of the big differences between different classes of goods. You can see from the numbers in the graph that inflation varies a good deal among countries and that it is a worldwide problem. For some countries, inflation is so high that the values would be off the scale of the graph shown. For example, in the same year, inflation was 2,148 percent in Brazil, 66 percent in Turkey, 49 percent in Peru, 38 percent in Venezuela, and 20 percent in Iran.

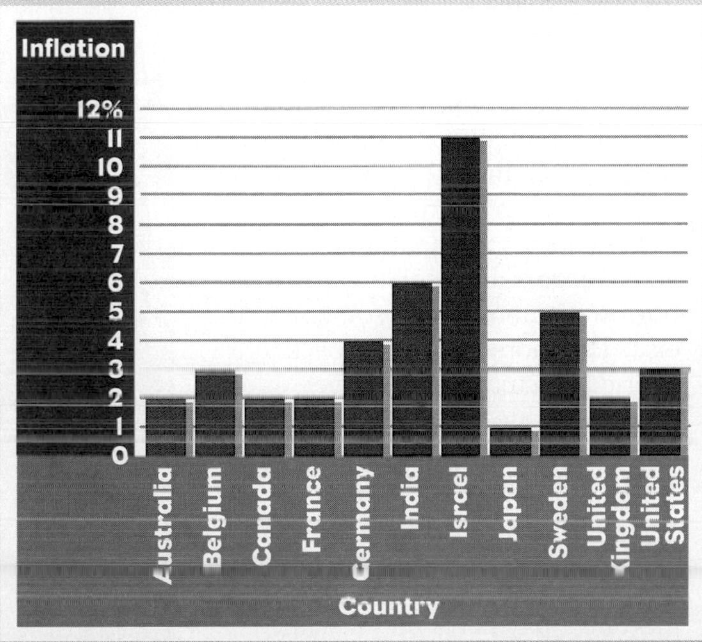

SOURCE: U.S. Bureau of the Census, *Statistical Abstract of the United States: 1994,* 114th ed. (Washington, D.C.: U.S. Government Printing Office, 1994), 868.

If inflation rises to higher levels, however, it may contribute to unemployment. Rapidly rising prices mean that workers' incomes decrease in real terms, and so they buy fewer goods. As workers make fewer purchases, the total demand in the economy falls. This falling demand, then, may result in unemployment. If wages go up faster than prices, businesses tend to hire less labor and so unemployment worsens.

Inflation also may distort the economic system. It causes prices to increase, and they often do not increase evenly. All goods do not have the same rate of increase in price. Consumers and producers react to price changes by buying and producing different amounts of goods. Thus, the distribution pattern of goods and the allocation of resources changes. It is hard to say for sure whether these changes lead to a less or more efficient economy. But, the pattern of allocation clearly can be changed by inflation, and many economists believe that this lowers economic efficiency.

speculation
when someone buys a large amount of a good and hopes to resell it at a much higher price

Inflation also may lead to speculation. This is especially true when prices increase rapidly for particular commodities. ***Speculation*** occurs when someone buys a large amount of a good and hopes to resell it at a much higher price. For example, during one period the price of antifreeze rose rapidly. Many people stocked their garages with antifreeze, intending to sell it later at a high profit. This type of speculation is generally nonproductive and causes distortions in the market distribution of goods. In the case of antifreeze, the price did not go up much more, and people were stuck with large amounts of antifreeze. In the meantime, they lost the use of the money that went for the speculation.

WHO BENEFITS FROM INFLATION?

Let's consider how inflation may benefit some groups of people. Inflation helps people whose incomes rise faster than the rate of inflation. For example, if a union can negotiate a pay increase that exceeds the rate of inflation, the union's members will benefit. However, this gain may be short-lived. The higher wages will result in higher prices. Then, other workers will get higher wages, which will result in more price increases. This cycle can continue on and on such that, in the end, few, if any, actually benefit.

debtors
people who have borrowed money from someone else

Debtors also benefit from inflation. ***Debtors*** are people who have borrowed money from someone else. The money they pay back at a later date actually has a lower value than the money they borrowed. Consider mortgage payments on a home. A fixed mortgage payment starting in 1967 may have been only $140 a month, which is quite a bargain in today's housing market! The mortgage payments on the same home bought today might be $1,000 or more a month.

Economic Spotlight

NOW THAT'S HITTING THE NAIL ON THE HEAD!

Can you imagine a company that builds an average of 23 homes a day and has hundreds of people on waiting lists for its homes? A company that conducts business in more than 900 cities in 40 countries? Believe it or not, such a company exists—and even though you'd expect it to be one of the world's biggest moneymakers, it doesn't even turn a profit. The company is Habitat for Humanity, a nonprofit organization dedicated to refurbishing or building affordable housing for individuals in need.

Through its efforts, Habitat helps low-income families turn their lives around to become responsible home owners involved in their communities. Habitat for Humanity's success can be attributed to two things: its skill in building houses and its skill in building relationships between people and for-profit corporations. But, how does this all come together? First, Habitat identifies people who are truly in need and want to work toward having better lives. Then, volunteers build a Habitat house or make an existing residence as good as new.

Still, these homes are by no means freebies. Buyers are given no interest loans, but they must make monthly mortgage payments and invest considerable "sweat equity"—300 to 400 hours of labor—into the building of their own and others' homes. A typical Habitat home is an average of 1,100 square feet in size and has three bedrooms and one and one-half baths. Final building costs average only about $40,000, thanks to companies who donate materials and individuals who volunteer their hard work.

One well-known Habitat for Humanity volunteer is singer-songwriter Amy Grant, who is also the spokesperson for Target Stores, a corporate sponsor of Habitat. Other famous and dedicated volunteers include former President Jimmy Carter and his wife, Rosalynn, who volunteer one day a week to the cause. Carter states, "You put maximum confidence in people's own intelligence and ambition, ability, [and] family values and share with them the responsibility of finding a better future. Then let them do their work and have control over what goes on."

Habitat for Humanity's goal is to empower people to improve their lives, and it's doing just that. As volunteers work around the clock to provide homes for those in need, thousands of families are learning that they can get by with a little help from their friends.

People who own property or assets that gain value at a faster rate than the rate of inflation also benefit. For example, suppose you own real estate that increases 10 percent a year in value, while the rate of inflation is 5 percent a year. You are better off and less harmed by inflation than those who do not hold similar assets. Home owners gain in at least two ways from inflation. Homes often appreciate more rapidly than the general level of price increases. Also, home owners often pay a constant dollar amount for their mortgage payments. Therefore, in real terms (or in buying power), the home owner pays less each year. Payments on some mortgages do change over time because the rate of interest is adjusted during the term of the loan.

WHO IS HURT BY INFLATION?

fixed income
an income that is set and does not change from year to year

People on a fixed income are hurt the most by inflation. A ***fixed income*** is an income that is set and does not change from year to year. For example, if your grandparents receive a retirement pension that is fixed at $9,600 per year, inflation could greatly damage their purchasing power. If the rate of inflation is 5 percent per year, what they could purchase for $9,600 one year would cost $10,080 a year later. (The $10,080 is obtained by multiplying $9,600 by 1.05.) Each year, they would be able to buy fewer goods with that $9,600 income.

Many workers retiring today face this problem. Their retirement programs were set up 30 or more years ago when a given income could buy much more. What was a good income at one time provides only limited buying power in retirement years. Many retirement and insurance programs as well as Social Security benefits now have cost-of-living adjustments. That is, they have automatic increases that protect against inflation to help reduce this problem of inadequate retirement income. People on semifixed incomes, or whose incomes are not adjusted often, also can be hurt by inflation.

creditors
people who have loaned money to others

Inflation also hurts people who have money in the bank or people who are creditors. ***Creditors*** are people who have loaned money to others. Suppose you have money in a savings account that pays a 5 percent rate of interest and there is a 4 percent rate of inflation. All but 1 percent of your earnings are eaten away by inflation. If inflation is greater than the interest rate you receive, you actually lose buying power by having your money in that savings account. Creditors such as savings and loans, banks, and credit unions can, therefore, be hurt by inflation. The money that debtors (the people who have borrowed) pay back in the future is worth less than the money that was originally lent.

Perhaps most importantly, many economists think that high inflation can lead to a high rate of unemployment. Businesses do not run as well in an unstable economy as in a stable one. With high inflation, businesses find it hard to plan for their production. Business growth is slower, fewer goods are produced, and fewer workers are hired. This means that the unemployment rate will likely go up. People can lose their jobs due to inflation. Or, those already unemployed may have less chance of finding jobs. In this way, inflation hurts nearly everyone. This is why so many people speak of the need to control inflation both in our country and in other countries.

Checkpoint

Content Check

1. Why is inflation called a rise in the cost of living?

2. Who benefits from inflation?

3. Who is hurt by inflation?

What Do You Think Now?

Reread *What Do You Think?* in the Section One Focus. Then answer the following question:

4. If Claudia keeps her $5,600 in a savings account that pays 4.5 percent per year, will she have increased her purchasing power at the end of one year?

FOCUS

Section Two
Measuring the Rate of Inflation

What Do You Think?

Janice and Eric Steinberg, along with their two teenage children, live on a farm in upstate New York. The Steinberg farm, which they inherited from Janice's parents, includes some dairy cows, a few sheep, and a very large vegetable garden. Much of the Steinbergs' food comes from the farm. Janice and Eric teach at the local high school. One evening, Eric, an art teacher, complained about how the high rate of inflation was eating away at their standard of living. Janice, a history and economics teacher, said that she didn't think the high rate of inflation was a problem for them. Who was right?

Terms to Know

price index

Consumer Price Index (CPI)

What's Ahead?

Inflation is usually measured by some type of price index. The index compares the average current prices for goods to the average prices of those goods in some previous period, called the *base period.* In this section, you will see how inflation is measured using the Consumer Price Index.

PRICE INDEXES

price index
a number that compares prices in one year with some earlier base year

Inflation is usually measured by using price indexes. A ***price index*** is a number that compares prices in one year with some earlier base year. There are many different kinds of price indexes. These include specific price indexes for particular industries, as well as the Producer Price Index (PPI) and the Consumer Price Index (CPI). These are calculated by the U.S. Labor Department's Bureau of Labor Statistics. In this chapter, we will focus on the Consumer Price Index.

Consumer Price Index (CPI)
a number used to calculate changes in the average level of prices for a number of items typically bought by urban families

What Is the Consumer Price Index?

The ***Consumer Price Index (CPI)*** is a number used to calculate changes in the average level of prices for a number of items typically bought by urban families. The CPI does not include every good and service produced in the economy. Instead, the Bureau of Labor Statistics chooses about 400 items that represent the goods and services that would be bought by typical city households. (Urban residents comprise about 80 percent of the population.) The Bureau sends people to several thousand retail stores and service establishments to find out the prices for each of these 400 items. The prices found for each item are then averaged.

The influence that each item has on the Consumer Price Index is found by a weighting process. This process is based on the importance of each item to families as determined by the fraction of their total spending that goes for that item. For example, families spend about 17.4 percent of their income on food and beverages. So, food and beverage prices make up about 17.4 percent of the final Consumer Price Index.

The way in which different items are weighted in the CPI is shown in Figure 17-1. You can see from that figure that housing makes up 41.2 percent and medical care makes up 7.3 percent of total expenditures. The percentages for apparel, transportation, and entertainment are also shown.

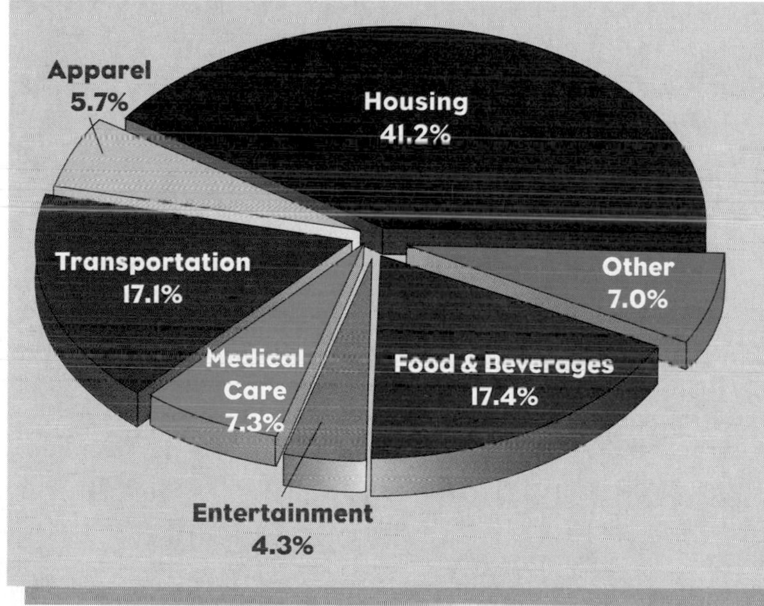

Figure 17-1

The Makeup of the Consumer Price Index

This pie chart shows the major kinds of consumer spending that are included in the CPI. The weight, or relative importance, for each type of spending is indicated by the percent in each slice of the pie. ***What percent of total consumer spending do the necessities of food, apparel, housing, transportation, and medical care represent?***

NOTE: These percentages change slowly over time as our pattern of consumption changes. If your library has the most recent CPI Detailed Report, you might want to look at it to see what changes have occurred.

What Does the Consumer Price Index Measure?

Once the price of the set of 400 items is determined each year, it is compared to prices in the base period. The other years are given as a percentage of the base period. For example, in Figure 17-2 on page 452, 1982–1984 is the base period. You can see in Figure 17-2 that the CPI for 1950 was 24.1. This means that, in 1950, prices were only 24.1 percent of prices in the 1982–1984 period. In 1985, prices were 107.6 percent of 1982–1984 prices, and prices in

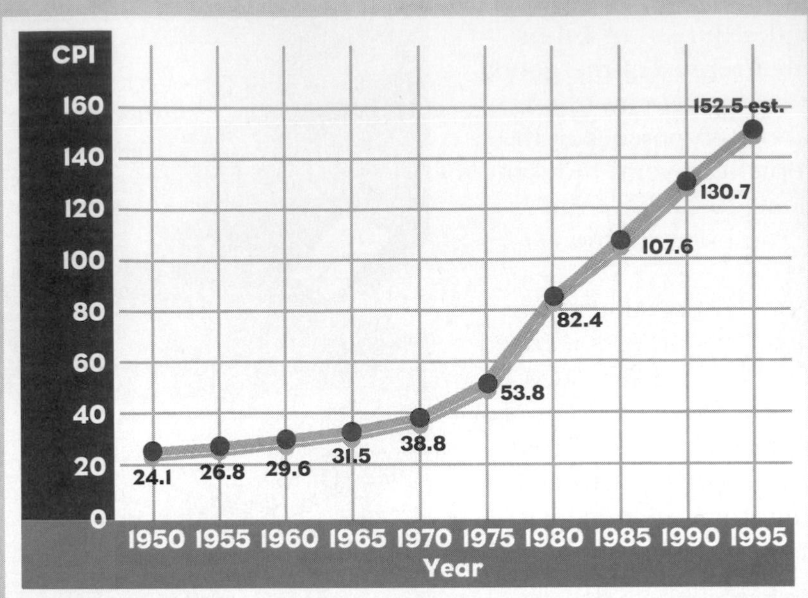

Figure 17-2

Consumer Price Index for Selected Years with 1982–1984 as the Base Period

This line graph of the CPI shows how prices have been increasing throughout the last half of the twentieth century. ***If a suit cost $100 in the base period, how much would it have cost in 1960? What about in 1995?***

SOURCE: *Economic Report of the President: 1995* (Washington, D.C.: U.S. Government Printing Office, 1995), 341.

1990 were 130.7 percent of 1982–1984 prices. By 1995, prices had risen to more than 150 percent of those in the 1982–1984 base period.

The numbers in Figure 17-2 show how the CPI has increased over the years. Using 1982–1984 as the base period, the CPI in 1995 was about 152.5. This means that, on average, prices in 1995 were at about 152.5 percent of the level of prices in 1982–1984. Consider a skateboard that cost $50 in 1982–1984. If its price increased at the average rate, how much would that skateboard have cost in 1995? To find out, multiply the $50 price by 152.5 percent, or 1.525. You can see from the following calculation that the skateboard that cost $50 in 1982–1984 would have cost about $76.25 in 1995:

$$\$50 \times 1.525 = \$76.25$$

USING THE CPI TO FIND THE RATE OF INFLATION

The Consumer Price Index can be used to find the rate of inflation. To figure the rate of inflation between two years, you start by finding the difference in the CPI for the two years. This is done by subtracting the CPI for the earlier year from the CPI for the more recent year. You then divide the difference between the price indexes by the first year's price index. Here is the formula:

$$\text{Rate of Inflation} = \frac{\text{More Recent Year's Price Index} - \text{Earlier Year's Price Index}}{\text{Earlier Year's Price Index}}$$

Calculating the Rate of Inflation

Suppose that you want to calculate the rate of inflation between 1989 and 1990. From Figure 17-2 you see that the CPI was 130.7 in 1990. In 1989, the CPI was 124.0. To find the rate of inflation between 1989 and 1990, you should subtract 124.0 from 130.7 and then divide the difference by 124.0. The rate of inflation is 5.4 percent. Here are the calculations:

$$\text{Rate of Inflation 1989 to 1990} = \frac{\text{1990 Price Index} - \text{1989 Price Index}}{\text{1989 Price Index}}$$

$$= \frac{130.7 - 124.0}{124.0}$$

$$= 6.7 \div 124.0$$
$$= 0.054$$
$$= 5.4\%$$

WHO'S THE CONSUMER IN THE CPI?

Does the Consumer Price Index (CPI) apply to you and your family? Perhaps yes and perhaps no. To answer this question, you need to think first about whether you live in an area that would be described as an urban area. If you live in the Bronx, the answer is yes, as it would be if you live in a suburb of San Francisco or St. Louis. If you live in Sugarcreek, Ohio, or in Circle, Montana, or in Holly, North Carolina, the answer is no.

Next, you should think about whether your family spends its money in approximately the same proportions as those shown in Figure 17-1. If it does, and if you live in what could be classified as an urban area, then the CPI probably does a pretty good job of measuring price changes for your family. If these things are not true, then the CPI is at best a rough approximation of the effect of price changes on your family.

The Inflation Rate Varies from Year to Year

The inflation rate in the United States has varied considerably from year to year. The graph in Figure 17-3 will help you to see this. Note that, in the early 1960s, inflation was less than 2 percent per year. Since that time, there have been ups and downs, but we have not been able to get the inflation rate back under 2 percent.

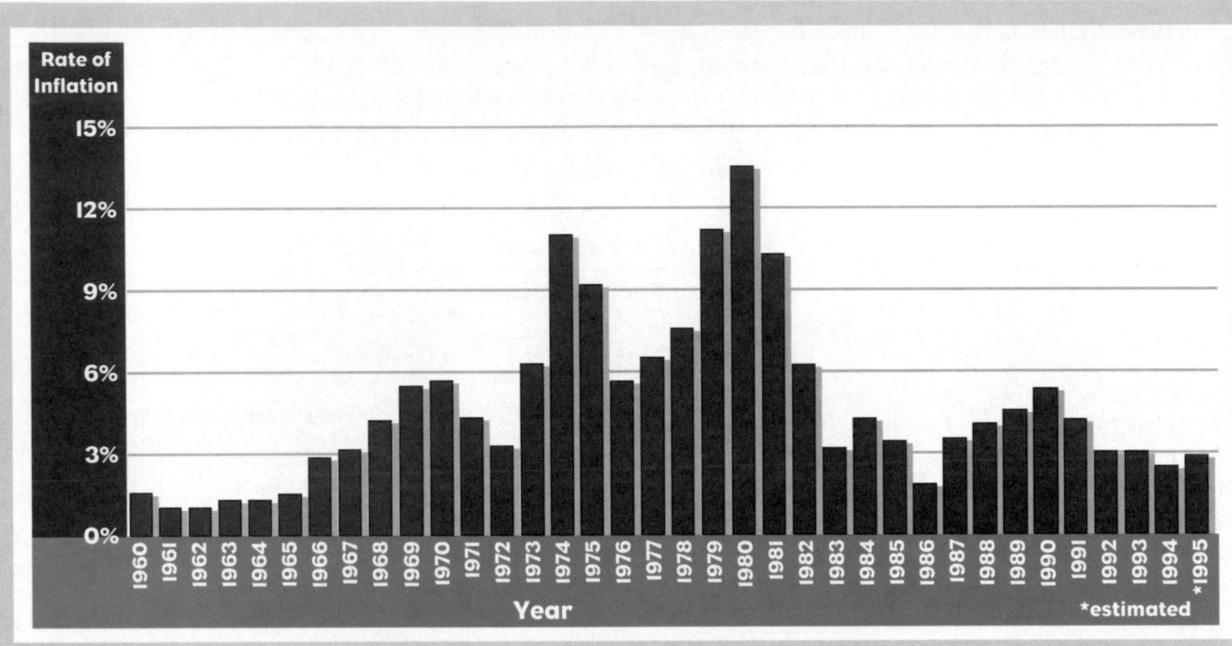

Figure 17-3

U.S. Inflation Rates

In the early 1960s, inflation was less than 2 percent per year. Since that time, there have been wide variations in the inflation rate. ***Since 1990, what has been the general trend in the rate of inflation in the United States?***

SOURCE: For 1960–1993: U.S. Bureau of the Census, *Statistical Abstract of the United States: 1994,* 114th ed. (Washington, D.C., 1994), 488. The value for 1994 was calculated from data in *Economic Report of the President: 1995* (Washington, D.C.: U.S. Government Printing Office, 1995), 341. The value for 1995 is the author's estimate.

The Inflation Rate Varies Among Types of Goods

The rate of inflation varies among certain kinds of goods. If you spend most of your money on items with lower price increases, you will not be affected as much by inflation. However, if you spend a higher percentage of your income on food, housing, or medical services, you may suffer more than the typical urban family that the CPI represents. To help see the different effects of inflation, look at the price indexes in Figure 17-4 for different types of expenditures.

These price indexes are based on 1982–1984 prices. (They all equaled 100 in 1982–1984.) You see that shelter and medical care have contributed most to inflation. Prices for transportation and apparel have increased less rapidly than the general level of prices as measured by the Consumer Price Index.

Year	Overall	Food	Shelter	Trans-portation	Medical Care	Apparel
1950	24.1	25.4	NA	22.7	15.1	40.3
1955	26.8	27.8	22.7	25.8	18.2	42.9
1960	29.6	30.0	25.2	29.8	22.3	45.7
1965	31.5	32.2	27.0	31.4	24.6	47.3
1970	38.8	39.2	35.5	37.5	34.0	59.2
1975	53.8	59.8	48.8	50.1	47.5	72.5
1980	82.4	86.8	81.0	83.1	74.9	90.9
1982–1984	100.0	100.0	100.0	100.0	100.0	100.0
1985	107.6	105.6	109.8	106.4	113.5	105.0
1990	130.7	132.4	140.0	120.5	162.8	124.1
1991	136.2	136.3	146.3	123.8	177.0	128.7
1992	140.3	137.9	151.2	126.5	190.1	131.9
1993	144.5	140.9	155.7	130.4	201.4	133.7
1994	148.2	144.3	160.5	134.3	211.0	133.4

Figure 17-4

Price Indexes for Selected Goods and Services

This table shows how prices have increased for five major types of spending, as well as the overall average. ***Calculate the rate of increase in prices for the medical care category between 1993 and 1994. (Hint: Use the same process as when calculating the overall rate of inflation between two years using the CPI.)***

SOURCE: *Economic Report of the President: 1995* (Washington, D.C.: U.S. Government Printing Office, 1995), 341.

LIMITATIONS OF THE CPI

The Consumer Price Index must be used carefully for several reasons. First, even though the CPI is often called the *cost-of-living index,* it doesn't measure the *cost of living* for any one person. It is unlikely that your market basket of goods exactly matches the one chosen by the Bureau of Labor Statistics. Therefore, the Bureau's figures on the rate of inflation will not apply exactly to you. This is especially true of farm workers and people with a fixed housing payment.

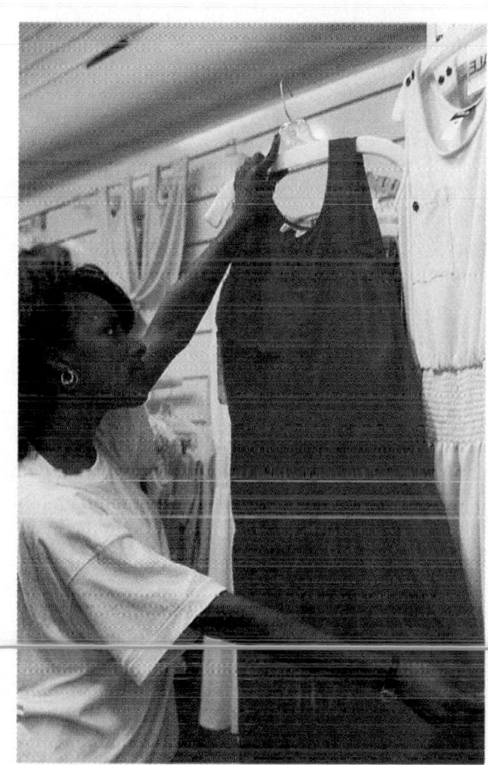

Second, the CPI includes only those items that can be bought and sold in the market. It does not include such factors as taxes or government services. Third, price indexes do not account for changes in the *quality* of goods. For example, compare a television set made in 1970 with a new television. The new set may have cost more, but are the two sets the same? The answer is no. There have been very significant changes in the quality of color televisions since 1970. Part of the increase in price reflects better quality. As you might think, it is difficult to measure what percentage of a price increase results from improved quality and what percentage is due to inflation.

Checkpoint

Content Check

1. What is the Consumer Price Index?
2. Calculate the rate of inflation for transportation between 1990 and 1991 using the price indexes in Figure 17-4.
3. Is the rate of change in prices the same for all goods and services? Explain.

What Do You Think Now?

Reread *What Do You Think?* in the Section Two Focus. Then answer the following question:

4. Is the CPI an appropriate measure of the cost of living for the Steinbergs?

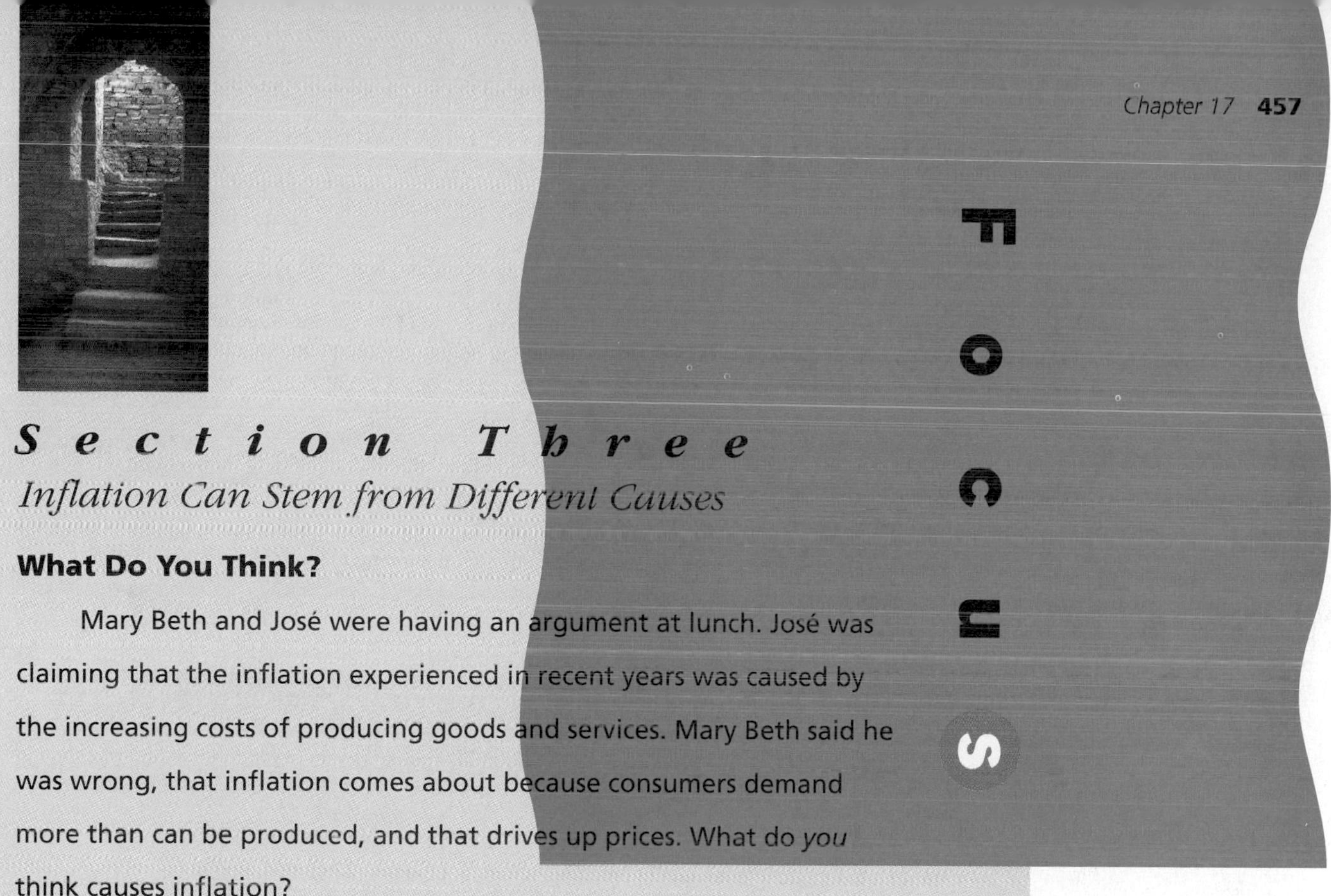

Section Three

Inflation Can Stem from Different Causes

What Do You Think?

Mary Beth and José were having an argument at lunch. José was claiming that the inflation experienced in recent years was caused by the increasing costs of producing goods and services. Mary Beth said he was wrong, that inflation comes about because consumers demand more than can be produced, and that drives up prices. What do *you* think causes inflation?

What's Ahead?

Inflationary pressures in the economy are often separated into two kinds based on their causes: demand-pull inflation and cost-push inflation. In this section, you will learn how inflation can be caused by demand-side factors as well as by supply-side factors.

Terms to Know

demand-pull inflation

cost-push inflation

deflation

DEMAND-PULL INFLATION

Demand-pull inflation is a rise in the general level of prices caused by too high a level of aggregate demand in relation to aggregate supply. The phrase *too many dollars chasing too few goods* is often used to describe this kind of inflation. *Too many dollars* means that the total demand in the economy is too high. *Too few goods* means that the total supply in the economy is too low in relation to that demand. Figure 17-5 on page 458 illustrates demand-pull inflation.

demand-pull inflation
a rise in the general level of prices caused by too high a level of aggregate demand in relation to aggregate supply

The original aggregate demand curve and the supply curve represent the level of demand and supply at some beginning point in time. The new demand curve shows the increase in demand that occurs during some period. You can see the amount of increase by comparing the distance between the original and new aggregate demand curves.

The equilibrium average price level of goods at the beginning of the period is at CPI_1. This is at the level where the original aggregate demand and the aggregate supply curves cross. CPI_2 represents the equilibrium average price level after the inflationary pressures of rising demand have been felt. The price level goes up from CPI_1 to CPI_2. In other words, inflation occurs.

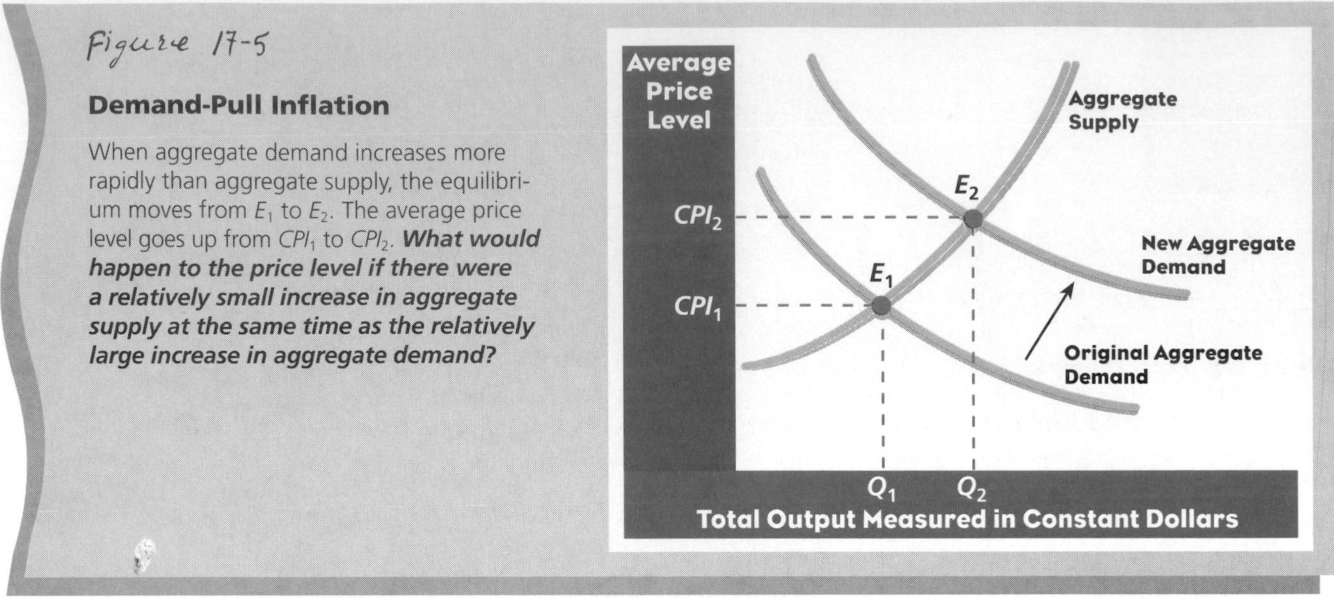

Demand-Pull Inflation

When aggregate demand increases more rapidly than aggregate supply, the equilibrium moves from E_1 to E_2. The average price level goes up from CPI_1 to CPI_2. ***What would happen to the price level if there were a relatively small increase in aggregate supply at the same time as the relatively large increase in aggregate demand?***

Historically, demand-pull inflation has accompanied the ends of wars and military conflicts. The large amounts of resources tied up in fighting wars can cause large increases in demand when resources return to the civilian economy. The inflation that followed World War II and the Korean conflict were examples of demand-pull inflation.

The inflation from 1965 to 1970 was related to a war, but had other causes as well. During the Vietnam conflict, high defense spending was accompanied by continued high consumer demand. There was also increased government spending on President Johnson's Great Society social programs. Much of this spending was financed by increasing the National Debt. The result: a steady increase in inflation during the years of the Vietnam War.

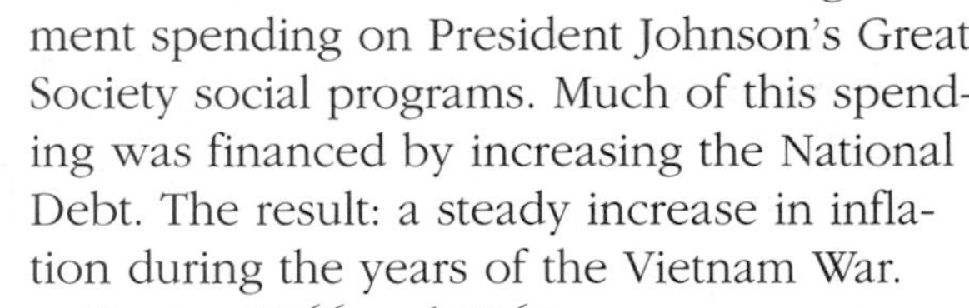

During 1966 and 1967, consumer prices only rose an average of about 3.0 percent. But, between 1967 and 1968, the increase was 4.2 percent. By 1970, the economy had edged into a recession. In December of that year, unemployment reached a level of 6.2 percent. Unemployment typically results in decreasing demand, since unemployed persons don't have as much money to spend as when they were employed. The decreasing demand usually eases the pressure of demand-pull inflation, and the inflation rate falls. But, inflation did not go down. In 1970, it was 5.7 percent. We faced the twin problems of inflation and recession. Later in the 1970s and in the early 1980s, the rate of inflation was more than 10 percent (in 1974, 1979, 1980, and 1981).

internet Connection

CURRENT INFLATION FACTS

Inflation is defined as a sustained increase in the general level of prices, but how do we measure the general level of prices? The answer is, "With a price index." A price index is an average of the prices of some type of good. There are indexes for the prices of energy, food, housing, and many other goods and services. The three broadest measures of prices are the Consumer Price Index (CPI), the Producer Price Index (PPI) and the implicit price deflator for GDP.

The CPI and PPI are calculated by the Bureau of Labor Statistics and are available from the *Statistical Abstract* at **http://www.census.gov/ftp/pub/statab/indicator/prices.txt.**

The GDP deflator is calculated by the Bureau of Economic Analysis and is available from Economic Bulletin Board in Table 701, line 8, at **gopher://una.hh.lib.umich.edu/00/ebb/nipa/nipacurr/nipa-a.prn**.

Inflation rates are more meaningful than price indexes. An inflation rate is the percentage change in some price index. When we talk about the inflation rate, we usually mean as indicated by the CPI or one of the other broad measures of prices. The inflation rate measured with the CPI is available from the *Statistical Abstract* at **http://www.census.gov/ftp/pub/statab/USAbrief/part2.txt**.

Using the *Statistical Abstract,* look at the inflation rates for the last three years. When was inflation the highest and when was it the lowest? Is the inflation rate increasing, decreasing, or staying about the same?

Economics/Internet Application: In Chapter 14, we discussed using a variety of economic statistics to evaluate the state of the economy. A well-known summary indicator is the "misery index." The misery index is the sum of the inflation and unemployment rates. A decrease in either is good news, so, when the misery index is declining, that is a sign of overall increasing economic health. Calculate the misery index over the last three years. When was it the highest? When was it the lowest? Is the misery index increasing, decreasing, or staying about the same?

COST-PUSH INFLATION

cost-push inflation
a rise in the general level of prices that is caused by increased costs of making and selling goods

Economists explained that this continuing inflation was partially made up of a second kind of inflation called *cost-push inflation*. ***Cost-push inflation*** is a rise in the general level of prices that is caused by increased costs of making and selling goods. Cost-push inflation does not result from pressures on demand. Instead, the pressures are on the supply side.

An increase in the cost of raw materials and capital equipment can cause firms to raise the prices they charge for the products they produce. Workers and unions may then demand pay increases to make up for real income they lose due to rising prices. Unions and laborers expect inflation, so they negotiate cost-of-living increases in their contracts. As a result, the costs of labor continue to rise. This adds to the cost of production and firms have even more reason to increase prices. Thus, inflation results from pressures on the supply side of the marketplace.

There is another factor that may contribute to cost-push inflation, but it is hard to prove. This factor is the increased concentration of economic power in the hands of a few companies and labor unions. Large, strong companies and unions can increase prices and wages if they have little competition. The costs of these higher prices and wages are paid by consumers and add to inflationary pressures.

Cost-push inflation can be explained by a graph such as the one in Figure 17-6. The demand curve in that figure represents the total demand in the economy. The original supply curve represents the total supply of goods in the economy at one point in time. The equilibrium price is at the level CPI_1. Suppose that something happens to cause production costs to rise. For example, perhaps raw material, energy, or labor costs go up. As costs go up, companies can afford to produce less at each price level. Therefore, the supply curve shifts to the left to the position of the new supply curve in the diagram. This results in the increase of the equilibrium price to the level CPI_2.

Figure 17-6

Cost-Push Inflation

An increase in production costs shifts the aggregate supply curve to the left. The equilibrium moves from E_1 to E_2, and the average price level goes up from CPI_1 to CPI_2. ***What would happen to the price level if, in addition to the shift in aggregate supply, there was a simultaneous increase in aggregate demand?***

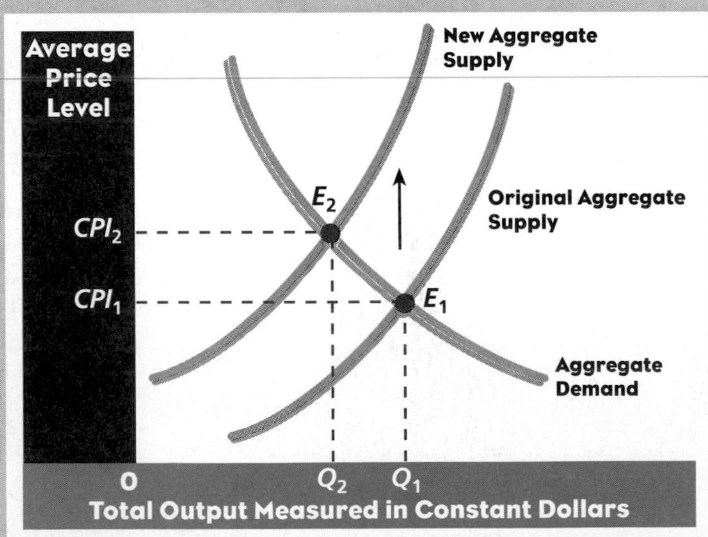

Economic Dilemma

THE AGGREGATE BALANCING ACT

Growth in aggregate demand is helpful in reducing unemployment. This is because an increase in aggregate demand increases the derived demand for labor. However, an increase in aggregate demand may at the same time stimulate demand-pull inflation. Thus, there is a problem of finding the right balance in the economy so that increases in aggregate demand result in increasing employment without causing inflation.

This balance involves both aggregate demand and aggregate supply. The accompanying diagram shows economic growth (both aggregate demand and aggregate supply shift to the right) along with a constant, noninflationary level of prices. Since the passage of the Employment Act of 1946, it has generally been accepted that the government has a responsibility to help the economy reach this balance of aggregate demand and aggregate supply such that noninflationary growth can result.

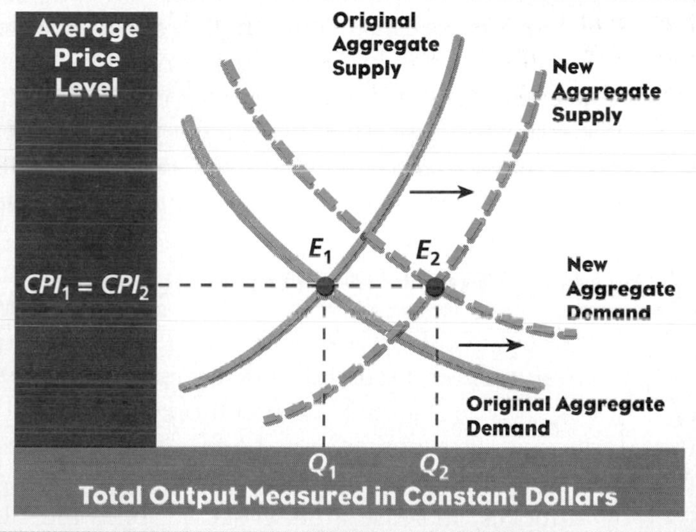

Some economists think that cost-push inflation may cause a continuing type of inflation. When higher costs cause prices to rise, the level of output may decrease. Look at Figure 17-6. At the equilibrium level E_2, the amount produced (Q_2) is less than the amount produced at the equilibrium level E_1 (Q_1). This happens because, at the higher price, people are willing and able to buy fewer of the goods. The reduction in output may cause unemployment. Government economists may interpret the unemployment as a sign that total demand is too low. They then might take steps to increase demand and thus may cause demand-pull inflation. The demand-pull inflation might start another round of cost-push inflation, and the cycle goes on and on.

CAN INFLATION BE CONTROLLED?

We try to control demand-pull inflation largely through monetary and fiscal policy. These will be discussed in detail in Chapters 19 and 21. The battle against cost-push inflation is a difficult one. To control this type of inflation, the supplies of all resources must be free from any artificial limits. Big companies and big unions must not have the power to lower supply levels and thereby artificially increase input costs. Supplies must be free to change in response to changes in demand. However, to free supplies from artificial controls is a hard, if not impossible, task. The United States cannot control the OPEC suppliers of oil, for instance. The concentration of economic power in a few large companies may be hard to correct using the present antitrust legislation. And, the power of large unions often proves hard to control. To stop cost-push inflation, the government must support policies that reduce the control over important raw materials by special interest groups. Such policies might include strongly enforcing present antitrust laws and perhaps passing stronger ones. The government also might pass laws to limit the power of unions.

Inflation is a real problem in our modern economy. Whether cost-push or demand-pull inflation, it must be controlled. The consequences of rapid inflation are dire. It lowers standards of living for many and distorts the functioning of the entire economy.

DEFLATION

Deflation is the opposite of inflation. ***Deflation*** is a decline in the average level of prices. During a period of deflation, some prices may rise but the general, or overall, level of prices falls. Deflation has not often been a problem in the United States. The most important deflationary period in the United States was the Great Depression of the 1930s.

deflation
a decline in the average level of prices

Checkpoint

Content Check

1. What does the term *demand-pull inflation* mean?

2. What is cost-push inflation?

3. How can inflation be controlled?

What Do You Think Now?

Reread *What Do You Think?* in the Section Three Focus. Then answer the following question:

4. Who is right in this debate, Mary Beth or José?

Concepts in Brief

1. Inflation is a rise in the average level of prices. It is as much of an economic problem as unemployment. Inflation can cause the allocation of resources in the economy to be inefficient. It also can cause labor to be less productive because people may use more time to find ways to reduce the impact of inflation on their lives. Perhaps most important, inflation makes it difficult for businesses and households to plan for the future. This can reduce economic activity and slow down economic growth.
2. Inflation is usually measured by using the Consumer Price Index (CPI). The Consumer Price Index is based on a typical market basket of goods and services consumed by urban families. It compares average prices for these goods to average prices of those goods in some base period, such as 1982–1984. The CPI shows what percentage the prices in any other year are of the base year prices.
3. All prices do not go up at the same rate. In the recent past, food, shelter, and medical care prices have risen faster than the overall average price level, as measured by the CPI. Some prices may go down even in periods of high inflation. But, overall, in inflationary periods, rising prices will outweigh falling prices.
4. Inflation can be categorized as demand-pull inflation or cost-push inflation. These can be explained using the concepts of aggregate demand and aggregate supply. Demand-pull inflation results from pressures on the demand side of the marketplace. The phrase *too many dollars chasing too few goods* is sometimes used to describe this type of inflation. Cost-push inflation comes from the supply side of the market. Factors that push up production costs can result in higher prices and inflation.

Economic Foundations

1. How does inflation distort the economic system?
2. What groups are hurt the least by (or benefit the most from) inflation?
3. What groups are hurt the most by inflation?
4. How does the Bureau of Labor Statistics determine the Consumer Price Index?
5. How is the rate of inflation between two years figured?
6. List three limitations of the Consumer Price Index.
7. In terms of aggregate demand and aggregate supply, what is the difference between demand-pull inflation and cost-push inflation?

8. How does government try to control demand-pull inflation?
9. How might government try to control cost-push inflation?

Your Economic Vocabulary

Build your economic vocabulary by matching the following terms with their definitions.

1. an income that is set and does not change from year to year
2. when someone buys a large amount of a good and hopes to resell it at a much higher price
3. a number that compares prices in one year with some earlier base year
4. a rise in the general level of prices that is caused by increased costs of making and selling goods
5. people who have borrowed money from someone else
6. a decline in the average level of prices
7. a rise in the general level of prices caused by too high a level of aggregate demand in relation to aggregate supply
8. a sustained rise in the general level of prices
9. people who have loaned money to others
10. a number used to calculate changes in the average level of prices for a number of items typically bought by urban families

Consumer Price Index (CPI)
cost-push inflation
creditors
debtors
deflation
demand-pull inflation
fixed income
inflation
price index
speculation

Thinking Critically About Economics

1. What does the term *inflation* mean? If meat prices go up, does this automatically mean that there is inflation? Explain your answer.
2. Give an example of who is hurt and who is helped by inflation. Briefly explain how inflation affects each group you have named.
3. How is the Consumer Price Index used to measure the rate of inflation?
4. Review the meanings of *demand-pull inflation* and *cost-push inflation*. Can one of these lead to the other? Explain your reasoning.

Economic Enrichment

In Figure 17-4, you saw that the rate of increase in prices varies among different types of goods and services. Because of this variability, the Consumer Price Index may not be a good indicator for the increase in the cost of living for different subgroups of the population. Explain why this may or may not be true.

Math and Economics

The Consumer Price Index was 118.3 in 1988. In 1989, it was 124.0. What was the rate of inflation between 1988 and 1989? Show your calculations.

Writing About Economics

The Wall Street Journal publishes a report on the level of prices as measured by the CPI every month, shortly after the Department of Labor releases the information. This usually occurs about midway through the month. *The Wall Street Journal* normally has a graphic on the front page and a story elsewhere in the same issue to discuss the current changes in the level of prices. Go to the library and find this information in a recent issue of *The Wall Street Journal*. Copy the graphic on a piece of paper and use the concepts you have read about in this chapter and the information contained in the article to explain the graphic.

A Graphical Look at Unemployment

Employment, or the lack of it—known as *unemployment*—is a very important factor in economics. We hear of the latest unemployment figures from Washington, D.C. We are told of the effects these figures can have on the rest of the economy, how a decrease in unemployment generally results in more housing starts and an increase in retail sales, and so forth. Many times, we see these unemployment figures in a table such as the following:

U.S. Unemployment Rates by Gender, Age, and Race

Years	All Workers	Workers 16–19	Male Workers 20 or Older	Female Workers 20 or Older	White Workers	Nonwhite Workers
1990	5.5%	15.5%	4.9%	4.8%	4.7%	10.1%
1991	6.7%	18.6%	6.3%	5.7%	6.0%	11.1%
1992	7.4%	20.0%	7.0%	6.3%	6.5%	12.7%
1993	6.8%	19.0%	6.4%	5.9%	6.0%	11.7%
1994	6.1%	17.6%	5.4%	5.4%	5.3%	10.5%

We can look at a table of numbers such as this one and make some observations. However, a bar chart can help us make some comparisons of unemployment rates quite quickly. As an example, let's create a bar chart with the civilian unemployment figures for All Workers, Workers 16–19, and Nonwhite Workers for 1990–1994.

Civilian Unemployment Rate

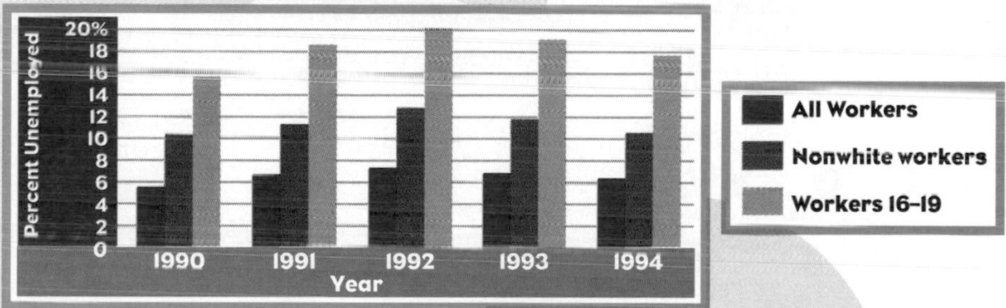

As you look at the bar chart, you can see some relationships quite easily. At a glance, you can tell that the unemployment rate for Nonwhite Workers is nearly twice the unemployment rate for All Workers, while the unemployment rate for Workers 16–19 is nearly three times as high as the rate for All Workers. Another term for these relationships is *ratio.* For example, the relationship of nonwhite workers to all workers is a ratio of about two to one. A ratio shows the relationship between two numbers reduced to its lowest common denominator. In this example, the ratio would be written as 2:1.

When reading magazines and newspapers, be on the lookout for bar charts. See if you can make any quick estimates of ratios just by looking at the charts. With practice, you'll find that you actually can become quite good at it and gain useful, quick insights into the facts behind the chart.

SOURCE: *Economic Report of the President: 1995,* (Washington, D.C.: U.S. Government Printing Office, 1995), 320.

Overview

Section One
Money

Section Two
Our Central Banking System

Section Three
Financial Institutions

Money, the Federal Reserve System, and Banking

Learning Objectives

18-1

Describe the three main functions of money.

18-2

Analyze the demand for and supply of money.

18-3

Explain the organization and functions of the Federal Reserve System.

18-4

Differentiate among the various types of financial institutions.

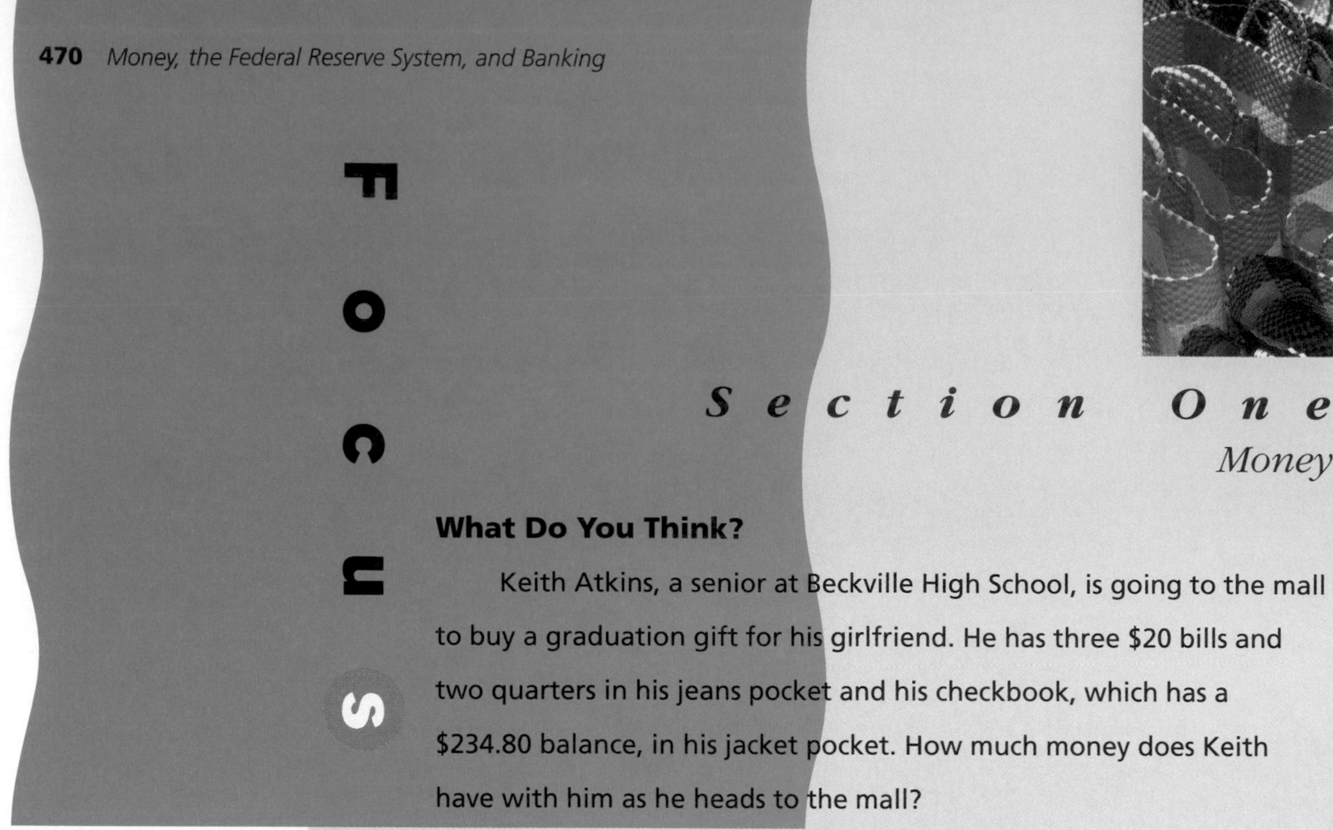

Section One
Money

What Do You Think?

Keith Atkins, a senior at Beckville High School, is going to the mall to buy a graduation gift for his girlfriend. He has three $20 bills and two quarters in his jeans pocket and his checkbook, which has a $234.80 balance, in his jacket pocket. How much money does Keith have with him as he heads to the mall?

What's Ahead?

Money: Everyone knows what that is . . . or do they? In this section, you will learn about what is considered money, the functions of money, and what determines the supply of and demand for money.

Terms to Know

- currency
- check
- transaction demand for money
- asset demand for money

WHAT IS MONEY?

So far in your study of economics, you have discovered many things that are measured in monetary terms. You have used money to measure price, the size of a business, total output in the economy, and income. But, we have not yet discussed money itself. What is money?

currency
coins and paper money

At first, this question may seem ridiculous. After all, we know what money is. Or do we? Every day we use coins and paper money, such as dimes, quarters, $1 bills, and $20 bills. Coins and paper money are called ***currency.*** People use currency daily. When you go to a movie, you probably buy a ticket with currency. If you buy snacks or soft drinks from machines, you use coins. If you borrow money from a friend, it is likely to be some kind of currency. Currency is sometimes referred to as *cash*. As important as currency is, it makes up less than 30 percent of the money that is actually used in the United States.

Coins and paper money work well for small purchases and when payment is made directly from one person to another. But, for large purchases or when the payment travels through the mail, currency is not practical. Very few people go to a car dealer with 500 $20 bills to pay for a $10,000 car. Most people do not pay the rent or house payment with coins or paper money. If you want to buy a $10 pocket calculator from a mail-order store, you should not send a $10 bill with your order. If your order were lost in the mail, there would be no way to get your money back. It is even possible that the clerk who opened your order would keep the $10 and never report the order. There would be no way to trace the money.

What kind of money is used for large purchases or purchases for which money must be sent through the mail? Checks are a common and widely accepted kind of payment. A ***check*** is a written order to pay money from amounts deposited. Therefore, deposits in checking accounts, credit union share draft accounts, and other similar accounts are considered money. Many stores and businesses accept checks as money as long as the person writing the check shows proper identification. Checks and related types of checkable deposits account for just over 70 percent of the money that is actually used in the United States.

check
a written order to pay money from amounts deposited

For most purposes, we think of currency and checking type accounts as money. Some definitions of money also include what is called *near money*. These items do not take the form of currency or checking accounts, but they easily could be changed into one or more of these. A savings account at a bank is an example of near money. If you have $200 in a savings account, you cannot use that money directly to buy a stereo. But, you can withdraw the $200, or have it transferred to your checking account, and then use that money to buy the stereo.

The question *What is money?* becomes more complex every year. As the line between money and different kinds of near monies becomes less clear, to define what should count as money becomes more challenging. Should certificates of deposit (CDs), money market funds, or insurance policies from which money can be borrowed be considered money? What about credit cards? It is often just as easy, or easier, to use credit cards to buy products as it is to use currency or a check. Credit cards are often called *plastic* money because we actually can buy things with them. Some people think that we will one day have a cashless society in which there are no coins or paper money. All paychecks will be sent directly to a bank account. Then the amount of all the products we buy will be deducted from our account and credited to the account of each seller. It is difficult to tell how far or how fast we may move in this direction. We certainly have started down that road. One fact seems clear. The answer to the question *What is money?* is likely to keep changing.

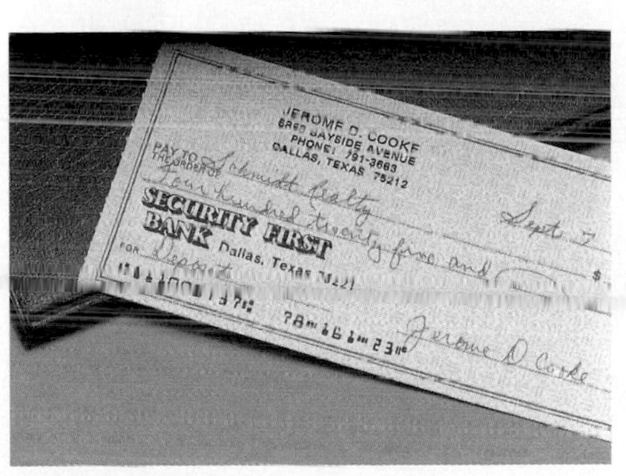

Economic Dilemma

PAY NOW OR PAY LATER, AND LATER, AND LATER

Getting a credit card these days is not difficult. It is very easy. Perhaps too easy. It is not uncommon for someone to receive several unsolicited application forms for credit cards in a single week. Many will have preapproved credit limits of several thousand dollars. Just fill in a few lines of a superficial application form and you are on your way to carefree shopping, followed by a big bill the next month.

While you may not yet be on these mailing lists, you soon will be. How many credit cards do you want? How many charges do you want to tally up? How far in debt are you willing to go? It seems so easy to buy on credit. You just hand the salesclerk a plastic card, sign your name, and off you go with a new bike. Or, you can sit in the comfort of your home and call 1-800-numbers to place an order and have the item shipped to you at home. You also can sit at your computer and order through cyberspace.

The problem is that you must pay for all those purchases. The credit card is not money and does not pay for the purchase. It just facilitates the "consume now–pay later" preference of many people. It operates like a loan, but it is much easier. It is so easy that some people get too far in debt and have trouble making the minimum monthly payment on their credit card balances. In fact, there are people who get cash advances on one credit card to make payments on others. Some people sign up for new credit cards that allow them to transfer balances from other cards, thus postponing payment for another month. This, of course, clears the balance on the old card and some consumers fall into the charging trap and start to build a new balance on the old card. And, on it goes.

There are situations in which consumers have outstanding credit card debt that is well above their annual income. This creates a financial hole that is difficult to climb out of. Who should be responsible to see that you don't fall into this trap? The banks? The government? Or, you? The Federal Reserve System publishes a booklet entitled *SHOP: The Card You Pick Can Save You Money*. To get a copy, contact the Board of Governors, Federal Reserve System, Washington, D.C. 20551-0001.

THE FUNCTIONS OF MONEY

Without money we would have to barter for the mix of goods and services we want, which would be difficult and confusing. Money makes the economics of exchange much easier. Money also serves as a measure of value and as a store of value. Let's look at each of these functions more closely.

Money as a Medium of Exchange

Money works as a medium of exchange. For example, suppose you worked for a bakery in an economy that used no money. At the end of a week's work, you might be paid in cakes or pies. Or, you might be paid 80 loaves of bread. You surely could not eat that much bread during the next week. But, you could trade it for other items, such as jeans, movie tickets, or gasoline. What if the person who sold jeans wanted milk instead of bread? You would have to trade your bread to someone else who had milk but wanted bread. Then, you could trade the milk for jeans. The use of barter in a modern society would limit the variety of goods to which we would have access. Your economic life would be much less complicated if the bakery paid you in money rather than in bread.

In order for something to function as money, it must be widely accepted in exchange for goods and services. What if you tried to buy a can of tennis balls with a $5 bill, but the tennis shop wouldn't accept it in exchange? When you tried to buy a cake, the baker wouldn't take the $5 bill either. If no one would take that $5, it would be worthless as money. But, what if you had a cow's ear that the baker, the tennis shop owner, and others would take in exchange for their goods? The cow's ear, then, would be a valuable form of money. The point is that anything readily accepted as a medium of exchange can work as money. Cows' ears are not money in our society because we do not accept them in exchange for goods or services. You certainly would not consider it a good payday if you were paid 500 cows' ears in return for your work!

Just because the government defines an item as money does not mean that it will function as money. For example, the government made $1 coins called Susan B. Anthony dollars in the 1970s. But, the coins did not become readily accepted for exchange. People often confused them with quarters, paying $1 for a $0.25 item. The Susan B. Anthony dollar had just as much value as a dollar bill. But, because they did not function well as a medium of exchange, Susan B. Anthony dollars never became a widely accepted form of money.

Money as a Measure of Value

Money functions in a second way by measuring the value of items. We count our income in monetary terms: $10,000, $25,000, and so on. We often measure the value of what we make or buy using a price expressed in monetary terms. The price of a tire is $60. The price of a can of tennis balls is $5. The price of a sweater is $80. The price of a house is $90,000. We express all prices in dollar amounts. This makes it easy to compare different prices since the measure used—dollars—is the same for everything.

Think about how confusing buying would be otherwise. What if we had a barter economy? Prices would have to be stated in terms of goods. The price

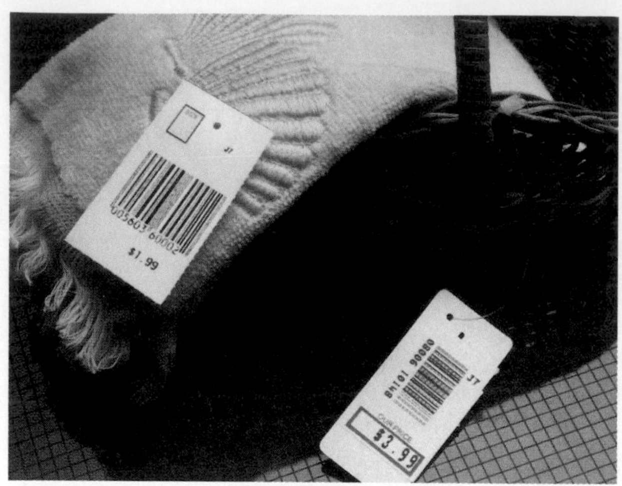

of a tire might be 22 cans of tennis balls, or 1.75 sweaters, or 1/1,500 of a house. There would have to be a cookie price for books, a book price for cars, and a fish price for steak. We would need a paper clip price for computers and a computer price for fish. Such a system would make a modern economy impossible. The use of money as a measure of value is essential to our society. Yet, we have come to take this for granted. You would never ask a salesclerk for the dollar price of a necklace. You would just ask the price and would expect the answer to be in dollars. You would certainly be surprised if the clerk told you that the price of the necklace was 251 pounds of butter!

Money as a Store of Value

Money also functions as a store of value. This means that if you choose not to buy something with your money today, you can save it to buy in the future. If money were a perfect store of value, you could buy the same items next year as you could today with the same amount of money.

But, money functions poorly as a store of value when there is inflation in the economy. If inflation occurs, next year $100 will not buy as much as $100 will buy today. For this reason, people often keep their savings in other assets, such as in savings accounts, in corporate stock, in gold, or in land. These may function better as stores of value, but there is some risk involved with each. This is true because their value could fall even faster than the value of money.

THE DEMAND FOR AND SUPPLY OF MONEY

The functions of money just discussed should give you some idea about why there is a demand for money and what might change that demand. There is also a supply of money in the economy. The demand for money and the supply of money interact to determine the level of interest rates in the economy. An interest rate can be thought of as the "price for money."

The Demand for Money

Remember that the most important function of money is as a medium of exchange. Therefore, one reason we demand money is to make exchanges. We can trade our labor for money and then trade the money for what we want to buy. This means that we have a transaction demand for money. The ***transaction demand for money*** is the demand for money to make exchanges. We need money to make economic transactions. We want to be paid in money, and we want to use money to buy goods and services. The main factor that affects the transaction demand for money is the level of income in the economy. The higher the level of income, the greater the demand for money and buying power.

transaction demand for money
the demand for money to make exchanges

Economic Spotlight

FROM STOCKBROKER TO "THE LADY OF LACE"

Watch out Victoria's Secret, Ralph Lauren, and Laura Ashley! Here comes Josie Natori. Born in the Philippines, Josie Cruz Natori came to the United States to study economics because it seemed like the logical thing to do, not because she had a keen desire to do so. Her first love was music. Considered a child prodigy at the age of nine, Natori played her first piano solo with the Manila Philharmonic. Still, economics seemed far more practical, so she came to New York.

After graduating from Manhattanville College, she became a registered stockbroker and traveled back to Manila to start a branch office for her employer. Two years later, Natori switched companies and returned to the United States where, in five years, she became Merrill Lynch's first female vice president of investment banking. A few years later, Natori found herself bored with Wall Street, so she left her $100,000-a-year job to start her own firm.

She began by importing products native to the Philippines that she thought might be marketable in the United States. Says Natori, "I tried baskets, furniture, and several other things before ending up by accident in [the] intimate apparel [market]." The entrepreneur says a buyer from Bloomingdale's suggested that she redesign into nightshirts the delicate, hand-embroidered blouses she was selling. The sleepwear was an instant success, launching the Natori label into additional markets, such as loungewear, bed-and-bath linens, fragrances, shoes, jewelry, handbags, and a variety of other accessories. But, this rapid expansion wasn't easy.

In need of help with her growing business, Natori convinced a top Wall Street businessperson to leave his executive vice president position to join her company as chairperson. Of course, it helped that the executive was her husband, Kenneth Natori. Today, this husband and wife team work side by side, overseeing a staff of more than 100 Natori Company employees.

Why is the company so successful? Natori credits her family (her father and grandmother owned their own businesses) and her heritage, which has made her a "fresh face" in business circles. "I make it work for me," Natori says. "Being female and Filipino . . . have been my greatest assets." Judging from Josie Natori's success, a great attitude is also a powerful tool.

asset demand for money
the demand for money in order to hold wealth in the form of money

You can see from the third function of money, as a store of value, that there is also a demand for money as an asset. The ***asset demand for money*** is the demand for money in order to hold wealth in the form of money. Some people will always want to hold some part of their wealth in the form of money. Many factors, including the rate of inflation, will affect the asset demand for money. One of the most important and most interesting of these factors is the rate of interest.

If we use money to buy an asset that pays interest, such as a government or corporate bond, we earn more money in the form of interest payments. The same can be said for money we put into a savings account. On the other hand, if we keep our money in $50 bills, we earn no interest on that asset.

When the interest rate is very low, we don't give up much by not putting our money in an asset that pays interest. Thus, when interest rates are low, we may hold money as an asset. But, when interest rates are high, we give up more in interest payments by holding money. So, we would want to hold less money as an asset. Therefore, the quantity of money we demand as an asset is inversely related to the interest rate. When interest rates rise, the quantity of money demanded as an asset falls. And, when interest rates fall, the quantity of money demanded as an asset increases.

Look at Figure 18-1. If everything, including income, except the interest rate stays constant, the demand for money might look like the solid black line that slopes down to the right. At high interest rates, the quantity of money demanded is less than at lower interest rates. You should be able to use this relationship to show your understanding of opportunity cost. When we hold money, we have an opportunity cost equal to the interest we could have earned with that money. If the interest rate is high, our opportunity cost of holding money is high. Therefore, we will desire to hold a relatively small quantity of money. But, if the interest rate is low, our opportunity cost of holding money is low, so we might desire to hold more.

Figure 18-1

Demand for Money

The quantity of money demanded depends on the interest rate. We will want to hold a greater quantity of money as an asset the lower the interest rate. ***What represents the price for money?***

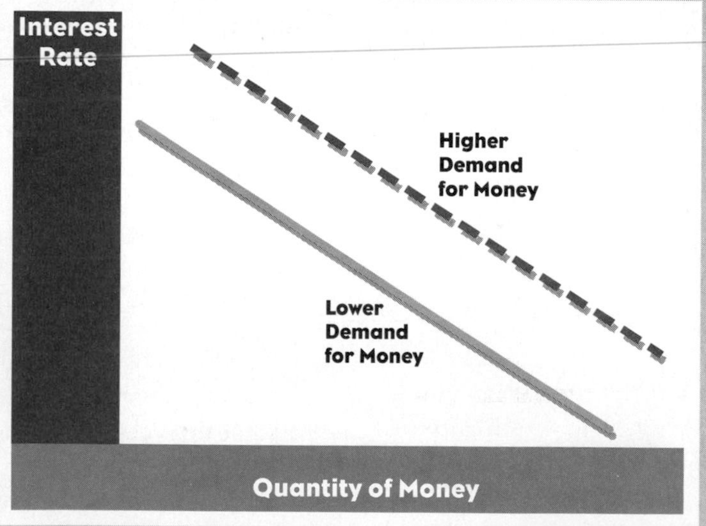

The dashed line in Figure 18-1 shows a higher demand for money than does the solid line. At any interest rate, people would prefer to hold more money along the dashed line than along the solid line. A shift from the lower demand for money to the higher demand for money could be caused by an increase in income. It might also be caused by a perception of greater risk in holding nonmoney assets.

The Supply of Money

In the United States, the Federal Reserve System controls the supply of money. The Federal Reserve System is the central banking system in the United States. It is frequently called *the Fed.* We will talk about the structure and functions of the Federal Reserve System in the next section of this chapter. You will learn how the Fed controls the money supply. For now, we will simply state that the Fed determines the supply of money in the economy. Therefore, at any given time, some fixed amount of money circulates through the economy. This is shown by the vertical lines in Figure 18-2.

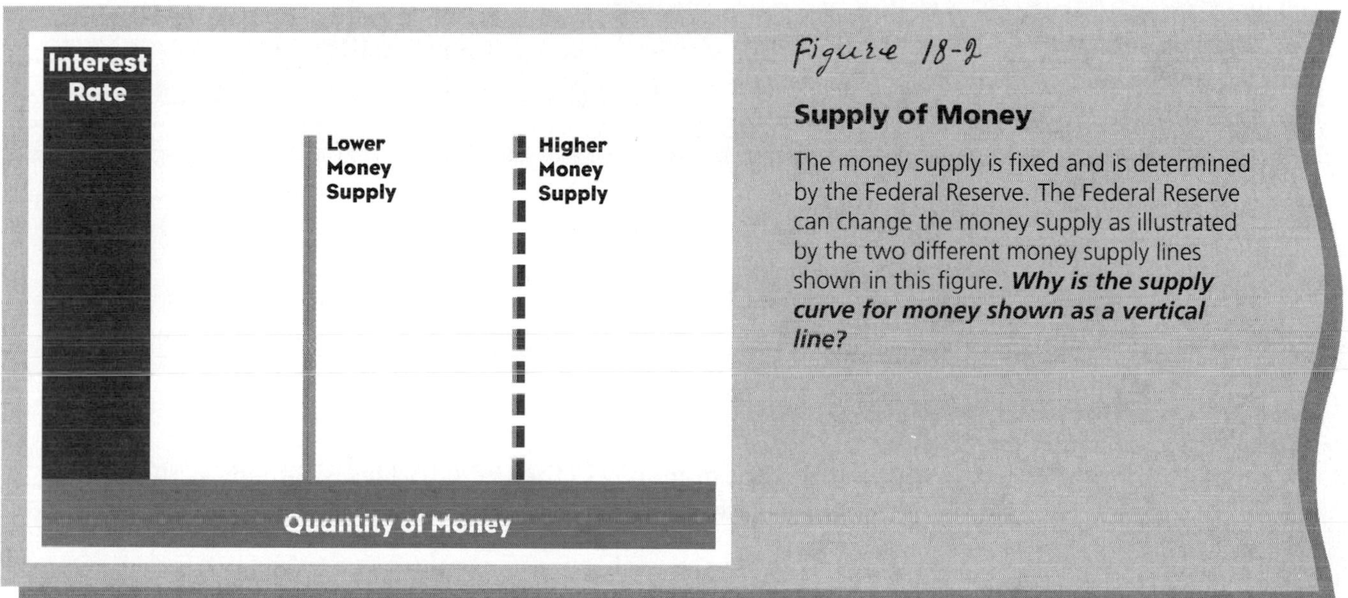

Supply of Money

The money supply is fixed and is determined by the Federal Reserve. The Federal Reserve can change the money supply as illustrated by the two different money supply lines shown in this figure. ***Why is the supply curve for money shown as a vertical line?***

Equilibrium in the Money Market

The market, or equilibrium, interest rate is at the level where the quantity of money demanded equals the quantity of money supplied. This is a general level of interest. There are many different interest rates and all tend to move up or down at about the same time. If this general rate changes, the individual specific rates are also likely to change.

What causes this interest rate to change? Anything that causes the money demand or the money supply to change also causes this general interest rate to change. Let us focus on the effect of a change in the demand for money at this point. In the next chapter, we will discuss changes in the supply of money.

Using Figure 18-3, see what happens if the demand for money goes up, such as a move from the solid demand for money curve to the dashed demand curve. The interest rate rises. The opposite occurs if there is a decline in the demand for money, such as a shift from the dashed line to the solid line. A fall in the demand for money causes interest rates to fall.

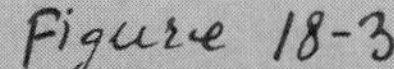

Equilibrium in the Money Market

The money supply is fixed and is a vertical line at the current money supply. The quantity of money we demand depends on the interest rate. The equilibrium interest rate is at the level where supply curve and the demand curve cross. Two such equilibrium interest rates are illustrated in this figure. ***Which interest rate is associated with the higher demand for money and which is associated with the lower demand for money?***

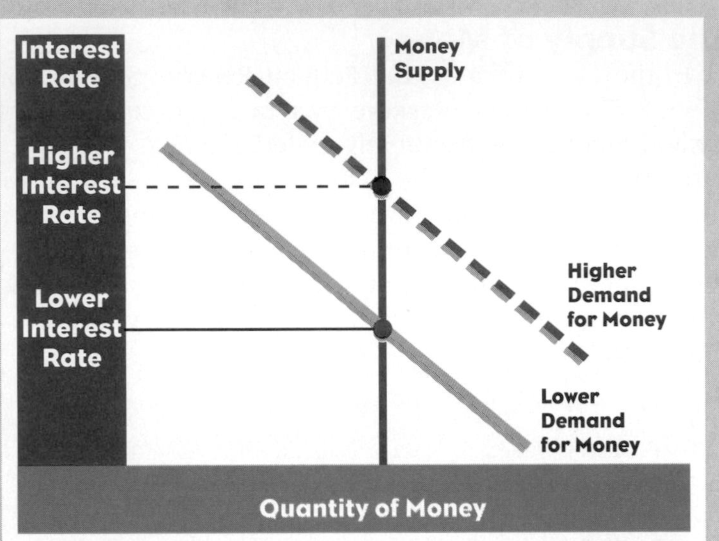

Chec k oint

Content Check

1. What percent of money in the United States is actually in the form of paper money and coins? What about various types of checking accounts?
2. Why don't we use candy canes as money?
3. What would cause a change in the quantity of money demanded?

What Do You Think Now?

Reread *What Do You Think?* in the Section One Focus. Then answer the following questions:

4. How much money does Keith have with him as he heads to the mall?
5. What percent of Keith's money is in the form of cash?

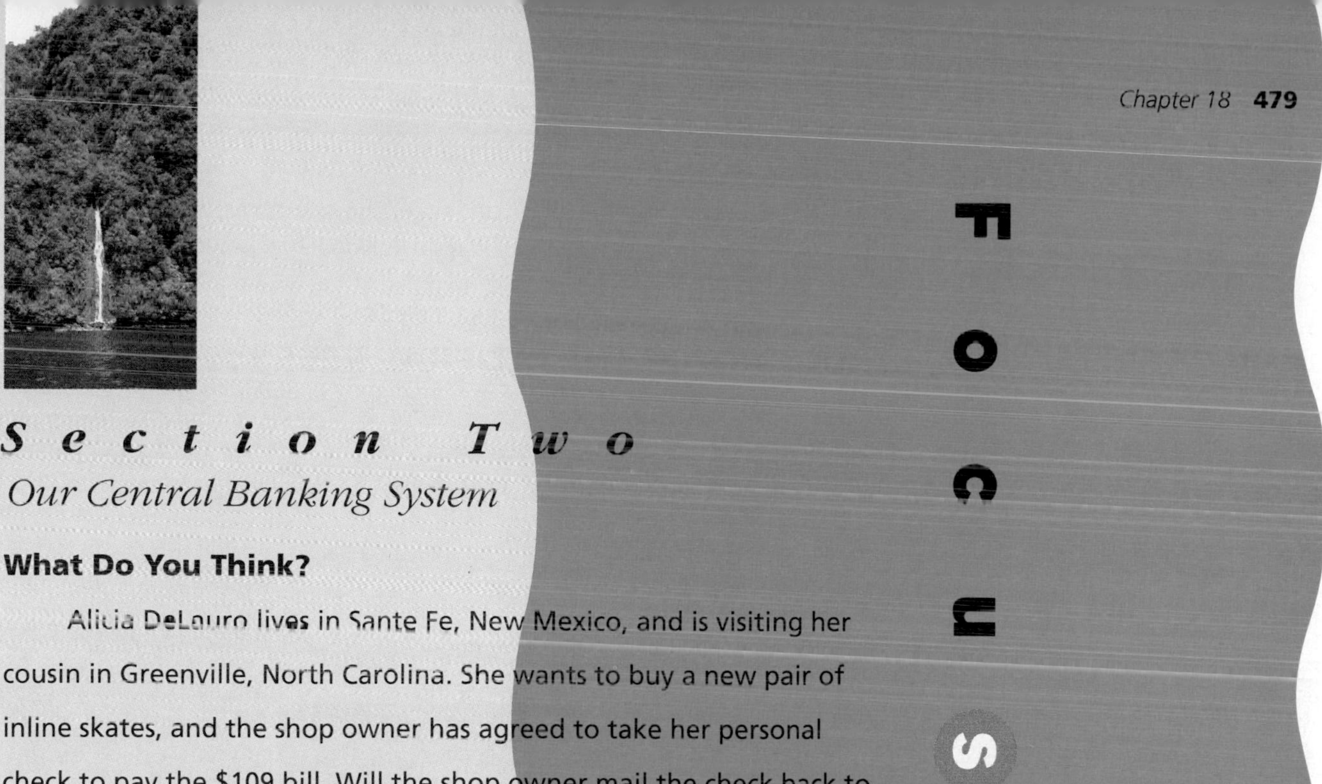

Section Two
Our Central Banking System

What Do You Think?

Alicia DeLauro lives in Sante Fe, New Mexico, and is visiting her cousin in Greenville, North Carolina. She wants to buy a new pair of inline skates, and the shop owner has agreed to take her personal check to pay the $109 bill. Will the shop owner mail the check back to Alicia's Sante Fe bank in order to get the $109?

What's Ahead?

The Federal Reserve System plays a very important role in our economy. In this section, you will learn about the structure of the Fed and some of the functions it performs.

Terms to Know

Federal Reserve System (the Fed)

member banks

Board of Governors

Federal Open Market Committee (FOMC)

Federal Advisory Council

THE FEDERAL RESERVE SYSTEM

As you learned in the previous section, the ***Federal Reserve System (the Fed)*** is the central banking system in the United States. The United States was slow to adopt a central banking system. Not until 1913 did Congress, under pressure from President Woodrow Wilson, pass the Federal Reserve Act of 1913. Many other countries had central banking systems long before this. The Bank of England was founded in 1694, the Bank of France in 1800, and the Bank of Japan in 1882. Americans, however, felt skeptical about having too much centralized authority in banking. So, when the Federal Reserve System was set up, it had 12 separate regional banks. Each of them was to act as the central bank for a given part of the country. Over the years since 1913, the 12 regional banks have become much less independent. They now act, for the most part, as one central bank.

Federal Reserve System (the Fed) the central banking system in the United States

The Federal Reserve System began as an independent agency. It was not controlled by the executive branch of the government, nor was it controlled by Congress. The Fed had to report to Congress each year, but for years this was just a formality. Only a weak relationship existed between the Federal

Reserve and the federal government. More recently, the government has tightened its control on the Fed. Now, the Fed reports to Congress on a more regular and formal basis.

THE STRUCTURE OF THE FEDERAL RESERVE SYSTEM

The structure of the Federal Reserve System is shown in Figure 18-4. Each section of this chart will be discussed in some detail. Try to keep the various parts of the chart in mind as you read the following discussion.

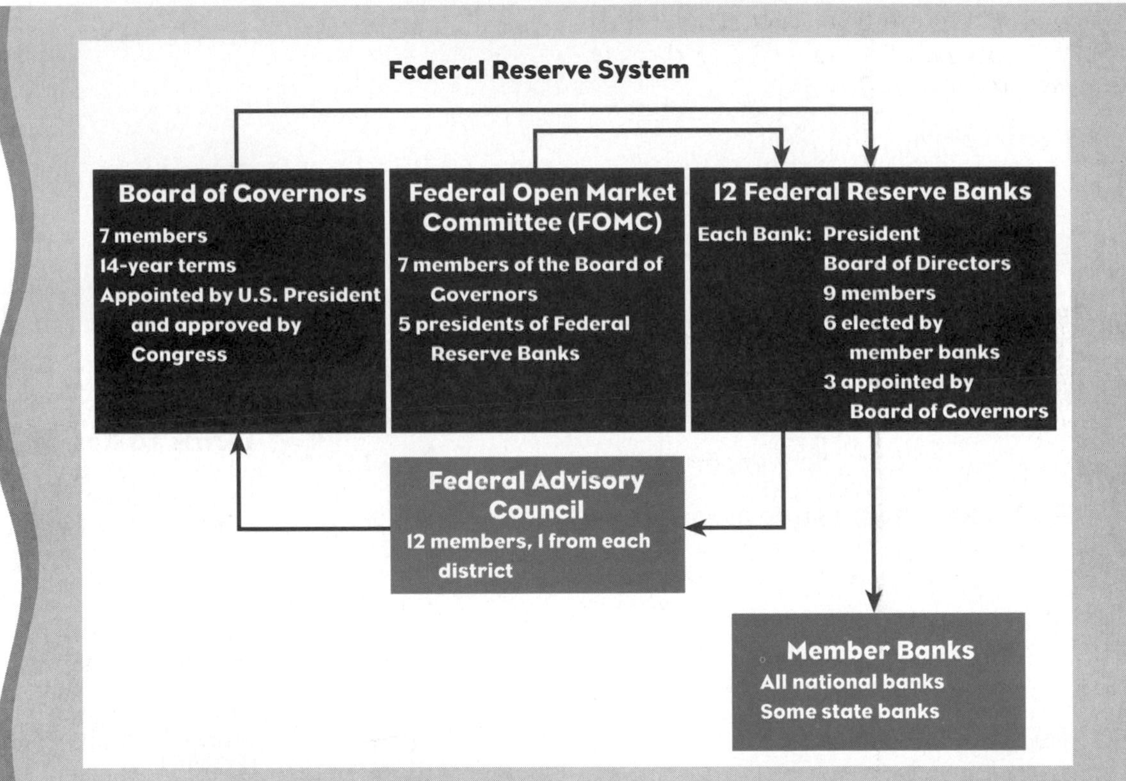

Figure 18-4

The Structure of the Federal Reserve System

The Board of Governors supervises the Federal Reserve System. The Federal Open Market Committee buys and sells U.S. government securities. The Federal Advisory Council has no real power but meets with the Board of Governors to discuss policy. The 12 Federal Reserve Banks are the central banks of their geographic areas and issue Federal Reserve notes (currency). ***Are all of the Federal Reserve districts represented on the Federal Advisory Council?***

Federal Reserve Banks

The Federal Reserve Act of 1913 divided the United States into 12 districts, each with a Federal Reserve Bank. The Federal Reserve Banks for each district are located in the following cities:

District	Federal Reserve Bank Location	District	Federal Reserve Bank Location
1	Boston, MA	7	Chicago, IL
2	New York, NY	8	St. Louis, MO

3	Philadelphia, PA	9	Minneapolis, MN
4	Cleveland, OH	10	Kansas City, MO
5	Richmond, VA	11	Dallas, TX
6	Atlanta, GA	12	San Francisco, CA

The Federal Reserve Banks in each district issue Federal Reserve notes (paper money) with the number of the district on each note. These districts are shown in Figure 18-5. Look at a dollar bill or any larger bill. On the same side as the president's picture, you will see the number of a Federal Reserve district about one inch in from each corner. If that number is 10, the money came from the tenth Federal Reserve district headquartered in Kansas City, Missouri. Most of the paper money you see in your area probably comes from the Federal Reserve district in that area. People in Pittsburgh, for example, are more likely to see paper money with a 4 on it than any other number.

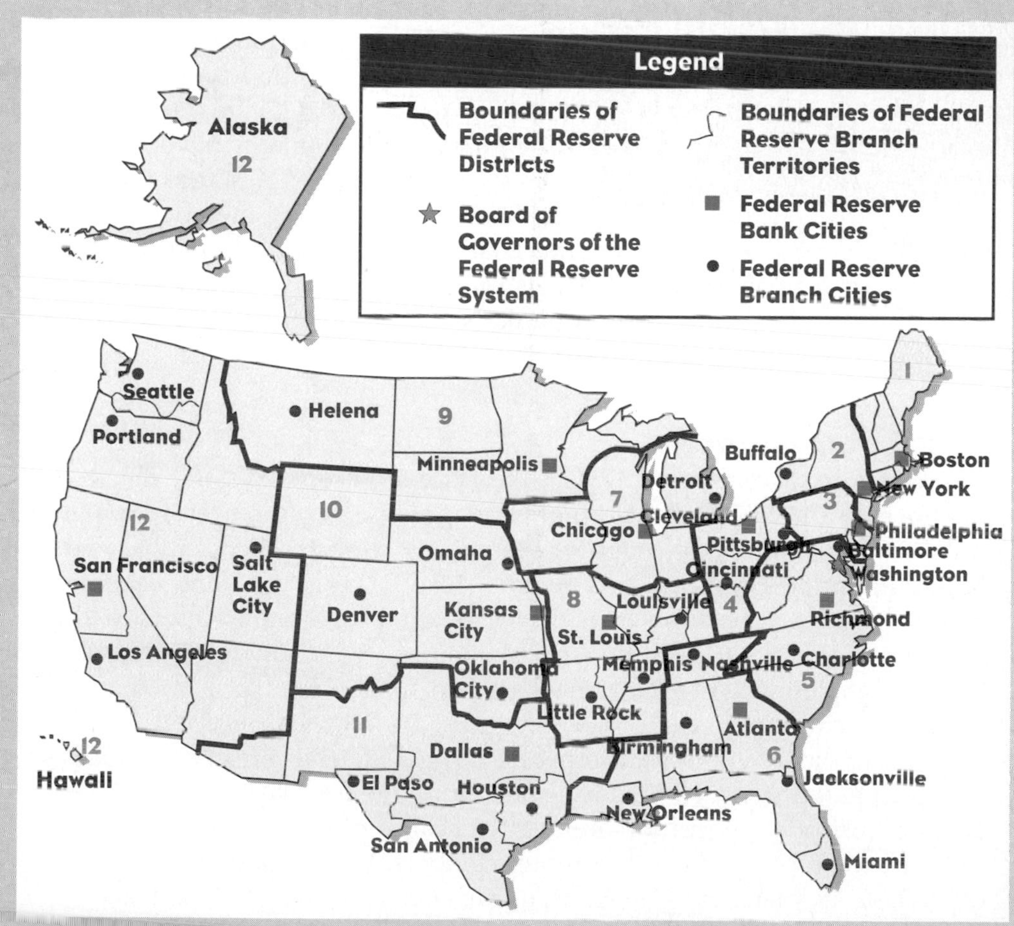

Figure 18-5

The Geographic Boundaries of the 12 Federal Reserve Districts

This map shows how the 50 states are divided into the 12 Federal Reserve districts. ***Find the Federal Reserve district in which you live.***

member banks
those banks that belong to the Federal Reserve System

Each Federal Reserve Bank operates as a private business with its own president and board of directors. The board of directors has nine members, six of whom are elected by member banks. ***Member banks*** are those that belong to the Federal Reserve System. The other three directors are appointed by the Board of Governors of the Federal Reserve System. Ten of the Federal Reserve Banks have branches that are closely controlled by the district banks.

Member Banks

Banks that are members of the Federal Reserve System also form part of the system's structure. Not every bank is a member of the Federal Reserve System. In fact, as you will see, only about half of the banks in the United States are members. All national banks must belong, and some state-chartered banks also apply for membership. Any bank with the word *national* in its name is a national bank. That makes it also a member of the Federal Reserve System. National banks must use the word *national* in their name or have *N. A.* following their name. *N. A.* stands for National Affiliation. Size among member banks varies quite a bit. For example, the First National Bank of Geraldine, Montana, is a small bank with assets measured in tens of millions of dollars. By comparison, the Mellon Bank, N. A., of Pittsburgh has assets measured in tens of billions of dollars.

Board of Governors

Board of Governors
a group that supervises the Federal Reserve System

A ***Board of Governors*** supervises the Federal Reserve System. The seven members of the Board of Governors are appointed by the president with the approval of Congress. In order for there to be equitable geographic representation on the Board, no two members can be from the same Federal Reserve district. A person serves on the Board for 14 years. A person also can be appointed to finish the term of someone who leaves the Board before completing a 14-year term. That person can then be appointed to a new 14-year term.

Because the seven 14-year terms are staggered, each president appoints two people to the Board of Governors during the four-year term of office. But, because some governors quit early because of old age or for financial reasons, some presidents select more members. Even though the term of office lasts 14 years, the average term runs between five and six years because people leave before their terms expire. Board members can be removed from office if there is cause, but this has never been done.

The president chooses the chairperson and the vice-chairperson of the Board of Governors, with the approval of Congress. Each serves a four-year term in these positions but can be reappointed. For example, President

Reagan initially retained Paul Volcker as the chairperson. In 1987, Reagan appointed Alan Greenspan as chairperson of the Board of Governors. Alan Greenspan was kept on by Presidents Bush and Clinton. Who is the current chairperson?

Members of the Board of Governors have their offices in Washington, D.C. They have a large staff of economists, lawyers, and other professionals who research the economy and the role of money and banking in the economy. The Board must rule on bank mergers and on many nonbanking activities in which banks may want to become involved. The Board also administers truth-in-lending laws and laws that relate to eliminating discrimination in lending. In addition, members of the Board of Governors have a great deal to say about the direction of monetary policy. You will read more about monetary policy in Chapter 19. You can see, then, that membership on the Board of Governors is an important and powerful position.

Econ & You

NOT ALL MONEY IS STORED IN THE BANK

Consumers generally pay for transactions with cash, a check, a credit card, or a debit card. A new method for paying is called a *stored value card* or an *electronic purse*. An electronic purse, or stored money card, might be thought of as electronic cash. A sum of money is "contained in the card" and is deducted from the card when the transaction is made.

Prepaid cards have been used for special purposes for some years. Examples include cards issued for mass transit; some long distance calling cards; and cards issued on college campuses for dining services, purchases at the college bookstore, and payment for concerts. These, however, are limited-use cards operating only in a closed system. You can't use your calling card to pay for a burger at Wendy's, for example.

An electronic purse, on the other hand, is an open system card used to buy fast food, go to a movie, get a soda from a vending machine, or buy groceries, for example. It provides a simple and compact way to carry purchasing power.

Here's how it works. Your financial institution issues the card to you. You then transfer money to the card using an ATM (automatic teller machine). Then, at the point of purchase, the card is passed through a terminal and money is taken off the card and transferred to the seller. When the card runs low, you go to an ATM and fill it up again. The mechanics of making such a system work are complex. But it can be done. Such cards have been successful in Denmark (the DANMONT card) and in Finland (the Avant card).

Federal Open Market Committee

Federal Open Market Committee (FOMC)
a group that acts on one important part of monetary policy: the buying and selling of U.S. government securities by the Federal Reserve Banks

The ***Federal Open Market Committee (FOMC)*** acts on one important part of monetary policy: the buying and selling of U.S. government securities by the Federal Reserve Banks. This group is a powerful part of the Federal Reserve System. There are 12 members on the FOMC, seven of whom are members of the Board of Governors. The chairperson of the Board of Governors also chairs the FOMC. The other five members of the FOMC are the presidents of five of the Federal Reserve Banks. The president of the New York Federal Reserve Bank is a permanent member of the FOMC. The other four slots are rotated among the remaining 11 Federal Reserve Districts. The monthly meetings of the FOMC take place in Washington, D.C., and usually all 12 Federal Reserve Bank presidents attend. All of them can participate in the meeting, but only the five official members can vote.

Federal Advisory Council

Federal Advisory Council
a group that consists of 12 members who meet four times each year with the Board of Governers to discuss the economic situation and policies of the Board

The ***Federal Advisory Council*** consists of 12 members who meet four times each year with the Board of Governors to discuss the economic situation and policies of the Board. The 12 members, one from each Federal Reserve district, usually are bankers who are selected by the Federal Reserve Banks. This gives the Board of Governors a chance to hear the concerns of the banks in each district. It also gives the bankers some direct contact with the Board. The Federal Advisory Council has no real power. However, it links bankers with the Board of Governors, which has much control over bankers' activities.

FUNCTIONS OF THE FEDERAL RESERVE SYSTEM

The Federal Reserve System functions as a *banker's bank* and as the bank for the government. The Fed acts as a banker's bank because banks use the Federal Reserve Banks much as you use your local bank. A bank can have an account with the Fed and keep money on deposit in a Federal Reserve Bank. In addition, banks can borrow from the Fed. In fact, the Federal Reserve is sometimes called a *lender of last resort*. This means that banks can always borrow from the Fed if they need money to satisfy withdrawals by bank customers. This function reduces the threat of panics and runs on banks. Thus, if everyone with a deposit at your local bank tried to withdraw their money at once, your bank could borrow from the Fed to meet this abnormal demand.

There have been no major runs on *national banks* in the United States since the Great Depression of the 1930s. Today, people can have great faith in national banks. One of the major reasons we always can get our money is that the bank can borrow from the Fed if necessary. For example, back in the 1970s, the Franklin National Bank in Philadelphia borrowed $1.75 billion from the Fed to help prevent a complete collapse of the bank.

As you have seen, each Federal Reserve Bank issues currency to meet our demand to hold money in the form of currency. If we want a greater fraction of our money in $20 bills, the Fed will make more $20 bills

available. If we want to hold most of our money in currency rather than in checking accounts, the Fed makes the necessary amount of currency available.

Another function of the Federal Reserve System is to provide a way for checks to flow from one part of the country to another. This is called the *check-clearing process*. Suppose you send a check drawn on your account at a bank in Great Falls, Montana, to a company in Freeport, Maine. There must be some way for that check to get back to your bank. Look at the upper right-hand corner of the check in Figure 18-6. You will see some numbers (other than the check number) called *routing numbers*. These are codes for Federal Reserve districts and individual banks that help to send checks easily back to the bank from which they originated.

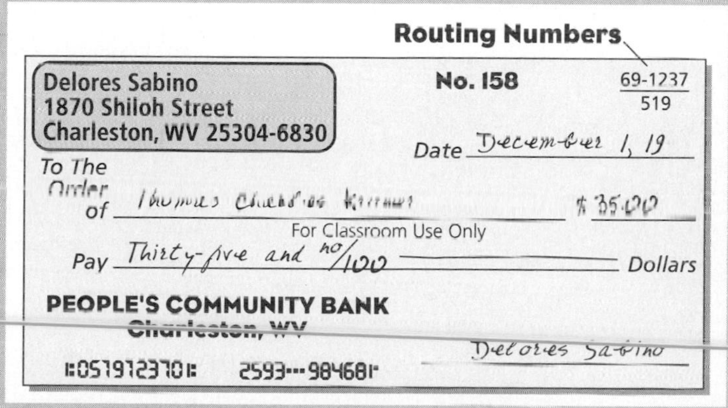
Routing Numbers
Delores Sabino
1870 Shiloh Street
Charleston, WV 25304-6830
No. 158
69-1237
519
Date December 1, 19
To The Order of Thomas Charles Kirrans
$ 35.00
For Classroom Use Only
Pay Thirty-five and no/100 Dollars
PEOPLE'S COMMUNITY BANK
Charleston, WV
Delores Sabino
⑆051912370⑆ 2593⑈984681⑈

Figure 18-6

A Personal Check Showing Routing Numbers

The routing numbers on this check help to move it through the banking system. ***Look at a check from a bank in your community and find the routing numbers. Compare the routing numbers with those found by other members of your class. Are they the same or different? Why?***

The Federal Reserve System also acts as the bank for the government. The government has accounts with the Fed and can write checks on these accounts. Also, the government can borrow from the Fed if necessary. These functions give the Fed control over the supply of money along with control of the banking system. Controlling the supply of money is the most important job of the Federal Reserve System and is the very heart of monetary policy. Because this function is so important, we will discuss it exclusively in Chapter 19.

Checkpoint

Content Check

1. What is the Federal Reserve System?
2. What are the major structural components to the Federal Reserve System?
3. The phrase *lender of last resort* was used to describe one function of the Fed. What does this mean?

What Do You Think Now?

Reread *What Do You Think?* in the Section Two Focus. Then answer the following question:

4. Will the shop owner have to mail the check back to Alicia's Sante Fe bank in order to get the $109?

FOCUS

Section Three

Financial Institutions

What Do You Think?

Pat Sandford, a nurse at Tri-City Memorial Hospital, has a checking account in a Norwest bank. His house is financed through Mutual Home Savings and Loan, where he also has a Christmas club account. His car is financed through the Tri-City Memorial Hospital Credit Union, where he keeps a share account. Do you think it would be possible for Pat to have all five of these financial accounts at one financial institution?

What's Ahead?

In the United States, we have a great many financial institutions that move money from those who wish to save to those who wish to borrow. Many people are both savers and borrowers. In this section, you will learn about some of the most important financial institutions for the majority of households.

Terms to Know

- commercial bank
- demand deposit
- share draft account
- Federal Deposit Insurance Corporation (FDIC)
- financial intermediary
- savings and loan association
- mutual savings banks
- credit union

COMMERCIAL BANKS

A ***commercial bank*** is a type of financial institution that was originally formed to serve businesses but now provides a large number of financial services to both business customers and individuals. Commercial banks offer a broad set of services. They make business loans, offer checking accounts and savings accounts, and rent safe-deposit boxes. They make loans to consumers for the purchase of cars, boats, home appliances, computers, and so on. They also make loans for the purchase of homes. They issue credit cards, sell travelers' checks, and often exchange foreign currency for U.S. currency. The term *full service bank* is used in some bank advertisements. This accurately describes most banks because they provide a broad range of financial services.

commercial bank a type of financial institution that was originally formed to serve businesses but now provides a large number of financial services to both business customers and individuals

Global Economy

CULTURAL INVESTMENT PAYS OFF

Would you like a tax-free, interest-free loan of $12,800? Do you need motivation to save? Perhaps you should join a rotating savings and credit association such as those that are common in some cultures. The Ethiopians call such an association an *ekub*. Bolivians call it *pasanaqu*. Koreans call it *keh*. Cambodians call it *tong-tine*. Whatever it is called, it functions in some ways like a savings bank.

Here's how a rotating savings and credit association works. You first organize a group that agrees on how much each member will contribute, how often contributions will be made, and how the money will be given out (by lottery or by need). After each member has collected money once, the distribution cycle starts over again. In January 1995, Solomon Teferra, a member of an Ethiopian *ekub* in the Washington D.C. area, was selected by lottery to receive $12,800, the amount that *ekub* distributes each month. His *ekub* has 16 members, each of whom contributes $200 a week. Thus, every four weeks there is $12,800 to distribute. All members eventually collect. In fact, Solomon postponed his distribution in favor of another member with a more urgent need.

For those who collect early in the cycle, it is like getting a bank loan with no interest. For those who collect late in the cycle, it is like having put money into a savings account—except there is no interest. However, belonging to the group and putting in the money every week provides motivation that may well stimulate more savings than one might have made otherwise.

The success of such arrangements depends on the commitment, honesty, and integrity of the members. You certainly don't want to form such a group by picking names from the phone book. Close friendships and cultural ties may be responsible in part for the success of many of these associations. The chairman of Solomon's *ekub* commented that in his group a member simply would not consider missing a payment. Someone who did not pay would lose his reputation in the community *forever*.

At one time, having the authority to establish checking accounts separated banks from other financial institutions. Economists usually call checking accounts *demand deposits.* A **demand deposit** is money that must be paid upon demand by the holder of a check. But, today other financial institutions can have accounts that do essentially the same thing as checking accounts. For example, a ***share draft account*** is an account with a credit union from which withdrawals easily can be made through a draft (a draft is a type of check). Most businesses accept all kinds of "checks" with equal willingness. Today, the differences between banks and the other financial institutions are slight. Nonetheless, some consumers have a strong preference for one type of financial institution over another, just as some people prefer McDonald's to Wendy's (or vice-versa).

demand deposit
money that must be paid upon demand by the holder of a check

share draft account
an account with a credit union from which withdrawals easily can be made through a draft (a draft is a type of check)

Some banks are chartered by the federal government and others are chartered by a state government. The federally chartered banks are called *national banks,* and the others are called *state banks.* About 30 percent of the insured banks in the United States are national banks. As stated earlier, national banks must be members of the Federal Reserve System. State banks may apply for membership if they meet certain qualifications. Only about 10 percent of state banks are member banks.

An important feature of the U.S. banking system is the role played by the ***Federal Deposit Insurance Corporation (FDIC),*** the agency that insures deposits of individuals and businesses for up to $100,000 in the event of bank failure. This insurance, along with the ability of banks to borrow from the Fed, has been responsible for much of the stability of banks since the 1930s. More than 98 percent of all banks belong to the FDIC, even though only national banks are required to belong. Since the founding of the FDIC in 1934, 99 percent of all depositors have been paid in full when banks have had to close. This means that there is almost no risk of losing the money you have deposited at an insured bank.

Federal Deposit Insurance Corporation (FDIC)
the agency that insures deposits of individuals and businesses for up to $100,000 in the event of bank failure

If you had more than $100,000 in an account at a bank that failed, you would get at least $100,000 from the FDIC. But, you probably would get back your full deposit. This is because the FDIC tries to merge a failing bank with a healthy bank so that no one loses money. You also can protect your deposits above $100,000 by putting the money in two separate accounts in the same bank. (By law, one must be a joint account with someone else in order to be protected.) Then, both accounts will be insured for the full $100,000. You also can protect yourself by having separate accounts in as many different banks as you choose. So, there is no reason to risk losing any money at all.

NONBANK FINANCIAL INTERMEDIARIES

At one time, banks were not interested in providing financial services to individuals and households. Their main interest was in businesses. Therefore, other financial intermediaries formed to serve the needs of special groups of people. A ***financial intermediary*** is an organization that helps the flow of money from people with money to save to people who need to borrow money.

financial intermediary
an organization that helps the flow of money from people with money to save to people who need to borrow money

Savings and Loan Associations

savings and loan association
a financial intermediary that mainly provides a place for people to save money and then lends that money to people to buy houses or other items

Savings and loan associations are some of the best-known of the nonbank financial intermediaries. A ***savings and loan association*** is a financial intermediary that mainly provides a place for people to save money and then lends that money to people to buy houses or other items.

Savings and loans were first formed by groups of people who needed a way to put together enough money to buy houses. A group of people pooled their savings until enough was collected to buy one house. A member of the group was selected to receive the money through some method that gave each member an equal chance of being selected. That member then used the money to buy a house and began paying back into the savings and loan association. Those payments, along with continued savings from the other members, built the pool of money up again until another member could buy a house. The savings and loan association did what no one person could do. It collected money from many different members and made that money available to one borrower.

Today, savings and loan associations operate much more formally and make many more services available to their customers. But, the principle is the same: Many people put money into savings accounts, while others borrow the money to buy homes or other items. Before 1980, savings and loans were very limited in how they could lend their money. More than 80 percent of their assets were in loans for housing. Now they can lend some money to businesses as well, and they have more flexibility to lend money to people for other (nonhousing) purposes. Since 1981, all savings and loans have been able to issue NOW (negotiable order of withdrawal) accounts, which are similar to bank checking accounts. These days, very little differentiates banks from savings and loan associations for most consumers. Both provide a full range of financial services.

Savings and loan associations, like banks, can be started with a state or federal charter. There are more state-charted savings and loans, but the biggest ones have federal charters. All federally chartered savings and loans must belong to the Federal Savings and Loan Insurance Corporation (FSLIC). The FSLIC insures deposits up to $100,000. State savings and loans also can belong to the FSLIC. In total, about 85 percent of all savings and loan associations are insured by the FSLIC. An important and further safeguard for savings and loans that was recently implemented allows them to borrow from the Fed much like banks can.

Mutual Savings Banks

mutual savings banks
banks that were first formed for the same reasons as savings and loan associations and that promote thrift in their members

Mutual savings banks are banks that were first formed for the same reasons as savings and loan associations and that promote thrift in their members. Their loans are used mainly for housing, and they usually appeal to the depositor with a small savings account. In fact, the names of many mutual savings banks give the idea that the banks began with small accounts. For example, one of the oldest mutual savings banks is the Boston Five Cent Savings Bank. Today, it is large enough to be listed in Dun & Bradstreet's *Million Dollar Directory*. Mutual savings banks are found mainly in the northeastern United States.

MONEY, BANKING, AND THE INTERNET

Few people would associate money and banking with cyberspace. Most people think of money as currency, but it consists of anything generally accepted as a means of payment, whether paper or electronic.

In Chapter 9, we introduced you to commercial uses of the Internet by drawing an analogy with mail order sales. To pay for a mail order purchase, you can use a credit card or check. Sending a credit card number over the Internet is risky, because computer hackers can get access to your number. And you can't send a check over the Internet. Or can you?

In fact, money and banking are coming to the Internet. Visa and Mastercard have Web pages at **http://www.visa.com/visa** and **http://www.mastercard.com**.

Many banks and other thrift institutions are also on the Internet and are listed at **http://rampages.onramp.net/~clawson/bank/#top** and **http://www.yahoo.com/Business/Corporations/Financial_Services/Bank** and **http://www.tiac.net/users/dstein/nw39.html**. These Web pages have links to hundreds of domestic and foreign financial institutions as well as related topics.

In the near future, we are likely to see several forms of online payments systems, including secure electronic credit card transactions, online debit cards, and electronic banking.

In order to make credit card sales more feasible in cyberspace, a number of firms are working on secure electronic payments systems. For an example, see **http://rampages.onramp.net/~clawson/bank/#ecash**, especially the link to Cybercash.

Once this problem is solved, you can expect to see online debit cards as well. Unlike credit card transactions, which still require you to make a payment to your credit card company at the end of the month, electronic debit cards will automatically deduct money from your bank account when you make a transaction, just like an ATM card.

Several banks are actively developing electronic banking. This will enable you to check your account balances, transfer funds from one account to another, and, eventually, pay bills. Two good examples are First Union Corporation at **http://www.firstunion.com** and Bank America at **http://www.bankamerica.com**.

Internet/Economics Application: Visit the Web page of a bank that serves your local area. If you can't find a local bank, visit some other bank. Write a description of what you find and e-mail it to your teacher.

credit union
a financial intermediary formed around something that its members have in common

Credit Unions

A ***credit union*** is a financial intermediary formed around something that its members have in common. Credit unions often originate from an occupational group, a labor union, or a religious group. They may be based on anything that a group has in common, including where the members live. The names of some sample credit unions give an idea of the bases upon which they can be founded: The Tulsa Teachers Credit Union, the Isabella County Employees Credit Union, The Great Falls Telephone Employees Federal Credit Union, and the Westside Federal Credit Union.

For years, credit unions have made most of their loans for consumer purchases such as appliances, cars, and furniture. Since about 1980, they have been allowed to change their financial services to the extent that they now resemble banks. Credit unions have share draft accounts that work almost exactly like bank checking accounts. Some credit unions will even finance the purchase of a house. To borrow from a credit union, you must be a member of that credit union. This usually means that you must have at least $5 in a share account. (A share account is like a savings account.) Accounts in credit unions may also be insured up to $100,000 by the National Credit Union Association (NCUA).

Other Financial Intermediaries

Many other kinds of organizations act as intermediaries between savers and borrowers. Life insurance companies, finance companies, pension funds, and investment companies are some examples in the private sector of the economy.

The Farm Credit Administration supervises a number of federal government financial intermediaries. These include 12 Banks for Cooperatives, 12 Federal Intermediate Credit Banks, and 12 Federal Land Banks, which make loans through 800 Federal Land Bank Associations. All these are aimed mainly at providing credit to the agriculture sector for equipment, marketing or storing crops, and housing.

C h e c k  o i n t

Content Check

1. What do checking accounts, share draft accounts, and NOW accounts have in common?
2. The Federal Deposit Insurance Corporation (FDIC) insures bank deposits of individuals and businesses for up to $100,000 in the event of bank failure. What are the comparable agencies for savings and loan associations and for credit unions?

What Do You Think Now?

Reread *What Do You Think?* in the Section Three Focus. Then answer the following question:

3. Could Pat obtain a checking account, savings account, car loan, home loan, and Christmas club account at one financial institution?

Concepts in Brief

1. Money can be anything that is generally accepted as a medium of exchange. In the United States, coins, paper bills, and checking accounts of various kinds are all forms of money. Small purchases are usually made with currency, while larger purchases are usually paid for by check. Currency is made up of coins and paper money. Checks include bank checks, credit union share drafts, and checks written on NOW (negotiable order of withdrawal) accounts.

2. Without money we would have to barter to buy products we want. That is, we would have to trade what we have for what we would like to have. Without money we would be paid for our work with some of the products that we made. A bakery worker's salary might be in bread or cookies. If you were paid in cookies and wanted to buy a bicycle, you would have to find someone with a bicycle who would trade it for cookies. Life in a barter economy would be complex. A modern society such as ours simply would not work without money as a medium of exchange.

3. Money has three functions. First and most important, money acts as a medium of exchange. For something to act as money, it must be readily accepted as payment for goods and services anywhere in the economy. Second, money is a measure of value. We measure such things as prices, income, and GDP in terms of money. Finally, money is a store of value. We can save money and use it to buy something at a later time. Inflation makes it difficult for money to work well as a store of value. Therefore, people sometimes trade their money for other items, such as gold, stocks, or land, to use as a store of value.

4. The supply of money is determined within the banking system. The Federal Reserve has the power to change the nation's amount of money, but at any time there is some given amount of money available. There are two kinds of demand for money. First, we demand money to make transactions; that is, to buy things. We need more money for this as incomes rise. Second, we may want to hold money as an asset. This kind of demand for money is related to interest rates. The higher the interest rate, the lower the quantity of money we would want to hold.

5. The Federal Reserve acts as the central bank in the United States. It was set up by the Federal Reserve Act of 1913. There are 12 Federal Reserve districts, each of which has a Federal Reserve Bank. All national banks must belong to the Fed, and state-chartered banks may apply for membership.

6. The Board of Governors is the group of people that manages the Federal Reserve. These seven people have a great deal of power over economic events in the United States. Each member of the Board is appointed by the president for a term of 14 years. In addition to their other duties, the members of the Board of Governors serve on the Federal Open Market Committee (FOMC). The FOMC controls the most important part of monetary policy: the buying and selling of U.S. government securities by the Federal Reserve Banks.
7. The Federal Reserve functions as a *banker's bank* and a *lender of last resort.* National banks can borrow money from the Fed. In general, banks use the Federal Reserve Banks much as we use our local banks. The Federal Reserve Banks also issue paper currency and help clear checks from one part of the country to another. Finally, the Federal Reserve acts as the bank for the government.
8. There are many financial intermediaries between people who want to save and those who want to borrow. These include commercial banks, savings and loan associations, credit unions, and mutual savings banks. All of these take in savings from some people and then loan that money to others. In recent years, these institutions have become increasingly similar. All of them now can offer a broad range of financial services to their customers.

Economic Foundations

1. What is money?
2. Why do we have money?
3. What three functions does money perform?
4. What determines the supply of money and the demand for money in our economy?
5. What happens to interest rates if the demand for money increases and the supply of money remains the same?
6. What are the functions of the Fed?
7. List three nonbank financial intermediaries that are used frequently by U.S. households. What has been the trend in recent years in the services they offer?

Your Economic Vocabulary

Build your economic vocabulary by matching the following terms with their definitions.

1. the demand for money to make exchanges
2. an account with a credit union from which withdrawals easily can be made through a draft (a draft is a type of check)
3. banks that were first formed for the same reasons as savings and loan associations and that promote thrift in their members
4. a group that supervises the Federal Reserve System
5. coins and paper money
6. the central banking system in the United States
7. the demand for money in order to hold wealth in the form of money
8. a written order to pay money from amounts deposited
9. money that must be paid upon demand by the holder of a check
10. a type of financial institution that was originally formed to serve businesses but now provides a large number of financial services to both business customers and individuals
11. the agency that insures deposits of individuals and businesses for up to $100,000 in the event of bank failure
12. those banks that belong to the Federal Reserve System
13. a financial intermediary that mainly provides a place for people to save money and then lends that money to people to buy houses or other items
14. a financial intermediary formed around something that its members have in common
15. a group that acts on one important part of monetary policy: the buying and selling of U.S. government securities by the Federal Reserve Banks
16. an organization that helps the flow of money from people with money to save to people who need to borrow money
17. a group that consists of 12 members who meet four times each year with the Board of Governors to discuss the economic situation and policies of the Board

asset demand for money
Board of Governors
check
commercial bank
credit union
currency
demand deposit
Federal Advisory Council
Federal Deposit Insurance Corporation (FDIC)
Federal Open Market Committee (FOMC)
Federal Reserve System (the Fed)
financial intermediary
member banks
mutual savings banks
savings and loan association
share draft account
transaction demand for money

Thinking Critically About Economics

1. Could we use paper clips as money? Why or why not? What problems might develop if people started using paper clips as money?
2. Review the three functions that money should perform. Which of these functions does U.S. money perform best? Which of these functions does U.S. money perform the most poorly? Explain your answer.
3. What does the term *barter* mean? Think of a recent purchase you made. How might that purchase have been made by using barter rather than by using money?
4. How do interest rates affect the quantity of money demanded?
5. Give the number of the Federal Reserve district in which you live. In what city is your district's Federal Reserve Bank located?
6. Write an essay in which you explain what the Board of Governors of the Federal Reserve is, what the Board does, and how the members are appointed. Who currently chairs the Board of Governors?
7. Explain the differences between commercial banks, savings and loan associations, and credit unions. Look in the *Yellow Pages* of your phone book and count the number of each in your area. Which ones are more numerous? Why?
8. What is the difference between the two terms in each of the following pairs: (a) national banks and state banks; (b) member banks and nonmember banks. Are there state banks and national banks where you live? List an example of each type of bank in your area.
9. What are the FDIC, the NCUA, and the FSLIC? Why are these an important part of the financial system in the United States?

Economic Enrichment

Most people prefer to use a checking account or a share draft account rather than rely solely on cash for making purchases. Contact three financial institutions in your area and find out how their checking or share draft accounts compare. Summarize the offerings of each financial institution on a chart and indicate which one you would choose. Be sure to cover the following points in your analysis:

- **Fees:** Is there a monthly service charge? What is the processing charge per check, if any? What is the overdraft fee? What is the charge for a returned check? How much do checks cost?
- **Restrictions that affect the account:** Is there a minimum balance required? How long is the holding period for checks you deposit in your account?
- **Special services:** Is there overdraft protection? Can you use an automatic teller machine (ATM) to access your account 24 hours a day? Is such access part of a network so you can get money from your account when you travel to other locations?

Math and Economics

The following table contains information about three fictitious credit cards: Passport, Traveler, and Explorer. This example assumes an average monthly balance of $2,500 (this is about the national average). On a separate sheet of paper, calculate the values for the Annual Finance Charge and Total Annual Cost to Consumer for each of the credit cards. Then, identify the card that is the best choice under these conditions.

Terms	Passport	Traveler	Explorer
Average Monthly Balance	$2,500	$2,500	$2,500
Annual Percentage Interest Rate (APR)	18%	17%	16%
Annual Finance Charge			
Annual Fee	$20	$20	$50
Total Annual Cost to Consumer			

Writing About Economics

Smart consumers must understand the "language" of credit when choosing a credit card. The cost and terms for credit cards vary and it is up to you to determine what mix of fees, charges, and benefits is best for you. The following terms appear on a typical credit card bill. Prepare a glossary that lists these terms alphabetically and provides a definition for each.

- closing date
- annual fee
- annual percentage rate (APR)
- periodic percentage rate
- transaction date
- finance charge
- average daily balance
- grace period
- fixed interest rate
- variable interest rate
- account number
- cash rebate
- purchase protection
- extended guarantee
- frequent flyer program
- credit line
- cash advance
- account balance
- payments
- credits
- minimum payment
- payment due date

The Social Security Act

Social Security is important because it addresses a universal human need. Throughout history, all people have faced uncertainties brought on by death, disability, and old age. Prior to the turn of the twentieth century, the majority of people in the United States lived and worked on farms. Economic security was provided by the extended family. This arrangement changed with the Industrial Revolution. The extended family and the family farm as sources of economic security became less common. Then, the Great Depression triggered a crisis in the nation's economic life. It was against this backdrop that the Social Security Act was passed.

On August 14, 1935, the Social Security Act was signed into law by President Franklin D. Roosevelt. In addition to offering several provisions for general welfare, the Social Security Act created a social insurance program designed to pay retired workers age 65 or older a continuing income after retirement.

Over the years, a number of amendments have been enacted to cover additional groups of people and situations. The most significant change took place on July 30, 1965, when President Lyndon Johnson signed the Medicare Bill. Nearly 20 million beneficiaries enrolled in Medicare in the first three years of the program.

From its modest beginnings, Social Security has grown to become a fact of modern life. One in seven Americans receives a Social Security benefit, and more than 90 percent of all workers are in jobs covered by Social Security. In 1940, slightly more than 222,000 people received monthly Social Security benefits totaling $35 million. Now, more than 42 million people receive benefits in excess of $316 billion.

As this growth in benefit payments continues, we must make some decisions about how we are going to handle the increased burden. Will we decide to increase Social Security taxes on those currently working? Will we decide to reduce benefits to the old, the poor, and the disabled? Will we be able, through efficiency, to stem the rising medical costs that have contributed to the cost of Medicare and to the Social Security program as a whole? Or, will it take a combination of all of the possibilities plus a few more ideas to put the Social Security program back on solid ground? Only time will tell.

SOURCE: *Social Security—A Brief History,* **http:/www.ssa.gov/60ann/history6.html**.

Overview

Section One
How Important Is Money to Our Economy?

Section Two
Changes in the Money Supply Influence the Level of Economic Activity

Section Three
Monetary Policy, Interest Rates, and Economic Activity

Monetary Policy

Learning Objectives

19-1
Explain the relationship between interest rates, quantity of money supplied, and quantity of money demanded.

19-2
Describe how the reserve requirement affects the supply of money.

19-3
Distinguish between tight monetary policy and loose monetary policy.

19-4
Identify three ways the Federal Reserve can cause the money supply to change.

19-5
Explain the relationship between monetary policy and interest rates.

19-6
Present different viewpoints about the role and effectiveness of monetary policy.

FOCUS

Section One
How Important Is Money to Our Economy?

What Do You Think?

In 1980, the supply of money in the U.S. economy was about $1,600 billion. By 1995, it was more than $4,300 billion. So, in 15 years, the amount of money circulating in the economy increased by more than two and one-half times. You may have heard someone say that "banks can create money." How do you think they are able to do this? Do you think that there are limits to how much money banks can create?

Terms to Know

fractional reserve banking system

reserve ratio

reserve requirement

excess reserves

What's Ahead?

Remember that the Employment Act of 1946 gave three goals for the national economy: full employment, price stability, and economic growth. Each of these is affected by the amount of money in the economy. In this section, you will learn more about what determines the supply of money. You also will see that the interaction between the demand for money and the supply of money influences the level of interest rates in the economy.

MONEY DEMAND AND SUPPLY: A CLOSE LOOK

How important is money in our economy? Surprisingly, there is much debate about this question. But, there is no doubt that the amount of money available for use affects our economy in several important ways. In particular, it can affect employment, inflation, and economic growth. If you follow the national news, you probably have seen or heard stories that cover these topics.

The amount of money in the economy, or the *money supply,* has important effects on the functioning of our economy. Many economists have spent much time studying how the supply of money affects the economy. But, there is not complete agreement about the exact role of money or about exactly how money affects employment, the growth rate, and the level of prices. On one point there is broad agreement, however. The balance between the demand for money and the supply of money is crucial.

The Demand for Money

You may think that there is no limit to our demand for money. After all, do you know anyone who would not like to have more money? However, this line of thinking confuses money with income. We all would like to have more income and be able to buy more things. But income and money are not the same. Income gives us the ability to buy things. Money is something we invented to help make buying and selling easier. The main function of money is as a medium of exchange. Although we get our income in the form of money, most people do not want to hold or keep all their income as money. If you earned $500, would you keep it all as money? Or, would you use some of it to buy other things? History shows that most people hold only a part of their income as money. They use the rest to buy food, clothing, housing, or cars or to add to their savings.

In Chapter 18, you saw that more money will be demanded in the economy at lower interest rates. Why is this? First, consider how people may change the amount of money they want to hold when interest rates change. When the interest rate is high, such as 15 percent in Figure 19-1, people will not want to hold a lot of money. This is because of the high opportunity cost in doing so. People would rather invest that money in an interest-earning asset. Holding on to money will have a high opportunity cost. At a lower rate, such as 3 percent, the opportunity cost of holding money is not high. We then would be willing to hold more money. Generally, the lower the interest rate, the greater the quantity of money we would demand.

How does the interest rate affect the demand for money by businesses? Businesses demand money mainly to invest in more capital, such as a larger plant or a new machine. Such capital investments earn a return for a firm that is usually expressed as a percentage. For example, an oil company might expect

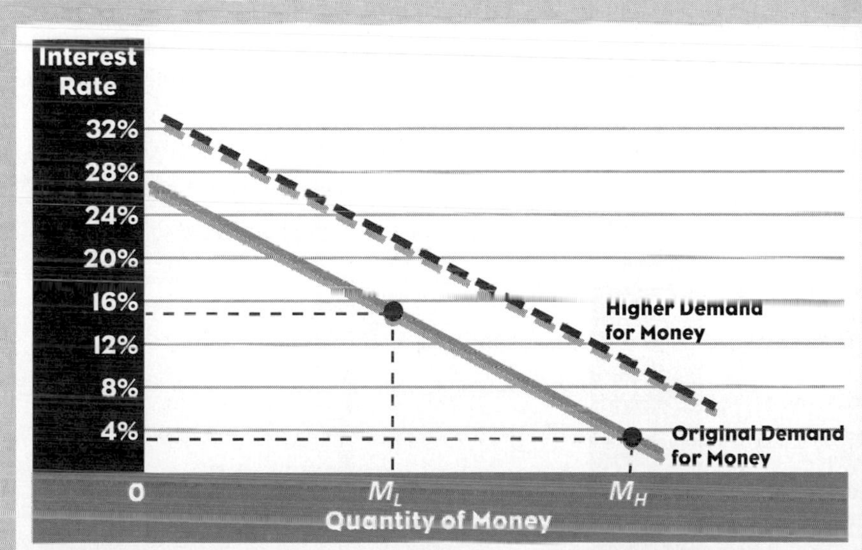

Figure 19-1

The Demand for Money

People and businesses will demand a greater quantity of money at lower interest rates than at higher interest rates. At an interest rate of 15 percent, a lower quantity of money would be demanded (M_L) than at a 3 percent rate of interest. ***What would happen to the quantity of money demanded if the interest rate increased to 20 percent?***

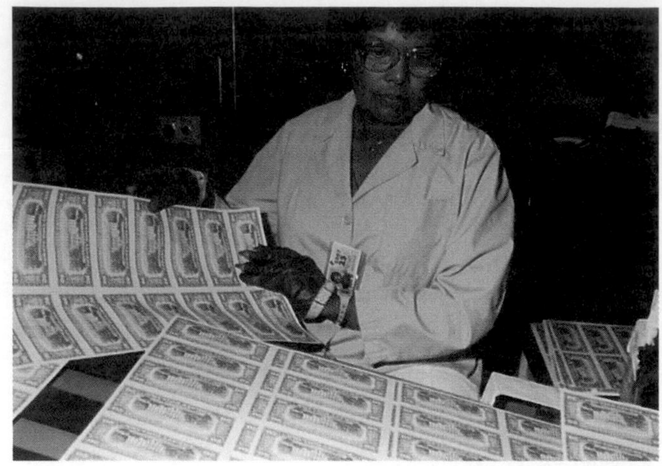

the investment in a new refinery to earn a return of 12 percent. Suppose the oil company had to pay 15 percent interest to borrow the money to build the refinery. The company would not build the new refinery because it would lose money. But, if it could borrow at 3 percent interest, the investment would be profitable. Therefore, at the lower interest rate, the oil company would borrow the money and build the refinery. Many business projects would be profitable at low interest rates but not at high interest rates. So, businesses' demand for money also slopes down to the right. This means that for the whole economy the demand for money looks like Figure 19-1. Both households and businesses will demand a greater quantity of money at lower interest rates than at higher ones.

The demand for money may shift to the right or to the left, depending on economic conditions. Shifts to the right are the more likely, since, as our economy grows, there are more people and businesses to demand money. Also, the wealthier we become, the greater our demand for money becomes. As you have seen in earlier chapters, our country has been getting richer over the years. An increase in the demand for money is shown in Figure 19-1 by the dashed line labeled "Higher Demand for Money."

You now know that interest rates affect the quantity of money demanded. But, what determines the rate of interest? The public always wants to know about the level of interest rates. Changes in interest rates are often featured in the news. But, before we can explore the level of interest rates, we need to look at the supply of money.

The Supply of Money

You will remember from the last chapter that the amount of money that exists in the economy is controlled by the Federal Reserve. This is why the money supply is drawn as a vertical line in Figure 19-2. At any given time,

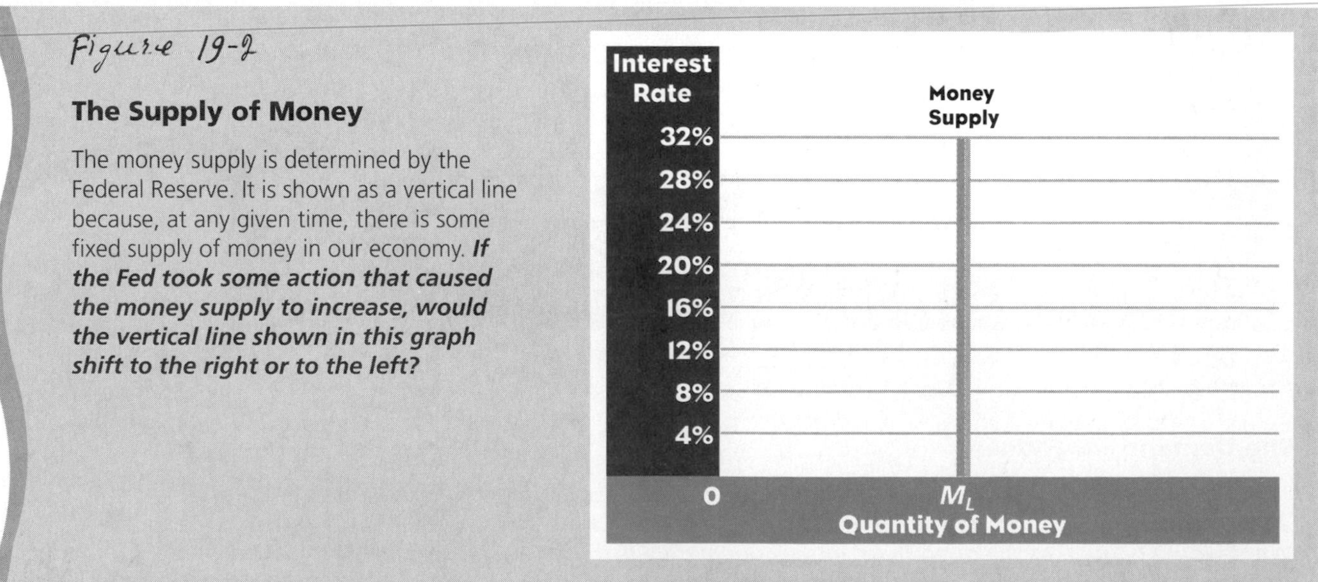

Figure 19-2

The Supply of Money

The money supply is determined by the Federal Reserve. It is shown as a vertical line because, at any given time, there is some fixed supply of money in our economy. ***If the Fed took some action that caused the money supply to increase, would the vertical line shown in this graph shift to the right or to the left?***

there is some fixed supply of money in our economy. But, this does not mean that the money supply never changes. The Fed may cause more money to be available. In fact, over the years, our money supply has grown greatly. It must grow in order for us to have enough money to allow a growing economy to function. For example, in 1980, the supply of money in the U.S. economy was about $1,600 billion and, in 1995, it was more than $4,300 billion. During that 15-year period, the amount of money circulating in the economy increased by more than two and one-half times.

The money supply grows as banks "create" more money. In order to understand the *creation of money*, you need to know that banks operate within a fractional reserve banking system. A ***fractional reserve banking system*** is a system that requires banks to keep some fraction of their deposits in the form of reserves. *Reserves* are the money a bank has in its vaults and on deposit at the Federal Reserve Bank. The ***reserve ratio*** is the fraction of deposits that the Federal Reserve determines banks must keep on reserve. The ***reserve requirement*** is the dollar amount banks must keep on reserve.

fractional reserve banking system
a system that requires banks to keep some fraction of their deposits in the form of reserves

reserve ratio
the fraction of deposits that the Federal Reserve determines banks must keep on reserve

reserve requirement
the dollar amount banks must keep on reserve

Suppose that the Fed sets a 20 percent reserve ratio. Twenty percent is the same as 0.20 or one-fifth. This means that, for each dollar a bank has in deposits, it must keep $0.20 in reserve. The reserve requirement equals 0.20 times the amount of deposits. A bank with $100,000 of deposits would have to keep $20,000 in reserves (0.20 × $100,000). A bank with $800,000 of deposits would need $160,000 in reserves (0.20 × $800,000).

Now, suppose you own a bank that is the only bank in the area. Suppose also that Gabrielle Alvarez has just put $10,000 of cash in a checking account at your bank. Your bank now has a $10,000 deposit. The Fed requires you to keep 20 percent of that amount, or $2,000, on reserve. What will you do with the rest of the money? As a banker, you wish to make money, so you might lend as much as possible to someone else. In this case, you have money that you could lend. This money is called *excess reserves*. ***Excess reserves*** is the difference between actual reserves and required reserves. That is,

excess reserves
the difference between actual reserves and required reserves

Excess Reserves = Actual Reserves – Required Reserves

Your bank has $10,000 in reserves (from the deposit made by Alvarez), but your reserve requirement is only $2,000. The difference, $8,000 in this case, is excess reserves.

By lending more money to other customers, your bank would earn money in the form of the interest paid on the borrowed money. So, bankers usually lend as much as possible, to earn money for the owners of the bank. Suppose Luke Fujimori comes in and asks you for a $4,000 loan to buy a new multimedia computer. If you lend him the money, you could open a $4,000 checking account for him or add $4,000 to his current checking account. It would be very unusual to give him the $4,000 in cash. Now, you would have checking deposits of $14,000 (Alvarez's $10,000 plus Fujimori's $4,000). How much do you have to have in reserves? At a reserve requirement of 20 percent, you need $2,800 to meet the reserve requirement (0.2 × $14,000).

Global Economy

READING ABOUT RATES

Interest rates in one country can have an impact on the economies of countries that are thousands of miles away. Businesses in the United States, for example, are interested in interest rates in other countries because they may borrow money in other countries to finance their global operations. The interest rates in countries also are used sometimes as indicators of how those economies are doing. Because people in the business community are interested in interest rates all over the world, *The Wall Street Journal* publishes a section on "Money Rates" in Section C of the paper. Many different interest rates are published, including the prime rates in a number of countries. An excerpt from this feature is shown in the accompanying illustration.

Money Rates

Monday, July 3, 1995

The key U.S. and foreign annual interest rates shown are a guide to general levels but don't always represent actual transactions.

PRIME RATE: 9%. The base rate on corporate loans posted by at least 75% of the nation's 30 largest banks.

DISCOUNT RATE: 5 1/4%. The charge on loans to depository institutions by the Federal Reserve Banks.

CERTIFICATES OF DEPOSIT: 5.31% one month; 5.29% two months; 5.31% three months; 5.22% six months; 5.16% one year. Average of top rates paid by major New York banks on primary new issues of negotiable C.D.s, usually on amounts of $1 million and more. The minimum unit is $100,000. Typical rates in the secondary market: 6.00% one month; 5.85% three months; 5.83% six months.

LONDON LATE EURODOLLARS: 6 1/8% - 6% one month; 6 1/16% - 5 15/16% two months; 6% - 5 7/8% three months; 6% - 5 7/8% four months; 5 15/16% - 5 13/16% five months; 5 15/16% - 5 13/16% six months.

LONDON INTERBANK OFFERED RATES (LIBOR): 6 1/8% one month 6% three months; 5 15/16% six months; 5 7/8% one year. The average of Interbank offered rates for dollar deposits in the London market based on quotations at five major banks. Effective rate for contracts entered into two days from date appearing at top of this column.

FOREIGN PRIME RATES: Canada 8.75%; Germany 4.59%; Japan 2.75%; Switzerland 5.62%; Britain 6.75%. These rate indications aren't directly comparable; lending practices vary widely by location.

TREASURY BILLS: Results of the Monday, July 3, 1995, auction of short-term U.S. government bills, sold at a discount from face value in units of $10,000 to $1 million: 5.53%, 13 weeks; 5.46%, 26 weeks.

FEDERAL HOME LOAN MORTGAGE CORP. (Freddie Mac): Posted yields on 30-day mortgage commitments. Delivery within 30 days 7.80%, 60 days 7.85%, standard conventional fixed-rate mortgages; 5.875%, 2% rate capped one-year adjustable rate mortgages. Source: Dow Jones Telerate Inc.

SOURCE: *The Wall Street Journal*

Since you have $10,000 of reserves from Alvarez's deposit and only need $2,800, you can still make more loans. This is because now you have $7,200 of excess reserves. By making still more loans you would create even more checking account deposits. Remember that checking account deposits are one kind of money. Some of the checking accounts might end up at other banks, which complicates the process but does not change the result for the banking system.

How many dollars' worth of deposits could the banking system support with $10,000 of reserves? The answer is $50,000. If there are $50,000 in deposits, there must be 20 percent of that amount in reserve. Twenty percent of $50,000 is $10,000 (0.20 × $50,000). So, the banking system could continue to loan out money by creating additional checking account deposits up to $50,000. Then the banking system would be *loaned up*. The banking system is loaned up when it has loaned all it can and still meets the required reserve.

The total amount of deposits that could be supported by any given amount of reserves can be found as follows:

Total Deposits = Reserves ÷ Percentage Reserve Requirement

In this example,

$50,000 = $10,000 ÷ 0.2

You now see that, with a reserve ratio of 20 percent, $10,000 of reserves can support up to $50,000 in total deposits.

As banks lend money by issuing additional checking account deposits, the money supply becomes larger. People have more money (in the form of checking accounts) to spend. Remember that most of our money takes the form of checking accounts. So, as the volume of checking deposits changes, so does the biggest part of the money supply.

Figure 19-3 shows that the interest rate does not directly affect money supply. Once the Fed decides that the money supply should be at the lower

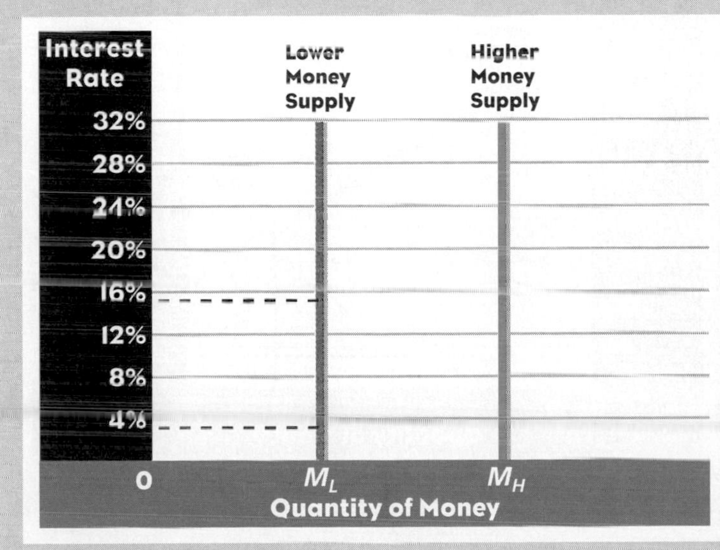

Figure 19-3

An Increase in the Supply of Money

The money supply is determined by the Federal Reserve. It stays the same until the Fed does something to make it rise or fall. ***Starting with the money supply labeled M_L what would happen to the money supply if the interest rate rose clear up to 28 percent?***

level, M_L, it does not matter what the interest rate is. If the interest rate is low, such as 3 percent, the money supply is M_L. If the interest rate rises to 15 percent, the money supply will still be M_L dollars. The money supply will change only if the Fed takes action to change the money supply. If some Fed action caused the money supply to rise, the money supply line will shift to the right. Such a larger money supply is shown by the vertical line at M_H.

You have seen that the reserve ratio can affect the amount of total deposits banks can have. You soon will see how the Federal Reserve can use changes in the reserve ratio and other actions to change the money supply. But first, let's look at how money supply and the demand for money interact to affect the rate of interest in the economy.

BALANCE BETWEEN MONEY SUPPLY AND DEMAND

You have learned that interest serves as a price for using money. You might then expect that supply and demand forces may affect interest rates much as they affect other prices. Suppose the quantity of money demanded exceeds the quantity of money supplied at the current interest rate. You will expect upward pressure on the interest rate. This will be true at the 3 percent interest rate in Figure 19-4. The quantity of money demanded is at M_3 but only M_2 dollars are being supplied by the Fed. The excess quantity demanded will put upward pressure on the price of money (the interest rate).

But, at high interest rates, such as at the 15 percent rate in Figure 19-4, there is a lower quantity of money demanded. The quantity demanded (M_1) is less than the quantity supplied (M_2); therefore, you can expect the interest rate to fall. Market forces tend to push the interest rate toward a level where the quantity demanded and the quantity supplied are in balance. This is true at Point *A* in Figure 19-4. If the money supply is at the level represented by M_2 dollars, a 10 percent interest rate will bring the

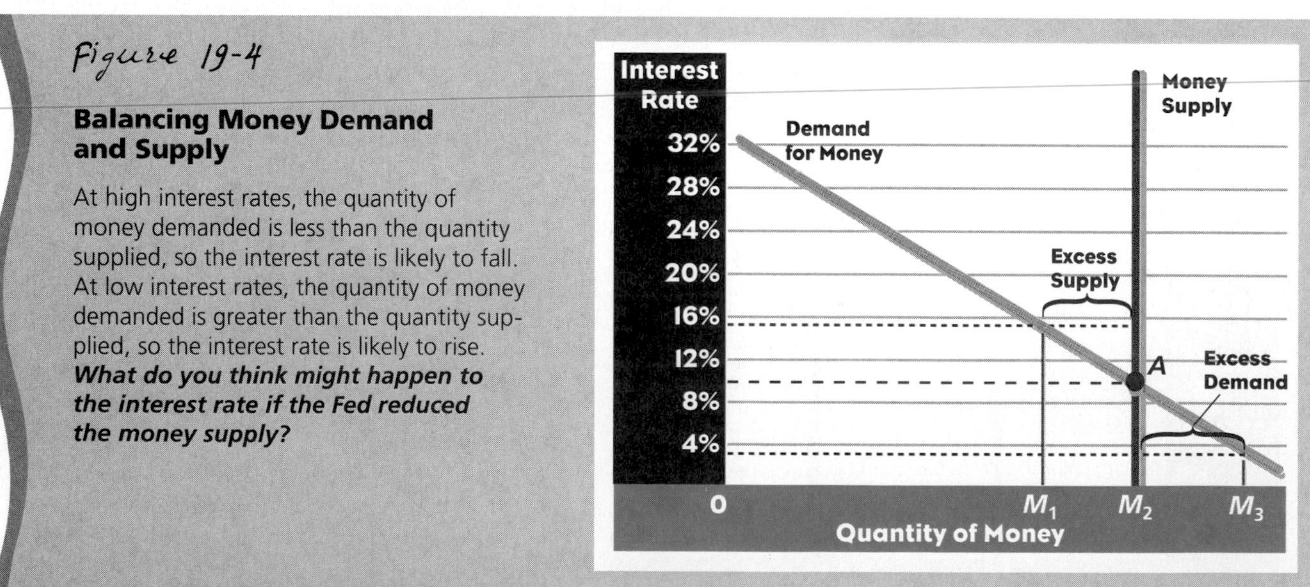

Balancing Money Demand and Supply

At high interest rates, the quantity of money demanded is less than the quantity supplied, so the interest rate is likely to fall. At low interest rates, the quantity of money demanded is greater than the quantity supplied, so the interest rate is likely to rise. ***What do you think might happen to the interest rate if the Fed reduced the money supply?***

quantity demanded into balance with the quantity supplied. At an interest rate of 10 percent, people and businesses will want M_2 dollars' worth of money, and M_2 dollars is the quantity currently supplied by the Federal Reserve. So, at 10 percent, the quantity of money demanded and the quantity supplied are in balance.

Checkpoint

Content Check

1. How is the quantity of money demanded related to the interest rate?
2. Is the quantity of money supplied related directly to the interest rate?
3. When are the quantity of money demanded and the quantity of money supplied in balance?

What Do You Think Now?

Reread *What Do You Think?* in the Section One Focus. Then answer the following questions:

4. How do banks "create" money?
5. How is the amount of money loaned by banks influenced by the reserve ratio that is set by the Fed?

FOCUS

Section Two
Changes in the Money Supply Influence the Level of Economic Activity

What Do You Think?

Suppose that Amy writes a $500 check to buy a U.S. Savings Bond. At the same time, Darrell writes a check for $500 to buy a new TV. Will these transactions have any effect on the money supply?

What's Ahead?

You have learned the Fed determines the size of the money supply. How does the Fed cause the money supply to fall or rise? What can the Fed do to cause the money supply line to move to the left or to the right? In this section, you will learn the answers to these questions.

Terms to Know

- monetary policy
- loose monetary policy
- tight monetary policy
- deposit expansion multiplier
- federal funds rate
- discount rate
- open market operations

MONETARY POLICY

Now, you know how the demand for and supply of money determine the rate of interest. You also have learned that the Fed controls the supply of money. This is accomplished through monetary policy. ***Monetary policy*** is the changing of the quantity of money in the economy in order to reduce unemployment, keep prices stable, and promote economic growth. The Federal Reserve watches over monetary policy with these objectives in mind.

monetary policy
the changing of the quantity of money in the economy in order to reduce unemployment, keep prices stable, and promote economic growth

In discussions of monetary policy, the terms *loose monetary policy* and *tight monetary policy* are often used. You should know what these terms mean. A ***loose monetary policy*** is a policy of the Federal Reserve that causes the money supply to increase. Such a policy tends to favor economic growth and more employment, but it also may cause inflation. A tight monetary policy is just the opposite. A ***tight monetary policy*** is a policy of the Federal Reserve that causes the money supply to decrease. This may help lower inflation, but, at the same time, it may cause higher unemployment. A tight monetary policy also may lower the rate of economic growth.

loose monetary policy
a policy of the Federal Reserve that causes the money supply to increase

The left side of Figure 19-5 shows that reducing the money supply causes the interest rate to go up. In the example shown, the interest rate goes up from 8 percent to 12 percent. This is an example of a tight monetary policy. A loose monetary policy means that the Fed causes the amount of money in the economy to rise. A loose monetary policy is shown in the right-hand graph in Figure 19-5. An increase in the money supply causes a movement of the money supply curve to the right. As the money supply increases, the interest rate falls. In the example shown, the interest rate goes down from 8 percent to 4 percent.

tight monetary policy
a policy of the Federal Reserve that causes the money supply to decrease

How does the Fed cause the money supply to fall or rise? What can the Fed do to cause the money supply line to move to the left or to the right? The information in the following pages will help you answer these questions; we'll look at the three main tools the Fed can use to change the supply of money.

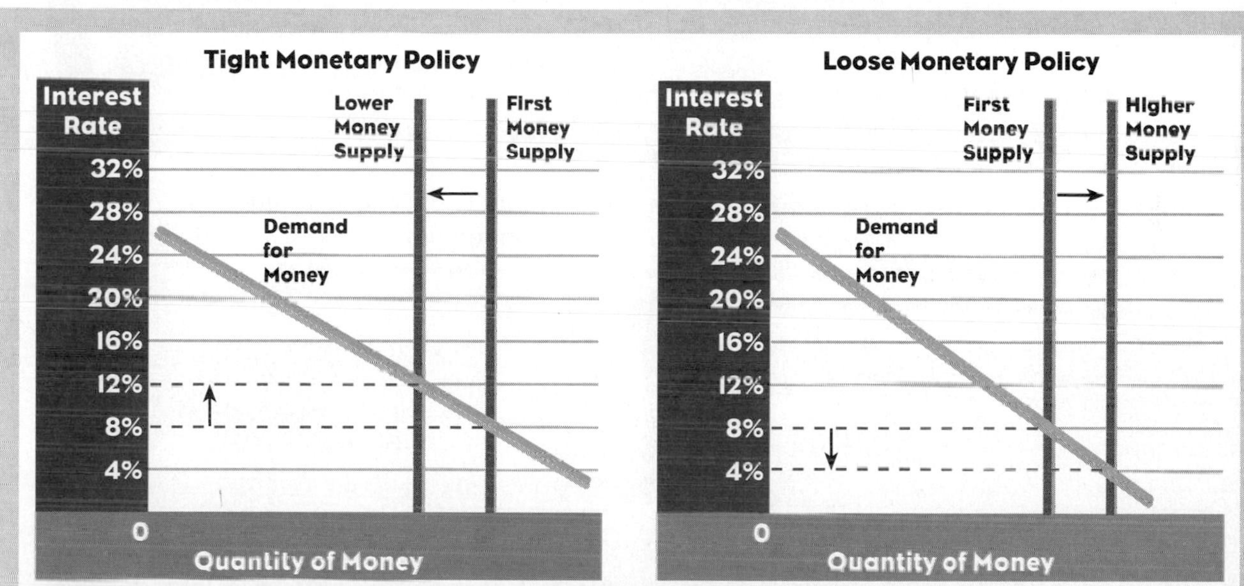

Tight and Loose Monetary Policies

The left-hand graph shows that interest rates go up when the Fed follows a tight monetary policy. The graph on the right shows that a loose monetary policy can cause interest rates to fall. ***Suppose the interest rate is 8 percent and the first money supply exists. If the demand for money shifts to the right (increases), will the Fed have to increase or decrease the money supply to keep the 8 percent rate of interest?***

Economic Spotlight

FINANCIAL MAGICIAN OR FRUSTRATED MUSICIAN?

Can a nod, a frown, or a raised eyebrow set the stock market into a tailspin? They can if it's Alan Greenspan, Chairman of the Federal Reserve, who's doing the nodding, frowning, or eyebrow raising. Greenspan is sometimes called the second-most powerful man in America, after the President.

When Greenspan, a Republican appointee, sat next to Democrat Hillary Rodham Clinton at President Clinton's first State of the Union Address, the shock waves were felt throughout the United States. What difference does it make where a person sits? As Chairman of the independent Federal Reserve that controls U.S. monetary policy, Greenspan quickly found out that the American public, especially the press, watches his every move and analyzes his every word. Greenspan jokes that he "learned to mumble with great incoherence" when President Reagan nominated him as Chairman in 1987. Says Greenspan, "If I seem unduly clear to you, you must have misunderstood what I said."

From the Fed's marble headquarters in Washington, D.C., Greenspan steers the U.S. economy, trying to maintain an annual growth pattern of between 2.5 percent and 3.0 percent while keeping inflation below 3.0 percent. He has found that controlling monetary policy today is a lot more difficult than in the past. Even the "normal" economic indicators are difficult to read because of changes in the ways people save money and because of the globalization of the U.S. economy. With this globalization, even a slight move by the Fed can be magnified into a worldwide shock wave. That's why Greenspan is careful to convey only a general mood about the economy, without much detail or specific information.

This numbers cruncher, who is known for his to-the-point communicating skills and his love of numbers and dry statistics, seems well-suited for the task. What you might be surprised to know is that Greenspan originally studied music at Juilliard School of Music. He even dropped out of school for a year to tour the country as a saxophone and clarinet player. When he returned to school, he studied economics at New York University and then went on to get his doctorate in economics and to become an economic consultant. It's a long road from musical notes to bank notes, but Alan Greenspan appears to feel right at home spouting off important numbers and percentages—even if he does mumble sometimes.

CHANGING THE RESERVE RATIO

You have learned that the Fed requires banks to keep part of their deposits on reserve, either in the bank or as deposits with the Federal Reserve. Earlier in this chapter, we used an example of a bank that was required to keep 20 percent of its deposits in reserves. In that example, the reserve ratio was 20 percent (or one-fifth).

With a reserve ratio of 20 percent, reserves of $10,000 would support $50,000 in deposits. The amount of deposits supported equaled five times the amount of reserves: 5 × $10,000 = $50,000. The 5 is called the *deposit expansion multiplier*. The **deposit expansion multiplier** is the number that expresses the relationship between a change in bank reserves and the change in the money supply. A deposit expansion multiplier of 5 means that a $1 increase in reserves could lead to a $5 increase in deposits. This, of course, also means a $5 rise in the supply of money.

deposit expansion multiplier
the number that expresses the relationship between a change in bank reserves and the change in the money supply

The size of the deposit expansion multiplier depends on the reserve ratio. Once you know the reserve ratio, you can calculate the deposit expansion multiplier by using the following equation:

Deposit Expansion Multiplier = 1 ÷ Reserve Ratio

For a 20 percent reserve ratio, the deposit expansion multiplier is calculated as follows:

Deposit Expansion Multiplier = 1 ÷ 0.20
= 5

Suppose the reserve ratio went up to 25 percent. What would happen to this multiplier? It would go down to 4. Check this yourself by solving this equation: 1 ÷ 0.25. If the deposit expansion multiplier is 4, a $1 increase in reserves will allow deposits and the money supply to rise by $4. With reserves of $10,000, only $40,000 of deposits can now be supported.

This relationship gives the Federal Reserve a great deal of power over the money supply. If the Fed raises the reserve ratio, banks will have to reduce the level of their deposits. In doing so, the money supply is reduced. Banks can cut the level of their deposits by not making new loans when old loans are paid off.

What would happen if the Fed lowered the reserved requirement? First, banks would have lower required reserves and more excess reserves. They would then make loans until they were loaned up. This would create new deposits and would, therefore, increase the money supply.

You see that changing the reserve requirement can cause a change in the money supply. However, the Fed does not often use this tool of monetary policy. One reason is that even small changes in the reserve ratio can cause large changes in the money supply because of the effect of the deposit expansion multiplier. Also, it is hard to predict exactly how long it will take for the entire change in the money supply to be completed.

Internet Connection

REAL WORLD MONETARY POLICY

Monetary policy is carried out by a nation's central bank. For the United States, the central bank is the Federal Reserve, or Fed. The Fed has several sites on the Internet that provide information about recent monetary policy, as well as a great deal of macroeconomic, industry, and financial data.

A good place to start is the Chicago Fed at **gopher://gopher.great-lakes.net:2200/11/partners/ChicagoFed**. This Gopher site contains background material on the Federal Reserve System, a glossary of banking and financial terms, and a guide to Federal Reserve regulations. It has an easy-to-use collection of macro and financial data. Under the link "Monetary Policy" are copies of the *Beige Book,* which summarizes current economic conditions in each Federal Reserve District of the country, as well as nationwide.

The Economic Bulletin Board at **gopher://una.hh.lib.umich.edu/11/ebb/summaries** contains the Minutes of the Federal Open Market Committee meetings, at which the current monetary policy is determined. This site also contains speeches by Fed officials that relate to monetary policy.

Another good site is the Minneapolis Fed at **http://woodrow.mpls.frb.fed.us**. This Web page has a number of useful links, including detailed data on interest rates, charts showing interest and exchange rates, information on publications, and the Kimberley Bulletin Board System, which provides data on hundreds of economic variables via dial-up access.

There are several other Fed sites on the Internet. The Philadelphia Fed at **http://www.libertynet.org** makes available a number of economic forecasts. The Federal Reserve Board Data Bank at **gopher://gopher.town.hall.org/11/other/fed** provides extensive statistics on economic and financial data, but, because it was designed for professional economists, it is not very user friendly. The Boston Fed at **http://econwpa.wustl.edu/EconFAQ/node17.html** has a fairly detailed collection of economic data for the New England states.

Internet Application: Visit the Internet site of your regional Federal Reserve Bank. If your regional Fed has no site, visit some other region's site. Find something interesting at the site and e-mail a description to your teacher.

Economics Application: Connect to the Chicago Fed and select a recent issue of the *Beige Book.* Look up the current economic conditions in your Federal Reserve District. E-mail a summary to your teacher.

CHANGING THE DISCOUNT RATE

The ***discount rate*** is the interest rate that banks must pay when they borrow money from the Federal Reserve. You might wonder why a bank would borrow money from the Fed. Remember that banks must keep enough reserves to meet the reserve requirement. Sometimes, bankers simply cannot know exactly when loans will be paid off. Therefore, they may need to borrow money in order to meet the reserve requirement. Banks may borrow from the Fed. When they do, they must pay the discount rate of interest on the money they borrow. Sometimes, banks will borrow from other banks, at an interest rate that is called the *federal funds rate*. The **federal funds rate** is the interest rate that banks pay for short-term loans that they make to one another.

discount rate
the interest rate that banks must pay when they borrow money from the Federal Reserve

federal funds rate
the interest rate that banks pay for short-term loans that they make to one another

You see that a bank could borrow from the Fed to increase its reserves. It could then make new loans based on these added reserves. This would cause the bank's deposits to rise and would increase the money supply. Banks would be more likely to borrow from the Fed at a low discount rate than at a high discount rate. In this respect, banks work like other businesses. So, by lowering the discount rate, the Fed could encourage banks to borrow more money. This would tend to increase the money supply.

Therefore, changes in the discount rate tell us about the type of monetary policy the Fed intends to follow. When it raises the discount rate, you know that it intends to follow a tight monetary policy. You can then expect other moves that will reduce the money supply. On the other hand, if the Fed lowers the discount rate, it can be expected to follow other loose monetary policies, as well. The money supply is then likely to rise.

In recent years, the Fed has used the discount rate to implement monetary policy more frequently than it did in the past. If you pay attention to the business news, you are likely to hear or read about changes in the discount rate from time to time.

OPEN MARKET OPERATIONS

Open market operations are the buying and selling of U.S. government securities by the Federal Reserve. These securities resemble the savings bonds you or your family might buy. They are the IOUs issued by the government when it borrows money to finance government operations.

open market operations
the buying and selling of U.S. government securities by the Federal Reserve

When the Fed buys or sells such government bonds, it has a direct effect on the country's money supply. Let us see why this is true. Suppose that the Fed buys a $1,000 government bond from you. You will trade the $1,000 bond to the Fed in exchange for a $1,000 check. When you cash the check or deposit it in the bank, the money supply goes up by $1,000. In this process, you have traded a nonmoney asset (the bond) for money. You cannot use the $1,000 bond to purchase anything. But, you can do so with the money you get in exchange for the bond.

Is that $1,000 all the money that is created when the Fed buys your bond? The answer is no. Remember the deposit expansion multiplier. If the required reserve ratio is 20 percent, the deposit expansion multiplier is 5 (1 ÷ 0.20 = 5). When the added $1,000 is deposited in the banking system, it represents new reserves. Those $1,000 of new reserves can then support $5,000 of new deposits (5 × $1,000). So, the money supply will go up by $5,000 when the Fed buys a $1,000 government bond.

What happens when the Federal Reserve sells bonds? The whole process is reversed. If the Fed sells you a $1,000 bond, you pay for it by check. Your checking account falls by $1,000. In exchange, you get a $1,000 government bond—a nonmoney asset. The Fed takes that check to your bank for payment. This makes the bank's reserves fall by $1,000. The bank then has to reduce its deposits by $5,000 due to the deposit multiplier. In this case, when the Fed sells a $1,000 bond, the money supply goes down by $5,000.

The Federal Open Market Committee (FOMC) that you learned about in Chapter 18 determines the amount of government securities to buy or sell. The FOMC has a great deal of power over the whole U.S. economy. Its decisions about buying and selling securities are carried out by the Federal Reserve Bank of New York.

Checkpoint

Content Check

1. Distinguish between loose and tight monetary policies.
2. If the reserve ratio were set at 40 percent, what would be the deposit expansion multiplier?
3. What is the discount rate?
4. If the Fed buys a $10,000 bond and the reserve ratio is 20 percent, how will the money supply be affected?

What Do You Think Now?

Reread *What Do You Think?* in the Section Two Focus. Then answer the following questions:

5. What effect does Amy's purchase of a $500 U.S. Savings Bond have on the money supply?
6. What effect does Darrell's purchase of a $500 television have on the money supply?

Section Three
Monetary Policy, Interest Rates, and Economic Activity

What Do You Think?

Rosemarie LeBaron is a salesperson at a car dealership in central Iowa. On the way to work one day, she was listening to "Morning Edition" on National Public Radio and heard a report that the Fed had lowered the discount rate by 0.5 percent the previous day. What effect, if any, do you think this would have on Rosemarie's job in the coming weeks?

What's Ahead?

The level of interest rates is very important in determining the level of economic activity. Interest rates affect nearly every part of our economy. In this section, we will look at the effect of interest rates on four major parts of the economy.

Terms to Know

inside time lag

outside time lag

MONETARY POLICY AND INTEREST RATES

One way to see how monetary policy affects the economy is to examine its influence on interest rates. Let's look at this with the help of Figure 19-6 on page 518. A loose or easy monetary policy is shown by a rise in the money supply from M_1 to M_2. This is a shift of the money supply line to the right. Such a rise in the money supply causes interest rates to fall. On the other hand, a tight monetary policy is shown as a move from M_2 to M_1. The movement of the money supply line to the left shows a move to a lower money supply. This decline in the money supply causes interest rates to rise. Note that the demand for money is being kept constant.

The level of interest rates is very important in determining the level of economic activity. Interest rates affect nearly every part of our economy. Let's look at the effect of interest rates on four major parts of the economy.

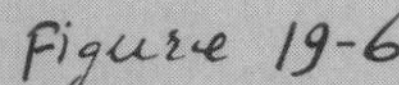

The Effect of Monetary Policy on Interest Rates

A loose monetary policy is a shift of the money supply from M_1 to M_2. The interest rate decreases with a loose monetary policy. A tight monetary policy results in a shift of the money supply from M_2 to M_1. The interest rate increases with a tight money supply. ***If the Fed wants to decrease interest rates, should it increase or decrease the money supply?***

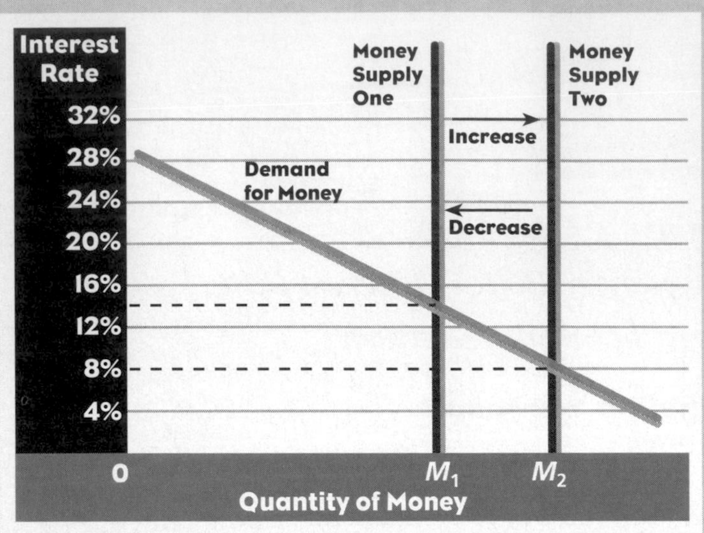

Interest and Investment in Factories and Equipment

Businesses will only invest in new factories and new equipment if they can expect to profit from doing so. An investment schedule like the one in Figure 19-7 is common for most firms. It shows that new factories and new equipment would be more profitable at lower interest rates than at higher interest rates. If the market rate of interest were 8 percent, businesses would invest an amount equal to I^* dollars per year.

This means that a loose monetary policy that lowers interest rates leads businesses to invest more than they would otherwise. This investment leads to more economic activity, greater employment, and a higher rate of economic growth. But, increasing investment by a loose monetary policy has a disadvantage: The added aggregate demand can cause inflation.

The opposite is also true. A tight monetary policy causes interest rates to rise. This leads businesses to cut back on investment spending. A potential

Figure 19-7

A Typical Business Investment Schedule

The lower the interest rate, the greater the quantity of money demanded for business investment. At 8 percent interest, business invests I^* dollars. ***If the interest rate were lower than 8 percent, would firms want to invest more or less than the amount shown by I*?***

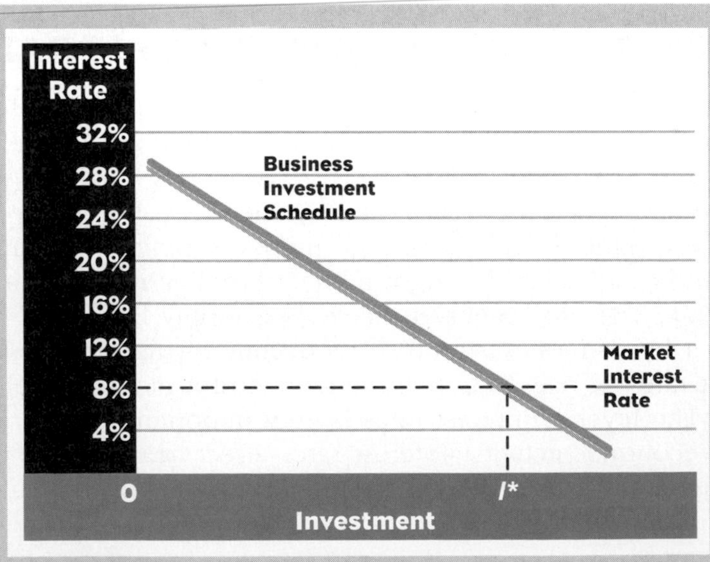

positive result of this action is that inflation will be reduced. But, at the same time, the level of economic activity will be reduced. This can increase unemployment and slow the rate of economic growth.

Exactly how much investment spending changes when the interest rate changes remains debatable. Some economists think that the investment line is steep. This means that even fairly large changes in the interest rate will have only a slight effect on investment spending. Others think the investment line is fairly flat, so small changes in the interest rate greatly affect the level of investment. The debate concerns only a matter of degree. Nearly everyone agrees that, other factors being equal, investment spending will be greater at lower interest rates than at higher rates.

Interest and Inventory Investment

Businesses would like to have enough products on hand to meet the demands of all possible customers. Suppose you want to buy a pink four-door car with a green interior. Your car dealer wants to have one for you to buy. But, you probably will not find that car on the dealer's lot. Your dealer would need an inventory large enough to have nearly every combination of colors. For several reasons, a business would not keep such large inventories. First, large inventories result in high storage costs. Second, there is the risk of costs that would be incurred if products spoiled, were damaged, or went out of date. A third and very important cost involves the interest rate.

Many firms have to borrow money to pay for their inventory. A high interest rate makes a firm's borrowing cost high, so it will carry less inventory. This means that the firm orders fewer products to sell, and so producers make less. Fewer people are hired and unemployment rises. At the same time, though, the rate of inflation may be reduced since aggregate demand is lower. During periods of high interest rates, many stores cut back on the number of alternate styles and colors that they carry.

On the other hand, when interest rates are lower, it costs businesses less to keep a large inventory. This results in more goods being ordered and in more production and employment. While this is good for businesses, the added aggregate demand may cause inflation.

Interest and the Housing Market

The market for houses is especially sensitive to interest rates. When interest rates rise, the cost of housing also rises. This affects both home buyers and renters. Suppose you wanted to borrow $60,000 to buy a house. If the interest rate increased from 9 percent to 12 percent, your monthly payment would go up by more than $130. Over 30 years, you would pay close to $50,000 more for the house at the higher interest rate than at the lower interest rate.

When the housing market falls off, construction also falls. So does the employment of construction workers, plumbers, electricians, and other skilled

Economic Dilemma

THE DIRECTION IS CLEAR

An important issue for the Fed in recent years involves determining what response the economy has to changes in interest rates. The effect that a change in the interest rate has on the growth of GDP is of particular importance. Estimates of this effect are dependent in part on the model used to measure that effect. Results for four such models are summarized in the accompanying table.

You can see that a 1 percent increase in the interest rate has an inverse effect on the growth of GDP according to all four models. This is indicated by the minus signs. You also see that the impact continues for the two years following the interest rate hike.

The differences in the estimates show that we really don't have a full understanding of exactly how monetary policy affects the economy. There is, however, a consensus on the direction of the effect: As the interest rate goes up, GDP growth goes down and vice versa. There is also agreement that this effect extends over a couple of years.

Model	First Year	Second Year
1	-0.2%	-0.7%
2	-0.47%	-0.53%
3	-0.24%	-0.25%
4	-0.55%	-0.19%
Average	-0.37%	-0.42%

The Effect That a 1 Percent Increase in Short-Term Interest Rates Has on GDP Growth

laborers. If fewer homes are built, other industries also are affected. People need fewer new appliances, less new carpeting, and less new furniture. You can see the ripple effects through other parts of the economy. The entire economy can be hurt by a decline in the housing sector. Higher interest rates due to a tight monetary policy can then greatly affect the whole economy through its effects on housing. While it causes unemployment to rise, it can reduce inflation.

When interest rates fall due to a loose monetary policy, the housing market usually picks up. The ripple effects work through the economy as activity in other parts of the economy rises as well. Employment goes up, but there is a danger of creating more inflation.

Interest and Personal Spending

Individuals tend to change their personal spending as interest rates change. With a tight monetary policy and higher interest rates, we are likely to cut back on those purchases we have to finance. This includes cars, appliances, computer equipment, furniture, some types of clothing, vacations, and some costly recreational items. Once more, this reduces employment, but it also eases inflationary pressures. A loose monetary policy will have the opposite effects. Employment will tend to rise, as will inflation.

EVALUATION OF MONETARY POLICY

You now may think that there is complete agreement about the role and effectiveness of monetary policy. This is far from true.

Some of our best economists believe that changing the money supply will have no lasting effect on output or employment. This group thinks that monetary policy has its main effect on price levels. These economists argue that we should only increase the money supply to match the rate of real growth in the economy. If average real economic growth is 3 percent a year, they say that we should increase the money supply at a steady 3 percent rate.

Other economists think that we should use monetary policy as the main tool to control the level and direction of our economy. They point to the great flexibility in monetary policy to make large or small changes. Such changes also can be made very quickly. The ***inside time lag*** is the time it takes to decide on a policy. Since relatively few people determine monetary policy, they usually can reach agreement quickly and make the changes almost at once. Therefore, the inside time lag for monetary policy is usually short. As you will see in a later chapter, other economic policies cannot be brought about nearly as quickly.

inside time lag
the time it takes to decide on a policy

Finally, some economists think we always should follow a loose monetary policy to keep employment growing and to keep a high rate of economic growth. These people believe that nearly all our inflation is the cost-push type. Therefore, they believe that increasing aggregate demand will not cause further inflation. However, empirical evidence suggests that a loose monetary policy does lead to higher inflation.

Concepts in Brief

1. Monetary policy is the changing of the quantity of money in the economy in order to reduce unemployment, keep prices stable, and promote economic growth. Monetary policy is under the control of the Federal Reserve.
2. There are three ways the Fed can change the money supply: by changing the reserve ratio, by changing the discount rate, and by buying and selling government securities on the open market.
3. The Fed follows a loose monetary policy when it allows the money supply to grow larger by lowering the reserve ratio, lowering the discount rate, and/or buying government securities. All these actions usually cause interest rates to fall and aggregate demand to rise. This helps reduce unemployment and stimulate economic growth. These results are desirable, but the same actions also worsen inflation, which is undesirable.
4. A tight monetary policy is the opposite of a loose monetary policy. If the Fed holds back on the growth of the money supply or decreases it, it is following a tight monetary policy. This can be done by raising the reserve ratio, raising the discount rate, and/or selling government securities. All these actions are likely to cause interest rates to rise and aggregate demand to fall. This reduces inflation, but it can cause higher unemployment and slow the rate of economic growth.

Economic Foundations

1. What is the relationship between interest rates and the quantity demanded of money?
2. How is the money supply determined?
3. How do money supply and demand affect the interest rate?
4. What effect does a tight monetary policy have on the money supply, economic growth, employment, and inflation?
5. What effect does a loose monetary policy have on the money supply, economic growth, employment, and inflation?
6. List three ways the Fed can control the money supply.
7. How does changing the reserve ratio affect the money supply?
8. List two reasons the Fed does not often change the reserve ratio.
9. How does changing the discount rate affect the money supply?

10. How do open market operations affect the money supply?
11. How do interest rates affect investment in factories and equipment?
12. How do interest rates affect investment in inventories?
13. How do interest rates affect the housing market?
14. How do interest rates affect personal spending?
15. Why do we say that the inside time lag for monetary policy is short?
16. Why do we say that the outside time lag for monetary policy is long?

Your Economic Vocabulary

Build your economic vocabulary by matching the following terms with their definitions.

1. the fraction of deposits that the Federal Reserve determines banks must keep on reserve
2. the number that expresses the relationship between a change in bank reserves and the change in the money supply
3. the buying and selling of U.S. government securities by the Federal Reserve
4. the time it takes for the effects of a policy change to be completely felt in the economy
5. the interest rate that banks pay for short-term loans that they make to one another
6. a system that requires banks to keep some fraction of their deposits in the form of reserves
7. a policy of the Federal Reserve that causes the money supply to increase
8. the time it takes to decide on a policy
9. the dollar amount banks must keep on reserve
10. a policy of the Federal Reserve that causes the money supply to decrease
11. the changing of the quantity of money in the economy in order to reduce unemployment, keep prices stable, and promote economic growth
12. the difference between actual reserves and required reserves
13. the interest rate that banks must pay when they borrow money from the Federal Reserve

deposit expansion multiplier
discount rate
excess reserves
federal funds rate
fractional reserve banking system
inside time lag
loose monetary policy
monetary policy
open market operations
outside time lag
reserve ratio
reserve requirement
tight monetary policy

Thinking Critically About Economics

1. What is a fractional reserve banking system? Write an essay in which you explain how the terms *required reserves, excess reserves,* and *reserve ratio* are related to each other.
2. Assume that the reserve ratio is 20 percent and that the total amount of deposits in the banking system is $8 million. How many dollars of reserves would be required in the banking system?
3. What is monetary policy? What are the objectives of monetary policy? Is there any conflict between these objectives? Explain your answer.
4. Explain the difference between a loose monetary policy and a tight monetary policy.
5. Why does aggregate demand go up when the money supply is increased? Include in your answer business investment in factories and equipment, business investment in inventories, the housing sector of the economy, and personal spending.
6. If the Fed sells bonds, how will the money supply change? How will it change if the Fed buys bonds? Which of these actions is most likely to cut down on inflation? Why?
7. A business has a project that is expected to earn a 10 percent rate of return each year. How will interest rates affect the business's decision about going ahead with the project?

Economic Enrichment

Draw the following chart on a separate sheet of paper. Determine the effects that a tight monetary policy and a loose monetary policy would have on each economic factor in the first column. If the effect is an increase, draw an up arrow (↑). If the effect is a decrease, draw a down arrow (↓).

Economic Factor	Tight Monetary Policy	Loose Monetary Policy
Supply of money		
Interest rate		
Unemployment		
Economic growth		
Inflation		
Investment in factories and equipment		
Investment in inventories		
Housing market		
Personal spending		

Math and Economics

The reserve ratio is 25 percent and in the Lakota National Bank there are total deposits of $5 million. Required reserves are $1.25 million. There are no excess reserves because Lakota National is loaned up. Based on this information, answer the following questions:

a. If the Fed lowered the reserve ratio to 20 percent, what amount of reserves would be required?

b. How many dollars of excess reserves would there be?

c. What volume of deposits could be supported with $1.25 million of total reserves and a 20 percent reserve ratio?

d. How much could the money supply increase due to the Federal Reserve action of lowering the reserve ratio from 25 percent to 20 percent? (Assume that Lakota National Bank is the only bank in the economy.)

Writing About Economics

Go to a library to find a recent issue of *Business Week* magazine. Near the end of each issue, there is a page with the title "Business Week Index" that has a section on "Interest Rates." Look at the federal funds rate, the mortgage rates, and the prime rate. Each of the rates is given for the latest week, one week before, and one year before. Based on this information, write a short explanation of what has been happening to interest rates and what you think this might say about the monetary policies that have been implemented.

Overview

Section One
Taxes Support Governmental Functions

Section Two
Principles of Taxation

Section Three
Evaluating Taxes in the United States

Taxes

Learning Objectives

20-1
Explain why taxes are necessary in a market economy.

20-2
List major sources and uses of revenue for the federal government.

20-3
List major sources and uses of revenue for state and local governments.

20-4
Compare the ability-to-pay principle of taxation to the benefit principle of taxation.

20-5
Discuss the effects of progressive, regressive, and proportional taxes.

20-6
Distinguish between direct and indirect taxes.

20-7
Evaluate seven major types of taxes in the United States.

Spending for Other Government Programs

Many other government programs give us different kinds of benefits. For example, most Americans felt national pride as Neil Armstrong took his first step on the moon several decades ago. In addition, the technology of the space program has brought us improvements in many products such as transistors, computers, and calculators. Even Tang and Teflon were first developed for use in the space program. Farm programs pay for research that makes crops better. Other government spending gives aid to people for job training and for school lunches. Some veterans receive health and educational benefits as well as housing loans on relatively favorable terms.

STATE AND LOCAL TAX REVENUES AND SPENDING

Individuals and businesses pay taxes to state and local governments to raise revenue for other kinds of public goods. These state and local government revenue sources and spending programs are important aspects of our economy.

Sources of Revenue

Most states depend heavily on sales taxes as a revenue source. Some states rely on income taxes as well. Local governments get most of their money from property taxes. Some local governments also use income taxes. The percentage distribution of state and local revenues by source is shown in Figure 20-2.

Figure 20-2

Percentage Distribution of State and Local Revenues by Source

The data in this table show the importance of the major sources of revenue for state and local governments. Sales taxes are most important at the state level and property taxes are most important at the local level. ***How does the percentage of revenue that comes from personal income taxes for state and local governments compare to that percentage for the federal government? (Refer to Figure 20-1.)***

SOURCE: Calculated from data in U.S. Bureau of the Census, *Statistical Abstract of the United States: 1994,* 114th ed. (Washington, D.C., 1994), 307.

Source	Percentage of Total Revenue
Revenue from federal government	15.1%
Sales taxes	16.5%
Property taxes	15.1%
Insurance trust revenue	12.7%
Personal income taxes	9.7%
Utility & liquor store revenue	5.3%
Corporate income taxes	2.0%
All other sources	23.7%

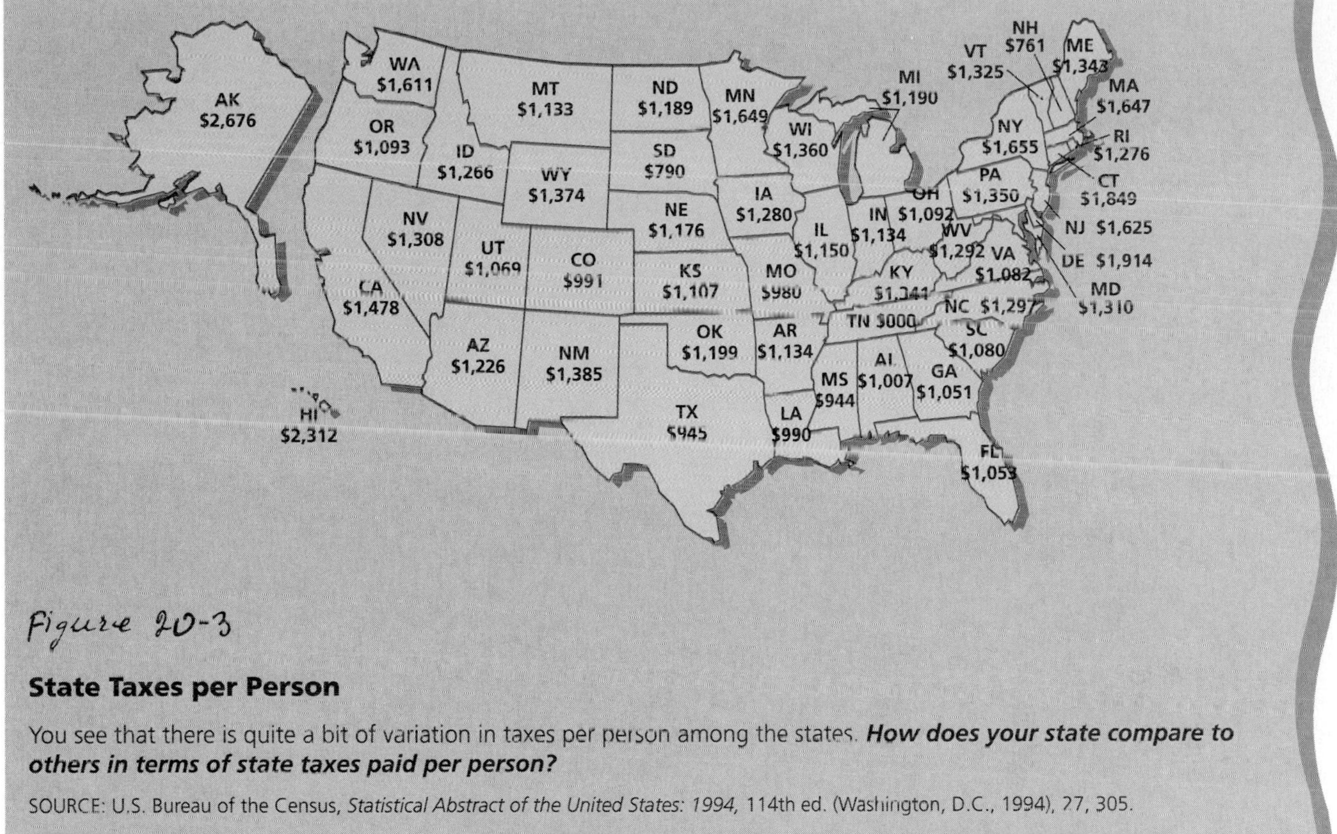

Figure 20-3

State Taxes per Person

You see that there is quite a bit of variation in taxes per person among the states. ***How does your state compare to others in terms of state taxes paid per person?***

SOURCE: U.S. Bureau of the Census, *Statistical Abstract of the United States: 1994*, 114th ed. (Washington, D.C., 1994), 27, 305.

These percentages represent an average for all states. More specifically, the map in Figure 20-3 shows how the amount of state taxes paid per person differs among states. Such differences sometimes affect a person's decision about where to live.

Spending Programs

State and local revenues are spent differently from federal revenues in several important ways. First, the federal government spends only a small part of its budget on education. On the other hand, state and local governments together spend about 30 percent of their money for education. Second, state and local revenues provide police and fire protection, sanitation services, parks and recreation, health programs, and highways.

The list of benefits we get from the spending of all tax dollars runs long. Some people believe that our tax dollars are wasted, spent unwisely, or stolen by corrupt politicians. There is some waste, dishonesty, and inefficiency. But, the public does receive many benefits from the spending of its tax dollars. The private sector would not be likely to provide national defense, highways, public education, or many of the other tax-funded programs already mentioned. Taxes are needed to provide these beneficial public programs.

Checkpoint

Content Check

1. What is the most important source of revenue for the federal government?
2. What are two important sources of revenue for state governments?
3. Name three important services that are supported by state and local taxes.

What Do You Think Now?

Reread *What Do You Think?* in the Section One Focus. Then answer the following questions:

4. Why are taxes necessary in a market economy?
5. If taxes are necessary, and even beneficial, why are elected officials hesitant to vote for new taxes?

FOCUS

Section Two

Principles of Taxation

What Do You Think?

Most everyone agrees that we must have some taxes. But, there is less agreement about who should pay taxes and how much each of us should pay. It seems as if many people think the best type of tax structure is one that places most of the burden on someone else. If you could make decisions about taxes, how would you decide what is a fair amount of tax for each person to pay?

What's Ahead?

You have seen that taxes are necessary and that we receive many benefits from the spending of our tax dollars. In this section, you will learn about some principles that often are used in deciding on policies that determine how taxes are distributed among people in the society.

Terms to Know

- benefit principle of taxation
- ability-to-pay principle of taxation
- progressive tax
- regressive tax
- proportional tax
- direct tax
- indirect tax

PRINCIPLES OF TAXATION

There are some basic principles that describe how taxes are distributed among groups of people. Understanding these principles will enable you to evaluate various types of taxes.

The Benefit Principle of Taxation

One answer to the question of how much each person should pay in any tax is called the *benefit principle of taxation*. The ***benefit principle of taxation*** is the concept that those who benefit from the spending of tax dollars should pay the taxes to provide the benefits. Our gasoline taxes are a good example of the benefit principle of taxation. The money collected from gasoline taxes is used primarily to repair and improve highways. The amount of gasoline bought is a good measure of the amount of highway services used. So, a tax on gasoline makes the heaviest users of the highways pay the most for their upkeep.

benefit principle of taxation
the concept that those who benefit from the spending of tax dollars should pay the taxes to provide the benefits

But, often the benefit principle of taxation cannot be used. Most public goods, such as national defense and social welfare programs, cannot use this principle. All people benefit from national defense spending, but all people cannot be charged directly for the benefit. People who benefit from social welfare payments cannot afford to pay for those benefits. If they could afford to pay for them, they would not need them.

The very nature of public goods often makes it hard to apply the benefit principle of taxation. It is often impossible to separate those who benefit from those who don't. Even when this is possible, it is difficult to find ways of charging only those who benefit. So, two conditions are necessary to use the benefit principle of taxation: (1) those who benefit from a particular good must be identified easily and (2) ways to charge only those who benefit must be found. However, when these conditions do exist, it is usually more efficient to have the private sector produce the particular good or service.

The Ability-to-Pay Principle of Taxation

ability-to-pay principle of taxation
the concept that those who can best afford to pay taxes should pay most of the taxes

The second principle of taxation is the ability-to-pay principle of taxation. The ***ability-to-pay principle of taxation*** is the concept that those who can best afford to pay taxes should pay most of the taxes. Generally, the rich or the economically better off can best afford to pay. Most economists believe that every extra dollar a person earns has value to that person. For a person earning only $10,000 a year, extra dollars of income mean more food, badly needed clothing, or medical care. On the other hand, a person earning $100,000 a year does not need the extra dollars to meet basic needs. This person would hardly notice an extra few dollars of income. Therefore, the extra dollars may not have nearly the value to that person as to the person earning $10,000 a year. The ability-to-pay principle of taxation would tax the person earning $100,000 a year more heavily than the person earning $10,000 a year.

TAXES IN RELATION TO INCOME

Closely connected to the ability-to-pay principle is the way the tax burden is distributed among people in relation to their level of income. Taxes often take a different percentage of income from the rich than they do from the poor.

Progressive Taxes

progressive tax
a tax that takes a larger percentage of higher incomes and a smaller percentage of lower incomes

A ***progressive tax*** is a tax that takes a larger percentage of higher incomes and a smaller percentage of lower incomes. For example, if a person earning $100,000 a year pays $25,000 for a particular tax, the tax is 25 percent of the person's income. If a person earning $10,000 a year pays $1,000 for that same tax, the tax is 10 percent of that person's income. This tax is a progressive tax because it takes a larger *percentage* of the richer person's income and a smaller *percentage* of the poorer person's income.

Regressive Taxes

Taxes can be regressive. A ***regressive tax*** is a tax that takes a larger percentage of lower incomes and a smaller percentage of higher incomes. Assume that a tax took $10,000 from a person earning $100,000 per year and $2,500 from a person earning $10,000 a year. The tax rate was 10 percent for the richer person and 25 percent for the poorer person. Such a tax would be regressive since the richer person paid a smaller *percentage* of income for that tax than did the poorer person. Regressive taxes go against the ability-to-pay principle of taxation. They take greater percentages of the incomes of those who can least afford to pay.

regressive tax
a tax that takes a larger percentage of lower incomes and a smaller percentage of higher incomes

Global Economy

SECURITY IS MORE THAN NATIONAL DEFENSE

Many people in the United States complain a great deal about paying too much in Social Security tax. Study the data in the accompanying table and you may get a different perspective. You can see here that people in some countries pay a good deal more than we do in the United States, while others pay less. It is also interesting to see how the total is divided between the employer and employee in different countries. In every country shown, the employee pays a lower percent than the employer. In Sweden, this is especially true.

Social Security Tax Rates

Country	Employee	Employer	Total
Austria	16.45%	24.55%	41.00%
Canada	5.50	8.20	13.70
France	18.27	31.61	49.88
Japan	11.23	13.39	24.62
Sweden	0.95	31.36	32.31
Switzerland	5.80	6.89	12.69
United Kingdom	11.00	10.40	21.40
United States	7.65	12.85	20.50

SOURCE: U.S. Bureau of the Census, *Statistical Abstract of the United States: 1994,* 114th ed. (Washington, D.C., 1994), 868.

Proportional Taxes

proportional tax
a tax that takes the same percentage of income from all taxpayers

Taxes can be proportional. A ***proportional tax*** is a tax that takes the same percentage of income from all taxpayers. For example, consider a tax that takes $10,000 from a person earning $100,000 a year and $1,000 from a person earning $10,000 a year. Both taxpayers must give up 10 percent of their incomes for that tax. The tax is proportional because it taxes all taxpayers at the same percentage rate.

Proportional taxes do follow the ability-to-pay principle of taxation. However, they are less strong in this regard than are progressive taxes. They take proportional amounts of income at all levels. The proportional amounts taken may have much more value to the individual at a lower income level than to the individual with a higher income. So, a proportional tax may take more dollars that are needed for basic necessities from lower income families than from higher income families.

TAX INCIDENCE

To evaluate whether each taxpayer pays a fair share of taxes, we must find out who really pays a certain tax. *Tax incidence* refers to the group on whom the tax burden actually falls. Sometimes the person on whom a tax is levied is able to pass the tax on to someone else.

Direct Taxes

direct tax
a tax paid by the person against whom the tax is levied

Taxes can be classified into two types: direct taxes and indirect taxes. A ***direct tax*** is a tax paid by the person against whom the tax is levied. The tax is levied against the individual taxpayer, and that taxpayer must pay the tax. Personal income tax is an example of such a tax.

Indirect Taxes

indirect tax
a tax that can be shifted, at least in part, to a party other than the one on whom the tax is levied

Sometimes the person against whom a tax is levied can shift the tax so that someone else must pay it. This is an indirect tax. An ***indirect tax*** is a tax that can be shifted, at least in part, to a party other than the one on whom the tax is levied. For example, property owners must pay property taxes. However, property owners who rent their property can shift some of the tax to renters by including it in the rent that they charge.

Taxes on a business often can be shifted to the people who buy the company's products. For example, businesses must pay taxes on the sale of certain items, such as cigarettes, liquor, and gasoline. Many times companies raise prices in order to cover part of the cost of new taxes. These taxes are indirect taxes because, although they are levied on the business, the consumer actually pays part of the tax in the price of the good. Other taxes on business, including property taxes, can be shifted in part to consumers as well.

The amount of a tax that a business can shift to consumers depends on how much importance the consumers place on the product. If people must have a certain product (or think they must), almost all of the tax can be shifted to the consumer. This might hold true for certain medicines. If a patient must have a certain medicine no matter what the price, any tax on that medicine can be shifted entirely to the patient.

Internet Connection

ELECTRONIC BULLETIN BOARDS ON THE INTERNET: LISTSERVS AND USENET NEWSGROUPS

In the fourth lesson, we pointed out that the commercial online services have discussion facilities (e.g. Electronic Bulletin Boards). Two similar services are available on the Internet: listservs and usenet newsgroups. Listservs are e-mail-based; usenet newsgroups are more sophisticated. Let's see how they work.

E-mail can be used to send messages to groups of people as well as to individuals. Most mail programs allow you to create mailing lists. Listservs take this idea one step further. A listserv is a discussion group to which people can subscribe by sending e-mail to the listserv address. The listserv creates a large mailing list consisting of all the "subscribers." Any subscriber can send messages to the discussion address. Messages also are called postings or articles. These messages will then be forwarded to all subscribers.

Some listservs are "moderated." A person who runs the listserv acts as an editor and decides which submissions will be sent out. Other listservs are "unmoderated," which means that everything sent in will be disseminated to the subscribers.

Usenet newsgroups are a more sophisticated type of discussion group. Unlike listservs, they don't run on e-mail. Rather, if they are available to your Internet site, you can subscribe to them by using a "newsreader" program.

Newsreaders allow you to read, save, and print articles, as well as send in your own articles. Newsreaders organize the articles by topics or "threads". When you use a newsreader, each article and all responses to that article are grouped together. By contrast, with a listserv there is no organization. The articles simply appear in chronological order. It is up to you to figure out which response goes with which initial comment. Another advantage of usenet newsgroups is that they don't fill up your e-mail account.

Internet Application: Find out if you have access to usenet newsgroups at your Internet site. If you do, subscribe to a newsgroup that interests you.

Economics Application: If you have access to e-mail, then you can subscribe to a listserv. Your teacher will give you an e-mail address to subscribe to a listserv that deals with the topic of economics.

If a tax is placed on a good not essential to a consumer, the producer cannot shift the tax as easily. Suppose a new tax is levied on the producers of chewing gum. If the producers of chewing gum raise the price of gum to cover the tax, many people will buy less chewing gum. Some may switch to candy or mints. Chewing gum producers cannot afford to have too many people stop chewing gum. Therefore, they will want to keep the price of gum low and pay at least part of the tax from their profits. If the good is not essential to a consumer, it is harder for the producer to shift the incidence of the tax (to add the tax to the price of the product).

Checkpoint

Content Check

1. How do the benefit principle and the ability-to-pay principle of taxation differ?

2. What determines whether a tax is progressive, regressive, or proportional?

3. What differentiates a direct tax from an indirect tax? Give an example of each.

What Do You Think Now?

Reread *What Do You Think?* in the Section Two Focus. Then answer the following questions:

4. Do you believe the benefit principle or the ability-to-pay principle is more fair?

5. What are some drawbacks to using a proportional tax?

FOCUS

Section Three

Evaluating Taxes in the United States

What Do You Think?

Our federal income tax code allows people who own their homes to deduct the mortgage interest and property taxes from their income before calculating their income tax. Families also get deductions for each child in the family. Do you think these deductions are fair?

What's Ahead?

The tax system in the United States is complex. We use many different kinds of taxes for different purposes and at different levels of government. In this section, you will learn more about these taxes and how they relate to the principles of taxation you just read about in the previous section.

Terms to Know

- personal income tax
- corporate income tax
- sales tax
- excise tax
- property tax
- Social Security tax
- estate and gift taxes

PERSONAL INCOME TAXES

A ***personal income tax*** is a tax on the income of individuals. The federal government gets about 44 percent of its revenues from personal income tax. State and local governments get about 10 percent of their revenues from taxes on personal income.

personal income tax
a tax on the income of individuals

For the federal income tax, the Internal Revenue Service (IRS) defines the tax base, or taxable income, as total income minus the following: (1) some excluded income, (2) certain adjustments, (3) deductible expenses (or a standard deduction), and (4) personal allowances. The income tax owed is then figured from this tax base.

The Federal Personal Income Tax Is a Progressive Tax

In general, people with higher incomes pay a higher percentage of their incomes for federal personal income tax than do people with lower incomes. At the low end of the income structure, the tax rate is the lowest. As income increases, added income is taxed at higher rates. Therefore, our federal personal income tax is a progressive tax. A progressive tax rate structure is shown in Figure 20-4 on page 546.

Effects of Sales and Excise Taxes

The concepts of demand, supply, and market equilibrium can help evaluate the incidence of sales or excise taxes. The graph on the left in Figure 20-5 shows the supply and demand for a product when no sales tax exists. The equilibrium price is $4 and the equilibrium quantity is 10,000 units. These values are determined by the intersection of the supply and demand curves at Point *E.*

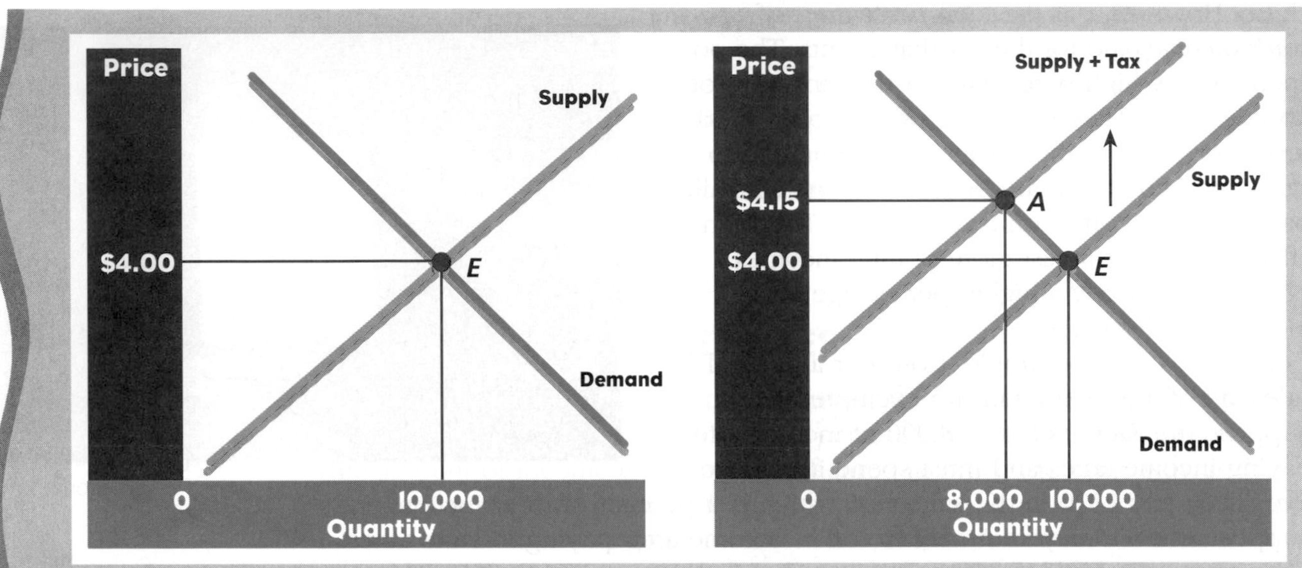

Figure 20-5

The Effect of a $0.24 Sales Tax

The supply curve shifts up to the *Supply + Tax* curve. The new equilibrium at Point *A* shows a drop in quantity demanded from 10,000 to 8,000 and a rise in price from $4.00 to $4.15. ***How much of the $0.24 tax is actually paid by the seller?***

Now, suppose that a sales tax of $0.24 per unit is placed on the sellers of this product. Such a tax will shift the supply curve up by $0.24 to the line labeled *Supply + Tax,* as shown on the graph on the right in Figure 20-5. The distance between the two supply curves represents the $0.24 tax. You can see that a new equilibrium results at Point *A.* On the vertical axis, you see that the equilibrium price rises to $4.15, while the equilibrium quantity falls from 10,000 to 8,000 units.

The sales tax of $0.24 has lowered the amount people buy and has raised the price. But note an important point about this example: Price went up by just $0.15 (from $4.00 to $4.15), even though the tax was $0.24. So, part of the tax is paid by the buyers ($0.15 per unit) and part is paid by the sellers ($0.09 per unit). It is the seller, such as a gas station owner, who really pays the tax money to the government. But, part of the burden of the tax shifts to consumers in the form of a higher price.

PROPERTY TAXES

Property taxes are most often used by local governments. A ***property tax*** is a tax levied on real estate, such as a home, land, and buildings. In general, the value of property is assessed, and then a certain percentage of the assessed value of the property must be paid in taxes.

property tax
a tax levied on real estate, such as a home, land, and buildings

Property taxes are often regressive because they are based on property value rather than on income. The regressiveness of the property tax shows most for senior citizens. They may have worked hard for many years in order to pay for their homes. However, after age 65 their incomes often drop sharply. Despite this drop in income, they must continue to pay taxes on their property which generates no income. In some areas, property taxes are lowered for people over 65 or some other age used as a cutoff point.

THE SOCIAL SECURITY TAX

The ***Social Security tax*** is a tax that provides disability and retirement benefits for most working people. Social Security taxes contribute a large part to federal tax revenues, as you saw in Figure 20-1. They pay for old-age and survivors' benefits, unemployment compensation, health care for the aged, and disability benefits. The Federal Insurance Contribution Act (FICA) provides the revenues for Social Security retirement payments. It taxes the yearly wages and salaries of workers. The amounts of wages and salaries subject to tax and the rates of taxation go up over time in order to allow for increased expenditures.

Social Security tax
a tax that provides disability and retirement benefits for most working people

Arguments for and Against Social Security Taxes

A common argument against the Social Security system is that it offers fewer benefits than could be attained by investing the same amount of money in a private insurance program. This may be true. However, Social Security payments have, on the average, amounted to more than the amount paid in by each taxpayer (including the employer's contributions).

There are benefits to Social Security. Since almost everyone must pay Social Security taxes, benefits for everyone are more certain. If no one paid Social Security taxes, some people might invest in private retirement insurance programs, but many would not. Sooner or later, the country would be faced with caring for these individuals without their having made any contribution to the system. Those people who did not buy insurance or start a retirement plan might starve or die from lack of good medical care. Society prefers not to let that happen, so other people must pay for their aid. The Social Security system began in part for this reason. Even though Social Security taxes may not provide a generous retirement benefit, they at least provide some benefit for most retired workers.

Our Social Security tax and payment system has become very complex over the years. There probably are very few people, if any, who really understand all aspects of the system. This is part of the reason that the Social Security system is often the focal point of political debate. Some people believe that the system will run out of money and that at some time there will not be enough money to pay the benefits that are due. Others say that is not true and that the system is solid. A lot depends on what assumptions one makes about the

growth in the economy, the number of workers paying into the system, how long people will live, and so forth. You can expect to hear a lot of debate about the Social Security system, especially in years when there are major national elections.

Principles of Taxation Applied to Social Security Taxes

In applying the principles of taxation to Social Security taxes, one must consider the employees' shares separately from the employers' shares. For employees, the Social Security tax is a direct tax. For employers, Social Security tax is probably best described as an indirect tax. Just as the burden of corporate income tax appears to be partly shifted to stockholders, employees, and consumers, the employer's share of the Social Security tax can be shifted the same way.

For employees, the Social Security tax is regressive. Those earning more than the highest income taxed pay a smaller percentage of their incomes than those earning less than the highest income taxed. For employers, it is difficult to say whether Social Security tax is proportional, progressive, or regressive.

For employees, Social Security taxes follow the benefit principle of taxation to a large extent. Those who pay the taxes will draw Social Security benefits at some time in the future. The employer, however, gets no direct benefit from paying Social Security taxes. Also, because the tax is not based on the employer's income, Social Security tax does not follow the ability-to-pay principle, either. Therefore, neither of these principles applies to the employer's share of Social Security tax.

estate and gift taxes
taxes levied on the wealth (money and property) passed from one person to another either at death or as a gift

ESTATE AND GIFT TAXES

Estate and gift taxes are taxes levied on the wealth (money and property) passed from one person to another either at death or as a gift. These taxes are designed to stop the passing of great fortunes from one generation to the next. Estate taxes would not be very effective without a gift tax as well. A gift tax prevents people from giving their wealth to their children before death in order to avoid the tax. People may receive a gift of up to $10,000 per year, however, without paying either tax.

Many people, mostly in lower income groups, say that estate and gift taxes should be higher, since they tax money for which the receiving person has not worked. Others, mostly in higher income groups, say that if people have worked hard to gather a lot of wealth, they should be able to pass all of it on to their heirs. These people would prefer to do away with or reduce these taxes. Doing so, they argue, would provide more reason to work and gather wealth, and greater productivity would result.

Estate and gift taxes tend to be progressive. In practice, most small estates pay no tax at all. Therefore, these taxes also follow the ability-to-pay principle. In addition, they are direct taxes. It is very difficult to shift such taxes to other parties.

Checkpoint

Content Check

1. How does our federal personal income tax relate to the ability-to-pay principle of taxation?

2. What is the difference between a sales tax and an excise tax?

3. Why do we have a Social Security tax?

What Do You Think Now?

Reread *What Do You Think?* in the Section Three Focus. Then answer the following questions:

4. Do you think it makes sense for home owners to be able to deduct mortgage interest and property taxes when calculating their federal income tax?

5. Do you think it make sense to give tax deductions for children?

Concepts in Brief

1. Taxes are necessary to raise the money needed for government activities. We receive many goods and services from the public sector in exchange for the taxes we pay.
2. The federal government gets most of its money from income taxes. These include personal income tax, corporate income tax, and Social Security tax. Most state governments rely heavily on sales taxes, with some income taxes. Local governments rely most heavily on property taxes.
3. The benefit principle of taxation is useful when you can identify those who benefit from a particular good and you can charge only those who benefit. The ability-to-pay principle taxes those who can afford to pay the taxes.
4. When describing the relationship between taxes and income, there are three categories: progressive, regressive, and proportional. A tax is progressive if the *percentage of income* paid for that tax goes up as income goes up. A tax is regressive if the *percentage of income* paid for that tax goes down as income goes up. A tax is proportional if the *percentage of income* paid for the tax is the same at all levels of income.
5. The incidence of a tax refers to who actually pays a tax. Sometimes, it is possible to shift a tax from one person to another. For example, if an excise tax is levied on the seller of a product, but part of the tax is shifted to the buyer of the product, that is an indirect tax.
6. Our federal personal income tax is a progressive tax that follows the ability-to-pay principle. A corporate income tax is collected from corporations. It is based on a firm's income after expenses and depreciation have been deducted.
7. The amount of sales and excise taxes we pay is based on our purchase of certain goods and services. Sales taxes are an important part of state tax revenues. An excise tax applies only to a specific good such as tires or gasoline. Both sales and excise taxes tend to be regressive.
8. A property tax is one that is levied on real estate. It tends to be regressive, especially for older people. Property taxes are important sources of revenue for local governments.
9. The Social Security tax provides disability and retirement benefits for most working people. It is a proportional tax up to the highest income taxed, but it is regressive beyond that level.

10. Estate and gift taxes are levied on wealth passed from one person to another. Estate taxes cover wealth that changes hands at the death of the wealth holder. Gift taxes cover transfers of wealth from one living person to another.

Economic Foundations

1. Give several reasons we have taxes.
2. List the four major sources of federal tax revenue.
3. List the two major uses of federal tax revenue.
4. What is the major source of state revenue for most states?
5. What is the major source of local government revenue for most local governments?
6. Compare the spending of the federal government with that of state and local governments on education, in terms of percentage of total spending.
7. List several benefits other than education that we receive through state and local government spending.
8. Copy the following chart onto a separate sheet of paper. Then, complete the chart by putting a check mark in the appropriate box if the tax:
   a. is progressive, regressive, or proportional;
   b. follows the benefit or ability-to-pay principle of taxation; or
   c. is an indirect or direct tax.

Type of Tax	Pro-gressive	Re-gressive	Propor-tional	Benefit Principle	Ability-to-Pay Principle	Indirect	Direct
Personal Income							
Corporate Income							
Sales							
Excise							
Property							
Social Security							
Estate and Gift							

Your Economic Vocabulary

Build your economic vocabulary by matching the following terms with their definitions.

ability-to-pay principle of taxation
benefit principle of taxation
corporate income tax
direct tax
estate and gift taxes
excise tax
indirect tax
personal income tax
progressive tax
property tax
proportional tax
regressive tax
sales tax
Social Security tax
tax

1. a tax that takes a larger percentage of lower incomes and a smaller percentage of higher incomes
2. a sales tax levied only on a specific item
3. the concept that those who can best afford to pay taxes should pay most of the taxes
4. a tax levied on real estate, such as a home, land, and buildings
5. a tax on goods that are bought
6. taxes levied on the wealth (money and property) passed from one person to another either at death or as a gift
7. a tax that takes a larger percentage of higher incomes and a smaller percentage of lower incomes
8. a tax that provides disability and retirement benefits for most working people
9. a tax paid by the person against whom the tax is levied
10. the concept that those who benefit from the spending of tax dollars should pay the taxes to provide the benefits
11. a tax on the income of individuals
12. a tax on the earnings of corporations
13. a tax that takes the same percentage of income from all taxpayers
14. a tax that can be shifted, at least in part, to a party other than the one on whom the tax is levied
15. a charge imposed by the government on people or property for public purposes

Thinking Critically About Economics

1. Refer to the most recent issue of the *Statistical Abstract of the United States.* Look up the current data on the pattern of federal tax revenues and federal government spending. Compare this pattern to the one in Figure 20-1 and write an explanation of the differences that appear. Refer to an issue of the *Statistical Abstract of the United States* from the early 1960s and make a similar comparison between the patterns that appear now and the patterns of the early 1960s.

2. Obtain a copy of the current federal income tax form and the instructions for completing it from the local Internal Revenue Office, the library, or a local accounting firm. Calculate the amount of tax paid by a single individual who earned $25,000 last year. Assume the person claims the standard deduction.

3. If two single people living in the same household each earned $25,000, they would each owe the tax you calculated in question 2. Now, suppose those two people were married. How much tax would they owe on the total $50,000 income? Assume they took the standard deduction. Use the same tax forms as you did in question 2.

4. Identify the major sources of revenue for your local government. Which of these correspond most closely to the ability-to-pay principle of taxation and which follow most closely the benefit principle of taxation? What are the major uses of these revenues? List at least ten services supported by your local government. Compare your list with those of other members of your class and compile a composite list.

Economic Enrichment

Would it be better for your state government to rely most heavily on a state income tax or on a sales tax as a revenue source? Research the pros and cons of each type of tax. Identify the type of tax you favor and create a poster that promotes your choice. Then, present your poster to a student who has studied economics and convince him or her that your position is the best for the economy.

Math and Economics

Kelly Smyth, a 22-year-old chemist, recently moved to the United States from Australia and became a U.S. citizen. She has a job with a major chemical company where she earns $32,000 per year. She wants your help in determining how much tax she owes. The following income tax table is appropriate for someone in her situation. How much income tax will Kelly pay on her $32,000 income? What is her average tax rate?

Taxable Income Bracket		Average Percentage Rate on Base Amount	Tax on Base Amount	Percentage Rate on Income Above the Base and Below the Upper Limit
Base	**Upper Limit**			
$8,000	**$15,000**	**0%**	**0**	**20%**
$15,000	**$30,000**	**9.33%**	**$1,400**	**30%**
$30,000	**and above**	**19.67%**	**$5,900**	**35%**

Writing About Economics

Using the library, a computer online service, or access to the Internet, find four articles that have been published in the last year that describe the Social Security system and how it is changing. Take notes about the main ideas in those articles. Then write a letter to your grandchildren in which you describe the current Social Security system and predict what it will be like when your grandchildren retire.

Overview

Section One
The Federal Government and Aggregate Demand

Section Two
Fiscal Policy Affects Unemployment, Inflation, and Economic Growth

Section Three
Government Use of Wage and Price Controls

Fiscal Policy

Learning Objectives

21-1

Identify two ways the federal government can change fiscal policy.

21-2

Distinguish between expansionary fiscal policy and restrictive fiscal policy.

21-3

Analyze the relationship between the federal budget deficit and the national debt.

21-4

Describe the effects of fiscal policy changes on unemployment, inflation, and economic growth.

21-5

Compare monetary and fiscal policies.

21-6

Explain why the government has used wage and price controls.

FOCUS

Section One
The Federal Government and Aggregate Demand

What Do You Think?

You have learned that the demand for labor is derived from the demand for goods and services. When the government increases spending, aggregate demand increases and there is a greater demand for labor. This can reduce unemployment. How else do you think the government can bring about an increase in aggregate demand and a reduction in unemployment?

What's Ahead?

At times, the federal government changes its spending and/or taxing in order to influence the level of economic activity. In this section, you will learn how changes in government spending and taxing affect the economy.

Terms to Know

fiscal policy

expansionary fiscal policy

multiplier effect

restrictive fiscal policy

budget deficit

national debt

crowding out

external debt

FISCAL POLICY CHANGES AGGREGATE DEMAND AND SUPPLY

An imbalance between the level of spending (aggregate demand) and the amount of production (aggregate supply) can cause inflation or unemployment. You have learned that monetary policy can be used to fight these problems through changes in the money supply. In this chapter, you will see that the government can use two other tools as well. These are fiscal policy and wage and price controls.

fiscal policy the changing of federal government spending and taxes in order to control the level of economic activity

Fiscal policy is the changing of federal government spending and taxes in order to control the level of economic activity. The government can raise or lower taxes to try to change the levels of aggregate demand and/or aggregate supply in the private sector. Also, changes in government spending can cause direct changes in aggregate demand. Such actions aim to achieve the goals stated in the Employment Act of 1946. Remember that these goals are full employment, stable prices (no inflation), and a good rate of economic growth.

Using fiscal policy to change aggregate demand and supply is an important economic concept. In this section, you will study it in a general way. Then, in the next section of the chapter, you will explore how fiscal policy can be used for specific purposes. But, first, a word of caution. As you know from your study of economics so far, economics offers few simple answers. The economy changes constantly. Also, a change in any one part of the economy is likely to affect many other parts. As society changes, so does the economy. The policies that work today may not work tomorrow. This makes the study of our economy frustrating but also very interesting.

Historically, the primary emphasis of fiscal policy has been on the demand side of the economy. In this chapter, these demand side effects of fiscal policy will be our principal focus. However, there are some effects on the supply side as well, and we will discuss them at the end of section two of this chapter.

EXPANSIONARY FISCAL POLICIES

Expansionary fiscal policies cause the economy to run more rapidly primarily by increasing aggregate demand. As you will see, the emphasis of fiscal policy is on the demand side of the marketplace. The diagram in Figure 21-1 shows the effect of an increase in aggregate demand. The point of balance between the forces of demand and supply moves from E_1 to E_2 as demand goes up. This change means that both the price level and the amount of goods produced will go up.

expansionary fiscal policies causing the economy to run more rapidly primarily by increasing aggregate demand

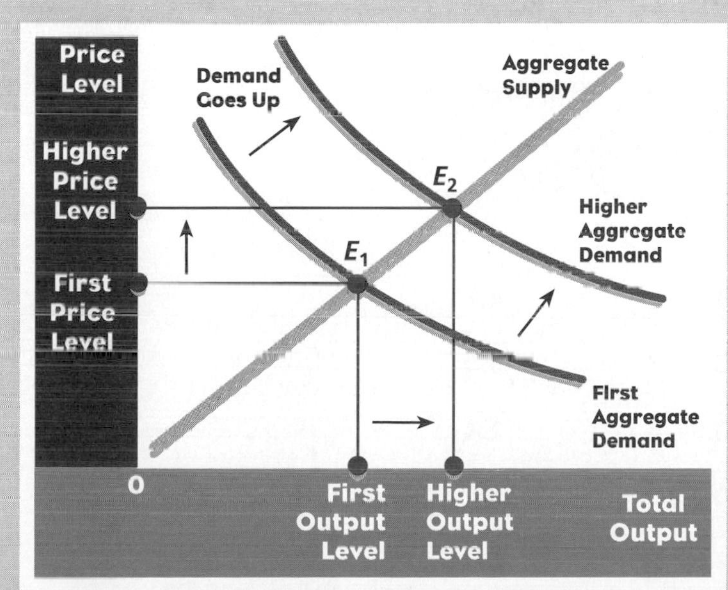

Figure 21-1

An Expansionary Fiscal Policy

A rise in aggregate demand causes a higher level of output. But, it also will put upward pressure on price. ***What action(s) by the federal government could cause an increase in aggregate demand?***

Increase Government Spending

What government actions will cause aggregate demand to rise? Remember that government spending is one part of aggregate demand. If the government spends more money, the total demand in the economy will go up. In fact, total demand will rise by more than just the added government spending.

To see why this is true, let's look at an example. Suppose the government adds $20,000 to its spending by buying a new car for the FBI. Part of that $20,000 becomes income to the person who sold the car. Other parts become income to an auto worker and income to a trucker who hauled the car from Detroit to Washington. These people will spend at least part of their added income on products such as food, clothing, appliances, and gasoline. The people who make and sell these products, then, have more income. And, they spend some part of their income. Each round of added spending increases

Global Economy

HOW DO YOU SAY "DEFICIT"?

Is the United States the only country with a national debt problem? In a nutshell, the answer is *no.* Many other countries also have large national debts and face similar problems in trying to reduce their deficits. Because of differences in the sizes of various economies, a direct comparison of the national debts and yearly budget deficits is not meaningful. Therefore, we might look at data that provides relative measures of the burden of the debt and deficit for different countries. This is done for seven countries in the accompanying table. You can see in this table that the United States has less of a problem with its national debt and yearly deficits than many of the other leading economies of the world.

Country	Net Debt Interest Payments (as a percent of GDP)	Budget Deficit (as a percent of GDP)
Britain	2.6%	4.7%
Canada	4.6	4.7
France	3.4	5.0
Germany	3.8	2.4
Japan	0.5	1.8
United States	2.1	1.8

SOURCE: Adapted from *Business Week*, (March 20, 1995): 51. Data are for 1995.

aggregate demand a little more. This is called the *multiplier effect*. A ***multiplier effect*** is the concept that any change in fiscal policy affects total demand and total income by an amount larger than the original amount of the change in spending or taxing.

multiplier effect the concept that any change in fiscal policy affects total demand and total income by an amount larger than the original amount of the change in spending or taxing

Cut Taxes

Can you think of any way other than by increasing spending the government could cause aggregate demand to rise? What about cutting taxes? Lowering taxes on personal income increases the amount of spendable income people have. If take-home pay goes up, we can expect that people will save and spend more than they did before the tax cut. The added spending helps increase aggregate demand directly. The added savings makes more money available for business investment and so may indirectly increase demand as well.

A tax cut for corporations also can cause demand to rise. After a tax cut, businesses have more money left to buy new equipment. They also may distribute more money to shareholders who, in turn, will spend at least part of it. Tax cuts also have a multiplier effect, but it is less than for government spending.

You see, then, that tax cuts and spending increases are expansionary fiscal policies. Both actions cause aggregate demand to rise. This results in more activity in the economy

RESTRICTIVE FISCAL POLICIES

Restrictive fiscal policies cause the economy to run more slowly primarily by reducing aggregate demand. Some restrictive fiscal policies also may slow the growth of aggregate supply. But, again, we will focus our attention on aggregate demand. In Figure 21-2, you see the effect of a fall in demand. The point of balance between demand and supply moves from E_1 to E_3. This change causes both the price level and the amount of goods produced to be lower.

restrictive fiscal policies causing the economy to run more slowly primarily by reducing aggregate demand

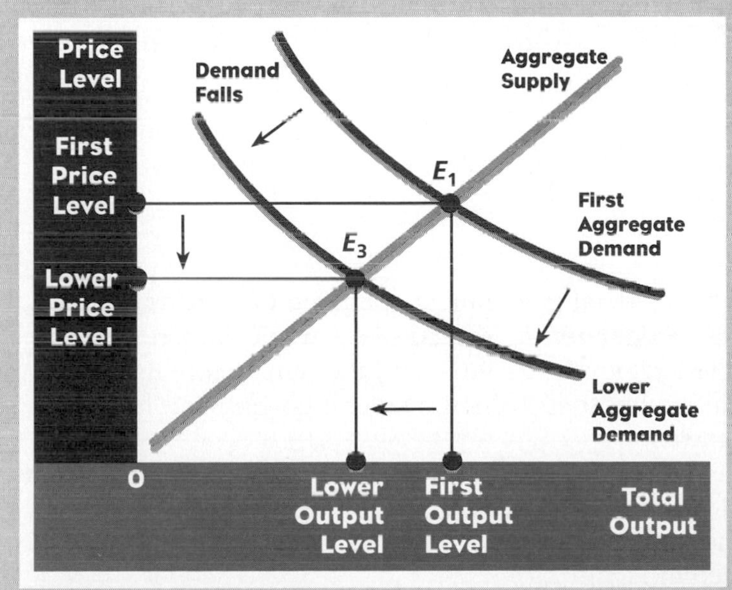

Figure 21-2

A Restrictive Fiscal Policy

A fall in aggregate demand can cause a lower level of prices. But, it also lowers the level of output. ***Name two actions by the federal government that could cause a decrease in aggregate demand.***

Reduce Government Spending

Two kinds of government actions will cause aggregate demand to fall. As you might have guessed, these are the opposites of the actions that cause demand to rise. One action is reducing the level of government spending. This reduces aggregate demand directly. It also has an indirect multiplier effect on government spending cuts. If the government buys fewer cars, fewer auto workers will be employed, so income in that part of the economy will be less. If income decreases, demand for the goods and services those workers would have bought also decreases. This means less income in other parts of the economy, and demand decreases even more.

Raise Taxes

The other government action that causes aggregate demand to fall is raising taxes. If people have to pay higher taxes, they will have less money to spend for goods and services. This causes them to cut back on the amount of goods and services they buy. As a result, businesses hire fewer people and total income in the economy falls. This further reduces demand. You can see the multiplier effect at work here also. Raising the corporate income tax will have the same general effect on the economy.

You see that both cuts in government spending and increases in tax rates represent restrictive fiscal policies. Both actions cause aggregate demand to fall, which lowers the level of activity in the economy.

THE BUDGET DEFICIT AND THE NATIONAL DEBT

The federal government takes in revenue, mainly from taxes, and uses that money for various types of government spending. The government does not necessarily have to limit spending to the amount it takes in as revenue. In fact, that rarely happens.

Budget Deficit

budget deficit
the amount by which federal government spending exceeds revenues each year

The amount by which federal government spending exceeds revenues each year is called the ***budget deficit***. The last year in which there was no budget deficit at the federal level was 1969, and the time before that was 1960. So, you see that in almost 40 years the federal government has had a deficit in all but two years.

The size of the annual budget deficit has been the subject of much discussion during the last four decades. It seems as if most politicians talk about wanting to reduce the yearly deficit, and yet it has grown fairly steadily since 1970. This is illustrated in Figure 21-3.

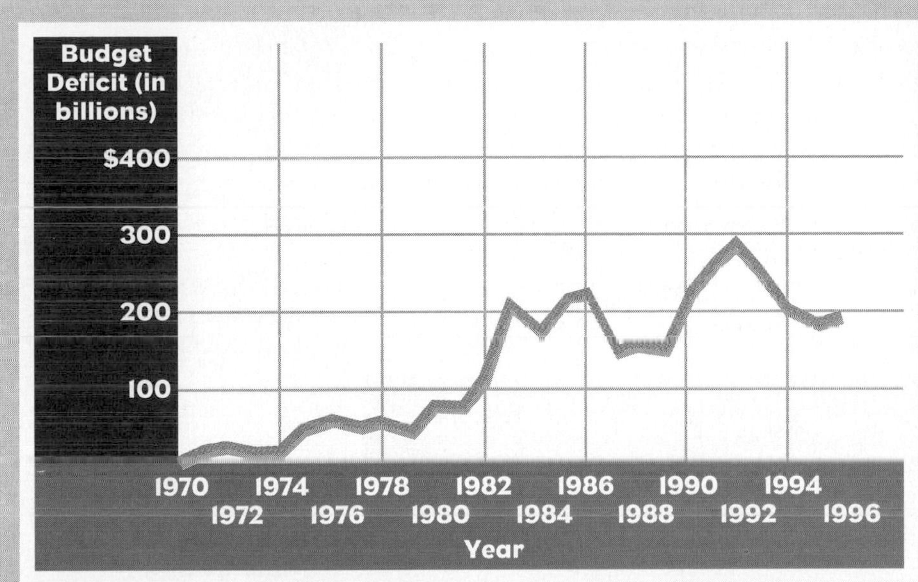

Figure 21-3

The Annual Federal Budget Deficit

The amount by which federal government spending has exceeded revenues in each year is shown by this graph. ***How do you think this annual deficit relates to the national debt?***

National Debt

The ***national debt*** is the amount of money that the federal government owes. It is the accumulation of yearly deficits. You have seen that the government has had big deficits in most years since 1970. This should lead you to expect that the national debt has been increasing steadily.

national debt the amount of money that the federal government owes

The Amount of Debt. The national debt began in 1790 and has fluctuated up and down over the years. But mostly, the debt has gone up. By 1929, it was $16.9 billion. In the next ten years, it grew to $48.2 billion. During World War II, the debt rose so rapidly that, in 1946, it was $271 billion. In 1975, the debt was $541.9 billion. During 1981, the national debt crossed the $1 trillion mark, or about $4,700 for every man, woman, and child in this country. Despite considerable comment by politicians that the debt was growing too rapidly, the government continued to spend more than it collected in taxes. During 1990, the national debt rose to over $3 trillion, which was close to $13,000 per person. In the 1995 *Economic Report of the President,* the authors lamented that the debt was approaching $20,000 per person. The growth in the national debt is illustrated by the upper graph in Figure 21-4 on page 568.

Debt as a Percent of GDP. The bottom graph in Figure 21-4 shows the national debt as a percent of GDP. For years, people argued that as long as the debt as a percent of GDP decreased or stayed constant it was not a problem. However, as you can see in Figure 21-4, during the 1980s and early 1990s this percentage grew substantially. The national debt as a percent of GDP began to level off again in the mid-1990s.

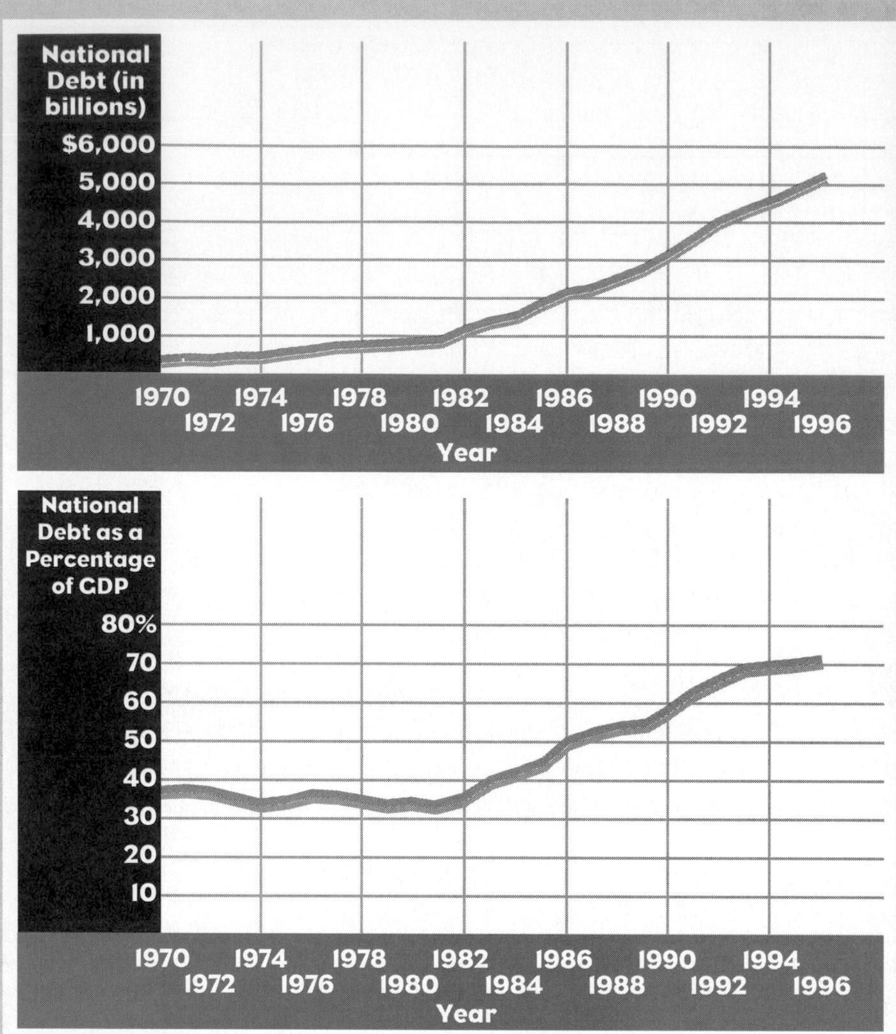

Figure 21-4

The National Debt

You see in the top graph that the national debt has been increasing rapidly, especially since the early 1980s. The bottom graph shows that the national debt as a percent of GDP also has been rising. ***To whom does the federal government owe this debt?***

Concerns About the National Debt

To whom does the government owe this money? In part, the government owes money to people like you. Do you own a government savings bond? If so, part of the national debt is owed to you. The Federal Reserve Banks also own part of the debt, as do other domestic investors such as insurance companies. Also, some of the national debt is owned by people or governments outside of the United States.

You may have heard people say things such as, "The government should not borrow money—the government should learn to live within a budget just like we do." Actually, borrowing money is often a wise thing to do. A family will probably have to borrow money to buy goods such as a home or a car. Businesses also need to borrow money to build new factories and to buy new machinery. Borrowing money, and the debt that results, is an important part of a modern economy.

In a similar way, it may make sense for the government to borrow. We have seen that, in periods of high unemployment, the economy may be healthier if government spending is increased without increasing taxes. This means the government has to increase its debt. What matters is whether the government can afford to pay the interest on the debt. Since the government has unlimited power to tax, it can always raise taxes enough to meet its interest payments on the debt.

People worry most about the effect the national debt has on business investment. When the government borrows large amounts of money, the flow of money to businesses may be reduced. In order for the government to sell bonds, it must pay an attractive interest rate on them. This may cause people to shift their money to government bonds and away from the kinds of savings that provide money to businesses. This shift is called *crowding out*. ***Crowding out*** is the effect on private businesses when increased government borrowing raises interest rates and reduces private borrowing. Private businesses may get pushed out of the money markets by the high interest rates caused by high government borrowing. This can reduce the amount of capital in the private sector, which can lower our productive ability. The degree to which crowding out actually occurs is not yet clear. A good deal of economic research is focused on this issue.

crowding out
the effect on private businesses when increased government borrowing raises interest rates and reduces private borrowing

Another concern about the national debt is the portion that is external debt. ***External debt*** is the part of the national debt that is owed to people or governments outside the United States. Interest paid on the external debt does not become income to people in the United States and therefore drains our economy. In the mid-1980s, more than 10 percent of the national debt was owned by foreign countries.

external debt
the part of the national debt that is owed to people or governments outside the United States

Economic Spotlight

Backing Fitness with Muscle and Style

If there's one message Arnold Schwarzenegger continually delivers to the young people of America, it's, "I'm going to *pump you up*" about fitness! Schwarzenegger's goal as chairperson of the President's Council on Physical Fitness and Sports (PCPFS) is to motivate students to train their bodies as well as their minds. According to the former Mr. Universe, "it's just as important to be fit as to be smart."

Schwarzenegger sends his message not only to kids but also to their teachers. Despite the fact that only one state, Illinois, requires daily physical education, he encourages teachers to commit to quality fitness training every day. The idea sounds simple enough but faces major obstacles. Because physical fitness classes do not directly challenge the brain, they are often the first targets for school budget cuts. Still, Schwarzenegger believes that fitness is possible without spending much money.

He has toured the country showing off his physically fit body and telling students, "I did not get like this by sitting down and playing video games. It's cool to exercise every single day." The PCPFS supports the idea that physically fit people are less inclined to use drugs, alcohol, and tobacco. And, Schwarzenegger emphasizes at every stop on his cross-country tours the need to "stay clean." He adds, "Sports teach kids lessons that are absolutely crucial to life—lessons about discipline, team work, and self-esteem." He stresses a can-do philosophy, telling kids that they should never say "can't."

This philosophy is shared by Schwarzenegger's co-chair, track superstar Florence Griffith Joyner. Joyner, an Olympic gold medalist, first became interested in running as a child growing up in Watts, a poor section of Los Angeles. With her first competitive victory at age seven, Joyner began her journey toward becoming the fastest female runner on earth. With her focus on sports, "Flo Jo," as she came to be known, never lacked the confidence she needed to succeed. Flo Jo's message to children everywhere is that sports can help you believe in yourself. Together with Schwarzenegger, she hopes to inspire young people to make fitness a priority in their lives and to make people sit up and take notice.

The national debt is not really an *economic* problem, however. It is a *political* problem. Politicians have not accepted the responsibility of carefully balancing the costs and benefits of the spending programs they consider. Politicians do not like to increase taxes enough to pay for increased spending. The result has been yearly deficits that continue to add to the national debt.

Checkpoint

Content Check

1. What are the objectives of fiscal policy?
2. Distinguish between expansionary and restrictive fiscal policies.
3. What is the difference between the budget deficit and the national debt?

What Do You Think Now?

Reread *What Do You Think?* in the Section One Focus. Then answer the following question:

4. What can the government do in the way of an expansionary fiscal policy besides increase government spending?

FOCUS

Section Two
Fiscal Policy Affects Unemployment, Inflation, and Economic Growth

What Do You Think?

You have learned a great deal about how the economy works. You know that fiscal policy can be used to affect the overall level of economic activity. One of the goals for the economy is to provide full employment, and yet there are people who are unemployed and who would like to work. Why doesn't the government just increase spending until everyone who wants a job is employed?

Terms to Know

inside time lag

outside time lag

inflationary bias in fiscal policy

What's Ahead?

You now understand the basics of fiscal policy. You know what expansionary policies and what restrictive fiscal policies are. In this section, you will learn how these policies can be focused on specific economic problems.

FISCAL POLICY AND UNEMPLOYMENT

If the government wants to use fiscal policy to lower the unemployment rate, an expansionary policy is needed. This means that government spending should be increased and/or taxes should be cut. Both of these actions will cause aggregate demand to rise. Whether this actually will help the employment picture depends on the kind of unemployment that exists.

In Chapter 16, you learned that there are several kinds of unemployment. The two most important kinds are cyclical (demand deficiency) unemployment and structural unemployment. The other types of unemployment, frictional and seasonal, are of less concern from a public policy perspective.

Increased Spending and Unemployment

A fiscal policy that causes aggregate demand to go up will lower demand deficiency unemployment. But, what about structural unemployment? Will an expansionary fiscal policy help alleviate this problem? Answers to these questions are not clear-cut. To some degree, we can expect a rising demand to help a little. Remember that one reason for structural unemployment is that many workers are unskilled. Businesses whose products are in high demand are more likely to help train new workers. This can help those workers get into the mainstream of economic life. Businesses also may offer to help people move from one area of the country to another. This may help to solve the geographic mismatch between workers and jobs, another problem associated with structural unemployment. So, a rise in demand may help to reduce structural unemployment.

The kind of fiscal policy used can make a difference in how well the program works to lower unemployment. The source of the increased demand (government spending, consumer spending, or business spending) also can affect the outcome of fiscal policy. Government spending is not evenly spread throughout the country. So, how much a program of higher government spending helps depends on where the spending takes place and where the unemployment is.

Tax Cuts and Unemployment

A personal income tax cut will have a fairly even effect across the country and will do less to change the mix of employment opportunities. If a corporate tax cut is part of the expansionary fiscal policy, the industrial regions of the country will be affected most.

We can be fairly sure that programs that cause demand to rise also will cause employment to rise. As long as this does not attract too many more people into the labor market, the unemployment rate will fall. Why, then, don't we just increase government spending until the desired level of unemployment is reached? (Remember that due to frictional unemployment we would not want to shoot for a zero rate of unemployment.) The reason is that the expansionary programs also may cause inflation. You will learn more about this trade off as you go through the rest of the chapter.

FISCAL POLICY AND INFLATION

Fighting inflation calls for restrictive fiscal policies. As you saw in Figure 21-2, the price level can be reduced by cutting back aggregate demand. But, we really don't want to cause prices to fall. We want stable prices. That is the real aim of a restrictive policy. Population growth and general economic growth push aggregate demand up every year. By following a restrictive fiscal policy, the government may be able at least to slow the rise in price levels. The kinds of actions that would lower inflation are cutting government spending and/or raising the level of taxes.

Once more, think back to the discussion of unemployment and inflation in chapters 16 and 17. You will remember that some inflation may result from demand-pull forces. But, part of our inflation may come from the cost-push side as well. The restrictive fiscal policies that we've looked at will only affect the demand side of the market. If demand is the cause of inflation, the policies will work. But, if inflation is cost-push, we cannot look for help from fiscal policy. For cost-push inflation, we need some other kind of program. Perhaps better antitrust laws and enforcement would help. Some economists also suggest using wage and price controls of some kind. Wage and price controls will be discussed later in this chapter.

THE UNEMPLOYMENT/INFLATION TRADE-OFF

At one time, people believed that there was a clear trade-off between unemployment and inflation. There was much talk about fine-tuning the economy by using monetary and fiscal policies to get exactly the unemployment rate and inflation rate we wanted. Today, we realize that we cannot reach such exactness. It is no longer true that, when inflation gets worse, unemployment gets better, and vice versa. The 1970s and 1980s taught us that both inflation and unemployment can rise to high levels at the same time. Our society faces the problem of finding policies that can lower unemployment and inflation at the same time.

From your understanding of how fiscal policy affects each problem, you know that what helps one hurts the other. An expansionary policy may reduce unemployment but increase inflation. A restrictive policy that reduces inflation can cause unemployment to rise. The same kind of trade-off results from monetary policies. A loose monetary policy may help unemployment but will raise prices. A tight monetary policy may keep inflation in line but will make unemployment worse.

So, from a monetary and fiscal policy point of view, the problem of the trade-off between inflation and unemployment remains unsolved. This problem will likely be the focus of much attention for a long time to come.

FISCAL POLICY AND ECONOMIC GROWTH

Only a stable and healthy economy can encourage economic growth. This means that inflation and unemployment must be kept down. This is clearly hard to do. But, the better we deal with these economic problems, the better economic growth will be.

An expansionary fiscal policy generally promotes economic growth better than a restrictive policy. However, this is true only if inflation does not get out of hand due to the high level of economic activity. Businesses find it hard to plan for the future in an inflationary economy and are likely to cut the spending that might lead to economic growth.

The government can use certain specific policies other than controlling unemployment and inflation to promote economic growth. One is to follow tax policies that make it desirable for businesses to invest in new plants and machines. Investment tax credits often have been used for this purpose. A business that spends money for investment is given a tax reduction under such a plan. This lowers the cost of investment to the business, which results in greater investment spending. Investment plays an important part in increasing the growth rate in the economy. Government spending on research and development also can promote growth. Tax cuts for businesses that spend more for research and development also can be used.

Economic growth will be spurred on by expansionary fiscal policies. This is particularly true of policies that encourage more savings, more investment, and more spending for research and development.

When the savings rate in the economy falls, the government can use tax policies to try to increase savings. This can make more money available for business investment, which then can be expected to help increase the rate of economic growth. Unfortunately, the rate of savings in the United States

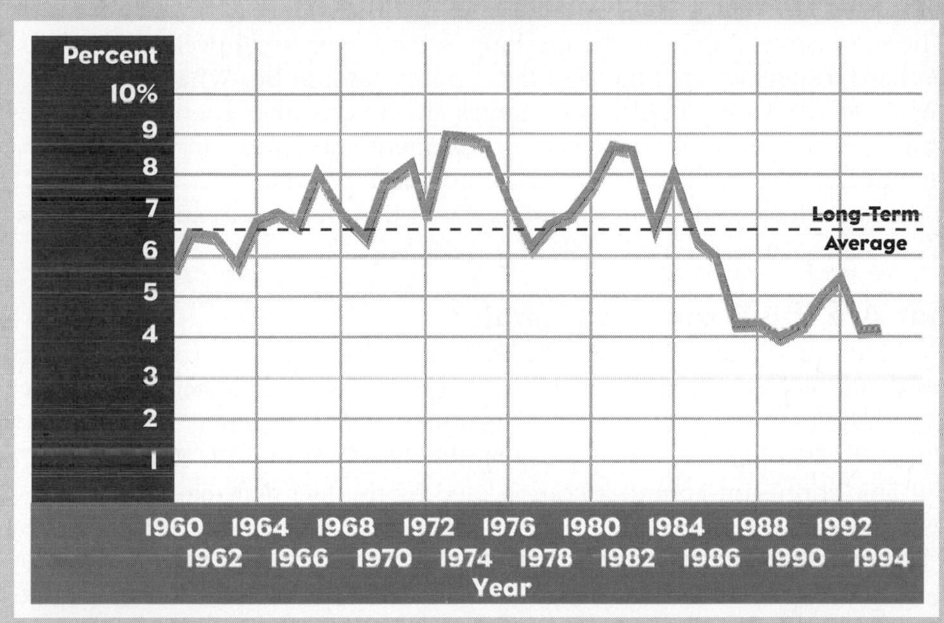

Figure 21-5

Savings as a Percent of Disposable Personal Income

The rate of saving in the United States has been low, especially since the mid-1980s. ***What might the government do to increase the savings rate?***

SOURCE: *Economic Report of the President, 1995* (Washington, D.C.: U.S. Government Printing Office, 1995), 306.

is relatively low and in recent years has dropped to below the already low long term average. This is illustrated in Figure 21 5.

PUTTING FISCAL POLICY TO WORK

Congress and the president should work together in forming fiscal policies. Failure to do so greatly reduces the chances of having timely and effective policies. But, the way Congress works makes it difficult to get quick action on fiscal policy. A lot of debate always occurs before fiscal policy can change.

What Time Issues Are Involved?

The ***inside time lag*** for fiscal policy is the time it takes to decide on a policy. The inside time lag for fiscal policy is long. This means that, at best, it takes months and often years for the president, the House of Representatives, and the Senate to agree on fiscal policy measures.

inside time lag the time it takes to decide on a policy

Consider the length of the outside time lag for fiscal policy. The ***outside time lag*** for fiscal policy is the time it takes for the effects of a policy change to be completely felt in the economy. Once agreement is reached on the kind of fiscal policy needed, the policy can become effective in the economy very quickly. Changes in taxes can be effected almost immediately by changing the amount withheld from paychecks. Many government spending programs also can be started, stopped, or modified quickly. For these reasons, we say that fiscal policy has a short outside time lag.

outside time lag the time it takes for the effects of a policy change to be completely felt in the economy

What Fiscal Policy Is Needed?

There are several reasons for the long debate over fiscal policy. First, it is often hard to decide what the best fiscal policy should be. What mix of tax changes do we want? Should the changes affect consumer spending, business spending, or both? What changes in government spending will work best? Which programs should change and by how much? Politicians, economists, and the president hold strong opinions about the answers to such questions. Thus, reaching agreement can take a long time.

What Are the Economic Signals?

Problems arise partly because the economy often sends unclear and sometimes contradictory signals. People who are more worried about the negative effects of inflation may interpret the economic signals one way. People who are more worried about unemployment may interpret the same signals differently. This confusion is further complicated by the fact that many politicians do not understand economics very well. Therefore, they may not understand the signals coming from the economy. Try to imagine answering a question asked by someone speaking in a language that you do not know. Any answer you give is more likely to be wrong than right. The same is true for economic policy made by people who do not understand economic reasoning.

What Risks Are Involved?

Also, remember that we elect politicians to office. If they vote for unpopular economic policies, they risk losing their jobs. It is always easier to get Congress to agree to tax cuts and more government spending than the reverse. Voters rarely object to a cut in their taxes or to getting federal funds for some local project. This confusion gives rise to an inflationary bias in fiscal policy. The ***inflationary bias in fiscal policy*** is the natural tendency for Congress to favor expansionary policies over restrictive policies. What might serve the economy best may give way to what will win votes in the next election. This results in long debates as our representatives and senators try to please the voters who elected them.

inflationary bias in fiscal policy
the natural tendency for Congress to favor expansionary policies over restrictive policies

How Much Do the Voters Understand?

An important message should surface from this discussion. If we, the voting public, want to have responsible fiscal policy, we must understand economic issues ourselves. And, we must let our representatives and senators know that we understand that higher taxes or lower government spending may be necessary to control inflation. They must know that we will continue to vote for them only if they vote for responsible, economically sound fiscal policy measures. By understanding the relationships summarized in the table in Figure 21-6, you are taking a step toward responsible fiscal policy.

	Government Actions		Effects on U.S. Economy			
	Government Spending	Taxes	Interest Rates	Inflation	Unemploy-ment	Economic Growth
Restrictive Fiscal Policy	Decreases	Increase	Could Decrease Indirectly	Lower	Increases	Slows
Expansionary Fiscal Policy	Increases	Decrease	Could Increase Indirectly	Higher	Decreases	Encourages

Figure 21-6

A Summary of Important Relationships Involving Fiscal Policy

This table shows how restrictive and expansionary fiscal policies can be implemented. It also shows the effects of such policies on the economy. ***Suppose the unemployment rate has started to increase. What fiscal policies might be used to reduce this unemployment?***

MONETARY OR FISCAL POLICY: WHICH IS BETTER?

There is a good deal of disagreement between people who favor monetary policy and those who favor fiscal policy. Those who argue for fiscal policy point out that it has a more direct effect than monetary policy. Government spending can increase demand directly. Tax changes can be made that are sure to increase or reduce demand in a fairly predictable way. Fiscal policy is probably more effective than monetary policy in getting the economy out of a recession. Government spending and/or tax cuts will increase total spending. But, a loose monetary policy can only make money available. Businesses may not increase borrowing because their leaders may feel pessimistic about the future due to their experiences during recession.

People who favor monetary policy may point out that monetary policy can effectively control inflation. If there is less money available, people have less to spend. Monetary policy certainly combats the kind of demand-pull inflation we speak of as *too many dollars chasing too few goods*. Some economists believe that monetary policy has greater flexibility than fiscal policy. They say using fiscal policy to control inflation is like a jeweler using a sledge hammer to cut a diamond. The wrong fiscal policy can damage the economy as surely as the hammer can ruin the diamond. Some who favor monetary policy think that fiscal policy should be used only in times of complete economic breakdown, such as during the 1930s.

Some economists and politicians believe that the best monetary policy increases the money supply at a steady rate equal to the rate of growth in real GNP. This makes a good deal of sense to many people. Suppose real GNP expanded to the extent that production doubled. It is likely that twice as much money would be needed to support transactions in the expanded economy.

Part of the debate about monetary policy versus fiscal policy concerns the time lags involved. Both the Board of Governors and the Federal Open Market Committee of the Federal Reserve System can act quickly on a policy change. Therefore, the inside time lag for monetary policy is short. But, once a change is made, it can take a long time for the entire impact to be felt in the economy. Some experts say that the effects of monetary policy may take two years to filter through the economy—quite a long outside time lag.

With fiscal policy you have seen that, once a policy is determined, changes can be put into effect quickly. If Congress and the president agreed on a tax change today, the results could show up in paychecks within the next couple of weeks. But, it takes a long time to achieve agreement on fiscal policy. In the House of Representatives, it takes time for the Ways and Means Committee to agree. Then, the whole House has to be convinced to pass the measure. Once this is done the Senate must act, and then the president must approve.

Econ & You

THE FISCAL IN YOUR FUTURE

National economic policy affects the entire economy, but it can affect you personally as well. Spending programs may open up new jobs in your area and/or provide new services that benefit you. For example, Congress might enact a law that provides a greater pool of low interest loans for postsecondary education, which might make it easier for you to attend college. Of course, budget cuts can have a direct impact on individuals as well. If you live in an urban area, a cut in funding for mass transit might mean that you will have to pay more to get to and from places for which you use mass transit. If you live in a rural area, a cut in agricultural subsidies may mean a lower standard of living for you and your family.

Changes in tax programs also affect individuals. If more tax dollars were collected because the government eliminated or reduced the tax break for having children, a family with children would have to pay more in tax than it did under previous tax law. This would leave them with less spendable income and a lower standard of living. If, on the other hand, a new provision were added to the tax law that gave families the ability to deduct all educational expenses from their tax bill, many families would have more spendable income and a higher standard of living.

Because fiscal policy does affect individuals and individual organizations, we see special interest groups lobbying for special treatment. You might join with others to convince Congress that your group deserves special treatment in terms of government spending or tax programs. Your tax break is what others might think of as a tax loophole. Spending on your special project might be seen by others as an example of wasteful government spending.

Any program may cycle several times through this process for changes and revisions. This often results in long delays between the time when the need for a new policy is recognized and when changes are made.

As you can see, there is no clear winner in this debate. The choice depends on the state of the economy at any particular time as well as on personal preferences. Many intelligent people may not agree on what is best for the economy at any moment. Very good economists, even Nobel Prizewinners, argue on both sides of the debate. You have to weigh the advantages and disadvantages of each kind of policy and decide for yourself.

SUPPLY SIDE EFFECTS OF FISCAL POLICY

While the primary aim of fiscal policy in the United States has been to influence the level of aggregate demand, there are potential effects on the supply side of the economy as well. For example, a cut in corporate income taxes may increase both demand and supply in the economy. Such a tax cut may encourage the creation of new jobs and an increase in investment of both physical and human capital. As a result, there may be increased productivity and, thus, an increase in supply.

Similarly, a cut in personal income taxes may increase savings, which can result in lower interest rates, greater investment, and a corresponding increase in supply. As firms produce more and hire more workers, the income tax base may increase, and some economists and politicians argue that more tax dollars may be collected even though the tax rate decreased. However, there is little concrete evidence to support these arguments at present.

Increased government spending may increase aggregate supply as well as aggregate demand. Suppose the government increases spending on the nation's infrastructure (highways, railways, water and sewer systems, airports, etc.) and on education. One result of such spending may be increased productivity, which will increase aggregate supply.

Checkpoint

Content Check

1. What kinds of fiscal policies would reduce unemployment?
2. If inflation is the primary concern, what kinds of fiscal policies do you recommend?
3. Does monetary policy or fiscal policy have a shorter outside time lag? Why?

What Do You Think Now?

Reread *What Do You Think?* in the Section Two Focus. Then answer the following question:

4. Why doesn't the government just increase spending until everyone who wants a job is employed?

FOCUS

Section Three
Government Use of Wage and Price Controls

What Do You Think?

Suppose that the rate of inflation crept up to 12 or 13 percent. Suppose that, at the same time, the unemployment rate was more than 10 percent. These are levels of inflation and unemployment that most people in the United States would find too high. If the economy were faced with these dual problems, why could we not use monetary and fiscal policies to reduce unemployment and make it illegal for prices to be increased? Would this solve the nation's economic problems?

Term to Know

wage and price controls

What's Ahead?

Wage and price controls are upper limits on wages and prices that are set by the government. This is done to keep prices from going up too fast. Some people think that using government controls to keep prices low can solve the problem of inflation. In this section, you will learn how the tools of supply and demand can be used to examine the effects of wage and price controls.

WAGE AND PRICE CONTROLS

wage and price controls government controls on the levels of wages and prices

Wage and price controls are government controls on the levels of wages and prices. Such controls also are called an *incomes policy* because they try to keep control over people's income and buying power. There are many kinds of wage and price controls. These include wage-price freezes, wage-price guideposts (voluntary controls), and mandatory wage-price guidelines with penalties for violators.

Why Use Wage and Price Controls?

We do not like to see unemployment rise when we try to slow inflation. As you have seen, monetary and fiscal policies result in a trade-off between inflation and unemployment. Policies that slow inflation tend to make the unemployment problem worse. The voting public is sensitive to unemployment, so the use of monetary and fiscal policies to lower inflation is politically unpopular. Therefore, the government sometimes turns to wage and price controls to guide the economy.

Another reason for using wage and price controls is that, at times, our economy faces inflation that is not caused by too much demand. This cost-push inflation is not easily corrected with the usual methods, and so controls are often suggested. Furthermore, many people believe that big businesses and big labor unions have too much power. They can raise prices or wages more than is necessary or desirable because they have some degree of power over the marketplace. Controlling price increases that are due to market power may necessitate specific government controls.

Past Uses of Wage and Price Controls

Throughout all of recorded history, there have been times when prices have risen rapidly. As early as 1800 B.C., wage and price controls were used by the Babylonians to keep prices from rising too fast. The Roman Emperor Diocletian controlled prices on many goods and controlled wages for many kinds of work.

Economic Dilemma

AMENDING FISCAL POLICY

Except for periods of war and depression, the federal government managed to balance the budget in most years until relatively recently. In the last 30 or 40 years, the norm has become the red ink of a budget deficit and the corresponding increase in our national debt. This has led to increased interest in the possibility of a constitutional amendment that requires the federal government to balance the budget. Such a measure was defeated twice in the early 1990s.

What would a balanced budget amendment do to fiscal policy? For one thing, it would reduce the government's ability to use fiscal policy, especially to curb a recession. Suppose the economy heads into a recession. With lower employment and lower incomes, tax receipts would fall. To maintain government programs, tax rates would have to rise, which is just the opposite of the appropriate fiscal policy to alleviate a recession. Similarly, with lower tax receipts, spending programs would have to be cut, which again would not help us out of a recession. A balanced budget law could allow for a deficit under certain conditions if approved by a substantial majority of Congress (such as 60 percent).

The advantage that many people see in a balanced budget amendment is that it would force Congress to be more responsible in its pursuit of spending programs. Congress has provided evidence that it will not control its spending without a balanced budget mandate. But whose fault is that? The responsibility lies in part with every citizen. How many people write to their representatives in government and ask for a tax increase or a cut in a spending program that would directly affect them?

In the United States, such controls were used during World War II. With the heavy demand caused by the production of war goods, inflation rose rapidly. President Roosevelt ordered the control of prices to keep inflation down. This meant that prices no longer provided accurate signals to business, and, as a result, the economy had many shortages. Many goods had to be rationed. Consumer goods such as gasoline, meat, sugar, and cigarettes grew scarce. To make them available to rich and poor alike, a rationing system was set up. In 1944, the banking system was handling 5 billion ration coupons each month. As you might guess, this rationing program needed many workers. The government had about 50,000 paid employees and more than 200,000 volunteers to manage the controls.

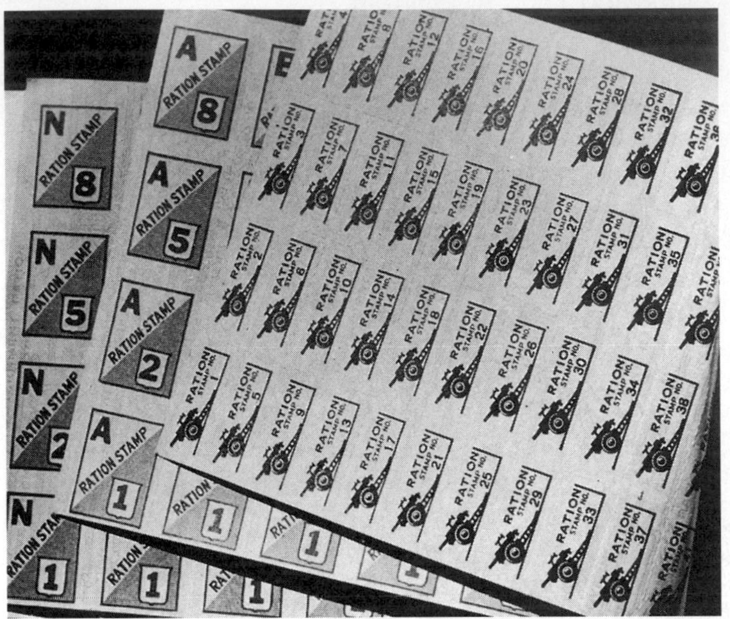

Overall, the controls worked well during the years of World War II. People were willing to cooperate with the program. The war gave people a sense of purpose, and they were willing to make sacrifices for the war effort. It is doubtful that in peacetime people would willingly go along with such controls.

Another attempt at wage and price controls came during the Nixon presidency. On August 15, 1971, President Nixon issued an order that froze wages, prices, rents, and salaries for 90 days. During this period, prices rose relatively little. This 90-day period was followed by a second phase that lasted 14 months. During this phase, wages could rise at a 5.5 percent rate, and prices could rise at a 2.5 percent rate. Then, in January 1973, a period of voluntary guidelines began. Prices and wages shot up rapidly. On June 13, 1973, President Nixon again froze prices for 60 days to try to "cool off inflationary expectations" in the economy. As soon as that 60-day period was over, prices once more started rising rapidly.

WAGE AND PRICE CONTROLS IGNORE MARKET FORCES

Wage and price controls block the price signals from the market. When this happens, supply and demand can get out of balance. To see why, look at the graphs in Figure 21-7.

The left-hand graph shows what would happen if the market were left to work by itself. At the market price, the amount people would want to buy would be exactly the same as the amount businesses would make. That is, the quantity demanded would equal the quantity supplied at the market price.

Now, suppose a control price were set below the market price. This is shown in the right-hand graph. At the lower control price, a greater quantity would be demanded than the quantity supplied. In a free economy, price would rise until a balance were obtained. But, with the control price, a shortage would result.

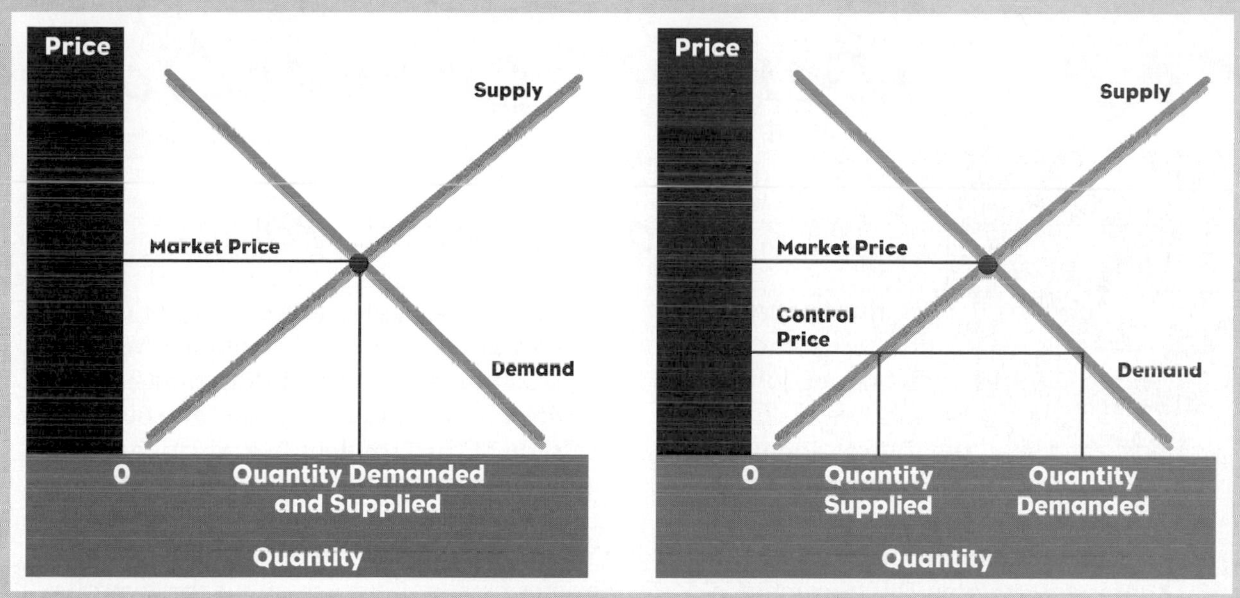

Figure 21-7

Supply and Demand Analysis of Price Controls

To be effective, a wage or price control must be below the equilibrium value determined by supply and demand. Such a control price is shown in the right-hand graph. ***At the control price, is the market in balance?***

When there is a shortage, people try to find ways around the system. A network of illegal markets usually develops. In such cases, it is often the rich and powerful people who end up with the limited amount of the good. In order to try to make the allocation of goods more fair, the government might use ration coupons. Of course, it is not easy to decide who gets how many coupons. Keeping prices below the market level is not easy. Doing so creates many new problems that may be as bad as or worse than the problem of high prices.

Wage and price controls of the kinds we have tried do not work well. Controls cause price signals to fail, and supply and demand get badly out of balance. People and businesses spend too much time trying to get around the controls and seeking special treatment. Time spent in this way is not productive.

Some economists believe that controls have not worked because we have used only short-term controls. They think that, if the controls operated on a long-term basis, the controls

Internet Connection

REAL WORLD FISCAL POLICY

U.S. fiscal policy is reflected in the federal budget, which covers two main areas: the sources and uses of government revenues.The U.S. budget for the most recent fiscal year can be obtained from **gopher://sunny.stat-usa.gov**. This document is extraordinarily detailed. A more managable source of information is the "National Income and Product Accounts" at **gopher://una.hh.lib.umich.edu/00/ebb/nipa/nipacurr/nipa-a.prn**, which we introduced in Chapter 14. Table 302 provides summary data for tax and other government revenues (lines 1–13) and government expenditures (lines 14–30).

A quick measure of the stance of fiscal policy is the size of the federal deficit. Traditionally, when the budget was in deficit, fiscal policy was described as loose or expansionary. When the budget was in surplus, fiscal policy was described as tight or contractionary. Given the string of budget deficits in recent history, fiscal policy might be better described as relatively tight or loose depending on whether the deficit is increasing or decreasing. An easy source of deficit information is the *Statistical Abstract,* **http://www.census.gov/ftp/pub/statab/USAbrief/part2.txt.**

There are several places to look for discussions of the stance of fiscal policy. With the U.S. budget in the first URL given in this activity, you can find the annual "The Budget Message of the President," in which the president gives his explanation and justification for the budget. Also at that site is "A Citizen's Guide to the Federal Budget." This reviews fiscal policy throughout the twentieth century as well as gives summary budget data dating from 1930. Another useful document is the "Economic Report of the President" (ERP), which is published annually. The first two chapters usually provide a statement of the administration's current fiscal policy. Chapter 1 tends to be more theoretical, while Chapter 2 explains the current state of the economy and where and how the administration expects the economy to proceed. The ERP is available online at **gopher://umslvma.umsl.edu:70/11/library/govdocs/erps**.

Economics Application: Connect to "The Citizen's Guide to the Federal Budget," **gopher://sunny.stat-usa.gov/00/BudgetFY96/bud96g.txt**. From the tables at the end, determine the last year the federal budget was a surplus.

Internet Application: Try to "balance the budget" using the simulation game at **http://garnet.berkeley.edu:3333/budget/budget.html**.

could keep inflation down. Others think that our mistake has been in trying to control too much. They say that we need only use controls for highly concentrated kinds of businesses and for a small number of the large labor unions. If we can keep wages and prices under control in these parts of the economy, maybe the rest will come under control, too. There is no way to know for sure unless these ideas are tried. Most economists, however, do not favor the use of controls.

Checkpoint

Content Check

1. Why do you think wage and price controls worked better during World War II than when they were tried again in the 1970s?
2. Use the concepts of supply and demand to explain the consequences of using wage or price controls.

What Do You Think Now?

Reread *What Do You Think?* in the Section Three Focus. Then answer the following question:

3. Why doesn't the government use wage and price controls to control inflation, along with a loose monetary policy and an expansionary fiscal policy to keep unemployment to an acceptable level?

Concepts in Brief

1. Fiscal policy is the changing of government spending and/or taxes in order to control the level of economic activity. The goal of fiscal policy is to keep unemployment and inflation at acceptable levels.
2. Expansionary fiscal policies raise the level of demand in the economy. When demand is increased, more people are likely to be hired to work and economic growth will increase. While this will reduce unemployment, it also may increase inflation.
3. Restrictive fiscal policies lower the level of demand in the economy. This will help lower the inflation rate but may make the unemployment problem worse.
4. Congress and the president are responsible for putting fiscal policies to work. Getting agreement within Congress and between Congress and the president is hard. For this reason, there is a long inside time lag in forming fiscal policy. But, once there is agreement, fiscal policy can be put into effect very quickly and can be felt in the economy almost at once. This means that there is a short outside time lag for fiscal policy.
5. The budget deficit is the amount by which the federal government spends more than it gets in revenue. The government borrows money when its spending projects cost more than the amount of money it gets from taxes. The national debt is the amount of money the federal government owes. The national debt is the accumulation of yearly budget deficits.
6. Wage and price controls are government controls over the levels of wages and prices. These controls are sometimes suggested as a way to get around the inflation/unemployment trade-off.

Economic Foundations

1. What is the effect of an expansionary fiscal policy on aggregate demand? on the level of prices? on the amount of goods produced?
2. What two actions can the government take for an expansionary fiscal policy?
3. What is the effect of a restrictive fiscal policy on aggregate demand? on the level of prices? on the amount of goods produced?
4. What two actions can the government take for a restrictive fiscal policy?
5. What is the relationship between the national debt and the budget deficit?
6. What are two major concerns about increasing the national debt?
7. Will an expansionary fiscal policy increase or decrease unemployment? Which kind of unemployment will it affect the most?
8. Will a restrictive fiscal policy increase or decrease inflation? Which kind of inflation will it affect the most?
9. Which kind of fiscal policy is better for economic growth? When might this not be true?
10. Besides changing the level of spending or taxes, what other actions can government take to promote economic growth?
11. Why is there a long inside time lag for fiscal policy?
12. Is the outside time lag for fiscal policy long or short? Why?
13. Why do we have such large budget deficits at the national level?
14. Give two reasons wage and price controls might be used. Have they usually been effective in controlling inflation?

Your Economic Vocabulary

Build your economic vocabulary by matching the following terms with their definitions.

budget deficit

crowding out

expansionary fiscal policies

external debt

fiscal policy

inflationary bias in fiscal policy

inside time lag

multiplier effect

national debt

outside time lag

restrictive fiscal policy

wage and price controls

1. causing the economy to run more slowly primarily by reducing aggregate demand
2. the time it takes to decide on a policy
3. the concept that any change in fiscal policy affects total demand and total income by an amount larger than the original amount of the change in spending or taxing
4. government controls on the levels of wages and prices
5. the amount by which federal government spending exceeds revenues each year
6. the part of the national debt that is owed to people or governments outside the United States
7. the time it takes for the effects of a policy change to be completely felt in the economy
8. the amount of money that the federal government owes
9. causing the economy to run more rapidly primarily by increasing aggregate demand
10. the effect on private businesses when increased government borrowing raises interest rates and reduces private borrowing
11. the natural tendency for Congress to favor expansionary policies over restrictive policies
12. the changing of federal government spending and taxes in order to control the level of economic activity

Thinking Critically About Economics

1. For each of the following parts of the economy, give an example of a fiscal policy that would reduce inflation: (a) consumer spending, (b) business investment, and (c) government spending. Draw a graph such as the one in Figure 21-2 to represent such fiscal policies and explain how each of your examples relates to the graph.
2. For each of the following parts of the economy, give an example of a fiscal policy that would reduce unemployment: (a) consumer spending, (b) business investment, and (c) government spending. Draw a graph such as the one in Figure 21-1 to represent such fiscal policies and explain how each of your examples relates to the graph.
3. Explain the multiplier effect. In your explanation, describe how this effect comes about when the government uses a fiscal policy of increased government spending.
4. "It is impossible to control both unemployment and inflation. The trade-off between the two is so strong that solving one problem *always* makes the other problem worse." In what ways do you agree with this statement? In what ways do you disagree?
5. The overall economy is always changing. Read recent issues of *Time, Newsweek, U.S. News & World Report,* and *The Wall Street Journal* to find out whether inflation or unemployment is the most important current problem. Based on what you find out, what type of fiscal policy would you suggest the government use? What evidence can you find that the government is following a path similar to the one you suggest? If there are differences, explain them.

Economic Enrichment

Use a graph of aggregate demand and aggregate supply to show how a fiscal policy of cutting income taxes might increase output and therefore increase employment. Are there any harmful effects of such a policy on the level of inflation? If so, explain why by using your graph. Write a paragraph that carefully explains your graph.

Math and Economics

The following table contains data about the U.S. population and the national debt for 1970 through 1995 (at five-year intervals). Copy this table on a separate sheet of paper. Then, use the data in the second and third columns to calculate the national debt per person. National debt per person is calculated by dividing the national debt by the population. In doing your calculations, be sure to remember that the national debt is given in billions and that income is given in millions. For example, $380.9 billion is $380,900,000,000 and 205 million is 205,000,000. The national debt per person for 1970 has been calculated and entered in the table as an example.

Enter your answers in the fourth column of your table. Draw a line graph that depicts the national debt per person for the years given. National debt per person should be on the vertical axis and years should be on the horizontal axis.

Year	Population (in millions)	National Debt (in billions of dollars)	National Debt per Person
1970	205	$ 380.9	$1,858
1975	216	541.9	
1980	228	909.1	
1985	238	1,817.5	
1990	250	3,206.6	
1995	262	4,961.5	

Writing About Economics

It has been suggested by some that Democrats and Republicans have different attitudes about the relative importance of unemployment and inflation. Republicans are often thought to have greater concern about inflation than unemployment. The opposite is thought to hold for Democrats.

To see whether people in your community reflect these opinions, conduct an informal survey of ten adults. Ask each one whether they think unemployment or inflation is the most important economic problem for the nation in the long run. For five of the interviews, phrase the question with unemployment first and for the other five mention inflation first. This helps to prevent a bias in the answers based on the wording of the question.

After each person answers the unemployment/inflation question, ask whether he or she would best be classified as a Democrat or a Republican. If the person says, "neither," continue doing other interviews until you have ten people who have said they would be best classified as Democrats or Republicans.

Summarize the results of your informal survey in a table. Use these results to write a short report in which you indicate whether you think the assumptions about the two parties are true.

Overview

Section One
Measuring Economic Growth

Section Two
Sources of Economic Growth

Section Three
Economic Growth Involves Trade-Offs

Economic Growth

Learning Objectives

22-1

Explain why real GDP instead of current dollar GDP is used as a measure of economic growth.

22-2

Chart various aspects of the record of growth in GDP in the United States.

22-3

Identify the contributions of natural resources, human resources, capital, and technology to economic growth.

22-4

Present the trade-offs involved in economic growth.

22-5

Describe how the government encourages economic growth.

FOCUS

Section One
Measuring Economic Growth

What Do You Think?

President Faulstich of Hopeland is running for reelection. As is often the case in a market economy, the state of the economy is the subject of much debate and controversy during the campaign. Hopeland's gross domestic product has increased by 452 billion sartobs (Hopeland's currency) during President Faulstich's four-year term of office. This represents an average growth rate of 3.4 percent per year. Does this sound like a good record of economic growth to you?

Terms to Know

- economic growth
- real GDP
- rate of growth
- depression
- real GDP per person

What's Ahead?

There are several ways to measure economic growth. In this section, you will learn about some of these alternatives and look at the record of economic growth in the United States.

ALTERNATE MEASURES OF ECONOMIC GROWTH

economic growth the change in the level of economic activity from one year to another

Economic growth is the change in the level of economic activity from one year to another. This may seem like a pretty straightforward definition. But, people don't always agree about whether our economy is growing, most likely because people use different measures of economic growth.

Current Dollar GDP Versus Real GDP

real GDP the value of gross domestic product after taking out the effect of price changes

One person may be looking at whether the current dollar value of gross domestic product (GDP) is going up. If it is going up, that person might say that the economy is growing. Another person may be looking at real GDP, removing the effects of price changes, to measure economic growth. ***Real GDP*** is the value of gross domestic product after taking out the effect of price changes. Real GDP is also called *constant dollar GDP.* Is it better to use real GDP or current dollar GDP to measure economic growth? To answer this question, consider three fictitious countries: Surat, Mahaly, and Galway.

Surat. Assume that in 1985 the economy of Surat produced a GDP of $1,000 million. The price index in 1985 was 1.00 (or 100). In 1995, Surat had a GDP of $1,600 million, and the price index was 1.80 (or 180). How much did Surat's economy grow during those ten years? The dollar value of GDP grew by $600 million ($1,600 – $1,000 million). That represents a 60 percent increase in GDP ($600 million ÷ $1,000 million = 0.60 = 60%). But, prices also went up during that same time. In fact, the price index of 1.80 in 1995 shows that prices went up by 80 percent (1.80 – 1.00 = 0.80 = 80%). To compare GDP in *real terms* you must take out the effect of inflation as follows:

Real GDP in a Given Year = Current Dollar GDP in that Year ÷ the Price Index

Applying this to Surat, you have the following:

Real GDP in 1985 = $1,000 million ÷ 1.00 = $1,000.0 million

Real GDP in 1995 = $1,600 million ÷ 1.80 = $888.9 million

So, you see that, in real terms, Surat's GDP fell $111.1 million ($1,000 million – $888.9 million) during this period. In real terms, the people of Surat had fewer goods and services to consume in 1995 than in 1985.

Mahaly. Now, assume that in 1985 Mahaly had a GDP of $800 million, and its price index was 1.10 (or 110). In 1995, Mahaly's GDP was $1,360 million, and the price index was 1.87 (or 187). How much did the economy in Mahaly grow during this period? The dollar value of GDP went up by $560 million ($1,360 million – $800 million). That is an increase of 70 percent ($560 million ÷ $800 million = 0.70 = 70%). Prices also increased by 70 percent, as shown by the increase in the price index [(1.87 – 1.10) ÷ 1.10 = 0.70 = 70%]. Let's see what happened to real GDP, since GDP and the level of prices both increased at the same 70 percent rate:

Real GDP in 1985 = $800 million ÷ 1.10 = $727.3 million

Real GDP in 1995 = $1,360 million ÷ 1.87 = $727.3 million

You see in this case that real GDP stayed the same. In terms of the amount of goods and services available for people to consume, there was no change in Mahaly's real output.

Galway. Assume that, in 1985, Galway had a GDP of $900 million and a price index of 1.20 (or 120). In 1995, Galway's GDP grew to $1,350 million, and the price index was 1.68 (or 168). How much did Galway's GDP grow during this period? The dollar value of GDP went up by $450 million

($1,350 million – $900 million). That is a 50 percent increase in GDP ($450 million ÷ $900 million = 0.50 = 50%). But, during this period, prices also increased, since the price index went from 1.20 to 1.68. This is a 40 percent increase in prices [(1.68 – 1.20) ÷ 1.20 = 0.40 = 40%]. Let's see what happened to real GDP in Galway:

Real GDP in 1985 = $900 million ÷ 1.20 = $750.0 million

Real GDP in 1995 = $1,350 million ÷ 1.68 = $803.6 million

In Galway, real GDP increased by $53.6 million during this period. In real terms, the people had more goods and services to use in 1995 than in 1985.

Analyzing the Results. Think for a moment about these results, which are summarized in Figure 22-1. In all three countries, GDP grew during the decade between 1985 and 1995. And, there was inflation in all three countries during this period. You can see that, when the percentage increase in prices was greater than the percentage increase in GDP, real GDP went down (Surat). What appeared to be an increase in GDP was really an illusion caused by rapidly rising prices. In Mahaly, the percentage increase in GDP was exactly the same as the percentage change in prices. So, all of the increase in Mahaly's GDP during that decade was caused by higher prices. No more goods and services were produced in 1995 than in 1985. But, in Galway, GDP went up more rapidly than prices (50 percent compared to 40 percent). Only part of the increase in GDP in Galway was due to inflation. The rest was actually a rise in the amount of goods and services produced.

Figure 22-1

Percentage Change in GDP in Surat, Mahaly, and Galway

An increase in GDP may not mean an actual increase in output. Whether there is an increase in real GDP depends on whether GDP increases at a faster rate than the rate of increase in prices. ***If prices increase at a faster rate than GDP, what happens to real GDP?***

	Surat	Mahaly	Galway
Percentage Increase in GDP	60%	70%	50%
Percentage Increase in Prices	80%	70%	40%
Change in Real GDP	Down	No Change	Up

You can see in these three examples that only Galway produced more in 1995 than in 1985. Without looking at changes in real GDP, you might have reached a different conclusion. So, you can see that real GDP is a better measure of economic growth than current dollar GDP.

Some Remaining Problems. Even using real GDP as a measure of economic growth presents problems. An increase in real GDP does not tell us about distribution of income among people. It says nothing about the quality of goods produced. And, it does not show the average amount produced per person. Suppose Galway, Surat, and Mahaly all started with the same number of people. Suppose the populations of Surat and Mahaly increased 10 percent over the period, but the population of Galway doubled. Would you still say that Galway was better off? Probably not. So, even using real GDP as a measure of economic growth can lead to mistaken conclusions if we are not careful.

The Rate of Growth in an Economy

Another way of looking at economic growth is to look at the *rate* of growth in an economy. The ***rate of growth*** is the percentage change in the level of economic activity from one year to the next. If in Year 1 real GDP is $200 million and in Year 2 real GDP is $210 million, the rate of growth will be as follows:

rate of growth
the percentage change in the level of economic activity from one year to the next

Rate of Growth = (Year 2 GDP – Year 1 GDP) ÷ Year 1 GDP

= ($210 million – $200 million) ÷ $200 million
= $10 million ÷ $200 million
= 0.05
= 5%

So, the rate of growth for this economy between Years 1 and 2 is 5 percent. In the news, you often hear reports about changing GDP in terms of a rate of growth. You now have seen how that rate of growth is determined.

Small Changes in the Percentage Growth in GDP Can Have a Great Impact

Have you ever wondered why so much fuss is sometimes made over a few percentage points of difference in the rate of economic growth? Why is it a news story if the rate of growth in real GDP goes up from 2.6 percent to 3.0 percent? The answer is that, over a number of years, small differences in the rate of growth are magnified and can have significant results.

Let's use two different growth rates to see what could happen to real GDP in the United States between 1960 and 2000. Real GDP in 1960 was $1,970.8 billion. At a growth rate of 2.5 percent, real GDP would grow to $5,292 billion in the year 2000. At a growth rate of 4.5 percent, real GDP would grow to $11,463 billion in the year 2000. The 2 percent difference between 2.5 percent and 4.5 percent would account for a $6,171 billion difference in real GDP in the year 2000.

Such changes in growth rates can affect you on a more personal level. Suppose you were offered either of two jobs, each with the same starting pay of $15,000 a year. In job A, you could expect an increase of 5 percent a year for each of the next ten years. In job B, you could expect an increase of 7.5 percent in each of the next ten years. How would your yearly earnings differ after the ten years? You might be surprised by the results that are shown in Figure 22-2. After ten years, your yearly income would be about $6,500 higher with job B. Even though the difference in the growth rates for income between the two jobs is not large, it could result in big differences in income.

Figure 22-2

Effect of Different Growth Rates on Yearly Income

The size of the annual percentage increase in a person's income can have a big effect over the years. ***Would you take a lower paying job if you thought the percentage increase in your earnings per year would be greater than in another job?***

	Job A 5.0% Income Growth Each Year	Job B 7.5% Income Growth Each Year
Yearly Income Now	$15,000	$15,000
Yearly Income in Ten Years	$24,433	$30,915

THE RECORD OF U.S. ECONOMIC GROWTH

There is a great deal of interest in economic growth in the United States. People in the business sector want a growing economy because that usually means more sales and higher profits. Government officials like a growing economy because it makes their jobs easier. There is less need for social welfare programs, and there are more tax dollars to be spent on public sector services. We like a growing economy because growth provides more jobs and more chances for better jobs, newer products, and higher incomes.

To evaluate our record of economic growth, look at two measures: real GDP and real GDP per person. Note that both measures use real terms, so the effect of inflation is taken out. We will look as far back as 1929 but will look more closely at the record in recent years.

Growth in Real GDP

Figure 22-3 shows how much real GDP has increased in the United States since 1929. The figure also shows the drop in real GDP during

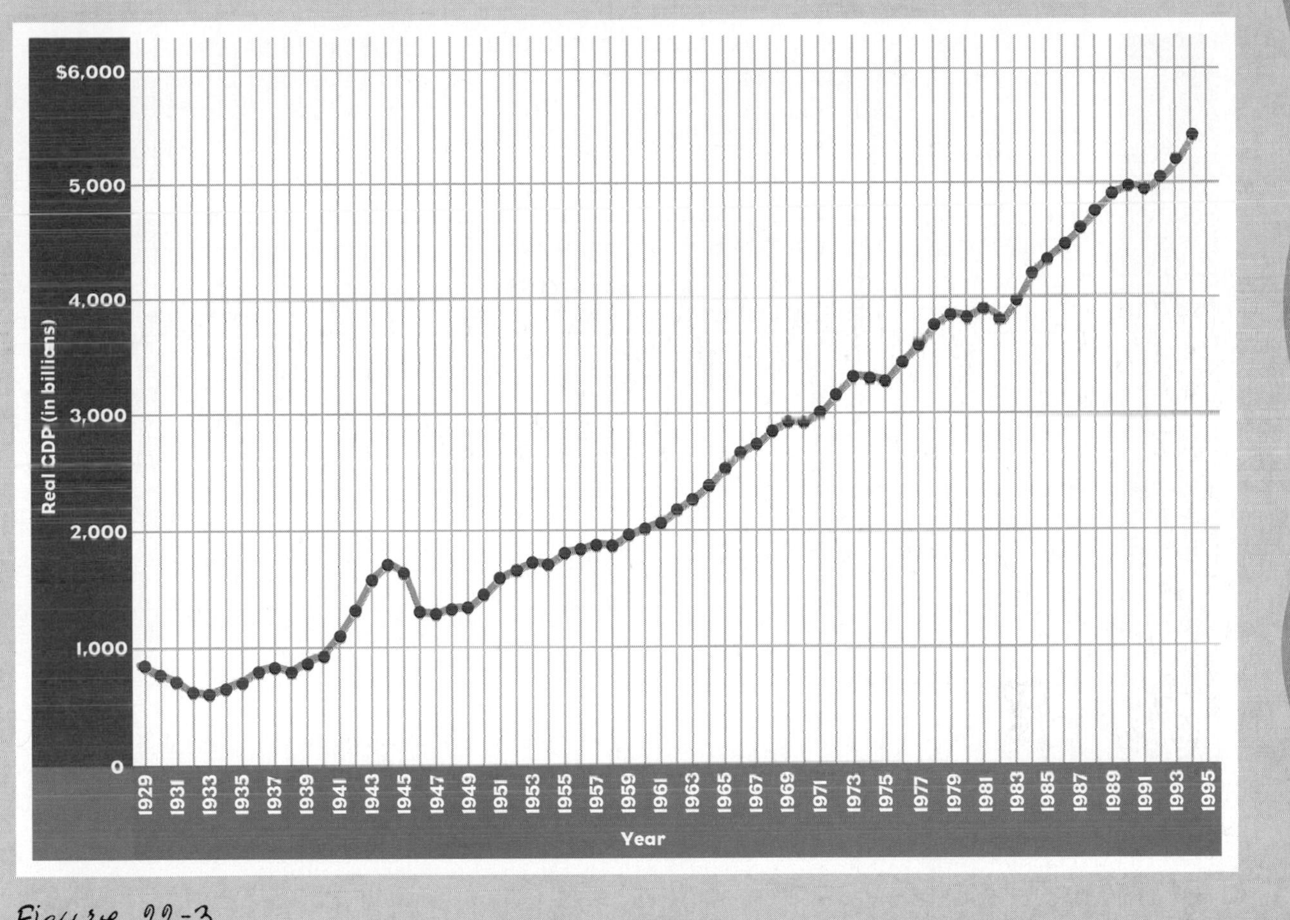

Real GDP in the United States for Selected Years

In this figure, you can see that real GDP has generally increased since the late 1940s. ***Does it look like the increases from year to year have been fairly steady?***

SOURCE: *Economic Report of the President 1995* (Washington, D.C.: U.S. Government Printing Office, 1995), 276, 406.

the Great Depression of the 1930s. A ***depression*** is a severe and prolonged decline in the level of economic activity. Except for during the early and middle 1930s, the U.S. economy has grown in almost every year. During those hard years of the Depression, real GDP fell from $821.8 billion in 1929 to only $587.1 billion in 1933. This negative economic growth made life difficult for most people. From 1929 to 1940, real GDP only increased by about $84 billion, a yearly average growth rate of only about 1 percent.

depression
a severe and prolonged decline in the level of economic activity

The great rise in production during World War II is shown by the jump in real GDP in the early 1940s. After World War II, there was a drop in real GDP. But, people may have been better off after the war, since more consumer goods than war goods were produced. In economic terms, the period from 1945 to 1950 was generally slow as we switched from a wartime to a peacetime economy.

During the 1950s, our economy grew, although more slowly in the last half of that period. Real GDP increased from $1,418.5 billion in 1950 to

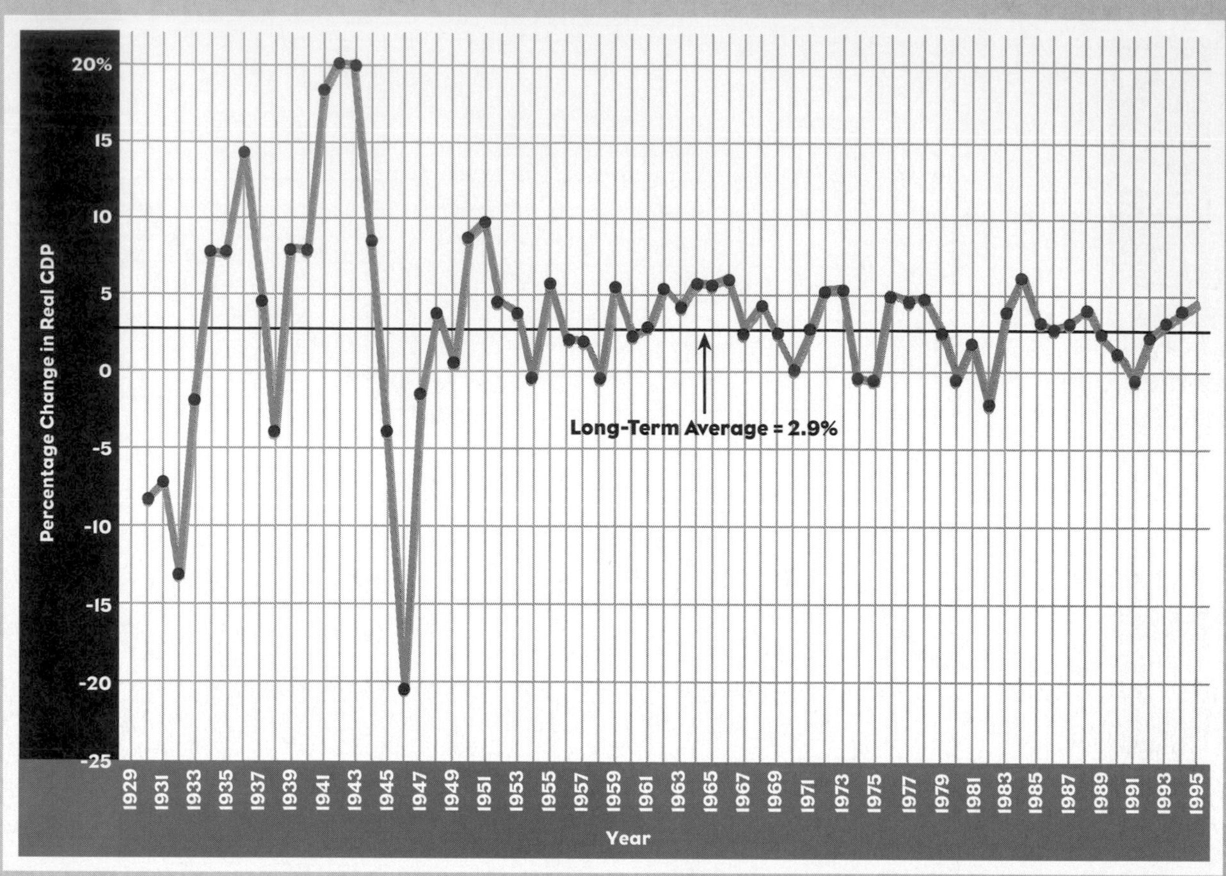

Figure 22-4

Average Yearly Percentage Increases in U.S. Real GDP

These percentages represent year-to-year changes in real GDP. ***Have we ever experienced negative growth in real GDP since 1950?***

SOURCE: *Economic Report of the President 1995* (Washington, D.C.: U.S. Government Printing Office, 1995), 276, 406.

$1,970.8 billion in 1960. This gave us an average yearly growth rate of 3.3 percent for the decade. Yearly growth rates are shown in Figure 22-4.

The 1960s were good years for economic growth. The average yearly growth rate for the 1960s was 3.8 percent.

The 1970s and 1980s showed a slowing in the rate of economic growth. The average rate of growth for the 1970s was 2.8 percent and for the 1980s it was 2.6 percent. As shown in Figure 22-4, the long-term growth rate in real GDP averaged 2.9 percent a year from 1929 to 1994. Keep this number in mind when you hear a politician say we should aim for a 5 percent rate of real growth. You will know that such a rate is well above our long-term average. Could we reach this high a rate? Use the history shown in Figure 22-4 to judge what growth rates seem likely for the United States.

Growth in Real GDP per Person

The population of the United States has been increasing. This means that production and the resulting income must be shared among more and more people each year. In countries where population grows faster than GDP, this can mean falling income per person. Fortunately, economic growth in the United States has risen faster than population growth, and average income has gone up.

To measure the effects of population growth on economic well-being, real GDP per person is frequently used. ***Real GDP per person*** is the real value of the total output of goods and services divided by the number of people in the economy. Real GDP per person is often called *real GDP per capita.*

real GDP per person
the real value of the total output of goods and services divided by the number of people in the economy

Let's look at the record of growth in real GDP per person in the United States. As you look at these values, remember that these data are in real terms per person. This means that inflation and population growth have been accounted for. So these values are comparable in terms of the amount of goods and services the average person could buy in each year. Figure 22-5 shows that, in 1929, real GDP per person was $6,743. This fell to $4,671 in 1933 but has generally gone up since then. By 1940, real GDP per person

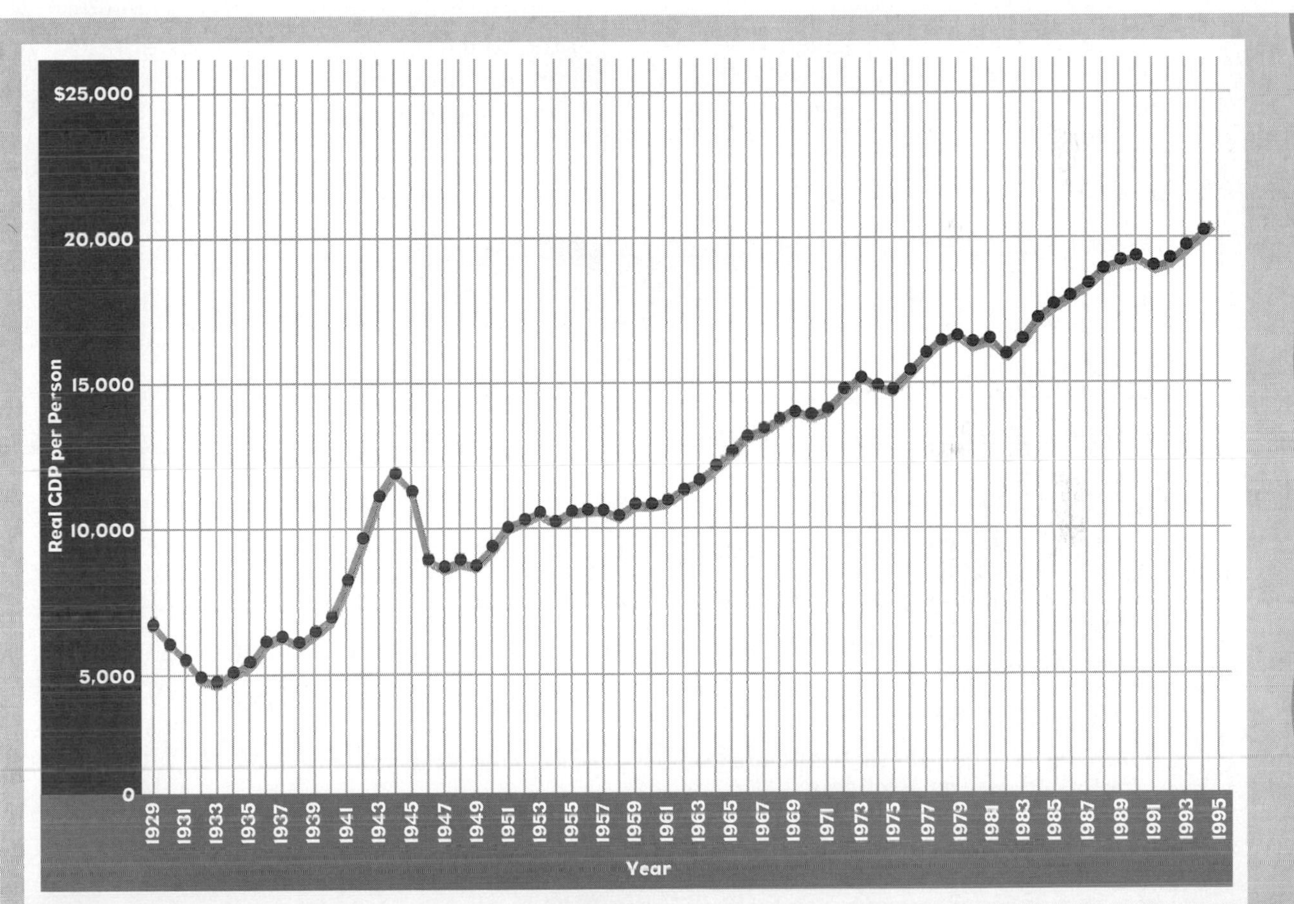

Figure 22-5

Real GDP per Person in the United States

This figure shows real GDP per person starting in 1929 and continuing into the 1990s. ***Have the periods of increase been longer or shorter than the periods of decline?***

SOURCE: Calculated from real GDP and population data in *Economic Report of the President 1995* (Washington, D.C.: U.S. Government Printing Office, 1995), 276, 311, 406.

Global Economy

A PAINFUL TRANSITION

The accompanying table shows how growth in real GDP has varied among selected countries. The countries selected are some of our most important trading partners and countries in which we have other important economic or political interests.

Data for Russia are not given in the earlier years because they would not be comparable with the new Russian economy. The negative economic growth in the two years shown for Russia is typical for "economies in transition" from command-oriented systems to market-driven systems. The process of transition is quite difficult because the social and economic infrastructure needed for a market economy is not in place. For example, in Russia, a legal system governing contracts was essentially nonexistent prior to the demise of the command economy. The government just directed what was to be done between economic agents.

Country	Average for 1976–1985	1986	1988	1990	1992	1994
United States	2.9	2.9	3.9	1.2	2.3	3.7
Canada	3.4	3.3	5.0	-0.2	0.6	4.1
Japan	4.2	2.6	6.2	4.8	1.1	0.9
France	2.3	2.5	4.4	2.5	1.2	1.9
Germany*	2.2	2.3	3.7	5.7	2.2	2.3
Italy	3.1	2.9	4.1	2.1	0.7	1.5
United Kingdom	1.9	4.3	5.0	0.4	-0.5	3.3
Russia*	NA	NA	NA	NA	-19.0	-12.0

***Data for Germany through 1990 are for West Germany only. Values prior to 1992 for Russia were not available.**

SOURCE: *Economic Report of the President 1995* (Washington, D.C.: U.S. Government Printing Office, 1995), 403.

was $6,857, and, in 1950, it was $9,352. Growth has generally continued since that time, and, by 1994 real GDP per person was $19,593. As you see in Figure 22-5, this upward trend has continued in the 1990s.

In Figure 22-6, the percentage growth rate of real GDP per person is shown in graphic form. This shows that in most years, there has been positive growth. However, there has been considerable year-to-year variation in the rate of growth. The periods of decline are indicated by negative percentages (those below the line at zero).

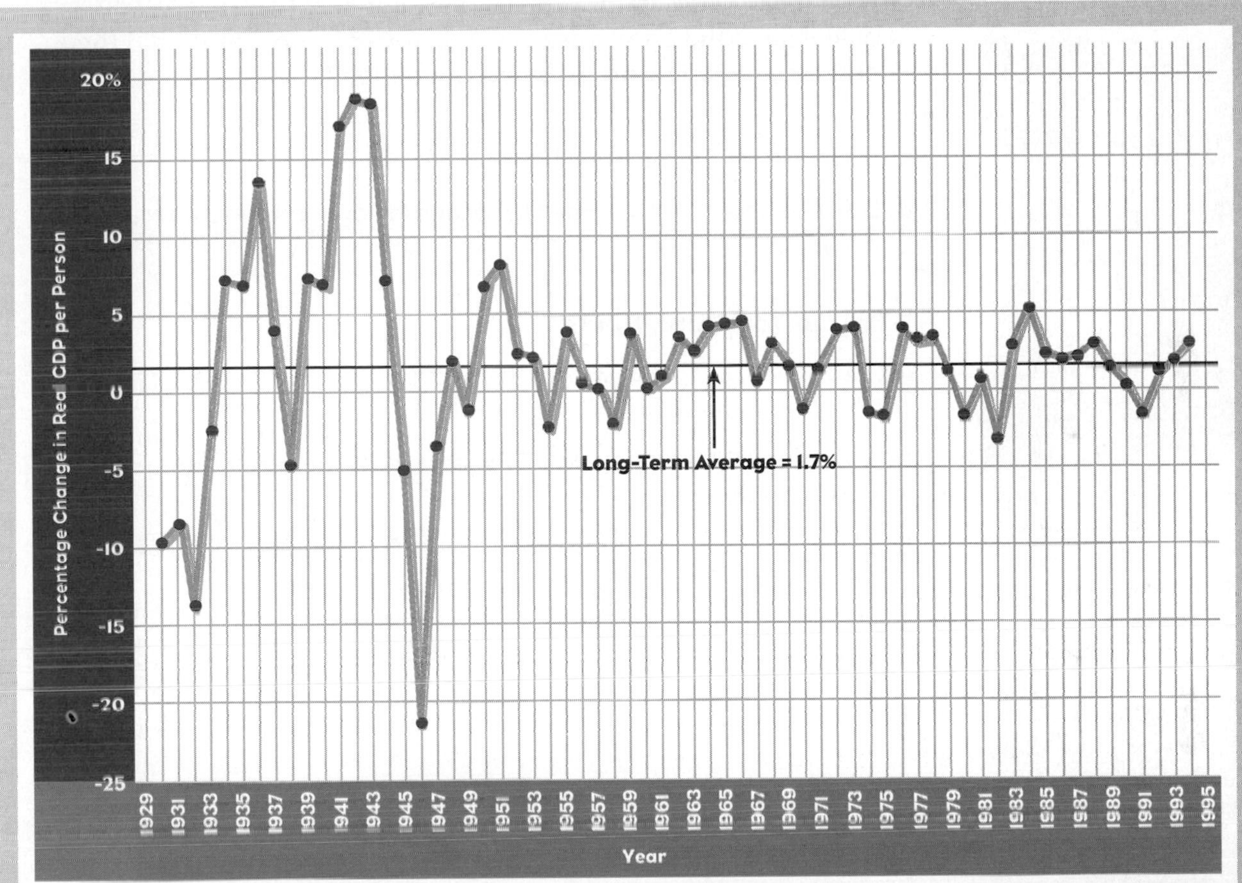

Yearly Percentage Changes in Real GDP per Person in the United States

These percentage changes show that there has been a lot of year-to-year variability in the rate of growth in real GDP per person. ***Why do you think the long-term average rate of growth in real GDP per person (1.7 percent) is less than the rate of growth in real GDP (2.9 percent) shown in Figure 22-4?***

SOURCE: Calculated from real GDP and population data in *Economic Report of the President 1995* (Washington, D.C.: U.S. Government Printing Office, 1995), 276, 311, 406.

Checkpoint

Content Check

1. Why is it important to take inflation into account when measuring economic growth?
2. In 1985, the country of Burlew had a GDP of $600 million, and its price index was 1.10 (or 110). In 1995, Burlew's GDP was $1,000 million, and the price index was 1.87 (or 187). How much did the economy in Burlew grow during this period?
3. How can you use GDP to compare the economies of countries with different populations?
4. Describe the growth in the U.S. economy over the last several decades.

What Do You Think Now?

Reread *What Do You Think?* in the Section One Focus. Then answer the following questions:

5. How much does Hopeland's GDP tell about the growth in Hopeland's economy?
6. What other economic information would you need to know before you voted in Hopeland's presidential election?

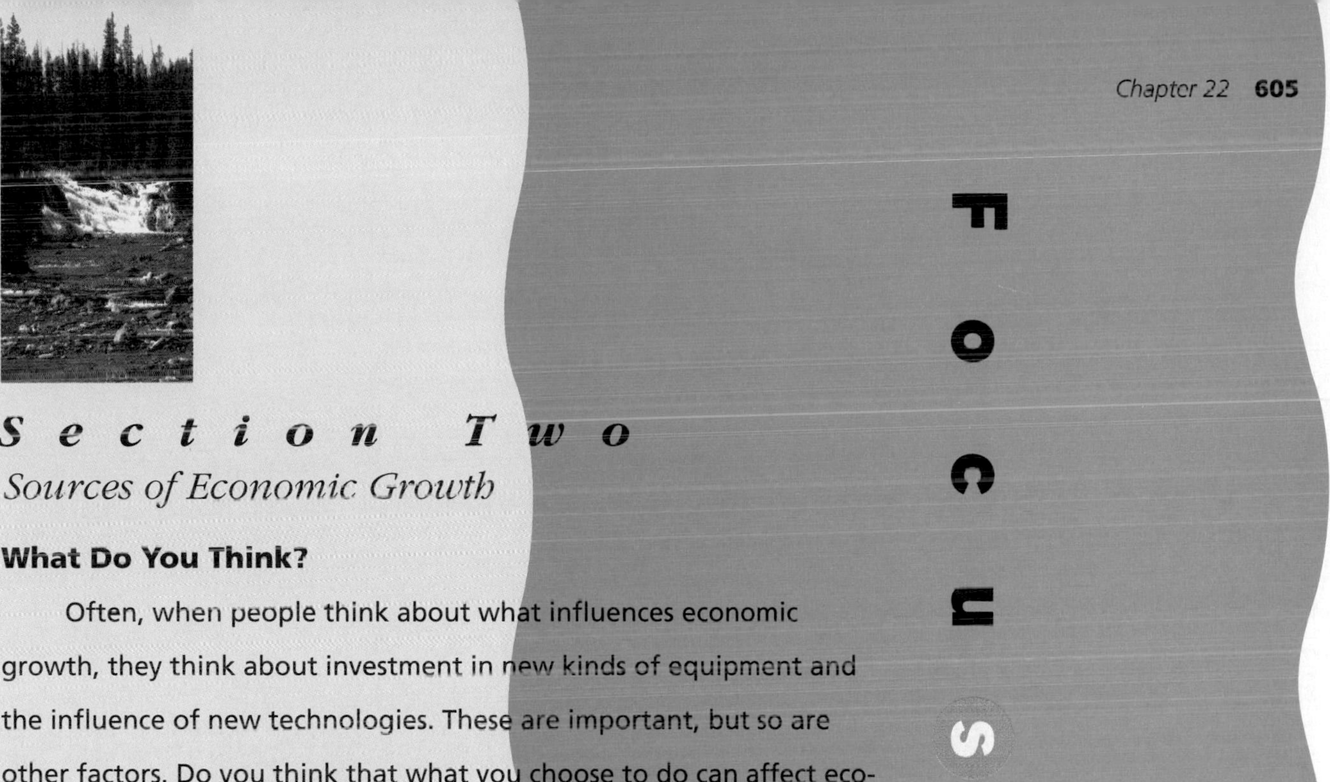

Section Two
Sources of Economic Growth

What Do You Think?

Often, when people think about what influences economic growth, they think about investment in new kinds of equipment and the influence of new technologies. These are important, but so are other factors. Do you think that what you choose to do can affect economic growth?

What's Ahead?

If, as a country, we would like to have continued economic growth, we should have an understanding of what factors influence growth in the economy. Four factors are usually thought to affect economic growth. These are natural resources, human resources, capital, and technology. In this section, you will learn about these sources of economic growth.

Terms to Know

natural resources

human resources

capital

technology

research and development

NATURAL RESOURCES

Natural resources are the total raw materials supplied by nature. Natural resources include land, minerals, water, timber, and wildlife. The base of natural resources that an economy has plays a significant part in the economy's growth. The United States has a rich supply of natural resources. But, even though the United States has rich resources compared to many other countries, those resources are limited. Early in the history of our country, it seemed that our natural resources would last forever. There were few people and great amounts of fertile land, clean water, green forests, and minerals. Much of our early economic growth stemmed from these resources.

natural resources the total raw materials supplied by nature

Not only are our resources numerous, but they are also of very high quality. Land that cannot be used to grow crops or raise livestock will not contribute as much to economic growth as fertile land. Coal deposits with soil and many unusable minerals mixed in have less value than pure coal. The

same can be said of all other natural resources. The U.S. economy has had a base of high-quality natural resources as well as fairly large amounts of them. Both the quantity and the quality of natural resources have impact on economic growth.

As we use natural resources, we need to find new ones to replace depleted supplies. New supplies of natural resources almost always cost more than the old ones. We have to drill deeper to find oil. We have to dig deeper and/or in more remote areas to find coal. And, water must be piped greater distances. This means that the use of such natural resources will cost more, which then can reduce economic growth. Some people feel that natural resource shortages may one day lead to zero, or even negative, economic growth. It is yet to be seen if this will prove true.

HUMAN RESOURCES

human resources the people who work or may be able to work

Human resources are the people who work or may be able to work. You are part of the human resources of this country. You personally can contribute to the economic growth of the country. So, you and others like you offer a potentially productive resource. People make up the stock of human resources without which production would be impossible. Human labor is needed to drive trucks, wait on tables in restaurants, teach classes, sell stereos, build houses, fly aircraft, and do thousands of other jobs.

At one time, the physical ability of labor made up the most important part of labor resources' productivity. Skill and mental abilities have received greater emphasis in recent years. Today, a person needs a good deal of skill and/or education to be a productive member of society.

Let's now look at the quantity and quality of our human resources. The quantity has been increasing because of population growth of about 1 percent a year. In 1940, there were about 132 million people in the United States. The population grew to nearly 181 million by 1960, to 228 million by 1980, and to about 261 million in 1995. This growth continues as we move through the 1990s.

Higher educational levels are an important change in the value of our human resources. In 1940, almost 28 percent of the population over 25 years of age had no more than an eighth grade education, but, now that percentage is well under 10 percent. Also in 1940, less than 5 percent of people 25 or older had finished college, and, now more than 21 percent of people 25 or older have done so. The number of high school and college graduates has risen steadily. The trend toward more education is illustrated by the bar chart in Figure 22-7.

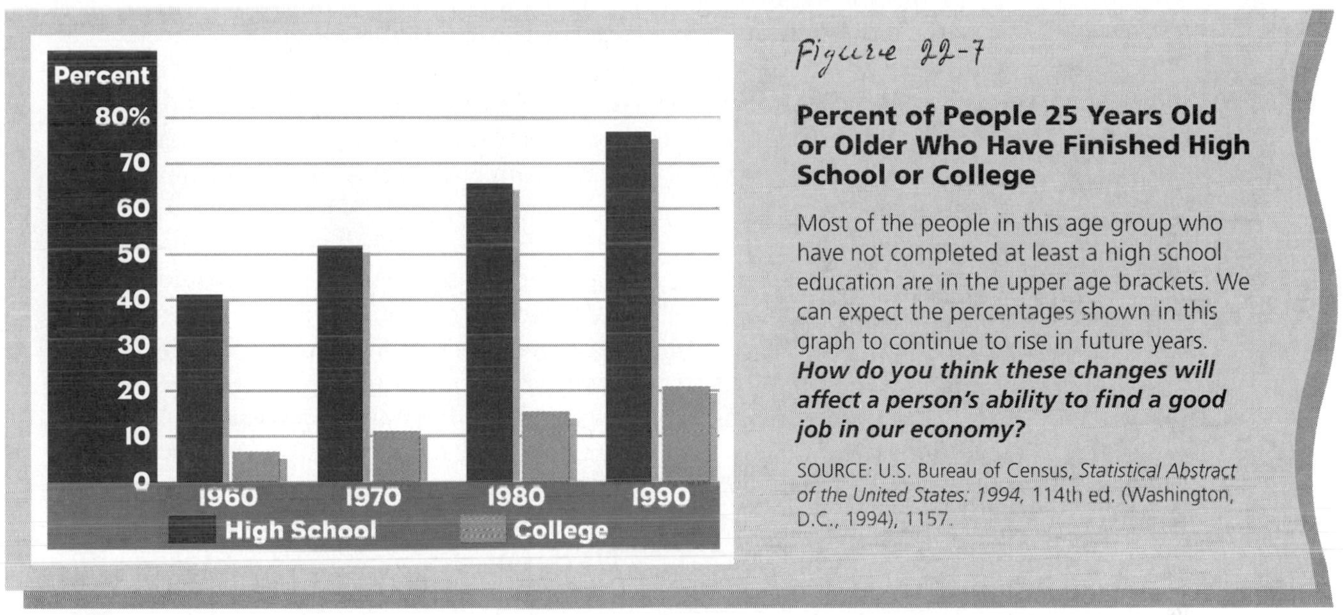

Percent of People 25 Years Old or Older Who Have Finished High School or College

Most of the people in this age group who have not completed at least a high school education are in the upper age brackets. We can expect the percentages shown in this graph to continue to rise in future years. ***How do you think these changes will affect a person's ability to find a good job in our economy?***

SOURCE: U.S. Bureau of Census, *Statistical Abstract of the United States: 1994,* 114th ed. (Washington, D.C., 1994), 1157.

Figure 22-7 shows that the quality of our human resources has been rising steadily. As people get more training and more education, they become better able to add to production. People who cannot read or write have less chance of becoming productive members of society. Unskilled workers also find few opportunities. The uneducated and/or unskilled members of our society are not high-quality resources in terms of economic productivity and growth. People with well-developed skills and more education have more ability to add to the country's economic growth. The trends graphed in Figure 22-7 show that the quality of our human resources is getting steadily better. This should help us to have continued economic growth.

Economic Spotlight

ST. JUNE OR THE IRON LADY?

Can a business leader be both caring and tough? June Rokoff, senior vice president of Lotus Development Corporation, seems to be able to be both with dignity and grace. Rokoff has earned the nickname "Iron Lady" because of her strong, decisive nature. A gifted motivator and manager, she also is known in her company as "St. June" because of her compassion for her coworkers and for rescuing the follow-up to Lotus's popular *1-2-3* program.

After six other managers had failed to produce *1-2-3* on time and without bugs, Rokoff volunteered to manage the development team. She took over just as morale was hitting rock bottom and many talented software developers were threatening to quit. Rokoff's calming effect helped build trust and commitment within the group. Several months later, the product was successfully released, and Rokoff had earned the undying respect of her team. However, Rokoff herself takes a humble view. "I still have so much I think I need to do," she says, "and I'm very hard on myself. I don't ever feel I'm done."

The oldest child in a middle-class Jewish-American family from Queens, New York, Rokoff was taught early that she could do whatever she set out to do. It's clear that Rokoff has passed this belief on to her coworkers at Lotus. After the first *1-2-3* release, Rokoff led her team to a much smoother release of *1-2-3 for Windows*. And, she's just getting started.

The key to Rokoff's continuing success seems to lie in listening to her employees and giving them what they need. After taking over her first project, Rokoff immediately set short-term goals for her team and met with programmers regularly to discuss complications. She also had their work area cleaned up and promised that meetings would never last more than an hour. Perhaps the most unusual but effective change she made was instituting a "guest chef night." Knowing that programmers are often forced to work all night, she began arranging a catered meal once a week. The programmers' steady diets of cold pizza and sandwiches were replaced with healthful, gourmet meals prepared by a different Lotus executive each week—including the CEO himself, Jim Manzi.

Rokoff also began rewarding the oft-ignored accomplishments of her employees with everything from small gifts to a full-page ad in the local newspaper. The result has been a renewed sense of camaraderie and accomplishment among team members. Judging from Rokoff's success as a leader, the "Iron Lady" and "St. June" may just be the perfect management team.

CAPITAL

In economic terms, ***capital*** means goods that are produced and can be used as inputs for further production. Each year, hundreds of billions of dollars are spent on capital in the United States. New machines, tractors, computers, factories, schools, and other forms of capital are put into use every year. As people have more capital to work with, they become more productive. A good stock of capital contributes to the mix of factors that add to a country's economic growth.

capital
goods that are produced and can be used as inputs for further production

Figure 22-8 shows the amount of money invested in new plant and equipment for representative years in five major sectors of our economy. In each year shown, there has been new capital put in place. In general, the figure shows an increase in spending on capital over time. This means that people have more and better machines to help them with their work.

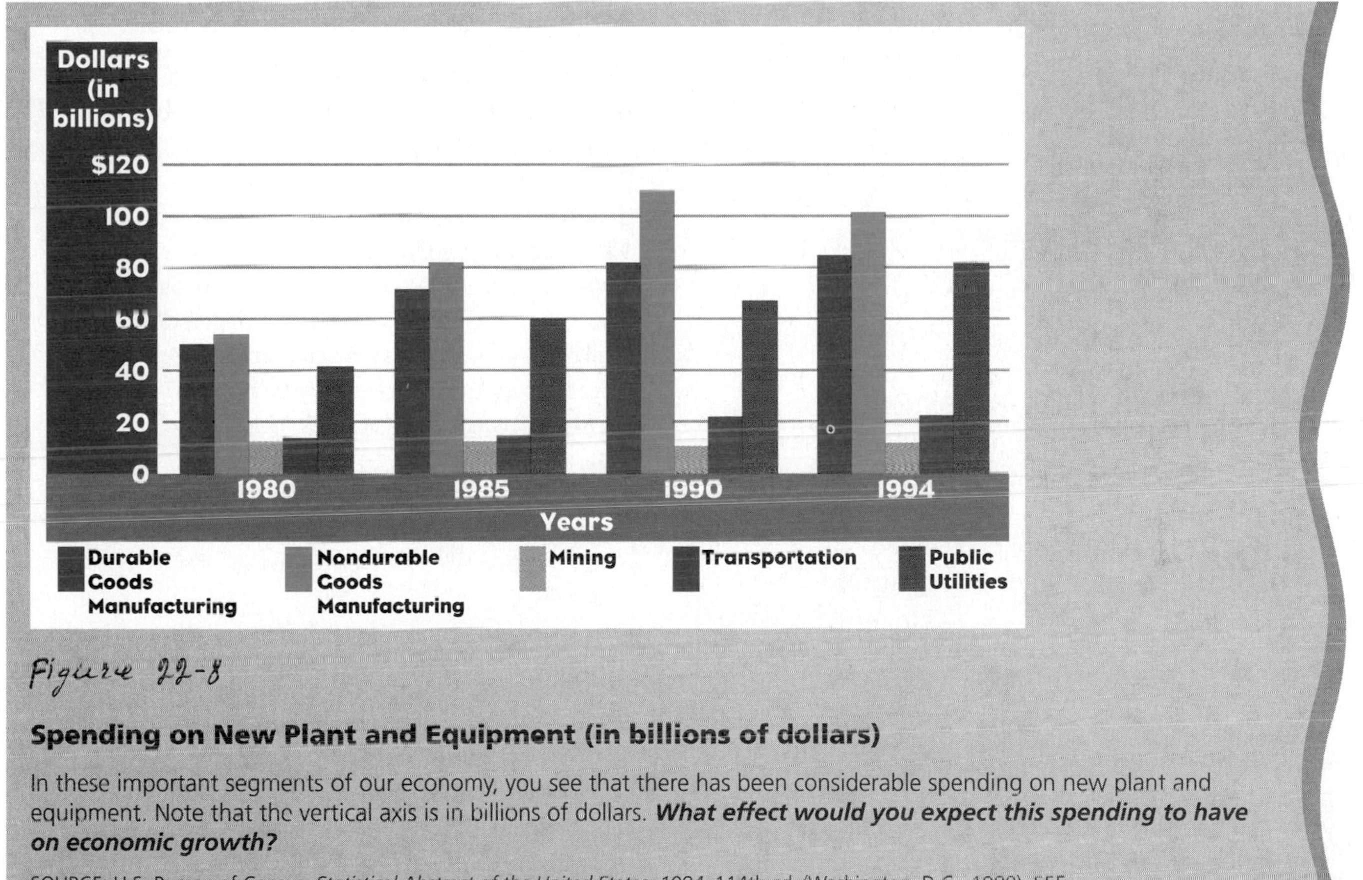

Spending on New Plant and Equipment (in billions of dollars)

In these important segments of our economy, you see that there has been considerable spending on new plant and equipment. Note that the vertical axis is in billions of dollars. ***What effect would you expect this spending to have on economic growth?***

SOURCE: U.S. Bureau of Census, *Statistical Abstract of the United States: 1994*, 114th ed (Washington, D.C., 1980), 555.

Continued investment in new capital equipment is important in order to keep a strong rate of economic growth. One measure of investment that is often looked at is the percentage of GDP that goes for investment goods each year. From 1960 to 1994, this investment was between 4 percent and 9 percent of GDP most of the time. A drop in the rate of investment means that lower productivity and lower economic growth may follow.

internet Connection

ECONOMIC PROGRESS AND THE INTERNET

Economic growth refers to the progress of the economy over the long term. It is the percentage increase in real GDP. Another measure of growth is the percentage increase in real GDP per capita (per person). GDP per capita is computed as GDP divided by the population. *The Statistical Abstract* at **http://www.census.gov/ftp/pub/statab/USAbrief/part2.txt** contains data on both real GDP and GDP per capita. Compute the percent change from one year to the next. The growth rate of GDP in 1993 is calculated as GDP at the end of 1992 minus GDP at the end of 1993, divided by GDP at the end of 1992.

The Statistical Abstract already mentioned lists data on the size of the labor force and labor productivity. How fast has the labor force grown over the last few years? How much has productivity increased?

Capital stock grows as a result of investment. Data on investment and GDP are available at **http://www.census.gov/ftp/pub/statab/indicator/gdp.txt**. To compute the investment share for the most recent year available, divide gross fixed domestic investment by GDP. Has the share been increasing or decreasing? What does that suggest about economic growth?

One way to measure technological improvement is by measuring spending on research and development. The National Science Foundation at **http://www.nsf.gov** publishes a variety of data on this topic.

Internet Application: Connect to **gopher://una.hh.lib.umich.edu/11/ebb/nipa/nipahist/cadata**. Using Table 102, line 1, compute the average annual growth rate of the U.S. economy since 1990. Compare the growth in the economy in the 1990s to the long-term average reported in this chapter. Connect to **http://www.census.gov/ftp/pub/population/estimate-extract/nation/intfile1-1.txt**. Find the U.S. population in 1990 and in the most recent year for which you have GDP data. Compute the average annual growth rate for GDP per capita since 1990.

Economics Application: *The Economic Report of the President* at **gopher://umslvma.umsl.edu:70/11/library/govdocs/erps** contains a great deal of information about U.S. economic growth and policies to stimulate growth. According to Chapter 1 of the 1994 ERP, what were the causes of the slowdown in economic growth during the early 1990s?

TECHNOLOGY

Technology is the body of knowledge that is used for the production of goods and services. People in the United States have become used to rapid technological change. We play complex computer games on high-quality monitors. We fly from place to place without thinking about what a wonder air travel really is. In the late 1960s, electronic calculators that could multiply, divide, add, subtract, and find a square root sold for more than $1,000. They weighed well over 30 pounds and were larger than a typewriter. Now, a calculator with even greater capabilities costs less than $20. It weighs but a few ounces and fits in a pocket or wallet. Technological advancement has influenced our economy greatly.

technology
the body of knowledge that is used for the production of goods and services

It is difficult to measure exactly how much of the rise in our standard of living is due to technological advances. But, technology probably has contributed a great deal. Many new and improved products are the results of technological advances. These advances grow out of research and development, which takes place in many fields all over the country. ***Research and development*** refers to the activities undertaken to find new and more efficient methods of production. Research and development often is called *R&D*.

research and development
the activities undertaken to find new and more efficient methods of production

Chemists, biologists, home economists, geologists, agricultural economists, and researchers in many other areas add to our technological base. Researchers contribute as much to our economy as workers in other fields. Their contribution is not obvious, however, because not all research results in technological application. Even for successful research, the actual applications may take years to be put to use in products we buy. Also, much research aims to improve present ways of making a product, to keep costs from rising as fast as they might otherwise. Consumers of the products usually are not aware of valuable research such as this.

Research and development spending results in most of the technological advances that are important in our daily lives. This spending leads to better products and methods of production. So, research and development greatly add to the economic growth of the country. Much of our research and development spending is supported by the federal government. In recent years, about one-half of all R&D spending has been government supported.

Research and development spending as a percentage of gross domestic product was relatively high in the 1960s but fell some in the 1970s. However, it rebounded in the 1980s and has held fairly steady in the 1990s. Research and development spending today is likely to lead to higher productivity and growth in the future.

Research and development, along with technological change, create change in our society. Change can be threatening to some people who might prefer the comfort of having things stay as they are. In our personal roles in the economy, change may make our particular jobs obsolete and they may be eliminated. This means that we should develop flexible skills and an attitude of flexibility about our work. The days when a person had one job for life are gone. Most people will make many job changes during their working years. This may involve periodic retraining to adapt to the changing economic environment.

Checkpoint

Content Check

1. Is it the quantity or the quality of natural resources that is important to economic growth?
2. Why is it important to invest in new plant and equipment?
3. Give two examples of ways in which changes in technology may have increased productivity in education.

What Do You Think Now?

Reread *What Do You Think?* in the Section Two Focus. Then answer the following question:

4. How do your personal decisions influence economic growth?

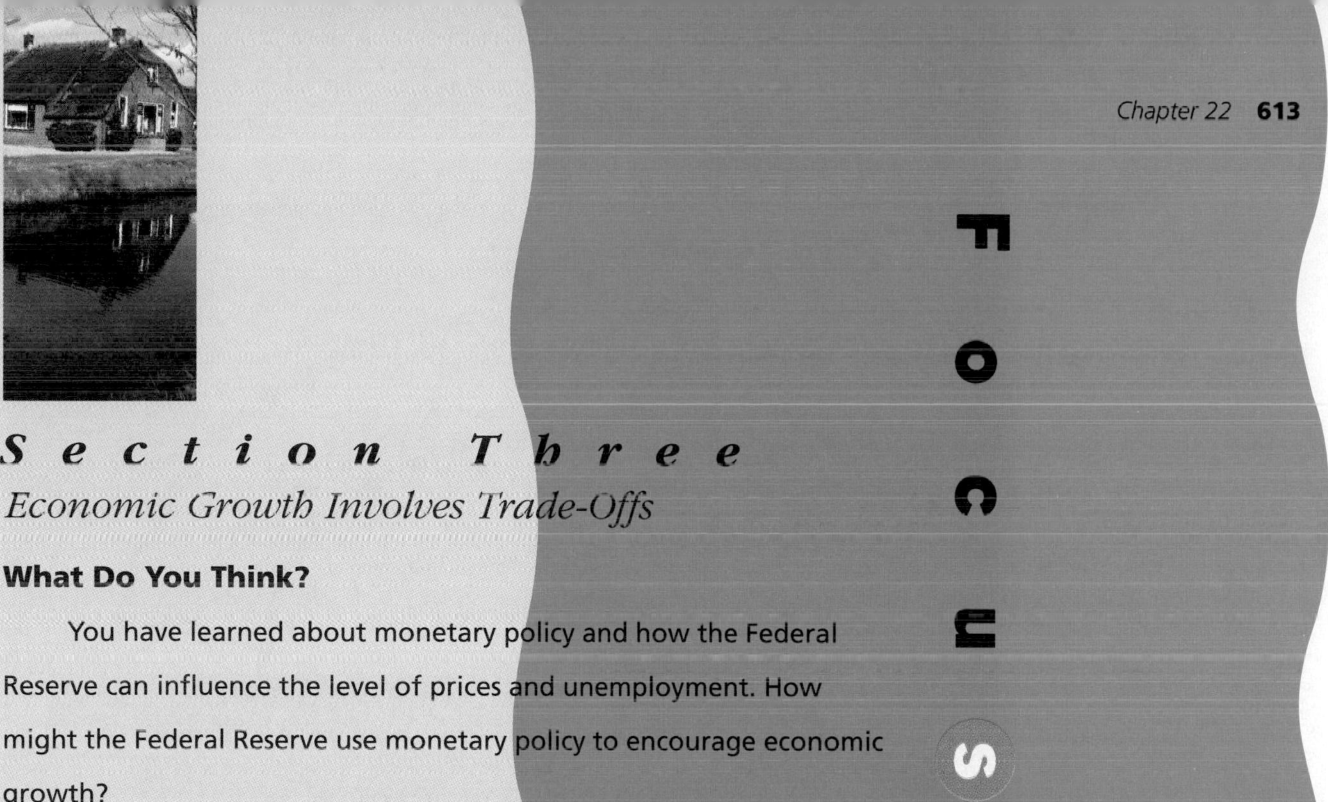

Section Three

Economic Growth Involves Trade-Offs

What Do You Think?

You have learned about monetary policy and how the Federal Reserve can influence the level of prices and unemployment. How might the Federal Reserve use monetary policy to encourage economic growth?

What's Ahead?

Economic growth may involve a cost in terms of current consumption and may not always progress as fast as some might hope. Economic growth may not even be desirable in the eyes of some. A smaller economy may be better than a bigger one if economic growth is accompanied by too much environmental damage, too much inflation, or other negative consequences. In this section, you will learn about some of the trade-offs involved in economic growth and about the government's role in promoting and controlling economic growth.

Term to Know

work ethic

TRADE-OFFS BETWEEN THE PRESENT AND FUTURE

In some ways, the goal of having continued economic growth conflicts with our desire for present consumption. Looking at a production possibilities curve helps to explain this relationship. The production possibilities curves in Figure 22-9 on page 614 show the trade-off between making products for current consumption and making capital goods. Making more capital goods will help to make the economy more productive in future years. But, making more consumer goods gives us more products now, for current consumption.

Suppose that the lower curve, labeled Curve *1*, shows the immediate trade-off between consumer and capital goods. If we decided to make the combination of goods represented by Point *A*, we would have many products for present consumption. But, by choosing this bundle of goods, we

Figure 22-9

Production Possibilities Curves for Consumer Goods and Capital Goods

As we produce more capital goods, fewer goods can be made for present consumption and vice versa. Economic growth, represented by the shift from Curve *1* to Curve *2*, relies on having a good stock of capital goods. ***What would be the cost to society of moving from Point A to Point C? What would be a benefit?***

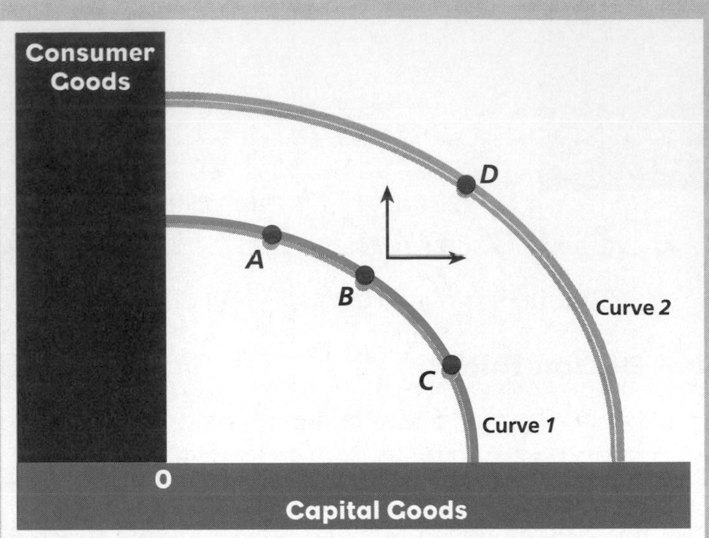

would make relatively few capital goods. This might mean that we would have fairly slow, or even zero, economic growth.

We could use more of our productive resources to make capital goods by moving from *A* to either *B* or *C*. Such a move would mean we would give up some consumer goods now. But, it also would mean we would be likely to have more economic growth and more goods to consume in the future.

The production possibilities curve labeled Curve *2* in Figure 22-9 represents economic growth compared to Curve *1*. An outward shift of the production possibilities curve would mean that the economy had a greater ability to produce goods and services. The point marked *D* shows a bundle of items that could not be produced given the production possibilities shown by Curve *1*. There is no point on Curve *1* that represents as many consumer goods and capital goods as Point *D*. But, with economic growth, this bundle could be produced in the future.

The amount of economic growth the economy has is shown by the distance between the two curves. If we made all consumer goods now but made no capital goods, the economy would not grow very much; output might even fall. Only by making some capital goods can we have continued growth. Of the points labeled *A*, *B*, and *C* in Figure 22-9, *C* would lead to the most growth. But, we would not want to make so many capital goods that we didn't have enough consumer goods to consume right now. This trade-off must be balanced in order to have the best allocation of resources for a prosperous present and a bright future.

SOCIAL ATTITUDES AND ECONOMIC GROWTH

work ethic
the belief that people should work hard and pull their own weight in economic life

Social attitudes in the United States generally favor economic growth. First, and perhaps most important, we have a strong work ethic. A ***work ethic*** is the belief that people should work hard and pull their own weight in economic life. If people expected a *free ride* or *to get something for nothing,* our economy would be much weaker. We also would have a lower rate of growth. A positive work ethic means that people want to be productive and contribute to the economy. Hard work pays off individually and for society. Also, people in the United States seem to think highly of successful business executives, inventors, and innovators. Their successes lead to a better standard of living for all of us.

Not everyone thinks we should seek economic growth. Some people think that economic growth will cause us to run out of natural resources more quickly than we would otherwise. Some also think that blind acceptance of the goal of economic growth has caused us to pollute our environment unnecessarily. It is difficult to either reject or support these arguments. The logic of economic thinking should help you reach your own decisions.

Econ & You

REEDUCATE TO RELOCATE?

There once was a time when it was a relatively rare occurrence for people to move far from the area in which they grew up. Now, it is fairly common. There are a lot of reasons a person may choose to move to another part of the country or the world. One reason is work related. You may find that jobs are scarce in your home area but plentiful elsewhere. Economic growth does not occur evenly across all geographic areas, and workers may have to move to where new jobs develop.

No matter what type of job you start out with, it is likely that you will change careers several times during your work life. Some people say that young people entering today's labor market will change careers four or more times. And, they mean change *careers* not just change jobs within one line of employment. Often, this means that a person has to get additional education and training as the years pass. It is now more true than ever that education is an ongoing part of life. It does not end when you leave the formal educational environment.

GOVERNMENT ENCOURAGEMENT OF ECONOMIC GROWTH

Economic growth is one of the goals that was mentioned in the Employment Act of 1946. The government tries to form policies that stimulate activities that promote economic growth. Such activities might include a variety of fiscal policies such as increasing federal spending for research and development, capital equipment, educating more people, and/or programs designed to help people use natural resources more efficiently. On the tax side, the implementation of tax incentives to increase investment and/or personal saving would promote economic growth.

Monetary policies also may influence economic growth. In general, monetary policies that lower interest rates promote economic growth. These are described as loose monetary policies. On the other hand, tight monetary policies slow economic growth.

The fiscal and monetary policies that promote economic growth tend to reduce unemployment. This is good. However, these policies also may contribute to inflation. Thus, there is another trade-off involved in promoting economic growth. We must guard against bringing on high inflation as we seek to promote economic growth.

Economic Dilemma

IMPROVED TECHNOLOGY MAY IMPROVE THE ENVIRONMENT

Most people prefer more economic growth to less. Growth means more opportunities for personal advancement, lower unemployment, and higher standards of living. These positive outcomes are partly responsible for government programs that support economic growth. Examples of governmental actions that promote economic growth at the national level include tax reductions for capital investment (often called *investment tax credits*), sponsorship of research and development programs, and support for education.

While economic growth is in many ways good for society, there may be negative consequences for the environment. As we produce more, we may at the same time generate more pollution as well. New technologies may offer alternative production methods that could allow production to grow without added environmental damage. But, often, such methods lower output per labor hour, driving up product prices.

As a country, we need to balance our desire for more goods and services with our desire for a clean environment. Both contribute to our overall satisfaction.

Since our economy is mainly a free enterprise system, most of the decision making that influences the rate of economic growth happens within the private sector. Many of your personal decisions may influence growth. You, and others like you, decide how much education or training to get, how much money to save, and how to spend your money. These decisions can affect the rate of growth of the economy.

Checkpoint

Content Check

1. If all of society's productive resources were used to produce goods for current consumption, what would happen to the rate of economic growth in the long run?

2. How does a positive work ethic relate to economic growth?

3. Can fiscal policy influence economic growth?

What Do You Think Now?

Reread *What Do You Think?* in the Section Three Focus. Then answer the following question:

4. How can the government use monetary policy to influence economic growth?

Concepts in Brief

1. The rate of change in real GDP is usually used as the measure of the rate of economic growth. Real GDP is used so that price changes do not cloud the view of what is really happening in the economy. Growth in real GDP per person gives an even better feel for how our economic well-being is changing.
2. A small change in the rate of growth can be important. Over a number of years, a small difference in the growth rate can become magnified into a big difference in our economic well-being.
3. Real GDP grew at an average yearly rate of about 2.9 percent between 1929 and 1994. Real GDP per person grew a bit more slowly, averaging about 1.7 percent during the 1929 to 1994 period.
4. A country with many high-quality natural resources can be expected to have better growth than a country with few natural resources or resources of a lower quality. The amount and quality of labor have a good deal of influence on economic growth. A well-educated and well-trained labor force is one of the real strengths of our economy. Capital equipment has been an important factor in economic growth in the United States. Technological improvements contribute to economic growth in the United States. Money spent for research and development programs helps to strengthen our technological base.
5. There is a trade-off between economic growth and current consumption. If we do not save, we have the ability to buy more today, but that may mean having less in the future. Investment in capital increases future economic growth; but, to invest in capital, we must give up some current consumption. The government can influence economic growth through fiscal and monetary policies.

Economic Foundations

1. Why is real GDP a better measure of economic growth than current dollar GDP?
2. If a country's GDP has increased 70 percent and its prices have increased 80 percent, how has real GDP changed?
3. If a country's GDP and prices have both increased 25 percent, how has real GDP changed?
4. If a country's GDP has increased 40 percent and prices have increased 20 percent, how has real GDP changed?

5. What was the average increase in our country's real GDP during the period between 1929 and 1994?
6. During what periods since 1929 did our country's real GDP suffer a large decrease?
7. Name the four factors discussed in the text that contribute to economic growth.
8. A large amount of natural resources can promote economic growth if the resources are of good quality. How does this statement apply to human resources?
9. If more capital goods than consumer goods are produced, what is the likely effect on economic growth? What is the effect on consumers?
10. Name three ways in which the government encourages economic growth.

Your Economic Vocabulary

Build your economic vocabulary by matching the following terms with their definitions.

1. the activities undertaken to find new and more efficient methods of production
2. the belief that people should work hard and pull their own weight in economic life
3. goods that are produced and can be used as inputs for further production
4. the real value of the total output of goods and services divided by the number of people in the economy
5. the people who work or may be able to work
6. the change in the level of economic activity from one year to another
7. the percentage change in the level of economic activity from one year to the next
8. a severe and prolonged decline in the level of economic activity
9. the value of gross domestic product after taking out the effect of price changes
10. the body of knowledge that is used for the production of goods and services
11. the total raw materials supplied by nature

capital
depression
economic growth
human resources
natural resources
rate of growth
real GDP
real GDP per person
research and development
technology
work ethic

Thinking Critically About Economics

1. Would using real GDP per person instead of total real GDP make any difference in our rate of economic growth? Why or why not?
2. Write a paragraph in which you explain how the educational level of the adult population of the United States has been changing. How will these trends affect our economic growth?
3. Is there any relationship between technological advance and the educational level of a country? Is a higher average educational level likely to lead to more technological advances?
4. Choose some type of production, such as farming, steel manufacturing, or education. Determine how the use of capital has changed in that field during this century. You will need to do research in your school library to answer this question. You also might talk with someone who works in the kind of production you chose.
5. Using a production possibilities curve, explain what is meant by the trade-off between current consumption and economic growth. How does the level of savings in the economy relate to your answer?
6. Is economic growth a good objective for the U.S. economy? Why or why not? List some reasons growth is desirable. List some reasons we might want to limit the rate of economic growth.

Economic Enrichment

A U.S. Senator once said, "To get rid of unemployment and poverty we need government policies that will guide the economy to a yearly growth rate of 6.5 percent." Based on our history of economic growth as described in this chapter, do you think we can achieve this rate of economic growth? Explain your answer.

Math and Economics

Using the information in the following table, analyze the economic growth in the countries of Trent, Rudan, and Alcore.

	Trent		Rudan		Alcore	
	1986	1996	1986	1996	1986	1996
GDP (in millions of dollars)	$1,000	$1,350	$1,000	$1,600	$1,000	$1,800
Price Index	1.00	1.70	1.00	1.60	1.00	1.50

How would your analysis change if you knew that Trent and Rudan had no increase in population from 1986 to 1996, but that Alcore's population increased by 40 percent?

Writing About Economics

The percent of GDP that comes from the goods-producing sectors of the U.S. economy has been declining from about 40 percent to about 20 percent in the last half of the twentieth century. Meanwhile, the percent originating in the service sectors has been rising. There appear to be more opportunities for technological advances that increase productivity in the manufacture of goods than there are in providing services. Write a story in which you follow the career of a new high school graduate in to the twenty-first century. Include appropriate background information on the trend of overall rate of growth in real GDP for the United States and how that affects your character's career options.

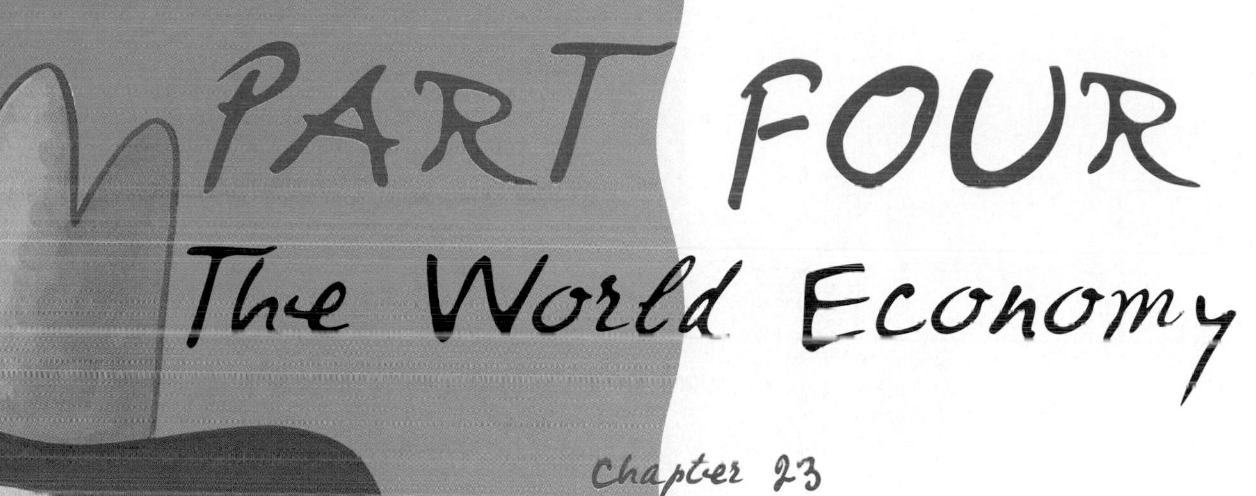

PART FOUR
The World Economy

Chapter 23
The Global Marketplace

Chapter 24
Economic Development:
A Global Economic Issue

Overview

Section One
Trading Among Countries

Section Two
Is Free Trade Always the Answer?

Section Three
Some Financial Aspects of International Trade

The Global Marketplace

Learning Objectives

23-1
List the major imports and exports of the United States.

23-2
Explain why countries trade with each other.

23-3
Present reasons for restricting world trade.

23-4
Present reasons for encouraging world trade.

23-5
Describe several examples of international trade cooperation.

23-6
Compare three different systems for valuing one country's money in relation to another country's money.

FOCUS

Section One
Trading Among Countries

What Do You Think?

You are the trade minister for Shaba, a country that produces personal computers and in-line skates. Your analysis shows that your country can produce one personal computer at a cost of $1,800 and one pair of in-line skates at a cost of $65. Ari, your largest trading partner, produces personal computers at a cost of $2,000 and in-line skates at a cost of $80. The products are of equal quality in both countries. Since Shaba can produce both products at a lower cost, do you think there is any reason to trade with Ari for these products?

Terms to Know

exports

imports

European Community (EC)

comparative advantage

absolute advantage

What's Ahead?

International trade between countries has become so common that we accept it as a natural part of our economic landscape. Hardly a day goes by that there is not mention of some aspect of international trade in the news. In this section, you will learn about the exports and imports of the United States and about why countries find it advantageous to trade with other countries.

U.S. EXPORTS AND IMPORTS

exports
goods and services that one country sells to another country

imports
goods and services that one country buys from another country

International trade consists of exports and imports. ***Exports*** are goods and services that one country sells to another country. ***Imports*** are goods and services that one country buys from another country. Exports go out of a country. Imports come into a country.

Exports account for about 10 percent of the GDP of the United States. In some countries, exports are an even larger percent of GDP. So, many people's jobs and incomes depend on world trade.

To see which U.S. jobs may be most sensitive to world trade, let's first look at what we export to other countries. In Figure 23-1, you can see that the high-technology electrical, scientific, and telecommunications industries are

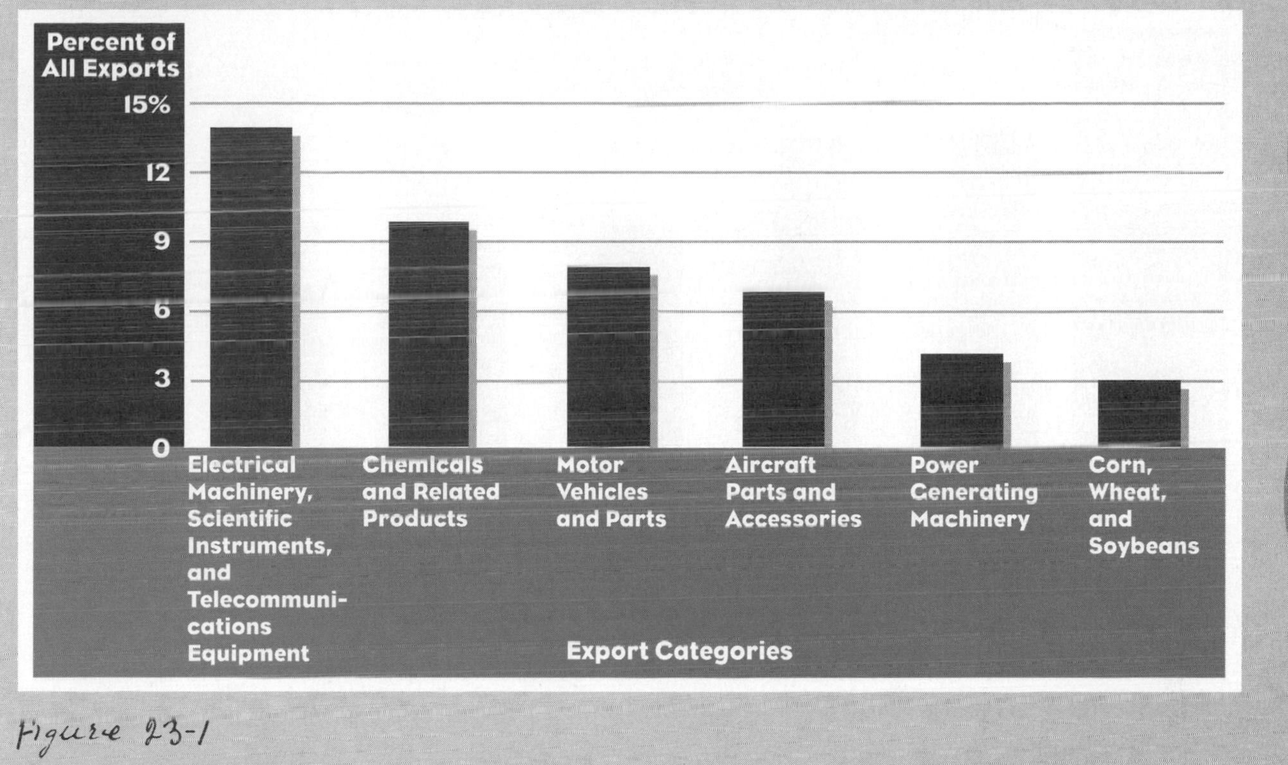

Figure 23-1

Some Major Exports of the United States

High-technology items are important exports of the United States. We also export many agricultural products, especially grains. ***If total exports were $464,767 million, about how many millions of dollars of chemicals and related products were exported?***

SOURCE: U.S. Bureau of the Census, *Statistical Abstract of the United States: 1994,* 114th ed. (Washington D.C., 1994), 827–828.

big exporters. The chemical and automotive sectors also export quite a lot. It probably is not surprising that we export a lot of high technology items and a lot of chemical products. These are areas in which the United States always has been a world leader. It is probably more of a surprise to see the high percentage of motor vehicles and parts we export. However, most of our exports in this category are auto parts rather than new cars. You also can see that corn, wheat, and soybeans are important exports. Many U.S. workers are employed making these products that are sold to other countries.

About half of our exports go to Canada, Japan, and countries in the European Community. The ***European Community (EC)*** is a group of European countries that have joined together and agreed on ways to improve trade among themselves.

European Community (EC) a group of European countries that have joined together and agreed on ways to improve trade among themselves

Imports also affect jobs for U.S. workers. The bar chart in Figure 23-2 on page 628 shows some of the products that we import from other

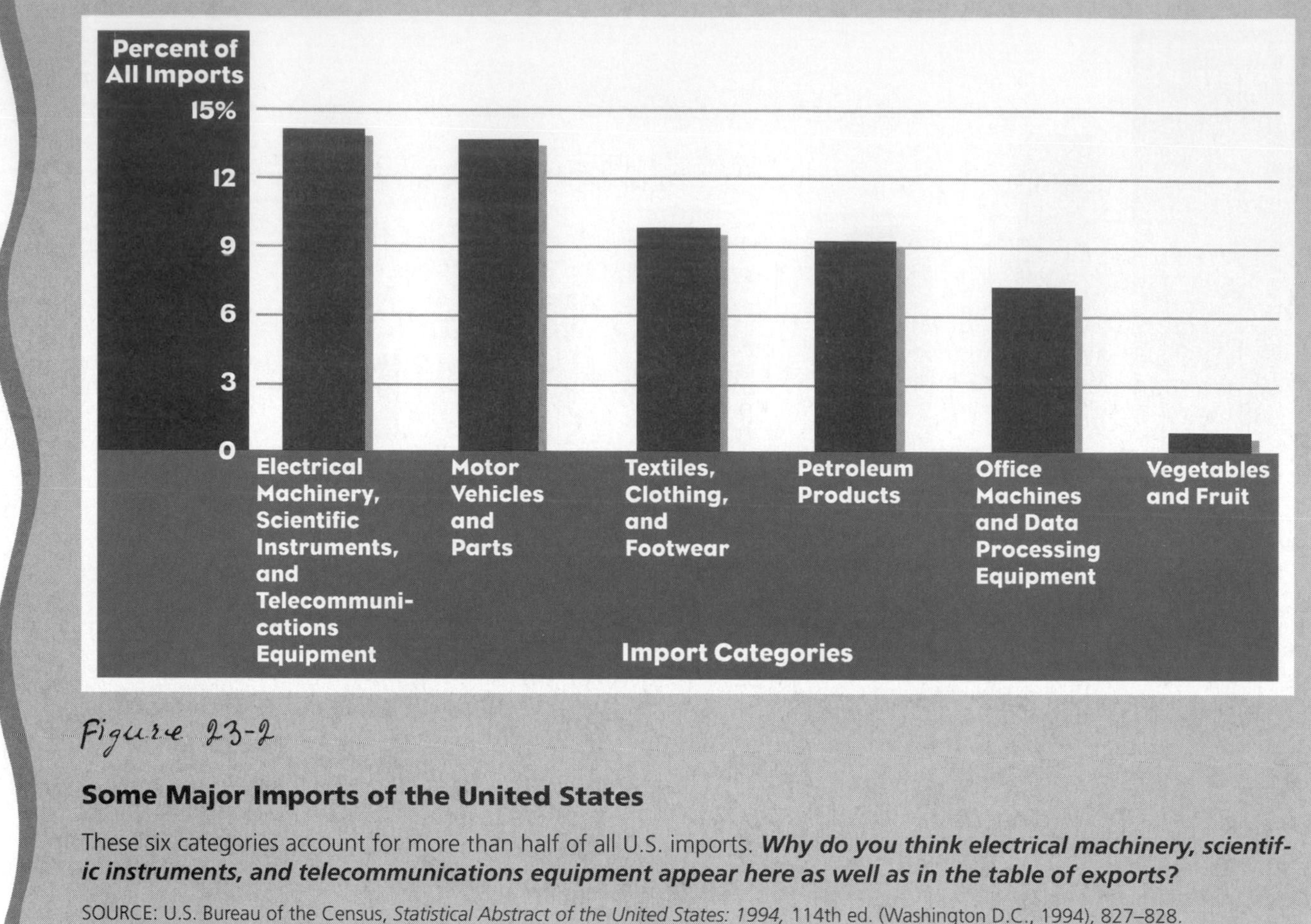

Figure 23-2

Some Major Imports of the United States

These six categories account for more than half of all U.S. imports. ***Why do you think electrical machinery, scientific instruments, and telecommunications equipment appear here as well as in the table of exports?***

SOURCE: U.S. Bureau of the Census, *Statistical Abstract of the United States: 1994,* 114th ed. (Washington D.C., 1994), 827–828.

countries. Electrical machinery, scientific instruments, and telecommunications equipment, as well as automobiles and parts, are the most significant of our total imports.

REASONS FOR INTERNATIONAL TRADE

Nations trade with each other because they can make some goods more efficiently than other goods. They use the money from the goods they can make most efficiently to buy those goods they cannot make as efficiently.

Comparative Advantage and Absolute Advantage

comparative advantage the principle that a country benefits from specializing in the production at which it is relatively most efficient

Trade makes nations economically better off. David Ricardo, an English economist, explained the reasons for international trade in 1817 by using the law of comparative advantage. The law of ***comparative advantage*** is the principle that a country benefits from specializing in the production at which it is relatively most efficient. This law holds true, even if one country is more efficient than other countries in all kinds of production. The law of comparative advantage explains why a country that can make everything at a lower cost than any other country still benefits from trade. This law shows that such a country should concentrate on making the goods for which its cost advantage is highest.

Economic Spotlight

DOMINO'S DELIVERS . . . TO JAPAN?

Is sushi a fair trade for pizza? Due to increased international trade and to entrepreneurs like Ernest M. Higa, Americans have increased their appetites for foreign food, and people in other countries have changed their eating habits to include some typical American fare, too. Originally intending to work in the family business back in Japan after graduating from The Wharton School and Columbia Business School, Higa returned home to find his three older siblings in charge of his family's business. So, Higa set out on his own.

After starting his own business importing lumber and neurosurgical medical devices from North America and adapting them for the Japanese market, Higa read about the fast-growing U.S. company Domino's Pizza. He knew immediately that he wanted to become a master franchisee, which involved setting up company units in a specific area. Higa already had adapted American products for the Japanese market, so he figured he could do it with pizza. He knew that there were more and more working couples in Japan who craved the convenience of fast food—and Higa wanted that fast food to be Domino's.

He was excited about the company's young, dynamic corporate culture. However, Domino's was skeptical. Other pizza chains had failed to crack the Japanese market due to the Japanese people's distaste for finger food. But, Higa knew that he could cross the cultural barrier between American food and the Japanese culture. He was convinced that his formula would sell in Japan and his "enthusiasm and passion for Domino's Pizza convinced them [Domino's]." He knew that "in Japan, one eats with one's eyes." So, he meticulously mapped out the placement of each pizza topping, made special perforations in the boxes to ensure perfectly uniform slices, and added local toppings such as squid and tuna. He also added other fare to the menu, including chicken and salads. Higa opened the first Domino's in 1985 in central Tokyo. Today, Higa Industries owns more than 100 Domino's in Japan with more than $140 million in sales annually.

Higa believes that, in addition to knowing how to match a product to a culture, the secret to his continuing success is motivating employees and maintaining high standards worthy of demanding consumers. After successfully growing Domino's in Japan, Higa has turned to Hawaii. There, too, he has become a master franchisee, taking over 18 company stores and four franchises with revenues in excess of $12 million. Just as he did in Japan, Higa is localizing and "Hawaiianizing" his Domino's stores. So, move over poi, here comes pizza!

To understand Ricardo's law of comparative advantage, assume there are only two countries in the world: Germany and England. Also, assume that there are only two products: steel and cloth. Suppose that Germany can make both steel and cloth more cheaply than England. Germany can make one unit of steel using 80 labor hours, while England can make one unit of steel using 120 labor hours. Germany can make one unit of cloth using 90 labor hours, while England can make one unit of cloth using 100 labor hours. Think of a unit of steel as one ton of steel and a unit of cloth as 50 yards of cloth. Figure 23-3 summarizes the production costs.

You can see from Figure 23-3 that Germany has an absolute cost advantage in making both goods. An ***absolute advantage*** exists in the production of a good when one country can produce that good more efficiently than another country. In our present example, Germany can make both goods using fewer labor hours than England. So, Germany has lower costs for a unit of steel and for a unit of cloth.

absolute advantage
when one country can produce a good more efficiently than another country

Figure 23-3

Production Costs of Steel and Cloth in Terms of Labor Hours

In this example, you can see that Germany can produce both steel and cloth at a lower cost (fewer labor hours) than England. ***For which product does Germany have the greatest advantage in production?***

	Germany	England
One Unit of Steel (1 ton)	80 Hours	120 Hours
One Unit of Cloth (50 yards)	90 Hours	100 Hours

Opportunity Costs of Making Cloth

Now let's look at the opportunity cost of making cloth. That is, what amount of steel must be given up when labor is used to make cloth rather than steel? As you read the next four paragraphs, refer to Figure 23-3 often. Make sure that you see how the numbers in this table relate to the numbers used in these paragraphs.

If you decide to use 90 labor hours to make one unit of cloth in Germany, you will not have those 90 hours to make steel. Since it takes 80 labor hours to make one unit of steel, those 90 labor hours could have made 9/8 (90/80) units of steel. So, Germany will have to give up 9/8 or 1.125 units of steel to make one added unit of cloth.

Now, if you decide to use 100 labor hours to make one unit of cloth in England, you cannot use those 100 hours to make steel. Since it takes 120 labor hours to make one unit of steel, those 100 labor hours could have made 5/6 (100/120) of a unit of steel. So, England will have to give up only 5/6 or 0.83 of a unit of steel to make one added unit of cloth.

The opportunity costs of making cloth are now a little more clear. To make an added unit of cloth, Germany has to give up 1.125 units of steel. But, England has to give up only 0.83 of a unit of steel. England gives up less steel to produce an additional unit of cloth. Therefore, England has a comparative advantage in making cloth. This is true even though Germany has an absolute advantage in making cloth.

Econ & You

TEENS LEAD THE WAY

There is some evidence that teens around the world are becoming much more homogeneous than they were 20 years ago. A New York advertising agency did an interesting bit of research in this regard. It videotaped the bedrooms of teenagers in 25 countries and concluded that "It's hard to tell whether the rooms are in Los Angeles, Mexico City, or Tokyo."

There appear to be two main reasons for the convergence of tastes and preferences of the world's teens, which has been made possible by the globalization of communications, especially television. Probably the most important contributing factor is music. MTV reaches millions of teens around the globe. Mexico, Brazil, and Argentina have 57 million teenagers. Japan, Korea, Singapore, and Vietnam have 42 million. Then, there is the rest of the world. As a result, the ads of Reebok, Coke, Pepsi, Levi's and Diesel jeans, Nike, and others reach around the globe, often dubbed into native languages. The second reason for convergence is sports, especially basketball and soccer. Games are broadcast internationally, and the message of sponsors reaches out to all who have access to the airwaves.

Opportunity Costs of Making Steel

Now, think about the opportunity cost of making steel. This is the cost of a unit of steel in terms of the amount of cloth that must be given up. Suppose you decide to make one more unit of steel. In Germany, you must give up 80 labor hours of cloth production to make one more unit of steel. Those 80 hours could have produced 8/9 (80/90) or 0.89 of a unit of cloth. So, to make one more unit of steel in Germany, you must give up 0.89 of a unit of cloth.

In England, you must take 120 labor hours away from cloth production in order to make one more unit of steel. Those 120 hours could have made 6/5 (120/100) or 1.2 units of cloth. So, in England you have to give up 1.2 units of cloth to make one unit of steel.

This analysis helps you to see the opportunity costs of making steel. In Germany, you only have to give up 0.89 of a unit of cloth to make an added unit of steel. In England, you have to give up 1.2 units of cloth. Since Germany has to give up less cloth to produce an added unit of steel, Germany has a comparative advantage in steel production. Figure 23-4 summarizes the opportunity costs of producing cloth and steel in Germany and England.

Figure 23-4

Opportunity Costs of Producing an Added Unit of Cloth and Steel

This table helps you see that England has a comparative advantage in the production of cloth. England has to give up less steel per unit of cloth (0.83 of a unit of steel per unit of cloth) than Germany does (1.125 units of steel per unit of cloth). ***Why does Germany have a comparative advantage in producing steel?***

	Cloth	Steel
England	0.83 of a Unit of Steel	1.2 Units of Cloth
Germany	1.125 Units of Steel	0.89 of a Unit of Cloth

Comparative Advantage Leads to International Trade

The law of comparative advantage shows that both countries could gain if they specialized in making the good for which they have the comparative advantage. England would be willing to trade cloth for steel if it could get more than 0.83 of a unit of steel for each of its units of cloth. Germany would be willing to trade steel for cloth if it could get more than 0.89 of a unit of cloth for a unit of steel.

If Germany and England agree to trade one unit of steel for one unit of cloth, both countries will be ahead. The one unit of cloth England trades gains a whole unit of steel from Germany. If England had tried to produce the steel itself, it would have had to give up 1.2 units of cloth. By trading, it has to give up only one unit of cloth. If Germany had tried to produce the one unit of cloth itself, it would have had to give up 1.125 units of steel. By trading, it loses only one unit of the steel. Both countries gain by trading. Nations trade because of this mutual benefit.

Checkpoint

Content Check

1. Explain the difference between the terms *exports* and *imports*.
2. Can a nation without an absolute advantage still have a comparative advantage? Why or why not?
3. How does the law of comparative advantage explain international trade?

What Do You Think Now?

Reread *What Do You Think?* in the Section One Focus. Then answer the following questions:

4. Which country has an absolute advantage in producing personal computers? in-line skates?
5. Which country has a comparative advantage in producing personal computers? in-line skates?

FOCUS

Section Two
Is Free Trade Always the Answer?

What Do You Think?

A company in California makes a critical component for a radar system used to identify air traffic that approaches the United States. Senator Bussman, from Oregon, has learned that this component can be purchased from a new factory in China at a lower cost than it can be produced in the United States. Senator Bussman wants the Department of Defense to start buying the product from the Chinese firm. Do you agree with Senator Bussman?

Terms to Know

tariff

quota

protectionism

General Agreement on Tariffs and Trade (GATT)

North American Free Trade Agreement (NAFTA)

What's Ahead?

Throughout your study of economics, you have seen the advantages of free competition. You also learned that sometimes laws are passed against restraint of trade. Why, then, would any country want to restrict international trade? In this section, you will learn about some reasons it may sometimes make sense to limit free trade between countries. You also will learn more about why free trade is favored by many economists.

PROS AND CONS OF FREE TRADE

You have seen that international trade accounts for about 10 percent of our GDP. Yet, some people would like to limit free trade. What are the reasons for limiting free trade? What are the reasons for promoting free trade? Let's take a look.

Limiting Free Trade

Two common barriers that are used to restrict trade are tariffs and quotas. A ***tariff*** is a tax on imports. A tariff makes imports more expensive for consumers to buy. This happens because producers must charge higher prices to cover

tariff
a tax on imports

the additional cost of the tariff. A ***quota*** is a limit on the amount of imports or exports. Quotas make it illegal to import or export more than a certain amount.

quota
a limit on the amount of imports or exports

protectionism
the idea that we should limit international trade to protect our own self-interest

Protectionism refers to the idea that we should limit international trade to protect our own self-interest. One of the reasons often stated for restricting international trade is the *national security argument*. This states that some goods are so vital to our national defense and security that we should not depend solely on other countries for them. Steel and aluminum may be such goods. The argument is that if too much is imported, our own producers will eventually go out of business. Then, in the event of war, we might not be able to import enough to defend ourselves. We might even be at war with the country upon whose imports we depend. The argument holds that tariffs and quotas should be used to protect defense-related industries. Then, these industries will remain strong.

The *infant industry argument* states that an industry in its infant or beginning stages may not be able to compete against better organized and more mature foreign industries. Therefore, tariffs or quotas should be used to protect the young industry.

The *diversified economy argument* also is used to justify tariffs and quotas. This argument suggests that it isn't safe to put all your eggs in one basket. If you rely on just one import source for a particular good, what happens if that source is cut off? This argument holds that domestic producers should be able to supply every kind of good. In other words, an economy should be fully diversified.

Labor leaders frequently use the *protection of domestic wages argument* to justify tariffs and quotas. They favor using tariffs and quotas so that domestic workers do not have to compete with workers who earn lower rates in some countries. They believe that importing goods produced using foreign labor will hurt domestic workers' wages. They also believe that imports can cause unemployment in the domestic labor force.

Promoting Free Trade

Most economists take a stand against the use of tariffs and quotas. First, they point out that tariffs and quotas hurt consumers by causing a rise in prices of goods. A tariff raises the costs for foreign businesses trying to sell products in the United States. When costs rise, businesses supply a smaller amount of goods at each price than they did before the tariff. This is because the tariff has the effect of shifting the supply curve up to the left. This is shown in Figure 23-5. If the demand remains constant, the equilibrium price of the good will rise from P_1 to P_2. Also, the equilibrium quantity will fall from Q_1 to Q_2. Quotas have a similar effect in that they decrease supply, resulting in an increase in price.

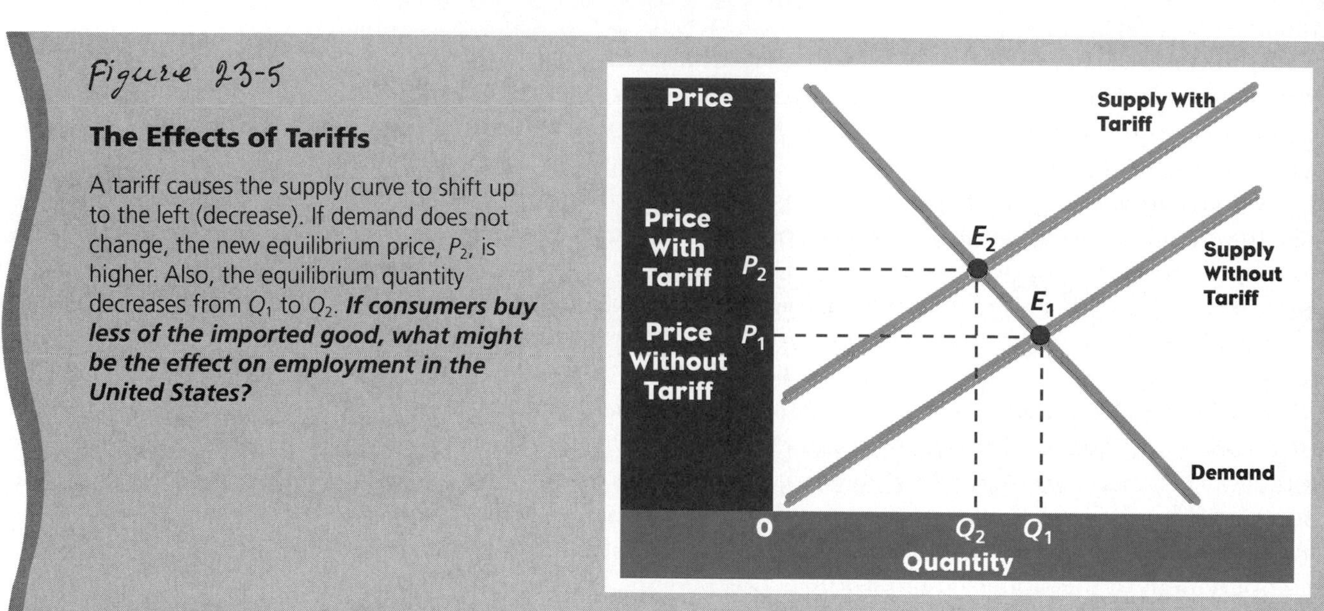

Figure 23-5

The Effects of Tariffs

A tariff causes the supply curve to shift up to the left (decrease). If demand does not change, the new equilibrium price, P_2, is higher. Also, the equilibrium quantity decreases from Q_1 to Q_2. ***If consumers buy less of the imported good, what might be the effect on employment in the United States?***

Second, economists point out that tariffs and quotas interfere with the efficient functioning of supply and demand. This may result in the misallocation of valuable resources. Think about the national security argument with respect to oil and petroleum products. Tariffs and quotas allow the domestic prices of oil and petroleum to rise. This encourages more rapid development of our domestic reserves of oil. As a result, we deplete our domestic supplies and become more and more dependent on foreign supplies in the future. Tariffs and quotas then have defeated the purpose of protecting our national security.

Third, economists say that some of these protectionist arguments have no validity for the United States. To argue for tariffs and quotas on the basis that the United States must maintain a diversified economy makes little sense. We already have a diversified economy. Labor unions' arguments for tariffs and quotas also sound weak. Members of the labor force sometimes think of labor as the only input into production. In reality, the capital supplied by businesses has a lot to do with labor productivity. Think about so-called cheap foreign labor being used to make a product. If a foreign business has less capital equipment than a U.S. business, it will have lower productivity.

Higher paid U.S. labor may have better capital equipment and may be more productive. The more expensive and productive labor may well be able to compete with cheaper but less productive foreign labor. In cases where U.S. labor cannot make products as efficiently, it is probably better to let other countries make the product. U.S. labor should be shifted to those areas or industries where it can be most productive. Like all countries, the United States should apply the law of comparative advantage to decisions about trade.

Fourth, tariffs and quotas are usually hard to change. For example, an industry may receive the benefit of a tariff or quota during its infant stage. But, due to the difficulty of repealing tariffs and quotas, the industry may become quite mature and still receive protection.

PROTECTIVE TARIFFS VERSUS REVENUE TARIFFS

So far, we have discussed tariffs as a means of limiting international trade in order to protect our own self-interest. When tariffs are used in this way they are called *protective tariffs*. Tariffs also can be used to raise money for the government, much like other taxes do. When tariffs are used primarily to raise money for the government, they are called *revenue tariffs*.

A protective tariff will reduce imports substantially only if demand is price elastic. When demand is price elastic, a given percentage increase in price causes a larger percentage reduction in quantity demanded. So, if we put a tariff on a product that has an elastic demand, we will succeed in substantially reducing imports of that product.

A revenue tariff, on the other hand, can raise substantial amounts of money for the government only if the demand is price inelastic. When demand is price inelastic, a given percentage increase in price causes a smaller percentage reduction in quantity demanded. In such a case, the increase in price to the consumer (due to the tariff) has little effect on the amount purchased. The result is that the government can raise a good deal of money. One U.S. president advocated a $0.10 a gallon tax on imported oil as a way to help reduce the government's deficit. Oil was a good product to tax, because the demand for oil is quite inelastic.

INTERNATIONAL TRADE COOPERATION

All countries can gain from free trade. Therefore, it should not be surprising to learn that there is a good deal of cooperation to improve trade.

General Agreement on Tariffs and Trade (GATT)

The most important move in the direction of free trade came in 1947. In that year, 23 countries, including the United States, signed the General Agreement on Tariffs and Trade (GATT). The ***General Agreement on Tariffs and Trade (GATT)*** is an agreement that gave broad international support to improving trade among countries. The countries that belong to GATT, now about 100, meet with each other to lower trade barriers.

General Agreement on Tariffs and Trade (GATT)
an agreement that gave broad international support to improving trade among countries

The most recent round of GATT meetings was called the *Uruguay round*. This round began in July 1986. The formal discussions began in September 1986, in Punta del Este, Uruguay. The Uruguay round included 108 countries. This time, the United States was especially interested in issues related to

The Bretton Woods system slowly broke down. In August 1971, the United States stopped its sale of gold. It announced that it would no longer buy or sell gold at $35 an ounce. In December 1971, the United States lowered the value of its dollar by about 9 percent. Several other nations also changed the values of their money. In 1972, the United States had the worst trade deficit in its history. It again lowered the value of the dollar in February 1973, and several other nations again changed the values of their money. The Bretton Woods system no longer worked.

exchange rate the rate at which one kind of money can be traded for another

Flexible Exchange Rates

An ***exchange rate*** is the rate at which one kind of money can be traded for another. The exchange rate between dollars and selected other currencies is published daily in *The Wall Street Journal.* Some representative examples from one day's paper are shown in Figure 23-6.

Let us look at two examples of how these values are interpreted. First, suppose that you have traveled to Canada and decide to purchase a new parka that you see while in Calgary. The price on the parka is $300 Canadian. How much would it be in terms of U.S. dollars? To find out, you would multiply the Canadian price by the U.S. dollar equivalent (.7437) from the exchange rate table shown in Figure 23-6. Thus, the price in terms of your U.S. purchasing power is: .7437 × 300 = 223.11 U.S. dollars.

Figure 23-6

Representative Exchange Rates

This table shows exchange rates for several different currencies. The *U.S. Dollar Equivalent* column indicates how many U.S. dollars it would take to buy one currency unit of the other country. The *Currency per U.S. Dollar* column indicates how many units of the other country's currency you would get in exchange for one U.S. dollar. ***How many Spanish pesetas can be exchanged for one U.S. dollar?***

Country (Currency)	U.S. Dollar Equivalent	Currency per U.S. Dollar
Brazil (Real)	1.0492	0.9531
Britain (Pound)	1.5710	0.6365
Canada (Dollar)	0.7437	1.3446
China (Renminbi)	0.1202	8.3194
Denmark (Krone)	0.1794	5.5750
France (Franc)	0.2019	4.9532
Germany (Mark)	0.6974	1.4340
Japan (Yen)	0.009949	100.51
Mexico (Peso)	0.1564	6.3950
Netherlands (Guilder)	0.6221	1.6075
South Korea (Won)	0.0013	769.25
Spain (Peseta)	0.008061	124.05

Now, consider a Canadian who buys a CD player for $300 (U.S.) while visiting the Mall of America in Minneapolis. It would take 403.38 dollars of Canadian currency to make that purchase (403.38 = $300 × 1.3446).

These rates of exchange are determined by a system of flexible exchange rates in which each country's money is treated like a commodity for sale.

A ***flexible exchange rate*** is a system in which the laws of supply and demand are allowed to set the prices, or exchange rates, between each kind of money.

flexible exchange rate
a system in which the laws of supply and demand are allowed to set the prices, or exchange rates, of each kind of money

The role of supply and demand in determining exchange rates is illustrated in Figure 23-7 for the Japanese yen and the U.S. dollar. With the given supply curve and the original demand curve, the equilibrium yen price of dollars would be P_1 (for example on October 4, 1994 the exchange rate was 99.94 yen per dollar). Now suppose that the supply stays the same but the demand for dollars increases to the new higher demand. The price would rise to P_2 (for example on October 4, 1995 the exchange rate was 101.17 yen per dollar).

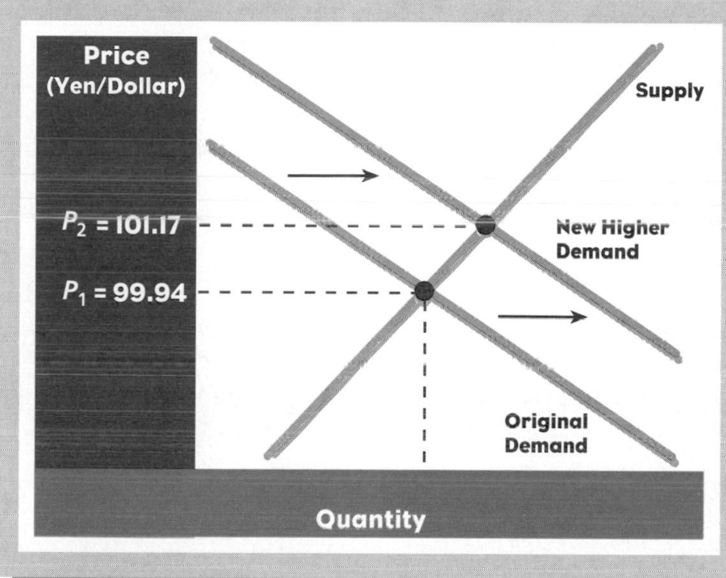

Figure 23-7

Supply and Demand Determine Exchange Rates

In this illustration, an increase in the demand for dollars brings about an increase in the exchange rate of yen per dollar, assuming supply remained constant. ***What would happen to the "value of the dollar" (i.e., its price) if demand stayed at the New Higher Demand but the supply of dollars in the world currency market declined (shifted to the left)?***

THE BALANCE OF TRADE AND BALANCE OF PAYMENTS

The ***balance of trade*** is the level of merchandise exports minus the level of merchandise imports. Sometimes, the phrase *net exports* is used instead of *balance of trade*. The balance of trade is considered favorable if a country has more exports than imports. If a country has more imports than exports, the balance of trade is unfavorable. In the United States, we have had an unfavorable balance of trade in recent years. An unfavorable balance of trade is often called a *trade deficit* when reported in the news.

balance of trade
the level of merchandise exports minus the level of merchandise imports

balance of payments the total flow of money into a country minus the total flow of money out of a country

Balance of payments is a more comprehensive concept. The ***balance of payments*** is the total flow of money into a country minus the total flow of money out of a country. The balance of payments includes, in addition to merchandise exports and imports,

- services imported and exported,
- travel by citizens in other countries,
- income from investments between countries,
- gold exports and imports, and
- other money movements between countries.

Checkpoint

Content Check

1. Differentiate between a trade surplus and a trade deficit.
2. What was the Bretton Woods agreement and why didn't it work?
3. What are flexible exchange rates?
4. Differentiate between balance of payments and balance of trade.

What Do You Think Now?

Reread *What Do You Think?* in the Section Three Focus. Then answer the following questions:

5. If you buy something in another country, how can you compare the purchase price to what you would have paid in the United States?
6. Use the exchange rates in Figure 23-6 to determine if Alex, Alicia, or An got the best buy.

Concepts in Brief

1. Trade can help two countries even if one of them has the capability to make all goods at a lower cost than another country. This is due to the law of comparative advantage. This law shows that a country should specialize in that activity for which it has the greatest relative cost advantage.

2. International trade is a very important part of the U.S. economy. It accounts for about 10 percent of our GDP. Our main exports are electrical machinery, scientific instruments, telecommunications equipment, and chemicals. Our main imports are machinery, scientific instruments, telecommunications equipment, and motor vehicles and parts.

3. Countries do not use barter to pay for goods that are traded between them, so they must agree upon some other method of exchange. At one time, countries used a gold standard in which each country's money could be exchanged for gold. The gold standard was too rigid, and any imbalance between exports and imports could lead to inflation or unemployment. We now use a flexible exchange system, which allows the supply of and demand for a country's money to determine its exchange rate.

4. Some people argue that trade should be restricted to protect infant industries, protect our national security, keep a diversified economy, and protect U.S. jobs and wages.

5. Economists almost always favor free trade. They realize that trade barriers raise prices for consumers and interfere with the functioning of the market system. This reduces efficiency and results in a misallocation of resources.

6. Since 1947, the General Agreement on Tariffs and Trade (GATT) has been a structure within which countries have been able to lower trade barriers. The result is more world trade and better living standards for all countries. In 1993, NAFTA (the North American Free Trade Agreement) was established between the United States, Canada, and Mexico. The aims of NAFTA include promoting economic growth and prosperity for all three economies by eliminating barriers to free trade.

Economic Foundations

1. How much of the U.S. GDP is accounted for by world trade?
2. What are the major exports of the United States?
3. What are the major imports of the United States?
4. Explain why countries trade with each other.
5. Give four reasons for restricting international trade.
6. Give four reasons for encouraging international trade.
7. What was the major reason for establishing the General Agreement on Tariffs and Trade?
8. What was the major reason for forming NAFTA?
9. How was money valued under the gold standard?
10. How was money valued under the Bretton Woods system?
11. How is money valued using flexible exchange rates?

Your Economic Vocabulary

Build your economic vocabulary by matching the following terms with their definitions.

absolute advantage

balance of payments

balance of trade

1. the rate at which one kind of money can be traded for another
2. trade agreement established between the United States, Canada, and Mexico to promote economic growth and prosperity for all three economies by eliminating barriers to free trade
3. the idea that we should limit international trade to protect our own self-interest

4. a tax on imports
5. the result when a country imports more than it exports
6. goods and services that one country sells to another country
7. a group of European countries that have joined together and agreed on ways to improve trade among themselves
8. a system in which the laws of supply and demand are allowed to set the prices, or exchange rates, of each kind of money
9. a bank established to promote economic cooperation by maintaining an orderly system of world trade and exchange rates
10. an agreement that gave broad international support to improving trade among countries
11. goods and services that one country buys from another country
12. the total flow of money into a country minus the total flow of money out of a country
13. the principle that a country benefits from specializing in the production at which it is relatively most efficient
14. a limit on the amount of imports or exports
15. the result when a country exports more than it imports
16. the level of merchandise exports minus the level of merchandise imports
17. a system in which each nation sets the value of its money in terms of a certain amount of gold
18. when one country can produce a good more efficiently than another country

comparative advantage

European Community (EC)

exchange rate

exports

flexible exchange rate

General Agreement on Tariffs and Trade (GATT)

gold standard

imports

International Monetary Fund (IMF)

North American Free Trade Agreement (NAFTA)

protectionism

quota

tariff

trade deficit

trade surplus

Thinking Critically About Economics

1. Why do most economists favor free trade and the elimination of tariffs and quotas?
2. Write an essay in which you discuss the major events since World War II that have led to better world trade. Which of these events seem most important to you? Why?
3. Recall the four reasons some people favor trade restrictions. Give an example from the U.S. economy that you think best fits each reason.
4. How important is world trade in the United States? Go to the library and find the most recent issue of the *Statistical Abstract of the United States.* Look up both *exports* and *gross domestic product* in the index. Compare their relative amounts for the most recent year given. Do exports still represent about 10 percent of GDP? If there has been a change, can you explain why?
5. Do you think the law of comparative advantage is as valid between states in the United States as it is between countries in the world? In what kinds of economic activities do you think your state has a comparative advantage? Why?

Economic Enrichment

Use the following table as the basis for answering this question. The table shows the cost of producing frozen foods and floor tiles in terms of labor hours in two countries. Notice that Country A can make both products with fewer labor hours than can Country B. Using the law of comparative advantage, explain why Country A can still benefit from trade with Country B. Would Country B also benefit from trade?

	One Unit of Frozen Food	One Unit of Floor Tiles
Country A	40 Labor Hours	100 Labor Hours
Country B	80 Labor Hours	120 Labor Hours

Math and Economics

Vicki Jahn recently took her two children on a two-week trip to Sweden. They spent 13 nights in a hotel where their bill totaled 7,366 kronas (the Swedish currency is the krona). They had meal expenses during the trip of 6,004 kronas and they bought 16,660 kronas of clothes and other souvenirs. The exchange rate during their visit to Sweden was 1 krona = $0.15. What was the U.S. dollar amount that they spent on these items?

Writing About Economics

Go to the library and look at a recent issue of *Business Week* magazine. Find the table of contents near the front of the issue and look for a section titled "International Business." Read one of the articles in that section and write a short report about the article. In your report, call attention to the issues in this chapter that relate to the article.

Foreign Currency Exchange Rates

In today's global economy, it is important to understand the way in which one country pays for goods produced in another country. In this example, we'll look at cars produced in Japan and sold in the United States. Japan would like to be paid for its goods in its own currency, which is yen. This makes sense since the people who perform the labor in the factory in Japan are paid in yen, as are the Japanese suppliers of raw materials and parts that go into the manufacture of the car. Because of these facts, companies that buy the vehicles in the United States must find a way to trade dollars for yen. The way this is done is through foreign currency exchange.

In the case of cars purchased from Japan, assume that, in order to cover the cost of production and a reasonable profit, the car manufacturer must receive 1,000,000 yen per car. What would be the dollar cost of the car? To answer this question, you need to know the foreign exchange rate. According to the accompanying bar chart, in 1970 the exchange rate was 358.16 yen for each and every U.S. dollar. In order to determine the number of dollars required, take the cost in yen and divide it by the number of yen per dollar:

$$\frac{1{,}000{,}000.00 \text{ yen}}{358.16 \text{ yen per dollar}} = \$2{,}792.00 \text{ (in 1970)}$$

Assume that, over time, the price of the car remains at 1,000,000 yen. What did this car cost in U.S. dollars in 1994?

$$\frac{1{,}000{,}000.00 \text{ yen}}{102.18 \text{ yen per dollar}} = \$9{,}787.00 \text{ (in 1994)}$$

To find today's foreign currency exchange rates for selected major world currencies, look in *The Wall Street Journal* on the front page of the "Money & Investing" section. Use the current foreign exchange rate to determine how much this car would cost today.

Exchange Rate Between Japan and United States

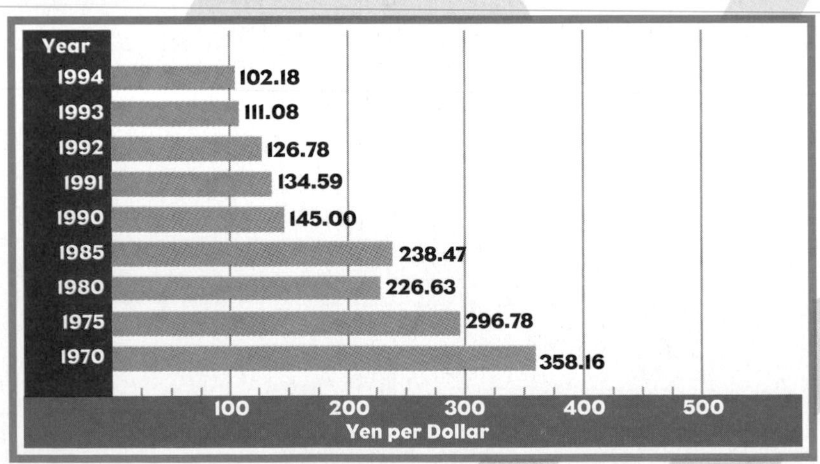

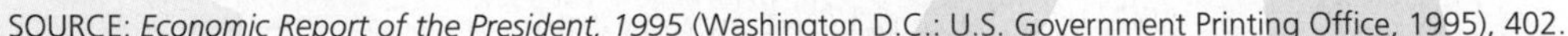
SOURCE: *Economic Report of the President, 1995* (Washington D.C.: U.S. Government Printing Office, 1995), 402.

NAFTA

The North American Free Trade Agreement (NAFTA), in effect since January 1, 1994, has increased the volume of trade within North America. U.S. companies are selling more high-value products, such as automobiles and computers, than they have in the past as NAFTA has reduced Mexico's and Canada's trade barriers. Reading the preamble to NAFTA will give you some idea of the scope of this historic agreement:

PREAMBLE

The Government of Canada, the Government of the United Mexican States and the Government of the United States of America, resolved to:

STRENGTHEN the special bonds of friendship and cooperation among their nations;

CONTRIBUTE to the harmonious development and expansion of world trade and provide a catalyst to broader international cooperation;

CREATE an expanded and secure market for the goods and services produced in their territories;

REDUCE distortions to trade;

ESTABLISH clear and mutually advantageous rules governing their trade;

ENSURE a predictable commercial framework for business planning and investment;

BUILD on their respective rights and obligations under the General Agreement on Tariffs and Trade and other multilateral and bilateral instruments of cooperation;

ENHANCE the competitiveness of their firms in global markets;

FOSTER creativity and innovation, and promote trade in goods and services that are the subject of intellectual property rights;

CREATE new employment opportunities and improve working conditions and living standards in their respective territories;

UNDERTAKE each of the preceding in a manner consistent with environmental protection and conservation;

PRESERVE their flexibility to safeguard the public welfare;

PROMOTE sustainable development;

STRENGTHEN the development and enforcement of environmental laws and regulations; and

PROTECT, enhance and enforce basic workers' rights;

HAVE AGREED as follows: . . .

After NAFTA went into effect, tariffs on goods traded between the United States, Mexico, and Canada were reduced, permitting more efficient trade. As a result, consumers in all three countries benefit.

As you think about this preamble, consider how these resolutions might positively affect the economies of the parties involved: Canada, the United States, and Mexico.

SOURCE: "Preamble" to *NAFTA*, **http://the-tech.mit.edu/Bulletins/Nafta/.**

Overview

Section One
Life in Less-Developed Countries

Section Two
Economic Development

Economic Development: A Global Economic Issue

Learning Objectives

24-1
Identify some income and population conditions in less-developed countries.

24-2
Describe some of the effects of poverty in less-developed countries.

24-3
Present five barriers to economic development in less-developed countries.

24-4
Explain why more advanced countries provide foreign aid to less-developed countries.

FOCUS

Section One
Life in Less-Developed Countries

What Do You Think?

In earlier chapters, you learned about the distribution of income in the United States. You have seen that the average income per person in the United States is more than $20,000. You also have learned that, even though we are a rich nation, there are people in the United States who live in conditions described as poverty. Most people would say that a family of four with a yearly income of only $12,000 is poor. That would be an income of $3,000 per person in the household. Do you think that there are many countries in the world where the average level of income per person in the entire country is less than $3,000?

Terms to Know

- less-developed country (LDC)
- infant mortality rate
- life expectancy
- dual economy
- foreign aid

What's Ahead?

Some people have been fortunate enough to have been born in places such as the United States, Japan, Norway, Canada, and France, countries that have relatively high standards of living. Not everyone is so lucky. If you were born in Pakistan, Uganda, Honduras, or one of many other countries, the standard of living you could expect would be far more modest. In this section, you will learn how desperate economic conditions are in some parts of the world.

LESS-DEVELOPED COUNTRIES

Living in the United States, you are among the richest of all the people in the world. You may not come from a family that is wealthy by U.S. standards, but in comparison to the entire population of the world you are rich. You almost surely wear shoes to school. You probably have at least one full meal each day. It is likely that someone in your family has a car. Somewhere in your home there is probably a television and one or more radios. Most people in the United States take these luxuries for granted. However, for much of the world's population, adequate food and clothing are not readily available. Cars, televisions, and radios are either unknown or only something heard of but never experienced.

Most of the poorest countries in the world are in Asia, Africa, and Latin America. These countries are often referred to as less-developed countries, or LDCs. A ***less-developed country (LDC)*** is generally defined as a poor country with a relatively low level of education and a largely rural population. Sometimes less-developed countries are referred to as *third-world countries*. There is no universally accepted definition of a less-developed country. However, economists often define a country as being less-developed if the annual income level per person averages $3,000 or less.

less-developed country (LDC)
a poor country with a relatively low level of education and a largely rural population

Comparing Income Data

To help you see how little that is, let us compare it to income per person in the United States. We will use real gross national product (GNP) per person as the measure of income. GNP is used here rather than GDP because GDP data are not as widely available for less-developed countries. In the most recent year for which comparable data are available, real GNP was more than $22,000 per person in the United States. That equals over seven times the $3,000 upper end of the per-person level of income for LDCs.

Econ & You

FOUNDATIONS OF GOOD HEALTH

Most people in the United States have excellent health care and live in a generally healthy environment—at least when compared to the less-developed countries of the world. You take for granted the availability of soap and water to wash with, especially prior to eating or preparing food to be eaten. This is not true in many less-developed countries. Basic habits of cleanliness are not widespread. As a result, diseases spread more rapidly.

Most students who read this book will have had immunizations for diseases such as polio and measles. Most young people in the less-developed countries do not have access to such immunizations.

In most of your homes, there is electricity and you probably have a refrigerator and perhaps a freezer in which to store foods until they are to be eaten. Many of your food products come in containers that are well designed to maintain the freshness and purity of the products. In the less-developed countries, refrigeration is a rarity for vast numbers of people. In addition, people in LDCs have less access to prepackaged foods that can be kept from spoiling.

Most of you have seen a medical doctor, or could have, in the last year or so. For young people in less-developed countries, medical care is scarce. Often, there is not even a single doctor in a person's hometown. So, you see that you live in a much healthier environment than do people in the less-developed countries.

Look at the first column of numbers in the table shown in Figure 24-1. You see that many countries have a level of income per person far below the $3,000 level. In Ethiopia, the yearly income is only $124 per person. In India, income per person is only $303. The countries listed in Figure 24-1 are not the only LDCs, but they are representative.

Comparing Population Data

You also see in Figure 24-1 that the LDCs represent more than just a few very small countries. Some have quite large populations. Look especially at Bangladesh, China, India, Mexico, Nigeria, and Pakistan. It should be clear to you that a great many people live in countries with very low income per person.

Country	1991 GNP per Person	1994 Population	1994 Population per Square Mile
Bangladesh	$195	125,548,000	2,421
China (Mainland)	$1,327	1,190,431,000	331
Colombia	$1,187	35,578,000	89
Egypt	$543	60,765,000	158
Ethiopia	$124	58,710,000	138
India	$303	919,903,000	801
Kenya	$310	28,241,000	128
Mexico	$2,506	92,202,000	124
Mozambique	$74	17,346,000	57
Myanmar (Burma)	$531	44,277,000	174
Nepal	$141	21,042,000	398
Nigeria	$242	98,091,000	279
Pakistan	$369	128,856,000	429
Peru	$2,090	23,651,000	48
Sri Lanka	$518	18,130,000	725
Sudan	$1,016	29,420,000	32
Tanzania	$96	27,986,000	82
Thailand	$1,618	59,510,000	301
Turkey	$1,790	62,154,000	209
Uganda	$157	19,122,000	248
United States	$22,550	275,327,000	74

Figure 24-1

Income and Population Data for the United States and 20 Less-Developed Countries

Mexico is the only one of these countries to share a border with the United States. ***How does our GNP per person compare with that of our southern neighbor?***

SOURCE: U.S. Bureau of the Census, *Statistical Abstract of the United States: 1994,* 114th ed. (Washington D.C., 1994), 862, 850–852.

The third column of numbers in Figure 24-1 shows the population density in these countries. Population density refers to the number of people per square mile. The United States has 74 people per square mile. You see that many LDCs are much more crowded than this. Bangladesh is the most crowded of the countries listed, with 2,421 people per square mile. That is almost 33 times more people per square mile than in the United States.

Being crowded is not the reason these countries are poor, however. Japan (821 people per square mile) and the United Kingdom (623 people per square mile) also seem crowded compared to the United States. But, both Japan and the United Kingdom are relatively wealthy countries. Japan's GNP per person is $27,300 and, in the United Kingdom, GNP per person is $17,400. However, being both poor *and* crowded magnifies the problems in the less-developed countries.

EFFECTS OF POVERTY IN LESS-DEVELOPED COUNTRIES

As you might expect, the poverty in LDCs has an important impact on people's lives. Poverty also can weaken the political stability of a country. In addition, the poverty that exists in LDCs can affect those of us who live in the richer countries of the world. As you read about some of the results of poverty in LDCs in the following sections, keep in mind how little income people have in these countries.

Individuals Have Fewer Goods and Services

The lives of people in less-developed countries are very different from yours. The depth of their poverty is hard for us to fully understand. Many people do not have the basic food, clothing, and health care that we take for granted.

Material Goods. Items such as televisions and radios, common in our households, rarely belong to households in LDCs. Figure 24-2 illustrates this.

The first column of numbers in Figure 24-2 shows how many people there are per car in the United States and some of the less-developed countries. The United States has so many cars that, on average, there is a car for every 1.7 people. Thailand has only one car for 69 people. In Ecuador, there is only one car for every 134 people. Think for a moment about how different your life would be if cars were not as readily available as they are in the United States.

The other two columns in Figure 24-2 provide information about the availability of radios and televisions. In the United States, there are 2,118 radios and 814 televisions for every 1,000 people. The numbers in Figure 24-2 show that these items, common to people in the United States, are very rare in LDCs. You probably own your own radio. Perhaps you own more than one. But, if you lived in China, that would be unlikely. In China, there are only 182 radios for every 1,000 people. This equals about 18 radios for every 100 people.

Similar comparisons can be made for televisions. You see that, in some of the countries listed in Figure 24-2, there are less than 100 televisions for every 1,000 people. Think about how different your life would be if cars, televisions, and radios were not common.

The three goods discussed here act only as examples to help you understand how poor many of the world's people are. If you lived in one of the LDCs, you would not have many other goods you may now enjoy: CDs or cassette players, skateboards, telephones, watches, movie theaters, new school clothes. You would be lucky to have shoes, basic clothing, and one full meal a day.

Country	Persons per Car	Radios per 1,000 People	Televisions per 1,000 People
Argentina	2.5	676	220
Chile	19.0	344	209
China	NA*	182	31
Dominican Republic	53.0	171	84
Ecuador	134.0	317	84
Panama	16.0	224	166
Thailand	69.0	191	114
United States	1.7	2,118	814
Uruguay	16.0	604	231

*NA = Data not available

Availability of Selected Products in the United States and Some Less-Developed Countries

The values in this table illustrate how much more people in the United States have than do people in less-developed countries. While only three products are shown here, similar comparisons could be made for a wide variety of products. ***Which country of those shown has the fewest televisions per thousand people?***

SOURCE: U.S. Bureau of the Census, *Statistical Abstract of the United States: 1994,* 114th ed. (Washington D.C., 1994), 865–866.

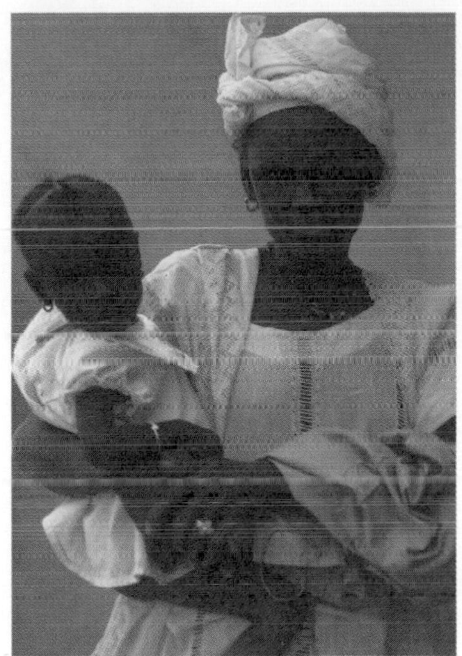

Health Care. In the less-developed countries, poverty goes beyond material goods. People generally suffer poor health as well. The level of health care available in the United States far exceeds what is found in LDCs. As shown in the first column of numbers in Figure 24-3, the infant mortality rate is much higher in the LDCs than in the United States. The ***infant mortality rate*** is measured as the number of deaths of children under one year of age per 1,000 live births. In our country, only about 1 percent of children born each year die within their first year. But, look, for example, at Ethiopia. There, about 106 of every 1,000 children born die in the first year, that is, more than 10 percent of the children born there die before their first birthday.

infant mortality rate
the number of deaths of children under one year of age per 1,000 live births

Country	Infant Mortality Rate*	Life Expectancy
Afghanistan	155.8	44.9
Bangladesh	106.9	55.1
China	52.1	67.9
Colombia	28.3	72.1
Egypt	76.4	60.8
Ethiopia	106.4	52.7
India	78.4	58.6
Kenya	74.1	53.2
Mexico	27.4	72.9
Myanmar (Burma)	63.7	60.0
Nepal	83.5	52.5
Nigeria	75.0	55.3
Pakistan	101.9	57.4
Peru	42.9	65.6
Sri Lanka	21.9	71.9
Sudan	79.5	54.3
Tanzania	109.7	43.3
Thailand	37.1	68.4
Turkey	48.8	70.9
Uganda	112.2	37.5
United States	8.1	75.9

***Number of deaths of children under 1 year of age per 1,000 live births.**

Figure 24-3

Health-Related Data for the United States and 20 Less-Developed Countries

The values in this table help to illustrate how much worse health conditions are in these less-developed countries compared to the United States. ***Which of these less-developed countries has the life expectancy that is the closest to that of the United States?***

SOURCE: U.S. Bureau of the Census, *Statistical Abstract of the United States: 1994,* 114th ed. (Washington D.C., 1994), 854–855.

life expectancy
the average age the people in a country reach

The last column of Figure 24-3 shows the life expectancy of people born in these countries. The ***life expectancy*** is the average age the people in a country reach. In the United States, people live an average of about 76 years, although some die much earlier and some at a much older age. As you look down the right column of numbers, you see that in the LDCs the average life span is less. In Afghanistan, for example, you see that it is only about 45 years.

The life expectancy of people may be the best overall measure of the population's general health. Based on this measure you see that people in less-developed countries suffer from poor health. This is due to many factors. Part of the reason is that they have neither a nourishing diet nor adequate clothing or shelter. In addition, they do not have the level of medical care that exists in more developed countries.

Political Problems Are Magnified in Less-Developed Countries

We enjoy living in a fairly stable social and political environment. Less-developed countries often generate social and political instability. Government control may rest in the hands of small groups of wealthy people. Corruption among political leaders emerges all too often. People with large amounts of money have a great deal of influence over policies formed by government officials. As different groups of wealthy citizens press for policies that favor them, conflict frequently results.

You may be asking yourself where these wealthy people come from since we have stressed the poverty that exists in these countries. Even though the average income is low, some people are quite rich. Often the distribution of income is very uneven in LDCs. There are a few very rich people and many, many very poor people. Unlike in the United States, in less-developed countries almost no middle class exists. As the rich segments push for government policies that favor them, the poor may be nearly forgotten.

The poor tend to stay poor, often living a life no better than that of their ancestors of a thousand years earlier. Meanwhile, the rich get richer. The result is what may be called a dual economy. A ***dual economy*** is one in which a modern market economy exists side by side with a primitive subsistence economy. In such a dual economy, the modern sector may resemble more advanced countries. Factories, retail shops, and restaurants may line urban streets. At the same time, in the subsistence sector, crude technologies are used in rural areas where goods are exchanged in a barter system. Almost no one advances into the wealthy sector. If you are born poor, you stay poor.

dual economy
an economy in which a modern market economy exists side by side with a primitive subsistence economy

Economic Spotlight

FROM HOMETOWN GIRL TO WORLD-CLASS WOMAN

Born and raised in Salisbury, North Carolina, Elizabeth Hanford was presumed to be such a "hometown girl" that she would never be happy anyplace else. In 1995, Elizabeth Hanford Dole was president of the American Red Cross, making herself at home in all 50 states across the nation.

After graduating from her home state's Duke University, Dole enrolled in graduate school at Harvard, majoring in education and government and later enrolling in law school there. With her law and education degrees, Dole easily won a job as staff aide to the Assistant Secretary of Education in Washington, D.C. This position turned out to be the first of many government jobs, including those of Secretary of Transportation and Secretary of Labor.

From the beginning of Dole's career, Washington leaders watched her carefully, knowing that this intelligent and politically savvy woman was destined to "go places." She hasn't let them down. In her role as president of the American Red Cross, Dole was the picture of leadership. Under her direction, the Red Cross successfully responded to a record-breaking number of natural disasters. Dole, along with 30,000 Red Cross staff members and 1.5 million volunteers, helped victims of Hurricanes Andrew and Iniki, the midwest floods, the California earthquakes, and the terrorist bombing in Oklahoma City, among other catastrophes.

But, the nonprofit organization doesn't limit itself to helping out in the United States. When international crises strike, the American Red Cross joins forces with the International Committee for the Red Cross to help people worldwide. Dole was honored with a World Citizen Award in recognition of her international efforts.

However, things were not always so rosy within the Red Cross. When Dole took over as president, the organization faced a crisis of confidence because of dangerous impurities in its blood supply. Dole promptly went to work raising the safety standards involved in collecting, processing, and distributing blood, which reestablished the good name and credibility of the Red Cross. She also gave up her $200,000-a-year salary for the first year to show her dedication to volunteerism. Dole stated that "the best way I can let volunteers know their importance is to be one of them." It's this kind of dedication and leadership that have helped Elizabeth Dole make a difference throughout the country and the world.

Since the poor have the least education and mobility, they tend to be largely ignored. The political system favors the wealthy few, while the subsistence economy continues as it has for decades.

Poverty in LDCs Affects Advanced Countries

The low level of income in LDCs has an adverse affect on advanced countries such as the United States. There are several reasons this is so. First, poverty in LDCs is an opportunity cost for advanced economies. If the buying power of less-developed countries were greater, there would be larger markets for products that we export. People in the LDCs would purchase clothing, appliances, computers, cars, and other products that are produced in the more developed countries.

A second way that wealthier countries are adversely affected relates to the failure of LDCs to repay loans. Many banks and other financial institutions have made large loans to the governments of less-developed countries. Often, when these loans are due for repayment, the countries do not have enough money to meet their obligations. This is a very real concern. Because of the complexity of international finance, it is difficult to judge the seriousness of this problem. Some economists believe that the stability of our domestic financial structure weakens when we lend money to LDCs.

foreign aid
the money that more advanced countries provide to help LDCs in their economic development

A third way in which the low level of income in LDCs affects us relates to foreign aid. ***Foreign aid*** is the money that more advanced countries provide to help LDCs in their economic development. For years, we have been willing to share part of our wealth with LDCs in the form of foreign aid. While this may be a good thing to do, we need to recognize the opportunity cost involved. We do give up the ability to use that money to improve education, to reduce domestic poverty, or to solve other economic problems in the United States. We will discuss foreign aid in more detail later in this chapter.

Checkpoint

Content Check

1. Name three LDCs and describe the economic and population conditions in each.
2. What do infant mortality rates and life expectancy tell us about life in less-developed countries?
3. How does poverty affect political stability in LDCs?

What Do You Think Now?

Reread *What Do You Think?* in the Section One Focus. Then answer the following questions:

4. Name five countries where the average income per person for the entire country is less than $3,000.
5. How would you compare the standard of living in the United States with the standard of living in less-developed countries?

Section Two
Economic Development

What Do You Think?

After watching a television news report about the plight of people in one of the poorer countries in central Africa, two customers at the Chatter Box Cafe were talking about possible solutions. They agreed that if the less-developed countries would adopt modern technologies in production, they could reap the same benefits the more developed countries have obtained. Do you agree?

What's Ahead?

For many years, there has been concern about the slow rate of economic advancement for much of the world's population. Economists, sociologists, anthropologists, and others have studied the problem. They have come up with many different potential solutions, none of which has worked well in all of the diverse, less-developed countries of the globe. In this section, you will learn about some of the reasons economic development has progressed so slowly for these countries.

Terms to Know

barriers to economic development

population explosion

World Bank

BARRIERS TO ECONOMIC DEVELOPMENT

Economic, social, and political characteristics that prevent an economy from developing are called ***barriers to economic development.*** Five main barriers to economic development exist in the less-developed countries. These are limited natural resources, low human capital, shortage of investment capital, rapid population growth, and unfavorable political environment. We will consider each of these in the remainder of this section. Every single less-developed country is not faced with all five barriers, but it is not unusual to see all five operating at once.

barriers to economic development economic, social, and political characteristics that prevent an economy from developing

Limited Natural Resources

Most of the LDCs have very limited natural resources. The resources they have are usually (but not always) agricultural. Often, even these resources are

very specialized. For example, in Uganda, coffee production is a major industry that accounts for almost all of the country's exports. In Colombia, the major industries are textiles, food processing, clothing and footwear, beverages, chemicals, metal products, and cement. Most of these are based on agricultural processing. The major exports from Colombia are coffee, fuel oil, cotton, tobacco, sugar, textiles, cattle and hides, bananas, and flowers. You see that these originate from the agricultural sector.

While LDCs do have some useful natural resources, the base of those resources is usually narrow. They do not have the diversity of resources that we see in the United States; nor have they developed their resources effectively. The result for many LDCs is that the limited resource base acts as a barrier to sustained economic development.

Low Level of Human Capital

A second barrier to economic development is the low level of human capital in the LDCs. By *human capital,* we mean the level of education and training that people have. In most of the less-developed countries, the level of public spending on education is quite low. Look at the first column of numbers in Figure 24-4. These numbers represent the percent of secondary school-age children (ages 12 through 17) who are enrolled in school. Consider how low those percentages are for most of the countries listed as compared to the 90 percent level for the United States.

Look also at the second column of numbers in Figure 24-4. These numbers show the percent of the adult population that is literate—that is, the percent that can read and write at a very basic level. In the United States, nearly all of the adult population is literate. But, you see that the percent of literate adults is much lower in nearly all of the LDCs listed.

People with low levels of education and training tend to have low productivity. They cannot do jobs that require them to read and understand written instructions. Often, the skills of the labor force in LDCs are appropriate only to an agricultural economy. They are not suited to the kinds of economic activities that will likely lead to substantial economic development.

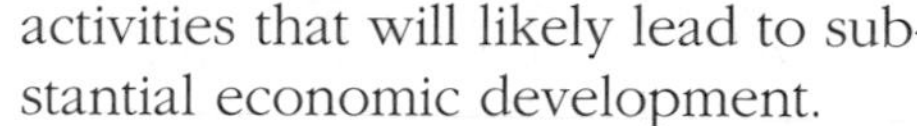

In part, this agricultural orientation is reflected in the rural living patterns we see in less-developed countries. Compared to the more advanced economic countries, fewer people in LDCs live in urban areas. Instead, they live in rural areas where they use what little skill and education they have to earn a subsistence income. You can compare the percentage of people living in urban areas of the United States to the percentage in LDCs by looking at the right-hand column of Figure 24-4.

Country	Percentage of Students Enrolled in School*	Adult Literacy**	Percentage Living in Urban Area
Afghanistan	NA***	29	NA
Bangladesh	19	35	18
China	51	73	27
Colombia	55	87	71
Egypt	80	48	44
Ethiopia	12	61–80 estimated	13
India	44	48	26
Kenya	29	69	25
Mexico	55	87	74
Myanmar (Burma)	20	81	25
Nepal	NA	26	12
Nigeria	20	51	37
Pakistan	21	35	33
Peru	70	85	71
Sri Lanka	74	88	22
Sudan	22	27	23
Tanzania	5	NA	22
Thailand	33	93	23
Turkey	51	81	64
Uganda	13	48	12
United States	90	over 95	76

* Percent of children 12 through 17 years of age enrolled in secondary school.

** Percent of the population over 15 who can read and write a simple statement about everyday life and do simple mathematical calculations.

*** NA = Data not available.

Figure 24-4

Education and Urbanization for the United States and Some Less-Developed Countries

The values in this table provide some insight into education and the relatively low level of urbanization in many less-developed countries. ***What do the values in this table tell you about the level of human capital in Pakistan?***

SOURCE: *The Development Data Book,* 3d ed. (Washington, D.C.: The World Bank, 1995), 12–18.

Shortage of Investment Capital

The third barrier to economic development is the less-developed countries' shortage of investment capital. You have learned that, in order to invest in capital equipment (such as machinery and factories), there must be savings. But, people with very low incomes need all of that income just for the basics of survival. There is little chance for them to save money. Typically, they live what is called a "hand-to-mouth" existence: When they earn money, it is spent immediately on food or other necessities.

Some investment does take place in the less-developed countries but not nearly enough to promote development. Money available for investment in capital usually comes from the government or from foreign-aid programs sponsored by countries such as the United States. Unfortunately, the projects undertaken with these monies often do not represent the best interests of the majority of people in the LDCs. Often, money is spent on the latest technological processes available when what is needed is an increase in the most basic technologies. The phrase "you need to learn to walk before you can run" is appropriate here. The less-developed nations need to develop basic production methods and human skills before trying to use the most modern and most difficult forms of production.

Rapid Population Growth

The fourth barrier to economic development for many of the less-developed countries is rapid growth of their populations. The number of people in these countries grows faster than the rate of growth in GDP. The result is that GDP per person stays very low or even falls despite all efforts at economic

Global Economy

INFORMATION ONLINE

You may have heard it said that "the world is becoming a smaller place everyday." Of course, this does not mean physically smaller. Rather, it means smaller in terms of the ability that people around the globe have to be in contact with one another. People travel to other countries with increased ease. Television and radio reach from continent to continent, largely ignoring geographic and political boundaries. Telephone and computer-based communications also are becoming widely available, even in many of the less-developed countries.

Virtually all of South and Central America have access to full Internet connectivity. The same is true for most of Asia. Of the less-developed parts of the world, Africa lags the most in terms of access to the Internet. Some countries have virtually no access, while others have access comparable to that of developed nations. Sudan has no Internet capability, while bordering countries are online. To the north of Sudan, Egypt is quite advanced in this regard, and to the east and south, Ethiopia and Kenya have only e-mail access to the Internet.

Access to information can be a powerful force. Electronic communications have the potential of speeding economic development, through improved education and awareness of what can be done. It can facilitate a sharing of ideas that have proven successful and that have failed.

development. Look at Figure 24-5, which shows the rate of population growth for representative LDCs. The rate of population growth for the United States also is shown for comparison. The number of years it would take for each country's population to double also is shown. These numbers should help you to see how rapidly populations are growing in many LDCs. This rapid growth in the number of people living in a country is sometimes referred to as a ***population explosion.***

population explosion
rapid growth in the number of people living in a country

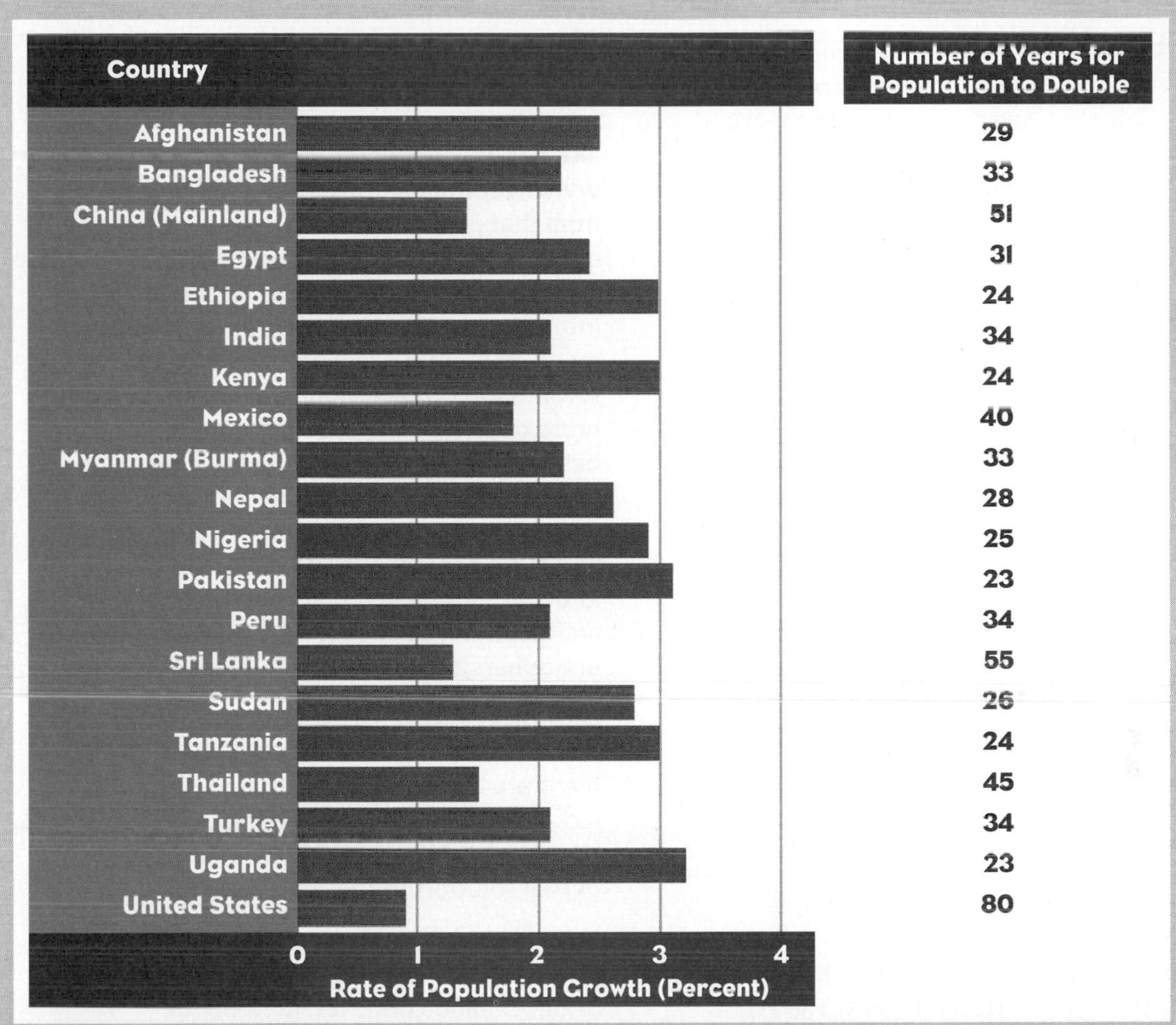

Growth Rates for Population and Number of Years for Population to Double

These values illustrate how much more rapidly population growth is in these less-developed countries than in the United States. ***Which of these less-developed countries appears to have the most rapid rate of population growth?***

SOURCE: *The World Bank Atlas* (Washington D.C.: The World Bank, 1995), 8–9. This source is for percentages only. The data on number of years for the population to double are based on the author's estimates. See the *Math and Economics* feature in this chapter to learn how such estimates can be made.

Internet Connection

THE NONINDUSTRIALIZED WORLD AND THE INTERNET

In this chapter, we have learned that much of the world's population has a lower standard of living than that of the United States, Canada, or other economically developed countries. An excellent source of economic, social, and political information about other countries is the *CIA World Factbook,* available at **http://www.odci.gov/cia/publications/95fact/index.html**.

Why are some countries less economically developed than others? In the last chapter, we discovered that a nation's standard of living depends on the quantity and quality of resources it has available. Developing countries tend to lack an educated workforce, capital, and technology. These countries are so economically poor that they must devote their limited resources to providing their people with a minimal standard of living. Unfortunately, that means they find it difficult to accumulate capital, technology, or training for their people.

For this reason, several international agencies have evolved to assist in the process of economic development. The World Bank was designed to provide technical and financial assistance to developing countries. The World Bank has Internet sites at **http://www.worldbank.org** and **gopher://ftp.worldbank.org/1**. The Web page contains a description of the Bank's activities, press releases, and speeches by Bank officials. It also has an Electronic Media Center at **http://www.worldbank.org/html/emc/Welcome.html** that provides current news in the form of audio, video, and text documents.

The United Nations has several relevant Internet sites. The United Nations Development Program (UNDP) has sites at **http://www.undp.org** and **gopher://gopher.undp.org**. The Web page provides a description of the UNDP, press releases, publications, and other information. The United Nations Conference on Trade and Development (UNCTAD) has sites at **http://gatekeeper.unicc.org/unctad** and **gopher://gopher.undp.org/11/ungophers/unctad**.

Economics Application: Two causes of economic underdevelopment are lack of technology and lack of an educated workforce. How might the Internet provide a partial solution to these problems?

Internet Application: *Figure 24-1* in this chapter lists a number of developing countries. Connect to the *CIA World Factbook* at **http://www.odci.gov/cia/publications/95fact/index.html**. to find examples of other developing countries. What is their national product per capita? What is their population growth rate?

Such rapid growth in the number of people coupled with low productivity means that many people live on the brink of starvation. An early economist, Thomas Malthus, predicted that populations would increase so fast that people would be kept at a subsistence level in the long term. He was wrong about the United States and other advanced nations, but, regarding LDCs, he may have been correct. People living in many of the LDCs today are no better off in economic terms than their ancestors of centuries past.

Unfavorable Political Environment

The unfavorable political environment in some less-developed countries is a fifth barrier to economic development. Sometimes, political leaders are corrupt and/or incompetent. Often, they follow policies that favor a small but elite ruling class. These policies may not promote economic advancement for the masses.

However, the best hope for economic development rests in proper governmental action. The provision of better education, for example, is probably best accomplished by the government. Further, the government can act as a strong guiding force in providing investment capital. To do so, the governments of less-developed countries often turn to the advanced countries for aid.

FOREIGN AID CAN PROMOTE DEVELOPMENT

Foreign aid is the money that more advanced countries provide to help the LDCs in their economic development. One reason that countries such as the United States provide foreign aid to the LDCs is that we believe in the

Economic Dilemma

SUPPORTING THE INFRASTRUCTURE

Most economists believe that the infrastructure of less-developed countries must be improved before meaningful advances can be made. The infrastructure of a country refers to its transportation system (roads, railways, etc.), buildings, water systems, power generating capabilities, and communications systems. Improving infrastructure is expensive, and so countries must make choices among many desirable projects. In addition, decisions are complicated by the fact that there are both good and bad outcomes from each. Consider the examples in the table below:

Leaving the good and the bad outcomes of infrastructure improvements aside, the decisions about what projects to support are difficult. The less-developed countries themselves have little money for infrastructure improvement, and so what they spend must be carefully rationed. Further, much of the money that is spent to improve the infrastructure comes from foreign aid provided by more developed countries. Some of this aid is direct and some comes by way of the World Bank or other international organizations. Often, foreign aid money is designated for particular types of spending that may not be the best use of the money for the local economy.

Infrastructure to Be Improved	Outcomes	
	Good	Bad
Roads	May increase rural families' incomes.	May encourage too much migration to cities and may cause environmental damage.
Hydroelectric Dams	Improve living conditions and productivity.	May flood thousands of acres of farmland and forests.
Telecommunications	Increase literacy and productivity.	May cause discontent as people learn about what they do not have.

morality of sharing a part of our wealth. A second reason is actually based on our own economic interest. If our aid can help less-developed countries become more prosperous, we may reap long-term benefits. Their development will open up more markets for the goods that we produce and thereby increase our own prosperity.

Figure 24-6 shows the amount of money that flows from selected developed countries to the LDCs. You see that the United States is one major source of such aid. Other countries such as Japan also provide large amounts of money.

Country	Flow of Money (in billions of U.S. dollars)
Canada	$4.0
Denmark	1.1
France	6.1*
Germany	13.1
Italy	7.6
Japan	25.0
Netherlands	4.4
Norway	1.4
United States	20.8

*This value was for 1990.

Figure 24-6

Net Flow of Money to Developing Countries from Selected Developed Countries in 1991

These values show that developed countries are making some effort to help the less-developed countries improve their economic conditions. ***In the year shown, what nation was the leader in terms of providing money to the less-developed countries?***

SOURCE: U.S. Bureau of the Census, *Statistical Abstract for the United States: 1994,* 114th ed. (Washington D.C., 1994), 884.

The World Bank also is a source of aid to the less-developed countries. The ***World Bank*** was established in 1944 to help finance reconstruction after World War II. Now the main function of the World Bank is to provide aid to LDCs. The World Bank borrows money from richer nations of the world and then lends the money to less-developed countries.

World Bank
an organization established in 1944 to help finance reconstruction after World War II

THE FUTURE OF LESS-DEVELOPED COUNTRIES

The future is not bright for most of the less-developed countries. Some of these countries are not very different today from how they were a thousand years ago. However, as we learn more about how economies work, the prospects for LDCs improve. Applying the "economic way of thinking" to the problems of economic development may provide insights that will lead to more economic progress for the LDCs in the years to come.

Checkpoint

Content Check

1. What role does education play in economic development?

2. How does population growth affect economic development in LDCs?

3. Why do developed countries provide aid to LDCs?

What Do You Think Now?

Reread *What Do You Think?* in the Section Two Focus. Then answer the following questions:

4. Do you think adopting modern technology in production is what LDCs need most?

5. Is there any one strategy or change that will solve the problem of slow economic progress for the less-developed countries? Why or why not?

Concepts in Brief

1. Countries are considered to be less developed if their level of income averages less than $3,000 per person per year. In the United States, income per person averages more than $20,000. The less-developed countries are not just small countries. Many are very large in terms of population and very crowded.
2. People living in the less-developed countries do not enjoy the same kinds of goods that we take for granted. Few people have such luxuries as cars, televisions, or radios. People in the less developed countries have little available health care. As a result, these countries have high infant mortality and low life expectancy rates.
3. Less-developed countries often have an unstable political environment. Further, those in power tend to promote policies that favor the few rich people at the expense of the majority of people, who are poor.
4. Rich countries such as the United States are affected by the poverty in LDCs because our export markets are more limited, loans are sometimes not repaid, and the large amounts of financial aid given to the LDCs are not invested at home.
5. The five major barriers to economic development in the LDCs are limited natural resources, low level of human capital, relatively little investment capital, explosive population growth, and unfavorable political environment.
6. Many of the world's most wealthy countries provide substantial money to the LDCs in the way of foreign aid. The World Bank also provides monetary support for economic development.

Economic Foundations

1. Describe the income and population conditions in less-developed economies.
2. Explain how poverty affects people in terms of material goods in less-developed economies.
3. Explain how poverty affects people in terms of health in less-developed economies.

4. Explain how poverty in LDCs affects people in the United States.
5. How does each of the following act as a barrier to economic development?
    a. low resource base
    b. low level of human capital
    c. low level of investment capital
    d. rapid population growth
    e. unfavorable political environment
6. Why does the United States provide foreign aid to less-developed countries?

Your Economic Vocabulary

Build your economic vocabulary by matching the following terms with their definitions.

barriers to economic development
dual economy
foreign aid
infant mortality rate
less-developed country (LDC)
life expectancy
population explosion
World Bank

1. economic, social, and political characteristics that prevent an economy from developing
2. rapid growth in the number of people living in a country
3. the average age the people in a country reach
4. an organization established in 1944 to help finance reconstruction after World War II
5. the money that more advanced countries provide to help LDCs in their economic development
6. a poor country with a relatively low level of education and a largely rural population
7. the number of deaths of children under one year of age per 1,000 live births
8. an economy in which a modern market economy exists side by side with a primitive subsistence economy

Thinking Critically About Economics

1. Write a one-page essay in which you describe what you think life is like for someone your age in Mexico.
2. Do you think the United States should continue to provide foreign aid to less-developed countries? Explain your answer.
3. When we evaluate economic conditions in the less-developed countries, we usually make comparisons to the United States or other more developed economies. Do you think this is a fair comparison? Explain why or why not.
4. Use the most recent issue of the *Statistical Abstract of the United States* to update either Figure 24-1, 24-2, or 24-3. Based on the data you find, determine if the countries have become more or less developed in recent years.

Economic Enrichment

You have certain expectations about your economic future. All of your expectations may not be realized, but for most people in the United States, there is a good chance that many of our expectations will come true. In less-developed nations, this is not true. Modern communications make people in less-developed countries aware of many goods that they are unlikely to ever have. The gap between expectations (hopes) and reality is often very large.

Identify five expectations that you and a person your age living in one of the LDCs listed in Figure 24-1 might both have. Describe how your plans to achieve these expectations might be different from the person living in the LDC. Then describe how they might be similar.

Math and Economics

In Figure 24-5, you saw information about the rate of population growth and how long it would take for a population to double at different rates of growth. There is a rule of thumb that can help you determine how long it will take for something to double in size if you know its annual growth rate. The rule is to divide the number 72 by the annual percentage growth rate to determine about how many years until the value will double. Consider the following example. You have $1,000 in a savings account that pays 6 percent a year in interest. Your $1,000 would double to about $2,000 in 12 years (72 ÷ by 6 = 12).

Use the information in the following table to calculate how long it will take for the populations to double.

Country	Population Growth Rate
Honduras	**3.3%**
Uzbekistan	**2.5%**
Namibia	**3.0%**
Viet Nam	**2.3%**

Writing About Economics

Pick one of the less-developed countries listed in Figure 24-1 and look up information on that country concerning the following topics:

a. natural resources

b. human capital

c. income

d. health measures

e. population level

f. economy

g. government

Write a booklet entitled *A Day in the Life of (insert your country's name here)*. Include a chapter on each of the seven topics listed. As a final chapter, compare life in the country you selected to life in the United States.

The Peace Corps: Helping Others Help Themselves

Many people in the United States feel that it is important to help those who are less fortunate in other parts of the world. During his inaugural address on January 20, 1961, President Kennedy verbalized what became the basic Peace Corps philosophy:

> "To those peoples in the huts and villages of half the globe struggling to break the bonds of mass misery, we pledge our best efforts to help them help themselves. . . ."

Later that year, President Kennedy issued an executive order creating the Peace Corps. Congress followed up on September 22, 1961, by approving legislation formally authorizing the Peace Corps with the mandate to "promote world peace and friendship" through the following objectives:

- to help the people of interested countries meet their needs for better trained men and women;
- to help promote a better understanding of the people of the United States on the part of the people served; and
- to promote a better understanding of other people on the part of people of the United States.

To achieve the first two objectives, the Peace Corps Partnership Program provides a link between U.S. contributors and requests for project assistance from the overseas communities served by the Peace Corps. This program has supported over 3,500 projects in more than 80 developing countries. These projects include such programs as helping to build schools, providing English language instruction and materials, and providing seed money and information needed to launch small businesses. For example, in Mali, a country in Africa, a small business entrepreneurial center was established to give people the opportunity to contribute firsthand to the development of a thriving market economy.

The third objective of promoting a better understanding of the peoples of the world by the people of the United States is accomplished by a program known as World Wise Schools (WWS) which is the Peace Corps' global education program. Each year, WWS links about 4,500 U.S. classrooms to Peace Corps Volunteers overseas. Through correspondence, U.S. students gain firsthand knowledge of the volunteer's country. The goals of the World Wise Schools Program are to encourage the study of geography, to promote cultural understanding, and to help our nation's youth recognize the importance of volunteer service.

Our social goal of helping others less fortunate than ourselves throughout the world has paid dividends by helping others develop the expertise necessary to participate in a market economy. At the same time, Peace Corps programs provide U.S. citizens the opportunity to learn about and participate in other cultures of the world.

SOURCES:
Lonardo, Brian P., "Peace Corps Chronological History," at **http://www.clark.net/pub/peace/History2.html** (August 1, 1995).
Lonardo, Brian P., "Peace Corps' Goals," at **http://www.clark.net/pub/peace/History6.html** (August 1, 1995).
Wilson-Jarrard, Maureen, "World Wise Schools," at **http:/www.clark.net/pub/peace/WWS1.html** (September 15, 1995).

Economic Measurement Concepts

Economists use several types of measurement tools to get data into a manageable form. You already may have learned some of these concepts in your mathematics classes. The focus of this appendix will be on how the following measurement concepts are used in economics: tables and graphs; averages and distributions; ratios and percentages; rates and absolute numbers; index numbers; and real and nominal values.

TABLES AND GRAPHS

Newspapers and magazines present economic information in the form of tables and graphs. Just pick up any newspaper or such popular publications as *The Wall Street Journal, Readers Digest, USA Today, Time, Newsweek,* and *U.S. News & World Report.* You will find examples in nearly every issue. Tables or graphs organize and display economic information in a clear and manageable form.

Tables Summarize Data

Assume you want to gather data on the distribution of income in a high school economics class. You could have all class members write on a piece of paper the income they earn each week, collect this data, and look at it piece by piece. However, the individual pieces of data would not, by themselves, tell you much about how income is distributed in your class.

If you were to look at this data in table form, your results would be much more meaningful. A *table* is a simplified way of showing numbers. Figure A-1 on page 682 is a table that summarizes weekly income for the economics class at Summit High School.

You could analyze this data by setting up some income categories. For example, you might arrange the incomes into the groups shown in Figure A-2 on page 682.

Graphs Show Relationships

From the information given in Figure A-2, you can create a bar graph. A *bar graph* uses the lengths of bars to represent the general relationship between variables. In the table in Figure A-2, the variables are *number of students* and *income categories.* To prepare a bar graph, label the vertical axis *number of students* and the horizontal axis *income categories.*

Student		Student		Student		Student	
No.	Income	No.	Income	No.	Income	No.	Income
1	$15	6	$27	11	$39	16	$57
2	15	7	33	12	45	17	63
3	15	8	33	13	48	18	63
4	21	9	36	14	51	19	69
5	27	10	39	15	51	20	75

Figure A-1

Income Data for Economics Students at Summit High School

This table summarizes student income for a class of 20 students.

Figure A-2

Categories of Income Data for Economics Students

These income categories further summarize the income data for economics students.

Category Number	Income Category	Number of Students in Category
1	$15–$27	6
2	$28–$40	5
3	$41–$53	4
4	$54–$66	3
5	$67–$79	2

The bar graph in Figure A-3 gives you several pieces of information at a glance. First, you can see that more students have incomes in the $15 to $27 range than any other income category. Second, you can see that the fewest number of students have incomes in the $67 to $79 group. Finally, you can see that the general relationship between income and the number of students who receive it is an inverse relationship. That means that, as income goes up, the number of students receiving incomes in that category goes down. And, as income goes down, the number of students receiving income in that category goes up.

A *line graph* is a diagram in which the relationship between variables is represented by a line. The bar graph in Figure A-3 can be converted into a rough approximation of a line graph by plotting a point in the center of the top of each bar and connecting the dots. This is shown in Figure A-4.

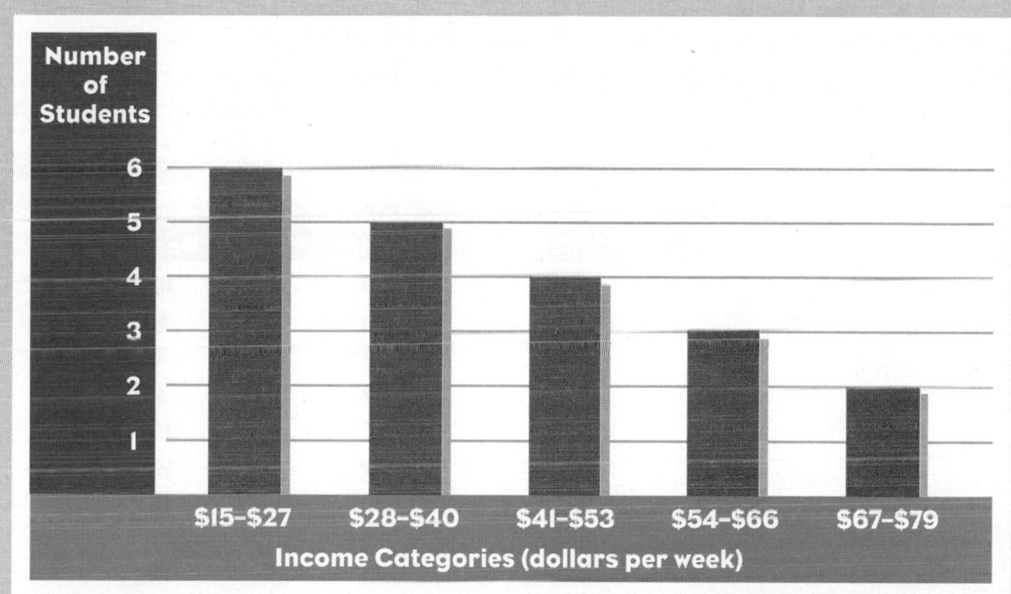

Figure A-3

Bar Graph of Income Data for Economics Students

This bar graph is a visual representation of the data summarized in Figure A-2

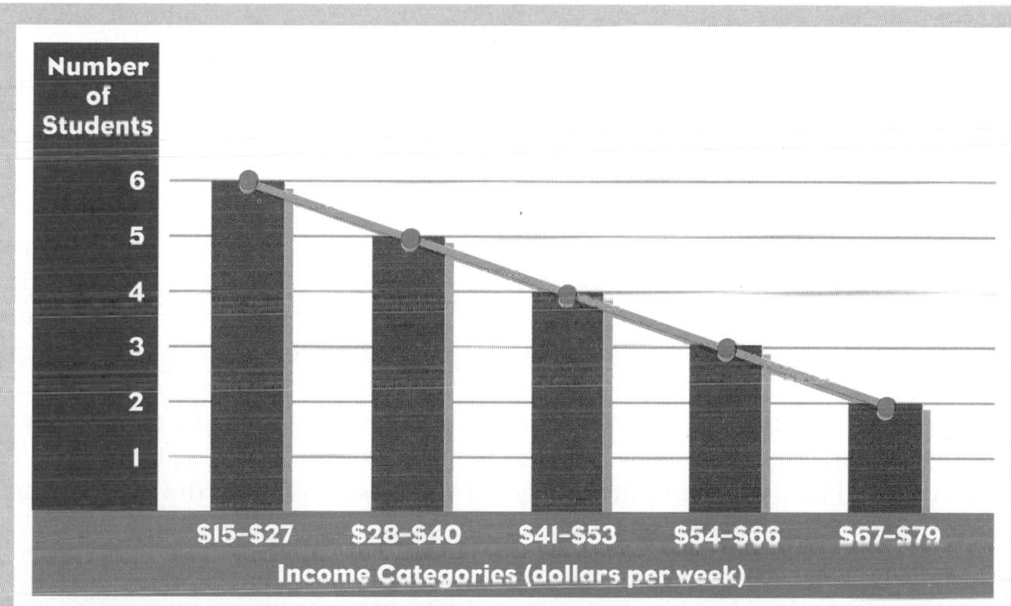

Figure A-4

Line Graph of Income Data for Economics Students

This line graph highlights the relationship between number of students and student income.

Now let's examine another type of graphical relationship. We will look at two variables that depend on each other. That is, the value or size of one variable depends on the size of the other. The information given in Figure A-5 describes the height and weight of ten clarinet players at Summit High School.

Figure A-5

Height and Weight Data for Clarinet Players at Summit High School

This table summarizes height and weight data for ten students.

Student No.	Height Inches	Weight Pounds
1	60"	105
2	61"	110
3	62"	117
4	64"	121
5	66"	128
6	67"	140
7	70"	152
8	72"	180
9	73"	192
10	75"	265
Totals	670"	1,510 lbs.

To graph these height and weight data points, the vertical axis of your graph should show weight and the horizontal axis should show height. Then, plot the points for the data and it will look like the graph in Figure A-6. From this graph, you can *see* a mathematical relationship. In general, the taller a person is, the heavier he or she is. While this is not always true, it does tell us the general relationship or rule.

AVERAGES AND DISTRIBUTIONS

It can be helpful to describe data points in more general terms. A *distribution* is a list of observations ordered from lowest to highest. In Figure A-5, the heights and weights for Summit clarinet players are presented as a distribution.

One way of summarizing data is to calculate the average or mean. The *average* or *mean* is the sum of the values for each variable divided by the number of observations. In our example, the mean height is the sum of the individual heights divided by the total number of students measured. The mean weight is the sum of the individual weights divided by the total number of students. The mean height and weight for clarinet players at Summit are calculated as follows:

$$\text{Mean height} = \frac{\text{Total height}}{\text{Number of students}} = \frac{670''}{10} = 67''$$

$$\text{Mean weight} = \frac{\text{Total weight}}{\text{Number of students}} = \frac{1{,}510\text{ lbs.}}{10} = 151\text{ lbs.}$$

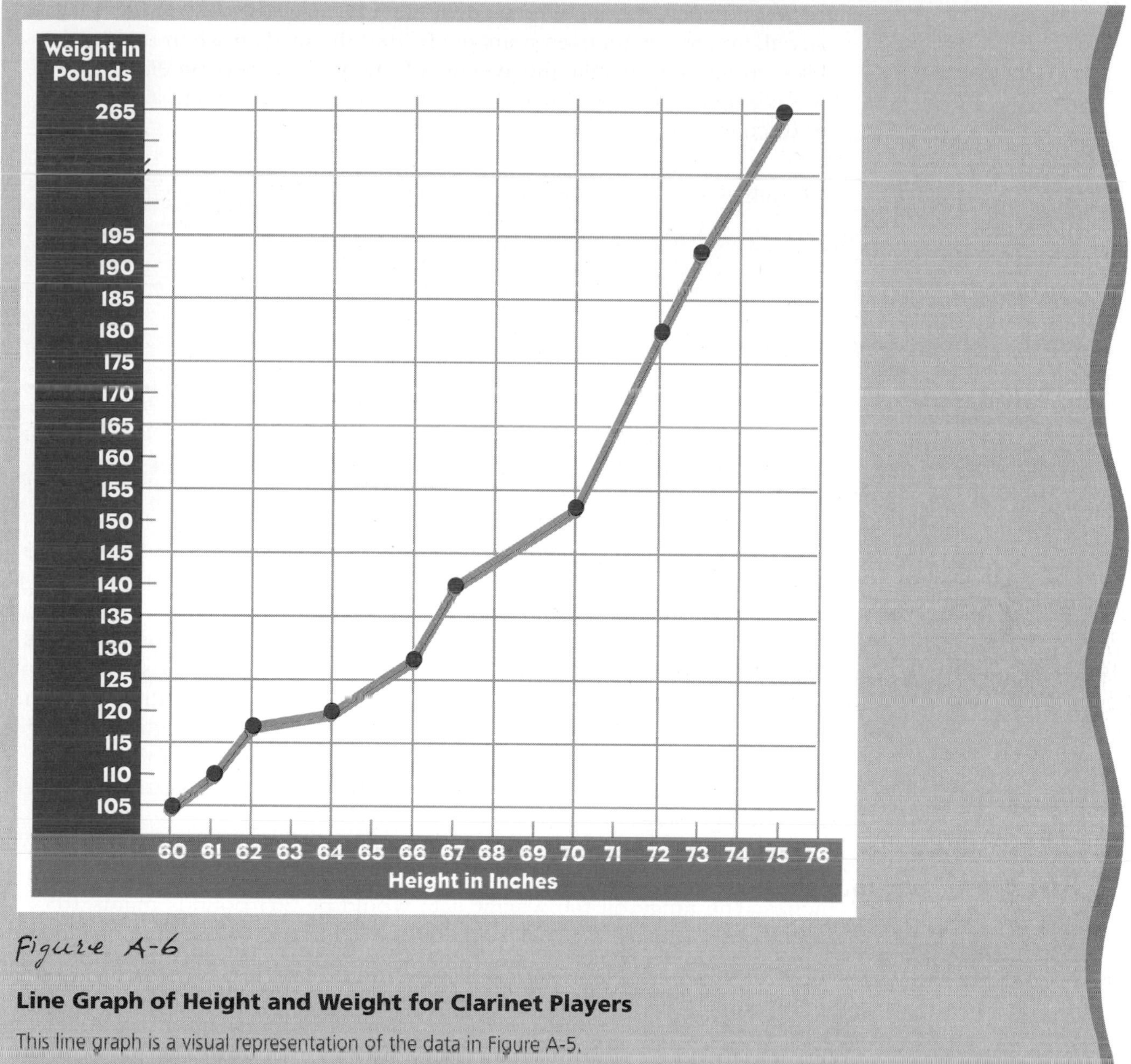

Line Graph of Height and Weight for Clarinet Players

This line graph is a visual representation of the data in Figure A-5.

The mean height, then, is 67 inches (5'7") and the mean weight is 151 pounds. These average measurements would be one way of describing all ten students at one time. However, it is important to notice that no clarinet player actually is 5'7" tall and weighs 151 pounds.

The median and the range are two other important measures of data. The *median* is the middle number in a distribution. One-half of all the numbers fall above the median, and one-half fall below. When there are an odd number of observations in the list, the median is simply the middle number when the numbers are listed from low to high. Consider the following five numbers:

		M		
13	16	20	28	35

As indicated by the M, the median is 20, the middle number.

How do you determine the median height and weight for clarinet players, since there are ten, an even number? To find the median when the number of observations is even, take the average of the two numbers on either side of the midpoint. For our clarinet players, then, the median height and weight are calculated as follows:

Height: 60 61 62 64 66 Midpoint 67 70 72 73 75

$$\text{Median height: } \frac{66'' + 67''}{2} = \frac{133''}{2} = 66.5''$$

Weight: 105 110 117 121 128 Midpoint 140 152 180 192 265

$$\text{Median weight: } \frac{128 \text{ lbs.} + 140 \text{ lbs.}}{2} = \frac{268 \text{ lbs.}}{2} = 134 \text{ lbs.}$$

Note that the median height and weight are a little below the average, or mean, height and weight. Can you look at the data and figure out why this is true? If you can, you will know something very important about averages. Note that the tallest student is 6'3" (75 inches) and weighs 265 pounds. This person is much taller and much heavier than the rest of the class. The mean is very sensitive to a single piece of information that is greatly different from the rest. This single tall and heavy person pulled the mean height and weight of the class above the median, or middle, weight and height of the class. There is a moral to this story: Averages can be misleading if you don't look at the other measures of the data.

The *range* is the largest number in a set of data minus the smallest number. The range of height would be 75 inches minus 60 inches, or 15 inches. The range on the weight data would be 265 pounds minus 105 pounds, or a range of 160 pounds. There is quite a wide range on both height and weight here. If the ranges were lower, what do you think would happen to the difference between the mean value and the median value? They would probably be closer to each other since there would not be individual pieces of data that were so much higher or lower than the rest.

When thinking about the concepts of mean, median, and range, it is important to understand how they are applied to economics. For example, you might see in the newspapers or on television that the median family income in the United States is approximately $35,000. Ask yourself why they chose to report the median income and not the mean income. The answer is simple. The range of family incomes in our economy is relatively large (from several thousand to millions of dollars per year). If the mean were reported, it might not give an accurate picture of what the "average" family earns. Since we have a large middle class in America, the median of $35,000 tells us that one-half of the families earns more and one-half earns less. The median gives us a more descriptive picture of family income in our economy.

RATIOS AND PERCENTAGES

A *ratio* shows the relationship of one numerical value to another numerical value. Ratios are often expressed in a form such as 5:1, which is pronounced, "5 to 1." A ratio is calculated by expressing two numbers as a fraction and then reducing the fraction to its lowest terms.

For example, consumers can do only two things with their after-tax incomes: They can spend (consume) or save them. In other words, consumers use their incomes for consumption and savings. Suppose that a family earns $30,000 after taxes and consumes (spends) $24,000. Savings, then, are $6,000. The proportion between these two activities is very important. In our example, the family spends four times as much as is saves:

$$\frac{\textbf{Consumption}}{\textbf{Savings}} = \frac{\$24{,}000}{\$6{,}000} = \frac{4}{1}$$

Our calculation reveals a consumption to savings ratio of 4:1. Another way of stating this proportion is that, on the average, for every $1 the family saves, it spends (consumes) $4. This concept of ratios can be extended to include income. What is the ratio of spending to after-tax income for this family? The answer is $24,000/$30,000 or 24:30 or 4:5. On the average, for every $5 earned, this family spends $4 and saves $1.

A *percentage* is a ratio that has been converted into a base of 100 equal parts. To get a percentage from a ratio, divide the numerator of a ratio by its denominator and multiply the result by 100. For example, what percentage of its income does this average American family consume? Divide consumption ($24,000) by income ($30,000) and multiply the result by 100. This average family consumes 80 percent of its income:

$$\frac{\$24{,}000}{\$30{,}000} = 0.80$$

$$0.80 \times 100 = 80\%$$

Percentages also can show how much a number has changed. For example, suppose you were making $5.00 per hour and then you received a raise to $5.50. The percentage change in your wage rate could be figured by finding the difference between your old wage and new wage, dividing by your old wage, and then converting the result to a percentage:

$$\frac{\$5.50 - \$5.00}{\$5.00} = \frac{\$0.50}{\$5.00} = 0.10$$

$$0.10 \times 100 = 10\%$$

Your new wage, then, would be 10 percent greater than your old wage.

RATES AND ABSOLUTE NUMBERS

Economic reports in the news media can be confusing because so many numbers are used. One of the most frequent mix-ups concerns percentage rates and absolute numbers. For example, you might hear that inflation is up 3 percent, or the money supply is growing at an annual rate of 5 percent, or the economy grew at 7 percent last year. The basic difference between rates and absolute numbers is that *rates* tell you how fast *absolute* numbers are changing. If you drive your car 200 miles at a speed of 50 miles per hour, then 50 miles per hour is the rate at which you are traveling. Two hundred miles is an absolute number that tells the distance you traveled.

The classic economic example of rate versus absolute numbers involves the rate of inflation. The rate of inflation tells us how fast prices are rising. When the headline in a newspaper reads, "Inflation increases to 15 percent," it means that prices are going up at a rate of 15 percent per year. If, in the next week, the same newspaper has a headline reading, "Inflation falls to 10 percent," it does not mean that absolute prices are falling. What it does mean is that absolute prices are rising at a slower rate (i.e., going up more slowly) than before.

To understand how relationships between rates and absolutes appear on a graph, look at the various graphs in Figure A-7 and read over the descriptions of what is happening under each graph. In each graph, the economic variable is some absolute number. Two examples of such absolute numbers would be Gross Domestic Product and sales of a company. The slope of the lines in the graphs tells you something about the rate of change in those absolute numbers.

INDEX NUMBERS

Index numbers are used by economists to show relative changes in factors such as consumer prices and gross domestic product. Index numbers set a base period and measure the changes from the base period to the present. The base period is usually considered to have an index value of 100 (or 100 percent). The other numbers, such as prices in the current year, are then expressed as a percentage of the prices in the base period. For example, for a typical market basket of goods in the 1982–1984 base period, the price index is set at 100. The remaining years' price indexes then show the percentage by which prices have increased over the base period. Figure A-8 on page 690 shows the price index of the same market basket of goods for the years 1980, 1985, 1990, and 1995.

Since the 1985 price index of 107.6 is greater than 100, it shows that 1985 prices were higher than prices in the base period. As you can see, the average level of prices rose steadily from 1980 to 1995. Index numbers are a quick and relatively accurate way to measure increases or decreases in any variable relative to a base period.

NOMINAL AND REAL VALUES

Dollar measurements in economics can be expressed in either nominal or real terms. For example, if you get paid a salary of $300 per week, your nominal income is $300 per week or $15,600 per year. If you receive the same

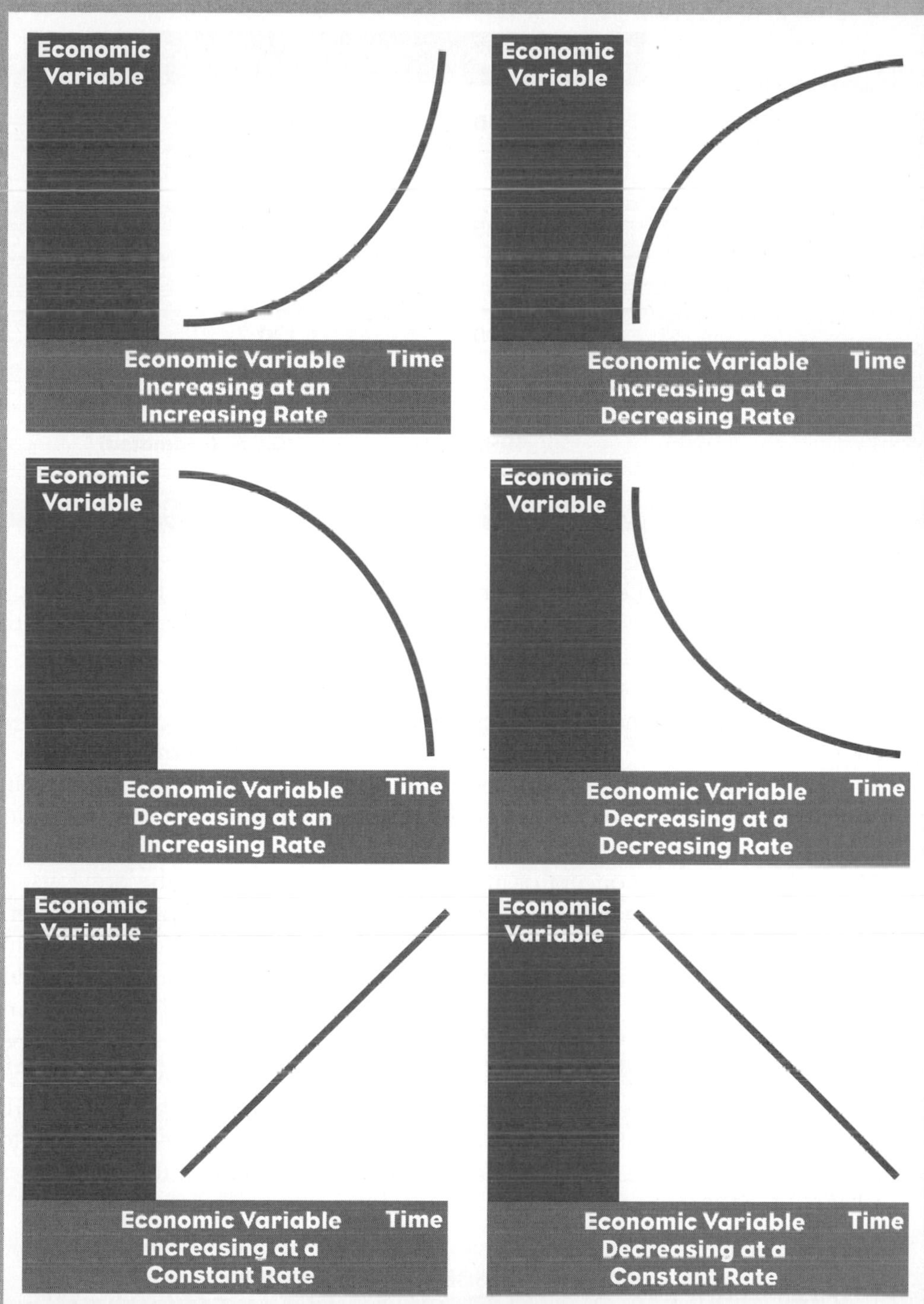

Figure A-7

Absolute Numbers and Their Rates of Change

These graphs are visual representations of a variety of different rates, both increasing and decreasing.

Figure A-8

Price Indexes for Selected Years

The price indexes in this table show the percentages by which prices have increased over the years shown.

SOURCE: *Economic Report of the President: 1995* (Washington, D.C.: U.S. Government Printing Office, 1995), 341.

Year	Price Index
1980	82.4
1985	107.6
1990	130.7
1995	152.5 (estimated)

salary next year, you'll earn another $15,600. But, let's take a closer look at your real income. If prices go up over the year by 10 percent and you get the same $15,600 nominal income, you will not be able to buy as much in the second year. In fact, your salary will buy 10 percent less. Your nominal income will be the same, $15,600, but your real income will decline by 10 percent to $14,040 ($15,600 – $1,560 = $14,040). Your *nominal income* is your income measured in dollars for this year. Your *real income* is the buying power of your nominal income. A real value in economics is a nominal value adjusted for changes in prices.

Economists use the concept of index numbers, discussed in the previous section, to adjust nominal values to real values. Recall that the price index for a market basket of goods in 1985 was 107.6, and, for the same market basket in 1990, it was 130.7. We can use this price index to adjust gross domestic product (GDP) figures. Suppose that GDP in 1985 was $4.0 trillion ($4,000,000,000) and that GDP in 1990 was $5.5 trillion ($5,500,000,000). At first glance, it might look as if GDP increased over the five years by $1.5 trillion. You know, however, that over the same period of time prices went up. To adjust both values of GDP to constant dollars—that is, dollars with the same buying power—you need to divide GDP for each year by that year's price index. (Note that the price index is divided by 100 when used in this equation.)

$$\text{1985 Real GDP} = \frac{\text{1985 Nominal GDP}}{\text{1985 Price Index}} = \frac{\$4,000,000,000}{1.076} = \$3,717,472,118$$

$$\text{1990 Real GDP} = \frac{\text{1990 Nominal GDP}}{\text{1990 Price Index}} = \frac{\$5,500,000,000}{1.307} = \$4,208,110,175$$

As the calculations show, real GDP did not go up $1.5 trillion. After adjusting for inflation, it "only" went up by about $491 million ($4,208,110,175 – $3,717,472,118 = $490,638,057).

APPENDIX B

United States Political Map

World Political Map

UNITED STATES
CANADA
Olympia
WASHINGTON
Columbia
River
MONTANA
Helena
NORTH DAKOTA
Bismarck
Red River
Salem
OREGON
IDAHO
Boise
SOUTH DAKOTA
Pierre
Minnesota
Snake River
WYOMING
Missouri River
Great Salt Lake
Cheyenne
NEBRASKA
Lincoln
Carson City
Sacramento
NEVADA
Salt Lake City
UTAH
Denver
COLORADO
Topeka
KANSAS
Arkansas River
CALIFORNIA
River
Santa Fe
OKLAHOMA
Oklahoma City
PACIFIC OCEAN
ARIZONA
Colorado
NEW MEXICO
Red River
Phoenix
Brazos River
TEXAS
Austin
MEXICO
Rio Grande
RUSSIA
ARCTIC OCEAN
ALASKA
CANADA
Yukon River
Juneau
PACIFIC OCEAN
Honolulu
HAWAII
PACIFIC OCEAN

POLITICAL

Projection: Transverse Mercator
MAINE
Augusta
VERMONT
Montpelier
NEW HAMPSHIRE
Concord
Boston
MASSACHUSETTS
Providence
RHODE ISLAND
CONNECTICUT
Hartford
Albany
NEW YORK
L. Ontario
Lake Superior
MINNESOTA
St. Paul
River
WISCONSIN
Madison
MICHIGAN
Lake Michigan
Lake Huron
Lansing
Lake Erie
PENNSYLVANIA
Harrisburg
Trenton
NEW JERSEY
Dover
DELAWARE
Annapolis
Washington, D.C.
MARYLAND
IOWA
Des Moines
ILLINOIS
Springfield
INDIANA
Indianapolis
OHIO
Columbus
WEST VIRGINIA
Charleston
Richmond
VIRGINIA
Ohio River
Frankfort
KENTUCKY
Jefferson City
MISSOURI
Raleigh
NORTH CAROLINA
Nashville
TENNESSEE
ARKANSAS
Little Rock
Mississippi River
MISSISSIPPI
Jackson
ALABAMA
Montgomery
GEORGIA
Atlanta
SOUTH CAROLINA
Columbia
ATLANTIC OCEAN
Tallahassee
LOUISIANA
Baton Rouge
FLORIDA
Lake Okeechobee
Gulf of Mexico
N
TROPIC OF CANCER

WORLD

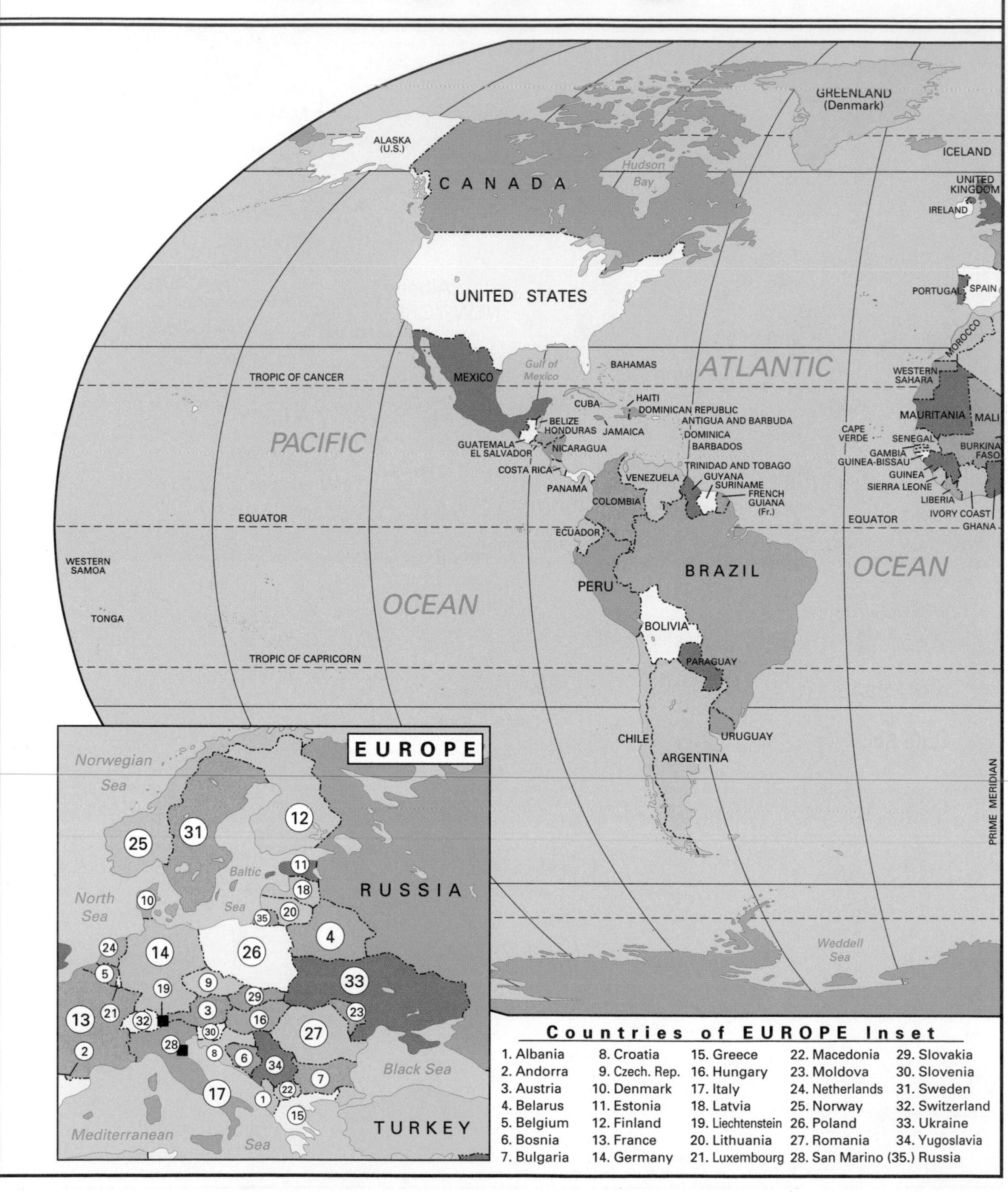
GREENLAND
(Denmark)
ALASKA
(U.S.)
ICELAND
C A N A D A
Hudson
Bay
UNITED
KINGDOM
IRELAND
UNITED STATES
PORTUGAL
SPAIN
MOROCCO
BAHAMAS
ATLANTIC
Gulf of
Mexico
MEXICO
TROPIC OF CANCER
WESTERN
SAHARA
CUBA
HAITI
DOMINICAN REPUBLIC
ANTIGUA AND BARBUDA
MAURITANIA
MALI
BELIZE
HONDURAS
JAMAICA
PACIFIC
DOMINICA
BARBADOS
CAPE
VERDE
SENEGAL
GAMBIA
GUINEA-BISSAU
BURKINA
FASO
GUATEMALA
EL SALVADOR
NICARAGUA
COSTA RICA
TRINIDAD AND TOBAGO
GUYANA
SURINAME
FRENCH
GUIANA
(Fr.)
GUINEA
SIERRA LEONE
LIBERIA
IVORY COAST
GHANA
PANAMA
VENEZUELA
COLOMBIA
EQUATOR
EQUATOR
ECUADOR
WESTERN
SAMOA
BRAZIL
OCEAN
PERU
TONGA
OCEAN
BOLIVIA
PARAGUAY
TROPIC OF CAPRICORN
CHILE
URUGUAY
ARGENTINA
PRIME MERIDIAN
Weddell
Sea
EUROPE
Norwegian
Sea
North
Sea
Baltic
Sea
RUSSIA
Black Sea
TURKEY
Mediterranean
Sea
Countries of EUROPE Inset
1. Albania
2. Andorra
3. Austria
4. Belarus
5. Belgium
6. Bosnia
7. Bulgaria
8. Croatia
9. Czech. Rep.
10. Denmark
11. Estonia
12. Finland
13. France
14. Germany
15. Greece
16. Hungary
17. Italy
18. Latvia
19. Liechtenstein
20. Lithuania
21. Luxembourg
22. Macedonia
23. Moldova
24. Netherlands
25. Norway
26. Poland
27. Romania
28. San Marino
29. Slovakia
30. Slovenia
31. Sweden
32. Switzerland
33. Ukraine
34. Yugoslavia
(35.) Russia

POLITICAL

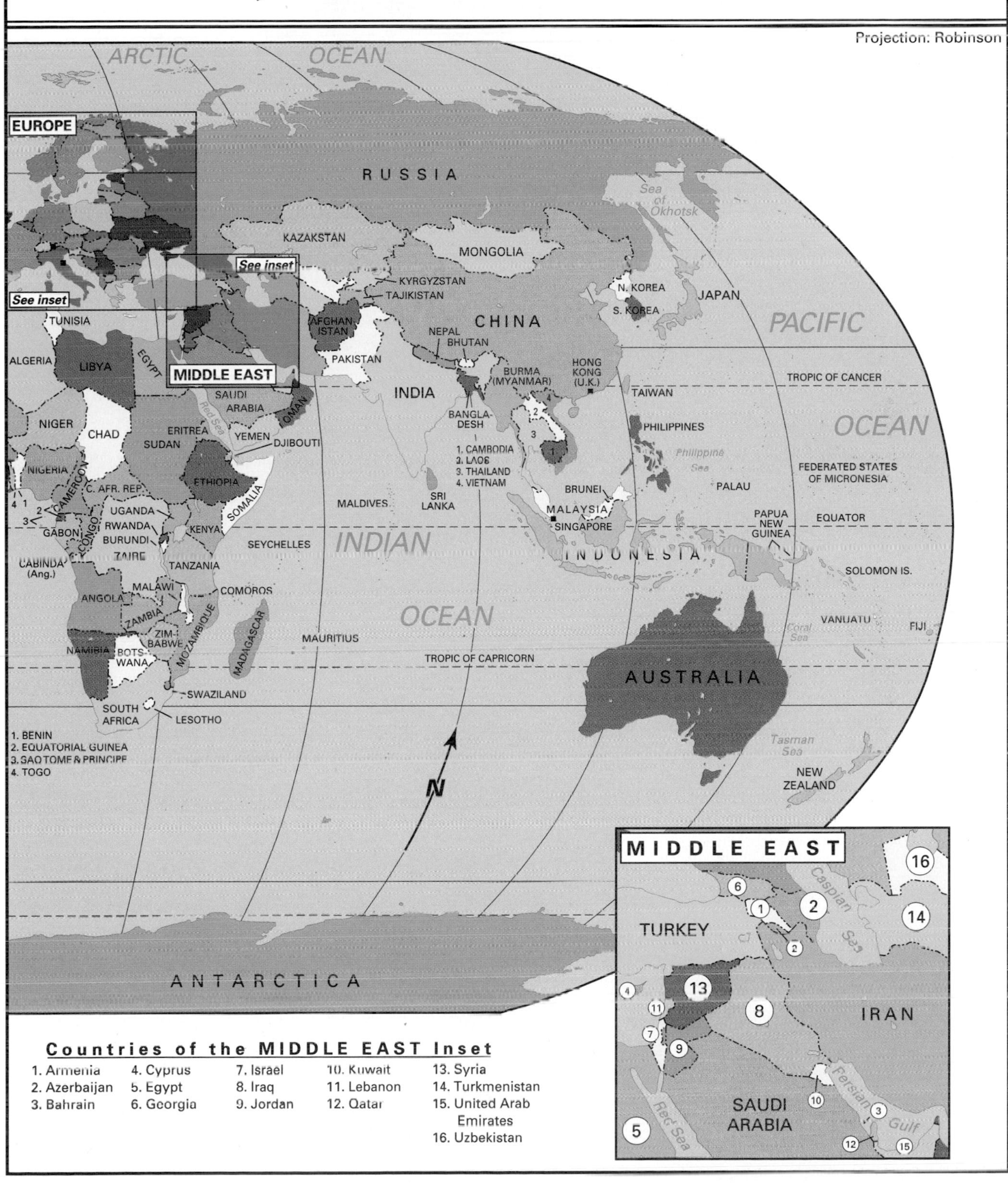
Projection: Robinson
ARCTIC OCEAN
EUROPE
See inset
RUSSIA
KAZAKSTAN
MONGOLIA
KYRGYZSTAN
TAJIKISTAN
N. KOREA
S. KOREA
JAPAN
Sea of Okhotsk
CHINA
PACIFIC OCEAN
TUNISIA
ALGERIA
LIBYA
EGYPT
MIDDLE EAST
AFGHANISTAN
PAKISTAN
NEPAL
BHUTAN
INDIA
BANGLADESH
BURMA (MYANMAR)
HONG KONG (U.K.)
TAIWAN
TROPIC OF CANCER
SAUDI ARABIA
OMAN
YEMEN
DJIBOUTI
Red Sea
NIGER
CHAD
SUDAN
ERITREA
ETHIOPIA
SOMALIA
NIGERIA
CAMEROON
C. AFR. REP.
UGANDA
RWANDA
BURUNDI
KENYA
GABON
CONGO
ZAIRE
TANZANIA
CABINDA (Ang.)
ANGOLA
MALAWI
ZAMBIA
COMOROS
ZIMBABWE
MOZAMBIQUE
MADAGASCAR
NAMIBIA
BOTSWANA
SWAZILAND
SOUTH AFRICA
LESOTHO
1. CAMBODIA
2. LAOS
3. THAILAND
4. VIETNAM
PHILIPPINES
Philippine Sea
PALAU
FEDERATED STATES OF MICRONESIA
MALDIVES
SRI LANKA
BRUNEI
MALAYSIA
SINGAPORE
PAPUA NEW GUINEA
EQUATOR
SEYCHELLES
INDIAN OCEAN
INDONESIA
SOLOMON IS.
VANUATU
FIJI
Coral Sea
MAURITIUS
TROPIC OF CAPRICORN
AUSTRALIA
Tasman Sea
NEW ZEALAND
N
1. BENIN
2. EQUATORIAL GUINEA
3. SAO TOME & PRINCIPE
4. TOGO
ANTARCTICA
MIDDLE EAST
TURKEY
Caspian Sea
IRAN
SAUDI ARABIA
Red Sea
Persian Gulf
Countries of the MIDDLE EAST Inset
1. Armenia
2. Azerbaijan
3. Bahrain
4. Cyprus
5. Egypt
6. Georgia
7. Israel
8. Iraq
9. Jordan
10. Kuwait
11. Lebanon
12. Qatar
13. Syria
14. Turkmenistan
15. United Arab Emirates
16. Uzbekistan

APPENDIX C

Careers in Your Future

Choosing a career is one of the most important decisions you will ever face. Preparing for the career of your choice through education and training is only part of successful career planning. You must also look at what tomorrow's job opportunities will be. In this appendix, you will read about projected trends in population and the composition of the labor force, the link between education and job opportunities, and growth in the service sector. Then, you will see some helpful job search hints. Finally, a variety of career choices are described to give you a broad overview of the types of jobs awaiting you.

The following additional career planning information is provided in the *Life Skills* worksheets, available from your teacher:

Chapter	Career Planning Topic
12	College application
15	Scholarship application
16	Job application
22	Résumé template

POPULATION TRENDS

Employment opportunities are affected in several ways by population trends. Changes in the size and composition of the population between now and 2005 will influence the demand for goods and services, which will affect the demand for jobs. For example, the percentage of the population who is aged 85 and over will grow about four times as fast as the total population, increasing the demand for health services. This may mean an increase in jobs in health services.

The U.S. civilian noninstitutional population, aged 16 and over, is expected to increase to about 219 million by 2005, growing more slowly than it has in the recent past. However, even slower population growth still will increase the demand for goods and services, as well as the demand for workers in many occupations and industries.

The age distribution will shift into the twenty-first century toward relatively fewer teenagers and a growing proportion of middle-aged and older people. The decline in the proportion of teenagers reflects the lower birth rates that prevailed during the 1980s; the impending large increase in the middle-aged population reflects the aging of the "baby boom" generation born between 1946 and 1964; and the very rapid growth in the number of old people is attributable to high birth rates prior to the 1930s and improvements in medical technology that have allowed most Americans to live longer.

Minorities and immigrants will constitute a larger share of the U.S. population in 2005 than they do today. Substantial increases in the number of Hispanics, Asians, and African Americans are anticipated.

Population growth varies greatly among geographic regions, affecting the demand for goods and services and, in turn, the number of workers required by various occupations and industries. Projections by the Bureau of the Census indicate that the West and South will continue to be the fastest growing regions, increasing 24 percent and 16 percent, respectively, by 2005. The Midwest population is expected to grow by 7 percent, while the number of people in the Northeast is projected to increase by only 3 percent.

COMPOSITION OF THE LABOR FORCE

Population is the single most important factor governing the size and composition of the labor force. The civilian labor force is expected to reach 151 million by 2005. America's workers will be an increasingly diverse group as we move toward 2005. White non-Hispanic men will make up a slightly smaller proportion of the labor force, and women and minority group members will comprise a larger share.

The changing age structure of the population will directly affect tomorrow's labor force. Compared to the pool of young workers, that of experienced workers will increase. In 1992, the median age of the labor force was 37.2 years; by 2005, it will be 40.5 years. Young people are expected to comprise roughly the same percentage of the labor force in 2005 as they did in 1992. The scenario should be somewhat different for prime-age workers (25 to 54 years of age). The baby boom generation will continue to add members to the labor force, but their share of the labor force peaked in 1985. The proportion of workers in the 25–34 age range will decline dramatically, from 28 percent to 21 percent in 2005. The growing proportion of workers between the ages of 45 and 54 is equally striking. These workers should account for 24 percent of the labor force by the year 2005.

EDUCATION AND JOB OPPORTUNITIES

In recent years, the level of educational attainment of the labor force has risen dramatically. In 1996, at least 27 percent of all workers aged 25 and over had bachelor's degrees or higher, while only 12 percent did not possess high school diplomas. The trend toward higher educational attainment is expected to continue. Projected rates of employment growth are faster for occupations requiring higher levels of education or training than for those requiring less.

Three out of the four fastest growing occupational groups will be executive, administrative, and managerial; professional specialty; and technical and related support. These occupations, which generally require the highest levels of education and skill, will make up an increasing proportion of new jobs. Office and factory automation, changes in consumer demand, and movement of production facilities to other countries are expected to cause employment to stagnate or decline in many occupations that require little formal education. Opportunities for those who do not finish high school will be increasingly limited.

Those who do not complete high school and are employed are more likely to have low-paying jobs with little advancement potential, while workers in occupations requiring higher levels of education will have higher incomes. In addition, many of the occupations projected to grow most rapidly are among those with higher earnings.

GROWTH IN THE SERVICE SECTOR

The long-term shift from goods-producing to service-producing employment is expected to continue. Service-producing industries, including transportation, communications, and utilities; retail and wholesale trade; services; government; and finance, insurance, and real estate are expected to account for approximately 24.5 million of the 26.4 million new jobs available between now and 2005. Expansion of service sector employment is linked to a number of factors, including changes in consumer tastes and preferences, legal and regulatory changes, advances in science and technology, and changes in the way businesses are organized and managed.

Continued expansion of the service-producing sector conjures up an image of a workforce dominated by cashiers, retail sales workers, and waiters. Although service-sector growth will generate millions of these jobs, it also will create jobs for financial managers, engineers, nurses, electrical and electronics technicians, and many other managerial, professional, and technical workers. As indicated earlier, the fastest growing occupations will be those that require the most formal education and training.

JOB SEARCH TIPS

It takes some people a long time to find the job they want. Don't be discouraged if you have to pursue many leads. Friends, neighbors, teachers, and counselors may know of available jobs in your area of interest. Read the want ads. Consult state employment service offices and private or nonprofit employment agencies, or contact employers directly.

Once you get an interview, keep the following recommendations in mind:

- Be prepared.
- Learn about the organization and review your qualifications for the job.
- Practice the interview with a friend or relative.
- Before you leave for the interview, gather your social security number, driver's license, a résumé (if required), and the names of three references (get permission from the references first).
- On the day of the interview, dress appropriately, arrive before the scheduled time of your interview, and do not chew gum or smoke.
- During the actual interview, answer the questions concisely, use good manners, and be enthusiastic. This is your chance to impress on the interviewer that you will be a good employee who is a benefit to the company.
- Always thank the interviewer and follow up with a letter.

DESCRIPTION OF JOBS

Occupation	Nature of Work	Education and Training	Job Growth Outlook	Earnings at Entry Level
Accountant	Prepare, analyze, and verify financial reports and taxes and monitor information systems that furnish this information.	Bachelor's degree; CPA recommended	Faster than the average	$28,000
Actor	Entertain and communicate through interpretation of dramatic roles.	Formal dramatic training or acting experience	Much faster than the average	Earnings vary greatly
Automotive mechanic	Repair and service automobiles.	High school education and formal training program	As fast as the average	$11,960
Bank Teller	Handle a wide range of banking transactions.	High school education	Declining	Federal minimum wage
Chef	Prepare food.	No formal requirement	Faster than the average	Earnings vary greatly
Computer Analyst	Conduct research, design computers, and discover and use principles of applying computers.	Bachelor's degree	Much faster than the average	$22,700
Economist	Conduct research, monitor economic trends, and develop forecasts. Study the ways a society uses scarce resources to produce goods and services.	Bachelor's degree	As fast as the average	$25,200

Occupation	Nature of Work	Education and Training	Job Growth Outlook	Earnings at Entry Level
Electrician	Install and maintain electrical systems.	4- or 5-year apprenticeship program	As fast as the average	$13,520
Engineer	Apply the theories and principles of science and mathematics to the solution of technical problems.	Bachelor's degree	As fast as the average	$34,000
Home Health Aide	Help elderly, disabled, and ill people live in their own homes instead of in a health facility.	Federal competency exam	Much faster than the average	Earnings vary greatly
Lawyer	Counsel clients as to their legal rights and obligations and represent parties in criminal and civil trials.	Law school and state bar examination	Faster than the average	$36,600
Occupational Therapist	Help individuals with disabling conditions to develop or maintain daily living and work skills.	Bachelor's degree	Much faster than the average	$30,470
Paralegal	Assist lawyers in preparing cases, investigating facts, conducting research, and preparing written reports.	Formal paralegal training programs, associate's degree, or bachelor's degree	Much faster than the average	$23,400

Occupation	Nature of Work	Education and Training	Job Growth Outlook	Earnings at Entry Level
Physician	Examine patients, obtain medical histories, and interpret diagnostic tests.	Medical school, residency, and licensing exam	Faster than the average	$28,618 (first-year resident)
Police officer	Prevent and investigate crimes.	High school education and written and physical exams	More slowly than the average	$18,400
Radiologic Technologist	Use radiation, ultrasound, and magnetic resonance scans to produce images of the interior of the body.	Certificate, associate degree, or bachelor's degree	Much faster than the average	$22,250
Reporter	Gather information and prepare stories about local, national, and international events.	Bachelor's degree	As fast as the average	$22,000
Retail Sales Worker	Assist customers in the selection and purchase of retail items.	No formal training required	As fast as the average	Federal minimum wage
Secretary	Perform and coordinate office activities.	High school education with office skills	More slowly than the average	$16,400
Teacher	Educate children in specific subject areas and teach abstract concepts, problem solving, and critical thought processes.	Bachelor's degree and state certification	Faster than the average	$24,000

Occupation	Nature of Work	Education and Training	Job Growth Outlook	Earnings at Entry Level
Travel Agent	Assist clients with personal and business travel plans.	Vocational training program or associate's degree	Much faster than the average	$12,428
Truck driver	Transport goods by truck.	Commercial driver's license	As fast as the average	$18,000
Veterinarian	Care for pets, livestock, and sporting and laboratory animals. Advise owners on care and breeding.	Doctor of Veterinary Medicine degree and state board exam	Faster than the average	$27,858
Visual Artist	Use a variety of methods and materials to communicate ideas visually.	No formal training required but demonstrated ability and appropriate training as shown in a portfolio	As fast as the average	$21,000

SOURCE: *Occupational Outlook Handbook 1994–1995 Edition* (Washington, D.C.: U.S. Government Printing Office, 1994)

APPENDIX D

Consumer Economic Issues

Consumers face many economic decisions in our complex world. This appendix will examine the importance of managing your money, using credit wisely, investing, managing consumer risk, and your role as a consumer in the marketplace.

MONEY MANAGEMENT

Money management is a plan for controlling and spending income. Money management requires personal application of the decision-making process first introduced in chapters 1 and 2. Money management involves scarcity and opportunity costs as you decide what tradeoffs will be made when you spend your limited income.

Budgeting

A *budget* is an estimate of expected income, expenses, and savings. It is a tool to help you reach your financial goals. Following a budget is a key to good money management. By using a budget, you can make good money decisions and spend your limited financial resources in ways that truly satisfy you.

The first step in preparing a budget is setting goals and priorities. Few people can afford to waste income. Setting consumer goals is a way to decide how to use limited income for the best results.

The second step in preparing a budget is estimating your income for a specific time period. You should estimate the amount of all income that you are sure you will receive, including wages, interest on a savings account or certificate of deposit, stock dividends, and gifts.

After you have estimated your income, the next step is estimating expenses. When your estimate of income is equal to your estimate of expenses, you have a balanced budget, but estimating expenses can be a very difficult step. It helps to separate regular expenses from those that can change from month to month.

Regular expenses such as rent or mortgage payments, telephone bill, loan payments, and insurance are called *fixed expenses*. Some people put a regular savings amount into this category. Although savings is not really an expense, if you save regularly, this fixed amount can be included in this category. Saving this way is a good idea.

Expenses that are likely to change from month to month are called *variable expenses*. These include items such as food, clothing, transportation, health care, and entertainment. Even these variable expenses can be estimated to an approximate amount.

Remember, a budget is a plan for estimating income and spending. Adjustments may be made within the budget. One purpose of a budget is to make sure that spending does not exceed income. The more realistic your budget is, the better you will be able to follow it. Self-discipline is also required to follow it and make it work for you.

Savings Accounts

A savings account gives you the opportunity to earn interest on money that you have deposited in it. A savings account can help you establish the habit of saving. Having your own savings account makes it easier for you to cash checks that you may receive. Different financial institutions offer different kinds of savings accounts. You should compare interest rates, bank location, bank business hours, automatic teller access, and the initial deposit amount required before choosing the financial institution for your savings account.

When opening a savings account, you will fill out a signature card. This card serves as the basic record for the account. It lists your name and address and the amount of the initial deposit. You then will be given a passbook in which all of your deposits and withdrawals should be noted.

Checking Accounts

Most financial transactions in the country involve checks. A *check* is a written order for payment. The dollar value of transactions handled by check is far greater than that of transactions involving cash. Checks provide a record of a transaction and are safer than using cash. Different financial institutions offer different types of checking accounts. It is important to find out what types are offered when you are choosing among different financial institutions.

To open a checking account, you will fill out a signature card and make an initial deposit. You then will be given a supply of checks and a *check register,* which is a booklet for record keeping. (Some checking accounts use check stubs or carbon copies of the checks for record keeping rather than check registers.)

Writing checks involves two procedures. The first is filling out the check register or check stub, if appropriate. It is very important to fill out the check register or stub first because you might forget to do it later. If this happened, you could easily lose track of how much money you had in the account. This might cause you to bounce a check, or write a check for money you did not have in the account, which is called *being overdrawn*. This can be both embarrassing and expensive, since most banks charge a fee for bounced checks or overdrawn accounts.

The second procedure in writing checks involves filling out the check itself. Be sure to use permanent ink. Never use a pencil or erasable ink, so that no one else can change the amount of your check in an effort to take money from you. To actually write the check, you should do the following:

1. write the date on the date line;
2. write in the name of the payee (the person or company being paid);
3. write in the amount of the check in numbers next to the dollar sign;
4. write in the amount of the check in words next to the word *dollars;*
5. write in the purpose of the check on the memo line; and
6. sign your name exactly as you signed it on the signature card.

When making a deposit to your checking account, either through an automatic teller machine, by direct deposit from your paycheck, or with the help of a teller at the financial institution itself, make sure you note the deposit in your check register or on your check stub. This will allow you to keep accurate checking account records.

The financial institution will send you a periodic report of the activity in your checking account. The report is usually made monthly and is called a *statement.* Some financial institutions also return your cancelled, or used, checks. The statement lists checks paid, interest payments, deposits, and any service charges made. The statement also includes the balance in your account the day the statement was prepared. This statement will not necessarily agree with your check register or stubs. There may be checks you have written that are still outstanding, some of your deposits may not have been received before the statement was prepared, or an error may have been made—by you or the financial institution. That is why it is very important to *reconcile* your statement, which means to try to make the statement agree with your records. A reconciliation form will be printed on the reverse side of the statement you receive. If you complete the reconciliation form and your statement and records still do not match, report the problem right away. The financial institution will compare your account records with its records and help you find the difference.

CONSUMER CREDIT

Credit is not a form of income. Credit is a borrower's promise to pay at some future time. When you use credit, you are actually borrowing against your future income. A seller or lender trusts you to pay later for goods or services you receive now. Whether the amount borrowed is large or small, the use of credit is an important part of a consumer's life. To use credit wisely, you must be aware of its advantages and disadvantages.

Advantages of Credit

To buy a major consumer good, such as a car, it would take years to save enough money to pay for the good outright. During the time when you were saving, you would not have the benefit of using the good. If you did not really need a car and had other options for transportation, it might be good to save the money. However, if you really needed a car, using credit to buy it would be an advantage. You could use the car when you needed it and pay for it in the future. For example, if you needed the car for a job, using credit would allow you to take the job where you could earn the income needed to buy the car. Another advantage of credit is that it allows you to carry less cash, which is both a convenience and a safety measure. Credit is also convenient when ordering over the telephone or by mail.

Disadvantages of Credit

For most arguments in favor of using credit, there are equally strong reasons for not using it. People tend to buy more when they use credit. They also tend to buy higher priced merchandise. Even though the bills for credit purchases must be paid eventually, some consumers buy on credit as if there is no tomorrow. Some consumers lose control of their spending when they use credit. Another disadvantage of credit is that it costs money. Credit is a financial service that you pay for in interest. This interest can add a great deal to the cost of an item if you carry a balance on your credit cards or loan.

INVESTMENTS

Millions of people set aside a portion of the money they do not spend for food, clothing, shelter and other needed items. Some people put this money into savings accounts, others put the money to work by investing it.

Many consumers invest their money by buying securities. Securities include stocks and bonds. People who buy securities hope that, over a period of time, the value of their investments will grow. They hope the money will earn more interest or dividends than it would in a savings account.

Many consumers choose not to buy securities because investing can be risky. The risk is that money may be lost—investments are not insured as are savings accounts. Securities can and do decline in price sometimes. The more you learn about the kinds of investments available, the better your decisions will be.

Stocks and Bonds

Corporations obtain the money they need to start and continue their operations by selling stocks and bonds. Buying corporate stocks and bonds is a common investment activity.

Stocks represent ownership in a company. When you buy common stock, you become a shareholder and part owner in the company that issues the stock. A *share* of stock is one of the equal parts into which the ownership of a company is divided. If things go well for the company, the price of the stock might increase, increasing the value of your stock investment. There is no limit to how much any stock can increase in price. This is one of the main reasons people buy common stock. *Dividend* is money earned as profits by the company and divided among the shareholders. If the company does well, dividends paid out will be high. So, stocks earn money for stockholders through dividends and through their increasing value. Over a long period of time, stocks have done better than other forms of investments, but this does not mean that every stock will do well. Therefore, it is necessary to know as much as possible about a company before investing in its stock.

A *bond* is a certificate representing a loan of money to a corporation or government. The organization that issues the bond agrees to pay back the money, with interest, within a certain time period. When you buy a bond, you lend an organization money, you receive interest, and you are repaid the money when the time period is up.

How to Invest

You can invest money individually or through a financial group. Either way, the more information you have about different investments, the better your decisions will be. Before investing in a company's stock or bonds, read a company's annual report. The *annual report* describes a company's type of business, sales and earnings, and financial condition. You also should read the financial sections of newspapers, where you will find articles and stock market reports that will increase your understanding. Special magazines and newspapers provide detailed information about stocks and bonds. *The Wall Street Journal, Money, Fortune,* and *Barrons* are all useful sources of investment information. The wise investor will follow the stock market averages to find out how the stock market is doing on a daily basis. The Dow Jones Industrial Average is probably the most widely watched stock market average. Other popular stock market averages are issued by the New York Stock Exchange, Standard and Poor's, and the Nikkei Index (from Japan).

In addition to being informed, you should follow three major investment principles:

1. set investment goals,
2. diversify your investments, and
3. review and revise your investments periodically.

Other Investments

You have a wide range of investment opportunities. Some people choose to invest in real estate, works of art, stamp or coin collections, rare books, antique cars, and thoroughbred horses. Some people invest in certificates of deposit (CDs), which are investments in which the investor agrees to leave money on deposit in a financial institution for a definite period, such as six months or several years. The interest paid is generally higher than that paid for regular savings accounts.

MANAGING CONSUMER RISK

A risk is the possibility of loss. As individuals and as consumers, we face many risks in life. All risks have an element of uncertainty. You do not know for sure that they will happen. You do not know if you will become ill, lose a wallet, or wreck your car. If you knew in advance, you would avoid the loss. It is impossible to completely remove all risks. But you can take steps to reduce them.

Insurance

Insurance is a system by which risks of loss are spread among a number of people. Many people who face similar risks, such as car owners, pay a relatively small amount of money, called a *premium,* to an insurance company. The insurance company, in turn, issues a policy to the consumer, who is the policyholder. The insurance company agrees to pay a certain amount of money if the policyholder suffers losses that are covered by the policy. Insurance policies can cover many different risks, such as automobile accidents, fire, and theft.

Types of Risk

One major category of risk that consumers face is property loss. Consumers are very concerned about the risk of damage to or theft of their property. People whose homes are damaged by fire often lose the use of their homes while they are being repaired or rebuilt. A driver who has been in an accident may lose the use of the car while it is being repaired. These risks of loss of the *use* of property, as well as the loss of property itself, can be covered by insurance.

A second major category of risk that consumers face is the risk of liability loss. To be liable means to be responsible. Most cases of liability are related to car accidents, but many cases involve accidents around the home. An injured person might sue the home owner and the home owner may have to pay an amount decided by the court. People who have been found liable for injuries to someone else are often not prepared to pay the large amount ordered by a court. If a person does not have enough cash to pay, the court can take away his or her home, car, and other property. Many liability lawsuits involve physical injury. Others involve damage to property. Liability insurance is the most important way to protect against risk of liability.

The risk of loss of income is the third major category of consumer risk. The sudden loss of income resulting from the death or disablement of a wage earner can cause financial hardship. Life insurance is intended to protect against the risk of loss of income due to unexpected, early death. Disability insurance is intended to protect against the loss of income due to serious injury or illness.

Finally, consumers face the risk of unexpected major expenses. The most common unexpected major expense consumers face is for health services. Hospital, medical, and dental costs are very high. Most consumers cannot afford to pay them on their own. Many employers provide insurance to protect employees against the risk of major medical expenses. Consumers can buy individual policies if they are not covered through work.

CONSUMERS IN THE MARKETPLACE

The relationship between buyer and sellers used to be described by the phrase *caveat emptor,* which means "let the buyer beware." As the marketplace changed, the relationship between buyers and sellers changed. By the beginning of the 1960s, the relationship could be described by the phrase *caveat venditor,* which means "let the seller beware."

Consumer Rights and Responsibilities

In 1962, President Kennedy proclaimed the Consumer Bill of Rights, which outlines the basic rights of all consumers. Along with these rights, consumers have certain responsibilities to themselves, the economy, society, and the environment. These rights and responsibilities include the following:

Consumer Rights	Consumer Responsibilities
The right to safety	The responsibility to use products safely
The right to be informed	The responsibility to use information
The right to choose	The responsibility to choose efficiently
The right to be heard	The responsibility to express satisfaction or dissatisfaction
The right to redress or remedy	The responsibility to seek a remedy to consumer problems
The right to consumer education	The responsibility to be an educated consumer

Consumer Legislation

The heart of consumer progress in the United States has been the passage and enforcement of laws that benefit consumers. The following is a sampling of consumer laws passed to protect consumers and provide for controls over producers and sellers:

Law	Major Provisions
Pure Food and Drug Act	Guards against unhealthy and adulterated food and drugs
Meat Inspection Act	Requires inspection of red meat products and establishes sanitation guidelines for meat and poultry processing
Federal Trade Commission Act	Established the Federal Trade Commission and declares unfair methods of competition to be illegal
Kefauver-Harris Amendment	Requires that all drugs be tested for safety and effectiveness before being sold to the public
Fair Packaging and Labeling Act	Requires manufacturers to provide specific information on packages
Consumer Credit Protection Act	Requires lenders to make full disclosure of actual annual interest rates and other costs of credit
Equal Credit Opportunity Act	Prohibits discrimination on the basis of age, gender, race, and religion when approving credit

Law	Major Provisions
Fair Debt Collection Practices Act	Prohibits unfair debt collection tactics
Clean Air Act	Requires the reduction of acid rain and pollution from auto emissions and from coal-burning utilities
Child Care Act	Gives tax credits to working parents and gives grants to states to increase the availability of child-care centers

Getting Help for Consumer Problems

If you are dissatisfied with a product or service, it is your responsibility to express your complaint to the merchant. But, what if the merchant will not resolve the problem? In that case, it is your right to report the problem to the appropriate regulatory commission or another consumer group. Working with a commission or an established consumer group is a very effective way to resolve consumer complaints.

Approximately 22 federal government agencies perform regulatory functions and have established programs designed to assist the consumer in dealing with problems and to involve consumers in the government decision-making process. Most government agencies do not handle individual problems. However, if the problem involves the violation of the law, the agency will be interested. Following is a list of some of the federal agencies that protect consumers through enforcement of federal legislation:

- Federal Information Centers
- Department of Agriculture
- Consumer Product Safety Commission
- Federal Trade Commission
- Food and Drug Administration
- Office of Consumer Affairs

In some communities, businesses collectively provide consumer assistance through such organizations as the Better Business Bureau. If there is a bureau in your community, you can ask about the reputation of a company before you do business with it. You also can report to the Better Business Bureau any problems you have with a certain business. Information about your complaint may then be made available to other consumers.

Some important consumer organizations are available to advance the interests of consumers in the marketplace. The National Consumers League, Consumer Federation of America, American Council on Consumer Interests, Consumers' Research, and Consumers Union are all consumer groups organized to push for changes when they feel the quality of life is being threatened.

SOURCE: Adapted from Joseph Bonnice and Rosella Bannister, *Consumers Make Economic Decisions,* (Cincinnati, Ohio: South-Western Publishing Co., 1990), and D. Hayden Green, *Consumers in the Economy,* (Cincinnati, Ohio: South-Western Publishing Co., 1993).

Understanding the Economic Numbers

ECONOMIC INFORMATION IS ALL AROUND YOU

An informed citizen should have a reasonable understanding of the economic data that are reported in both the business and popular media. Many people watch one of the morning or evening network news shows, listen to a radio news program, and/or read a daily newspaper on a somewhat regular basis. From such exposure to the world in which we live, almost anyone probably can name at least a few economic measures that he or she has heard or seen reported. As a student of economics, you probably can name more of them than most people. If you read *The Wall Street Journal, Time, Newsweek,* or *Business Week,* you might be able to name dozens of important measures of the economy. The ones you name might be different from those named by a classmate because each of you is likely to focus on one that for one reason or another is of particular interest.

In this discussion, some of the economic measures many economists and businesspeople think are important are described, and some information about their publication schedule is provided. Determining which measures to include was difficult because there are so many measures. As you read through the following paragraphs, you almost certainly will recognize most of the measures as being reported regularly in the mass media.

It is impossible to provide *current* economic data in a printed textbook that will be used in a classroom for several years. The data quickly will become outdated. For this reason, throughout this appendix there are references to online sources of economic information. If you have access to the Internet, you can use these addresses to find the most current data available. For example, the *Economic Report of the President,* which can be accessed online at **gopher://umslvma.umsl.edu:70/11/library/govdocs.erps**, contains much of the economic data you might need. Many economic indicators are updated by the Fed at **http://great-lakes.net:2200/0/partners/ChicagoFed/econind**.

However, it is the nature of the Internet that addresses change and a Web site that is here today might be gone tomorrow. If that should happen, simply contact the Web site for South-Western ECONOMICS at **http://www.thomson.com/swpco/internet/hb29da1.html** for current information on address changes in this text.

GROSS DOMESTIC PRODUCT

Gross domestic product (GDP) is the most broad-based measure of economic activity within the country. You can read about GDP in detail in Chapter 14, Measuring Aggregate Economic Activity. GDP is reported by the Department of Commerce on a quarterly basis. The quarterly report of GDP often makes it into the popular news media and is always reported in *The Wall Street Journal,* usually during the third week in January, April, July, and October. You can obtain current GDP figures online from the Census Bureau at **http://www.census.gov/ftp/pub/statab/indicator/gdp.txt** or at **http://www.census.gov/ftp/pub/statab/USAbrief/part2.txt**.

LABOR MARKET REPORTS

The Bureau of Labor Statistics releases data on employment and the unemployment rate on a monthly basis. The employment data are based on a survey of employer payroll records, while the unemployment rate data are based on a broader survey of households. This series is watched closely by businesspeople because of the relation to potential consumer demand. Demand for durable goods and luxury items is particularly sensitive to the unemployment rate.

Employment data are usually reported in the national news media and appear regularly in *The Wall Street Journal,* usually on Monday of the second week of the month. You also can get current employment figures online from the Bureau of Labor Statistics at **http://www.bls.gov/** or from the Census Bureau's *Statistics in Brief* at **http://www.census.gov/ftp/pub/statab/USAbrief/part2.txt**. To examine local and regional unemployment rates, access the Economic Bulletin Board at the University of Michigan at **gopher://una.hh.lib.umich.edu/00/ebb/employment/laus-5.bls**.

PERSONAL INCOME

Personal income includes the income of households from employment (including self-employment), investments, and transfer payments (such as social security). *Disposable personal income* is personal income minus various taxes. These values are important measures of purchasing power.

Data on the level of personal income are provided by the Department of Commerce on a monthly basis. These data are common fare on the evening network news and are always published in *The Wall Street Journal,* usually during the third or fourth week of each month. You can access the Department of Commerce online at **http://www.doc.gov/**. Income information is also available online from the Census Bureau's *Statistics in Brief* at **http://www.census.gov/ftp/pub/statab/USAbrief/part2.txt**.

NEW HOUSING STARTS

New home construction is often viewed as a precursor of things to come because so many other economic activities are tied to housing starts. For example, when a housing start is recorded, construction workers will soon be on the job, new materials (such as lumber, glass, cement, roofing supplies, and heating equipment) will be purchased, and new appliances for kitchens, baths, and laundries will be needed. Private housing starts are counted in the month during which excavation for the foundation begins, while public housing starts are counted when the contract is awarded.

During the third week of each month, the Bureau of the Census publishes data on housing starts for the previous month. This series is published in *The Wall Street Journal* about three weeks into the month following the month for which the data are reported. The Bureau of the Census can be accessed online at **http://www.census.gov/**.

RETAIL SALES

Retail sales are considered to be an indicator of the demand-side strength of the economy. The Bureau of the Census collects monthly data on retail sales using a voluntary survey of retail establishments.

The results are reported in a monthly release of the Department of Commerce titled "Retail Sales." These results are then frequently reported in the popular press, especially around the Christmas holiday shopping season, and they are routinely published in *The Wall Street Journal* during the second week of the month. The data are in nominal terms and are seasonally adjusted. Typically, the reporting focuses on which retail segments were particularly strong or weak in the previous month and offers some explanation of possible reasons. You can reach the Bureau of the Census and get current retail sales data at **http://www.census.gov/**.

CONSUMER ATTITUDES

There are several measures of consumer attitudes, of which the two most commonly cited are probably the Consumer Confidence Index and the Consumer Sentiment Index. The Consumer Confidence Index (CCI) is a monthly series developed by the Consumer Research Center of the Conference Board. The Conference Board publishes the index in two publications: the *Consumer Confidence Survey* and its *Statistical Bulletin*. The Consumer Sentiment Index (CSI) comes from the Survey Research Center at the University of Michigan and is published monthly in its *Survey of Consumer Attitudes*.

The CCI and CSI are both reported in *The Wall Street Journal* from time to time but not on a regular basis. You also may recall them being reported in the popular news media. Both are considered indicators of the future level of consumer spending. You can get information about the CCI online at **http://www.mlinet.com/bci/catBCI.html**. Information about the CSI is available online at **http://www.mlinet.com/bci/pages/u0m058.html**.

PRICE LEVELS

The two most commonly reported measures of prices in the economy are probably the consumer price index (CPI) and the producer price index (PPI). Both are considered measures of inflation, with the PPI being used as an indicator of what might be in store at the consumer level in the future. The CPI and the PPI are based on extensive surveys of consumers and producers, respectively, by the U.S. Department of Labor.

Each month, you can expect to see the CPI and PPI reported in *The Wall Street Journal*. You can find current data on CPI and PPI online at **http://www.census.gov/ftp/pub/statab/indicator/prices.txt** or **gopher://una.hh.lib.umich.edu/00/ebb/indicators/ei.prn**.

THE MONEY SUPPLY

The Federal Reserve is the agency that controls the money supply, and so it is natural to expect that it would be the provider of money supply data. M1 is the most basic measure of the money supply. It is defined to include currency and checking accounts. M2 is a broader measure (including M1 as well as savings deposits, CDs, and money market funds) and is usually considered the best overall measure of the money supply. The money supply data are closely watched by people in business because of the potential impact of the money supply on purchasing power, interest rates, real GDP, and inflation.

Each Thursday, the Fed releases data on the money supply. You might find it interesting to know that it waits to release data until after the New York financial markets have closed to circumvent knee-jerk reactions to the news. *The Wall Street Journal* reports money supply data in a section titled "Closely Watched Reports." The gopher site at **gopher://gopher.great-lakes.net:2200/00/partners/ChicagoFed/finance** provides current information on the money supply.

INTEREST RATES

Notice that the heading for this subsection uses the plural *rates,* not *rate*. This is because there are many interest rates, each of which is important for specific reasons. It may be hard to get universal agreement on which two or three interest rates are the most important, but the prime rate, the federal funds rate, and the discount rate would be high on the list for many business professionals.

The *prime rate* is the rate that large commercial banks charge their best corporate customers. This rate is often viewed as an indicator of the supply and demand conditions in capital markets. The *federal funds rate* is the rate that banks charge one another for very short-term loans (such as overnight) that are used to cover reserve requirements. This rate is also seen as an indicator of the state of money markets. The *discount rate* is the rate that the Federal Reserve charges banks to borrow from the Fed and is one of the instruments of monetary policy. Changes in the discount rate are therefore policy based rather than based on supply and demand conditions as are the prime and federal funds rates. Changes in the discount rate represent what the Fed's intention is with respect to monetary policy and thus may be indicative of an expansionary or restrictive policy.

These, and other interest rates such as mortgage rates, foreign prime rates, and CD rates, are reported daily in *The Wall Street Journal*. Up-to-date information on the federal funds rate, prime rate, and discount rate can be found at **http://great-lakes.net:2200/partners/ChicagoFed/finance/rates_cw.prn**.

INDUSTRIAL PRODUCTION INDEX

This index is released monthly by the Federal Reserve Board. The industrial production index includes agriculture, construction, transportation, communication, trade, finance, service, and government. It is sometimes seen as a gauge of general business fluctuations.

While it is published in *The Federal Reserve Bulletin,* it also is available in a timely manner in the more widely accessible *Wall Street Journal*. For current Industrial Production Index information, travel to **http://great-lakes.net:2200/0/partners/ChicagoFed/econind/indpro_c.prn**.

INDEX OF LEADING ECONOMIC INDICATORS

The index of leading economic indicators is developed by the Bureau of Economic Analysis of the U.S. Department of Commerce. This index is generally accepted as a reasonably good predictor of the future state of economic events, especially unemployment and industrial production. The eleven items that make up the index follow:

1. average weekly hours worked for manufacturing production workers;
2. average initial claims for unemployment insurance;
3. manufacturers' new orders for consumer goods and materials (constant dollars);
4. vendor performance—percentage of companies receiving slower deliveries;
5. contracts and orders for new plant and equipment (constant dollars);
6. index of new private housing units authorized by local building permits;
7. change in manufacturers' unfilled durable goods orders (constant dollars);
8. change in sensitive materials prices;
9. index of stock prices, 500 common stocks;
10. Index of consumer expectations; and
11. money supply (M2 in constant dollars).

The Bureau of Economic Analysis has a Web site at **http://www.bea.doc.gov/beahome.html**, where you can access the Index of Leading Economic Indicators. The index is also published every month in *The Wall Street Journal*.

EXCHANGE RATES

Published exchange rates reflect current trade in currencies between major banks and between banks and their corporate customers. The number of different exchange rates published is large and gives testimony to the truly global nature of today's business world. *The Wall Street Journal* publishes exchange rate data on a daily basis based on what is referred to as an "interbank market." Exchange rate data also are available from the Fed at **http://great-lakes.net:2200/0/partners/ChicagoFed/finance** and at **gopher://una.hh.lib.umich.edu/00/ebb/monetary/noonfx.frb**.

OTHER INTERNET SOURCES OF ECONOMIC DATA

There are many interesting economic sites on the Internet that you might want to visit. Here is a list of some favorites:

Census Bureau

- **http://www.census.gov/ftp/pub/foreign-trade/www/top10.html**
- **http://www.census.gov/ftp/pub/statab/indicator/**
- **http://www.census.gov/ftp/pub/population/www/**

CIA World Factbook

- **http://www.odci.gov/cia/publications/95fact/index.html**

World Bank

- **http://www.worldbank.org/**

GLOSSARY

ability-to-pay principle of taxation
the concept that those who can best afford to pay taxes should pay most of the taxes

absolute advantage
exists in the production of a good when one country can produce a good more efficiently than another country

aggregate demand
the total demand of all people for all goods and services produced in an economy

aggregate supply
the total supply of all goods and services in an economy

allocation
the process of choosing which needs will be satisfied and how much of our resources we will use to satisfy them

alternative
a possible course of action

articles of incorporation
a written application to the state requesting permission to form a corporation

asset demand for money
the demand for money in order to hold wealth in the form of money

average product
the number of units of output produced per unit of input

balance of payments
the total flow of money into a country minus the total flow of money out of a country

balance of trade
the level of merchandise exports minus the level of merchandise imports

barriers to economic development
economic, social, and political characteristics that prevent an economy from developing

barter
a direct trade of goods or services

benefit principle of taxation
the concept that those who benefit from the spending of tax dollars should pay the taxes to provide the benefits

Board of Governors
a group that supervises the Federal Reserve System

bond
a certificate stating the amount the corporation has borrowed from the holder and the terms of repayment

budget constraint
the mix of goods that can be purchased with a limited amount of income

budget deficit
the amount by which federal government spending exceeds revenues each year

capital
goods that are produced and can be used as inputs for further production

cartel
a formal organization of firms in the same industry acting together to make decisions

change in supply
a change in the number of units supplied at every price

change in the quantity supplied
change in the number of units made available for sale due to a *price change*

charter
the legal authorization to organize a business as a corporation

check
a written order to pay money from amounts deposited

civilian labor force
the total number of people in the working age group (16 years and over) who are either employed or actively seeking work

closed shop
a business that agrees to hire only those who are members of a union

collective bargaining
the process of having the union negotiate with management to determine the terms of employment for all workers rather than having each worker negotiate separately

collusion
the situation of firms acting together rather than separately

commercial bank
a type of financial institution that was originally formed to serve businesses but now provides a large number of financial services to both business customers and individuals

common stock
a type of stock that gives the holder a partial ownership of the corporation

comparative advantage
the principle that a country benefits from specializing in the production at which it is relatively most efficient

competition
the rivalry between two or more parties to gain benefits from a third party

complementary products
products that are used together

conglomerate
a firm made up of many divisions and/or subsidiaries that may not have much in common in their lines of business

conglomerate merger
a merger of two companies that are in different businesses

constant dollar GDP
the value of gross domestic product after taking out the effect of price changes

consumer goods
items that are made for final consumption

Consumer Price Index (CPI)
a number used to calculate changes in the average level of prices for a number of items typically bought by urban families

contract
a legally binding agreement between two or more competent persons

corporate bond rate
the interest rate paid on corporate bonds

corporate income tax
a tax on the earnings of corporations

corporation
an organization of people legally bound together by a charter to conduct some type of business

cost-push inflation
a rise in the general level of prices that is caused by increased costs of making and selling goods

creditors
people who have loaned money to others

credit union
a financial intermediary formed around something that its members have in common

criteria
the characteristics of a group of alternatives that will be judged to make a choice

crowding out
the effect on private businesses when increased government borrowing raises interest rates and reduces private borrowing

currency
coins and paper money

cyclical unemployment
unemployment resulting from too low a level of aggregate demand

debtors
people who have borrowed money from someone else

decision matrix
a table comparing possible decisions

deflation
a decline in the average level of prices

demand
the quantities of a good that consumers are willing and able to purchase at various prices during a given period of time

demand curve
a graphic illustration of the relationship between *price* and the *quantity demanded* at each price

demand deposit
money that must be paid upon demand by the holder of a check

demand for labor
the amount of labor that firms would want to hire at various wage rates

demand-pull inflation
a rise in the general level of prices caused by too high a level of aggregate demand in relation to aggregate supply

demand schedule
a listing of the quantities that would be purchased at various prices

deposit expansion multiplier
the number that expresses the relationship between a change in bank reserves and the change in the money supply

depression
a severe and prolonged decline in the level of economic activity

derived demand
demand for an input that is dependent on the demand for the product that the input helps to produce

determinants of demand
the factors that determine how much will be purchased at any given price

differentiated oligopoly
an oligopoly in which the product is differentiated

diminishing marginal product
the principle that as more of one input is added to a fixed amount of other inputs, the marginal product decreases

diminishing marginal utility
the principle that as additional units of a product are consumed during a given time period, the additional satisfaction decreases

direct tax
a tax paid by the person against whom the tax is levied

discount rate
the interest rate that banks must pay to borrow from the Federal Reserve System

disposable income
the income that is left after deducting tax payments

distribution effect
the way the benefit or inconvenience of a social issue is spread among the members of the society

dividends
that part of a corporation's income paid to its stockholders

dual economy
an economy in which a modern market economy exists side by side with a primitive subsistence economy

economic growth
the change in the level of economic activity from one year to another

economic incentive
the increase in personal satisfaction that may result from some economic activity

economic profit
total revenue minus total costs

economics
the social science that deals with how society allocates its scarce resources among its unlimited wants and needs

economic system
the combination of social and individual decision making a society uses to answer the three economic questions

economies of scale
the concept that some economic activities become more efficient when done on a large scale

efficiency
achieving the maximum benefit from a given amount and combination of resources

Employment Act of 1946
states that the federal government should take responsibility for full employment, price stability, and economic growth

entrepreneurs
individuals who take the risk of producing a product for a profit

entrepreneurship
the managerial ability and risk taking that contribute so much to a productive economy

equilibrium price
the price at which the quantity demanded equals the quantity supplied

equilibrium quantity
the quantity that is both demanded and supplied at the equilibrium price

equilibrium wage
the wage rate at which the quantity of labor demanded equals the quantity of labor supplied

equity
dealing fairly and equally with all concerned

estate and gift taxes
taxes levied on the wealth (money and property) passed from one person to another either at death or as a gift

European Community (EC)
a group of European countries that have joined together and agreed on ways to improve trade among themselves

excess reserves
the difference between actual reserves and required reserves

exchange
giving one thing in return for some other thing

exchange rate
the rate at which one kind of money can be traded for another

excise tax
a sales tax levied only on a specific item

exclusion principle
the principle that one person can keep others from benefiting from a private good

expansionary fiscal policies
causing the economy to run more rapidly primarily by increasing aggregate demand

explicit costs
payments made to others as a cost of running a business

exports
goods and services that one country sells to another country

external debt
the part of the national debt that is owed to people or governments outside the United States

externality
a cost or benefit passed on to people not directly involved in a transaction

factor of production
anything used to produce a good or service

Federal Advisory Council
a group that consists of 12 members who meet four times each year with the Board of Governors to discuss the economic situation and policies of the Board

Federal Deposit Insurance Corporation (FDIC)
the agency that insures deposits of individuals and businesses for up to $100,000 in the event of bank failure

federal funds rate
the interest rate that banks pay to borrow from each other on a short term basis

Federal Open Market Committee (FOMC)
a group that acts on the most important part of monetary policy: the buying and selling of U.S. government securities by the Federal Reserve Banks

Federal Reserve System (the Fed)
the central banking system in the United States

financial intermediary
an organization that helps the flow of money from people with money to save to people who need to borrow money

fiscal policy
the changing of federal government spending and taxes in order to control the level of economic activity

fixed income
an income that is set and does not change from year to year

flexible exchange rate
a system in which the laws of supply and demand are allowed to set the prices, or exchange rates, of each kind of money

foreign aid
the money that more advanced countries provide to help LDCs in their economic development

fractional reserve banking system
a system that requires banks to keep some fraction of their deposits in the form of reserves

franchise
a contract between a parent company (franchisor) and some other business or individual (franchisee) that details the terms under which the franchisee does business with products, names, or other services of the franchisor

freedom of choice
the individual power to choose and receive both the costs and the benefits of a choice

free rider
a person who benefits from a public good without sharing its cost

frictional unemployment
unemployment of people who are temporarily between jobs

full employment
employment of about 95 percent of the labor force

functional distribution of income
the way in which income is divided by economic functions

G

General Agreement on Tariffs and Trade (GATT)
an agreement that gave broad international support to improving trade among countries

gold standard
a system in which each nation sets the value of its money in terms of a certain amount of gold

gross domestic product (GDP)
the total dollar value of all final goods and services produced by resources located in the United States (regardless of who owns them) during one year's time

homogeneous product
a good or service that varies little from producer to producer

horizontal merger
a merger of two companies in the same industry

human resources
the people who work or may be able to work

I

imports
goods and services that one country buys from another country

income effect
the effect that increasing or decreasing prices has on the buying power of income

indirect tax
a tax that can be shifted, at least in part, to a party other than the one on whom the tax is levied

individual choice
decisions made by people acting separately

infant mortality rate
the number of deaths of children under one year of age per 1,000 live births

inferior goods
goods for which demand goes down as income goes up

inflation
a rise in the average level of prices

inflationary bias in fiscal policy
the natural tendency for Congress to favor expansionary policies over restrictive policies

injunction
a court order to stop someone from doing something (or to make someone *do* something)

inside time lag
the time it takes to decide on a policy

interest
the price paid for the use of money

International Monetary Fund (IMF)
a bank established to promote economic cooperation by maintaining an orderly system of world trade and exchange rates

investment
an increase in the amount of productive capital in an economy

invisible hand
the incentive for individuals to choose in the best interest of society by pursuing their own self-interests

job discrimination
the refusal to hire certain people because of their gender, race, or other characteristics that have nothing to do with their ability to do a job

labor
the human factor of production

labor union
an organization of workers formed to give workers greater bargaining power in their dealings with management

land
a broad measure representing all the basic natural resources that contribute to production

law of demand
the quantity demanded of a good will be greater at lower prices than will be the quantity demanded at higher prices

law of supply
states that the quantity of goods supplied will be greater at a higher price than it will at a lower price

less-developed country (LDC)
a poor country with a relatively low level of education and a largely rural population

life expectancy
the average age the people in a country reach

limited liability
the concept that owners of a business are only responsible for its debts up to the amount they invest in the business

limited resources
the condition of there not being enough resources to fulfill all wants and needs

line of credit
an arrangement through which a business can quickly access needed cash from a bank

lobbying
the act of communicating with government representatives to influence their votes on a specific issue

long run
a period during which the amounts of all inputs can be changed

loose monetary policy
a policy of the Federal Reserve that causes the money supply to increase

Lorenz curve
a graphic method of showing the amount of income inequality that exists in society at any point in time

M

macroeconomic equilibrium
what results when the sum of savings and taxes equals the sum of investment and government spending

macroeconomics
that part of economics that examines the behavior of the whole economy

marginal private benefit (MPB)
the added benefit that individuals directly involved in an activity get from increasing the activity by one unit

marginal private cost (MPC)
the added cost individuals directly involved in an activity pay to increase the activity by one unit

marginal product
the amount that total product increases or decreases as a result of adding one additional unit of input

marginal social benefit (MSB)
the added benefit that society gets from increasing an activity by one unit

marginal social cost (MSC)
the added cost that society pays to increase an activity by one unit

marginal utility
the amount of satisfaction a person gets from *one* additional unit of a product

market
exchange activities between buyers and sellers of goods and services

market economy
an economy in which the economic questions are decided mostly by individuals in the marketplace

market organization
the way participants in markets are organized and how many participants there are

member banks
those banks that belong to the Federal Reserve System

merger
the combining of one company with another company it buys

microeconomics
the branch of economics that examines the choices of individuals concerning one product, one firm, or one industry

minimum wage law
a law that sets the lowest wage that can be paid for certain kinds of work

model
a simplified form of reality that shows the relationship between different factors

monetary policy
the changing of the quantity of money in the economy in order to reduce unemployment, keep prices stable, and promote economic growth

monopolistic competition
a market organization in which many firms produce goods that are different but similar enough to be substitutes

monopoly
a form of market organization in which there is only one seller of a product

monopsony
a market in which there is only one buyer

multinational business
a firm that sells and produces products in multiple countries

multiplier effect
the concept that any change in fiscal policy affects total demand and total income by an amount larger than the original amount of the change in spending or taxing

mutual savings banks
banks that were first formed for the same reasons as savings and loan associations and that promote thrift in their members

national debt
the amount of money that the federal government owes

natural monopoly
a situation in which it is not practical to have competition

natural resources
the total raw materials supplied by nature

negative externality
the result when *costs* are shifted to people who are not directly involved with the production or consumption of a good

nonprofit organization
an organization that does not have profit as its objective

normal goods
goods for which demand goes up as income goes up

North American Free Trade Agreement (NAFTA)
trade agreement established between the United States, Canada, and Mexico to promote economic growth and prosperity for all three economies by eliminating barriers to free trade

objectivity
ruling out aspects of a problem that seem important only because of your strong emotions about them

oligopoly
a form of market organization in which there are relatively few firms

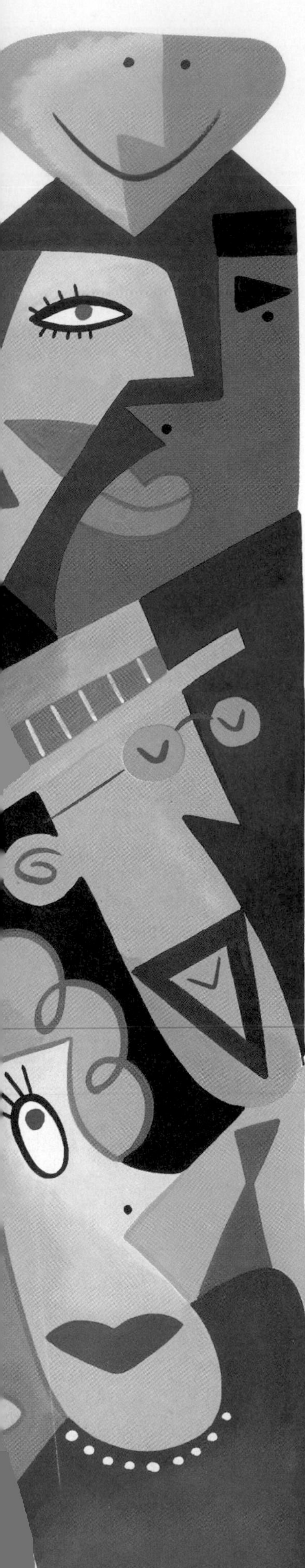

open market operations
the buying and selling of U.S. government securities by the Federal Reserve

opportunity benefit
what is gained by making a particular choice

opportunity cost
the value of any alternative that you must give up when you make a choice

outside time lag
the time it takes for the effects of a policy change to be completely felt in the economy

partnership
a type of business organization in which there are two or more owners

partnership agreement
a legally binding document that specifies how the responsibilities and profits or losses from a partnership will be split between the partners

patent
a legal protection for the inventor of a product or process that gives that person or company the sole right to produce the product or use the process for up to 17 years

per capita income
the average income per person

perfect competition
a form of market organization in which a great many small firms produce a homogeneous product

personal distribution of income
how income is shared among people in our society

personal income tax
a tax on the income of individuals

population explosion
rapid growth in the number of people living in a country

positive externality
the result when *benefits* are shifted to people who are not directly involved with the production or consumption of a good

poverty
the condition in which people do not have enough income to provide for their basic needs, such as food, clothing, and shelter

price ceiling
a maximum price set by government that is *below* the market equilibrium price

price elasticity of demand
measures the relative responsiveness of the change in quantity demanded as a result of a change in the product's price

price elasticity of supply
measures the responsiveness of the quantity supplied to changes in the product's price

price floor
a minimum price set by government that is *above* the market equilibrium price

price index
a number that compares prices in one year with some earlier base year

price setter
a firm that has some control over the price at which its product sells

price taker
a firm that takes a price determined by forces outside the firm's control

prime rate
the interest rate that banks charge their best corporate customers

private enterprise
a system in which individuals take the risk of producing goods or services to make a profit

private goods
goods that are privately owned and used to benefit only their owners

private sector
the part of an economy that is owned by individuals and operated for their personal benefit

product differentiation
the concept that the product of one firm can be distinguished from the products of other firms

production possibilities curve
a graphic illustration of the combinations of output an economy can produce if all of its resources are utilized and utilized efficiently, given the state of technology

progressive tax
a tax that takes a larger percentage of higher incomes and a smaller percentage of lower incomes

property rights
the rules that government has established to define who owns what property and how owners may use their property

property tax
a tax levied on real estate, such as a home, land, and buildings

proportional tax
a tax that takes the same percentage of income from all taxpayers

proprietorship
a form of business in which there is one owner

protectionism
the idea that we should limit international trade to protect our own self-interest

psychic income
the nonmonetary reward we get from taking some action

public goods
goods and services available to the whole society

public goods rationale
the argument that some public goods can be produced more efficiently by the government

public institutions
publicly owned organizations established by government to serve the wants and needs of a whole society

public sector
the part of an economy that is owned by the whole society and operated for its benefit

pure oligopoly
an oligopoly in which the products are the same for all firms

quota
a limit on the amount of imports or exports

rate of growth
the percentage change in the level of economic activity from one year to the next

real GDP
the value of gross domestic product after taking out the effect of price changes

real GDP per person
the real value of the total output of goods and services divided by the number of people in the economy

recession
the condition in which unemployment is high and GDP falls for two or more consecutive quarters

regressive tax
a tax that takes a larger percentage of lower incomes and a smaller percentage of higher incomes

research and development
the activities undertaken to find new and more efficient methods of production

reserve ratio
the fraction of deposits that the Federal Reserve determines banks must keep on reserve

reserve requirement
the dollar amount banks must keep on reserve

restrictive fiscal policies
causing the economy to run more slowly primarily by reducing aggregate demand

returns to scale
the relationship between changes in the scale of production and the corresponding change in the amount of output

S

sales tax
a tax on goods that are bought

savings and loan association
a financial intermediary that mainly provides a place for people to save money and then lends that money to people to buy houses or other items

scale of production
the overall level of use of all factors of production

scarcity
the condition that occurs because people's wants and needs are unlimited, while the resources needed to produce goods and services to meet these wants and needs are limited

seasonal unemployment
unemployment of people who are out of work because of factors that vary with the time of year

share draft account
an account with a credit union from which withdrawals easily can be made through a draft (a draft is a type of check)

shortage
the condition in which the quantity demanded is greater than the quantity supplied at a certain price

short run
any period during which the usable amount of at least one input is fixed while the usable amount of at least one other input can change

social benefits
the benefits received by a society from a social choice

social choice
decision making by government in the interest of society

social costs
the costs to a society of a social choice

social economy
an economy in which the major economic questions are determined by a government representing the interests of the entire society

social goals
the goals of an entire society

Social Security tax
a tax that provides disability and retirement benefits for most working people

special interest group
an organization of people who are bound together by a common concern

speculation
when someone buys a large amount of a good and hopes to resell it at a much higher price

stock
shares of ownership in a corporation

structural unemployment
unemployment resulting from skills that do not match what employers require or from being geographically separated from job opportunities

subsidy
a payment made by the government to encourage some activity

substitute products
products whose uses are similar enough that one can replace the other

substitution effect
the change in the mix of goods purchased as a result of increasing or decreasing relative prices

supply
the quantities of a product or service that a firm is willing and able to make available for sale at different prices

supply curve
a graphic representation of the quantities that would be supplied at each price

supply of labor
the amount of labor that would be available at each wage rate

supply schedule
a table that shows the quantities of a good or service that would be supplied by a firm at different prices

surplus
the condition in which the quantity supplied is greater than the quantity demanded at a certain price

T

tariff
a tax on imports

tax
a charge imposed by the government on people or property for public purposes

technology
the body of knowledge that is used for the production of goods and services

test of the market
being able to provide goods that satisfy consumers' needs and desires at prices consumers are willing to pay

theory
a simplified description of reality

tight monetary policy
a policy of the Federal Reserve that causes the money supply to decrease

total product
all the units of a product produced in a given period of time

total revenue
the total amount of money a company receives from sales of a product

trade deficit
the result when a country imports more than it exports

trade surplus
the result when a country exports more than it imports

transaction demand for money
the demand for money to make exchanges

U

unemployment
the condition of those who are willing and able to work and are actively seeking work but who do not currently work

unemployment rate
the percentage of the civilian labor force that is considered unemployed

union shop
a business that requires workers to join a union shortly after taking a job

unlimited liability
the concept that an owner's personal assets can be used to pay bills of the business

unlimited wants and needs
the human characteristic of never having all wants and needs satisfied

util
the unit of measurement for utility

utility
the satisfaction one receives from the consumption, use, or ownership of a good or service

V

vertical merger
a merger of two companies that are at different stages in the same production process

W

wage and price controls
government controls on the levels of wages and prices

wage rate
the price paid for each unit of labor

work ethic
the belief that people should work hard and pull their own weight in economic life

World Bank
an organization established in 1944 to help finance reconstruction after World War II

INDEX

A

B

C

D

F

N

Q

T

V

W

Z

ACKNOWLEDGMENTS

Chapter 1

p. 5: Jeff Greenberg, Photographer; **p. 7:** Jeff Greenberg, Photographer; **p. 9:** Jeff Greenberg, Photographer; **p. 11:** Jeff Greenberg, Photographer; **p. 15:** Jeff Greenberg, Photographer; **p. 21:** Jeff Greenberg, Photographer.

Chapter 2

p. 30: Photograph by Paul Couvrette, Ottawa, Canada; **p. 32:** Jeff Greenberg, Photographer; **p. 33:** The Bettmann Archive; **p. 38: top:** Jeff Greenberg, Photographer; **p. 38: bottom:** Jeff Greenberg, Photographer; **p. 39:** Jeff Greenberg, Photographer; **p. 43:** Jeff Greenberg, Photographer.

Chapter 3

p. 53: Jeff Greenberg, Photographer; **p. 55:** The Bettmann Archive; **p. 58:** Jeff Greenberg, Photographer; **p. 61:** Jeff Greenberg, Photographer; **p. 62:** Jeff Greenberg, Photographer; **p. 65:** Jeff Greenberg, Photographer; **p. 67:** Jeff Greenberg, Photographer.

Chapter 4

p. 77: Jeff Greenberg, Photographer; **p. 79:** Jeff Greenberg, Photographer; **p. 80:** USDA Photo by Doug Wilson; **p. 83:** Jeff Greenberg, Photographer; **p. 85:** Jeff Greenberg, Photographer; **p. 89:** Jeff Greenberg, Photographer; **p. 90:** Scott Willis ©1989 San Jose Mercury News.

Chapter 5

p. 105: Alan Brown/Photonics; **p. 106:** Jeff Greenberg, Photographer; **p. 109:** Oil Spill Public Information Center; **p. 110:** Jeff Greenberg, Photographer; **p. 112:** Photograph by William P. McElligott, Ottawa, Canada; **p. 115:** Photo courtesy of the American League of Lobbyists.

Chapter 6

p. 124: Photograph by Les Amis du Jardin Botanique de Montreal, Montreal, Canada; **p. 125:** Jeff Greenberg, Photographer; **p. 129:** Jeff Greenberg, Photographer; **p. 130:** Jeff Greenberg, Photographer; **p. 133:** Photograph by Paul Couvrette, Ottawa, Canada; **p. 135:** Jeff Greenberg, Photographer; **p. 139:** Jeff Greenberg, Photographer; **p. 141:** Jeff Greenberg, Photographer; **p. 142:** Jeff Greenberg, Photographer.

Chapter 7

p. 154: Jeff Greenberg, Photographer; **p. 160:** Florida Citrus Growers; **p. 163:** Jeff Greenberg, Photographer; **p. 164:** Jeff Greenberg, Photographer; **p. 166:** Jeff Greenberg, Photographer; **p. 168:** Jeff Greenberg, Photographer.

Chapter 8

p. 190: Photograph by Harold Davis, New York, NY; **p. 191:** Jeff Greenberg, Photographer; **p. 192:** Jeff Greenberg, Photographer; **p. 193:** USDA Photo by Doug Wilson; **p. 196:** Jeff Greenberg, Photographer; **p. 198:** Jeff Greenberg, Photographer; **p. 206:** Alan Brown/Photonics.

Chapter 9

p. 216: Jeff Greenberg, Photographer; **p. 218:** Jeff Greenberg, Photographer; **p. 222:** Jeff Greenberg, Photographer; **p. 224:** Erik Von Fischer/Photonics; **p. 225:** Jeff Greenberg, Photographer; **p. 230:** Photograph by Robert Lear, Toronto, Canada; **p. 233:** NYSE; **p. 234: top:** Jeff Greenberg, Photographer; **p. 234: bottom:** Photo courtesy of Pizza Hut, Inc.

Chapter 10

p. 245: Jeff Greenberg, Photographer; **p. 247:** © Jose Carrillo, Ventura, CA; **p. 253:** Jeff Greenberg, Photographer; **p. 261:** Jeff Greenberg, Photographer; **p. 264:** Jeff Greenberg, Photographer.

Chapter 11

p. 273: top: Jeff Greenberg, Photographer; **p. 273: bottom:** Jeff Greenberg, Photographer; **p. 276:** Jeff Greenberg, Photographer; **p. 281:** Photograph by Malak, Ottawa, Canada; **p. 283:** Jeff Greenberg, Photographer; **p. 285:** Jeff Greenberg, Photographer; **p. 289:** Hoffmann-La Roche, Nutley, N.J.

Chapter 12

p. 304: USDA; **p. 305:** Jeff Greenberg, Photographer; **p. 307:** Jeff Greenberg, Photographer; **p. 310:** Jeff Greenberg, Photographer; **p. 317:** Photograph by Al Greening, San Francisco, CA.

Global Economy: p. 313: Adapted from Sharon Begley et al., "Ice Cubes for Penguins," in *Business Week* (April 3, 1995): 56.

Chapter 13

p. 327: Jeff Greenberg, Photographer; **p. 333:** Courtesy of Apple Computer, Inc.; **p. 335:** Jeff Greenberg, Photographer; **p. 339:** Jeff Greenberg, Photographer; **p. 341:** Photograph by Helen Cohen Rimmer, Pincourt, Quebec, Canada.

Chapter 14

p. 359: left: Photograph by Larry White, New York, NY; **p. 377:** Alan Brown/Photonics; **p. 379: left:** Photograph by Larry White, New York, NY; **p. 379: center:** Architect of the Capitol; **p. 383:** Jeff Greenberg, Photographer.

Chapter 15

p. 393: Jeff Greenberg, Photographer; **p. 399:** Photograph by Christine Dameyer and Anne Xu; **p. 405:** Photograph by Harold Davis, New York, NY; **p. 406:** National Archives Trust; **p. 408:** Jeff Greenberg, Photographer; **p. 409:** Jeff Greenberg, Photographer.

Chapter 16

p. 422: Jeff Greenberg, Photographer; **p. 425:** Jeff Greenberg, Photographer; **p. 428:** Jeff Greenberg, Photographer; **p. 429:** Jeff Greenberg, Photographer; **p. 433:** Courtesy of Apple Computer, Inc.; **p. 435:** Photograph by William P. McElligott, Ottawa, Canada; **p. 437:** Jeff Greenberg, Photographer.

Chapter 17

p. 457: Photograph by Christine Dameyer and Anne Xu;
p. 458: The Bettmann Archive.

Chapter 18

p. 470: Photograph by William P. McElligott, Ottawa, Canada; **p. 482:** Jeff Greenberg, Photographer; **p. 485:** Photograph by Lee Paris, Belmont, MA; **p. 486:** Jeff Greenberg, Photographer; **p. 487:** Photograph by Jack Parsons (Los Gatos, CA), Alan D. Harkrader Jr. (Peoria, IL) and other photographers; **p. 490:** Jeff Greenberg, Photographer.

Econ & You: p. 483: Based on John Wenninger and David Laster, "The Electronic Purse," *Current Issues*, Federal Reserve Bank of New York (April 1995).

Global Economy: p. 488: Based on Lena H. Sun, "A Cultural Bank and Trust," in *The Washington Post National Weekly Edition* (February 27–March 5, 1995): 9.

Chapter 19

p. 504: Bureau of Engraving and Printing; **p. 516:** Jeff Greenberg, Photographer; **p. 517:** Photograph by Robert Lear, Toronto, Canada; **p. 519:** Jeff Greenberg, Photographer.

Chapter 20

p. 536: Photograph by NASA; **p. 540:** Jeff Greenberg, Photographer; **p. 542:** Jeff Greenberg, Photographer.

Chapter 21

p. 569: The Bettmann Archive; **p. 576:** Jeff Greenberg, Photographer; **p. 580:** Photograph by Al Greening, San Francisco, CA; **p. 582:** The Bettmann Archive; **p. 583:** The Bettmann Archive.

Chapter 22

p. 594: Photograph by Lee Paris, Belmont, MA; **p. 597:** Photograph by Lee Paris, Belmont, MA; **p. 598:** Photograph by Lee Paris, Belmont, MA; **p. 606:** Photograph by Esther Mugar and David Ryan, San Francisco, CA; **p. 607:** Jeff Greenberg, Photographer; **p. 613:** Photograph by Jack K. Blonk, Laval, Quebec, Canada.

Chapter 23

p. 626: Photograph by Esther Mugar, San Francisco, CA; **p. 627:** Photograph by William P. McElligott, Ottawa, Canada; **p. 634:** Photograph by Gordon Barbery and Esther Mugar, San Francisco, CA; **p. 640:** Photograph by William P. McElligott, Ottawa, Canada; **p. 644:** Jeff Greenberg, Photographer; **p. 645:** Photographs by Lee Paris, Belmont, MA.

Econ & You: p. 631: Shawn Tully, "Teens: The Most Global Market of All," in *Fortune* (May 16, 1994): 90–97. Cyndee Miller, "Teens Seen as the First Truly Global Consumers," in *Marketing News* (March 27, 1995): 9.

Global Economy: p. 641: Dom Del Prete, "Latin America Is a Marketer's Dream Come True," in *Marketing News* (October 10, 1994): 7–8.

Chapter 24

p. 656: Jeff Greenberg, Photographer; **p. 662: top:** Photograph by France Pepper, Montreal, Canada; **p. 662: bottom:** © TSM/Sally Wiener Grotta; **p. 666: bottom:** Photograph by Robert Chadwick, Montreal, Canada; **p. 671:** ICRC/Red Cross.